24 50/EC

D1123441

RHYME AND REVOLUTION IN GERMANY

RHYME AND REVOLUTION
IN GERMANY

A STUDY IN GERMAN HISTORY, LIFE,
LITERATURE AND CHARACTER
1813-1850

By J. G. LEGGE

LIBRARY

JUL 2 1974

UNIVERSITY OF THE PACIFIC

AMS PRESS
NEW YORK

LIBRARY

JUL 2 1974

UNIVERSITY OF THE PACIFIC

282440

Reprinted with permission of Constable & Company, Ltd.
From the edition of 1918, London
First AMS EDITION published 1970
Manufactured in the United States of America

International Standard Book Number: 0-404-03947-2

Library of Congress Catalog Card Number: 72-126646

AMS PRESS, INC.
NEW YORK, N.Y. 10003

TO THE MEMORY OF

CAPTAIN W. E. GREIG

5TH KING'S (LIVERPOOL REGIMENT)

WHO DIED ON 27TH MAY 1915

OF WOUNDS RECEIVED AT NEUVE CHAPELLE

ONE OF THE GLORIOUS HOST

WHO FOUGHT FOR CONSCIENCE' SAKE AND FELL

TO RISE AGAIN AS WE BELIEVE AND TO RAISE US

THIS BOOK IS AFFECTIONATELY AND ADMIRINGLY

INSCRIBED

1817

Again the judgment-scales are trembling,
 The old, old strife again is born,
The great Assize is now assembling
 Will separate from chaff the corn.
On this side and on that are parted
 Now and for aye truth and deceit,
The coward and the lion-hearted,
 The half-man and the man complete.

UHLAND.

PREFACE

THIS book is the outcome of a desire to place in the hands of the British Public the means of studying German history and the German character at first hand. Of recent years, and particularly since the outbreak of war, many books have been published in this country giving the writers' opinions about the enemy, and reasons, more or less convincing, to justify those opinions. Such judgments are apt to be coloured by the writer's political opinions and national prejudices, and do not always agree. So that the layman, apart from the helpless feeling of dependence on others, is perplexed by the variety of opinions offered to him.

Of German history during the last century accounts are to be found in excellent text-books by English scholars, but even the best of text-books is, from conditions essential to its form, far from easy reading. And the same must be said of the *Cambridge Modern History*, where the fullest account in English is to be found. The debt owed by latter-day students of modern history to that monumental work cannot well be exaggerated, but the plan of the work, justified by its purpose, gives but little scope for picturesque narration, and requires the student of a particular thread in the skein of world-history to exercise much patience in unravelling it from others. To Sir A. W. Ward, and Professors Alison Phillips and Pollard, who are mainly responsible for the chapters in the *Cambridge Modern History* devoted to Germany since the Congress of Vienna, I have to acknowledge my obligations.

My study of Modern Germany began with a visit to Berlin in the autumn of 1888, soon after the accession of the present Kaiser. A kindly chance gave me exceptional opportunities of seeing and hearing, not so much the fussy, self-important politician, or the domineering, self-satisfied official, whom it is in Germany a crime to criticise, or again the plausible diplomatist, but soldiers, men of affairs, leaders in colonial enterprise, and others who represented the seething mass of middle-class opinion in the capital of Imperial Germany. I recorded the impressions left on my mind in an article published in *Macmillan's Magazine* in April 1889. The article was, it must be confessed, written in an undergraduate vein, but, after pointing out that Berlin was becoming the European centre of disturbance, it ended with these words : ' the military fever and commercial greed, which are at present the stimulating influences in Berlin, have already, on his own confession, forced even Prince Bismarck's hands in East Africa ; and the future is dark indeed, if, encountering less resistance in dealing with his successors, these unlovely forces drag the whole Empire behind them on a career of unscrupulous aggression.'

A desultory but voluminous reading, during the last fourteen years, of German literature, classical and popular, and of historical works, including memoirs, autobiographies and correspondence, treating of the nineteenth century, could not fail to lead to the conviction that the real foundation of modern Germany was laid in the period before Bismarck. The architectural design of the edifice of Empire which he reared was his, and it was part of his greatness that he acted as his own clerk of works in supervising every detail of the work ; but the order to build came rather from the people than their princes, and the people cleared the ground, and dug the foundations on which he set to work. It is a profound mistake to conceive of the German of to-day as representing a peaceful, guileless stock perverted by the evil influence of Bismarck. The German type of to-day, sprung from a stock not as peaceful and guileless as is supposed, was developed in most of its present characteristics between the War of Liberation, 1813, and the Revolution of 1848.

To one who thought it important that now, of all times, this truth should be brought home to the British Public in the most convincing manner, *i.e.* by the testimony of Germans themselves, the obvious resource seemed to be the translation of a German book. There has been during recent years a large output of German works dealing with the revolutionary period, for men's minds, not altogether satisfied with the present, have been turning to the ideals of the past. *The German Revolution,* 1848-1849, by Hans Blum, one of Bismarck's historians, and the son of Robert Blum, the republican leader shot by the Austrians, seemed a useful book for the purpose. The Jubilee edition of this, published in 1898, is remarkable, even among the many admirable German publications of the kind, for the wealth of illustrations and documents in facsimile with which it is garnished. As a means of bringing this somewhat ponderous tome into reasonable compass the idea occurred of making the substance of the book so far as possible a series of quotations from the authorities drawn upon and the documents given by Blum, amplified from my own resources, and connected by a thread of narrative in which I should follow not merely Blum, but also recognised historians with whose writings I was acquainted, notably Ranke, Treitschke, Sybel, and Carl Biedermann. But the work seemed hopeless in view of the shortness of time at one's disposal, and the difficulty of obtaining access to many of the works from which it was desirable to make extracts. However, before the day came when it was impossible to order such books from abroad, I obtained a copy of Dr. Tim Klein's *Der Vorkampf,* a book published early in 1914 in the well-known series *Die Bücher der Rose.* This proved to be a compilation, giving just the sort of documents required, including quotations from many of the books impossible to get hold of, and supplementing the popular broadsheets and ballads given in Blum's work by invaluable additions from the Friedländer Collection in the City Library, Berlin. Dr. Klein is to be congratulated on his keen appreciation of the foibles of his countrymen and the humour of the revolutionary period. I have made free use of both Klein and Blum. In a number of cases where I have

made selections from the same authors as Klein I have given
way to his choice, for it is to be clearly understood that the
immense majority of the citations given in this work are passages
selected by Germans themselves as typical of an event, an
occasion, a temper or a mood ; many of them indeed are to a
German what may be called stock quotations.   Where I have
not been able to obtain access to authorities quoted by Klein,
I have indicated the fact by giving his initial in addition to the
reference.

The endeavour then has been to provide more than a mere
miscellany, and, while making each book, and indeed each
chapter, so far as possible, self-contained, to provide a thread
of narrative and comment that may serve to bind all together.
I venture to indulge the hope that I have not entirely failed to
present even those who are not versed either in the German
language or in German history with a graphic picture of a people,
as well as of a period of national reconstruction, the lessons of
which for ourselves I have at times made bold to suggest.
The appearance, while this book was passing through the press,
of the first instalment of a great scheme of reconstruction on
which our government is understood to be engaged, encourages
the hope that the last paragraph of the Introduction is not
ill-timed.   The new Education Bill promises the long-hoped-for
boon of continued education during adolescence, but at what a
price !   Local authorities are to be reduced to the position of
agents of the central government ; nay more, under the Bill
as drawn, representative bodies elected by the people may, at
the discretion of the State, be supplanted by associations
nominated by the State, the executive is placed above the law,
and a hand steals out to grasp the functions of the legislature
itself.   There will come the usual bland, official *démentis*, the
customary protests from injured innocence, the inevitable suggestions that no points of principle, only points of draftsman-
ship, are involved.   Denials, protests, suggestions, all, humanly
speaking, in good faith !   For the idea undying the bureaucratic system is dazzling enough to blind mere mortal eyes.

It signifies control, wisely administered by a class elect, a lay priesthood with human weaknesses veiled in mystic attributes, and the idea in operation is as subtle, as elusive and, at times, as stupefying as a drug. The Bill may be modified, but if its administrative provisions are a sample of what is in store for us in the general scheme of reconstruction, we may yet see erected in our country the terrible machine of which we have pictures, drawn by German hands, on pages 48, 50 and 85.

A word may be added with regard to the amount of verse which is given. Germans rhyme with a fatal facility. The mass of German political poetry during this period of passion, resentment, and excitement, is great, and much of it is good. Arnold Ruge's *Politische Dichter unserer Zeit*, 1847, has been useful where a poet's complete works have not been accessible. It may be that doggerel, in German, remains doggerel in English, but I hope that the versions given of fine German originals do not wholly traduce them. Generally, of course, the attempt has been made to follow the original metres. The double rhyme, so common in German with its wealth of inflections, one may perhaps be excused from attempting too often in English. But at times the double rhyme is of the very stuff of the poem ; the poem is not the poem without it.

In the comparatively few cases where I have used existing prose translations I have not scrupled to correct obvious lapses, and to modernise spelling, and even forms of expression, where that seemed desirable. My thanks are due for assistance in the work of translation to my sister Miss H. E. Legge of Oxford, to whom is due the spirited rendering of the Viennese revolutionary song À *la Lanterne*, and to my colleagues associated with the work of the Liverpool School of Commerce, and of the School of Languages in particular, Messrs. John Montgomery, R. F. Jones and A. R. Turton. Mr. R. F. Jones has not only rendered great service in unravelling difficult passages, in tracing more recondite allusions, and in providing several apt illustrations, he has also placed at my disposal his unfinished translation of Fichte's *Reden*, which some day, it may be hoped, release from military duty will enable him to complete. Mr. John Montgomery has been generous of his assistance in the general work of translation. Many of the verse translations are due to him, and without the reinforcement of his happy gift the work could not have been completed. His help has been invaluable.

My thanks are also due to Messrs. T. and T. Clark of Edinburgh for permission to use Dr. Hastie's translation of Kant's *Philosophy of Law*, to Messrs. G. Bell and Sons and Professor Dyde, of Robertson College, Edmonton, Canada, for permission to use the latter's translation of Hegel's *Philosophy of Right*, to Mr. John Murray for permission to print certain letters from *Queen Victoria's Letters*, to Messrs. Doubleday, Page and Company of New York for permission to make excerpts from *The Reminiscences of Carl Schurz*, and to my publishers for permission to print a long extract from Wagner's *Autobiography*.

Since the work is, in a measure, an enterprise associated with the School of Languages in Liverpool, it is a pious act to inscribe it to the memory of one of the School's keenest students, a business man, whose interests outside his business were the School and his duties as a Territorial officer, who did his day's work at his office and learnt three languages in his evenings, and who, when the call came, made the supreme sacrifice for his country. Had he lived, his genial interest in the work would have been a constant source of encouragement. But his type will persist, and, in the new England of our hopes, may there be many another of his honest sort !

J. G. LEGGE.

LIVERPOOL, 14th October 1917.

CONTENTS

BOOK I

GATHERING CLOUDS

1813-1830

CHAPTER I

FREDERICK WILLIAM THE THIRD'S PROMISE OF A CONSTITUTION—
THE WARTBURG FESTIVAL

CHAPTER II

THE MURDER OF KOTZEBUE

CHAPTER III

THE CARLSBAD DECREES—GÖRRES' ATTACK ON REACTION

CONTENTS

CHAPTER III

HEGEL, THE APOSTLE OF BUREAUCRACY

CHAPTER IV

PRUSSIA AS THE HOPE OF GERMANY—THE HAMBACH FESTIVAL

CHAPTER V

THE SECRET CONFERENCES AT VIENNA—THE GERMAN RAILWAY SYSTEM

CHAPTER VI

POLITICAL POETRY OF THE THIRTIES

BOOK III
The Roaring Forties

CHAPTER I
ACCESSION OF FREDERICK WILLIAM IV

CHAPTER II
FOREIGN COMPLICATIONS

CHAPTER III
SOCIAL CONDITIONS AT HOME

CHAPTER IV
PHILOSOPHY AND THE MOB

CONTENTS

CHAPTER VII

THE KING'S HUMILIATION

CHAPTER VIII

THE KING DRINKS THE DREGS

BOOK V

THE FIRST GERMAN PARLIAMENT

1848

CHAPTER I

THE PRELIMINARY PARLIAMENT—HECKER'S REBELLION IN BADEN

CHAPTER II

OPENING OF THE NATIONAL ASSEMBLY

CHAPTER III

ELECTION OF ARCHDUKE JOHN AS REGENT

CHAPTER IV

DEBATES ON FUNDAMENTAL RIGHTS, ON POLAND, AND
ON HECKER'S ELECTION

CHAPTER V

THE BUILDING FESTIVAL AT COLOGNE, AND THE LIGHTER
SIDE OF LIFE IN THE NATIONAL ASSEMBLY

CHAPTER IV

CONFUSION IN AUSTRIA AND VIENNA THROUGHOUT SPRING AND SUMMER

CHAPTER V

THE REVOLUTION IN VIENNA

CHAPTER VI

THE MAILED FIST IN VIENNA AND IN HUNGARY

BOOK VII

THE LAST ACT

1849

CHAPTER I

THE NATIONAL ASSEMBLY ELECTS A GERMAN KAISER

CONTENTS

CHAPTER II

FREDERICK WILLIAM REJECTS THE IMPERIAL CROWN

CHAPTER III

SUPPRESSION OF THE NATIONAL ASSEMBLY

CHAPTER IV

THE REVOLUTION IN DRESDEN

CHAPTER V

THE FINAL REVOLUTION IN BADEN

CORRIGENDA

Page x. l. 35: for "undying" read "underlying."

„ xi. l. 13: for "*Dichter*" read "*Lyriker*."

„ 40 l. 19: insert "not" before "only."

„ 237 l. 9: for "March" read "February."

„ 255 l. 1: for "prize" read "prise."

RHYME AND REVOLUTION IN GERMANY

INTRODUCTION

THE history of Germany since the War of Liberation in 1813, when the German peoples rose as one nation to shake off the yoke of Napoleon, may be conceived of as a vast trilogy, the subject of which is more tremendous even than that of Thomas Hardy's *Dynasts*. The first part dramatically complete is that which covers the period between 1813 and 1850, the period during which the consciousness of Germans in every German state was roused to the need of national unity and constitutional government, and a contest raged between the peoples and their princes for the redemption of promises made by the latter while still shivering under the Napoleonic terror, and repudiated by them as soon as they began to recover strength and courage. The struggle failed to achieve German unity on a popular basis, but did achieve a certain measure of constitutional reform. The second part covers the Bismarckian regime, when the constitutional strife died down, but by blood and iron a German unity was achieved, a lesser German unity, for the German provinces of Austria were deliberately excluded. Moreover the basis was not popular but dynastic, with one dynastic rod, the Hohenzollern, turned serpent, and devouring the others. The third great drama is now unrolling itself before our eyes.

This work covers the first of these periods, and is an attempt to give a sketch of the history of the period between 1813 and 1850. The historical passages and the comments connecting the various documents quoted form but the mere framework within which Germans speak and act for themselves. Little more indeed has been done by the English author than to provide, as it were, a series of stage directions, which give for the various actors and speakers the setting necessary for an

A

understanding of their characters and the purport of what they do or say. His purpose is accomplished if a true and lively picture of a lively time is presented by the German people themselves. It may be claimed that an understanding of this period is vital if Englishmen are to appreciate the magnitude of the problems involved in the issues of the present war. They will realise that it was during this period, and not under the Bismarckian regime, that the German character as we see it displayed to-day was really formed. They will realise, moreover, that they have before them the spectacle of a great nation under reconstruction, and that Great Britain and the British Empire, now on the threshold of an era of social, industrial, and political reconstruction, have much to learn from a study of Germany's portentous efforts successful and unsuccessful, good and bad.

Here, in this work, is offered evidence enough to enable any English reader, even though he knows not a word of German, to make up his own mind as to what the German is. The bombastic utterances of the present Kaiser excite our mingled disgust and derision. We learn in these pages that the gift is a hereditary one, nay, more, that it is a national one. His great-uncle, Frederick William IV., with intellectual gifts superior to his, had an exalted eloquence no less remarkable. Read the speeches and letters of his that are given in profusion, and admire the fantastic figure of this most gifted of his race. For a specimen of the courtly jargon common in Germany turn to page 168, and laugh at Hoffmann's skit upon it, which shows that Germans of a past generation could laugh at it with us. For demagogic talent of the same bombastic sort turn to Siebenpfeiffer's speech on page 107, and to the extracts from the *Text-book of Demagogy* to be found on page 441, which may cheer the jaded journalist with fresh suggestion. There is evidence enough of the kinship of Kaiser and people in speech and thought.

The two, speech and thought, cannot be separated ; and sympathise as we may with the constitutional struggle of the German people from 1813, when they, and not their princes, delivered their country from a foreign yoke, we cannot fail to detect in the swelling phrases of their leaders in the council-chamber, on the platform and in the study, the underlying thought of insolent domination. They were a strong people ;

they were conscious of their strength ; they realised how their strength was rendered ineffective by want of unity. They were also a speculative people, and their thoughts dwelt with insistence on what the German people could be and could do, were the German people one. Their politicians, their philosophers and their poets taught them *Deutschland, Deutschland über Alles,* and so Freedom to them came to imply dominion over others. Unity and constitutional government were but stepping-stones to preponderance in the world's counsels. In the debate in the National Assembly at Frankfort on the question as to who was to be over-lord of United Germany, Dahlmann, grim oracle of truth and a man entitled to all respect, declared in his speech (page 511) in favour of a Hohenzollern Kaiser : ' The path of power is the only one that will appease and satisfy the fermenting passion for freedom, a passion that has hitherto not recognised its own nature ; for it is not only freedom it desires, it is power, the greater half, which it has hitherto lacked, for which it craves.' It will be news to most of us that in the forties of last century Germany was aflame for a fleet, and that Germans were nursing jealousy of ourselves (page 159), that Prussian officials were already hugging the idea of a Colonial Empire, and news to most Americans that as a step to that end the purchase of California from Mexico (page 162) was under consideration. Why not ? Why should not Germans expand as others have done and are doing ? It is the spirit that matters, the spirit in which a nation expands. The spirit of insolent domination must go ; the spirit of hate must be exorcised. And let any one who doubts that Germans have been reared on hate as a virtue read the evidence adduced on page 208, and the following pages.

Of what German and Austrian fanaticism and brutality are capable the amateur of murder as a fine art will find much to shock him in the graphic accounts of the murders of Kotzebue (page 33), of Lichnowsky and Auerswald (page 417), of Count Lamberg (page 477), of Latour (page 481), and of Pastor Weidig (page 116), for this last was the most refined murder of all. Too numerous to quote are the examples of military, official, and bureaucratic arrogance and cruelty ; this work is full of them. But we learn incidentally how the German universities, once the home of freedom (as understood in Germany), have become the strongholds of reaction in politics, and the tame servants of the bureaucratic state. We read, to the confusion of the well-regulated municipal mind, how a young Prussian lieutenant felt entitled to damn mayors and town-clerks. We learn too how Prussians can treat their own flesh and blood (page 307) and, from the testimony of Gottfried Keller, a Swiss and a neutral, how the Baden rebels, in July 1849, killed their own wounded to prevent their falling into the hands of the Prussians (page 564).

A study of this period will give us a clue to the understanding of one of the most astonishing revelations of the present war, viz. the prodigious extent of a system of intrigue without parallel in history, a system laboriously devised and ruthlessly applied, foul and unscrupulous in its choice of methods and means, inhuman in its contempt of that law of hospitality which from time immemorial has rendered possible the intercourse of man with man, of nation with nation. The Central Powers have been a nest of intrigue, espionage, bribery and corruption for a century ; Prussia intriguing against Austria, Austria against Prussia, over the *Zollverein*, over the German hegemony; the other German kingdoms and the lesser states dealing in secret with one, and then with the other, or with both at the same time ; princes and their bureaucratic bodyguard conspiring against their subjects, their subjects conspiring against them ; German exiles scheming and plotting, with paid German spies from the Fatherland in their midst. It was a vast and well-drilled army of which Bismarck took control, and developed on a grander scale, until he succeeded in bribing a German king with £15,000 a year, and at least attempted to buy a majority in a foreign parliament with £50,000 of Prussian bonds.[1] His successors have probably paid higher, and sunk lower.

There is a lighter side to the book. Apart from examples of Hoffmann von Fallersleben's genial satire, there are specimens of the pawky humour of Berlin, which show the existence there of a precious quality much needed to redress the balance against the ruthlessness of the official machine, the sentimentality of enthusiasts, and the turgid eloquence of demagogues and philosophers alike. That quality existed in Berlin up to the middle of the last century, and it would be a useful exercise to trace what became of it during the Bismarckian period. Of stories against the censorship few equal that told on page 564 of

[1] Lord Acton's *Historical Essays and Studies*, pp. 204, 214.

the sapient individual who ruled that no ' author ' could legiti-
mately be described as an ' authority.' What a racy impression
too we get of many a revolutionary hero, notably of Michael
Bakunin, the Russian !

In the full account given of the first German parliament it
will be seen that caricature and satire played their human part.
But the chief value of this section of the book lies in the opportunity it affords for studying the German in a setting so familiar
to us as that of the parliamentary stage, with the limelight on
face and figure, the sense of self-importance which it develops
in the actors, the ' make-up ' in dress, facial expression, carriage
and gesture which it encourages in the public men who bear the
burdens of state, and are grave with a responsibility for secrets,
guilty and innocent, not vouchsafed to ordinary men, nor even
to all journalists.

To many readers, however, the culminating interest will lie
in the full account given in Book IV. of the actual revolution
in Berlin in March, 1848. They will find there contemporary
accounts, by eye-witnesses of and participants in the struggle,
of the fierce fighting at the barricades, of the humiliation of
Frederick William IV., and of the flight to London of the Prince
of Prussia, later the ' hero-Kaiser,' William I. The spectacle
of a Hohenzollern eating dirt as if he liked it is more than we
may be prepared for, and even unofficial and liberal German
historians, for all their courage and conscientiousness, have
generally shrunk from telling the story down to the last degrading detail. Here, however, are authentic accounts of the
present Kaiser's great-uncle riding through the streets of Berlin
with the revolutionary colours round his arm, making bombastic
speeches of congratulation to the rebels, and paying homage,
with bared head, to the mutilated corpses of the men whom his
soldiers, in his defence, had shot down. True that he played
the rogue, on the scale that kings and statesmen have played
the rogue before him, but no king and few statesmen have played
the coward in the conspicuous fashion of this Hohenzollern.
And yet, as we read the flaming lines of Freiligrath's ' The Dead
to the Living,' do we think only of a stupid German mob and
a craven German king ? Must not the sudden thought come
home to us that some day our dead will speak to our politicians,
and to ourselves ?

This book is to be read in no Pharisaic spirit. It has many

lessons for us. When we realise *quantae molis erat Germanam condere gentem*, and when we realise the nature of the people who accomplished that stupendous task, we shall appreciate better the quality of the enemy we are battering down, and the gigantic task before us even when the walls of this Jericho have fallen, a double task, to secure guarantees for reform in Germany and to set our own house in order. No candid mind can ponder over German weaknesses as they reveal themselves in this book without an uncomfortable feeling that many of them are our own. The brilliant satires and epigrams of which the book contains not a few hit us at times as well as their German objects. The same sort of talk goes on, not quite so strident perhaps, in parliament and congresses here as went on in the first German parliament and congresses (page 435) there ; the type of Herr Piepmeyer (page 406) flourishes here as there. The cry for the ' great man ' (page 436), and the hysterical welcome of the supposed great man, are to be heard here as there. And when qualities and not defects are under review we shall find something to envy. What English stateman excels, in the very qualities we admire, the great Stein ? Read what he has to say on bureaucratic rule (page 50). What English soldier ever united strength with tactfulness more successfully than ' old Wrangel ' in the pacification of Berlin ? What Englishman ever said a finer word on freedom of the press than Bunsen's quoted on page 176 ? Are there not great and fine qualities, for all its crudity, in Adolf von Zerzog's letter to his son (page 423) ? Does it not recall at least the temperament of an old fox-hunting English squire, a patron of the prize-ring maybe, but honest, just, and generous, never afraid to strike a blow with the naked fist when honour and humanity are at stake ? Does any plain Englishman to-day prefer the type of the Conscientious Objector to that ? Are not men such as Uhland, Heinrich von Gagern, Ludolf Camphausen, Victor von Unruh and Carl Mathy akin in tone and temper to the best men of their kind whom we can produce ?

Let us repeat that the task the German peoples have been in stages accomplishing, gigantic though it be, is not greater than the one confronting our race to-day, the form and content of the British Empire after the War, the social, economic, and political conditions which we are to lay down for ourselves after the War. We shall do well to study the vicissitudes of the

German struggle, the varying conditions of a settlement or what seemed a settlement at this stage or at that, the characteristics of the protagonists, and of the rank and file. From such a study will emerge the silent moral and economic forces that are irresistible, and that ultimately determine human destinies, however brilliant the diversion effected for a time by the will-power or the cunning of king, statesman, or soldier.

On the German side there is this to be said, viz., that there has been of recent years a growing discontent in Germany with a political system which provides no government responsible to the people. We have mentioned the great output of literature on the subject of the revolutionary period. The object of much of that literature has been to spread throughout the country the truth about the constitutional struggle between 1813 and 1850, and to drive home the lesson that all has not yet been won in the domain of politics which men strove for then. Take the case of Carl Biedermann's popular but scholarly histories that cover the period, and have served the author of the present work in good stead. Though they are clearly written from the liberal point of view, they are admitted by German critics to be impartial and reliable authorities. In the preface to the earlier one, published in 1881, there is not a word said of latter-day discontent. But in the other, the preface, dated 1889, contains this significant sentence : ' Certainly to-day, when so many are dissatisfied with our political conditions and complain of " retrogression," " oppression," and the like, one may well refer them to the stage of our development that followed 1818 ! Then may they learn what " reaction " really is, and be forced to acknowledge, if they are honest, how much better off we are to-day.' Then proceed to Klein's compilation, of which, again, so much use has been made in the present work. The book was published in the spring of 1914, a few months before the outbreak of war. In a note printed—characteristically enough printed on the slip-cover, not in the book itself—the author states its purpose thus : ' We neglect a duty both of gratitude and of national pride so long as we misjudge or allow to remain suspect a movement which is damned to-day by some as " insolent rebellion " or disowned as " the German shame," and by others unreasonably extolled, even in its excesses, while current historical text-books treat it as a rule with the brevity of embarrassment. This movement was not, in point of fact, the cause of a "radical party," not the cause of "blood-thirsty conspirators," not the cause of "impractical professors"—it was the cause of the best of the German people in overwhelming majority. It touched all, as it still touches all to-day. For it was the fore-fight for German Unity and Freedom.'

At the end of the book, after some bitter words on the reaction that followed the restoration of the Federal Diet in 1851, he hails the rising of Bismarck's star. And he goes on : ' Bismarck had passionately fought the revolution because it seemed to him to shake the foundations of the state founded by Frederick the Great, which he saw to be destined at that very moment to fulfil its high mission for Germany. Bismarck's way was the way of might. His genius and his audacity assumed the right, first of forcing back the popular movement with its "ideas born on the nation's heights," and then of guiding them on the road he had himself chosen. He accepted those ideas, and in the edifice of empire which he reared gave them the place which is their due for all time. But with might and wealth alone the German is not to be satisfied. The highest political possessions are and remain for him, as for his fathers, might tempered with justice, and unity with freedom.'

Klein's book was designed to be a popular book, and we may presume that his views in the winter of 1913-14 were shared by many thousands of the middle-class in Germany. The embers of the old fire of 1848 were still smouldering, and it depends on the result of the present war whether these embers are fanned into a flame or not. Whatever be the fate of the Hapsburg and the Hohenzollern dynasties, whatever the degree to which militarism is discredited, we may count on this much at least, that the people's sufferings in Germany and Austria will nerve them to accomplish what they failed to do in 1848, and to secure a system of government responsible to parliament and the people.

Parliament ! What of our own situation to-day ? An Englishman living in a year when the constitution has been virtually suspended, obeying laws made by a Long Parliament, whose members from time to time co-opt themselves for a further spell of acquiescence in ministerial and quasi-ministerial government, does not utter the word ' parliament ' with the same bland confidence as of yore. And if we leave out of account the peculiarity at the moment of the parliamentary position, which is supposed to be rendered necessary by the state of war, there still remains room for doubt whether the House of Commons, as it stood in the early summer of 1914, was playing anything like the part in the government of the country that it did twenty-five years, or fifty years ago. Bound up with this is the further question whether the power of the cabinet has been growing at the expense of parliament, and the two questions together lead up to one of tremendous importance : is the goal a cabinet autocracy in alliance with a bureaucracy that has been forming itself on the Prussian model ? Few persons not in some way associated with the central or local administration of government in this country realise to what an extent, of quite recent years, the poison of the Prussian system had permeated Whitehall before the war, and how surely the franchises of local government, one of the bulwarks of English liberty, were being sacrificed to aggrandise a bureaucrary of the very sort denounced by Stein a hundred years ago. It will be strange indeed if, after this war, in which the nation has risen as did universal Germany in 1813, we find that our constitutional development of more than a thousand years has landed us where Germany stood in 1813, with an apparatus of government like that against which Germans fought in vain, and died, in 1848.

BOOK I
GATHERING CLOUDS
1813-1830

CHAPTER I

FREDERICK WILLIAM THE THIRD'S PROMISE OF A CONSTITUTION—THE WARTBURG FESTIVAL

In 1813, at the close of the War of Liberation, the various German peoples were in a mood of high enthusiasm, such as ours may possibly be when the present great war is over. They had risen as one great people, and, in alliance with Russia and ourselves, shaken off the yoke which Napoleon had fastened upon them. They had risen spontaneously, and had the proud consciousness that it was they themselves, and not their princes, who had wrought salvation. It was they who had roused their princes, not their princes who had animated them ; it was they who had saved their princes' names ; they had, as a caricature of the period indicates, dragged their princes from under the table, set them on their feet, patted them on the back, and when the great Stein and Marshal Yorck, of English stock, by audacious *coups de main*, diplomatic and military, had forced their princes' hands, offered themselves freely as the stuff which the genius of Scharnhorst and of Gneisenau should weave into the web of victory. They, the peoples of Germany acting as one people, had triumphed, and hearts beat high as the twofold prospect unfolded itself of (1) unity, whereby the German peoples should now at last weld their thirty-eight separate governments into one, and (2) freedom, freedom at home, whereby having shaken off a foreign tyrant they should free themselves from absolutism and the tyranny of their own princes, and secure the blessings of constitutional government. That freedom some felt they owned by right, the right based on Rousseau's social contract between prince and people, others, little worried by philosophical theories or political formulas, felt that they had earned.

There was bitter disappointment in store for all their enthusiasm. The Congress of Vienna in 1815, which was to bring about a millennium, did little more as regards Germany and Austria than stereotype monarchical and territorial conditions as they obtained at a moment when princes and soldiers and those ' honest brokers,' the diplomats, had done their best or worst. ' Men had promised themselves,' wrote Friedrich von Gentz, ' an all-embracing reform of the political system of Europe, guarantees for peace ; in one word, the return of the Golden Age. The Congress has resulted in nothing but restorations, which had been already effected by arms . . . ; quite arbitrary alterations in the possessions of the less important states ; but in no act of a higher nature, no great measure for public order or for the universal good, which might compensate mankind for its long sufferings, or reassure it as to the future.' [1]

A German Federation was established, with a diet sitting at Frankfort, a twofold diet, an inner and an outer diet, both representing princes and their entourage of ministers, not the people, with Austria presiding over each. This was the substitute for unity, for the National State, offered to German enthusiasm. The scheme betrayed the hand not of a Stein who had more than any German the qualities of a Chatham, but of Metternich, the arch-manipulator, who balanced states and kingdoms for over thirty years as other politicians have balanced parties, who believed in the absolutism of princes as others believe in that of Cabinets or the bureaucracy, who had no scruple in using every means of repression, secrecy, the censorship and the police, and who doubtless was regarded up to the moment of his sudden fall in 1848 as indispensable. The old particularism was buttressed by absolutism ; neither unity nor freedom could be achieved save by the gracious condescension, the self-abnegation of thirty-eight or thirty-nine independent German princes, and behind all lowered the grim menace of Austrian and Prussian rivalry for the hegemony of Germany, the German question which gradually emerged above all others and was not to be settled until 1866.

Among German poets one seer discerned the troubles and the struggle of the future before the settlement of Vienna had come into effect, the stalwart Swabian, Uhland, first and perhaps greatest of German political poets of the period, and one free from the brutal arrogance and spirit of hate that

[1] *Cambridge Modern History*, x. p. 2.

give a taint of sulphur to the bombastic speeches of Kaiser and
demagogue and the writings of poets, historians, and journalists
all through the half-century. In October, 1815, he began one
of his rousing odes with the lines

> ' The nations' warfare now is over,
>   From foreign foe the land is free,
> But yet our fields, though free, discover
>   Signs of the earlier tyranny ;
> As men dig up in desert places
>   Statues of hero and of god,
> Of sacred rights we 'll find the traces
>   Tho' hid beneath the trampled sod.'

No finer or more exalted illustrations can be given of the feelings
that animated the popular leaders who strove to fan the flame
of true German patriotism and national feeling, of democratic
right, in the first days of disillusionment, than Uhland's odes,
every line like the clink of hammer on anvil. Examples will
be given in the next few pages. German poets, even those
whose reputations have extended far beyond the limits of
German-speaking peoples, have studied the *volkstümlich*, the
popular, more assiduously perhaps than any poets of high
standing save the Scottish, and the success of German political
poetry is largely due to this quality in singers such as Arndt,
Uhland, and Hoffmann von Fallersleben, author of *Deutschland,
Deutschland über Alles*. The same quality distinguishes many
of the patriotic war songs of the Napoleonic period, and student
songs of all times ; and the dignity compounded of simplicity
and directness of appeal which has given such poetry its popularity and power in Germany is hard to match in France, Italy,
and our own country, even at a time of stress. True, few
countries have gone through so long a period of stress, when
national feelings are strung up to the pitch of resonance, as did
Germany during the first half of last century ; what in the way
of soul-stirring verse may be born for the Belgians, the French,
and ourselves out of the present crisis we have yet to see in its
fulness.

Each German people, not the German nation as a whole, had
to carry on its own struggle for constitutional freedom ; this
book will illustrate in the main the struggle in Prussia, but
enough will be given to show how the same fight went on in
Austria and all over Germany. Advantage had been taken by

Stein, and other liberal-minded statesmen, of the collapse of Frederick William III. and his military and official bodyguard before Napoleon, to free Prussia from many of the vestiges of feudal tyranny, notably oppressive land laws and even serfdom. Modern Germans, who point the finger of scorn at Russia where serfdom was abolished in 1861, may fairly be reminded that this is little more than fifty years later than the abolition of serfdom in Prussia ! Stein's was too noble a nature to win appreciation from so small-minded a man as Frederick William III., the present Kaiser's great-grandfather, and his benign influence was withdrawn too soon from Prussian affairs. But his collaborator and successor, Hardenberg, an aristocrat who combined with a good deal more than Fox's libertinage much of his liberal sentiment, continued his work. As Prussian Chancellor he attended Frederick William at Vienna in 1815 and induced him even there and then to issue an Order in Council promising representative government to his excited people.   This took the following form : [1]

1. A Representation of the People shall be formed. . . .
3. The Assembly representing the country shall be selected from the Provincial Diets, and shall have its seat in Berlin.
4. The authority of the country's Representatives extends to Deliberation upon all matters of legislation which affect the rights of person and property, including taxation.
5. Without loss of time a Commission, which is to be composed of sagacious State-officials and Persons domiciled in the Provinces, is to be established in Berlin. . . .
7. The Commission shall meet on the 1st September of the present year.

Given under our Royal Hand and Seal, Vienna, the 22nd May 1815.

FRIEDRICH WILHELM.
C. FÜRST VON HARDENBERG.

Thus was confirmed the manifesto issued by Frederick William III. and his brother princes at Kalisch, in 1813, after Napoleon's defeat in Russia, calling the German people to arms, and promising them a new national unity and a constitutional form of government.

The royal deliverance cheered not Prussians only, but Germans generally, for the Prussian government was well known to be as absolutist in sentiment as the Austrian.   The promise

[1] Klein.

of representative government was clear enough, a promise to be redeemed ' at no distant date,' to use a time-dishonoured parliamentary term. But it was the failure of the Hohenzollerns to redeem that promise, made in 1815, that led to the Revolution in Berlin in 1848. Months passed in Prussia without any step being taken by the king to give effect to his words ; in other German states the situation was similar. One can imagine the saturnine smile on Metternich's lips when he heard such promises made, and when they recurred to his mind as time rolled on. The people were lulled by them at first, and their supineness roused Uhland to his indignant remonstrance against princes and their peoples for their apparent forgetfulness of what the struggle of 1813 and the crowning mercy of Leipzig ought to have meant for Germany. In the autumn of 1816 he published a scornful appeal to all classes and all German states :

ON 18TH OCTOBER 1816

If now a Spirit from Heaven descended,
    A hero and a singer too,
One who a holy cause defended,
    And fell as happy warriors do ;
He 'd sing a song to make us wonder,
    Sharp-edged, as who a sword should swing,
A song of Heaven and loud as thunder,
    Not such as I should feebly sing.

' Time was you spoke of church-bells ringing,
    Of bonfires blazing far and wide,
But what the message joy was bringing,
    Is there a soul can now decide ?
'Tis well that I from Heaven descended,
    In hope the highest to achieve,
And wounded hands to all extended,
    That they might touch them and believe.

Speak first, ye princes here assembled,
    Have you forgot that day of fight,
When beaten to your knees you trembled
    And bowed before a higher might ?
To save your fame the people rallied,
    They proved them loyal to the core,
Therefore 'tis yours, who still have dallied,
    To grant them now what once you swore.

B

And you, ye peoples sorely stricken,
  Have you forgot that fiery day,
The noblest day that pulse could quicken ?
  Why should its grace so soon decay ?
You trod the foreign hordes to powder,
  But here at home is no more light,
And Freedom rears her head no prouder ;
  You 'stablished not the freeman's right !

To you, ye wise, be this imparted,
  Since all you 'd have in black and white,
That lowly men and simple-hearted
  With blood bought what was theirs by right.
Think you that in the furnace glowing
  Our Phœnix-age is born anew,
To hatch from eggs of your bestowing
  Another busy brood like you ?

Courtiers and counsellors, with orders
  That flicker dim on breasts so cold,
Since of the fight on Leipzig's borders
  Even to this day you 've not been told,
Now learn from me how God Almighty
  Came down for that great Judgment Day—
You listen not, to ears so flighty
  No ghostly voice may win its way.

I 've sung the song that earthward brought me,
  And back to Heaven my thoughts aspire,
All that my stay with men has taught me
  I 'll tell to the celestial quire ;
No boast be mine, no curse malignant !
  Though little comfort I descry,
Yet many an eye flashed forth indignant,
  And many a heart I heard beat high.'

This was followed in 1817 by an appeal to the members of
the Würtemberg Diet, the first and third verses of which might
have been sung at every recruiting meeting in our own country
during the first eighteen months of this war :

TO THE DIET

Again the judgment scales are trembling,
  The old, old strife again is born,
The great Assize is now assembling,
  Will separate from chaff the corn ;
On this side and on that are parted
  Now and for aye truth and deceit,
The coward and the lion-hearted,
  The half-man and the man complete.

No Highness shall that style inherit,
  Save one who high example sets,
And rank as knight but he shall merit,
  Who ne'er his knightly word forgets ;
Mid priests, His Reverence we 'll hail him
  Whose spirit ranges free as light ;
No rights as citizen shall fail him
  Who for his land has learnt to fight.

Quit you like men for honour's guerdon,
  Stand up and make the manly choice,
Lest friends but curse you for a burden,
  And foemen mock you and rejoice.
Enough of haggling and of dealing,
  Of speeches that like rivers run,
Enough of writing and of sealing,
  Speak one word more, and then have done.

And if you fail in high endeavour,
  Find refuge in the People's heart,
For who his rights surrenders never
  May feel he plays the hero's part.
O strong, who in this truth confideth :
  'Tis Freedom's light proclaims the day,
And God Himself the sun who guideth
  On its unhalting, changeless way.

In the same year he wrote his famous *Nachruf*, a call that may ring in German ears once more :

A CALL

There is no prince so high in station,
  So high-elect none formed of clay,
That when for freedom thirsts a nation,
  A royal hand its thirst can stay.
Is one alone with greedy fingers
  The riches of all rights to grasp,
While, for a dole, the people lingers
  Till slow the royal fist unclasp ?

Favours may wait on princes' pleasure,
  Our rights are of the common good,
All sons of earth own this one treasure
  That thrills them like the heart's warm blood.
And were we now, as freemen, risen
  To pledge our honour, hand in hand,
Our in-born rights would burst their prison,
  And on that oath take firm their stand.

The oath we swear one to another
    Will lay our rights' foundation sure ;
That bond more close than love of brother
    'Twixt Prince and People shall endure.
Soft hands may rock in princely houses
    The cradles of the princely born,
But none the King's right first espouses
    Till he the People's right has sworn.

Tho' bitter foes around assail us,
    This truth invincible shall stand.
The warrior's wreath that shall avail us
    Is woven with victory for a strand.
And as the ensign saves from capture
    The flag wound round his bleeding breast,
Let us, through tears, behold with rapture
    The rights for which we pledge our best.

No herald shall this message flourish
    With beat of drum and trumpet-call,
But time the seed we sow will nourish
    Mid German peoples great and small :
There 's none so wise our rights can banish,
    No ease so soft can take their place,
From Swabian hearts will never vanish
    The rights, the oath we once embrace.

These appeals seemed, perhaps, to fall on deaf ears, but the
leaven was none the less at work, and in no class more actively
than among the constituencies of the universities, students
and professors alike.   The part played by the universities
both of Germany and Austria all through the troubled period
leading up to the Revolution of 1848, and during the Revolution
itself, is surprising to an Englishman, who knows of our universities giving birth to nothing more exciting than a Tractarian
Movement in England, or a heresy hunt in Scotland.   But the
German universities had played a leading part in the War of
Liberation ; in lecture-room, platforms and benches had alike
been deserted ; even Froebel, godfather of the modern infant
school, shouldered a musket and fought for his country ; and
records may be searched in vain for the name of a single conscientious objector.   The young intellectuals and not a few of
their professors came back with a passion for unity and freedom,
politics became a fever with them, and nothing says more for
Prussian and Hohenzollern craftiness than the skill with which
a force so ardent, which up to 1848 was against absolutism and

bureaucracy, was after that date converted into one of the main buttresses of the Hohenzollerns and the Prussian system. It will be curious to note in years to come the effect of the Great War on our own universities : they have responded as nobly now as the German universities did then. When our young intellectuals, and their tutors and professors, come home, what will be their view of the government of our empire ?

It was from the young intellectuals of Germany in 1818 that the first shock was to come for Metternich, the King of Prussia, and German princes generally. In 1815 the *Burschenschaft*, a great Students' Union, was formed, with branches in every German university. Its object was to substitute a pan-German organisation for the clubs which had hitherto split up the students into their various German ' nations.' The leader of the movement was Jahn, a hero of the War of Liberation who set himself to regenerate the youth of Germany, physically by gymnastics (*turnen*) and spiritually by politics ; he was, indeed, the founder of German gymnastics, and earned the affectionate soubriquet of Turnvater Jahn. He suffered, as will be seen later, for his temerity in giving the Government a lead. The colours of the Union, sufficiently indicating its political complexion, were, in distinction from the Prussian black and white, the old German colours, black, red, and gold, which Jahn interpreted, with the true German instinct for swelling phrases, as signifying ' out of the black night of slavery through bloody strife to the golden dawn of freedom.' On 19th October 1817, at the Wartburg, the scene of Luther's encounter with the devil, was held a great students' festival, to celebrate jointly the Reformation and the battle of Leipzig. The account of the proceedings which is here given was published by a Jena professor, Lorenz Oken as he called himself, thus mitigating the crudeness of his original name, Ockenfuss. He edited a paper called *Isis*, in which, among encyclopædic matter of scientific interest, he inserted political items which might not otherwise see the light of day. The number containing this account of the Wartburg proceedings was confiscated by the authorities and destroyed, and copies became of extreme rarity. Indeed, the grandson of Brockhaus, the publisher of the sheet, states in his life of his grandfather that he had never been able to set eyes on a copy. Facsimiles, however, will be found in Hans Blum's jubilee edition of his history of the German

Revolution and many other illustrated commentaries on the period.

THE STUDENTS' FESTIVAL ON THE WARTBURG

Assured of the permission of His Royal Highness, our Grand Duke, the authorities and citizens of Eisenach took all necessary measures to make cheap, comfortable and agreeable the visit of the students who thronged to the sacred festival. They were quartered in the town for three days, the 17th, 18th and 19th October; the Hall of the Knights in the Wartburg was bedecked with wreaths, and provided with tables and benches to seat seven hundred to eight hundred men. Such was the total number present at the midday meal on the day of victory, the rest of us included. Representatives had come from Berlin, Erlangen, Giessen, Göttingen, Halle, Heidelberg, Jena, Kiel, Leipzig, Marburg, Rostock, Tübingen and Würzburg.

On the 19th at 9 A.M. the students, who had assembled in the market-place, marched to the Castle, banners and a band at their head. We accompanied them. Of the professors who had this festival at heart, who saw in it the germ of some great and fruitful tree, and had come designedly to judge, from the proceedings, the students' conduct, and events that passed, what might be expected of its blossoming, there were four of us, Fries,[1] Kieser, Schweitzer and myself. We were shown to a place opposite the speakers. When general silence was obtained a student delivered a speech on very much the following lines : he spoke of the aim of this assembly of educated young men from all circles and all races of the German Fatherland ; of the thwarted life of the past ; of the rebound, and the ideal that now possessed the German people ; of hopes that had failed and been deceived ; of the vocation of the student and the legitimate expectations which the fatherland founded upon it ; of the destitution and even persecution to which a youth devoting himself to science had to submit ; finally, how they must themselves take thought to introduce among them order, rule, and custom, in a word, student-form, must earnestly and together take thought for the ways and means of facing worthily the duties of their calling, to divert in their direction the regard, at once comforted and encouraging, of grown up people who unfortunately could attain to nothing more themselves, and to be to them in days to come what they would that young men should be. The audience, and we men among them, were moved to tears, tears of shame that we had not so acted, of pain in that we were cause of such distress, of joy over this intellectual message, so beautiful, so pure, so clear, joy too for that we had so brought up our sons that they should one day win the victory where we in our folly had failed.

By one and another further encouraging speeches were delivered,

---

[1] For Hegel's savage attack on Fries see page 91.

and then the company made for the courtyard of the Castle until the tables were spread. There they formed themselves into groups large and small, some moving about, others standing still. . . .

In one of the groups a speech of the following tenor was delivered : Dear friends, you must not let this moment of emotion and exaltation pass in smoke. It will not return. Now or never must you be united. You must not let the matter rest at mere emotion, you must not allow any one to depart from the Wartburg without taking some real possession with him. . . . What is the situation now ? What have we gained ? Are our relations different from what they were before ? Are the ' nations ' dissolved ? Are we members of a greater society ? Does each of us only represent the Students' Union of his individual university, or do we together form branches of a universal German Students' Union ? Have we pledged ourselves thereto ? Have we laws and regulations determining our pledge ? . . .

Therefore must you give the students a handsel. Only a few laws, but if you want them in words—all students are one ; they all belong to one single nation, the German ; they all follow the same precepts and customs. . . . The university man, come he whence he may, can find occupation and a position in Austria, Prussia, Bavaria, Hanover, Saxony, in Swabia, Franconia, Thuringia, Hesse, Mecklenberg, Holstein, on the Rhine, in Switzerland. He speaks no more the speech of his village, of his town ; he is not one who understands only this or that trade which ties him to a particular workshop or to the soil ; he is a universal man ! It is a shame, not to have advanced oneself further by study than to be a Thuringian, a Hessian, a Franconian, a Swabian, a Rhinelander !—If the university man is by nature no provincialist, so is it unnatural to try and force him to be one by means of an artificial institution. . . . You should only be by your precious institution that which you are as students, universal.—But universality does not extend over the whole world. You . . . can and will (and the German people, including its princes, will) be nothing other than educated Germans, who are like one to the other, and whose business everywhere is free. For that very reason you must give yourselves no name which conflicts with this universality. Let your name be what you are alone and exclusively, namely, the Students' Union or the League of Youth. Thereto you all belong, and no one else. But be on your guard, against wearing a badge and so sinking to party distinctions, proof that you do not realise that the status of the educated class reproduces in itself the whole state, and therefore destroys its being by breaking up into parties. Also beware of the vain thought that it is on you that Germany's being, and continuance and honour depend. Germany depends only on itself, on Germany as a whole. . . . . Your duty is indeed to act firstly as parts of the head ; but the head is powerless when the limbs and the entrails refuse their office. Now you stand for Youth, which has no other proper business than so to maintain itself that it grows in beauty, educates itself, does not wear itself out in dissipation, and therefore concentrates itself on the goal, and bothers itself about nothing else save in so far as it keeps clear in sight the goal which man should pursue. Yours is not to discuss what should or should not happen in the State ; what alone is seemly for you to consider is, what your business shall one day be in the State, and how you can prepare yourselves to be fit for it. . . . Ponder on that ! Do not depart as you came ! Make certain firm resolutions, and take them home with you. A written word has marvellous power ! . . . To meet again, but not for three years !

Then trumpets gave the signal for dinner. 'Twas a merry meal. Wine warmed the feelings and the good resolutions that beamed from every countenance. Some toasts were proposed which did not seem to us in the spirit of the feast ; therefore we kept our good wishes in our hearts.

After dinner, about 3 P.M., the procession made its way downhill and shoulder to shoulder with the Landsturm, like friends, into the city church, where the sermon aroused general emotion. Then followed a display of gymnastic exercises in the market-place, after which darkness fell. Thus every moment was passed in praiseworthy activity.

At 7 the students, some six hundred of them, each with a torch, marched up the hill to the triumphal bonfire where the Landsturm were already assembled. On the hill-top songs were sung, and another speech delivered by a student.

Afterwards trial by fire was held over the following articles, which were first displayed high in the air on a pitch-fork to the assembled multitude, and then with curses hurled into the flames. The articles burnt (indicated in the paper by vignettes) were these : a bag-wig, a guardsman's stays, a corporal's cane. . . .

At 12 there was a move to bed.

Next day the students again assembled during the forenoon at the Wartburg, and there was much discussion anent the student-form of the future, especially as regards a limit to duelling. The students from Giessen who had hitherto been split up by nationalities into hostile camps threw themselves into each other's arms and made friends. Thus did a sacred moment of freedom, when only the voice of youth was heard in counsel, accomplish what the Court of Darmstadt with all its soldiers, the whole Senate with all its laws and periwigs, could not bring about—had rather fanned the flame more fiercely ! If courts and senates do not know how to handle students, there is real need that they should learn how in their policy of intimidation (there is a more expressive word, emasculation) they should conduct themselves. Force is always, as a remedy, the wrong end of the stick, and governance by soldiers will never more be endured.

Thereafter a number took their departure, but many remained for supper. Thus did the students of Germany celebrate the Festival of the Wartburg !

Many of those who manage the affairs of Germany, and still more, those who mismanage them, might well take the conclave on the Wartburg as an example.

Jahn incited the undergraduates to follow up the auto-da-fè described above by burning a number of reactionary books, including Kotzebue's *History of the German Empire*, the *Police Code*, the *Code Napoléon*, and works by Haller and Schmalz. The whole course of proceedings reveals to us the mixture of turbulent passion and maudlin sentimentality which forms a German characteristic. Goethe's unsympathetic attitude to the students' performance is indicated in a letter to Zelter of 16th December 1817 : ' In this innocent way I live my quiet life, and allow the horrible smell of the Wartburg fire, at which all Germany is taking offence, to pass off ; it would by this time have evaporated here, had it not been driven back by the north-east wind, and smothered us a second time.' But the effect of the festival on the public was considerable, for it roused the slumbering discontent all over Germany, and enabled Metternich to apply his tools of repression, Frederick William of Prussia and the German princes. Petitions and demands began to pour in upon Frederick William, calling for the redemption of his promise to grant a measure of representative government. Prominent among petitioners was the Rhine Province, then, from its proximity to France, the most politically intelligent district in Germany. Stein looked out from his watch-tower, and wrote to his friend Gagern in November : ' Think you that the Chancellor (Hardenberg) intends to visit the Rhine ? His latest botch in the way of government control is a multiplication of official boards, faulty in principle, faulty in execution.' But there was to be no comfort for the old statesman ; the king replied to all petitions on 21st March 1818, by a rescript [1] which shows clearly enough that the present Kaiser's gift of bombastic language is not original, but a family inheritance. The reader is likely enough to draw the conclusion before he has done with this book that the gift is a racial one.

Neither in the Edict of 22nd May 1815 nor in Article 13 of the Federal Act is a time fixed when the national constitution shall come into being. Not every time is the right time for the intro-

---

[1] Quoted by Klein.

duction of a change in the constitution of the State. The Sovereign has given these assurances quite of his own free will, and whoever reminds him of them casts sacrilegious doubt on the inviolability of his word, and forestalls his judgment as to the right time for the introduction of this constitution. . . . The call on people to petition cannot, however, be allowed, and a demand of the kind is evidently to hand when a petition is circulated in a district and the question is asked, who of the inhabitants will sign it. Such a remonstrance can therefore only awake my well-founded displeasure. I shall determine when the promise of a national constitution shall be fulfilled, and shall not allow myself to be hurried by untimely remonstrances in my due progress to that end. It is my subjects' duty, in reliance on a resolution freely adopted by Myself, who gave that assurance, and inspired the relevant article in the Federal Act, to await the precise moment, which I, guided by my survey of all circumstances, shall consider appropriate for its fulfilment.

CHAPTER II

THE MURDER OF KOTZEBUE

WITH Austria, and German governments generally, Prussia was now committed to repressive measures. Evanescent indeed had been the reflection in the cold hearts of princes and bureaucrats of that popular enthusiasm, kindled by hopes of a constitutional and unified Germany, which had rendered possible the triumphs of the War of Liberation. The people were not represented at the Congress of Vienna ; this aristocratic capital was thronged by an ardent crowd of reactionaries gathered from all over Germany.

As early as 1815 reactionary sentiments found voice, from a Berlin professor among others, one Schmalz, a horrid fellow with an odious name. To his hard, narrow intelligence it was intolerable that the patriotism of ' the people ' should carry off the honours of the War of Liberation, and that men like Stein and Arndt should be counted as heroes. The old League of Virtue which had done so much to bind German patriots together in the days of the French occupation was denounced by him as the progenitor of a whole series of secret societies whose aims and intrigues were subversive of law and order. Even so loyal a friend of the king as Niebuhr was moved with other men of moderate opinions to protest against so abominable a travesty of justice and of fact. The dispute grew hotter and hotter until the king himself had to intervene. He imposed silence on all parties—and decorated Schmalz ! Treitschke, in vol. ii.[1] of his *History of Germany in the Nineteenth Century*, does his best to whitewash, or rather to cleanse with benzine, the Schmalzian reputation. He ' was Scharnhorst's brother-in-law,' ' during the period of French dominion he had preserved his patriotic courage,' ' beyond question, as even the professor's opponents admitted, the unhappy man was acting in good

---

[1] E. and C. Paul's translation. Jarrold & Sons.

faith.' But Treitschke is less kind to a more dangerous apostle of reaction who made his appearance in the following year. This was C. L. von Haller, a distinguished German-Swiss professor at Berne, who published in 1816 his *Restoration of Political Science*. Therein he demolished all arguments in favour of natural rights or the social contract, even as transformed by Kant, or the sovereignty of the people, and founded the state, as Treitschke tells us, solely upon the right of the stronger, and made of it a mere caricature of the ancient feudal state. ' Land belongs to a prince, a corporation, or a church ; upon this property of a suzerain lord, and under his protection, settlers appear ; if the people should disappear, the state would still continue to exist in the person of the prince, who can readily find new subjects. Consequently the state resembles any other association based on civil law, differing from others only because it is more powerful and independent, and because its prince is an "owner, a man equipped with absolutely independent rights " ; he rules the nation through the instrumentality of his personal servants, is entitled to regard (it is even his duty to regard) himself and his house as the principal aim for which the state exists, but he must resist the dispersion of his own property and must protect his subjects with his own soldiers.' A few years later Haller followed a number of those who found it convenient to accompany the passage from liberal to reactionary sentiments with a change of the Protestant for the Roman Catholic habit, and Treitschke, the doughty champion of the Protestant north, lashes out at him. ' Enlightened Protestants had long become accustomed to these numerous conversions, and they were first startled out of their thoughtless indifference when it was reported that C. L. von Haller of Berne had gone over to Rome. Who could take it amiss in the case of the valiant publicist, the passionate enemy of the Revolution, that as a logical outcome of his political views he should be forced to a change of faith ? But Haller kept his conversion secret, with the approval of the bishop of Fribourg. Subsequently, as member of the Council of Berne, he took the official oath which pledged him to the protection of the Reformed Church ; and, when the unsavoury secret was at length disclosed by others, in an open *Letter to my Family* (1821) he declared unashamedly that he had remained silent on excellent grounds, in order that his new volume, *Die Geistlichen Staaten*, might exercise a stronger influence upon its readers, " because it was apparently written by a Protestant ! " '

Metternich is justly hailed as the reactionary hero who dominated German policy up to the revolution of 1848, but his fame ought not to be allowed to obscure that of his hench-man, Friedrich von Gentz, one of the most brilliant publicists that ever lived. Gentz was born at Breslau and was thus politi-cally a Prussian. He began his public career as a liberal. A brief enthusiasm for the French Revolution cooled down, under the influence of Burke, to an admiration of English constitutional-ism, and ultimately, when he left the Prussian for the Austrian service and was taken up by Metternich, congealed into that statesman's view that ' in an age of decay the sole function of a statesman was to " prop up mouldering institutions." ' [1] No pen in Europe did more to undermine the Napoleonic regime than that of Gentz, and in selecting him for guide, philosopher and friend, in appointing him secretary to the Congress of Vienna, Metternich displayed that greatest of a great man's gifts, the selection of the most serviceable instrument for his purpose. What does not appear to be generally known is that Gentz was a Jew. This circumstance provoked Disraeli to a remarkable deliverance in chapter xxiv. of his *Life of Lord George Bentinck.* The passage is worth quoting at some length, as an appreciation of the part an ancient race has played in directing the political movements of modern Europe, and an antidote to Treitschke's phrenetic depreciation of Judæo-Germanism, a force that has yet to be fully and fairly explored.

The Jews represent the Semitic principle : all that is spiritual in our nature. They are the trustees of tradition and the conser-vators of the religious element. . . . All the tendencies of the Jewish race are conservative. Their bias is to religion, property, and natural aristocracy. . . . But existing society has chosen to perse-cute this race which should furnish its choice allies, and what have been the consequences ?

They may be traced in the last outbreak of the destructive principle in Europe. . . . secret societies . . . form provisional governments, and men of Jewish race are found at the head of every one of them. . . . When the secret societies, in February 1848, surprised Europe, they were themselves surprised by the unexpected opportunity, and so little capable were they of seizing the occasion, that had it not been for the Jews, who of late years,

[1] Alison Philips in *Encylopædia Britannica,* Gentz.

unfortunately, have been connecting themselves with these unhallowed associations, imbecile as were the governments, the uncalledfor outbreak would not have ravaged Europe. If the reader throws his eye over the provisional governments of Germany, and Italy, and even of France, formed ʋt that period, he will recognise everywhere the Jewish element. Even the insurrection, and defence, and administration, of Venice, which from the resource and statesmanlike moderation displayed, commanded almost the respect and sympathy of Europe, were accomplished by a Jew—Manini,[1] who by the bye is a Jew who professes the whole of the Jewish religion, and believes in Calvary as well as Sinai, ' a converted Jew,' as the Lombards styled him, quite forgetting, in the confusion of their ideas, that it is the Lombards who are the converts—not Manini.

Thus it will be seen that the persecution of the Jewish race has deprived European society of an important conservative element and added to the destructive party an influential ally. Prince Metternich, the most enlightened of modern statesmen, not to say the most intellectual of men, was, though himself a victim of the secret societies, fully aware of these premises. It was always his custom, great as were the difficulties which in so doing he had to encounter, to employ as much as possible the Hebrew race in the public service. He could never forget that Napoleon in his noontide hour had been checked by the pen of the greatest of political writers ; he had found that illustrious author as great in the cabinet as in the study ; he knew that no one had more contributed to the deliverance of Europe. It was not as a patron, but as an appreciating and devoted friend, that the high Chancellor of Austria appointed Frederick Gentz secretary to the Congress of Vienna— and Frederick Gentz was a child of Israel.

In the next chapter he goes on to make a claim not easy to substantiate : ' It may be observed that the decline and disasters of modern communities have generally been relative to their degree of sedition against the Semitic principle . . . Austria would long ago have dissolved but for the Semitic principle, and if the north of Germany has never succeeded in attaining that imperial position which seemed its natural destiny, it is that the north of Germany has never at any time been thoroughly converted.'

Gentz, as we shall see, had the true official mistrust of freedom in the expression of thought as well as of mere opinion, and the foolish bureaucratic belief in the possibility of repressing it. The first step taken by his master and himself was to increase the stringency of the censorship. It is difficult for us, even in days of a censorship of our own, to realise how wide were the ramifica-

---

[1] Commonly called Manin, the heroic defender of Venice against the Austrians.

tions of a system which was designed to fetter freedom in philosophical speculation as well as in political propagandism.[1] The spectre of the censorship haunted the student as well as the journalist. When negotiating with Brockhaus about the publication of his *magnum opus, The World as Will and Idea,* Schopenhauer touches in a letter dated 3rd April 1818, on the censorship :

Moreover, the work cannot fail to pass the censor. Though not a syllable in it refers to governments or anything connected with them, nothing again is to be found in it which conflicts with good morals ; on the contrary in the last book a moral principle is developed which agrees well enough with Christianity proper. Still the whole scheme of philosophy presented stands in contradiction, never, indeed, expressed in so many words, but tacitly and undeniably implied, to the dogmas of Jewish-Christian religious instruction. On this point people have certainly become extremely tolerant with philosophers, inured, one might say, to the acceptance of things that fifty years ago would have brought trouble in their train ; and the Church is nowhere directly attacked in my book ; so that I have every hope of passing the censorship. However, I am not fully acquainted with the principles it goes on, and one cannot tell how their lordships may be pleased to interpret this or that.

I cannot bring myself to tolerate alterations in this, to me, most important manuscript. But, if the worst comes to the worst I think you could get the book printed in Jena or Merseburg ; still I hope it won't come to that. For the rest it is well known that it is no misfortune for a book to be suppressed.

But before reaction had recovered from the effect of the Wartburg Festival in 1817 came the shock of an event tragic enough to raise to fever point an already excited public opinion. In March 1819, all Germany was startled by the news of the murder of the dramatist Kotzebue by a fanatical student at Jena, Carl Sand ; one of the famous murders of history, Sand's own account of which reads like a chapter out of Dostoevsky. Kotzebue is dismissed by Professor Pollard in the *Cambridge Modern History* as ' a sentimental poetaster,' but Professor Robertson has more to say for him in his *History of German Literature* : ' When the worst has been said of Kotzebue, he remains one of the most fertile and ingenious writers for the theatre that have ever lived ; and he has influenced, as no other playwright, the entire development of the drama to the present

---

[1] See also pages 40 f., 117 f., 172 ff.

day.' Kotzebue, who had once posed as a liberal, was now editor of a reactionary journal, and was suspected of being a paid Russian spy on the journalists of Germany. Hence he had incurred the peculiar hatred of hot-headed reformers. His murderer, Sand, was like several other German apostles of hate a student of theology. At Jena he came under the influence of ' the uncompromising ' Carl Follen, one of a family of firebrands, a *Docent* or lecturer of the extremest views, and endowed with a gift of inflammatory speech exceptional even for a German. Specimens [1] of his eloquence in prose and poetry may be given : ' What ! Are we to shoot down without scruple the robber who tries to steal our purses in the street, and is not the people's freedom worth more than our purses ? In war murder, treachery, and all means are valid, and are not tyrants at home worse enemies than foreign soldiers who only fight against us under compulsion ?   Are not Timoleon, Brutus, Tell and others glorified in history as heroes and martyrs ? . . . And shall I, because I sought to save my people, be damned ? Nevertheless, better that one man should be damned than that a whole people should sink into slavery.' And in poetry :

> Their country's need stirs all,
> They hear the Lord God's call :
> Strike till your tyrants fall,
> O save the land !

and in what he called ' A New Year's Hymn for Free Christians ' :

> Now brandish the claymore that freedom hath blest,
> And, ho, for a dirk in the gullet hard prest !
> In purple gown,
> With fillet and crown,
> By the altar of vengeance the victim stands drest.

Follen was largely responsible for Kotzebue's murder, as a brother of his was for the attempted murder of one President Ibell at Wiesbaden. Under his pernicious influence the morbidly excitable Sand soon began to see red. Nearly a year before the murder on 5th May 1818, he wrote in his diary : ' When I brood thus, I often think there must come some one who will boldly undertake to thrust a sword into the stomach of Kotzebue or another such traitor.' Before setting forth from his lodgings at Jena on his fatal journey to Mannheim

---

[1] Furnished by Biedermann and Treitschke.

he wrote out the following farewell [1] to the Students' Union;
it was found among his papers after his arrest :

As it may easily occasion our dear Students' Union grievous
trouble, and as I can well imagine that many of our number may
receive a shock when for the Fatherland I come to die on the gibbet,
I would anticipate any movement that may be made on their
part, and desire to be allowed even before I leave (Jena) to retire
from the Students' Union. Salaried bloodhounds among us here,
who, as we can only conclude, report our trivial student-proceed-
ings to Weimar, Vienna, St. Petersburg and who knows where,
may if they please announce this in addition, that I am about to
wreak the vengeance of the people on the traitor Kotzebue !—With
the few among us of his sort I have no concern ; I wish I could
scent them out and denounce them openly. But so much the more
am I rooted in the deepest affection, even until death, towards all
those who mean well by the dear German Fatherland.

CARL SAND of Fichtelgebirge.

Klein's account of the murder, incorporating Sand's own
deposition, runs as follows :

The entrance to the living-room (in Kotzebue's house at Mannheim), where the deed took place, is opposite the staircase. From
this room a door leads on the left to the nursery, which adjoins
the drawing-room where at the time Kotzebue's family was, as
usual, gathered together. Sand's account (according to the depositions) runs : ' The servant waited some minutes in the room,
walking about or talking : then he called me in but stood in the
doorway speaking in subdued tones to some one inside the room.
At last I was admitted and Kotzebue entered from the door on the
left. I saw him through the half-open door enter, and, as the door
was opened wide, retire. I took some half-dozen steps forward
into the room and greeted Kotzebue, who came a little nearer to
the door. Then, keeping him in front, I turned my back towards
the entrance door. The worst of it was that I had to dissemble.
I said to him that, passing through the town, I wished to pay him
a visit. After some commonplaces I said : ' I take no pride '—
meanwhile I drew my dagger and went on—' in you, no none.
Here, you traitor against your fatherland,' and with the last cry
I struck him down. I gave myself the name of Heinrichs of Mietau,
because I did not think that Kotzebue would admit me if I gave
myself out as a native German. This was more likely to happen
to one bearing the name of a Courlander. And as a matter of
fact Kotzebue did ask me : ' Are you from Mietau ? '—How many
blows I gave him I can't remember, and, as little, which was the
first blow ; it happened so quickly. I drew the dagger from the
left sleeve of my coat, where I had kept it in a sheath, and stabbed

---

[1] Quoted by Klein.

him several times on the left side. Kotzebue said nothing at all during the attack, but merely uttered a wail even when he saw I was on to him with upraised arm. He only held his hands in front of him and collapsed right at the entrance of the room to the left, about three steps from it. Whether I wounded him in the face, I know not. Quite possibly it may have happened, for he held his hands and arms in front of him and waved them about. I held the dagger in such a fashion that the edge pointed to the back of thumb and fist. I struck him straight, neither up nor down. Kotzebue collapsed in a sitting posture, and I looked once again at him right in the eyes, in order to see how it was with him. I wanted to see what the effect of my attack had been, and above all to see him again face to face. I think there was still a continual quivering of the eyelashes, so that one saw now the whites of the eyes, now nothing at all. Thereupon I concluded he wasn't dead yet, but I didn't wish to do anything more, since I thought I had done enough. As I turned round I noticed a little child which had run into the room by the door on the left, during the murder. Its screams induced me, in the highly strung condition of my mingled feelings, to offer it some sort of atonement by giving myself a blow with the little sword. The blow entered the left breast and went several inches deep ; I drew the blade out again. The result was an instantaneous loss of blood ; as I went out and descended the staircase I felt the pain and the rush of blood more keenly.'—Sand went down the staircase without a pause. It is true the cook and the housemaid met him as he came out, but as he strode along holding his little sword, as he calls it, at the thrust, they made not the slightest attempt to stop him. Nevertheless they followed the unknown down the steps and called for help. Sand, who had reached the house door without hindrance, found there several people who had run up in answer to the cries. Meanwhile several ladies, who were paying Frau Kotzebue a call, had shouted from the window for help, and called on people to seize the murderer. Thereupon the stranger standing in the street looked up at them and cried : ' Yes, I did it : so shall all traitors die ! ' Then Sand called out in a loud voice to the hurrying crowd : ' Long live my German fatherland, and among German people all those who strive to promote the dignity of Man ! ' Sand knelt down and said half aloud the words : ' I thank thee, O God, for this victory,' prayed, placed with both hands the little sword to his left breast, and drove it slowly straight in until it stuck fast. Then he let go with his hands and fell forwards on to the right side. Such is his description of what passed. That he did, sinking on one knee, call out before the blow the words, ' I thank thee, O God,' is attested by neighbours who came up before Sand gave himself the second blow. . . . People hurrying to the scene found Sand lying in his blood, the dagger standing up in his breast. A shoemaker's apprentice who lived opposite drew it out, and threw it on the roadway. A midwife ran to him, tore open his waistcoat, called for vinegar, which was handed out from Kotzebue's house, and washed his wounds, whereupon the heavy bleeding diminished. As his face was also being washed with vinegar, Sand turned his head round and sighed and gave further signs of life. Meanwhile watchmen and police had hurried up ; and, under a covering, Sand was carried on a stretcher to the general hospital.

Sand recovered from his self-inflicted wounds, and on 20th May 1820, the Saturday before Whitsuntide, he was beheaded outside the Heidelberg gate. During his last few days he wrote to his parents : ' God is as near to me as ever He was ; He makes me, the weak, strong to endure all that may still come over me.'
Klein goes on to tell us :

After the execution the spectators forced their way on to the scaffold and dipped their handkerchiefs in Sand's blood ; the chair of execution was, as the story goes, smashed up and the pieces distributed. Sand's grave was often strewn with flowers, and the populace named the place of execution ' The place of Sand's Ascension.' It is characteristic of the feeling of the time that Sand became the object of a sentimental idolatry. A famous landscape painter of the period painted landscapes with ruined Gothic cathedrals, on whose last altar a youth with long hair and in German dress deposited his dagger. Another artist chiselled in black marble and alabaster a monument in Sand's honour. Nor was there any lack of poems and ballads. Varnhagen von Ense wrote this epigram :

Grimly a cynical fate heaps horror on horror of madness ;
　False was the star whose beams urged thy unhappy career !
Here in a pitiful tangle is ev'rything twisted and tortured,
　Deed, aim, means and success, thine and thy enemy's fate.

' The results of Sand's deed are incalculable and tremendous,' wrote at the time a student in his enthusiasm, ' and the Spirit of the Universe, which stands for eternal progress, will turn them to good.' Things turned out otherwise. The consequences of this deed lay like a load on the universities, on the press, on the national consciousness and on the ardent enthusiasm of the German youth.

Certainly the impression produced by this murder was prodigious. The attempt that followed to murder President Ibell at Wiesbaden, instigated, as we have said, by a brother of Carl Follen at Giessen, failed, and it was attended by fantastic and gruesome details which helped to spoil the effect of it. When Paul Follen, a certain pastor, and an apothecary had resolved on Ibell's death, the three set about drawing lots for the honour of rivalling Sand. But Ibell was a Nassauer and the apothecary came from Nassau, so that his claim to kill his countryman was one the others could not resist and the distinction fell to him. A poor, bungling druggist, he was no artist in murder and made but a sorry show with a dagger in place of a phial in his hand ; and then he revolted the hardiest aspirant after like honours by the shocking means he adopted for suicide—the swallowing of small fragments of broken glass. Sand stood alone as a knightly figure. The great Stein bewailed ' so noble and pious a youth whom political fanaticism had tempted to such a deed of horror.' Stein's coadjutor, Joseph Görres, in his *Germany and the Revolution*, said of the murder :

The youth took it upon him to write out himself the commission for the deed, and to execute it with his own hand. When his measure was filled to the brim, and ready to flow over on his head, he whom he sought was delivered into his hands. He himself, however, gave his own life as a propitiation to the enraged Nemesis ; according to the ancient doctrine, that blood demands blood.

The deed struck the people like lightning. Since the years of our rising, nothing had taken place which they could comprehend ; but what had long remained unintelligible, and struggled for meaning, now found a language. A bloody deed had again become the point in which the thoughts of all were collected, and opinion was soon agreed respecting this event. Disapprobation of the act, with approbation of the motives, a renovated feeling of the presence of eternal justice in all human things, a clear light thrown over the condition of the country, and a keen interest in public affairs, were the results of the general agitation which followed in a short space. Public opinion had passed a grand climacteric ; a profound seriousness came over the age, which, up to that period, had entered into public affairs with less earnestness.

But the most remarkable tribute of all was that paid by a famous theologian, De Wette,[1] in a letter to Sand's mother, quoted by Biedermann. ' The deed he committed had its source in error and was not without passion ; but what man can boast that he is free from error and passion ? Error is excused and in a certain measure abrogated by the strength and candour of one's conviction, and passion is sanctified by the goodness of the source from which it flows. I am persuaded that in your son's case both of these conditions obtained. He held it for right, to do what he did do, and therefore he did right. It was the purest of inspirations which absorbed him, but which borrowed from his youthful strength a momentum that drove

---

[1] Frequently quoted by Strauss in his *Leben Jesu.*

him beyond the limits of this life.   Without some share of this sort of enthusiasm scarcely any great deed could be achieved ; the light of inspiration must always glow until it becomes red hot. . . . So, as the deed has come to pass through this pure and pious youth, with this belief, with this confidence, it is a beautiful sign of the times. . . . That a youth should hazard his life, to extirpate a man whom many reverence as an idol—can this be without any effect ? ' The letter was published through a breach of confidence, and the result was De Wette's instant dismissal from his academic position.   But the whole theological faculty rose as one man in his behalf.

Curt and business-like, after the above parsonic deliverance, was the exclamation of Hardenberg, Prussian chancellor and co-signatory with Frederick William III. to the promise of 1815, when he heard of the murder : ' Now a constitution is impossible ! '

CHAPTER III

THE CARLSBAD DECREES—GÖRRES' ATTACK ON REACTION

METTERNICH, with his henchman Gentz, was, as we have said, busy over measures of repression even before the murder of Kotzebue, but that event helped him to speed up the machinery necessary for this purpose, since no difficulty was now to be encountered in playing on the fears aroused among German princes. It was against the universities and the intellectuals, against the liberal spirits still warm with the enthusiasm of the War of Liberation, and against the press that Metternich decided to direct his guns. Gentz had a useful coadjutor in another renegade from the Prussian to the Austrian service, his intimate friend Adam Müller, to whom a large section of his voluminous correspondence is addressed. Müller had gone over to Rome from Protestantism and joined a circle of converts who were, according to Treitschke, the most vigorous defenders of the German policy of Austria. 'But in talent, activity, and fanaticism,' says Treitschke,[1] 'Adam Müller excelled all the rest; it seemed as if the brilliant but fundamentally false sophist desired to wipe out the stain of his Berlin origin by his raging fury against heretics; his hand was at work wherever there was evidence of Jesuit intrigues throughout the north.' A glance at a few of the letters [2] exchanged between the pair gives one a good insight into the workings of the reactionary mind. Said Gentz to Müller at the end of 1818: 'Things cannot stay as they are. In the first place the gymnastic movement must be done away with; this I regard as a sort of ulcer that must be utterly removed before we can proceed to a radical cure.' In April 1819 he sees in Protestantism the root of all evil: 'Protestantism is the original, the true and

---

[1] E. and C. Paul's translation.   Jarrold & Sons.
[2] See the published correspondence between the pair.

only source of all the monstrous ills from which we suffer to-day. Had it remained merely an intellectual exercise, we must, and could, have borne with it, for its essence lies deep in human nature. But when governments were pleased to acknowledge Protestantism as a permissible kind of religion, as one form of Christianity, as a human right, to come to terms with it, to assign to it a position beside the true authentic Church, or rather, indeed, on the ruins thereof, the religious, moral, and political order of the world was at once dissolved. What we have experienced is only a necessary consequence and the natural development of that first incalculable offence. The whole French Revolution, and the still worse one which confronts Germany, have flowed from the one identical source.'

Müller replies in May by an expression of the hopes he draws from the jealously guarded isolation of the army : ' Governments are powerful only through their armies ; that these armies belong in the last instance to the system which was definitely established at Aix, and that the armies' principle of absolute personal obedience . . . keeps them of late sharply isolated, differentiates them from all other industrial and intellectual professions, I regard as one of the greatest and most effective steps that make for good.'

In October Gentz declares : ' I stick to my maxim : " As a preventive measure against the abuse of the press absolutely nothing shall be printed for—years. Full stop ! " With this maxim as a rule, and with the fewest possible exceptions which should be specified by a tribunal of acknowledged position, we should in a short time get back to God and the Truth.'

With these two worthies to help him, Metternich set to work in the secrecy general among statesmen and officials in his uncontrolled position. During August and September 1819, the so-called ' Carlsbad Decrees ' [1] were settled by him at Teplitz and Carlsbad in concert with Prussia and other German states, and passed by the Federal Diet. A plenipotentiary extraordinary was charged with the supervision of the universities, professors as well as students. The Confederated States pledged themselves to discharge, and never again reappoint, teachers who by their instruction endangered ' public

---

[1] The quotations given are taken mainly from Beidermann ; some from Klein. Details of persecution are given by Biedermann, Klein, Blum, and Treitschke.

order and peace ' or ' undermined the foundations of existing
state institutions.' The Universal Students' Union, founded
on 1st October 1818, was proscribed afresh in the strongest
terms. Students had to produce ' satisfactory guarantees for
their good behaviour.' As regards the press, the preliminary
censorship was introduced, to which were subjected all publications of under twenty sheets. The Federal Diet had in its own
hands power, without appeal, to suppress every piece of printed
matter. No editor of a suppressed publication was, for a period
of five years, to take up an editorship.

In the sitting of the Federal Diet on 20th September it was
unanimously resolved to set up a Central Inquiry Commission.
The purpose of this nineteenth-century German Inquisition
was thus described : ' The aim of this Commission is a concerted
and as thorough and comprehensive as possible, examination
and collection of evidence on the origin and manifold ramifications of revolutionary intrigues and demagogic associations
directed against the existing constitution, as well as against
the internal peace only of the Federation as a whole, but also
of each individual state, indications of which, direct or indirect,
are already to hand, or may reveal themselves in the course of
the inquiry.'

The Commissioners reported in 1822 that political activity
' expresses itself less in actual performance than in enticement,
preparation and preliminaries. . . . They had endeavoured
to measure the degree of certainty or the greater or less probability of individual facts, not according to standards prescribed
in this or that enactment, but by the principles of historic
credibility, and their personal, subjective convictions. They
believed themselves entitled to put aside any fine distinction,
at best but relative, between the conceptions of revolutionary
intrigue and demagogic association, and had therefore in their
representation of the facts taken account of each and every
effort which came to their knowledge, and which had for its
object to procure, against the will, or at any rate without the
concurrence, of the governments, changes in the existing constitutions by popular pressure and by methods not approved
by existing laws. In so doing they had not considered themselves entitled to ignore anything which, even unintentionally,
caused, encouraged, or promoted such efforts. They had
therefore no hesitation in citing by name such persons as,

without having been either involved in any proceedings or called up for examination, were nevertheless mentioned in the documentary evidence before them.'

Among the persons who were thus, though unindicted and untried, charged with 'having even unintentionally caused, encouraged or promoted revolutionary efforts' appear in the list men like Arndt, Stein, Gneisenau (the brains of Blücher's army), Yorck, Eichhorn, Schleiermacher, even Fichte, and others! 'It is significant,' says Biedermann, 'of the impartial point of view taken by the Commission that among the efforts which had for object to procure "without the concurrence of the governments, changes in the existing constitutions by popular pressure and by methods not approved by existing laws," efforts which therefore in the Commission's opinion came under the rubric of "revolutionary intrigues," it included the dissemination of addresses and petitions for the active recognition of a land's constitution, that is to say the exercise of the most primitive of human rights, the trustful petition of subject to prince, a petition in this case for something that all the German princes had collectively promised their peoples by Article 13 of the Federal Act.'

It is agreeable to find that even in Germany such an inquisition as this did not always find either the laws or the courts in the various states sufficiently complacent for its purpose. The Commissioners complained that 'the diversity in the character of penalties inflicted seems expressly designed to confuse estimates of the culpability of parties to intrigue, and generally to weaken the effect of sentences passed.' They found the chief reason for this diversity 'in the deficiency of legislation on the subject of high treason,' since in most of the Federal States no new penal law under this head had been enacted since the days of Charles v.

In fairness, also, prominence should be given to the fact that in the Prussian ministry there was a party, headed by Wilhelm von Humboldt, scholar, diplomat, educational reformer, and most humane of German humanists, which was hotly opposed to the Carlsbad Decrees. Humboldt protested against them while in process of incubation, and was bluntly ordered by the king 'to obey.' When they were hatched, he denounced them as 'shameful, anti-national, provocative to the people.' On the last day of 1819 he was, with two friends like-minded,

Boyen and Beyme, dismissed from office, and in him fell the warmest, the most upright and unflinching friend of reform in high place.

A dismal period of repression followed, for the official mind in bureaucratic countries is conscientious enough in ruthlessness. Many youths and grown-up men, suspected of demagogic intrigue, were haled before this new Inquisition and imprisoned. In May 1825, forty-two Bavarian subjects, professors, students, clergymen, doctors, etc., were tried and given long terms of imprisonment. Among them were the practising physician, Dr. Eisenmann of Würzburg (who got fifteen years), Professor C. W. Feuerbach, Adolf von Zerzog,[1] Anselm Feuerbach, a student from Ansbach, and his brother, Edward Feuerbach. In Würtemberg twenty-two young students were tried ; they got from fourteen days to four years' imprisonment in Hohenasperg. The author, Wilhelm H. Hauff, then a medical student, got two and a half years ; he was handed back to his family in February 1825, half dead. The subsequent church historian, Carl August Hase, then a lecturer in theology, got two years' confinement in a fortress. The High Court at Wiesbaden sentenced a teacher, C. R. Hildebrandt, to nineteen years' confinement in a fortress. Among the most barbarous were the punishments inflicted in Prussia. There, in the case of seventeen young men, found guilty of active membership of proscribed associations, no sentence of less than twelve years' confinement in a fortress was pronounced. Collectively they got two hundred and forty-one years. Another eight in addition, sentenced for merely sympathetic adhesion, got collectively sixty-one years. Among those sentenced were Arnold Ruge and the theologian Wislicenus, who received fifteen years each. One German prince, only a little one to be sure, but Goethe's friend, Carl August of Saxe-Weimar, deserves honourable mention, for he allowed his three subjects found guilty of high treason to escape.

Not only was the *Burschenschaft* proscribed, but the gymnasia and gymnastic clubs established by Jahn were also closed. Turnvater Jahn himself was arrested in July 1819, torn from the death-bed of a child and conveyed to Spandau, thence in chains to Küstrin, and so on from fortress to fortress. In 1825 he was acquitted of the charges against him by the Court of Appeal at Frankfort. But notwithstanding this the King of

[1] See page 423

Prussia placed him under police supervision, banished him from Berlin, and from every city containing either a university or a high school (*gymnasium*). On a strict compliance with this condition was to depend the continuance of his salary as gymnastic teacher. The authorities indeed seemed determined, now Napoleon was out of the way, to lay the hated ghost of the War of Liberation. After Jahn, Arndt was their next prominent victim. He was, like others less famous, suspended from the exercise of his professorship at Bonn, the full rights of which were only restored to him twenty years later on the accession of Frederick William IV.

Another case that cast a gloom over academic circles was that of Friedrich List. List had been professor of political economy at Tübingen, but had to resign his chair in consequence of a difference of opinion with the Würtemberg government over a memorandum of his on the question of the *Zollverein*. He was in 1820 elected by his native town, Reutlingen, to the Würtemberg Diet, and at the instance of his constituents presented a petition, stigmatising a number of administrative abuses and calling for drastic reforms. The result was his expulsion from the chamber, and, in 1822, a sentence of ten months' hard labour. He served a portion of his time, but was released on undertaking to emigrate to America. How well he used his time there we shall learn later.

Such a recital as we have given affords one simple explanation why the universities of Germany, the champions of popular rights and representative government during the first half of last century, became in the second half the servile instruments of militarism and bureaucracy. Who shall say after this that force is no remedy ?

Gentz was satisfied with the course of events. He wrote cheerfully to Müller in December 1819 : ' Our conferences go gaily on. The main questions—the relationship of the individual states to the Federation—the powers of the Federation, and Article 13—are as good as settled. According to (my judgment) yesterday—a date more memorable than those of Leipzig and Waterloo—has irrevocably overthrown, so far as Germany is concerned, not only the revolutionary system, but also every representative system that rests on the basis of the distribution of power, in so far as this can be achieved by an arbitrary principle.'

And his master, too, was pleased on the whole, for he wrote in May 1820 to the Baden Minister, Berstett : ' The times move on amid storms. To attempt to stay their tempestuous career by force were an idle endeavour. Only by firmness, moderation, and wisdom, by a united and well-calculated combination of force, to mitigate the ravages of their working : that alone is left over for the guardians and friends of order. . . . This aim can be very simply indicated, it is to-day neither more nor less than the maintenance of the *status quo*. So may all be saved, and even a portion of what has been lost be recovered, if on that aim are concentrated all the efforts of individuals and all the general measures of those who are bound together by common sentiments and interests. . . . The conferences at Carlsbad, and the decrees drafted there, have worked more effectively and more beneficially, than perhaps even we, in full consciousness of still existing claims . . . are disposed to believe.' [1]

One sign of discontent revealed itself in a strange little diversion in the world of politics. One of the most arrogant of Absolutists among German princes, King William I. of Würtemberg, hoping to profit by the dislike of repressive Prussia and Austria, conceived the idea in 1820 of setting up against Austria and Prussia a Constitutional Triad, consisting of Würtemberg, Baden, and Bavaria, and thus forming the confederation of a ' purged and constitutional Germany.' He got one Lindner, a Courlander, to float the idea in a document called the ' Manuscript from South Germany.' The pamphlet was published in London, and the author styled himself George Erichson ! But Bavaria would have nothing to do with the scheme, and it fell still-born. Its purport is thus described by Klein. 'The manuscript defended the Confederation of the Rhine and the Continental System, rejected the Carlsbad Decrees, pictured the contrast between the repulsive north and the glorious south of Germany in glowing colours, and proposed the exclusion of the two great powers from the Confederation.' Here is an extract from the manuscript :

Austria and Prussia may be desirable allies for the Confederation, as members of the Confederation they are dangerous. . . . Austria and Prussia pursue separate ends. The problem for the remaining states must be : to keep themselves clear of these aims, and so secure the independence of Germany. . . . Austria is as

---

[1] Quoted by Klein.

much as France an independent state. Just as the German possessions of the King of France are no longer contained in the Germany
of to-day, even so we may concede a similar right to Austria. . . .
Since Prussia acknowledges herself a European power, and has
specifically declared in public documents that her provinces in
matters of political rights must be treated as Prussian and not
as German, so is Prussia, like France and Austria, an independent
monarchy, and belongs as little as Alsace to Germany.

Far more effective than this foolish attempt of an autocrat
to fish in troubled waters was the protest made by Joseph
Görres, a stalwart warrior for freedom, and second only to
Gentz as a publicist. Görres, a native of Coblentz, had in his
youth been an admirer of the French Revolution, but during
the War of Liberation his part in rousing his countrymen
against the French was no less conspicuous than Arndt's.
He sobered down from republicanism to a reasoned desire for
a unified Germany in the form of a constitutional empire. In
1814 he founded a paper called *Der Rheinischer Merkur*, whose
columns Stein himself was glad to avail himself of, and which
became so influential a force that Napoleon styled it *la cin-
quième puissance*. The paper was disliked by the Prussian
Government, for Görres had no love for Prussia, and inclined
towards an Austrian figure-head for his constitutional empire ;
so the Prussian Chancellor took in 1816 what seemed to him the
natural step of suppressing it. When Görres realised what this
step, and the Carlsbad Decrees, meant for freedom, he hit back
with his *Germany and the Revolution*,[1] a blow more heavy-
weighted than any dealt by our own Cobbett. In a preface to
the French edition he roundly attacked the sovereignty of the
German princes as itself a usurpation :

In Germany . . . it is not the third Estate which has produced
a revolution ; on the contrary, the cabinets have effected a revolution under the protection of a foreign power. They have expelled
the superior clergy from the empire, and have shared among them
their possessions. They have, in the same manner, destroyed the
high immediate aristocracy of the empire ; they have possessed
themselves of their estates. As to the nobility, they have, for a
long time, been in a state of complete subjugation ; the ancient
liberties of the third Estate have been unable to resist the encroachments of power, aided by foreign bayonets. By the same means
the princes also have succeeded in destroying the unity of the

---

[1] English translation by J. Black, 1820.

empire. To the totality of these usurpations, and these acts of
despotism, they have given the name of *Sovereignty*.

Such was the situation of things in Germany, when, in 1813,
the German nation rose against this yoke of foreigners. Having
freed themselves from the yoke, they soon found out that these
usurpations of power, which the usurpers wished to defend at all
hazards, formed the principle obstacles to their prosperity and their
future safety.

From that moment began the struggle which agitates Germany
in all its elements, the struggle between the ancient and historical
liberties of the third Estate, and the pretensions of that *Sovereignty*,
which defends with all its strength, and with all its means, its
history of a few weeks, against that which has endured for several
centuries, and which the people claim along with unity and liberty.

Görres denounces in his book the infamies of Schmalz and
his kind, and ruthlessly analyses the causes that conduced to
the murder of Kotzebue, and were leading on to revolution at
large. It opens with a gloomy description of the situation in
Germany which is worth studying, not only as a picture of the
time, giving the very atmosphere of it, but also as a specimen
of that ponderous solemnity, that turgid eloquence of which we
shall presently have glorified examples from Fichte :

After a violent party struggle of four years, a blind and foolish
opposition to the claims of the age, and partial concessions to them
on the one hand, and exaggerations of various descriptions on the
other, things have at length come to such a pass, that the minds
of men throughout all Germany are in a state of the most violent
excitation ; and that disposition has become universally prevalent,
which is usually seen to preceed great catastrophes in history.
What the most active, the most crafty and deceitful demagogues,
with all their intrigues, could never of themselves have effected
from below, has been successfully accomplished by the dexterous
co-operation of those who have taken the business in hand by the
long arm of the lever from above ; and thus the peaceful, the tran-
quilly disposed, the sober-minded and moderate people of Germany,
have been agitated in all their elements and all their depths, and
worked up to the utmost degree of bitterness and rage. And that
these agitators may, with the utmost justice, lay claim to the
greatest part of the honour of this achievement, they are now
preparing with the utmost joy and alacrity to supply, in a short
space, what little may yet be wanting to give the last finish to
the whole ; that the work, in all its parts, may exhibit the hand
of a master. As whenever the agitated passions seemed in any
measure to subside, they have always, at the suitable moment,
supplied new incentives to discontent and irritation ; as with in-
imitable dexterity they have contrived to find out the weak side

of every one, and availed themselves of every occurrence of the
times to apply its sharp edge to the sore, or yet imperfectly cica-
trised places; they have thus actually discovered a secret for
rousing the whole body of the people, so that a common feeling
of discontent prevails from one end of the country to the other;
and the governments are at this time entangled in a hopeless contest
with all that is good and noble and energetic, and are lost in errors
from which they will never be able to extricate themselves by the
ways they have hitherto pursued. As in a sultry and oppressive
summer heat, when the sky begins to overcast, the dread of the
dark and boding tempest is unable to extinguish the inward longing
of nature for the refreshing coolness which follows in its train;
in like manner public opinion has now almost reconciled itself to
all that is most dreadful in events, if they only promise to relieve
us from our present ignominy, and open to us a source of pure
hope in the heavens, the face of which is now obscured by a vapour
which veils every happy star from our sight. Hence those birds
of presage, harbingers of the approaching tempest, the youths
who, to remove out of the way the base and unworthy in its organs,
devote themselves to death, fill it not with alarm, nor was it surprised when the discovery of a great and widespread conspiracy
for the establishment of a German Republic was announced from
Berlin, because the experience of the last age has sufficiently in-
culcated the knowledge of the universal law in nature, that every
extreme has a necessary and inevitable tendency to produce its
opposite. Only one thing amidst the alarm created by the breaking open of trunks and boxes, the going and coming of gendarmes
and police agents, the precaution which seemed to have been taken,
purposely, as it were, to trample on all judicial forms, the trouble
and uneasiness given to peaceable men, whom the least tact or
knowledge of the world would at once have acquitted beforehand,
the examinations and sealings of papers, arrests, and discharges
from arrest; only one thing was wondered at in the midst of all
these fearful movements, that, while searching for traces of secret
conspiracies carried on in the dark, these profound politicians
should see nothing of a grand conspiracy, which spreads its extensive ramifications over all Germany, throughout every rank and
age and sex; which sits murmuring by every hearth, which raises
its voice aloud in markets and highways, which is easily perceived
in all its members without any sign, and which, without secret
heads, and without impulse from a common centre, works constantly in concert and with the very best understanding to promote one common end; which stares with many thousand open
eyes into the most hidden recesses, and which has many thousand
arms constantly at command; that conspiracy, namely, in which
the irritated feelings, the disappointed hopes, the wounded pride,
the sufferings and oppression of the nation, have associated themselves together against the rigid obstinacy of arbitrary power, the
mechanism of lifeless forms, the devouring poison of despotic

maxims of government unconsciously acted on, the fruit of the corruption of the times, and the blindest prejudices, and which conspiracy, powerful and formidable to a degree that no former one ever yet reached, and growing every day in power and activity, is so sure of attaining its object, that the danger will not certainly arise from the tardiness, but from the excessive rapidity of its progress.[1]

He inveighs against the new machinery of bureaucratic control which Prussia had imposed upon his native Rhineland, in a passage which recalls the paragraph printed on page 85 where Fichte gibbets as non-German the very Art of the State which Görres denounces as now the accepted German method. Contrasting the old, stiff, slow and stupid officialism with the new, he says of the latter :

As they have not even a conception of the still, quiet, and easy way in which Nature unfolds her works, their impatience has recourse to mechanism, and the State becomes in their hands a great steam-engine, in which they themselves ascend and descend as a hot vapour, impelling, with deafening noise, an immense lever, at once serving to put in motion works for the coining of money, for raising of water, for hammering, spinning, and writing, and, at last, producing another machine like itself. In this mechanism, in which everything becomes lines and numbers, all the lines must terminate in one central point, and all the numbers must form one unit, that arbitrary power may, from the centre, calculate and control the different movements at pleasure, and no human or municipal relations may presume to assert an opposing and destructive independence.

Speaking of the persecution of the press he says in another fine passage :

Diplomatic campaigns were commenced against the journalists, in which, as in grand hunting-matches, the noble animal is provoked by dogs, teased with hallooings, and chased by pursuing hunters, till at last he falls down breathless, or sees himself under the necessity of plunging into water or bogs. The German forms of judicial proceedings were precisely such a bog to the persecuted writers in the state, in which a freedom from censorship had lately been established ; the most ardent of these writers, after remaining a very short time in this mud-bath, found the cooling quite sufficient to deter them from exerting themselves any longer with an over-abundant zeal in the cause of their country.

Others, foreseeing this fate, and having too much self-regard to expose themselves in such a manner to the rage of the agitated

---

[1] This last sentence is a good example of how much a German can pack between one full stop and another.

elements, had prudently adopted a safer course, and entered into an amicable arrangement with power for mutual satisfaction. To speak of liberty and liberal sentiments in general terms, while in practice they glossed over and justified every act of despotic violence, and every detestable institution, seemed to them the only course compatible with an age in which all regard for justice was laid aside. It was allowable to exhibit on the parade all the heroes of Plutarch, provided every man were held up as insane who wished, in any manner, to imitate them. . . . On the other hand, they were ready to cover with the cloak of love the most infamous acts of tyranny of him whose bread they eat, to concede to him, with the most affectionate kindness, every exception from elevated principle, and to put themselves forward on all occasions as his champions.

Plain speaking of this kind was intolerable to the King of Prussia, who issued the following rescript :

To LIEUTENANT-GENERAL VON HACKE, and the Minister of State VON INGERSLEBEN

' The culpability of Professor Görres, who, in his work committed to the press, entitled *Germany and the Revolution*, notwithstanding he enjoys from the liberality of the State a salary of 1800 rix-dollars, has not refrained from making use of the most disrespectful language towards his own and foreign sovereigns ; and, under the appearance of warning the people against revolution and illegal violence, and recommending peace, has endeavoured, by the most audacious censure of the measures of government, to fill the people with rage and discontent, is so evident, that I hereby commission you to seize the whole of his papers, and to transmit them under Seal to the minister Von Schuckmann.'

' FREDERICK WILLIAM.'

BERLIN, 30*th September* 1819.

The king had hoped to secure not only the papers but also the person of so pestilent a fellow as this Rhenish journalist ; but Görres skipped, if so light a motion is possible to a German, across the frontier to Strasburg, and thence to Switzerland. In 1827 Ludwig of Bavaria recalled him from exile to occupy a professorial chair at Munich, where the ardent Roman Catholicism to which he was no pervert, but in which, unlike Haller and Adam Müller, he was born and bred, gave him fresh scope for his combative energies. Princess Metternich wrote with warm appreciation of him in 1834 as of one who ' from being an abominable Jacobin has become one of the best men in the world.' [1]

[1] *Cambridge Modern History*, x. p. 380.

CHAPTER IV

MORE CRITICISM OF REACTION

IN this chapter will be brought together a further series of excerpts which give a clear indication of the feeling aroused among various classes of the community by the ruthless application of the Carlsbad Decrees. And we may best begin by giving some account of the attitude of Stein, the real hero of the War of Liberation, a statesman whom Englishmen may be proud to honour, though, for all his genuinely English conceptions of social and political reform, of freedom and of liberalism, he had no great admiration for their country. Stein was no Prussian ; he came from Nassau to the rescue of Prussia when she lay crushed beneath the heel of Napoleon. He acted for a time as Prime Minister of the distracted country, and his sagacious eye recognised in the Prussian bureaucratic system one of the most serious obstacles to the development of a free and self-reliant political Germany on which he set his hopes. As early as 1807, when embarking on his great scheme of social reform and reconstruction, he wrote to his colleague Hardenberg : ' I think it important to break the fetters with which the bureaucracy hampers the development of human capacity. We must destroy this spirit of greed, of mean advantage, of dependence on machinery, to which our form of government is subject. The nation must be accustomed to manage its own business and to emerge from this state of childhood, in which an ever-restless, officious government would keep grown men.' Too soon he was relegated by the jealousy of the Prussian nobility, and the reactionary instinct of the reigning Hohenzollern, to the position of a mere observer and commentator on events, though respect for his great accomplishments, his character and ideals, made his a name to conjure with among all true German patriots. In his old age he made warm friends with a fellow Rhinelander, and like himself an Imperial Knight,

Hans Ernst Chr. von Gagern, father of Heinrich von Gagern the real founder of the Frankfort Parliament of which we shall hear presently. In Stein's letters to Gagern will be found the terse and pithy expression of his views on men and things all through the period of repression associated with the Carlsbad Decrees and the Central Inquiry Commission. He was an honest liberal and would have no truck with abuse of the freedom of the press, or disloyal propaganda in the universities, but the right way to deal with evils like these was, in his judgment, to get quit of them by removing their causes. In 1818 he wrote to Gagern : ' It is terrible that freedom of the press should be so abused. This would cease if properly devised representative constitutions came into existence ; when men know and manage their own public business, then the shallow loquacity of demagogues makes no further impression.' In 1819, after the issue of the Carlsbad Decrees, he wrote : ' The most effective measure that can be taken for the maintenance of peace in Germany is to put an end to the reign of despotism, and to found and set going the one legal constitution ; in the place of bureaucrats and demagogic pamphleteers, of whom the former oppress the people by too much, and bad, government, while the latter irritate and perplex it, to set the influence and co-operation of the property-holders.' And again : ' Almost every one in the country wants peace, order, and the maintenance of the princely houses, but equally the provision by means of representative institutions of a guarantee against abuse of power. One must show confidence in the good sense of the people, strengthen the governments by rallying all interests about them, keep an eye on agitators, remove mischief-makers, punish the guilty. But what will be the result of oppressive measures of restraint, of the continuance of a system of bureaucratic ordinances, which receives its impulse from an empty, ignorant charlatan (Metternich), full of confidence in his own talents, and a frivolous, dissolute, arrogant, insincere old man (Hardenberg), always anxious lest he lose his place ? '

He admitted that in his opinion the universities were not free from reproach. He thought ' that among many German scholars a revolutionary and democratic tendency prevailed,' and that they ' abused the respect that their position secured for them by disseminating perverted principles among their youthful charges.' But at the same time he denounced the pains and penalties threatening the universities. Thereby, said he, students and professors were robbed of an independence which the former needed for the development of their characters, the latter for the pursuit of truth.

In 1821 he returned in a famous letter to Gagern to the charge against bureaucracy :

I have no more to say of the events of the time than that I have little trust in their immediate director, but absolute confidence in Providence, . . . and that we are governed by officials, salaried, lettered, uninterested, unpropertied officials; which will continue as long as it does. These four words contain the essence of our own, and similar, soulless government machines. Salaried, therefore striving for the maintenance and the increase of the salaried; lettered, therefore living not in the real world but in a world of the alphabet; uninterested, for they stand in association with no class of citizens, making up the State; they form a caste of their own, the clerking caste; unpropertied, therefore all the concerns of property do not touch them; the rain may fall or the sun may shine, taxes may rise or fall, old and traditional rights may be taken or left, all our peasants may be changed by theorists into day-labourers, and for dependence on landlords, dependence on money-lenders and Jews be substituted—all that troubles them not. They draw their pay from the Treasury, and write, and write, and write in their quiet offices well furnished with sound-proof doors, unwept, unhonoured, and unsung, and rear their children after them as similarly useful clerking machines. One machine (the military) I saw fall in 1806, on the 14th October; perhaps the clerking machine will also have its 14th October.

In 1825 he wrote of the Central Inquiry Commission : ' The whole of this inquisitorial apparatus is ridiculous and ineffective in the highest degree ; it is a veritable institution for fighting with windmills.'

Surely no statesman ever expressed himself more frankly in his dislike of policy or of persons. But there is nothing in any of his letters which might not, so far as the limits of expression go, be found in the private correspondence of an English statesman, nothing that can fairly be called undignified. Very different is it with the specimen of academic spleen which may now be given in illustration of the high professorial point of view when a colleague is summarily dismissed from his chair. Letter after letter in this book goes to show how impossible it is for a German intellectual to preserve his dignity even when expressing a well-founded resentment. We have told how

Arndt, on a charge of democratic intrigue, was dismissed from his professorship at Bonn, Arndt, the poet of the War of Liberation, the author of *Was ist des Deutschen Vaterland*. When the news reached Berlin of the charge brought against him, a letter of sympathy in the following terms came from Schleiermacher, the great Protestant divine of the period, Arndt's comrade in arms during the old days of stress, a philosopher of distinction as well as a leader of the people, and, last not least, the clergyman who confirmed Bismarck : [1]

BERLIN, *27th January* 1819.

I am very sorry, my dear brother, that I did not reply to you at once, with the announcement that you have still something very disagreeable to face, to wit, a great and Royal rap on the knuckles. As it is, I fear you've had to face the pretty business without any preparation ; for this very evening we've had read to us a ministerial rescript full of all-round warnings and threats, which, from the whole tone of it, is founded on the same Order in Council. I only wish I had let you know of it beforehand, since you are still something of a novice as regards the stricter side of the state service. However, I send you after the event my most friendly greetings on our joint and intimate acquaintance with the great Rap. For you probably know that I too had in the year 1813, à propos of an article in the *Prussian Correspondent*, to face just such a knock as fairly corresponds with yours. So soon as I made bold to mix myself up again with matters political (N.B. as editor of a newspaper) there spread rumours of the inevitable cancelling of all my official appointments. . . . But I gaily shook the pother off and now I'm simply storing up my political activity like a ham in pickle. Let us hope, my dear brother, you'll manage to do the same, and when you get a second rap, as I did soon afterwards, and that a rap from a Lord High Chancellor on account of a censorship dispute with Le Coq, save that one up too. All good things, I fancy, come by threes, but for all the trouble I've taken I've not yet succeeded in bringing it to a third. Altenstein (Minister of Public Worship) will certainly silver the pill more politely for you than Schuckmann (Minister of Police) did for me. In his oral examination he clawed me with all his bearishness, but I so tamed him by what I said, that he goes about since quite decently in a muzzle. There is nothing more pitifully mean for a king than getting the better of one in this petty way, and we can wish him well of it. The good man rolled himself sadly in the dirt a few days ago. At the Coronation Festivities, Eylert (Evangelical Bishop, Privy Councillor in the Ministry of Public Worship) delivered himself from the Cathedral pulpit of some wretched twaddle on the shocking spirit of the age, how

---

[1] Max Lenz, *Geschichte der Universität Berlin,* iv. K.).

all the forces of society had broken bounds, how the demand was on all sides for freedom and equality, how all respect for persons in a superior position had vanished, and how all knightly gentlemen must band themselves together to put an end to the scandal. So that our knightly gentlemen came to a determination : if the revolution broke out on Monday, they would give it a bold rap over the knuckles, but should it not make its appearance even on Tuesday, they would search for it at night with a lantern ! After service the good man (the King) walked about the court exclaiming : ' Fine words to listen to ! Very much to the point ! Must sting many consciences ! '—But why should one waste another word on such silly rubbish ?

Many people had dreamed that on the 18th or the 24th a whole hotch-potch of preliminaries on the constitutional question would be published ; but all dwindled down to little ministerial changes, which can only be regarded as important if (Wilhelm von) Humboldt attacks his business with a more exceptional earnestness that I can confidently ascribe to him.

How the students regarded the restriction of their liberties, and particularly the suppression of the *Burschenschaft*, is shown by a poem by A. Binzer, published at Jena in November 1819, which became famous at once, and was famous in the German universities in 1914, though the spirit that prompted it no longer existed :

' WE HAD BUILT US AN HOUSE '

We had built us an house
So stately in form,
Where we trusted in God
Through trouble and storm.

We lived there so snugly,
United and free ;
No chance for the Tempter,
So loyal were we.

The lying, the spying
Informer's jack-boot,
With slanders and curses,
Trod down the green shoot.

What God in us planted
The world took unkind ;
Good folk feared our motto,
' One heart and one mind,'

Who thought to condemn it
Deceived himself sore :
Love's mould may be shattered,
Love's self never-more !

The mould, it is shattered,
In fragments is broke ,
But what the spies sniff at
Is but vapour and smoke.

The band, it is severed—
'Twas black, red, and gold—
And God, in His wisdom,
Looked down to behold !

The house may be ruined—
Who fears storms that lower ?
Our spirit lives on in us,
And God's our strong tower !

The feeling among students was also evinced in prose by such an entry [1] as this in one of the albums which they, like so many German associations, are fond of keeping :

How can the works of the light be done in the darkness ? Our first effort must be for publicity. For only in publicity can a fuller life arise. As a matter of fact we all have one wish, and we have only ourselves to blame when we avoid a free understanding. A free spirit of criticism is our prime necessity. In the second place this publicity can only be attained if we are united. Our fatherland can give us a sad picture of all the misery that springs from our passion for Particularism. Our student life should give us more than mere rights ; it should give us a code. We should make ourselves a picture of the Fatherland State, to whose service we would devote our whole existence. In that we can only succeed when we allow a common spirit to grow up in us, sensitive to our fatherland's weal and woe, to freedom and justice. But how can this come about, when we, even as students, separate ourselves one from another, when we, even as students, prefer the interest of one to the interest of another ? Only unity can bring us salvation, all separatism is deadly, for it rouses a feeling of egoism even in the best of causes.

R. L. Schmid, of the Faculty of Law, Jena.

But perhaps the most drastic, pungent, incisive comments, certainly the two most remarkable prophecies in this work, we owe to a pair of Judæo-Germans, Ludwig Börne and Heinrich

[1] *Die deutschen Stammbücher des 16 bis 19 Jahrhunderts.* R. und R. Keil, 1893 (K.).

Heine, both of them men of genius, the latter of transcendent genius. Börne, the son of a banker, was born at Frankfort in 1786. All that money could do to provide education for a clever youth was lavished on him. But when he reached man's estate the official avenue of promotion in Frankfort was closed to him because he was a Jew. Of the oppression of his race in Germany before and during the revolutionary period F. A. Brockhaus gives a gloomy picture in his account [1] of their treatment in Frankfort :

In the reign of Carl von Dalberg, Grand Duke of Frankfort (under Napoleon), the Jews had to purchase equality of rights with Christian citizens by payment of a ransom of not less than 440,000 florins. At the Congress of Vienna the conclusion of Article 16 of the German Act of Confederation was drafted as follows : ' Until then [*i.e.* pending a general law] the adherents of this [the Jewish] faith shall retain the rights *in* individual states of the Confederation which have hitherto been conceded to them.' In one of the last sessions the word ' in ' was altered to ' of.' . . . The Jews became the victims of a squabble like the quarrel over a disputed cabbage-patch, and finally the protection of their rights was commended to or enjoined upon the (Frankfort) Senate, not as well-grounded but as ' well-earned,' according as any one liked to interpret terms. A commission had recommended, as guaranteed, the grant of equality of rights in the capacity of private citizens, but this view was rejected by the Senate. . . . The Jews appealed to the Federal Diet, and through its intervention a law was finally passed in 1824, whereby most of their rights as private citizens were acknowledged, but marriage was forbidden to Jews, as Börne puts it pointedly. In the case of only fourteen couples annually (twelve native couples, two where one party was of foreign birth) was an exception to be made. This Pharaonic decision was not revoked by the legislature until ten years later (1834), and then so far as regarded purely native couples. After a further thirteen years (31st October 1847) even semi-foreign couples might exceed two ; but this ' favour ' was limited to the following ten years. Not to accord to Jews nor withhold from them the title of citizen, they were to be styled ' Israelitish Citizens.' In this way a species of hawk-moths was created, with just so much light allowed as enabled them to burn their wings.

During a slight lull in the hardship of the conditions under which a Jew laboured, Börne did receive, in 1811, a public appointment as police actuary. But in 1814 the old measure of repression revived and he had to send in his resignation. Only one profession was now left open to him, that of journalism,

[1] *Die Gegenwart* (K.).

and he embraced it in the militant spirit born of righteous indignation. From 1830 to his death in 1837 he lived in Paris, and there he was inspired to even more brilliant satire than in his native land. The following passage from one of his dramatic sketches and criticisms, a form of journalism which he developed into a fine art, dates from his German period :

WORDS AND DEEDS.[1]

We think well and speak badly, speak much and do little, do much and finish nothing. But our indifference to business does not arise from our preference for words, rather the other way round, our preference for words arises from our dread of business. The coy German turns his eyes away from every naked act. Something happens without circumstance—pah ! how disgusting ! . . . But words are the clothing of actions. With us words make not only clothes, they also make people. This horror of action has its basis in the mania for secrecy which is born in us, which we have inherited. We gladly do nothing, for what has never taken place is most easily buried in silence. Our God is a secret, our religion reticence. We love silence and a shudder. With us every one has, or invents, his secrets, beggar as well as king. A Minister would gladly swathe every bomb in warfare in cotton-wool, so that one cannot hear it fall, and the Inspector of Police thinks that the State will collapse if a citizen learns that his good neighbour has hanged himself in the morning. Whoever among us lives to see the last day will find plenty to laugh at. Whatever God says, under twenty sheets in content, will be censored, and when the world catches fire and the fat begins to melt off the upper classes, the Police will make the announcement : ' Alarmists have spread the rumour that the World is overheated. This is an insidious fabrication : the weather was never cooler or finer. All people are cautioned against making ill-considered remarks and lounging idly about the streets. Parents should keep their children, teachers their pupils, and employers their work-people indoors. Keep the peace ! To keep the peace is the citizen's first duty.' . . . And then will the whole world be engulfed and keep the peace, and then will the whole world become German.

Heine wrote a sketch [2] of his compatriot's life and opinions, which, to say the least, contains less of the milk of human kindness [3] than most biographical essays, but it gives a number

---

[1] *Dramaturgische Blätter : Das Trauerspiel in Tirol.*
[2] English translation by T. S. Egan, 1881.
[3] Heine's reflections by Börne's grave provoke one of the most audacious flights of his cynical imagination: ' Whether we one day rise again ? My waking thoughts would negative this question, and out of pure spirit of contradiction my dreams at night say yes. For instance, I dreamed not long since : I had walked out early in the morning to the churchyard, and there, to my greatest

of examples of a genius which Heine recognised as akin to his own. Of the sort of ironic persiflage of which both were masters and for which, when turned against themselves, Germans naturally find it hard to forgive them, the following is not a bad example. Said Börne one day : ' I have just been reading . . . that the Mahommedans there (on the north coast of Africa) consider themselves warranted by their religion to treat all the Christians who suffer shipwreck, and fall into their hands, as slaves. They divide these unfortunate persons among them, and make use of each according to his abilities. Thus an Englishman who was lately travelling on that coast found there a learned German, who had been shipwrecked and made a slave, but being fit for nothing else, they put eggs under him to be hatched ; he belonged, of course, to the theological faculty.'

But of the more serious side of his genius take this little fragment of dialogue dating from early days in Paris ; it contains a prophecy which Bismarck fulfilled :

You can read it here, here it stands in print : ' Germany is pregnant with great things ! ' Yes, that is true, Germany is big with great events ; but there will be a difficult labour, and we require a man-midwife, who will have to operate with iron instruments. What do you think ?

' I do not think that Germany is pregnant.'

No, no, you are mistaken. An abortion may perhaps be brought into the world, but Germany will give birth.

This prophecy is only to be paralleled by one of Heine's own, a little later in date, but which ought for completeness sake to be printed here. The passage occurs near the end of his *Religion and Philosophy in Germany*, which was written in Paris. Addressing the French he says :

Christianity has to a certain degree moderated that brutal lust of battle, such as we find it among the ancient Germanic races who fought, not to destroy, nor yet to conquer, but merely from a fierce demoniac love of battle itself ; but it could not altogether eradicate it. And when once that restraining talisman, the cross, is broken, then the smouldering ferocity of those ancient warriors will again blaze up ; then again will be heard the deadly clang

---

surprise, I saw a pair of brightly polished boots standing by the side of every grave, as we see, it may be, at the room doors of travellers in an hotel. . . . It was an astounding sight ; a quiet stillness reigned throughout the church-yard, the weary pilgrims of the earth were sleeping, grave beside grave, and the brightly polished boots, standing there in long rows, shone in the fresh light of morning, rich in hope, full of promise, a proof of the resurrection clear as the sun at noonday.'

of that frantic Berserker wrath, of which the Norse poets say and sing so much. That talisman is rotten with decay, and the day will surely come when it will crumble and fall. Then the ancient stone gods will arise from out the ashes of dismantled ruins, and rub the dust of a thousand years from their eyes ; and finally Thor, with his colossal hammer, will leap up and with it shatter into fragments the Gothic cathedrals. . . . Smile not at my advice as the counsel of a visionary warning you against Kantians, Fichteans and natural philosophers. Scoff not at the dreamer who expects in the material world a revolution similar to that which has already taken place in the domain of thought The thought goes before the deed, as the lightning precedes the thunder. True, the German thunder *is* German, is rather awkward, and comes rolling along rather tardily ; but come it surely will, and when ye once hear a crash the like of which in the world's history was never heard before, then know that the German thunderbolt has reached its mark. At this crash the eagles will fall dead in mid air, and the lions in Afric's most distant deserts will cower and sneak into their most royal dens. A drama will be enacted in Germany in comparison with which the French Revolution will appear a harmless idyl.

. . . That hour will come. As on the raised benches of an amphitheatre the nations will group themselves around Germany to behold the great tournament. . . . Ye have more to fear from emancipated Germany than from the whole Holy Alliance, with all its Croats and Cossacks.

What was it gave these Jews this uncanny gift of prophecy ? In any country in which the chosen people are to be found Jews take their place among the intellectual aristocracy, as in commerce among its captains. They form the purest of races to this day, and we, above all nations, have to repudiate indignantly the German suggestion that no Jew can be in his adopted country a patriot in the full sense of the term, and have in honour and reason to admit the claim that he can be of, as well as in, the political tradition of what has become to him his homeland. But the Jew has and retains the intrinsic qualities that form the inheritance of his race ; he is thus enabled to look at life and all its concerns great and small, from a different angle from others, and may become on occasion the shrewdest of critics, the wisest of counsellors and the most inspired of prophets. So it was with Börne and Heine. Far more keen-witted than any of their German contemporaries, less passionate, less emotional, they were not permitted to embark on the main current of German life, but had from the bank a better sight of whither the stream was tending and the shoals or rocks ahead.

A not unnatural admixture of malice in their state of mind would not dim perception nor restrain anticipation of an evil fate for the ship of state on which they were not allowed to serve. Treitschke in the third volume of his monumental history does scant justice to the value of the literary influence of Börne and Heine ; their effect on German prose was enormous, and to Börne as the older man, and first in the field, is due most of the credit. His brilliant articles and sketches, and above all his *Letters from Paris*, captivated young Germany. The heightened sense of individuality, the suppleness, the adaptability, in short the genius of his race gave him the faculty of writing German that had the crystalline clearness, the sparkle, the terseness, and the epigrammatic force of French. Treitschke exhibits the German fault of ingratitude. Had it not been for Börne he might have been in style another elephantine Joseph Görres. To Börne he owes the flashing, sometimes flashy, style with which he is justly credited.

But we have been anticipating the next decade, and, as lame authors do, digressing. It is time to end this brief survey of Germany between 1813 and 1830 on an authentic German note. The period was one of disappointment, and the prestige of the Prussian nation sank with the spirits of the people. Prince William of Prussia (later Kaiser William I.) exclaimed in 1824,[1] ' Had the nation known in 1813 that of a degree of glory, reputation, and prestige, that might then be reached, and was actually reached, nothing would remain eleven years later but the memory, who would then have sacrificed all for such a result ? '

Stein in his old age came near to despair. In 1830 he wrote to Gagern : ' I plant, I build, I read ; but for whom do I plant, for whom do I build ? Who in these stormy, boisterous times can answer the question ? Here with us reign loyalty, love, and fear of God.' Goethe died, as he had lived, serene. His conversation with Eckermann, dated 23rd October 1828, is well known, but the concluding sentence merits attention, for it proves that the old seer had a foreboding of what Prussian ambition was nursing for Berlin, and his foreboding has been realised :

I have no fear that Germany will not become one ; our good roads and future railways will play their part. But above all may it

---

[1] Quoted by Klein.

be one in mutual love ! And may it ever be one against a foreign
foe ! May it be one, so that the German thaler and the German
groschen may have one value throughout the whole country ; one,
that my travelling-bag may pass through the six-and-thirty states
without being opened. May it be one, that the municipal passport of a citizen of Weimar be not treated by the frontier officials
of some great neighbour state as invalid, as being the passport
of a foreigner. May there be no more talk among German States
anywhere of *inland* and *outland*. Moreover may Germany be one
in weights and measures, in trade and intercourse and a hundred
similar things that I cannot and must not mention.—But if
any one supposes that the unity of Germany demands as a condition that the vast country shall have one single great Capital, and
that this one great Capital will conduce both to the development
of the great talents of individuals and to the welfare of the great
mass of the people, he is wrong.

BOOK II
STAGNATION
1830-1840

CHAPTER I

THE POSITION OF PRUSSIA IN 1830—THE POLITICAL TREND OF GERMAN PHILOSOPHY FROM KANT THROUGH FICHTE TO HEGEL

THE year 1830 marks a period in European history, for in July of that year broke out in Paris the revolution which drove out in exile from France the last of her Bourbon kings, Charles x. The effect of this revolution on discontent in Germany, and Prussia in particular, was not so great as might have been anticipated, and that for several reasons. Though a large section of the intellectuals was still seething with the wild hopes roused by the national uprising in 1813, there was a conservative section which was only confirmed in conservatism by any outburst of revolutionary violence either at home or abroad ; the business classes in Prussia were beginning to reap the reward of the skilful financial administration of the new Prussian bureaucracy, and the growing commercial prosperity of Austria's great rival could not be without its effect on other German states, where the way was opening for the entry of Prussia's administrative methods ; the population at large was still rooted in the dynastic tradition, and the figure of Frederick William III., now sixty years of age, had become venerable in the eyes of all Germany as the one comparatively amiable personality among the princes that counted. The opportunity afforded by the French Revolution of 1830 was, it is true, utilised in several of the more reactionary states, such as Brunswick, Hesse-Cassel, Saxony, and Hanover, to wring from the governments further instalments of constitutional reform, but Prussia herself was undisturbed. Until the end of 1830 opinion in Germany was slowly and surely working for conservatism and the ascendancy of Prussia. Then came a change which is well indicated by C. T. Perthes in his life of his father, the publisher, the tentacles of whose correspondence reached far and deep :

E

Towards the close of 1830, Perthes received communications from all parts of Germany, clearly showing that the former confidence in Prussia had passed into distrust and aversion. Thus a letter from the north of Germany : ' Many far-seeing men, who consider Prussia destined to promote our national progress, are not so sure that she understands this mission, and is able to fulfil it in the sense of the majority. This much is certain, that all the governments will do their utmost to maintain the *status quo*, and that their endeavour will be only in part successful ; for the *status quo*, properly speaking, fits but a single moment ; the very next takes away or adds something, so that the party of progress always wins in the long run, even when for the time it seems to be paralysed. Germany is at present a perfect chaos, in which, however, the usual functions still proceed regularly—as production, industry, population, and exchange. Only the higher functions suffer ; we can see that they are enfeebled, or are working with a fever pulse, and that greater men than have yet appeared are necessary for the restoration of this body to perfect health and regular action. The usual recipes have been used up ; the mystics, terrible people in our days, after exhausting their Latin, have bethought themselves of a radical cure, in the Last Day, which they announce as at hand. Let me hear soon what you expect.' Again : ' I don't doubt but that, if France attack the Rhenish frontier, she will be stoutly opposed ; but in present circumstances, to excite hatred of the French, and to kindle enthusiasm for Germany as a whole, would be alike impossible. At present the Germans feel that they have no country to defend, but that every man has to defend himself against spoliation and ignominy. The Prussians, the thorough-going ones, I mean, think more than they say, and see little else in a war with the French than a means of their own aggrandisement in Germany.' Again : ' For a long time at least I give up hopes of Prussia doing for Germany what I once expected. The peoples can be won only by going ahead, and the governments only by inspiring confidence. Now to take a proverb from my old French, *On ne prend pas les mouches avec du vinaigre* ; but Prussia has given all her neighbours an abundant foretaste of vinegar, and then what a state of matters in her own interior ! Her own servants are fretting under the starched formality of her administration, and complaining bitterly that no scope is given to civic life and local independence. You would almost think it had been decreed that the state alone has understanding, consequently that nothing shall be done but through its councillors, and that the citizen has only one duty, viz., to do as he is bidden. Men are tired of this, and now that the government confines itself to negative action, and that the machinery is getting stiff, the worst consequences may ensue.' Again : ' Great distance may account for much of the misinterpretation concerning Prussia, but the calumnies are unpardonable with which her every movement and purpose are blackened at present. I myself heard a man of high consideration say in the presence of several, that he should like to see a war with France, in order that despotic Prussia might be punished by the loss of the Rhenish provinces, and so be no longer able to resist constitutionalism.'

Perthes himself represented the conservative point of view, as the following extracts from prophetic letters of his written late in 1830 will serve to show :

'I can recall the time of Frederick the Great, when Prussia stood so high in the public opinion of Germany, that a word spoken against her was regarded as blasphemy.'

'As for the smaller states, the year 1830 might well be the beginning of the end, or rather the beginning of the beginning for them ; they cannot remain as they are, and on that very account Germany must be moulded anew. Sooner or later Prussia must enter on a great struggle for the status and unity of Germany ; and should she prove victorious, then are we Germans saved— we shall have a fatherland ; but if otherwise, a dark future lies before us.'

'The more I know of Prussia, the more am I convinced that her intellectual development and power must give her an influence in Europe far beyond that of material force, which may in time transcend even that of France and England. In consequence, however, of the disproportion between intellectual and material power in Prussia, strong convulsions may be expected.'

Nevertheless we may conclude that the prevailing view among the educated classes in the Germany of this period was not that of Perthes, but is rather that indicated in this pungent extract from one of his correspondents : 'Vengeance is now overtaking the princes for their offences in 1814 and 1815 ; they cared not a straw for the people then, though the people had just delivered them from the profound abasement into which they had fallen by their own folly and weakness. God is in the storm, judging kings and princes by His thunders.'

Certainly the prospects of Prussia in 1830 were not, to all appearances, hopeful, and it is necessary for us, before we proceed with any narrative of events during the thirties to realise clearly, and appreciate, the tremendous forces working for Prussia which enabled her in the course of the next fifty years to triumph over every difficulty and to establish herself as mistress of the German world. One of these forces, the bureaucratic system introduced into Prussia, has already been indicated, and we shall see how she absorbed into that system the cleverest brains in Germany, and how by her fiscal and commercial policy she brought Germany into economic earlier than political union. Another, her military power, will clearly demonstrate itself at the end of this volume. A third has now to be described, and in detail, viz., the part played by philosophy in consolidating the Prussian system. At the very outset of this work the claim of German poetry as one of the inspirations animating Germans in the first part of last century has been asserted, and the claim will be substantiated as the history of the time proceeds. But German philosophers played an even more powerful part than German poets, and a part which became more powerful as it became less popular, and developed from the metaphysical, critical, and ethical standpoint of Kant, through the surging Germanic enthusiasm of Fichte, into the hard, cold, reactionary, political dogmatism of Hegel, who ran his truck-load of philosophical ideas along the bureaucratic rails. It is intended in this chapter and the two following to illustrate this period of transition, which resulted in the elaboration by Hegel of a German political philosophy as distinct from all others as the German conception of *unser lieber Gott* is from the God of the universe. And the method employed will be that adopted in the rest of this book, viz., to let Germans speak for themselves. The view presented may shock the small class of those in our own country who read philosophy. Our professors have not laid much stress on the political side of philosophic thought in Germany ; after-war lecturers on the subject, even in the most mossy lecture-room, will not leave this aspect unillumined. For one who is not a professor, either in the academic sphere or in that of legerdemain, to attempt to break ground in this direction may bring down on his head the scorn of the hierophants of what has almost become an occult science, but he may console himself with a passage from Heine. Near the commencement of his *History of Religion and Philosophy in Germany* [1] he says : ' Distinguished German philosophers who may accidentally cast a glance over these pages will superciliously shrug their shoulders at the meagreness and incompleteness of all that which I here offer. But they will be kind enough to bear in mind that the little which I say is expressed clearly and intelligibly, whereas their own works, although very profound, unfathomably profound—very deep, stupendously deep—are in the same degree unintelligible. Of what benefit to the people

[1] English translation by J. Snodgrass, 1882.

is the grain locked away in granaries to which they have no key ? '

Sophistication apart, the story is very simple, and we shall begin it with Kant, the first great figure in modern German philosophy. Two facts with regard to him are of great moment, (1) he came of Scottish stock, (2) he flourished during the last portion of the eighteenth century. Both of these circumstances are significant when we come to consider what he has to say on the state and on political concerns. To the first are in some measure due the comparatively high flash-point of the blood coursing through his veins, and his freedom from any predisposition in favour of the autocratic or paternal government established in Prussia ; with him the dynastic tradition was not bred in the bone. The second gave him as food for thought two historical events of the first magnitude, the French Revolution, and the birth of the greatest republic the world has ever seen, the United States of North America. Every man accepted by subsequent ages as a leader of his time will be found to have reflected either the dominant among the forces of his time, which his keen eyes have been early to discover, or the first rays of some new light dawning on a chaos in which the world is involved. Kant's political views were undoubtedly influenced by a consideration of the victorious struggle of the British colonists across the ocean, and the rapid rise to importance of a new nation governed with success on lines strange to Europe, just as the trend of Fichte's thought in matters social and political was set by the humiliation of the Napoleonic regime and a passionate fervour for the redemption of his country, and as Hegel twisted philosophy into an apologia for the Prussian system.

In his views of the origin of society and the functions of the state Kant floated securely down the main stream of European thought. He accepted Hobbes's view of the origin of society out of a state of war, and he followed Locke and Rousseau in adopting the sovereignty of the people as the fundamental principle of the state. An elaborate exposition of his conclusions is to be found in his *Science of Right*, published in 1796.[1] He thus defines the state, and lays down the principles

[1] The quotations are from W. Hastie's translation under the title of *The Philosophy of Law*, by kind permission of Messrs. T. & T. Clark of Edinburgh. The style of the printing has been retained ; it brings into a German atmosphere a pleasant reek from the lums of the Old Town.

that should govern the legislative power and the attributes
that should belong to the members of a state :

45. A State (*Civitas*) is the union of a number of men under
juridical Laws. These Laws, as such, are to be regarded as necessary *à priori*,—that is, as following of themselves from the conceptions of external Right generally,—and not as merely established by Statute. The FORM of the State is thus involved in the
Idea of the State, viewed as it ought to be according to pure principles of Right ; and this ideal Form furnishes the normal criterion
of every real union that constitutes a Commonwealth.

Every State contains in itself THREE POWERS, the universal
united Will of the People being this personified in a political triad.
These are *the Legislative Power, the Executive Power,* and *the Judiciary
Power*.—1. The *Legislative* Power of the Sovereignty in the State
is embodied in the person of the Lawgiver ; 2. the Executive
Power is embodied in the person of the Ruler who administers the
Law ; and 3. the Judiciary Power, embodied in the person of the
Judge, is the function of assigning every one what is his own,
according to the Law (*Potestas legislatoria, rectoria et judiciaria*). . . .

46. The Legislative Power (viewed in its rational Principle)
can only belong to the united Will of the People. For, as all Right
ought to proceed from this Power, it is necessary that its Laws
should be unable to do wrong to any one whatever. Now, if any
one individual determines anything in the State in contradistinc-
tion to *another*, it is always possible that he may perpetrate a wrong
on that other ; but this is never possible when *all* determine and
decree what is to be Law to themselves. ' *Volenti non fit injuria.*'
Hence it is only the united and consenting Will of all the People
—in so far as Each of them determines the same thing about all,
and All determine the same thing about each—that ought to have
the power of enacting Law in the State.

The Members of a Civil Society thus united for the purpose of
Legislation, and thereby constituting a State, are called its CITIZENS ;
and there are three juridical attributes that inseparably belong
to them by Right. These are—1. Constitutional FREEDOM, as
the Right of every Citizen to have to obey no other Law than
that to which he has given his consent or approval ; 2. Civil
EQUALITY, as the Right of the Citizen to recognise no one as a
Superior among the people in relation to himself, except in so
far as such a one is as subject to *his* moral power to impose obligations, as that other has power to impose obligations upon him ;
and 3. Political INDEPENDENCE, as the Right to owe his existence
and continuance in Society not to the arbitrary Will of another,
but to his own Rights and Powers as a Member of the Commonwealth ; and, consequently, the possession of a Civil Personality,
which cannot be represented by any other than himself.

Regarding the state as representing the united will of the

people, Kant will have nothing to do with resistance to the
supreme legislative authority in the state. There is no right
of sedition, and still less of rebellion, belonging to the people.
The formal execution of a monarch by his people excites his
horror. But he reconciles liberal sentiment with respect for
law and order in the following way :

An alteration of the still defective Constitution of the State may
sometimes be quite necessary. But all such changes ought only
to proceed from the Sovereign Power in the way of *Reform*, and
are not to be brought about by the people in the way of *Revolution* ; and when they take place they should only affect the *Executive* and not the *Legislative* Power. A political Constitution which
is so modified that the People by their Representatives in Parliament can legally *resist* the Executive Power and its representative
Minister, is called a Limited Constitution. Yet even under such a
Constitution there is no Right of *active* Resistance, as by an arbitrary
combination of the People to coerce the Government into a certain
active procedure ; for this would be to assume to perform an act
of the Executive itself. All that can rightly be allowed is only a
negative Resistance, amounting to an act of *Refusal* on the part of
the People to concede all the demands which the Executive may
deem it necessary to make in behoof of the political Administration. And if this Right were never exercised, it would be a sure
sign that the People were corrupted, their Representatives venal,
the Supreme Head of the Government despotic, and his Ministers
practically betrayers of the People.

The supreme authority in the state has the right, according
to Kant, to distribute offices, *i.e.* public and paid employ-
ments, to confer dignities, such as unpaid distinctions of rank,
and also to administer punishment. But in his discussion of
the second point, the conferring of dignities, his democratic
sympathies peep out, and also a pawky humour denied even
to his Scottish commentators. He says :

It may happen, however, that such an anomaly as that of Subjects
who would be more than Citizens, in the manner of born Officials
or hereditary Professors, has slipped into the mechanism of the
Government in olden times, as in the case of the Feudal System,
which was almost entirely organised with reference to War. Under
such circumstances, the State cannot deal otherwise with this error
of a wrongly instituted Rank in its midst, than by the remedy
of a gradual extinction through hereditary positions being left
unfilled as they fall vacant. The State has therefore the Right
provisorily to let a Dignity in Title continue, until the Public
Opinion matures on the subject. And this will thus pass from the

threefold division into Sovereign, Nobles, and People, to the two-fold and only natural division into Sovereign and People.

When we come to administration we have to remember that Kant lived before the development of the new bureaucracy which was one of Prussia's great achievements in the nineteenth century. It is idle to speculate as to what his judgment would have been of it, or the subtle imitation of it which has been permeating our own constitution during the past twenty-five years, but a shrewd conclusion may be drawn from what he has to say in his *Science of Right* on administration. The sweet simplicity of government by an autocratic bureaucracy, which has beguiled even some who style themselves Socialists, makes no appeal to him, as the following passage indicates clearly enough :

As regards the Administration of Right in the State, it may be said that the simplest mode is also the best ; but as regards its bearing on Right itself it is also the most dangerous for the People, in view of the Despotism to which simplicity of Administration so naturally gives rise. It is undoubtedly a rational maxim to aim at simplicity in the machinery which is to unite the People under compulsory Laws, and this would be secured were all the People to be passive and to obey only one person over them ; but the method would not give Subjects who were also Citizens of the State.

Consideration of the rights of one nation as against another, and of international relations, naturally lead him to discuss the problems raised by war, and his views, particularly his definition of an ' unjust enemy,' furnish a grim commentary on the proceedings of the Germany of the twentieth century. The airy bridge of wire-drawn metaphysical speculation that spans the gulf between Kantian theory and German practice one hundred and twenty years later will be found on pages 96 and 97 to have been dangled by Hegel before his crowd of budding bureaucrats. However, thus says Kant :

57. . . . Defensive measures and means of all kinds are allowable to a State that is forced to war, except such as by their use would make the Subjects using them unfit to be citizens ; for the State would thus make itself unfit to be regarded as a person capable of participating in equal rights in the international relations according to the Right of Nations. Among these forbidden means are to be reckoned the appointment of Subjects to act as spies, or engaging Subjects or even strangers to act as assassins,

or poisoners (in which class might well be included the so-called
sharpshooters who lurk in ambush for individuals), or even employing agents to spread false news. In a word, it is forbidden to use
any such malignant and perfidious means as would destroy the
confidence which would be requisite to establish a lasting peace
thereafter.

It is permissible in war to impose exactions and contributions
upon a conquered enemy ; but it is not legitimate to plunder the
people in the way of forcibly depriving individuals of their property. For this would be robbery, seeing it was not the conquered
people but the State under whose government they were placed
that carried on the war by means of them. . . .

60. The Right of a State against an *unjust* Enemy has no limits,
at least in respect of quality as distinguished from quantity or
degree. In other words, the injured State may use—not, indeed,
any means, but yet—all those means that are permissible and in
reasonable measure in so far as they are in its power, in order to
assert its Right to what is its own. But what then is an *unjust*
enemy according to the conceptions of the Right of Nations, when,
as holds generally of the state of Nature, every State is judge in
its own cause ? It is one whose publicly expressed Will, whether
in word or deed, betrays a maxim which, if it were taken as a
universal rule, would make a state of Peace among the nations
impossible, and would necessarily perpetuate the state of Nature. . . .

He concludes with a discussion of the possibility of bringing
about peace between nations, and while indulging in no rhapsodies on the subject, indicates this as an ideal to be aimed
at. His allusion to the Assembly of the States-General at The
Hague in the first half of the eighteenth century must provoke
a sardonic smile when we bethink us how in these latter days
the mailed fist of Potsdam has resisted the attraction of the
steel magnate of Pittsburg, and how the philosophy of events
will clip even an angel's wings and make of the Great Illusion
itself confusion worse confounded.

61. . . . A *Union of States*, in order to maintain Peace, may be
called a Permanent Congress of Nations ; and it is free to every
neighbouring State to join in it. A union of this kind, so far at
least as regards the formalities of the Right of Nations in respect
of the preservation of peace, was presented in the first half of this
century in the Assembly of the States-General at The Hague. In
this Assembly most of the European Courts, and even the smallest
Republics, brought forward their complaints about the hostilities
which were carried on by the one against the other. Thus the whole
of Europe appeared like a single Federated State, accepted as
Umpire by the several nations in their public differences. But in
place of this agreement, the Right of Nations afterwards survived

only in books ; it disappeared from the cabinets, or, after force had been already used, it was relegated in the form of theoretical deductions to the obscurity of Archives.

By such a *Congress* is here meant only a voluntary combination of different States that would be *dissoluble* at any time, and not such a union as is embodied in the United States of America, founded upon a political constitution, and therefore indissoluble. It is only by a Congress of this kind that the idea of a Public Right of Nations can be established, and that the settlement of their differences by the mode of a civil process, and not by the barbarous means of war, can be realised.

Conclusion

. . . It may be said that the universal and lasting establishment of Peace constitutes not merely a part, but the whole final purpose and end of the Science of Right as viewed within the limits of Reason.   The state of Peace is the only condition of the Mine and Thine that is secured and guaranteed by *Laws* in the relationship of men living in numbers contiguous to each other, and who are thus combined in a Constitution whose rule is derived not from the mere experience of those who have found it the best as a normal guide for others, but which must be taken by the Reason *à priori* from the ideal of a juridical Union of men under public laws generally. For all particular examples or instances, being able only to furnish illustration but not proof, are deceptive, and at all events require a Metaphysic to establish them by its necessary principles.   And this is conceded indirectly even by those who turn Metaphysics into ridicule, when they say, as they often do, ' The best Constitution is that in which not Men but Laws exercise the power.' For what can be more metaphysically sublime in its own way than this very Idea of theirs, which according to their own assertion has, notwithstanding, the most objective reality ?   This may be easily shown by reference to actual instances.   And it is this very Idea which alone can be carried out practically, if it is not forced on in a revolutionary and sudden way by violent overthrow of the existing defective Constitution ; for this would produce for the time the momentary annihilation of the whole juridical state of Society.   But if the idea is carried forward by gradual Reform, and in accordance with fixed Principles, it may lead by a continuous approximation to the highest political Good, and to Perpetual Peace.

The idea of perpetual peace occupied Kant much during the last years of his life.   What he says above follows the lines of a treatise he published in 1795 on *Perpetual Peace*,[1] in which, after a sly allusion to the title as once found above the picture

---

[1] See English translation, with an invaluable historical introduction, by Miss M. C. Smith.   Heineman, 1903.

of a churchyard, he dealt so systematically with the subject as to draw up two series of preliminary and definitive ' Articles of a Perpetual Peace between States.' Kant's freedom from the prejudice, nursed subsequently by Hegel, in favour of Prussian autocracy is shown by the first of his definitive articles, viz. : ' the civil constitution of each state shall be republican.' It is true that he distinguishes republicanism from despotism simply by declaring that ' republicanism is the political principle of severing the executive power of the government from the legislative,' while ' despotism is that principle in pursuance of which the state arbitrarily puts into effect laws which it has itself made,' and he recognised as republicanism any form of government in accordance with a representative system, so that a constitutional government under a limited monarchy, such as our government was until the autumn of 1914, is covered by the term. But his endorsement of Frederick the Great's remark, passed though it may have been with his tongue in his cheek, that he was ' merely the highest servant of the state ' shows how abhorrent to the philosopher of 1795 would have been the claim of Frederick William III. as set out on page 25, of his son as set out on page 150, and indeed the whole attitude of the Hohenzollerns during the nineteenth century. He died with the eighteenth century, and was mercifully preserved from the educative processes of the nineteenth. What that century did for German culture is well indicated in the following paragraph from Professor Paulsen's study of Immanuel Kant [1] :

In order to become conscious of the interval that separates the views of the nineteenth century from that of the eighteenth, one may read a discussion of war in H. von Treitschke's treatise on constitutional monarchy.[2] Here we find war called ' a necessity of political logic,' that is implicit in the very concept of a state. ' A state that renounces war, that subjects itself at the outset to a tribunal of nations, yields up its own sovereign power, i.e. its own existence. He who dreams of everlasting peace demands not only something that is unattainable, but also something nonsensical, and commits a schoolboy fallacy.' And not only with logic, but also with ethics is the demand for an everlasting peace in irreconcilable conflict. ' The hope of banishing war from the world is not only senseless, but deeply immoral. If it were realised it would transform the earth into a great temple of egoism.'

---

[1] Translation by Creighton and Lefevre. J. C. Nimmo, 1902.
[2] *Historische und politische Aufsätze*, iii. pp. 533 ff.

CHAPTER II

FICHTE THE APOSTLE OF GERMANISM

I<small>T</small> is no part of our purpose here to indicate how Fichte, Kant's greatest disciple, differed in method from his master, and how his philosophy, in form and content, assumed a character of its own. What does concern us is to show the tremendous influence he exercised in diverting political speculation in Germany out of the main stream of European thought that Kant had followed. Here Fichte but reflected the emotions and the passions of his time. Before the mind of Kant had been vividly brought the French Revolution and the birth of the United States ; Fichte was to experience in his own person the humiliation of Napoleon's conquest of Prussia, and, in fierce resentment, to nurse a consuming desire to rouse his countrymen to a patriotic realisation of the greatness of their race, its achievements and traditions, to nerve them to redeem their country, and then to win for it the promises vouchsafed to a chosen people. Few oratorical campaigns have left so abiding an impress as the famous *Addresses to the German Nation* delivered by him in Berlin during the French occupation in the winter of 1807-8. There are fourteen of these addresses, and one essential feature of them has been little studied in our country. It is true that no history of the War of Liberation can be written without referring to them, but attention has been limited in the main to the development of the fine argument in favour of the Pestalozzian pedagogy, and to the last of a series of glowing perorations. Seeley in his *Life of Stein* gives perhaps as full an analysis of the *Addresses* as exists in English, and he says : ' I should not have lingered so long over this book if it did not strike me as the prophetical or canonical book which announces and explains a great transition in modern Europe.' But even he did not recognise that the most vital content of the book was a revelation of the insanity of self-exaltation, that German megalomania, which, preached as a gospel throughout a whole century, was to bring about something more than ' a great transition,' was indeed to provoke the very crack of doom. The writings of philosophers are full of special pleading ; if the facts do not square with theories, so much the worse for the facts ! Let us away with them, for to the philosopher there are no facts, only phenomena. When, as in Fichte's case, the philosopher is a rhetorician, and a German rhetorician, special pleading reaches a degree of violence which is best, perhaps, qualified as a passionate attempt, in Madame de Staël's phrase,[1] to bring enthusiasm into accord with reason.

The argument in support of German megalomania is developed in the fourth and fifth of the *Addresses*, in which the philosopher, doubling the rôle of prophet, proceeds to characterise the fundamental difference between the Germans and other peoples of Germanic origin, and to show the intrinsic superiority of the former. He has not the candour to admit that he has but one people in his eye, viz., the French, but begins with a flourish in which, conveniently forgetful of Germanic mythology, he claims for the Germanic stock the credit of imbuing the new social order established in Europe on the ruins of antiquity with the true religion which had been preserved in Asia time out of mind. Races such as the Slavs he dismisses as ' new European nations ' which have not yet developed characteristics definite enough to enable a precise description to be given of them. The Scandinavians, and other Germanic races, to whom his argument as against Latinised Germans will not apply, are, we are bluntly told, undoubtedly Germans, and his conclusions are to apply to them willy-nilly.

The main difference between the Germans and other peoples of Germanic origin he takes to be this, viz., that the Germans have continued to dwell in the home of their ancestors and to use and develop the language of their ancestors, while the others have sought pastures new, and adopted a strange tongue which they have modified to suit them. Change of climate he dismisses as of no importance. Of like unimportance is intermarriage with other races such as the Celtic, ' for, after all, the Germans alone were the conquerors, the masters, and

---

[1] *De l'Allemagne*, iii. cap. 3.

the builders of the new race that sprang from such inter-marriage.' He adds naïvely that the Germans themselves intermarried with Slavs, so that to-day no one German race can say that it is purer than others.

The question of language, however, is capital. The fact that the Germans have retained their own language means this, that they use to express ideas in the world of thought words, or sounds that were originally sense-impressions of things. To express metaphors they build up words from native roots that are all the more *conceptual* because they are *perceptual*. Two important deductions follow therefrom : (1) the Germans move more freely in the conceptual region than other Germanic races ; (2) a people whose language is not the free development of their own original tongue, but is based on a dead language (Latin), foreign to their stock, must at a certain stage come to a full stop in their development. To illustrate his point he takes three words of which we select two, popularity and liberality. ' These words pronounced before a German who has learnt no other language have the effect on him of an utterly meaningless noise, that recalls nothing to him that might be known by affinity of sound, and forces him out of the circle of his own ideas and indeed of any possible ideas.' Then he goes on :

Further, if I should use in speaking to the German, instead of the words Popularity (*Popularität*) and Liberality (*Liberalität*), the expressions ' striving for favour among the great mob ' and ' not having the mind of a slave,' which is how those words must be literally translated, he would at first not obtain the clear and lively sensual image such as the Roman of old days certainly obtained. The latter saw every day with his own eyes the flexible politeness of an ambitious candidate to all and sundry, and saw outbursts of the slave-mind also ; and those words represented these things to him in a living fashion. The change in the form of government and the introduction of Christianity took away even from the Roman of later days these sights and shows ; and then, too, his own language was beginning to die away to a great extent in his own mouth, this being more especially due to Christianity, which was alien to him and which he could neither ward off nor incorporate with himself. How could this language, already half dead in its own home, have been transmitted alive to a foreign people ? And how should it now be capable of transmission to us Germans ? Further, with regard to the sensual image of a mental thing that lies in both those expressions, there is in Popularity even at the very beginning something base, which became perverted to a virtue in the mouth of the nation, owing to their corruption and their constitution. The German never falls into this perversion so long as it is presented to him in his own language. But when Liberality is translated by saying that a man has not 'the soul of a slave,' or, to bring it into accordance with modern custom, ' a lackey's way of thinking,' he answers once more that when this is said it means very little too.

. . . Now supposing that what those . . . foreign words must really be intended to mean, if they mean anything at all, had been expressed to the German in his own words and in his own circle of sensual images as follows : . . . *Leutseligkeit* (condescension or affability), and *Edelmut* (noble-mindedness), he would have understood us ; but the base associations we have named could never have been slipped into those designations. In the range of German speech a wrapping-up in incomprehensibility and darkness of the kind mentioned arises either from clumsiness or evil design ; it can be avoided, and the means always ready to hand is to translate into right and true German. But in the Romance languages this incomprehensibility is natural and primitive and there is no means of avoiding it, for [those using] these languages are not in possession of any living language at all by which they might examine the dead one, and if one looks at the matter closely, are entirely without a mother tongue.

So much for the fourth *Address*; in the fifth Fichte ingeniously develops his argument to show the reaction upon thought itself, upon the thinking power of a race, of the use of a living as against what he terms a dead language. With a people in possession of a living language, he says, intellectual culture takes firm hold of life ; with the others intellectual culture and life go their several ways. But science, or knowledge, only becomes a self-reliant force in life when thought is at once the practical intelligence and the mental disposition of the thinker, so that without effort, instinctively as it were, he directs vision and action by fundamental thought. Never can thought become life and mental disposition when it is conceived of as thought in a sphere of life foreign to one. Then he goes on, so far forgetting in the heat of argument the dignity of the philosopher and the cunning of the rhetorician as to taunt the French with regarding *Tartuffe* as their greatest philosophical work :

Now this living effectiveness of thought is very much furthered, and indeed, where the thinking is of the proper depth and strength, even necessitated, by thinking and designating in a living language. The symbol in such a language is itself direct, living and sensual ; it represents all the life it stands for and so takes hold of and exerts

an influence on life.   To the possessor of such a language Spirit
speaks face to face and reveals itself to him just as a man does.
But the symbol of a dead language does not produce any direct
reaction ;   in order to attain the living stream of such a language
one must first recapitulate knowledge acquired by the study of
history from a world that has died, and transport oneself into a
strange or foreign manner of thought.   How super-abundant must
the impulse of one's own thinking be, if it does not grow weary in
this long and wide field of History, and in the end modestly decide
not to go beyond it !   If the thinking of the possessor of a living
language does not become alive, he may rightly be accused of not
having thought at all and of having merely indulged in reverie.
The possessor of a dead language, however, cannot be similarly
accused without hesitation in a similar case ;   it may be that he
has ' thought ' after his own fashion, *i.e.* developed the conceptions
deposited in his language.   Only he has not done what, if he succeeded in doing it, would be accounted a miracle.

It is evident in passing that the impulse to thinking, in the case
of a people with a dead language, will be most powerful and produce the greatest apparent results in the beginning, when the
language has not yet become clear enough to every one.   It is
also evident that as soon as the language becomes clearer and more
definite, this impulse to thinking will tend more and more to die
away in the chains of the language.   It is further evident that in
the end the philosophy of a people of this kind will consciously
resign itself to the fact that it is only an explanation of the
dictionary, or, as un-German spirits among us have expressed it
in a more high-sounding fashion, a Metacritic of language ;   and
finally that such a people will acknowledge some mediocre didactic
poem in comedy form on the subject of hypocrisy to be its greatest
philosophical work.

Science or knowledge being the first branch of the intellectual culture of a people, poetry is claimed by Fichte as the
second, and the passages in which he develops this theme are
among the most eloquent in what is perhaps the most eloquent
book in German.   Here the blend of philosopher and rhetorician
gives a result splendid enough, despite all the lapses in logic,
the passionate advocacy of counsel in his own case, that vitiate
the serious argument.   The hot-blooded youth and manhood
of intellectual Germany may well have steamed like horses on
a frosty day as they heard these burning words at a time when
their country lay in the cold grip of the foreigner.   Anæmic
beside this are all other criticisms or interpretations of poetry :

Of the means of extending the thought that has begun in the
life of the individual to the life of all, the highest and best is Poetry,
and hence this is the second main branch of the intellectual culture

of a people. The thinker designates his thought in language, and this, as we have said above, cannot be done except by images of sense, and moreover, by an act of creation extending beyond the previous range of sensuous imagery. In so doing the thinker is himself a poet; if he is not a poet, language will fail him when his first thought comes, and when he attempts the second, thought itself will depart from him. To take this extension and amplification of the language's range of sensuous imagery, thus begun by the thinker, and to send it streaming through the whole field of sensuous images in such a way that every image may receive its due share of the new spiritual ennoblement, and that the whole of life down to its deepest depth of sense may appear steeped in the new ray of light, yield well-being, and in unconscious deception ennoble itself as if by its own might—this is the work of true poetry. Only in a living language is poetry of this kind possible, for only in it can the sphere of sensuous imagery be enlarged by creative thought, and only in it does what has already been created remain living and open to the influence of kindred life. Such a language has within itself the power of infinite poetry, refreshing and renewing its youth, for every stirring of living thought in it opens a new lode of poetic enthusiasm. To such a language, therefore, poetry is the highest and best means of flooding the life of all with the spiritual culture that has been attained. It is quite impossible for a dead language to have poetry in this higher sense, for none of the conditions requisite to poetry are existent in it. Such a language, however, can have a substitute for poetry, though only for a limited period, in the following way. The outpourings of the art of poetry in the original language will attract attention. It is true that the people that has come into existence is unable to continue poetry in the path that has been opened up, for the latter is foreign to its life, but it can connect its own life and its new circumstances with the sphere of sensuous imagery and poetry in which the preceding age expressed its own life in some such way as this; it can dress up its knights as heroes and *vice versa*, and make the ancient gods exchange raiment with the new ones. It is precisely this arraying of the commonplace in borrowed vesture that gives it a charm akin to that produced by idealisation, and the result will be quite pleasing shapes and figures. But the original language's sphere of sensuous and poetical imagery on the one hand and the new conditions of life on the other are finite and limited quantities. At some point their mutual penetration is completed, and when that point is reached the people celebrates its golden age and the source of its poetry has run dry. Somewhere or other there must be a highest point in the adaptation of fixed words to fixed ideas and of fixed imagery to fixed conditions of life. When this point has been reached this people must do one of two things. It can either repeat its most successful masterpieces in a different form, so that they look as if they were something new although they are in fact nothing but the old familiar things.

F

Or else, if it is determined to achieve something new, it can seek refuge in the unbecoming and the unseemly. In this case their poetic art will mix together the ugly and the beautiful and have recourse to caricature and humour, while their prose will be compelled to confuse ideas and to jumble virtue and vice together. This they must do if they seek new forms of expression.

At this point he is pulled up by the necessity of explaining away certain awkward circumstances connected with the German civilisation and speech familiar to his audience, viz., the admiration in Germany of foreign customs, an aping of them, indeed, and the unfortunate fact resulting therefrom that whenever two words have the same meaning the one with a Germanic root denotes almost without exception the ignoble and base thing, and the one with a Latin root the nobler and more distinguished :

This failing, just as if it were an endemic disease of the whole Teutonic race, attacks the German in the mother country too, if he is not armed against it by a high earnestness. Even in our ears it is easy for Latin to sound distinguished, even to our eyes Roman customs appear nobler and everything German on the contrary vulgar. And as we were not so fortunate as to acquire all this at first hand, so we take much pleasure in receiving it at second hand through the intermediary of the Neo-Latin or Romance nations. As long as we are German we appear to ourselves men like any others ; when half or more than half our vocabulary is non-German, and when we adopt conspicuous customs and wear conspicuous clothes which seem to come from foreign parts, then we fancy ourselves distinguished. But the summit of our triumph is reached when we are no longer taken for Germans but actually for Spaniards or Englishmen, whichever of the two happens to be the most fashionable at the moment. We are right. Naturalness on the German side, arbitrariness and artificiality on the foreign side, are the fundamental differences. If we keep to the former we are just like all our fellow-Germans, who understand us and accept us as their equal ; only when we seek refuge in the latter do we become incomprehensible to our fellows, who take us to be of a different nature. This unnaturalness comes of itself into the life of foreign countries, because their life has deviated from nature at the beginning and in a matter of the first importance. But we Germans must first seek it out and accustom ourselves to the belief that something is beautiful, proper, and convenient which does not appear so to us by the light of nature. The main reason for all this in the case of the German is his belief in the greater distinction (almost ' stylishness ') of non-German and Romanised countries, together with the craving to be just as distinguished, and artificially to create in Germany too that gulf between the upper classes and the people which came about naturally in foreign countries. I shall content myself with having indicated the main source of this love of foreign things which is to be found among Germans ; on another occasion I shall show how widespread its effects have been and how all the evils which have now brought us to ruin are of foreign origin. Of course it was only when united with German earnestness and the resulting influence on life that such evils were bound to bring destruction in their train.

But the recoil is only to obtain purchase for a bolder and loftier flight. If the German to his own self be true, then will originality of thought, animating a peerless people in the full enjoyment of a living language, bestow on it a creative power strong enough not only to build up a future for the world, but also to appropriate lessons drawn from antiquity by others, and incorporate them, as another cannot do, in life :

So we may say that genius in foreign lands will strew with flowers the well-trodden military roads of antiquity and weave a becoming robe for that wisdom of life which it will easily take for philosophy. The German spirit on the other hand will open up new shafts and bring the light of day into their abysses, and hurl up rocky masses of thought out of which ages to come will build their dwellings. The foreign genius will be a delightful sylph which hovers in graceful flight above the flowers that have sprung of themselves from the soil, settles on them without causing them to bend and drinks up their refreshing dew. Or we may call it a bee, which with busy art gathers the honey from the same flowers and deposits it with charming tidiness in cells of regular construction. But the German spirit is an eagle, whose mighty body on strong and well-practised wing thrusts itself on high and soars into the empyrean, that it may raise itself nearer to the sun whereon it delights to gaze.

That part of the vigorous nation which has gone abroad and adopted the language of antiquity thereby acquires a far closer relationship to antiquity. At the beginning it will be far easier for this part of the nation to grasp the language of antiquity in its first and unchanged form, to penetrate the memorials of its culture and to bring into them enough fresh life to enable them to adapt themselves to the new life that has arisen.   In short, it will be from these migrants that the study of classical antiquity will have taken its way over modern Europe.   In their enthusiasm for the unsolved problems of antiquity they will work at them, but of course only in the way that one works at a problem that has not been set by the needs of life but by mere curiosity. They will take them lightly and not whole heartedly, merely grasping them with the power of imagination and solely in this medium giving them as it were an airy body. The very wealth of material bequeathed by antiquity and the ease with which the work can be carried on in this fashion will enable them to bring an abundance of such pictures into the field of vision of the modern world. Now when these images of the ancient world in their new shape reach that part of the original stock which by its retention of the language has remained in the stream of original culture, they will arouse the attention of the people, and stimulate them to activity on their own part, though perhaps these images, if they had remained in the guise of antiquity, would have passed before them unheeded and unperceived. But as soon as they have really grasped them and not, as it were, merely passed them on from hand to hand, they will grasp them as their nature impels them to, not merely learning of them about foreign life but making them a part of their own life. So they will not only derive them from the life of the new world, but also bring them into contact with it again, incarnating the hitherto airy shapes in solid bodies that will endure in the element of real life.

These figures, thus transformed in a way that would never have been possible to foreign countries, the latter now receive from them again. Only by means of this transition is a development of the human race on the path of antiquity possible, a union of the two main portions and a regular continuance of human evolution. In this new order of things the mother country will not actually invent, but in the smallest as in the greatest matters it will always have to acknowledge that it has been stimulated by some hint from abroad. The foreign countries themselves were stimulated in their turn by the ancients, but the mother country will take earnestly and bring into contact with life what other countries have only superficially and hastily sketched out.

Thus does Fichte work up to a peroration before whose effulgence the limelight flashes of Hohenzollern eloquence grow pale. The pretence is dropped with which the fourth *Address* opens, viz., that the burden of his discourse is to be the superiority of Germans over other peoples of Germanic stock. His message is a grander one, the superiority of Germans over all other peoples in the world, and the message is crashed out as in some tremendous orchestral climax with throbbing drums, wauling strings, whistling fifes, blaring brass and booming wood:

Non-German countries are the earth, from which fruitful vapours detach themselves and arise to the clouds, and by which even now the old gods condemned to Tartarus keep in touch with the sphere of life. The mother country is the eternal sky enveloping the earth, the sky in which the light vapours are condensed to clouds, which, impregnated by the lightning flash of the Thunderer from the other world, descend in the form of fertilising rain, which unites sky and earth, and causes the gifts whose home is in the sky to germinate in the lap of earth. Do new Titans want to take our heaven by storm? It will not be heaven for them, for they are earth-born, and the very sight of heaven, and its influence too, will be taken from them. Only their earth will remain to them, a cold, gloomy, and unfruitful habitation. But, says a Roman poet,[1] what could a Typhœus do, or the mighty Mimas, or Porphyrion with his threats, or the rash hurler of uprooted tree-trunks, Enceladus, if they flung themselves against the resounding shield of Pallas ? Ay, it is this very shield that without a doubt will cover us if we understand how to betake ourselves to its protection.

But we are not done with Fichte when we have read this message of German megalomania that struck a responsive chord in German hearts, and set the tune to which the nation has danced ever since. There is a curious passage in the seventh *Address*, dealing with the Art of the State, which shows how false a prophet a man becomes when passion usurps the place of reason. In contrasting the foreign and the German Art of the State he begins with a dismal, terrifying description of the former :

In holding that the erection and government of states should be looked upon as an independent art having its own fixed rules, non-German countries have undoubtedly served us as fore-runners, and they themselves found their pattern in antiquity. But what is it that will be regarded as the Art of the State by such a non-German country, which in the very element of its thinking and willing, *i.e.* its language, is supported by something fixed, closed, and dead ? And what too will all who follow its example regard as the Art of the State ? Undoubtedly the art of finding a similarly fixed and dead order of things, from which condition of death the living movement of society is to proceed, and to proceed according to their intention. This intention is to make the whole of life in society into a large and ingeniously constructed pressure machine with inner wheels ; and in this machine every single part will be continually compelled by the whole to serve the whole. They intend to do a sum in arithmetic with finite and given quantities and produce from them a concrete result : and acting on the assumption that every one is willing to find his well-being in that way, to compel every one against his wish and will to promote the general well-being. Non-German countries have repeatedly enunciated this principle and produced ingenious specimens of this art of social machinery.

Then follows as drastic a criticism of this view of government as could be written by any opponent of bureaucracy :

If at any time there is a stoppage in the work of society as it has hitherto been carried on, such artists of the State can give no other explanation than that perhaps one of the wheels may have

---

[1] Horace, *Odes III.*, iv. 53.

been worn out, and they know no other remedy than to remove the defective wheels and insert new ones. The more deeply rooted any one is in this mechanical view of society, and the better he understands how to simplify the mechanism by making all the parts of the machine as alike as possible and treating them all as if they were of the same material, the higher is his reputation as an artist of the State in this time of ours ; and rightly so, for things are even worse when those in control hesitate and come to no decision and are incapable of any definite view of affairs.

This view of the Art of the State enforces respect by its iron consistency, and by a halo of majesty which falls upon it ; and up to a certain point, especially when the whole tendency is towards a monarchical constitution, and one that is always becoming more purely monarchical, it renders good service. But when it reaches that point its impotence is apparent to every one. I will suppose that you have made your machine as perfect as you intended, and that in it each and every lower part is unceasingly and irresistibly compelled by a higher part, which is itself compelled to compel, and so on up to the top. But how will your final part, from which proceeds the whole compelling power present in the machine, be itself compelled to compel ? Suppose you have overcome absolutely all the resistance to the mainspring that might arise from the friction of the various parts, and suppose you have given that mainspring a power against which all other power vanishes to nothing, which is all you could do even by perfection of mechanism, and suppose you have thus created a supremely powerful monarchical constitution ; how are you going to set this mainspring itself in motion and compel it without exception to see the Right and to will it ? Tell me how you are going to bring eternal movement into your clock-work, properly designed and constructed though it is, when it stops. Is perhaps, as you sometimes say in your embarrassment, the whole machine itself to react and to set its own mainspring in motion ? Either this happens by a power that itself proceeds from the motion of the mainspring, or it happens by a power that does not proceed from that but is to be found in the whole thing independent of the mainspring. No third way is possible.

Finally comes his fanciful picture of the genuine German Art of the State :

Altogether different is the genuine German Art of the State. It too seeks fixity, surety, and independence of blind and hesitating nature, and in this it is quite in agreement with foreign countries. But unlike these it does not seek a fixed and certain thing as the first part, which may give the Spirit as the second part fixity or certainty ; on the contrary, it seeks from the very beginning, and as the very first and only part, a firm and certain Spirit. This is for it the mainspring, whose life proceeds from itself and which has eternal movement, the mainspring which will regulate and continually keep in motion the life of society. The German Art of the State understands that it cannot bring out this spirit by threats of punishment to adults who are already spoilt by neglect, but only by the education of the young, who are still unspoilt. And moreover with this education it does not seek to address itself, as foreign countries do, to the highest point, the prince, but to the broad plain which is the nation, for indeed the prince will without doubt be one of the nation. Just as the State in the persons of its adult citizens is the continued education of the human race, so must the future citizen himself, in the opinion of this Art of the State, first be educated up to the point of receiving and responding to that higher education. So this German and most modern Art of the State becomes once more the most ancient Art of the State, which among the Greeks founded citizenship on education and trained such citizens as succeeding generations never saw again. Henceforth the Germans will do what is the same in form, though its content will be made not in a narrow and exclusive, but in a universal and cosmopolitan spirit.

Now the odd thing is that the very Art of the State which Fichte denounces as non-German was in point of fact to become the new German Art of the State, of which Joseph Görres complains in the remarkable quotation from his *Germany and the Revolution* printed on page 48. There can be no reasonable doubt that Fichte's very words were in Görres' mind when he wrote. And thus it was the doom of the man who planted in the German mind the insanity of self-exaltation to indicate, while denouncing it, the machinery that was to afford an outlet for the energies of a monster of his own creation. Nothing, in truth, was further from Fichte's own mind than the Prussian system. He was a disciple of Kant and wrote in 1796 a review of the *Treatise on Perpetual Peace* in which he gave a general endorsement of the master's conclusions. In sympathy with pure republicanism he went further than Kant himself, as witness the glowing passage in his sixth *Address* where he hymns the praises of the German burghers of the Middle Ages and the Imperial cities they founded.

And with what spirit did this German burgher class bring forth and enjoy this period of bloom ? With the spirit of piety, of honour, of modesty, and of the sense of community. For themselves they needed little, for public enterprises they set no limits to their expenditure. Seldom does the name of an individual stand forth or distinguish itself, for they were all of like mind and alike in sacrifice for the common weal. Under precisely the same external conditions as in Germany free cities had arisen in Italy as well. Compare the histories of both ; contrast the continual disorders, the inner conflicts, nay, even wars ; the constant change of constitutions and rulers in the latter with the peaceful unity and concord in the former. What clearer expression could there be of the fact that there must have been an inward difference in the dispositions of the two nations ? The German nation is the only one among the neo-European nations that has shown in practice by the example of its burgher class for centuries that it is capable of enduring a republican constitution.

So difficult is it in Fichte's case to decide where the rhetorician leaves off and the philosopher begins, that it is not unfair, perhaps, to conclude this exposé of a great man's contribution to the culture of mankind with Heine's caustic remark : ' I once saw a caricature of a Fichtean goose, which had so large a liver that it no longer knew whether it was a goose or a liver.'

CHAPTER III

HEGEL, THE APOSTLE OF BUREAUCRACY

HEGEL, the one rival to Kant for supremacy in modern German philosophy, was a philosopher of very different sort from Fichte. In his composition there was no trace of the rhetorician ; no pulse of enthusiastic emotion throbbed through his brain ; head and heart were equally cold. He was, in Heine's fine phrase, ' the intellectual world-navigator who has fearlessly penetrated to the north pole of thought, where one's brain freezes amid abstract ice.' But his hard, cold, keen intellect, if without enthusiasm, was not without guile. His reserve, his academic pride, his anxiety never to give himself away, made natural to him a style in which every artifice for hedging in a man's opinions is utilised with infinite ingenuity. The obscurity of his writings was such that after his death his disciples streamed off right and left into two camps, the right, including Hegel's pious confidant and editor, Dr. Gans, a true denizen of the Hegelian *basse-cour*, claiming the support of his system for orthodoxy in religion and the accepted combination of autocracy and bureaucracy in the government of the state ; the left marching off to attack, with Strauss and Feuerbach, the gospel history and accepted Christianity, and with Arnold Ruge and Carl Marx, not only the existing political order, but even the social order itself.

The obscurity of Hegel has been stigmatised by many critics. Heine, a pupil of Hegel's, was never tired of girding at the obscurity of German philosophers in general. We have given his opinion on page 68. Of Hegel himself he says : ' I will confess honestly that I never understood Hegel, and only through later reflection did I arrive at an understanding of his words. It is my conviction that he did not wish to be understood, and hence his method of exposition, clause by clause ; hence, too, his preference for people of whom he felt certain that they could not understand him, and to whom therefore he vouchsafed all the more readily the honour of his closer acquaintance.' Heine goes on to describe Heinrich Beer, one of these brainless familiars of the great philosopher, and gives an illustration, etched in acid, of the master's chill reception of any youthful outburst of sentiment, and his ever-present dread of giving himself away : ' One beautiful starlight night Hegel stood with me at an open window. I, being a young man of twenty-two, and having just partaken of a good dinner and coffee, naturally spoke with enthusiasm of the stars, and called them abodes of the blest. But Hegel muttered to himself : "The stars ! H'm, h'm ! The stars are only a glistening eruption on the firmament." "What !" cried I, "then there is no blissful spot above where after death virtue is rewarded ? " But he, glaring at me with his dim eyes, remarked sneeringly : "So you want a recompense because you have supported your sick mother and have not poisoned your brother ? " At these words he looked anxiously around, but was reassured when he saw that it was only Heinrich Beer who had come in to invite him to a whist-party.'

It is idle to suggest, what is not true, that Heine was a cynic whenever he touched on politics, philosophy, or religion, or, what is true, that racially he was not a German and had none of the attributes of the Fichtean German. Schopenhauer, as we shall see later, was an even more savage critic ; and his attack was full-bloodily German in all conscience. We have, indeed, to admit that Hegelian obscurity made Hegelian philosophy for many years popular in this country, as in Germany between 1820 and 1830, among professional metaphysicians and lecturers on philosophy. It is an agreeable sensation in the course of one's studies to discover that previous investigators have failed ; and to commence a discourse on the high plane of philosophy with an exposure of other great and good men's misinterpretations of the point at issue is not only an attractive process in itself but also helps to eke out the lecturer's store of original thought. Nevertheless, English-speaking philosophers of not wholly academic type, from G. H. Lewes to Professor William James, have criticised Hegel severely as much for the difficulty at times of extracting any meaning whatever from his words, as for an opinion or judgment itself when doubtfully ascertained. Even so devoted a student as Hutchison Stirling is driven to exclaim : [1] ' The very cry of the hour is, Fichte and Schelling are dead, and Hegel, if not clotted nonsense, is unintelligible ; let us go back to Kant.'

But Hegel made his political attitude quite clear ; and it must seem to an Englishman, devoid of that earnestness amusingly urged by Fichte on page 83 as accounting for the magnitude of German shortcomings, that only the perversity natural to one of Germanic origin, inhabiting the home of his ancestors, and enjoying the living language he has inherited, could have made his disciple, Arnold Ruge, claim to be at once a red-capped republican and a ' Young Hegelian.' A series of extracts from Hegel's *Philosophy of Right* [2] and *Philosophy of History* [3] will enable the reader to form his own judgment in the matter.

In the first place he will note that Hegel, like Kant and Fichte, had his political outlook influenced by the circumstances of his time. In 1816 he was appointed to a professorship at Heidelberg, and the next year the lecture-room rang with echoes of the speeches delivered at the Wartburg Festival. In 1818 he was transferred to Berlin, and in 1819, next year again, all professorial chairs in Germany rocked at the news of the murder of Kotzebue. The passions and emotions stirring young Germany were repugnant to one who had blandly gazed on Napoleon in the streets of Jena, could wish well to the ' world-soul ' on horseback, and the principle of whose mature judgment was: 'What is is Reason.' In the preface, written in 1820, to his *Philosophy of Right* he attacks bitterly the most conspicuous of Kant's living disciples, Fries of Jena, who had ventured not only to attend the Wartburg Festival, but even to harangue the students :

In point of fact the pretentious utterances of recent philosophy regarding the state have been enough to justify any one who cared to meddle with the question, in the conviction that he could prove himself a philosopher by weaving a philosophy out of his own brain. Notwithstanding this conviction, that which passes for philosophy has openly announced that truth cannot be known. The truth with regard to ethical ideals, the state, the government and the constitution ascends, so it declares, out of each man's heart, feeling,

---

[1] *Mind*, No. xxxvi., quoted by Hastie in his translation of Kant's *Philosophy of Law* (*Rechtslehre*).

[2] Professor Dyde's translation, which breaks up Hegel's complicated German prose into crisp, clear English sentences, an achievement which it is easier to admire than to imitate.

[3] J. Sibree's translation in Bohn's Philosophical Library. G. Bell & Sons.

and enthusiasm. Such declarations have been poured especially into the eager ears of the young. The words ' God giveth truth to his chosen in sleep ' have been applied to science ; hence every sleeper has numbered himself amongst the chosen. But what he deals with in sleep is only the wares of sleep. Mr. Fries, one of the leaders of this shallow-minded host of philosophers, on a public festive occasion, now become celebrated, has not hesitated to give utterance to the following notion of the state and constitution. ' When a nation is ruled by a common spirit, then from below, out of the people, will come life sufficient for the discharge of all public business. Living associations, united indissolubly by the holy bond of friendship, will devote themselves to every side of national service, and every means for educating the people.' This is the last degree of shallowness, because in it science is looked upon as developing, not out of thought or conception, but out of direct perception and random fancy. Now the organic connection of the manifold branches of the social system is the architectonic of the state's rationality, and in this supreme science of state architecture the strength of the whole is made to depend upon the harmony of all the clearly marked phases of public life, and the stability of every pillar, arch, and buttress of the social edifice. And yet the shallow doctrine, of which we have spoken, permits this elaborate structure to melt and lose itself in the brew and stew of the ' heart, friendship, and inspiration.'

Hegel in becoming professor at Berlin had obtained an official position at the very centre of the Prussian system. He was selected, indeed, for the position because he was judged likely to prove a useful adviser to the bureaucracy, the man to shepherd the erring youth of the academic flock into the government fold. His old suspicion of the Prussians, his contempt for them, alive in the days when he saw Napoleon at Jena, and wished the ' World-soul ' on horseback well, was dead. He realised that the old type of Prussian official was gone, and he approved the new type depicted, in Fichtean language, on page 48. Thus his preface proceeds from a personal attack on Fries to a denunciation of his doctrines as implying the hatred of law, and to suggest that liberty allowed by the state to philosophy may be abused :

The particular kind of evil consciousness developed by the wishy-washy eloquence already alluded to, may be detected in the following way. It is most unspiritual, when it speaks most of the spirit. It is the most dead and leathern, when it talks of the scope of life. When it is exhibiting the greatest self-seeking and vanity it has most on its tongue the words, ' people ' and ' nation.' But its peculiar mark, found on its very forehead, is its hatred of law.

Right and ethical principle, the actual world of right and ethical life, are apprehended in thought, and by thought are given definite, general, and rational form, and this reasoned right finds expression in law. But feeling, which seeks its own pleasure, and conscience, which finds right in private conviction, regard the law as their most bitter foe. The right, which takes the shape of law and duty, is by feeling looked upon as a shackle or dead cold letter. In this law it does not recognise itself and does not find itself free. Yet the law is the reason of the object, and refuses to feeling the privilege of warming itself at its private hearth. Hence the law, as we shall occasionally observe, is the Shibboleth, by means of which are detected the false brethren and friends of the so-called people.

Inasmuch as the purest charlatanism has won the name of philosophy, and has succeeded in convincing the public that its practices are philosophy, it has now become almost a disgrace to speak in a philosophic way about the state. Nor can it be taken ill, if honest men become impatient, when the subject is broached. Still less is it a surprise that the government has at last turned its attention to this false philosophising. With us philosophy is not practised as a private art, as it was by the Greeks, but has a public place, and should therefore be employed only in the service of the state. The government has, up till now, shown such confidence in the scholars in this department as to leave the subject matter of philosophy wholly in their hands.

Thinking inflames him, and he goes on to suggest that Kantian doctrine as preached by Fries is as likely to prove subversive of the ethical system in private persons, as of public order, and to invoke the repressive hand of the state :

Yet this shallowness, notwithstanding its seeming innocence, does bear upon social life, right and duty, generally advancing principles which are the very essence of superficiality. These, as we have learned so decidedly from Plato, are the principles of the Sophists, according to which the basis of right is subjective aims and opinions, subjective feeling and private conviction. The result of such principles is quite as much the destruction of the ethical system, of the upright conscience, of love and right, in private persons, as of public order and the institutions of the state. The significance of these facts for the authorities will not be obscured by the claim that the holder of these perilous doctrines should be trusted, or by the immunity of office. The authorities will not be deterred by the demand that they should protect and give free play to a theory which strikes at the substantial basis of conduct, namely, universal principles, and that they should disregard insolence on the ground of its being the exercise of the teacher's function. . . .

Finally he propounds the cardinal principle on which, in his judgment, should be based a philosopher's attitude to politics. He is not to dream dreams ; observation may be his, but not vision, because ' What is is reason : '

This treatise, in so far as it contains a political science, is nothing more than an attempt to conceive of and present the state as in itself rational. As a philosophic writing it must be on its guard against constructing a state as it ought to be. Philosophy cannot teach the state what it should be, but only how it, the ethical universe, is to be known,

ἰδοὺ ʽΡόδον, ἰδοὺ καὶ τὸ πήδημα.

Hic Rhodus, hic saltus.

To apprehend what is is the task of philosophy, because what is is reason. As for the individual, every one is a son of his time ; so philosophy also is its time apprehended in thoughts. It is just as foolish to fancy that any philosophy can transcend its present world, as that an individual could leap out of his time or jump over Rhodes. If a theory transgresses its time, and builds up a world as it ought to be, it has an existence merely in the unstable element of opinion, which gives room to every wandering fancy.

So much for Hegel's important preface, dated, as we have said, in 1820. The body of his *Philosophy of Right* is built up of lectures [1] delivered between 1820 and 1830, and very different from Kant's clear-cut, straightforward analysis of the political state is the sophisticated account we get from Hegel. The state is the embodiment of an *universal* will which is not a *common* will postulating a number of individual wills each conscious of itself. No, he will have none of Rousseau's or Kant's or Fichte's individual wills acting in combination ; the notion of a social contract leads the understanding to deduce consequences which are blasphemous.

257. The state is the realised ethical idea or ethical spirit. It is the will which manifests itself, makes itself clear and visible, substantiates itself. It is the will which thinks and knows itself, and carries out what it knows, and in so far as it knows. The state finds in ethical custom its direct and unreflected existence, and its indirect and reflected existence in the self-consciousness of the individual and in his knowledge and activity. Self-consciousness in the form of social disposition has its substantive freedom in the state, as the essence, purpose, and product of its activity. . . .

258. The state, which is the realised substantive will, having

---

[1] In the canonical edition the paragraphs are Hegel's own, and so are the *notes*, while the *additions* are from students' notes accepted as giving a faithful version of the master's expansions.

its reality in the particular self-consciousness raised to the plane of the universal, is absolutely rational. This substantive unity is its own motive and absolute end. In this end freedom attains its highest right. This end has the highest right over the individual, whose highest duty in turn is to be a member of the state. . . .

Note—. . . To Rousseau is to be ascribed the merit of discovering and presenting a principle, which comes up to the standard of the thought, and is indeed thinking itself, not only in its form, such as would be a social impulse or divine authority, but in its very essence. This principle of Rousseau is will. But he conceives of the will only in the limited form of the individual will, as did also Fichte afterwards, and regards the universal will not as the absolutely reasonable will, but only as the common will, proceeding out of the individual will as conscious. Thus the union of individuals in a state becomes a contract, which is based upon caprice, opinion, and optional, explicit consent. Out of this view the understanding deduces consequences, which destroy the absolutely divine, and its absolute authority and majesty. Hence, when these abstractions attained to power, there was enacted the most tremendous spectacle which the human race has ever witnessed. All the usages and institutions of a great state were swept away. It was then proposed to begin over again, starting from the thought, and as the basis of the state to will only what was judged to be rational. But as the undertaking was begun with abstractions void of all ideas, it ended in scenes of tragic cruelty and horror.

Was ever a piece of special pleading so signally, so calamitously falsified by the course of events as the argument with which the above extract concludes ? The view he denounced led, says he, to the tragedy of the French Revolution. But the state based on the principles he advocated has led to a spectacle even more tremendous. For what is the revolution which the Prussian system is now bringing about ? The revolution in France convulsed Europe, the present one will convulse the world.

The dry metaphysical elements into which Hegel resolves the state, and which find their realisation as universals in the constitutional prince as understood in Prussia are well worth comparing with Kant's paragraphs set out on page 70. The Hegelian sophistication runs as follows :

273. The political state is divided into three substantive branches :
(*a*) The power to fix and establish the universal. This is legislation.
(*b*) The power, which brings particular spheres and individual cases under the universal. This is the function of government.

(c) The function of the prince, as the subjectivity with which rests the final decision. In this function the other two are brought into an individual unity. It is at once the culmination and beginning of the whole. This is constitutional monarchy.

275. The function of the prince contains of itself the three elements of the totality, (1) the universality of the constitution and the laws ; (2) counsel, or reference of the particular to the universal ; and (3) the final decision, or the self-determination, into which all else returns and from which it receives the beginning of its actuality. . . .

Hegel is bound to proceed in his discussion of the nature of the state to consider the relation of one independent state to others, and we are now to be presented with his famous defence of war :

224. *Note.*—It is a very distorted account of the matter when the state, in demanding sacrifices from the citizens, is taken to be simply the civic community, whose object is merely the security of life and property. Security cannot possibly be obtained by the sacrifice of what is to be secured.

Herein is to be found the ethical element in war. War is not to be regarded as an absolute evil. It is not a merely external accident, having its accidental ground in the passions of powerful individuals or nations, in acts of injustice, or in anything which ought not to be. Accident befalls that which is by nature accidental, and this fate is a necessity. . . . Necessity becomes in this way exalted to the work of freedom, and becomes a force which is ethical.

. . . It is often said, for the sake of edification, that war makes short work of the vanity of temporal things. It is the element by which the idealisation of what is particular receives its right and becomes an actuality. Moreover, by it, as I have elsewhere expressed it, ' finite pursuits are rendered unstable, and the ethical health of peoples is preserved. Just as the movement of the ocean prevents the corruption which would be the result of perpetual calm, so by war people escape the corruption which would be occasioned by a continuous or eternal peace.' . . . This principle is found in history in such a fact as that successful wars have prevented civil broils and strengthened the internal power of the state. So, too, peoples who have been unwilling or afraid to endure internal sovereignty have been subjugated by others, and in their struggles for independence have had honour and success small in proportion to their failure to establish within themselves a central political power ; their freedom died through their fear of its dying. Moreover, states, which have no guarantee of independence in the strength of their army, states, *e.g.*, that are very small in comparison with their neighbours, have continued to subsist because of their internal constitution, which merely of itself would seem to promise them neither internal repose nor external security. These phenomena are illustrations of our principle drawn from history.

But we are to take comfort. War, says this German philosopher, is recognised as containing the possibility of peace. Ambassadors are to be respected, and so too private persons. Modern wars are carried on humanely. There is no hate.

338. Although in war there prevail force, contingency, and absence of right, states continue to recognise one another as states. In this fact is implied a covenant, by virtue of which each state retains absolute value. Hence, war, even when actively prosecuted, is understood to be temporary, and in international law is recognised as containing the possibility of peace. Ambassadors, also, are to be respected. War is not to be waged against internal institutions, or the peaceable family and private life, or private persons.

Addition.—Modern wars are carried on humanely. One person is not set in hate over against another. Personal hostilities occur at most in the case of the pickets. But in the army as an army, enmity is something undetermined, and gives place to the duty which each person owes to another.

339. For the rest, the capture of prisoners in time of war, and in time of peace the concession of rights of private intercourse to the subjects of another state, depend principally upon the ethical observances [1] of nations. In them is embodied that inner universality of behaviour, which is preserved under all relations.

Addition.—The nations of Europe form a family by virtue of the universal principle of their legislation, their ethical observances, and their civilisation. Amongst them international behaviour is ameliorated, while there prevails elsewhere a mutual infliction of evils. The relation of one state to another fluctuates ; no judge is present to compose differences ; the higher judge is simply the universal and absolute spirit, the spirit of the world.

340. As states are particular, there is manifested in their relation to one another a shifting play of internal particularity of passions, interests, aims, talents, virtues, force, wrong, vice, and external contingency on the very largest scale. In this play even the ethical whole, national independence, is exposed to chance. The spirit of a nation is an existing individual having in particularity its objective actuality and self-consciousness. Because of this particularity it is limited. The destinies and deeds of states in their connection with one another are the visible dialectic of the finite nature of these spirits. Out of this dialectic the universal spirit, the spirit of the world, the unlimited spirit, produces itself. It has the highest right of all, and exercises its right upon the lower spirits in world-history. The history of the world is the world's court of judgment.

Truly German civilisation has developed since 1830, and,

---

[1] *Sitten,* whence *Sittlichkeit,* the now notorious German word of which Lord Haldane gave so appreciative an account in his *Higher Nationality.*

were he not a German, even an advocate so acute and ingenious as Hegel would find himself hard pressed to devise before that higher judge, the spirit of the world, a defence of his countrymen's contraventions of Hegelian precept. It is of unctuous platitudes such as the above that our politicians have been the dupes for over half a century, and not only our politicians. Our philosophers too have maintained, like so many Sancho Panzas, an attitude of foolish receptivity. Where the politician and the philosophic Sancho have been combined in the same individual, it has been possible in this mad world for a man to earn the reputation of a statesman.

Side by side with his lectures on the Philosophy of Right, Hegel delivered between 1822 and 1830 courses on the Philosophy of History.[1] The compilation made of these lectures by his editors contains striking illustrations of the application of his metaphysical theories to actual historical conditions. We learn how he regarded events, and how on his principles he interpreted them. The world has for him four Ages, the Oriental, the Greek, the Roman, and the German. He begins his account of the German world almost in the strain of Fichte : ' The German Spirit is the Spirit of the New World. Its aim is the realisation of absolute Truth as the unlimited self-determination of freedom. . . . The destiny of the German peoples is, to be the bearers of the Christian principle.' When he reaches the latter half of the eighteenth century, and the French Revolution in particular, he encounters for the first time that modern portent, the political force known as Liberalism. This is how he deals with it :

Not satisfied with the establishment of rational rights, with freedom of person and property, with the existence of a political organisation in which are to be found various circles of civil life, each having its own functions to perform, and with that influence over the people which is exercised by the intelligent members of the community, and the confidence that is felt in them, *Liberalism* sets up in opposition to all this the atomistic principle, that which insists upon the sway of individual wills ; maintaining that all government should emanate from their express power and have their express sanction. Asserting this formal side of Freedom— this abstraction—the party in question allows no political organisation to be firmly established. The particular arrangements of the government are forthwith opposed by the advocates of Liberty

---

[1] Translation by J. Sibree in Bohn's Library. G. Bell & Sons.

as the mandates of a particular will, and branded as displays of arbitrary power. The will of the Many expels the Ministry from power, and those who had formed the opposition fill the vacant places ; but the latter having now become the Government, meet with hostility from the Many, and share the same fate. Thus agitation and unrest is perpetuated. This collision, this nodus, this problem is that with which history is now occupied, and whose solution it has to work out in the future.

This outburst is followed after a few pages by a naïve account of the Prussian system as it presented itself to the philosopher and was approved by him :

Germany was traversed by the victorious French hosts, but German nationality delivered it from this yoke. One of the leading features (*Hauptmoment*) in the political condition of Germany is that code of Rights which was certainly occasioned by French oppression, since this was the especial means of bringing to light the deficiencies of the old system. The fiction of an Empire has utterly vanished. It is broken up into sovereign states. Feudal obligations are abolished, for freedom of property and of person have been recognised as fundamental principles. Offices of State are open to every citizen, talent and adaptation (*Brauchbarkeit*) being, of course, the necessary conditions. The government rests with the official world, and the personal decision of the monarch constitutes its apex ; for a final decision is, as was remarked above, absolutely necessary. Yet with firmly established laws, and a settled organisation of the State, what is left to the sole arbitrament of the monarch is, in point of substance, no great matter. It is certainly a very fortunate circumstance for a nation, when a sovereign of noble character falls to its lot ; yet in a great state even this is of small moment, since its strength lies in the Reason incorporated in it. Minor states have their existence and tranquillity secured to them more or less by their neighbours ; they are therefore, properly speaking, not independent, and have not the fiery trial of war to endure. As has been remarked, a share in the government may be obtained by every one who has a competent knowledge, experience, and a morally regulated will. Those who know ought to govern, οἱ ἄριστοι, not ignorance and the presumptuous conceit of ' knowing better.' . . .

Among the most brilliant of Hegel's pupils was Frederick William IV., and we shall have on page 354 a diatribe of his against Liberalism which is worth comparing with his master's, which was doubtless in the kingly mind. The presumptuous conceit of ' knowing better ' was a favourite expression with his Majesty, and the amusing passage printed on page 121 shows how thoroughly the Hegelian teaching had occupied the bureaucratic soul, if such a thing exists.

The criticism of Hegel to be found in this chapter is not to be dismissed as merely the outcome of insular prejudice. Hegel's own words are given ; they speak for themselves. But the sharpest of Hegel's critics was Schopenhauer, a brother German and an eminent philosopher, who, when he wrote in German, was gifted with a more brilliant style than any of his fellows. Hegel himself, as we have seen from his attack upon Fries, had all a philosopher's vanity and spleen, but that attack pales before Schopenhauer's castigation of Hegel. The cudgel was not the only weapon at Schopenhauer's command ; he could use steel as well, and his onset then had edge and point as well as weight. In a long letter, dated 21st December 1829, and written in the English of which he considered himself a master, he proposed to undertake a translation into English of the works of his master, Kant. He remarks incidentally : ' I will not mention the numberless monstrous and mad compositions which were called forth by Kant's works as " the sun, being a god, breeds maggots kissing carrion "—but so much did by and by degenerate our German philosophy that we now see a mere swaggerer and charlatan, without merit, I mean Hegel, with a compound of bombastical nonsense, and positions bordering on madness, humbug about a part of (the) German public, but the more silly and untaught part, to be sure, yet by personal means and connections he contrived to get a philosopher's name and fame.' More to the point here are the following quotations from Schopenhauer's attack on what he calls ' University philosophy.' [1] He says : ' Let any one who retains any doubt over the spirit and aim of university philosophy observe the fate of the spurious wisdom of Hegel. Has it been injured at all by the facts that its principles are the absurdest of conceits, that it builds up a topsy-turvy world, a philosophical harlequinade, that its content is the hollowest, most nonsensical verbiage that ever gave satisfaction to a noodle, and that the presentation of these principles in the works of the originator himself is the most tiresome and senseless gibberish, that even recalls the delirium of a madhouse ? Oh no, not in the least ! On the contrary it has, for twenty long years and more, flourished and grown fat as the most famous of academic philosophies ; that is to say, has been vaunted all over Germany, in hundreds of books, as the finally attained pinnacle of human wisdom and as

[1] *Parerga und Paralipomena.*

the philosophy of philosophies, ay, has been exalted to heaven
It has been the basis for the examination of students and the
nomination of professors. Who would not join the ring, has
been declared " a fool in his own right " by the disciples, grown
bold, of a master as pliable as he was brainless, and even the
few who dared to raise some feeble opposition to this scandal,
came forward but coyly, with full acknowledgment of " the vast
intellect and exuberant genius "—of this preposterous philoso-
phist.'   After this tirade we come to the main point of Schopenhauer's criticism, and it goes home.   It was, he says, the state
aims of university philosophy that procured for Hegelianism
so unexampled a favour from ministers.   ' For it regarded the
state as " the absolute, complete, ethical organism," and made
the whole aim of human existence lead up to the state.   Could
there be a better direction for future probationers for the civil
service than this, in accordance with which their whole nature
and existence, body and soul, was forfeit to the state, as the
bee's to the hive, and they had no other object to work for,
either in this world, or in another, than that they should become
serviceable cog-wheels, and co-operate in keeping the great
machine of the state, *ultimus finis bonorum*, in motion ?   Man
and probationer for the civil service were thus one and the same.
It was the proper apotheosis of Philistinism.'

With this we may leave the philosopher, to observe the
operation of his principles in practice.

CHAPTER IV

PRUSSIA AS THE HOPE OF GERMANY—THE HAMBACH FESTIVAL

HEGEL died of the cholera in 1831. At the time of his death there appeared to be a kind of lull in the internal affairs of Germany. People had been dazed, perhaps, by the hammer blows of repression, and as these tended to become less severe a growing material prosperity rendered the masses less accessible to the appeals of the restless elements in journalism, the universities, and the professions. The lull was to be brief, but, while it lasted, the thoughts of excitable Germans were half diverted in 1832 from their own wrongs by the call for sympathy with the Poles, on whom had fallen the heavy hand of Russia. Poets like Platen, Lenau, Gottfried Keller the Swiss, and others, poured forth Polish laments, ' Poland's cause is not yet lost,' and ' Think'st thou thereon, my hero Lajenka.' Their poetry reeked of sentimentality, and was mercilessly satirised by Heine in his *Krapulinski und Waschlapski*, which may be rendered as ' Dish-cloth and Sick-headache.' Nevertheless the Poles became popular heroes in Germany, and they remained so right up to the Revolution of 1848, in which, as will be seen, they played a spectacular if not an effective part. A good account of the sentiments agitating the German public about this time is given by Otto von Corvin in his *Reminiscences*. Corvin was an aristocratic adventurer, claiming descent from the Roman Valerii, and Matthew Corvin, King of Hungary. He began life as a Prussian officer, joined the revolutionaries, took to journalism and literature, held high command in the rebel army at Rastatt in the final struggle in Baden, was captured at its surrender, and was condemned to death, but the sentence was commuted into one of imprisonment, six years of which he passed in solitary confinement ; then he made his way to England as a political refugee, and continued his adventurous career as special correspondent of the *Times*, the *New York Times*, and the

Augsburger Allgemeine Zeitung. An English version of his *Reminiscences* was published in three volumes by Bentley in 1871 under the title of *A Life of Adventure.* The book deserves to be better known than it is, for it has perhaps more of the qualities of a good picaresque novel than any book of last century ; it brims over with dash, devilment, egotism, fun, frolic, love and wine, fighting and full-blooded life generally. And yet, despite the air of romance that pervades it, the book, with its vivid pictures of men and things, is a valuable historical document. There is plenty of evidence in publications more staid of the substantial accuracy of Corvin's lively stories and by no means modest claims. Here is his account of feeling in his first garrison town, Mainz, in 1832 :

The people of Mayence were at this time very much excited. The revolution of July 1830 had stirred up old sympathies with France, whilst, on the other hand, German patriots were of the opinion that the Germans had also outgrown the ' paternal,' despotic government, and were desirous of a constitution. Many young men in the city put on the French cockade and sang the ' Marseillaise,' and applauded in the theatre at every sentence expressing hatred of tyrants and love of liberty. Several pieces were prohibited on this account by the government of the fortress ; for instance, *The Dumb Girl of Portici,* because, when the soldiers were repulsed by the people in the market-place, the audience cried bravo like mad, and sang the ' Marseillaise.' *William Tell* was also prohibited for similar reasons. For a time this excitement found an outlet in the enthusiasm for the Poles. All the young ladies at their harps were singing ' Poland's cause is not yet lost,' when it was lost already ; and the exiled Poles were received everywhere like conquering heroes. Everybody did his best to do them honour ; and the women were wildly enthusiastic about them. Many a rascal put on a Polish uniform and spoke broken German, as it helped him better through the country than even a passport from the chief of police himself would have done.

We officers also caught this enthusiasm, for we admired the bravery the Poles had shown. Some Polish officers were not only received in a friendly manner in our casino, but even chummed with Prussian comrades. This, however, came to an end when our superiors discovered or received information from Berlin that the Poles after all had committed high treason, and that it was therefore improper for Prussian officers to associate with them.

It was, however, inevitable that we should meet them at public balls and other places of amusement ; and as they had nothing else to do, they were to be found everywhere, and mostly drunk. It seemed to be an affair of honour with the Mayence citizens not to suffer a sober Pole in their city. I, at least, never saw one

The Polish enthusiasm was followed by the black, red, and gold fever. The old German colours were then the badge of Liberalism, and he who laid claim to the title of a patriot wore a cockade of these colours. The German Confederation looked, however, with a very suspicious eye on these aspirations ; the princes were perfectly satisfied with the existing state of things ; they wanted no change, and as they had the military power in their hands, they used it to suppress all demonstrations. The soldiers, therefore, became very unpopular, and conflicts between officers and citizens occurred frequently. Officers were insulted, and made use of their arms ; and the excitement grew from day to day. One of these conflicts took place at a casino ball. Young citizens, sitting at the same table with Prussian officers, began to sing Liberal songs, and proposed corresponding toasts. The officers behaved very well ; in order not to create any disturbance they even touched the glasses of the young citizens with theirs, if requested ; but once, when the young men presumed too much on this forbearance of the officers, one of the latter rose and proposed a toast to the King of Prussia, by his look compelling one of the loudest to join him in it. . . .

The order was given to all guards to arrest every one wearing the German colours, and that the soldiers might be acquainted with them, a black, red, and gold cockade was pasted in every guard-book. This measure did much to increase the excitement instead of quelling it, as was intended. The persons arrested were conveyed to the citadel, where an officer on special duty had to receive and dispose of them. . . .

As I must needs always put my nose foremost, wanting to show my contempt in some striking manner, one Friday, when thousands were assembled for the concert in the new ' Anlage ' I appeared there with my little dog, Hélène, which proudly wore a large German cockade attached to its little stump of a tail. The joke was immensely applauded by all officers, both Prussian and Austrian, and my colonel laughed much about it, but warned me to take care lest my little dog should be killed. I told him, however, that I was ready to defend my dog's tail with my life. At that time neither my colonel nor myself imagined that both of us, and even the King of Prussia, would one day wear this then despised cockade.

But in spite of the lethargy of large masses of the population, the vagaries of sentimentalists, and liberal resentment against Prussia as the backbone of reaction in Germany, the forces making for her advancement to the German hegemony were too strong to be suppressed for long in the consciousness of calculating politicians. Strangely enough it was from South Germany, where Prussia was most unpopular, that there came in 1832 the apostle of a united Germany under Prussia, not

Austria, as the sovereign power. This was P. A. Pfizer, a Würtemberger and a leading liberal, who in his *Thoughts on the Aim and the Task of German Liberalism* argued as follows : [1]

To fulfil the sentiment and the inspiration of the century, the instrument that will make of Germany a single organisation, and convert a confederation of her princes into a confederation of her peoples, a diplomatic confederation of States into a National Federal State, there can only be a Representative Assembly of the German Nation, and the stimulus thereto and the main impulse must come from Liberalism. . . . (But) we must not build too confidently on the hope that the confederation of a constitutional Germany, in virtue of its inborn moral supremacy, will draw all Germany in its wake, and hurry it along with it, chained to its banner. So soon . . . as the time of excitement and intensity of feeling, which Liberalism must use for its objects, is over, and the strain of battle between Liberalism and Absolutism, which gives the former its strength, is relaxed, the confederation, if it does not of itself fall to pieces, will look about for some protection and some support, and must lean on some one strong Power. If the Confederation (of constitutional German States) chooses its protector from among the great powers of Germany, its choice will undoubtedly fall on that one which then exhibits most German sentiment. But that the rôle of Protector should ever fall to the lot of Prussia will strike many as quite incredible, in view of the decided prejudice against North German fashions and ways, and the bitter hatred that Prussia has recently incurred in Germany, mostly through her own fault. But the favours of public opinion are changeable . . . and as soon as Prussia realises her advantage better and decides to become German, as soon as the various German national assemblies are confronted with Provincial Diets under the Prussian Crown which have won a real existence, that prejudice will disappear, or at least will be much softened, so that it will remain no obstacle to a union between Germany and Prussia, just as despite national animosity between English and Scotch the Union of Great Britain exists. It was even this Prussia that succeeded during, and after, the War of Liberation in gaining friends for herself all over Germany, and the return to her motto ' Light and Right,' to the principles of a Stein and a Hardenberg, would soon without doubt evoke a similar friendly feeling. . . .

Pfizer was a poet as well as a publicist, and two examples from his *Correspondence between Two Germans* [2] may here be given, the first a glowing forecast of Germany's future under the Hohenzollerns, the second as lively a satire on German

---

[1] Klein.   [2] *Briefwechsel zweier Deutschen.*

demagogues and their extravagance as any good Briton could
desire to read :

THE GERMAN FUTURE

Night falls on the hills of my homeland,
Flooding valleys of oak and of pine ;
From the stars slowly over them wheeling
'Tis the eyes of our heroes that shine.
Our heroes, they all are departed,
Our glorious past, it is dead !
From the peace of the grave to the sunrise
Thy flight, O my soul, must be sped—
Like the Erne from the rock of the Staufens
Who once shook his wings to be free,
And wafted the fame of the Zollerns
To the Baltic's far easterly sea.
Spread o'er us thy covering pinions,
Great Frederick's eagle of gold :
We yearn for the sun where we linger
Like orphans in hunger and cold.
With the rush of thy wings strike them earthward,
Croaking raven and owl, kite and crow,
For the goal of thy flight is the morning,
Sunlit eye with adventure aglow !

THE DEMAGOGUES

The whole week through the bottle flew from dusk till daylight gaily ;
A drunken sun went down at night, a drunken sun rose daily.
When Saturday took leave of us with ruddy cheeks a-glowing
The bottle still went round and round ; the red wine still kept flowing.
The Sabbath day began this way, and set, with fresh libations,
The seal of an eternity on our week-long potations.
Spring burst for us and joyous bloomed amidst the winter hoary ;
The chill north wind blew soft, perfumed by youthful dreamland's
    glory ;
Aflame with strength and courage all, we felt like young immortals ;
For us the sunshine blazed on earth, the stars at Heaven's portals.
The birds their pæan sang, the trees their flowery favours showered,
Until Earth fainted, with their weight of kisses overpowered.
Then every maid a beauty was and filled us with love's madness,
And none to pine e'er gave us cause, each thrilled our hearts with
    gladness.
Then opened wide a mighty tide o'er life and death victorious,
And trumpet-call bade one and all to battles great and glorious,
Where wounds and pain would count as gain, and all to death aspired.
Our glances fly from eye to eye with wine-lit lightnings fired.
We clutch the sabres from the wall and shout amidst much cheering
Wild freedom's song the whole night long till daylight is appearing.

The new republic stands complete ere the last star is failing,
And fierce our challenge rings afar while the still east is paling :
   ' Come on, ye kaiser cohorts, ay, come prince from every region,
   We stand unconquerable here, immortal, Freedom's legion ! '

Again, however, the current of ideas in favour of Prussia was
to receive a check, for the brief lull in the agitation for constitutional reform was soon terminated by a festival at the castle of
Hambach, near Neustadt-on-the-Haardt, a picturesque spot
not far from Ludwigshafen. The ancient castle, like so many
of its kind in Germany, was consecrated in a more enlightened
age to the purposes of a restaurant. Two colleagues in the
editorship of a democratic newspaper, Wirth and Siebenpfeiffer,
the latter a retired Bavarian civil servant, issued invitations
broadcast to a meeting to be held at Hambach on 27th May 1832,
for the celebration of a ' German May Day on the anniversary
of the Bavarian Constitution.' This Hambach Festival was
to become an event almost as startling to Metternich and the
German princes as the Wartburg Festival fifteen years earlier,
for the turgid ideas surging in many German minds were well
illustrated by Siebenpfeiffer's speech. A crowd of well over
30,000 men assembled. There was the usual procession, with
flags Polish, German, and black, followed by a series of speeches.
Siebenpfeiffer's rang thus [1] :

. . We devote our lives to Science and Art, we measure the
stars, scrutinise sun and moon, we give poetical representations
of God and man, heaven and hell, we probe the world of body
and mind : but we are ignorant of the pulse of patriotism, the
investigation of which (just what the Fatherland needs) is high
treason, even the faint wish only to attain to a Fatherland, a home
for free men, is a crime. We help to free Greece from the Turkish
yoke, we drink to the resurrection of Poland, we are indignant
when the despotism of kings damps the ardour of the people in
Spain, in Italy, and in France, we follow with our regard England's
Reform Bill, we praise the strength and the wisdom of the Sultan,
who busies himself over the regeneration of his peoples, we envy
the North American his happy lot that he has boldly carved out
for himself ; but we slavishly bow our necks under the yoke of
our own oppressors. . . .
The day will come, the day of noblest pride of victory when
Germans from the Alps to the North Sea, from the Rhine, the
Danube and the Elbe will embrace like brothers, when custom-
houses and toll-bars, and all the princely insignia of division and
restraint and oppression will disappear, with the little constitu-

---

[1] Klein.

tions which have been granted like playthings to a few cantankerous children in the great family ; when free roads and free waterways give evidence of the free circulation of all national activity and strength ; when princes will exchange the particoloured ermine robes of Feudalism and the Divine Right of Kings for the manly toga of Germany's national dignity, and officials and warriors will deck themselves, not in the lacquey's uniform of their lord and master but with the People's sash ; when not thirty-four towns or townlets, receiving alms from thirty-four courts, as the price of a doglike subjection, but when all towns, blossoming free in sap of their own, wrestle for the prize of patriotic deed ; when every branch of our stock, with internal freedom and independence, develops with civic freedom, and a strong, homespun bond of brotherhood enfolds all in political union and strength ; when the German flag, instead of carrying tribute to barbarians, convoys the products of our industrial toil to foreign quarters of the globe, and no more catches guiltless patriots for the executioner's axe, but bears the kiss of brotherhood to all free peoples. . . . Ay, there will come the day when a universal German Fatherland arises, that greets all its sons as citizens, and encompasses all citizens with equal love, with equal protection ; when Germania, sublime, stands on her brazen pedestal of freedom and of justice, in one hand the torch of enlightenment, which sends its civilising light to the furthest corner of the world, in the other the scales of justice, dispensing among the contending peoples the self-sought law of peace, those very peoples who impress on us the law of force and the stamp of scornful contempt. . . .

Long live the free, the united Germany !

Long live the Poles, the German allies !

Long live the French, the Germans' brothers, who honour our nationality and independence !

Long live every people that breaks its chains, and swears with us the Bond of Freedom !

Fatherland, Sovereign People, Union of Nations, all hail !

Could any one but a German have delivered himself of so bombastic an utterance ? It was too much for his colleague Wirth, who endeavoured to soften down Siebenpfeiffer's peroration. He declared that friendly relations with France were his desire, and they could not fail to follow on the German reforms he was striving after ; then he went on [1] :

But the French have no wish for reform in Germany, or only at the price of the left bank of the Rhine. It is only at this price that even liberal propagandists in France will support the efforts of a League of Freedom in Germany. That we for our part will not purchase freedom itself by the cession of the left bank of the Rhine to France, that, on the contrary, any attempt of France

---

[1] Biedermann.

to rob us of a single sod of German soil will and must silence all internal opposition and rouse all Germany against France, that the re-birth of freedom in our German Fatherland, then to be hoped for, will probably have a result that turns the tables in the reincorporation of Alsace and Lorraine in Germany—on all these points there can be among Germans but one voice. . . . Only when guarantees have first been given for the inviolability of German territory can a union of German patriots enter into a bond of brotherhood with the patriots of all other nations.

Wirth, like Siebenpfeiffer, ended his speech with a ' Hoch ! ' but ' to the United Free States of Germany and a consolidated, republican Europe ! ' A Frenchman followed him with (1) a defence of his country against the charge of lust of conquest, and (2) a glorification of ' the victorious French army, that had pitched its camp on the banks of the Arno, the Rhine, and the Nile.' Then a couple of Poles called on Germany to ' win freedom for itself and other peoples,' and finally a German orator let fall the equivocal declaration : ' The liberation of Poland must depart from the ruins of Hambach.'

After this orgy of speeches the crowd disappeared, and a day or two later Prince Wrede and the military turned up to suppress a revolution that did not exist. Proceedings were taken against Siebenpfeiffer, the one who piped for seven, and he was ultimately sentenced to two years' imprisonment for the heinous offence of ' contempt of an official.' He managed, however, to escape, and found a congenial outlet for his eloquence in a professorial chair at Berne.

Among those who took part in the Hambach Festival was Ludwig Börne. In Heine's very Heinesque sketch of his compatriot's life is to be found the following passage :

The festival of Hambach denoted a great step in advance, especially when one compares it with that other festival which once took place upon the Wartburg, equally in glorification of the interests of the people. The two mountain celebrations are really similar only in externals and accidental circumstances ; by no means in their deeper signification. The spirit which manifested itself at Hambach is fundamentally distinct from the spirit, or rather the spectre, which haunted the Wartburg. There, at Hambach, modern time shouted its sunrise songs, and drank brotherhood with all mankind ; but here upon the Wartburg the past croaked its raven ditty, and follies were spoken and enacted which were worthy of the silliest days of the middle ages !

Granted that at Hambach French Liberalism preached its wildest doctrines, and granted that much was said which was unreasonable, yet reason was nevertheless recognised as that highest authority which binds and looses, and prescribes to the law her laws ; on the Wartburg, on the contrary, there prevailed that narrow-minded Teutomania, which whined about charity and faith, but whose charity was nothing else but hatred of the stranger, and whose faith consisted only in irrationality, and which could find, in its ignorance, no better employment than the burning of books. . . . Have these impenetrable fools, the so-called Germanists, entirely disappeared from the scene of action ?   No.   They have only laid aside their black coats, the livery of their imbecility.   Most of them have even laid aside their lamentable, brutal jargon, and disguised in the colours and rhetoric of Liberalism, they became all the more dangerous to the new Opposition, during the political fire-and-fury period which followed the three days of July.   Yes, the camp of the German men of revolution swarmed with these former Germanists, who with unwilling lips lisped out the modern password and actually sang the ' Marseillaise ' . . . they made horrible grimaces over it . . . but the object in view was a common fight for a common cause, the unity of Germany, the only idea of progress which the older Opposition had brought to market.

Börne had an unfortunate experience at the festival ; his watch was stolen.   On this he remarked, quite in Heine's vein : ' I should very much have liked to discover the patriot who eased me of my watch ; when we came into power I should at once entrust him with the police and diplomacy.   But I shall get at him, the thief.   I mean to advertise in the Hambach paper and offer to give the respected finder of my watch the sum of 100 louis d'or.   The watch is worth it, if only as a curiosity : you see it is the first watch stolen by German freedom. Yes, we too, Germania's sons, we too will wake up from our drowsy honesty . . . tremble, tyrants, we can steal as well ! '

Official equanimity, disturbed by this Hambach Festival, received a few months later a fresh shock, occasioned by the storming of the Frankfort guard-house by a handful of graduates and students, not more than fifty in all, from the universities of Heidelberg and Göttingen.   The object was, apparently, to abolish the Federal Diet sitting at Frankfort, to seize the treasury-chest, and so to redeem a pledge made at a Students' Day at Frankfort in September 1831, when it was resolved that every student should bind himself to bring about, even by force, a free and equitable political existence, founded on the unity of the people.   The ringleaders thought they had the soldiers safe, but were deceived, and after an inglorious display on the part of all concerned, for neither students nor soldiers liked

being shot at, the affair resolved itself into one of the series
of fiascos which marked the whole revolutionary period in
Germany. Nevertheless the event did, like the Hambach
Festival, bring grist to Metternich's mill. Repression, which
had slumbered, awoke to fresh life, and Hegel, had he been alive,
would have had fresh opportunities for developing the doctrine
of his master, Dr. Pangloss, that all is for the best in the best
of all possible worlds.

An unfortunate Frankfort teacher [1] had, after the Frankfort
affair, to emigrate to Switzerland, and there he wrote a song
which became immensely popular with the crowds of German
refugees. This ' Song of the Fugitive,' pathetic enough, is not
a great song, though it may candidly be admitted that the
original is rather better than the translation. The author died
in misery, after lying for years in hospital at Lyons, where he
held a tutorship for a short time. He was only brought back
to his native city, Frankfort, to end his days in a hospital.

THE FUGITIVE'S SONG

When the princes ask you
' Absalom, how 's he ? '
You can answer truly
' Oh ! he 's hanging free ;
Hanging to no tree, nor
Slip-knot sliding slick,
Hanging to the vision
Of a Republic.'

If they ask you further
' How 's the refugee ? '
Say : ' In rags and tatters,
As your eyes can see.
Give your purple garments,
They will make aright
Trews for freedom's soldiers
Marching to the fight.'

Ask they, more in comfort,
' Seeks he amnesty ? '
Say, in fitting accents,
' He 'll not bend the knee ;
He had nothing left, 'mid
Thoughts that overwhelm,
But to strike a blow for
One free German Realm.'

---

[2] Wilhelm Sauerwein. See Freytag's *Carl Mathy*.

A conspicuous figure among those who suffered at this time was Fritz Reuter, the famous Platt-Deutsch author. He was but twenty-three years old when he was arrested at Berlin for democratic intrigue, 'attempt at high treason.' After being under remand for three years he was, in 1836, condemned to death, though the sentence was commuted to thirty years' detention in a fortress. Notwithstanding the fact that he was a Mecklenburg subject the Prussian government kept savage hold of him, and only grudgingly allowed him at last to languish in a prison in his native state. He was finally pardoned by Frederick William IV. in 1840. Klein says : ' He came back to freedom a half-broken man and carried with him through life a thorn in the flesh. Reuter succeeded in forcing his way up again. Many others, poisoned in the bloom of youth by the breath of the prison-house, came as refugees to rack and ruin.'

Reuter told the story of his imprisonment in a work called *My Prison Days*. The blessed God, he says, only knows why he was shut up ; he had not stolen, nor lied, nor cheated. ' What then had we done ? Nothing, nothing at all ! At our meetings we had only spoken of things that now (after 1866) are freely cried aloud in the open street, viz., the freedom, and the unity of Germany ; but for action we were too weak, for writing too stupid, and therefore we followed the old German use, and merely spoke about these matters. That, however, was enough for the cunning of an examining magistrate.'

Two pathetic documents are the beautiful letter [1] of Reuter's father to his son, and the latter's account, from his *Ut miner Festungstid*, of his departure from the Sheriff's Bridewell in Berlin :

STAVENHAGEN, *4th November* 1833.

DEAR FRITZ !—I know not if these lines will reach thee. The humanity of thy judge will nevertheless, I hope, permit it. This morning I received the sad news of thy arrest. Away with reproofs, they cannot here help thee. If thou hast erred, bear the consequences of thy crime with courage. Rise superior to thy guilt, whatever it be. Lenient judges have always been Germany's pride. They will also be lenient to thee, I hope to God. Convinced with all who know thee, of the goodness of thy heart, I forgive thee, shouldst thou have done wrong. Count therefore on the continuance of my love for thee, and my sympathy with thee. This only do I ask in return : seek to preserve thy health,

---

[1] *Briefe von Fritz Reuter an seinen Vater.* F. Engel (K.).

as far as possible, and spend in hard work thy isolation and time as profitably as circumstances and the goodness of thy judge permit, and give me, when thou may'st, news of thee. May God direct all for the best! Thy most devoted father greets thee.

REUTER'S DEPARTURE FROM THE SHERIFF'S BRIDEWELL IN BERLIN [1]

. . . The door was opened and in the doorway stood the Gendarm Res'(ervist) who had so often conducted me for these five years to be examined by the Herr Kriminalrath. He was an old lanky dried-up fellow, his face pitted with pockmarks and sprinkled with freckles. Thin grey hair hung from his cheeks, and on either side of his nostrils dangled a ' Frederick William the Third ' like a grey tallow candle. Pretty to look at he was not, but, all the same, when the good God sends me His angel of release in the hour of death may it just be an old ' Gendarm Res'.' There he stood in the doorway in his royal Prussian angel-uniform and called into our miserable abode : ' Gentlemen, get ready ; we start in half an hour.' Ah! Kapteihn! (Reuter's fellow-prisoner) Charles Douze! What a joy it was! Away! Away! Whither ? We did not know ; but away! Away from the churl who had made our life a misery—away from the curmudgeon who without rhyme or reason had tortured us body and blood (Kriminal-direktor Dambach). ' But,' many will say, ' much better people have had to suffer much worse things. Think of the levies of eighteen hundred and thirteen.' Yes, but those men did not have to sit still and endure, they *did* things and that is a very different matter. We young people whose breath of life it is to be working and doing, we feel it to hear merely of ' enduring ' and ' suffering.' We feel it to have to allow ourselves to be talked limp by such fellows as Count H—— or a Kriminal-direktor Dambach at their good pleasure. Yes! Gendarm Res' and Providence delivered us then from our suffering, and I will not reckon it to the account of Kriminaldirektor Dambach, just as I have drawn a thick line through the score of the persecutions he inflicted on me while in prison on remand. On one point, however, I shall hold him to account— he is dead and in this world there is nothing to be done, but for one thing he shall answer me in the world beyond. When my old father, full of grief for his only son, came to Berlin to see what he could do towards obtaining that son's freedom, why did Kriminaldirektor Dambach not allow that old father to traverse the twenty paces which separated him from my prison, so that the son might lay his head on a father's breast and weep his heart out for once ?

---

[1] *Ut miner Festungstid*, c. 12.

H

CHAPTER V

THE SECRET CONFERENCES AT VIENNA—THE GERMAN RAILWAY SYSTEM

GENTZ was no longer alive in 1833 to assist his master Metternich in renewing and refurbishing the machinery of repression, and inventing new devices. But Metternich had not to depend on his own unaided wits. Inspiration came to him from Prussia's Foreign Minister, von Ancillon. The two arranged a meeting at Teplitz, and in August 1833 they sent out a joint circular inviting all German governments to send representatives to a series of secret conferences at Vienna. Remembering the difficulties experienced in 1820 in getting the Federal Diet to grant the force of law to the Carlsbad Decrees, they resolved that on this occasion there should be no attempt of the kind ; there were only to be ' understandings,' which, however, the governments were to pledge themselves to carry out in all severity. The result of five months' work was a programme, sixty articles long, covering the whole area of governmental activity. Not only were there drastic measures against the press and the hated universities, but several articles involved infringements of the internal rights of states composing the German Federation, and aroused the keenest resentment among such representative assemblies as existed in them, a feeling which only culminated in the revolution of 1848. The final protocol was settled in June 1834, but as the authors dare not give their resolutions publicity by bringing them before the Diet they never received sanction as Federal law. Not until 1844 were the resolutions published in Germany, though a United States newspaper published the gist of them earlier. Professor Pollard in the *Cambridge Modern History*, x. p. 378, attributes the secrecy ' to the hostility of France and England to this repressive policy.' And he says : ' The Frankfort conspirators were probably affiliated to the secret societies of

114

which Mazzini was now the moving spirit. A general conspiracy needed as general a system of police as possible ; and in June 1833, at Metternich's instance, the Diet appointed a central commission to supervise the prosecutions in individual states, to collect results, and to concert preventive measures. . . . A fresh series of ministerial conferences was held at Vienna in the spring of 1834. . . . The principal suggestions appear to have been the appointment of five committees to act as probouleutic councils for the Diet, and the institution of courts of arbitration—to be selected by the sovereign—to decide in legislative and financial disputes between the sovereigns and their estates.' It is doubtful whether there was any connection between the Frankfort disturbance and the system of secret societies controlled by Mazzini. The affair was engineered by academic hot-heads, such as those who contrived a student-riot staged at Göttingen in 1831. And the secret conferences at Vienna did more than what is suggested above. They laid the foundations of a whole reactionary system, interference with the rights of representative bodies, persecution of the press, dragooning of the universities, and infringement of the liberty of the subject.

A series of outrageous prosecutions followed, and the performances of the twenties were easily outdone in the thirties. There was, indeed, more to get hold of now, for Heine's contrast between the festivals of the Wartburg and of Hambach is largely true ; the Wartburg was thronged by boys, at Hambach there were grown men. Nevertheless the task of an inquisitor was as much beset as of old with the need for refinement in the estimation of guilt. Actual cases of high treason were hard to find, and the courts had to distinguish between ' a state of preparation for high treason,' ' an attempt at high treason,' and ' an actual case of high treason.' So there was the same variety in the severity of sentences imposed. While some defendants escaped with a short term of imprisonment, on others, where the facts were identical, even the death sentence was passed. ' In Prussia,' says Biedermann, ' the latter was the rule ; there the High Court at Berlin passed the capital sentence on thirty-nine members of the *Burschenschaft*, on four of them without any recommendation to mercy.' Their gracious king commuted these sentences, the last to imprisonment for life, the rest to terms of thirty years. The *Burschenschaft* had raised its head again, and a much more dangerous one than in the days when the lament printed on page 54 was written.

Three particular cases may be described in some detail, in order to show how brutal was the procedure of the authorities. A leading liberal in the Bavarian Landtag of 1819, one Behr by name, was a professor in the University of Würzburg. He was a few years later elected burgomaster of Würzburg. The sturdy liberal himself saw no objection to the part of pluralist, but the conscience of an autocratic government was shocked, and it succeeded in driving him not only from his professorial chair, but also from his seat in the chamber. Later the unfortunate burgomaster fell under the ban of this new Inquisition, languished for fifteen years in prison, and had to beg pardon on his knees before a portrait of King Ludwig I.!

Professor Sylvester Jordan of Marburg, a much loved personality, was first placed for several years under police supervision, then on the evidence of most unreliable witnesses he was arrested; for more than five years he lay in prison, and was then sentenced to five years' internment in a fortress for supposed high treason. Finally the Court of Appeal at Cassel entirely acquitted him.

But the case that shook the country to its depths was that of one Pastor Weidig, who was found to have committed suicide in the bridewell at Darmstadt, after awaiting trial for five years. Weidig had been headmaster of a grammar school in Hesse, and was known to be a man of free opinions, but not a revolutionary. An inquiry showed that his suicide was due to the inhuman torture, physical as well as mental, to which he had been subjected by his examining judge, Councillor Georgi of the High Court of Hesse, a notorious drunkard.

Few more poignant documents have ever been penned than this letter of Weidig to his wife, written in prison :

DARMSTADT, 5th March 1836.

DEAR WIFE OF MY HEART . . . I must tell you that since the end of last year, I have with little intermission been sick in body and mind, that my health is still very uncertain, and that though the doctor promises recovery, I am prepared for anything. But you and the children are well and that is what I have prayed to God for every hour of the day, and many an hour of the night too. My birthday poems to Wilhelm and Friedegarde I have already mentioned (Weidig had sent his wife two poems full of longing).

May the Almighty soon fulfil them ! I carry about in my head, as comforting society for my solitude, some forty poems from the days when my poor brain was clearer. My head is now, you see, very bad, and I see pictures and apparitions of the most discordant kinds. (Weidig had hallucinations ; he saw twice, for instance, while wide awake at night, coffins 'built up out of nothing but false indictments.') To-night came Friedegarde (born during his imprisonment) and her nurse, so that I saw them in the body and greeted them.—For the rest, I am unchanged and I reiterate the promises I gave you on leaving Friedberg ; I can and do repeat them so long as the breath remains in my body. I . . . repeat the request . . . that you, as my proxy, will contradict anything that may be said to my disparagement and believe no one but myself and your own heart, for people are fond of lying about others and especially about those who are buried alive. . . . I must close now, the raging pain in my head and breast, though often numbed, is again fiendish. So I greet you and our children with the sincerest unchangeable love.   THY FRITZ.

To this document Klein appends a grim note : ' This and other letters were never to reach the wife of the sick and despairing man. They were even suppressed for many years afterwards, for " police reasons of state." We understand the reasons, and we understand also why the nation demanded public trial.'

The circumstances [of the time had wellnigh expelled the ghost of romanticism from the literature of the thirties, and the younger writers, engrossed by the stern realities of the present, became more and more political in their message. The school thus formed was known as ' Young Germany,' and the following is the fulmination against it of the Federal Diet on 10th December 1835—with what success we shall see when we come to consider the political poetry of the forties :

Whereas there has recently sprung up in Germany a school of literature known of late under the name of ' Young Germany ' or the ' New Literature,' whose open and declared aim it is, in literary productions within the reach of every reader, to attack the Christian religion in the most insolent manner, to bring existing institutions into contempt and to subvert all discipline and morality, the German Federal Diet . . . has come unanimously to the following determination :

All German governments undertake the duty of enforcing with the greatest stringency the criminal law and police regulations of their respective countries against the authors, publishers, printers and vendors of the publications issued by the literary school known as ' Young Germany,' or the ' New Literature,' to which belong namely, Heinr. Heine, Carl Gutzkow, Heinr. Laube, Ludolf Wienbarg and Theodor Mundt, and to prevent the distribution of the above indicated publications . . . by all the legal means in their power.[1]

The publishers, and particularly those who dealt in the wares of Young Germany, or ventured to publish anything of political significance, had hard times. The life of Brockhaus, publisher of the great *Konversations-Lexikon*, affords ample evidence of the bitterness of the struggle against the censorship, a struggle which shortened men's lives. Campe, Heine's publisher, was, according to Klein, ' an absolute genius in guerilla warfare with the censorship, and carried it on with gusto and frequent success.' No doubt the impish side of Heine's brain was fertile in ingenious suggestion to his friend.

But reaction soon soared above such petty concerns as books and the men who wrote or published them, for Hanover was to furnish in 1837 a sensation on an elevated political plane. On the accession of Queen Victoria the operation of the Salic law severed the personal union between Great Britain and Hanover. Ernest, Duke of Cumberland, the new king and a reactionary of the worst type, revoked within a few days of his accession the liberal constitution which his elder brother had granted. Seven professors of the University of Göttingen, including Dahlmann, the great draftsman of constitutions, of whom we shall hear more, Gervinus, the great Shakespearean critic, and the well-known philologists, the brothers Grimm, whose name the famous fairy tales have made a household word in England, protested against this violation of a kingly oath. They were dismissed from their professorships, and three, Dahlmann, Jacob Grimm, and Gervinus, were expelled from the country. The result was that the seven professors became almost as famous as our seven bishops. Their expulsion moved Anastasius Grün, the aristocratic Viennese, to write a bitter epigram worth recording :

> Surely, where men like these go forth,
>   Banished from hearth and home,
> 'Tis exile into such a land,
>   Not out of it, to roam.

Jacob Grimm wrote a letter of protest [2] against his dismissal and expulsion in which he gave free vent to his feelings of

---

[1] *Corpus juris Confoederationis Germanicae*, ii. (K.).
[2] Quoted by Klein.

indignation, and yields yet another example of that curious egotism and want of self-restraint in the expression of one's feelings which is a German characteristic. Thus writes the German professor :

The thunderbolt which has fallen on my peaceful home has stirred the hearts of a wide circle. Is it merely human sympathy, or has the lightning flash that struck me affected others with its shock and made them fear that their own possessions are threatened. Not the arm of justice but that of violence compels me to leave a country in which I was invited to settle, and to which I have rendered eight years' loyal and honourable service. 'Give the gentleman a hand ; he is a fugitive,' said a grandmother to her grandson as, on the 16th December last, I stepped across the frontier. And where was I thus called a fugitive ? In my own country, which the same evening unwillingly admitted me, but rejected my companions. . . . I am of no such plastic nature as to sacrifice my rights without striking a blow, or allow myself to be driven about hither and thither by every fitful change in current opinion. My cause, however unimportant it may appear to the world, enshrines for me the essence of all I have achieved, and as such I shall maintain it unblemished and undefamed. Truth alone will prevail, and even the ill-disposed and the weak, who will not acknowledge it openly, must feel it throbbing in their inmost hearts. . . . Neither I nor my brother have ever received from any government either marks of distinction or means of support. I have sometimes felt the need of the latter ; of the former never. This independence has steeled my soul ; it is unaffected by imputations intended to asperse the purity of my feelings.

What kind of event is this then which, knocking at the door of my secluded chamber, scene of harmless and even-flowing occupation, enters rudely and casts me forth ? Who, even a year ago, could have persuaded me that such a retired and inoffensive existence as mine should ever be the object of invasion, insult and injury ? The reason of it all is that I would not be disloyal to the duty entrusted to me, without any prompting of mine, by a country which had granted me its hospitality, and did not hesitate to follow the dictates of my conscience when met by a threatening command to do what I could not do without perjuring myself. Now something that never occupied my heart or soul has with the force of irresistible necessity clutched me and torn me away. As a quiet wayfarer, suddenly finding himself in the midst of a fray from which rises a cry for succour, feels driven to respond on the instant, so I, involved in a public cause the claims of which I dare not shirk by a handsbreadth, must uphold it without first looking about me to see what the myriads of others, equally bound to maintain it, are doing or not doing. . . .

No other class in the whole kingdom could be more deeply and violently affected by this occurrence (the abrogation of the constitution by the King) than the University. The German seats of learning, so long as their proved and excellent constitution exists, must remain extremely sensitive to everything good or evil that happens in the state, and that not only because of the tide of students flowing constantly in and out of their class-rooms, but also because of the special qualities of the teachers which are so carefully adjusted to their duties. Were it otherwise the Universities would not be fulfilling their vocation as in fact they have done. The frank and unspoiled spirit of youth demands that their teachers shall answer their questions regarding life and politics from the purest and most moral point of view, and with sincerity and truth. No hypocrisy will serve. So strong is the power of justice and virtue on the still unprejudiced spirits of the students that they incline thereto spontaneously and resent any misrepresentation. Nor can there be any suppression of free teaching (which should be subject alone to conscientious convictions) regarding the essential conditions and consequences of beneficent government. . . . Knowledge is the bulwark of the noblest acquisitions of Man, the highest of earthly goods, but what is it compared with that foundation of existence—an inflexible reverence for the laws of God ? Knowledge if divorced from this resembles those marble fruits Italians carve, deceptive imitations indeed to the eye, but mere table ornaments that neither satisfy nor nourish. . . . History shows us frank and noble men who dared to speak the whole truth to the King's face. That is the privilege of those who have the courage for it. Sometimes their confession of faith has borne fruit ; sometimes it has proved fatal to them, though not to their reputations. . . . On the 11th of December the King after a short inquisitorial investigation into the publication of the protest (my first appearance before a court) decreed that the seven professors should be not merely suspended from their offices but actually dismissed from his service. Banishment within three days under penalty of imprisonment was the sentence on three of them who had communicated it to outsiders. Who, however, would care to languish, innocent, in prison ? . . .

I do not consider myself as yet to be deprived of my title to my post, and the well-earned salary attached to it, by this decree of dismissal, pronounced without law or justice by the King, in violation of the procedure prescribed by his own charter, and I intend to proceed legally against this order with all the means at my disposal. I was obliged to yield to force. . . . So long as I breathe, however, I shall rejoice to have acted as I did, and I feel, with consolation, that whatever part of my work survives me will not lose, but gain by this action of mine.

Two amusing examples of official arrogance may fitly follow. One of the Göttingen professors, Albrecht, was a native of Elbing, and when a number of his townsmen addressed a public letter of approval to the seven martyrs they were solemnly reprimanded by Rochow, Prussian Minister of the Interior :

It is not becoming for a subject to apply to the actions of the Head of the State the standard afforded by his own limited intelligence, and in his purblind arrogance to presume to give a public judgment on their legality. The signatories of the address should not have regarded the conduct of the Göttingen professors as a defence of established institutions, but as an act of audacious rebellion and a presumptuous undertaking on their part.[1]

And here is the sort of petty tyranny that went on in Hanover :

Privy Councillor von Schele knew how to persecute sharply officials who had even the most distant connection with any opposition tendencies. It is related, for instance, by Albert Oppermann, brother-in-law of Robert Prutz,[2] that his nomination as advocate was refused time after time, in spite of the highest recommendations. At last he addressed his request to the Councillor himself, basing it on the fact that want of means prevented his settling elsewhere to found a practice. Schele interrupted him with the question : ' What is your father ? ' ' A book-binder.' ' Then you ought to have been one too.'[3]

No wonder Jacob Grimm sent to Dahlmann the following poem by Hoffmann von Fallersleben[4] as an expression of his feelings :

OUT WITH THE BIG STICK !

(' *Facit indignatio versus* ')

Of all the wishes in my breast
The one that pleases me the best
Is ' Oh for the Great Big Stick ! '
If God would only grant me power,
Then every day and every hour
I 'd brandish my Big Stick.

Then neither goods nor gold I 'd need
To put the world all right with speed,
But only my Big Stick.
I 'd victor be and hero too,
The best and greatest the world knew,
If I had my Big Stick.

---

[1] Biedermann, *Dreissig Jahre deutscher Geschichte.*
[2] See page 199.
[3] Oppermann, *Geschichte des Königreichs Hannover* (K.)
[4] See page 197.

I 'd soon bring freedom, peace, and law
And happy life to all I saw,
    By means of my Big Stick.
And if I wanted to be gay,
Then great and small should dance all day
    To the beat of my Big Stick.

O dream of mine, could you come true !
For but one day could I wield you,
    My Great Big Stick !
Oh what would I not give to lay
About me, for but one long day,
    On rootling hogs
    And yapping dogs
        With my Big Stick !

Of the indignation which such facts as those set out in the
foregoing recital occasioned throughout Germany we shall have
some fine specimens in the next chapter, which treats of the
political poetry of the thirties.   A man may well wonder why
the nation did not, long before 1848, break out into rebellion
against so atrocious a system of tyranny and oppression.   But
we have to remember that, as has already been pointed out, the
section of the public that suffered in their own persons was comparatively small, viz., the academic and literary class that counted
for little more in the Germany of those days than the same
class does in England to-day, and the interest of large numbers
of the middle class was engaged in the development of industry
and commerce, opportunities for which were rapidly presenting
themselves.   We shall speak of the *Zollverein* later, but this is
the appropriate place to say a word on one of the great economic
enterprises that did as much as the *Zollverein*, or the Prussian
army, or the brain of Bismarck, to bring about the unification
of Germany, viz., the inauguration of the German railway
system.   Up to 1834 the only railway line in Germany was a
tiny little line connecting Nuremberg with Fürth.   In 1834 was
begun the important line between Leipzig and Dresden ; this
was completed within five years, and all over Germany the
example was followed.   The man who did more than any one
to rouse his countrymen to the importance of the railway
question was Friedrich List, of whose persecution by the government as a liberal politician we have already heard.   During his
exile in the United States in 1824 and the next few years he
watched with keen eyes the immense development of railway

enterprise going on all around him ; in one undertaking he
himself took an active part. After the July revolution in 1830
he returned to Germany and endeavoured unsuccessfully, first
in Hamburg and then in Munich, to win sympathy for his ideas.
But Leipzig at last responded to his message, and a body of keen
young business men took up the matter in real earnest. List's
active pen did much to educate the keen intelligences throughout his country to the great issues involved. But despite the
growing enthusiasm of his supporters among business men the
political jealousy between German states, the selfishness of land-
owners, the obstinacy of dull, unimaginative Philistines, like
similar adverse influences in our own country, prevented anything like a full realisation of List's dream. Money was wasted
over the building of roundabout inconvenient lines that had to
be duplicated later by others more direct, and states seemed to
take a perverse delight in selecting here and there different
gauges from their neighbours'. But before the thirties were
over, German emotion was touched, and gave vent, as German
emotion so often does, in verse. Carl Beck, a poet glowing with
the enthusiasm of youth, was moved by the excitement over
speculation in railway shares to celebrate the higher significance
of the railway in the following lines :

> How the shares upon the market
>   Rise and fall ! Oh aspect mean !
> Bank notes of our Bank of Union,
>   So by me the shares are seen.
> For these rails are bridal bracelets,
>   Wedding rings of purest gold ;
> States like lovers will exchange them,
>   And the marriage-tie will hold.

These charming verses provide an easy transition to the
subject of the next chapter.

CHAPTER VI

POLITICAL POETRY OF THE THIRTIES

THE Parisian revolution of 1830 was the mildest that ever graced the queen of revolutionary cities, and the shock it communicated to Germany was, as has been pointed out, less severe than might have been expected. The event did not inspire the poets of Austria and Germany to rhapsodies on a happy future about to dawn on the free peoples of Europe. They were faced by the cold realities of Austrian and Prussian repression at home, a repression only aggravated by the alarm created in reactionary minds at Vienna and Berlin ; and if a ray of light came in 1830 from the west, gloom settled down next year on the east, with the fall of Warsaw and the suppression of Poland by Russia. But the early thirties did evoke poetry that was fine, despite its political burden ; and the message it conveyed was one of despair rather than of hope. The most eminent of German poets poured out their souls in verses, now despondent, now satirical. Notable among these were three poets of aristocratic family, Platen (Count von Platen-Hallermünde), and the Austrians, Lenau (Niembsch von Strehlenau), and Anastasius Grün (Count A. A. von Auersperg). A few examples of their work will show clearly how stirred were the noblest natures of the time by forebodings for the future, and by fierce resentment against reaction and its apparatus of espionage, penal laws, and the censorship, while they denounced the vagueness that clouded the reformers' aims, and shrank from traffic with the demagogue or the assassin.

The most conspicuous figure of the three is that of Platen ; indeed, by many he is regarded as the greatest stylist German literature has produced. In his youth he passed through a romantic phase, but the romanticism of the literature of his time soon revolted him and he satirised mercilessly its formlessness and turgidity of language. Goethe was early in recognising his gifts, but there is an interesting passage in his *Conversations with Eckermann* in which he denounces a polemical tendency among poets :

In Count Platen there are nearly all the chief requisites of a good poet ; imagination, invention, intellect and productiveness, he possesses in a high degree ; he also shows a thoroughly technical cultivation, and a study and earnestness, to be found in few others. With him, however, his unhappy polemical tendency is a hindrance. That amid the grandeur of Naples and Rome he could not forget the trivialities of German literature, is unpardonable in so eminent a genius. The 'Romantic Œdipus' shows that, especially with regard to technicalities, Platen was just the man to write the best German tragedy ; but now in this piece he has used the tragic motives for purposes of parody, how will he write a tragedy in good earnest ? And then (what is not enough kept in mind) these quarrels occupy the thoughts ; the images of our foes are like ghosts which interrupt all free production, and cause great disorder in a nature already sufficiently susceptible. Lord Byron was ruined by his polemical tendency ; and Platen should, for the honour of German literature, quit for ever so unprofitable a path.

There is this much truth in Goethe's criticism—Platen did fail as a dramatist ; his fame rests on his sonnets, of which he wrote the finest sequence that exists in German, his odes, often in severe imitation of classical metres, and his lyrics. He has been described as cold and statuesque, but in 1831 he published his burning ' Address to an Ultra-Reactionary,' and in 1832 his noble verses, unrhymed, ' To a German State,' a poem that was much in German minds for the next sixteen years :

TO AN ULTRA

Dost praise an age, in which thy titled kind
    Enjoyed a peaceful prime ?
But, save a powder-puff, what 's left behind
    From all that gold-bespangled time ?

Can but the past thy feelings set ablaze,
    Not what the young years show ?
Why, like Apostate Julian, turn thy gaze
    Back to false gods we hardly know ?

'Tis Freedom's golden dawn, with sun-rays dowered.
    Now lights the western sky !
In darkness, say'st thou, she must long have cowered :
    That was the fault of Tyranny.

Who dared speak out, when there a despot stood
　　To close the mouths of all ?
Even Christ's word, that all the world finds good,
　　For long remained a secret call.

Not only evil works behind a veil,
　　Round Virtue one is thrown :
The Fatherland, by traitors put on sale,
　　Weeps in the market-place, alone !

Let sceptred king, thou say'st, rule without let,
　　Unchecked his fiat run,
As if he were a man by beasts beset,
　　Wild beasts he covers with a gun !

Wouldst thou have speech within safe limits brought,
　　Imprison tongue and pen ?
In vain ! 'Twill out, man's ever-glowing thought,
　　And like a Mænad dance again !

In vain, thou fossil, thou rail'st at novelty,
　　Too strong the ascendant star :
A virtue fair indeed is loyalty,
　　But simple justice fairer far !

And is that new, which could on us bestow
　　Free cities of renown,
Ere Charles the Fifth blazed forth, and his fell foe
　　Francis, who trod the people down ?

And must I once, like Ulrich Hutten, die,
　　Forsaken and alone,
I 'll tear the cowl from off Hypocrisy :
　　'Tis not worth while, the knave shall own !

TO A GERMAN STATE

Thou wak'st, but who can pledge himself
　　That thou wilt never sleep ?
That courage and love of Fatherland
　　Will always stay awake ?

Thou liest on the dizzy verge,
　　With danger all around,
And woe betide thee, shouldst thou sleep
　　But for one instant there.

Heed not that which the moment brings,
　　In life's deep essence see !
The future's compass, lies it not
　　Within thy breast alone ?

We 've seen the world for centuries
  Bemused with stupid sleep,
And to a wild tempestuous time
  A sluggish age succeed.

But even in an age of ease,
  Tell me, who kept awake ?
Why, even in an age of ease
  Free peoples kept awake.

Freedom it is we call that pulse
  That ever beats alive,
That ever drives a folk to fight
  For its own hearth and home.

She never lacks defence of man,
  She never wants a sword,
For he who knows her, what she is,
  Will face e'en death for her !

Who 'd rob me of her, were I free ?
  Lost I right hand and left,
Yet should I hold my weapon still
  Between my teeth clenched fast.

Thou fearest wine so strong as this,
  In ferment while it seethes ;
But set the beaker to thy lips,
  'Twill make thy soul grow strong.

And hast thou kept this impulse down
  (Thou wilt not, well I know !)
Naked and weaponless thou stand'st,
  Like some greybeard unmanned.

Whenc'er this impulse dies, as died
  It has in many a folk,
Well, may'st thou stir them, the dry bones,
  Nor stir them till they rise.

Preserve it as a sacred thing,
  Like yonder quenchless lamp,
That hanging by the high altar
  Lights all the vault above.

'Tis vain to gaze admiringly
  On peoples here and there :
Admire them not ! It lies with thee
  To be as great as they.

Oh throw away these stilts at last
Of courtly make-believe ;
Let man be true, no worm is he,
Else he 's past praying for.

Within our hearts dwells fear of God ;
And but a tyrant's self
(We 're sure of that) would spread it out
And flaunt it like a robe.

Did every mother's son with thee
His rights and duties own,
To thee would Europe lower her sword,
Asia [1] her headsman's axe.

Platen, out of sympathy with the German literature of his time, and consumed with a fiery indignation against the attempt to fetter by the censorship thought and its expression, made his permanent home in Italy, where he died, too young, in 1835. Had he lived during the next decade, his would probably have been the name that stood highest among the brilliant band of political poets of the forties.

On finally leaving Germany, in despair of freedom, he wrote a poem which only a German could have written, so fierce is the feeling indulged, so unrestrained its expression in the last verse. Treitschke and Biedermann have denounced the Judæo-Germans, Börne and Heine, for saying things of their stepcountry which no German would say of his Fatherland, but did either ever say so bitter a word in so deadly earnest a mood ?

ON LEAVING GERMANY

All that I have I pack together,
The thoughts that in my bosom glowed,
For, ah ! too soon, have reached their tether
The gifts a kindly God bestowed.

Was it in vain my inspiration ?
Vain the high hopes my fancy planned ?
The sorriest bungler in creation,
Wields he the pen with master-hand ?

---

[1] The Germans have always been fond of describing Russia as an Asiatic power. The allusion is to the suppression of Poland.

So must I roam, my thoughts concealing,
That I may cheat the mean man's view,
And, past the surly bailiff stealing,
With head erect my way pursue.

The savage censor crouches, thumbing
In cushioned ease my poetry,
The music of my song benumbing,
And jangling all its harmony.

And so must I give over singing,
Yield up, perforce, my fond desire,
To spend myself in sweetness bringing
To men who wallow in the mire !

Come, poet, take a view serener ;
The world unmoved thy loss will see ;
Thou know'st, on earth there 's nothing meaner
Than that one should a German be.

The melancholy Lenau wrote lyrics of almost intolerable
pathos, such as the prayer :

Turn not from me, eye of darkness,
All thy store of magic spend,
Night austere, dream-laden, tender,
Night, thou sweetness without end !

In thy sable cloak mysterious
Hide the world away from me,
O'er my beating heart for ever
Hovering may I know but thee.

Hungary was the land of his birth, and through the poems on
which rests his fame as the greatest of Austria's modern lyric
poets, all the voices of the nature he knew so well in youth
whisper their message of the passing of things temporal. His
sensitive spirit was roused to wrath by the tyranny of the
Metternichian system. As Platen was driven to Italy, so
Lenau sought escape from the gloom about him by emigration
to the United States, only to find disillusionment there. He
returned to Europe, and wrote epics like ' Savonarola ' and
' The Albigenses ' in which he pleaded for liberty of conscience
and in life. In 1844 his reason gave way, and he spent the
last six years of his unhappy life in an asylum.

Here are two of his indignant outbursts against princely misrule and the censorship :

A PROTEST

When I despise conspiracy's black mask,
    And when I hate the assassin's bloody trade ;
    When rogues transmogrified and heroes made,
Styled Saviours of the People, my patience task ;

When Kingship as a Heaven-sent boon I hail,
    Giving the fatherless a father's care,
    Therefore think not I count as treasure rare
What sort of king may here and now prevail.

Think not I keep no store of tinder dry
    To set ablaze my passion's noble flame,
    When prince as tyrant puts his folk to shame ;
A bandit crowned I may not glorify.

Mine honour will not mount a knacker's jade ;
    Its steed has wings ; and if, men's scorn, I sing
    A courtier's song, God's wrath a bolt may fling
To blast the minstrel hand the tune that played.

SHAME !

Shame that the Cross, that sacred sign
    That stood on Golgotha of old
    To free us all from Satan's hold,
Should serve a Censor to blot a line !

The symbol is perverted now ;
    It stands to mock man's fondest vow,
    And tells how long the years must be
Ere we from Wrong may find us free.

His pathetic farewell to his Fatherland, less bitter than Platen's, on seeking the ' fertile, flowery strand,' the ' coast ' in plain prose, the ' shores ' in journalistic English, of the United States was as follows :

THE EMIGRANT'S SONG

For the last time thy name I greet,
    O fallen so low, my Fatherland,
Who stoop'st to kiss a despot's feet,
    In dull obedience to command.

Thine arms may rock a child to rest
For thou hast gifts that children heed ;
And love-sick youth may call thee blest ;
But where is freedom, the strong man's need ?

The hunter in the wilds forlorn
Takes sudden cover, 'neath the press
Of panic-driven hoof and horn ;
And gasps, the danger past, no less.

Even so, my Fatherland, dost thou
Start when thy master's step draws near,
And, as he passes, cringe and bow
And hold thy breath in craven fear.

Oh speed, thou ship, like clouds that scud,
There, where the fires of God burn free,
And bridge the gulf, O roaring flood,
The gulf 'twixt me and liberty.

O thou new world, and Freedom's world,
Against whose fertile, flowery strand
The tyrant's wrath in vain is hurled,
In thee I greet my Fatherland !

The popular success in political poetry, and a success which
was prodigious, was reserved for Anastasius Grün.   In 1831 he
published his *Ramblings of a Vienna Poet* with a dedication
to Uhland, the first three verses of which run as follows :

For a people loyal-hearted,
    And the freeman's cherished right,
Flame to fuel thy songs imparted,
    Fought like heroes in the fight.

Man-at-arms, with sword victorious,
    Not the only hero he !
'Twas a hero just as glorious
    Made me of thy fireside free.

Each has arms he 's trained to handle,
    Sword and lance the soldiers choose,
Priests the bell and book and candle ;
    Song and rhyme the arms *we* use.

It is not easy to understand how it was that Grün's poems
should arouse the enthusiasm they did, for their style and the
burden of them have little of the simple and direct appeal of
Uhland's homespun verse.   At first glance they remind one of
the best of our own political verse of the period, such as Praed's.

His lines on the Whigs, in 1839, quoted in Trevelyan's *Life of Macaulay*, chapter viii., lines for which some might seek to find a modern application, have much of the point and brilliance that marks Grün's polished satire :

> ' And, truth to say, it must be pleasant
> To be a Minister at present :
> To make believe to guide the realm
> Without a hand upon the helm,
> And wonder what with such a crew
> A pilot e'er should find to do ;
> To hold what people are content
> To fancy is the government,
> And touch extremely little of it
> Except the credit and the profit ;
> . . . To hear demands of explanation
> On India, Belgium, trade, taxation,
> And answer that perhaps you 'll try
> To give an answer by and by ;
> . . . To promise, pause, prepare, postpone
> And end by letting things alone ;
> In short, to earn the people's pay
> By doing nothing every day ;
> These tasks, these joys, the Fates assign
> To well-placed Whigs in Thirty-nine.'

But Grün had a more serious purpose, and the hated minister at whose odious system he lunged in true fencing form was no place-hunting Englishman, but the master of central European diplomacy, Metternich himself. That the aristocratic poet of Vienna should draw his inspiration from the humble Swabian shows how ill the seer of Weimar, not wholly right about Platen, appreciated the value of Uhland as poet and politician to the German nation.

Speaking of Uhland, Goethe said to Eckermann in 1823 : ' When I see great effects I am apt to suppose great causes ; and, with a popularity so great as that of Uhland, there must be something superior about him. However, I can scarcely form a judgment as to his poems. I took up his book with the best intentions, but fell immediately on so many weak and gloomy poems that I could not proceed. I then tried his ballads, where I really did find distinguished talent, and could plainly see that there was some foundation for his celebrity.' Almost his last word to Eckermann was a condemnation, in 1832, of Uhland's political course. ' Mind,' said he, ' the politician will devour the poet. To be a member of the States, and to live amid daily jostlings and excitements, is not for the delicate nature of a poet. His song will cease, and that is in some sort to be lamented. Swabia has plenty of men, sufficiently well-educated, well-meaning, able, and eloquent, to be members of the States, but only one poet of Uhland's class.'

Here is an example of what Grün had to say—in answer to Goethe a man might suggest, if he wished to be severe :

QUESTION AND ANSWER

' Poet, tend thy garden-flowers ! No rude hands upon the throne !
When a prince's crown inspires thee more than lily's newly blown,
Celebrate, as many modest, patriotic singers do,
Royal birthday, royal name-day : raise thy voice in chorus too ! '

Shame I count it ! Such poor tribute must I pay a prince's fame ?
Say that he was born one morning, and was christened by a name ?
Any fool could sing such praises ! Silent let my accents stay
Till I hail some deed of daring, catch a flash of freedom's ray.

' Tiresome art thou ! Freedom always, nought but Freedom, thy
refrain !
Always harping on one motive ! Know'st thou not another strain ?
Wilt thou whine and whimper always ? Why not seek, in change,
relief ?
Change the key and change the burden, for the world's too full of
grief ! '

Shall I then my Land belittle ? Where another like it find ?
And my Folk, shall I defame them, who are good and true and kind ?
One thing lack they, one thing only, but 'tis Freedom that they need ;
Therefore in my heart one feeling, in my mouth one song I heed !

' Thou art welcome to thy grievance : But why spoil the others' joy,
As they climb the sunny mountain, wander through the woodlands
coy,
In the ripening corn rejoicing, for the sparkling wine-cup fain ?
Why disturb these simple pleasures with the clanking of the chain ? '

Just because in this rejoicing, where the sprays of blossom twine,
Mid the yellow corn a-rustling, mid the clusters of the vine,
In the forest's green recesses, neath the lark on airy wing,
Men should shudder as they hear them, clanking chain and fetter, ring.

This fencer could draw blood ; the point of his satire gets

well home in the following lines on Metternich, the lines, be it
remembered, of an aristocrat upon an aristocrat :

A BALL-ROOM SCENE

Evening comes, and in the ball-room bright the flaming lustres gleam,
Thousandfold the crystal mirrors multiply each dancing beam ;
In the sea of radiance swirling, presses on a festal crowd,
Powdered dames of ancient lineage, youth and beauty just as proud.

In amongst them move discreetly those whom princes decorate,
Here the rough-hewn sons of Mavors, there slim ministers of State ;
One I see who wanders slowly, every eye is in his wake,
Few the chosen ones who venture, at a nod, his hand to take.

He it is who guides our galleon, to his trade of pilot true,
Who, when princes meet in conclave, settles what they think and do.
Now regard him, O how modest, how complacent with it all,
How polite to all and sundry, courteous both to great and small !

On his breast the stars burn dimly, poor the glimmer that they shed,
But his mobile lips are smiling and a genial radiance spread,
Whether from youth's swelling bosom light he plucks a flower that glows,
Or a kingdom pulls in pieces, like a withered autumn rose.

Fascinating, when to beauty tribute on his tongue he bears,
Or from some anointed forehead suddenly the crown he tears ;
Surely 'tis the bliss of Heaven that the happy man attends,
Whom a word from him to Elba, or a nearer prison, sends.

Ah, could Europe now behold him, see how gracious he can be,
See the Church's pious servants, soldiers in their bravery,
High officials, star-bedizened, hanging on his lightest word,
Every woman, young or ancient, fascinated like a bird !

O thou statesman, wise in counsel, since thy humour 's now so good,
Since this interval of pleasure finds thee in a kindly mood,
Cast thine eyes towards the portal where a thirsty client stands,
Yearning for one sign of favour from thine all-compelling hands.

Start not, there 's no cause for terror ! He 's as harmless as the day,
In the folds of his poor mantle there 's no dagger hidden away ;
Austria's people stands there, peaceful, full of sense and loyalty,
And their prayer is simply : May we make so free as to be free ?

Different as were the two men, Uhland and Grün, Grün was
to the poetic youth of Germany, who made the next decade
ring, the inspiration that Uhland had been to him ; his phrase
' May we make so free as to be free ? ' became a catch-word.

But the poet, under his proper designation Count A. A. von Auersperg, became more or less reconciled to the duties expected of one in his social position. The following notice appeared in the *Leipziger Allgemeine Zeitung* in the year 1840 : ' Vienna, February 3, 1840. Anastasius Grün has been here for some days, seeking a post as chamberlain, since his wife, *née* Countess Attems, has obtained a Court appointment and nevertheless cannot go to Court alone. The Count seems quite to have renounced the poet.' This provoked from Herwegh an attack on Grün, which concluded with the verse :

> Profane the temple for a woman's fee,
> And dance with her the Golden Image round !
> No more you 'll make so free as to be free ?
> In place of sword, a ribboned cross you 've found ?
> I seek no poet outside *our* company.
> Farewell ! I leave you cringing to the ground,
> I hear your call : ' My heart, beat not so warm !
> For now we go to Court ; Countess, your arm ! '

The two poets met years afterwards, in 1861. Grün alluded to the poem, chuckled, and said, ' But it wasn't true ! '

A fitting close to this discussion of the political poetry of the thirties is furnished by an epigram of Grillparzer's. We deal with this great poet in connection with the following decade, but the epigram now given was written in the thirties and affords yet another example of the almost savage criticism of his own countrymen in which a German, albeit an Austro-German, thought fit to express himself :

> ' To strength alone the meed of honour 's due,'
> In youthful exaltation Germans cry ;
> Meantime, since strength comes slowly and to few,
> They rest content with mere brutality.

BOOK III
THE ROARING FORTIES
1840-1847

CHAPTER I

ACCESSION OF FREDERICK WILLIAM IV

THE eight years now under review are so full of material illustrating events in Prussia, and the psychology and performance of the Prussian people, that they will be dealt with in a series of chapters each concerned with one aspect of a crowded period. A commencement will be made in the present chapter with a study of Frederick William IV. and his treatment of the constitutional question.

Frederick William III. died on 7th June 1840, after a reign of forty-two years. He was a poor creature, though a Hohenzollern, but there clung to him a certain halo as the figure-head of the Prussian people through the humiliations of the Napoleonic conquest and the triumphs of the War of Liberation, and the memory of his Queen, Louise, was enshrined in Prussian hearts. The general attitude of the community during his last years was not unlike that of a charitable or statutory committee awaiting the demise of a venerable but masterful chairman for the inauguration of reforms which his middle-aged colleagues had espoused in their callow youth. High hopes were founded on his eldest son, Frederick William IV. He was known to be dowered with the most brilliant intellectual gifts, to be graced with a bombastic eloquence remarkable even in a Hohenzollern and a German, to indulge in mystic and romantic visions of a Christian state, and was fondly imagined to entertain liberal sympathies. It is impossible to read Leopold von Ranke's edition of Frederick William's correspondence with Bunsen, his ambassador at London, without being astonished by the evidence it affords of an intellectual endowment sufficient to confer distinction even on some darling of democracy. In one of his letters to Bunsen, on his project of a joint Prussian-English Bishopric of Jerusalem, a project which aroused the hostility of Newman and Pusey, this versatile monarch turns

his attention to the plan of the church to be erected, demands
a basilica, and illustrates the right and wrong form of a basilica
by sketches drawn with his own royal hand. His grand-nephew
could do no more. But for all his intellectual endowment he
died mad, for his brother William assumed the regency in
1857, nearly four years before his death. It is difficult to
resist the conclusion as one studies his restless mentality
expressing itself in amazing performance, that a strain of
insanity ran through his nature from birth. The reader cannot
fail to notice many striking points of resemblance between the
characters of the present Kaiser and his great-uncle.

Of Berlin and the accession festivities an unkind but amusing
glimpse is given us by Michael Bakunin, a most diverting and
attractive personality in the guise of a Russian revolutionary,
who seems to have assisted at every revolution that occurred
during his lifetime, including the Paris Commune in 1871.
Wagner knew him well. He first made his acquaintance at the
time of the revolution in Dresden, and was ' immediately struck
by his singular and altogether imposing personality. . . .
Everything about him was colossal, and he was full of a
primitive exuberance and strength.' Here is what Bakunin
has to say of Berlin in the autumn of 1840 :

> Berlin is a good town to live in : excellent music, cheap living,
> a very decent theatre, many newspapers in the cafés—and I read
> them all in turn—in short everything is good—very good. The
> Germans are frightful Philistines. If they carried into practice a
> tenth part of their spiritual aspirations they would be splendid
> people, but as it is they are a most ridiculous race ! Here are two
> inscriptions which I read on houses during the recent festivities
> (connected with the accession). In one case the Prussian eagle
> was painted and beneath it a tailor ironing. Under the tailor are
> the words :

> > ' Underneath this mighty wing
> > Peaceful is my ironing.'

> On another transparency :

> > ' Long may the royal consorts live,
> > Two thousand years were 't mine to give ;
> > And though my wish I can't fulfil,
> > It 's here as pledge of my goodwill.'

> On a third :

> > ' A Prussian heart and first-rate beer,
> > What more can be expected here ? '

The new King began his reign well by granting an amnesty to political offenders. Arndt was restored to the full rights of his professorship at Bonn, old Turnvater Jahn was relieved of police supervision, the brothers Grimm were called to Berlin, and Leopold von Boyen [1] was made Minister for War. But the monarch's vacillating mind drove him to vacillation in action. Within a few months of his accession he declined categorically to redeem the promise of a constitution made by his father in 1815. The City Council of Breslau proposed in March 1841 that the Silesian Provincial Diet should humbly petition his Majesty for the redemption of the old promise. Thereupon the King ordered the following reply to be communicated to the petitioners :

His Majesty had deigned to express himself most emphatically to the effect that on the occasion of his Gracious Majesty's intended visit to Breslau this autumn, he will not accept a civic reception or any festivity whatever from the town, because the petitioners through their deputies in the provincial diet had proposed to present a petition asking for a constitutional assembly, and his Majesty could not do otherwise than regard the proposition . . . as an act of open opposition.

This was the man who said a year later to Herwegh : ' I love a convinced opposition.'

Later, he went halfway towards liquidating the bill so long over-due, by calling together a United Landtag, and finally, in 1848, promised all—too late, for the revolution of 1848 had begun. There is no doubt that among his romantic dreams was a Prussia, rejoicing in some sort of representative government, and gathering other German states under her wing. What he succeeded in doing was to make Prussia hated as the most reactionary state in Germany. The feathery old hen of his dreams materialised into something like a porcupine.

German writers have indulged in many pen-portraits of this enigmatical monarch. The most epigrammatic is that of Treitschke, as elaborate as any similar exercise of Macaulay's, which, though written without any personal knowledge of his subject, is confirmed by the testimony of King Frederick William's friends and contemporaries. After a dazzling summary of his gifts and accomplishments Treitschke concludes :

And yet this brilliant intellect, with all its fascination for so many distinguished men, lacked the primary condition of creative

---

[1] See page 42.

power and, therewith, the secret of all human greatness, an inward unity. In the rich abundance of his gifts there was not one with the authentic stamp of genius, not one that dominated all others and could indicate the straight road to be followed throughout life. In the mirror of history his character appears not as a statue of bronze, in which many metals are molten in one, but as a cunningly compacted picture in mosaic. The kingly greatness of the Hohenzollerns, from the great Elector downwards, lay in the fact that all of them, great and small, were simple men, who in the hurlyburly of events in Germany pursued a clearly recognised end with stubborn tenacity ; for even in Frederick the Great's dual nature the German statesman was still incomparably stronger than the amateur of things French. Now for the first time there appeared in this princely house a contradictory, problematical character for whom the tragic fate was reserved, to remain a riddle to himself and to the world, to misunderstand his age and to be misunderstood of it, a true German nature, the superabundance of whose inspiration was paralysed by hastiness of decision, a prince capable of raising the highest expectations without wholly satisfying a single one.

This portrait evidently owes much to the daguerreotype of his patron executed by the historian, Leopold von Ranke : [1]

The peculiar destiny of Frederick William IV. was determined by the fact that his actions had widespread effects without procuring any satisfaction to himself. He was endowed with a comprehensive foresight, the gift of regarding from several sides all the warring elements in the world. His sympathies extended in many directions, but were accompanied by a conscientious maintenance of his own point of view. He united an extraordinary flexibility in detail with unswerving adherence to his main object. It was these qualities, perhaps, which enabled him to sustain the revolutionary storm without renouncing the monarchy. This fact was fraught with consequences still greater for future times than for his own. . . .

We shall not inquire whether King Frederick William might not have resisted the storm of the 18th of March still better than he did. He often said later to the writer of these lines : ' At that time we all crawled on our stomachs.' The moment arrived when he stepped out on the balcony of the palace and gave, as it were, recognition to the popular movement.

It was for him at one and the same time alluring and perplexing that the question of United Germany, which he had always had at heart, should of a sudden become more urgent than ever and susceptible possibly of decision by him. The King believed for a moment that he could master the situation not only in Prussia but throughout Germany by summoning again the United Diet. But how futile this effort proved to be ! . . .

---

[1] See pages 157, 161, 165 of his *Frederick the Great and Frederick William IV.*

If I might be allowed to add something further from my recollections, it would be this : when I saw the King again for the first time in the summer of 1848, he left the impression on me of a young man full of intelligence and knowledge who, excuse the professor in me, has by some mischance failed in his examination.

Equally frank was Bunsen's account to Perthes [1] of one who was to him more than a master—an intimate friend :

Many people talk of the approach of a great revolution and but few believe in it. Yet the existing state of things has no partisans, not even the princes. It is a strange cluster of embryonic parties which strive to make headway against the existing State. The dynastic party demands sanctimonious devotion to highly unsanctified princely personages. Much kindliness of disposition and good-will, but little kingly will and little kingly force in the princes themselves. The Conservatives are well intentioned but don't know what they want. Their demands also are negative in substance though positive in form. They have the strength of the child, the intelligence of the boy, the fantasy of the youth and little of the man save his years. Wishing to build for all time they do not build at all. The Constitutionals want political forms which are neither demanded by the conditions of life nor the outgrowth of our national character. Our King is endowed with powerful, stimulating and exciting force ; he is conscious of it, rejoices in it, and loves to exercise it and observe its results. It is dangerous in default of a definite aim and is used like a toy. The child rejoices when the bird it holds by a string behaves like a bird that is really free, but at no price would it cut the string and turn the resemblance into a reality.—The King regards himself absolutely as inspired of God. In 1844 he said privately to Bunsen : ' You all mean well by me and are serviceable instruments, but there are things one can only know as a king, things I did not even know as crown prince, and have only learned since I became king.' The King believes that everybody else only gets a one-sided view of things and that the King alone takes a bird's-eye view. During the last six or eight years the King has become narrower, more circumscribed, and more stubborn in ecclesiastical as in political matters. He is narrower now than ever.

The King had surrounded himself with thorough-going Conservatives, but his most trusted and intimate adviser was Radowitz, a man of the most brilliant talents. Of Hungarian origin on his father's side, he came of aristocratic Saxon stock on his mother's. He fought at Liepzig, and was wounded there.

[1] Quoted by Klein. Clement Theodor Perthes left notes of the year 1848 which are amongst the most valuable historical material of the time. The sources of his information were persons in the royal entourage, leading generals, statesmen and diplomats, and included the Crown Prince, the late Emperor Frederick III.

He joined the Prussian General Staff in 1828, and was admitted to the aristocratic clique known as the ' Christian-Germanic ' party, of which the Gerlachs, friends to Bismarck in his political youth, were members. He was a Catholic, and his mystic piety struck a responsive mediæval chord in the breast of Frederick William. Bismarck [1] termed him ' a skilful keeper of the mediæval wardrobe in which the King dressed up his fancies.'

Here is the view of Leopold von Gerlach, one of the King's confidants, [2] of the relation between the two men :

The King's admiration for Radowitz is founded on two things : first, his apparently clear cut, logical, mathematical reasoning, in spite of which his indifference, based on want of ideas, makes it possible for him to avoid every conflict of opinion with the King. Now the King sees in this mode of thought, which differs so entirely from his own train of ideas, the proof positive of the sum that he has worked out for himself, and so feels certain of his result. Secondly, the King considers his ministers and me also as so many animals, because we wish to transact with him the practical business of the day, which never suits his ideas. He does not credit himself with the ability to render these ministers docile or replace them by others ; so he gives up this line, and thinks he has found in Rado-witz a means of reforming Prussia by way of Germany at large, as Radowitz actually admits in *Germany and Frederick William IV*.

Two comments on the general situation, the first a moderate expression of opinion by William Grimm, the second a fine passage on Communism by Gottfried Keller, the great Swiss poet, show the uneasy, uncertain feelings of the intellectuals of the time.

WILHELM GRIMM TO DAHLMANN [3]

(BERLIN, 8*th October* 1842)

Under the long reign of the late King all expression of opinion regarding public affairs fell into abeyance. The feelings of not a few have thereby grown really indifferent and blunted while most of the rest still consider themselves too superior and too judicious to betray any opinions on such matters. Every one wishes to cover his retreat before daring to express any views, and thinks of the conclusions which may be drawn from any frankness of speech on his part. Only the extremists, like little pith figures with leaden feet, always stand up again when overturned, always act in unison, thus making up in pertinacity what they want in numbers, while those opposed to them, doubtless more numerous,

---

[1] *Reflections and Reminiscences.*   [2] *Denkwürdigkeiten*, i. p. 514.   [3] Klein.

are distracted by their endless variety of opinions. We see them recoil before the terrorising assertion : ' This amounts to a French constitution ' without seeing that in spite of all their faults the German constitutions have never followed in the track of the French, and the German chambers, if we consider their operation as a whole and during the past ten years, have ever shown themselves moderate and reasonable, nay, in many instances have proved far too docile.

GOTTFRIED KELLER ON COMMUNISM [1]

(ZURICH, 10th July 1843)

A vexed and pessimistic mood. And added to this comes the pernicious ferment and discontent of communism and its impudent and open expression. Reflecting on this soon to be important social question leaves one at a loss what to think. One thing appears to me certain, viz., that there is more misery in the world than ever and that communism has and is gaining many adherents. . . . One of its apostles, the journeyman tailor Weitling who has written a book about it with spirit and fire—*Guarantees of Harmony and Freedom*—has been arrested here. His arrest has aroused dissatisfaction amongst the liberal party because it was carried out with aristocratic high-handedness, and because the free press was insulted at the same time by a midnight inquisition. Meanwhile I can see no good side to the communism of Weitling and his friends, as it consists on the one hand of chimeras which it is impossible to realise without augmenting the existing misery, . . . and on the other hand appears to me to be only the consequence of a growing passion for luxury and ease. But indeed it seems to me to be chiefly animated by a short-sighted and covetous envy of the rich of this world. They do not merely want, as Weitling clearly says, to eat, they want to eat abundantly, luxuriously and well. They want their turn. O ye fools and blind ! Did you demand perfectly equal education by the state, state recognition of the right to live, state provision for the unemployable—then I am with you body and soul ! But away from me with your utterly fanatical world-storming ideas ! To the mad-house with you if you are sincere, and to the Devil if you are tempted by the belly you honour !

Early in 1844 Freiligrath published his great poem ' Germany is Hamlet,' describing as only a poet can the state of irresolution in which Germany seemed to be sunk. The dramatic commencement *Deutschland ist Hamlet !* reverberated through the nation like a deep-toned bell.

---

[1] Baechtold's *Life.*

K

HAMLET

(St. Goar, *April* 1844)

Germany is Hamlet! Elsinore
Is here, and nightly at her gates
The ghost of freedom, now no more,
To greet our sombre Hamlet waits.
The tall dim form in gleaming steel
Upbraids his hesitating fear :
' Go forth, let them thy vengeance feel
Who poured their poison in mine ear.'

And Hamlet hears with trembling limb,
The truth has dawned, the night is past ;
His soul is fired with vengeance grim.
Ah, will he venture it at last ?
He thinks till the pale cast of thought
His resolution has o'erspread,
Until his courage is as naught,
And all his resolution dead.

He sits too much beside the fire,
He lies and reads too long in bed,
His sluggish blood is thick with mire,
He 's scant of breath and too well fed.
'Tis learned oakum all he picks
With little work and too much thinking,
Too long in Wittenberg he sticks,
Frequenting lecture-halls, and drinking.

His courage knows no sticking point ;
His wrongs have doubtless driven him mad,
He says the times are out of joint,
Drones monologues and verses sad ;
He plays at grief in pantomime,
Has fighting fits, both short and few,
Then without reason, without rhyme,
Slays poor Polonius-Kotzebue.

So dreamily he hugs his woe,
And scorns himself in secret heart ;
And when abroad they make him go
Returns with store of sayings smart ;
And with his armoury of scorn
Assails ' these kings of shreds and patches ' ;
Says for great deeds he was not born,
So that no blame to him attaches.

And when at last his sword he grasps,
To keep the ghostly oath he swore,
'Tis the last act, and soon he gasps
His dying words upon the floor,
Amongst the dead whom in a mass
His hate has slain. His chiefest merit
Is—to make way for Fortinbras
Who comes his kingdom to inherit.

Thank God our Hamlet's not so far!
Four acts have passed, to Shakespeare true;
But, hero of our hearts, beware
Lest his fifth act you follow too.
We 've hoped in you both night and day;
So up and with determination
Our ghostly freedom, while you may,
Help to a swift reincarnation.

Now is the moment! Waste it not!
There still is time : Oh play thy part
Ere French Laertes' steel has got
Its poisoned point into your heart;
Ere, thundering down, a Northern host
Thy heritage find undefended.
Look whence it comes! From Norway's coast
It would be strange if this descended.

The way is free; be of good heart.
Enter the lists; be bold and strong,
Think of thine oath and play thy part,
Revenge our buried freedom's wrong.
Yet, dear old dreamer, should I blame
Because you love to shilly-shally?
No. In my heart I am the same—
A creature of delay and dally.

We know well how Germany has absorbed Shakespeare. It
is interesting to compare with Freiligrath's play on the character
of Hamlet at this period of irresolution the sonnet written by
an equally distinguished poet, Eichendorff, in 1810, in torment
as to what a poet could do to aid his country in shaking off the
Napoleonic tyranny.

1810

Full many a one, whose German heart the spite
Of this wild whirling time has sorely vext,
May with Prince Hamlet ask himself perplext
Alas, why was I born to set it right?

Weak and inclined to song and pastime light,
Easy were timely compromise his text;
But after joyful day, calls vengeance next;
His father's ghost stands ever there at night.
Fatal the flashy gift a false god gave:
Thy father's nod, it thrills thy very bones,
Gives thought free rein—not strength to fight and endure.
Resolve thee how thou may'st; of this be sure:
At need who can but strike his lute's soft tones,
His hand will point a warning from the grave.

In contrast to these poems, in which two full-blooded
Germans poured out their souls, may be presented one in which
Heine squeezed out the venom of his sardonic humour:

A SEDATIVE

As Brutus slept, we also sleep—
But he awoke and buried deep
In Cæsar's heart the keen cold steel!
Of tyrants Romans made a meal.

No Romans we, who smoke cigars;
Tastes are various under the stars,
And every nation has its boast;
Our Swabian dumplings rule the roast!

We 're genial Germans, ay, and brave,
And sleep the sleep to plants God gave,
And when we wake, we thirst, 'tis true,
But not for blood however blue.

Loyal are we as linden-wood
Or heart of oak, so staunch our mood;
In a land of lindens and of oaks
To Brutus ne'er an altar smokes.

And could a Brutus here have been,
No Cæsar surely had he seen;
He 'd look in vain for Cæsar's head;
The best we bake is gingerbread.

We 've princes up to thirty-six!
And on their tunics stars they fix,
To guard their bosoms stiff as starch;
No need to fear the Ides of March!

We call them father, and fatherland
Is what we call that self-same land
Princes inherit with the gout ;
We love them, sausages and sauer-kraut !

And when our father takes the air,
In reverence our heads we bare ;
A children's play-room is Germany,
No Roman shambles certainly.

Not until 1847 did Frederick William give expression to the liberal sentiments on the constitutional question with which so many at the time of his accession believed him to be animated. His scheme was to summon committees of the various Provincial Diets in Prussia to meet as a United Diet in Berlin. Professor Meinecke of Freiburg, writing in the *Cambridge Modern History*, vol. xi. p. 56, says of this step of the King's : 'On 3rd February 1847, the Order summoning the Combined Diets was published. It was the King's own political action, an attempt conceived on a large scale, but poorly executed, meant to achieve something different and better than the model constitutions of ordinary Liberalism, something original sprung from Prussian soil and suited to her special needs. The King hoped that Liberalism would be put to shame and conquered by a deeper insight. In reality it was a mongrel creation, in which absolutist ideas were mingled with the old theories of the representation of classes and privileges, and in which modern constitutional principles received very inadequate recognition. The result was a most inharmonious medley.' An artificial House of Lords was created, sometimes deliberating apart from and at other times with the rest of the Diet. The King specially reserved the right of summoning the United Diet in future, only when any special occasion made this desirable. Control over finance was made as indirect, complicated, and illusory as perverse ingenuity could contrive. One useful thing for his country, though not for himself, the King did achieve. He provided both the actors and the stage for the play of an organised opposition.

The following anecdote [1] illustrates the spirit in which the King seems to have acted :

King Frederick William iv. occupied himself zealously with the arrangement and decoration of the hall in the castle which was being prepared for the sittings. When everything was completed

---

[1] Klein.

he took his brother, the Prince of Prussia, round and showed him the arrangements made. ' Very fine,' the prince is said to have remarked, ' but not very airy ! ' The King retorted. immediately : ' I don't want the gentlemen to give themselves airs ! '

At the opening ceremony on 11th April 1847, the King delivered his famous ' scrap of paper ' speech : [1]

The noble edifice reared on class franchises (*der edle Bau ständischer Freiheiten*) whose eight mighty pillars [2] a King of blessed memory has set deep and immovable in the peculiar characteristics of his country is to-day by your union completed. . . . I know that many fail to appreciate this jewel, that many are not satisfied. A section of the press, for example, demands of me and of my government nothing short of revolution in church and state. . . . May the example of the one fortunate land, whose constitution the centuries and an inherited wisdom without parallel, but no scrap of paper, have built up, not be lost on us ! Other lands may find their happiness by way of constitutions ' made and given ' ; where this is so, it is our duty and our inclination frankly and in brotherly good-will to congratulate them. . . . But Prussia, gentlemen, cannot endure conditions such as these. It has pleased God to make Prussia great by the sword, abroad by the sword of war and at home by the sword of the spirit, not indeed the sceptic spirit of the age, but the spirit of order and discipline. I say it openly, gentlemen, as in war not without the greatest danger and the greatest folly can any will but one be allowed to rule, so the destinies of this country can only be guided by one will if it is not suddenly to fall from its high position. . . . I am impelled to the solemn declaration that no power on earth shall ever move me to transform into a conventional and constitutional relationship that bond between prince and people whose intrinsic truth it is which renders us so mighty, and that neither now nor ever will I allow a scribbled sheet of paper to intervene like a second Providence between our God in Heaven and this land of ours, to rule us by paragraphs and oust our time-honoured and sacred fidelity to each other. Let us be quite frank with each other. Of one weakness I know myself entirely free. I do not strive for vain popularity. . . . I strive only to do my duty to the best of my knowledge and of my conscience, and to deserve the thanks of my people, whether this be accorded me or not. Verily, I and my house will serve the Lord !

This swelling outburst of Frederick William's did not meet with the success that has attended similar efforts on the part of his great-nephew. The Berlin deputies wanted to walk out and were only persuaded to remain by the Rhinelanders.

---

[1] Peterdorff's *König Friedrich Wilhelm IV.*, and Klein.
[2] The several Provincial Diets of the eight Prussian provinces.

Jacob Grimm gave a frank expression of his views to his old colleague Gervinus : [1]

BERLIN, *20th April* 1847.

I must confess to you that the King's speech from the throne left me so confounded for three days that all the work in which I am so deeply immersed seemed to me shallow and insipid, and I felt more acutely than ever how necessary to us in the background is freedom and a fatherland of which we may be proud, without which we possess neither security nor hope. I am firmly convinced that the only Prussian constitution which can ever be called a success is one which will attract the loyalty of every German heart, and that the King has not yet fully understood his rightful place.

Two fine declarations were made in the course of debates in the Diet by members of an opposition that was soon formed. Said Count Schwerin : ' I am no forger of weapons either for the government or against it, but a free and independent member of this house, called here to say " Ay " or " No " according to my free and conscientious convictions. If then I have said " No " nobody is entitled to say to me that I have less trust in the crown than he has.' And Georg von Vincke, who in later years fought a duel with Bismarck, exclaimed anent the soldier's profession : ' Profession of soldier ! The profession of soldier is no profession ; it is only a calling, but the call comes to a man as—citizen of a state.'

The speech,[1] however, that summed up the general impression left by the King's effort to escape from an honourable obligation by offering a stone for bread was that delivered in the United Diet on 18th January 1848, by Ludolf Camphausen, a banker in Cologne and a magnate in the world of German railway construction and shipbuilding :

The ministry must know that the gulf between actual conditions and former legislation has not been bridged, as their organ has endeavoured to persuade the country. I hold it to be all the more my duty to leave the ministry in no doubt on this point, since the course they have adopted at and after the close of the United Diet fills me with profound grief for the past and deep concern for the future. A great event had occurred ; after thirty years of waiting the representatives of the whole country were assembled in one hall, and any one who knows how rarely and with what difficulty great assemblies succeed in exercising self-restraint awaited their proceedings with a tension not unmixed with anxiety. What was

---

[1] Klein.

the result ? The whole country was astonished and surprised at
the moderation of the assembly, at its loyal devotion to the sovereign. The country was indeed in doubt whether to praise it for
its restraint or blame it for its weakness. It considered the King
was to be envied for having been able to summon such an assembly
under such conditions, and for being in a position to show the
world such a splendid example of the loyalty and devotion of his
people. In Prussia, however, where the estates advanced to the
utmost limit and even leaning far beyond it, stretched forth the
hand of compromise, that hand has been rejected with scorn. In
Prussia the estates have encountered on the part of the government nothing but censure and neglect, nothing but expressions of
displeasure and ill-will, little in consonance with the principles of
a monarchical government which wishes nothing but advice from
the representatives of the people, and will not accord them the
right of offering anything else. A word would have sufficed to
end for ever the constitutional strife in Prussia. That word has
not been spoken. History will judge between the government
and us !

Exactly two months after the delivery of this speech occurred
the revolution in Berlin, and ten days later the outspoken man
of the middle class, who dared to give expression in words so
dignified to the feelings animating, not revolutionaries, but the
friends of reform in the English sense, was called by the King
to the head of the new ministry he was compelled to form.
Meantime the old regime persisted, with the mistrust of constitutionalism and reform that animated it. To many reactionaries the standing menace was the example of constitutionalism
in England constantly paraded before German eyes, and of the
effect of this menace on the bureaucratic mind an illustration
may be given. From time to time advice was freely tendered
to the ministers of the greater German powers by those of the
smaller fry. Thus a Privy Councillor in Reuss, one Dr. Jakob
Eduard Singer, favoured Bodelschwingh, the most liberal mind
in the pre-March ministry, with a memorandum, early in 1847,
in which he complained that one could hardly take up a paper
without finding a comparison between England and Prussia.
The memorandum [1] is interesting in particular as indicating a
suspicion of Bunsen's Anglicising influence :

England has certainly much for which we may envy her, but
all the elements for which we may envy her are the very ones that
would bring the monarchy to the position it occupies in England,

---

[1] Poschinger's *Unter Friedrich Wilhelm IV.* (Manteuffel's *Memoirs*), p. 17.

i.e. the king there is a shadow. From such a conclusion may God preserve us! For the rest we are no Englishmen; they are cold, calculating egoists, we are full of impracticable day-dreams, and our press will never be an English, but a Swiss, press, *i.e.* a mean one. When England is in the mood to flatter, then is she most dangerous; and she is flattering us now. Prussia has become great through the policy she has hitherto followed; by stepping in not at all (or late) she gains more than through doing business for (or by) herself.

And should Prussia act alone in giving freedom of the press, she would remain alone, as she must remain alone, if she is taken in tow by England the egoist. If Prussia remain alone with freedom of the press (or in a minority—and I can answer for the lesser German princes) then she would be as little in a position to allay the agitation that would arise, as she would be to escape the humiliating consequences of an over-hasty rapport with the country in which Herr von Bunsen has taken up his residence.

But if Prussia desires to win the sympathies of the Liberals she must give a real constitution. She will then satisfy the demands of the irresistible spirit of a modern age, though she will gain nothing thereby in power, for these sympathies must first bring about the collapse of the remaining governments that object! That, however, cannot be Prussia's wish!

Prussia for the past seven years has stirred up too much, only stirred up, without settling anything. She can only bring calm when she makes a clear end to unrest by a decisive resolution, a resolution, a system as to the meaning of which no one can feel a doubt, though he would if he could. The fatal lust for popularity must have its head trodden on without delay; that is the serpent, the most poisonous of serpents.

It seems to me a very happy thought to keep the members of the Diet as much together as possible, even outside the house, at meals and evening receptions. But that involves, to be sure, as short a session as possible, for otherwise the passion for change, and boredom, will invent all manner of devilry.

Finally, I venture to call attention to the growing danger of gatherings of citizens, clubs, etc., for they have their origin in a spirit of opposition, like most combinations nowadays, and once they are allowed, they must grow one out of another. 'Tis union that makes our enemies strong.

CHAPTER II

FOREIGN COMPLICATIONS

THE accession of Frederick William IV. coincided with an outburst of patriotism which rekindled the embers of national enthusiasm still left from the days of the War of Liberation. This outburst was provoked by the threats of Thiers, irritated by opposition from Germany among others to the Turko-Egyptian policy of France, a policy designed in the interests of her *protégé* Mehemet Ali. French writers began to discuss the question of acquiring the left bank of the Rhine. The whole of Germany was roused, and three famous songs were written, two of which, Max Schneckenburger's ' Die Wacht am Rhein,' 1840, and Hoffmann von Fallersleben's [1] 'Deutschland, Deutschland über Alles,' 1841, have become national anthems. The third was equally popular in early days, Nicolas Becker's

> ' Sie sollen ihn nicht haben
> Den freien deutschen Rhein.
>
> They shall not ever have it,
> The free, the German Rhine.'

A caricature of the time represents the French on one side of the river with a German band in full blast on the other, blaring forth Becker's song.

But Hoffmann wrote in 1841 a wonderful little War Song which shows that with national enthusiasm went some misgiving :

WAR SONG OF 1841

(*Chorus*)

> List to the beat of the drum !
> See the people stir. We come !
> Flags in the van !
> We follow man on man :

---

[1] See page 197.

Come forth, come forth
From house and hearth!
Wives and children all, good-night!
Forth we march into the fight,
With God for King and fatherland!

(Night-Watchman of 1813 alone)
My God! yet why?
For prince's whim and fame and might
Into the fight?
For palace-vermin, junker gay,
Into the fray?
To keep the people's will in thrall
To fight and fall?
For tax on wages, wine, meat, flour,
This battle hour?
For royalties and bridled press
Through storm and stress?
Yours most obediently has fought—
And yet he thought!

(Chorus)
List to the beat of the drum!
See the people stir. We come!
Flags in the van!
We follow man on man.
When the guns we prime
'Tis not a time
To reason why, to reason why!
Rub-a-dub, rub-a-dub, the drums beat high,
With God for King and fatherland!

Jacob Grimm's comment [1] to Gervinus on the French war
scare was as follows:

The vain and wicked war-cry now raised by the French shows
us indeed what we need, but confirms the difference between their
ways and ours. For it is fitting we should cry out for Alsace,
but not that they should shout for the bank of the Rhine. Vanity
under defeat urges them, as it did certain races in our own ancient
history, to store up a bloody revenge.

Metternich took the new King of Prussia very carefully in
hand over this business. He wrote to him on 9th October a
long letter [2] in which he discusses the possibility of France

---

[1] Klein.
[2] *Mémoires de Metternich, publiés par son fils*, vol. vi. No. 1402. See also
Dispatch No. 1405.

declaring war. In connection with the Eastern question he can see no *casus belli*, for Germany, he argues, has no interest in that dispute. No reliance is to be placed on Palmerston ' who, for once in his career of whig, has recognised where the true right lies, but wishes to exploit it like a gambler who seeks to break the bank.' The France they have to do with is ' a France whose weaknesses approximate to madness.' He urges, therefore, the importance of solidarity between Austria and Prussia, and begs the King to instruct his representative in London to support his Austrian colleague's *démarches*. Interesting excerpts from the letter are the following :

. . . Whether France wishes for war or not, it is certain that on either hypothesis the people of that country consider this land of Germany as an arena where every French acrobat is free to come and show off his cleverness. M. Thiers, who is a great artist in this line, speaks of war as if it were the legitimate means for France to extricate herself from difficulties and to teach others how to behave. The day will come when this great master must be asked with whom he proposes going to war. If it is with Germany, he must explain why he wishes to fight ; for there is no satisfaction to be derived from being a neighbour of France if one is to offer one's back to receive the blows which she is pleased to administer, or to open one's purse and pay any contribution that she deigns to demand. If he will not acknowledge it, his silence must be interpreted in an unfavourable sense, for a great political body cannot be put off with silence. . . .

. . . What then is the war with which M.Thiers threatens Europe? Is it enough that a President of the Council should set out to acquire the glory of a Napoleon, for a country, at the head of whose government he is placed, to be authorised to look upon Europe as a fencing-room where the parties can make proof of their skill. If such a pretension is absurd, the countries which should lend themselves to such an experience would not be less so ; now, the most important of the countries of Europe is certainly the territory of the German Federation. . . . To-day, everything depends on the firm union of Austria and Prussia, for these two powers form the central power in Europe, and that assuredly is bound up with the geographical position of the two states, their independent situation and the part they play as the principal members of the German Federation. . . .

The result of this letter was that military measures were quietly taken by Austria and Prussia in conjunction, setting the whole forces of the German Federation in readiness to meet France if the occasion arose.

Fortunately, perhaps, for France the trouble died down.

More serious for Germany was the Schleswig-Holstein question which was raised on 8th July 1846, by the ' Open Letter ' of Christian VIII. of Denmark, declaring inseparable the union with Denmark of Lauenburg and Schleswig, the position of Holstein being left untouched for the moment. What was the German view of this letter is shown by the following quotations from the indignant comment[1] of Ludwig Häusser, a contemporary historian :

In this ' Open Letter ' undisguised war is declared on the inalienable rights of the peoples of Schleswig-Holstein. . . . With a stroke of the pen Denmark overthrows the ancient German law of succession in Schleswig and promises to do the same for Holstein. . . . Denmark threatens, then, formally and avowedly to wrest three German lands from Germany, and does not even think it worth while to remember either the German law of succession or the fundamental laws of Schleswig-Holstein. She appeals to treaties with foreign powers who appear to have cast lots for our coat. Of German political opinion, which one would naturally expect to have been consulted first, she does not think it necessary to speak. . . . The whole of Germany looks with confidence to the inhabitants of these duchies who have shown that German honour and their German origin are still dear to them ; but the whole of Germany, princes and people, is in duty bound to treat the matter as one that concerns it personally and intimately. . . . The matter of these German duchies is for Germany a question of life and death. . . . If the Danes succeeded in making even a single village Danish, it would amount to playing pitch and toss with German rights ; and our country's name might appear at once in the obituary column of European nations.

The German interest in the vexed question of these duchies, a question which helped to break up the National Parliament of 1848, which was not settled until the Danish War of 1864, and which may yet be reopened, was a two-fold one. There was a sentimental view, and a very practical view. To the sentimental view eloquent expression was given by a song published by Friedrich Chemnitz in 1844 :

SCHLESWIG-HOLSTEIN OCEAN-BOUNDED
Schleswig-Holstein, ocean-bounded,
Fore-front of the German line,
Hold the fort thy fathers founded
Till a happier sun shall shine ;
Keep thy battlements bemanned,
Schleswig-Holstein, Fatherland !

---

[1] Klein.

God is mightiest in the meekest,
Feeble none where faith is fast.
Trust! for faith will waft the weakest
Storm-tossed bark to port at last.
Faithful to thy fathers stand,
Schleswig-Holstein, Fatherland!

From where billows charge curvetting
Through the Belt with rush and roar
To where silver seas are fretting
On thy westland's golden shore,
Keep the trust from strand to strand,
Schleswig-Holstein, Fatherland!

Where across the Marches sheening
Gazes dreamy Königsau,
Where the proud ships foam careening
Up the Elbe to Holstengau,
Keep the fires of freedom fanned,
Schleswig-Holstein, Fatherland!

Double oak whose boughs together
Mingle in one summer crown,
Breast the blast of wintry weather,
Let no north wind cast thee down.
See! Thy summer is at hand,
Schleswig-Holstein, Fatherland!

The song was sung far and wide in Germany, and its popularity shows what strides Germany had made towards a realisation of the real national sense aroused by the War of Liberation in 1813. The practical view regarded the question of German rights in Schleswig-Holstein as bound up with the question of sea-power. Each question reacted on the other. A fleet was needed to make Schleswig and Holstein secure as units in the German system; Schleswig and Holstein were necessary as affording harbourage for a German fleet. The agitation in the forties of last century for a German fleet is evidence not merely of such over-bearing arrogance as is illustrated by Siebenpfeiffer's speech on page 107, but also of a growing sense of power in the nation and of the desire to exercise that power by the application of force. The modern standpoint of Germany dates back further than has been realised; it certainly was not the invention of Bismarck, who found a weapon already forged which he knew well how to use. Contemporary poets harp on the string of sea-power. Ludwig Seeger, a Würtem-

berger, domiciled in Switzerland, like so many free-thinking
Germans in these days, wrote an ode to ' The Steamship ' which
concludes with this verse :

> Here on the quay before the storm we cower,
>   And watch her go, the mistress of the sea ;
> High overhead we saw the tall mast tower,
>   That now a lance, now but a finger might be.
> She beckons to us by the quay-side standing,
>   ' Why linger there, put forth and cross the bar !
> Up, up, ye Argonauts, loose from the landing !
>   Our quest is Freedom's Golden Fleece, hurrah ! '

And very significant are Heine's lines in his ironic ' Night-
watchman's Arrival in Paris,' [1] which reviews the situation in
Germany :

> And God will grant a fleet to us,
>   Our patriots' superfluous strength
> Shall sail the sea in German ships.

But the most striking quotation that can be given is a selection
of stanzas from Georg Herwegh's [2] ode, ' The German Fleet,'
published in 1841, to celebrate the anniversary of the foundation
of the Hanseatic League. It is not to be supposed that the
growth of a desire for sea-power in so truculent a people as the
German should be possible without leading to jealousy of
England. It did.

THE GERMAN FLEET

> Wake, land of mine, new life begin !
> Search with thine eyes Fate's book of gold,
> And read the tale the stars unfold :
>   The world is thine to win !
> Wake, land of mine, make all thy daughters spin !
> Good store of German sailcloth gather in,
>   The swelling gale to hold.
>
> Throw off the garb of slavery ;
> Crawl from thy shell, a wider sphere
> Shall to thy gaze, grown bold, appear,
>   And thine the world shall be !
> In thee their shepherd mighty nations see,
> The whole world sets its eager hope on thee ;
>   Cast anchor far or near !

---

[1] See page 194.   [2] See page 203.

Was Greece of better stock than thine ?
Held Rome of right a prouder place ?
Lest Hermann, father of the race,
    Curse his degenerate line—
Wide o'er the sea the Cross, thine emblem, shine !
Be man, no nursling now, but, like the Rhine,
    Once launched turn not thy face !

The sea shall wash from off thy soul
The last red stain of tyranny,
Its breath shall break thy chains for thee,
    Thy wounded heart make whole.
Oh, toss thy locks there where the storm clouds roll,
Free as the lightning choose for thee thy goal ;
    The sea, the sea set free !

On eagle's wings the tempest brave,
Till unrestrained thy fancy streams
Where man to man a hero seems,
    Nor bends his back a slave.
Still broods the Creator's spirit on the wave,
And down the track long since Columbus drave
    The German future gleams.

To thee all lands their tribute bear ;
The sea shall as thy fief be known,
And every tongue in benison
    One Empire shall declare.
A tradesman shall no more the purple wear—
Who dares the purple from the Kaiser tear ?
    Seize it, it is thine own.

Seize it, and grip the steersman's oar ;
Firmly the great world's history guide ;
With timbers rent tho' low she ride,
    The ship of Fate restore !
God's chosen one, His trust, thee we implore,
Speak to us, when shall German ships once more
    Belch forth a full broadside ?

Hear, land of mine, thy poet's stave ;
On many a hill the trees grow tall
And straight, to build thy ships withal,
    Thy liberty to save ;
Thine own true flag, the German colours, wave,
Crouch not for ever as the Leopards' slave,
    Nor heed their greedy call !

My soul surveys a sight unseen,
Swells sail-like with our hopes' increase,
Stout German ships without surcease
    Drive on their course serene ;
And, like a German Argonaut, I lean
Against the mast, and with my lute-strings keen
    Win the world's Golden Fleece.

Marcel Herwegh informs us that in his pencil draft of the poem
the poet made the following marginal comments against the
seventh and eighth of the above stanzas : ' Is it only the English
spirit that is to be planted abroad ?   Does not the tide strike a
warning note upon thy coast ?   Every German ship built is a
death-arrow in England's heart.'

Palmerston said, or Germans believe that he said, the British
fleet would treat the German colours, black, red and gold, on
the high seas as a pirate flag, and Germans have never forgotten
it.   Irritation was not allayed by the newspapers.   Bunsen
wrote to his English mother-in-law on 1st July 1848, ' the
English press has done but too much to make the name of
England an object of hatred ' (*Memoir*, ii. p. 185).

Jealousy of England was not confined to wild young revolutionary poets like Herwegh.   Here are two bitter epigrams by
Grillparzer, at English expense :

ENGLISH GODFATHERSHIP

' Your eyes are aglow, and your sympathy spills,
    For the freedom of lands—without factories or mills.'

ENGLISH !

' Cling too long to what is old,
    You 'll decay, no longer young ;
Of your freedom all you hold
    Is the foul and slanderous tongue.'

More refined as an expression of German jealousy of England
is the following remarkable sonnet by Anastasius Grün, written
in 1850 :

HELIGOLAND

Who is this island's master ?   What the name ?
No painted post is here to make it known,
No sentry-box, no scutcheon carved in stone ;
No brazen mortar speaks with tongue of flame :

L

Only on Sunday, to the bells' acclaim,
Aloft the British flag is proudly flown :
' I 'm here, on German coasts my shadow thrown ! '
But there the greeting is but grief and shame.
How at this Sunday show my tears restrain ?
Another's strength and glory can I see,
Rejoicing as if both belonged to me ?
At evening down the flag will come again,
And leave six days to ponder o'er in pain
Why this is so, and how it may better be.

If further proof be needed of the surging passion for expansion
now agitating German breasts, a passion which undeniably
implied strength, and a consciousness of strength, it will be
found in quotations from a letter of Bunsen's to a Hamburg
friend and one to Bunsen from the Prussian Ambassador at
Washington in 1842, which form a striking commentary on
Herwegh's lines given above,

' And down the track long since Columbus drave
The German future gleams.'

Among Bunsen's correspondents was the Syndic Sieveking of
Hamburg.   To him Bunsen wrote from London on 8th
September 1846, as follows [1] :

. . . I hail, with you, the emigration of our countrymen to North
America (the land of the Anglo-Saxons and of our own kindred),
towards the Pacific Ocean and the Gulf of Mexico. I have daily
the map before me, and contemplate the Rio del Norte, of which
I take possession from Santa Fè and San Felipe, and then the two
Californias and the fine desert land between North California
and the Rio del Norte as the connecting tract ; and then I draw a
line southwards, if possible to the 25th degree (instead of the 42nd),
as my boundary on the Pacific, and I feel the joy of the human
race, that God should have granted to it the length and breadth
of the earth.
' Canada is not worth keeping long,' is becoming here more and
more the general feeling.

A note to this passage by Bunsen's widow gives a glimpse of
what was going on behind the scenes in Prussia, as early as 1842,
in the direction of colonial expansion. This very significant
note runs thus :

Whenever the *curiosities* of Bunsen's diplomatic life in London
see the light of publicity, his plan of accepting the offer made by
the rulers of Mexico in 1842, to *purchase California for the King of*

---

[1] *Memoir*, ii. p. 112.

Prussia will be reckoned among the most original. Humboldt dissuaded His Majesty, and the matter was dropped. The Prussian Envoy at Washington, Baron Rönne, on the other hand, warmly applauded the project. ' The time has come,' he said in a letter to Bunsen, ' when we ought to take a grand and independent attitude. For this we must be united, and we must possess a fleet and colonies. Your idea of purchasing California is excellent. I never ventured to express such far-stretching desires. But I pointed out in 1837 already, when reporting upon the condition of German emigrants here, that Mexico would perhaps resolve upon ceding a portion of California. Your plan of purchasing the whole is better in every respect.'

But it was not only to the West that German eyes were turned. During this lively decade we get an early glimpse of German ambitions in the East, the very ambitions that have loomed so large of recent years. As a young man Prince Hohenlohe, German Chancellor at the end of the nineteenth century, travelled in the East in 1849 on a diplomatic mission from the short-lived National Government at Frankfort. Surveying the situation of Turkey, he says in his journal (see *Memoirs*, i. pp. 52, 53): 'If Germany is unified, strong and armed, she will be able to secure Cyprus and more besides.' And he goes on : ' If, however, by peaceful negotiations with the Turkish Government, or the explosion of the Eastern question, we acquire Rhodes or Cyprus, or whatever else, we shall thereby obtain a splendid outlet for thousands of the proletariat, we shall gain a sea-board and a mercantile navy, marines and sailors. Nor must Syria and Asia Minor be forgotten. We must do all we can to check the Russians and English there, to which end it is essential to send out no Protestant bishops and missionaries, but to make it a station for the Catholic world in the East. German consulates filled by efficient men are among the most pressing tasks of the Imperial Executive.' Germans have shown themselves to be possessed of long memories. Prince Hohenlohe never forgot his early dreams and the time came when he was in a position commanding enough to assist very effectively in making them a reality.

It is impossible to withhold all admiration from the great German official machine which could, even at a time when the country was split into fragments, and seething with discontent, set wheels in motion for enterprises such as these. According to Baroness Bunsen it was Alexander von Humboldt's opposition that brought the Californian scheme to nothing. Doubtless there was no more certainty in those days than now that the United States were too proud to fight. As for ourselves, Bunsen's remark with regard to Canada raises a flush of shame when we recall that there was a time when British statesmen, placemen, and others took so mean a view of the destinies of our colonies and of ourselves. And, in a measure, we have ironically to thank Germany for the impulse to larger ideals.

There remains for mention the agitation that arose in Neuchâtel, then a personal appanage of the King of Prussia, for incorporation as a democratic unit in Switzerland. English sympathy was with Neuchâtel, and Frederick William IV. addressed a letter [1] to Queen Victoria which contains several of his characteristic *obiter dicta* :

25th November 1847.

. . . . I hear with delight and thankfulness that it has pleased your Majesty to agree to a Conference for regulating the dreadful Swiss quarrels. I took the liberty to propose my beloved and truly amiable town of Neuchâtel, as the place for the Conference, not only because its position in neutral territory and in Switzerland herself qualifies it above every other place for that purpose, but *particularly* because this meeting of the representatives of the great Powers there would protect it and the courageous and faithful country of Neuchâtel from indignities, spoliation, and all the *horrors* which oppress at this moment the unfortunate and far from courageous Fribourg. I am afraid that your Majesty has not a full appreciation of the people and the partisans who fill Switzerland with murders and the miseries of the most abominable Civil War. Your Majesty's happy realms have centuries ago passed through the ' phase ' of such horrors, and with you the state of parties has been (as one says here) grown in bottles, under the glorious Constitution given by God and History, but *not* ' made ' ; but there, in Switzerland, a party is becoming victorious ! ! ! which, notwithstanding the exercise of Christian charity, can only be called ' *Gottlos und Rechtlos* ' (without God and without right). For Germany, the saving of Switzerland from the hands of the Radicals is *simply a vital question*. If they are victorious there, in Germany likewise torrents of blood will flow ; I will answer for that. The murder of Kings, Priests, and Aristocrats is no empty sound with them, and Civil War in song, writing, word and deed, is their watch-word. ' Toute charité bien entendu commence par soi-même.' So they begin with their own country, true to this ' Christian ' (!) motto. If they are allowed to proceed, surely they *won't stop there* Thousands of emigrated malefactors wait only for a sign (which their comrades and allies in Germany will not be backward in

---

[1] *Queen Victoria's Letters.*   John Murray.

giving) to pour forth beyond the German frontier. In Germany
the PEOPLE are just as little fond of them as they were in Switzerland, but the experience of Switzerland teaches us that that alone
cannot stem their victorious march, if circumstances are favourable
to them. The German people rely upon their Governments, and
do nothing, but Governments are weakened by the modern Liberalism (the precursor of Radicalism, as the dying of chickens precedes the Cholera), and will have to take the consequences of their
own negligence. Notwithstanding people and princes, that godless
band will march through Germany, because, though small, it is
strong through being united and determined. All this I have
pondered in my head and heart (led, so to say, by the hand of
History), and that has prompted me now to propose that the German
Confederation (which *en parenthèse* includes a population of more
than forty millions) should appear as one of the great Powers of
Europe at the settlement of the Swiss dispute, and should be
admitted as such by the other great Powers. *Would your Majesty
do justice, and give* PROTECTION *to this idea ?* . . .   F. W.

It is not surprising, with Palmerston as Foreign Secretary,
that certain difficulties attended the delivery of this ' private '
letter by Bunsen, and of them we have a full account from
Bunsen himself in a letter [1] to his wife :

OSBORNE HOUSE,
Sunday, 5th December 1847.

MY BELOVED,—God be thanked ! All right ! Better than could
be hoped ! I delivered my letter last night, in private audience,
to Her Majesty—not speechless, but without a speech—after eight,
before dinner.

I had desired Lord Palmerston to tell me what he wished me to
do. As an abstract Whig, he said, ' It was unheard-of, quite
unusual, that a foreign Sovereign should write to the Sovereign of
England on *politics.*' ' But,' said I, ' you praised the Queen and
Prince Albert for their excellent letter on politics to the Queen of
Portugal.' ' Yes, but that was between relations.' ' And this
between friends. But you are informed of the arrival, and of the
contents of the letter and will learn all that is in it. I shall, in
handing over the letter to the Queen, say nothing but a few com-
plimentary phrases, and plead the King's cause in the way the
Queen will direct, in your presence the next day. Will that do ? '
' Perfectly,' he replied. And so I did. The Queen read the letter
before dinner, and came down ten minutes before nine. After
dinner, Prince Albert told me that the Queen and he had had Lord
Palmerston with them after dinner (from six to eight), and that
we should to-morrow settle the answer. In the morning, the
prince translated the political part of the letter into English, and
then discussed with Lord Palmerston the heads of an answer.

---

[1] *Memoir of Baron Bunsen,* ii. p. 150.

Then I was called in to see the letter, and plead the King's cause, for which I was quite prepared. We all agreed :—

1. That conferences on Swiss affairs, on the basis of mediation between contending parties, were out of the question now. But the Queen wished to say (and Lord Palmerston saw no harm in it) that she *would* have accepted Neuchâtel in preference to London, as a place of conference, if it could still be thought of.

2. That (as I had proposed) *the Neuchâtel affair* was now the object with respect to which Her Majesty would try to be of use to her friend and brother. (I had demanded mediation, with arbitration, between Neuchâtel and the Federation ; but Palmerston observed, ' That could only be done upon the ground of general treaties, and then the three other Powers would come in too, and spoil the whole.') So I was to be satisfied with ' *bons offices*,' in consequence of the instructions already given to C., ' based upon the detailed Memoir written by your Majesty's faithful *Bunsen*, as your Majesty allows me to call him.' Circumstances would show what further could be done.

This the Queen will write *in English*, beginning and end in German. I ought to add, that she answers, besides, to the point, on the coming forward of the German Confederacy in a worthy manner on this occasion. She says, ' She and her Government wish nothing better ; but as the only point now in discussion resulted from general treaties not regarded by the Confederacy, this was perhaps not the right opportunity. (Of course there are weighty reasons against it besides.) But that she was sure the English public would with great sympathy see the German Confederation take a prominent part in European affairs—only that it would make a very material difference in their eyes, if the councils of Germany were directed by the enlightened Cabinet of Berlin, and not by Prince Metternich.'

All this is now already written out fair, by Prince Albert, under Lord P.'s revision, for the Queen, who will write it herself to-morrow, when the letter will be despatched by express messenger. As soon as we hear what the Diet of Berne has decreed against Neuchâtel, Lord P. and I shall confer further.

The Queen's reply [1] to the King of Prussia's letter gives expression to the sympathy with which Germany's striving for unity was regarded in Great Britain, though she indicates in her frank way a free country's mistrust of Metternich :

OSBORNE, *5th December* 1847.

Since your letter was written events have followed each other so rapidly, that at this moment the war in Switzerland may be considered as terminated ; by the capitulations of the Cantons formerly constituting the Sonderbund, *two* parties, between which

---

[1] *Queen Victoria's Letters.*   John Murray.

mediation of the great Powers could have taken place, have ceased
to exist, and consequently mediation and the Conference resulting
from it are in fact no longer necessary or possible. I had proposed
London as the place of conference, but should with pleasure have
waived this proposition to adopt the place which you have expressed
a wish of seeing fixed for that purpose, viz. Neuchâtel, and I should
have felt truly happy if by so doing I could have met your wishes,
and given further protection to the principality against possible
aggressions on the part of the Federal Government of Switzerland.
As matters now stand, the only complication which might arise
is that between Neuchâtel and the Diet. I have, in anticipation
of any such event, instructed Sir Stratford Canning to exert himself
to his utmost to dissuade the Diet from any plan of aggression
on your territory, and he has been furnished with an able and
elaborate state paper for his guidance, which Chevalier Bunsen
had drawn up, discussing the legal merits of the case. Should
events prove that Sir S. Canning did not arrive in time, or had not
the power of averting a hostile step against Neuchâtel, you may
rely upon my readiness at all times to put my good offices at your
disposal. Should a conference upon Swiss affairs still become
necessary, I conceive that the only plea upon which the great
Powers could meet in conference, would be their having guaranteed
the independence and neutrality of Switzerland, and by implica-
tion the Federal Compact amongst the Cantons. This has not
been the case with regard to the German Confederation, and I do
not readily see in consequence how the Confederation could be
admitted into this Conference, however much I confess I would like
to see Germany take her place amongst the Powers of Europe,
to which her strength and population fairly entitle her. I may
say that my Government are equally impressed with me with the
importance of German unity and strength, and of this strength
weighing in the balance of power of Europe ; I am sure that the
English public generally share this feeling, but I must not conceal
from your Majesty that much would depend upon the manner in
which this power was represented. Much as the English would
like to see this power represented by the enlightened councils of
your Majesty, they would be animated with very different feelings
in seeing it in the hands of Prince Metternich. . . .

VICTORIA R.

CHAPTER III

SOCIAL CONDITIONS AT HOME

In this chapter and the following we shall give a review of the social conditions that marked the early years of Frederick William's reign. We shall have to touch again on the arrogance of the princely and the military castes, and on the censorship on philosophy and on the miseries of the poor, on the *Zollverein* and on the scarcity of potatoes. Nevertheless we have a topic to commence with that is not without its amusing side. The hauteur of German princes is a feature that marks the forties of last century as it did the thirties. As a royal stickler for principle Prince Henry the seventy-second of Reuss-Lobenstein Ebersdorf, most insignificant but longest-named of German principalities, stood out among his fellows. In 1844 he issued the following order : [1]

EBERSDORF, *12th October* 1844.

I hereby command the following to be entered in the Register of Orders and the Register of Special Orders.

For twenty years past I have rigidly maintained one principle viz., that every one shall be called by his proper title. This does not always happen. I shall therefore as an exceptional measure fix a fine of one thaler on whoever is in My service [*sic*] and does not call another who is in My service by his proper title or office.

In the official Gazette for the Principality appeared in 1845 the following notice : [1]

His most Serene Highness has most graciously deigned, His All-Highest Self, most graciously to praise before the assembled troops those militiamen, six in number, who hastened to the fire which broke out in Tonna and gave their services there with the most self-sacrificing alacrity, and then with his own All-Highest hand to shake that of the oldest (on proof by birth certificate that he was so) as a mark of His All-Highest highest satisfaction.

On this a delightful skit by Hoffmann von Fallersleben

[1] Klein.

appeared, for Germans in those days could laugh at the bombastic jargon of courtly circles.

HONOUR TO WHOM HONOUR IS DUE

Great things do happen truly
    In our stupendous time ;
List while I tell you duly
    The tale of one in rhyme.

Quite recently in Reusse
    Militia at a fire,
(I 'm sure it will rejoice you)
    Great credit did acquire.

When this through a memorial
    Their gracious Prince by Right
Had learned ; those territorials
    He to him did invite.

And when the good men shyly
    Stood up before him, each
His Gracious Highness highly
    Praised in a Gracious speech.

A solemn affidavit
    With parents' names and date
Each then produced and gave it,
    —His birth certificate.

His Highness then demanded
    The oldest of the band,
And clasped that horny-handed
    With His All-Highest Hand.

Now this great deed recorded,
    Who would not dwell for choice
Where heroes are rewarded
    As in the land of Reuss ?

In whatever Elysium German princes congregate this Prince Henry of Reuss must have found a congenial spirit in the Elector William I. of Hesse, who died in 1821, and of whom the following story [1] is told :

The Elector William I., who amid his many outstanding qualities was born, as the saying goes, a hundred years too late, inspected

---

[1] General Garland's *Zwei Menschen alter Kurhessischer Geschichte.* (K.).

on parade not only the front but also the rear of the ranks, in order to examine the pigtails, less perhaps on account of the pigtails themselves, than because he saw in any deviation from pattern in this symbol of the past the indication of a criminal passion for change. So strong, indeed, was he on this point that an artillery-man who had lost all his hair as the result of an illness, so that a pigtail could not be plaited on him, was obliged to have a pigtail attached to a band round his head ; for which reason his comrades preferred to leave him at home.

The arrogance of German princes, who had quite recovered from the humiliating experiences of the Napoleonic regime, was reflected in a change in the spirit of the army, and its relation-ship to the civilian population, which became more and more marked.   In 1798 Frederick William III. had issued an Order in Council in the following terms :

I have with great displeasure noted how officers, especially the younger officers, endeavour to assert the privileges of their calling in the presence of civilians.   I shall know how to maintain the dignity of the military when it is to their real advantage to do so, and that is in the seat of war, where they have to defend their fellow-citizens with body and life ; but for the rest, no soldier, whatever his position or rank, must presume to snub any one of my subjects.   It is these, not I, who maintain the army ; it is they who employ the troops entrusted to my command.   Arrest, dismissal or death can alone be the consequence which any recalci-trant has to expect from my inflexible stringency.

Scharnhorst and Gneisenau had imbued the great army they raised for the War of Liberation with the feelings that should animate a national army.   Their spirit was Stein's, who said a noble word for National Service when he wrote in 1822 : ' It is fine that there should be an institution which nourishes in all the military spirit, which develops military skill, and which accustoms all to sacrifice, to effort, and to equality in obedience.' But reaction had worked its hardest to exalt its instrument into an isolated and privileged caste.   The idea animating reaction-aries finds expression in Adam Müller's letter quoted on page 39. And Klein tells us :

Promotion was made difficult for the untitled middle class ; the military schools were only open to scions of the aristocracy. The army lists of those days show how the middle-class element fell off.   The natural consequence was a serious cleavage between civilians and military in most of the garrison towns.   In society, the civilian avoided the officer or the officer refused admission to the civilian. This rendered possible that class hatred of the officers which prevailed in the time of revolution, and sharpened and embittered political dissensions. As early as 1846 it had brought about serious friction between the military and the civil element. In August 1846 bloody encounters took place in Cologne, although the public had offered to secure by itself the restoration of order and had in reality done so. A memorial from the municipal authorities was bluntly rejected by the King. In order that no more cordial understanding should arise between citizens and garrison it was decreed that every regiment should change its quarters every four years.

Of the new spirit in the Prussian army, and of the arrogance with which it expressed itself Corvin [1] is a good witness :

The views of a Prussian officer, as generally and openly professed formerly, and still secretly entertained by a great number of them, are about as follows :—The king is by Divine right the hereditary absolute master of the people and of the country, and all the revenues are his personal property. To speak of *rights* as opposed to the king is inadmissible ; for whatever liberty he grants to the people is done by way of grace, and he may revoke as much of it as he likes, and whenever he likes. The laws are only regulations prescribed by him for the behaviour of the people, with a final view to his own interest, which prevails above everything else, for ' *L'état c'est moi.*' The police, the ministers, and other employés are servants of the king, and have to look to his interest first, and to that of the people only so far as by injuring it that of the prince may be injured. The army is the actual bodyguard of the king, and his defence against danger wherever it may come from, and absolute obedience to all his orders is its most sacred duty. To utter a different opinion is infamous in an officer, and he who does so must be kicked out of the army. Such was the political creed of a Prussian officer of 1830, and hundreds of officers of 1869 still subscribe to it.

Corvin proceeds to give an account of how he himself as an officer felt entitled to behave even to the highest civic authority :

In Soest in Westphalia, therefore in Prussia, my assistant-sergeant reported to me that the authorities of the town refused to furnish the horses which I had ordered to be ready next morning. I was furious, and went at once to the town hall. When I arrived there and inquired rather loudly for the mayor, a fellow like a beadle whom I found in the antechamber held up his hands and said in a solemn whisper, ' The magistrates are in session,' and placed himself before the door. I have already explained the estimation in which citizens of any rank were held by officers ; I therefore

---

[1] *A Life of Adventure.* R. Bentley.

cried, ' D—— your magistrates and their session ! ' and uncere
moniously pushing the beadle aside, I rushed into the room where
I found all the elders of Soest sitting at a large table covered with
green cloth. With my shako on my head, and all the arrogance
of a Prussian lieutenant within it I asked harshly, and without
greeting, ' Where is the mayor ? ' An old gentleman rose, and I
said, ' I ordered six horses for to-morrow morning ; you refused
to furnish them ? '

The mayor, of course, knew nothing of it and appealed to the
town-clerk opposite him ; but I interrupted him with a rude,
' D—— the town-clerk ! I have nothing to do with clerks ; you are
the mayor, and I tell you the horses must be forthcoming to-morrow
morning at six o'clock, or I will report you in Berlin.' With that
I left. The horses were ready, however, next morning, and I
imagined I had acted quite properly. At that time a lieutenant
thought himself above the mayor of any city.

Corvin's statement of the Prussian officer's creed is a true one.
And to Frederick William IV. like a true Hohenzollern, that
creed commended itself. It was therefore impossible for him
to persist in the high spirit of tolerance that marked the opening
of his reign. Difficulties soon began over the vexed question of
the censorship. Here his attitude was, as always in face of a
practical difficulty, one of vacillation ; he hovered from affability to arrogance like a majordomo, or a civil servant of the
new model. First he issued instructions very moderate in tone,
and, to protect the press from the caprice of individual censors,
set over them a High Court of Censorship which acted with some
regard to judicial forms. He abolished the censorship of
caricatures, and from this source trouble was not long in arising.
The foibles of the King, not to speak of his dumpy person, were
too tempting a mark for the caricaturist, and the German caricaturist of those days was as heavy-handed, coarse and rude as
he is to-day. But the King himself, as we may gather from the
anecdote on page 149, loved to indulge his wit at the expense of
others, though, like so many men gifted with a sarcastic tongue,
he could not understand a laugh at his own expense. It pained
him. And as caricaturists and the press exercised their new
privileges somewhat freely pain soon turned to resentment.

Among the first to whom the worried King turned for advice
was Radowitz,[1] who communicates to us himself the views he
submitted, ingenious enough to give a fair indication of the
subtlety of his mind.

[1] Hassel's *Radowitz.*

My proposals, in their general outline, were as follows : when those of the effusions of the bad press are discounted which are merely unpleasant, vexatious and inconvenient, and must therefore be either refuted or ignored, there still remain some in face of which we cannot and ought not to remain passive. But with these again there are two categories absolutely distinct, the *dangerous* and the *criminal*. In the present state of things literature proper, *i.e.* books, is never really dangerous ; books call therefore for no preventive measure, no censorship in advance. But a book may, in virtue of its content, be criminal in the highest degree ; in such a case judicial proceedings and punishment provide the remedy. I should therefore lean to the view that literature proper should be entirely freed from the censorship, did not the Federal acts and the scruples of numbers of well-disposed persons stand in the way. My proposal accordingly suggests the introduction of a selective censorship. All persons whose official or academic standing provides them with a guarantee should keep in their own hands the censorship of their own works. But they should have, in addition, the privilege of granting, on their own responsibility, permission to others to print their works. Any one who cannot find a guarantee of this sort for his work would be subject to the police-censorship as heretofore. In this way I hope to secure more than one end : to distribute the business of the censorship, to make it honourable, and always to place it in the hands of experts. But I reckon on even more than this, viz., on thus creating a literary relationship like that of patron and client, and introducing some sort of organisation into the chaotic condition, the buccaneering methods, of the writers of to-day.

In the case of newspapers, and pamphlets, which are akin to newspapers, the position is quite different ; they are dangerous. They form no part, be it remembered, of real literature, but are a trade, and certainly one of the so-called dangerous trades, which, like the making of gunpowder, the mixing of drugs, we do not allow to be practised without constant police supervision. Therefore the measure suitable for them, in the first place, is the preventive censorship. Nevertheless one must strive even here to provide a bridge from police conditions to legal process. The way to do this is to make all newspapers depend upon concessions, and to grant these only to truly respectable men for whom one can vouch, even though they are of the most diverse political complexions. Such agents could then, as above, have the privilege, on their own responsibility, of acting as their own censors. Punishment should begin with fines and proceed after a given number of lapses to withdrawal of the concession. The main point in the whole question is to secure a firm foundation for legal process.

Radowitz claims that the King fought hard in support of these views, but could not prevail against the scruples of his ministers. The censorship was stiffened again, and a series of confiscations and prohibitions followed in which good and bad were alike confounded. The *Leipziger Allgemeine Zeitung* was banned from Prussia for daring to publish Herwegh's open letter to the King. A similar ban was placed on all the publications of Campe of Hamburg, Heine's publisher. Arnold Ruge had to transfer the issue of his *Annals* from Prussia to Saxony, but was pursued there until through pressure on the Saxon government he was forced finally to shut them down. Hoffmann von Fallersleben, author of the skit on page 169, was dismissed from his professorship. Even philosophers did not escape. In April 1843 the police made a domiciliary visit to the house of Ludwig Feuerbach. His letter of complaint [1] is egotistical enough, like everything professorial to be found in this volume, save, perhaps, Schopenhauer's letter quoted on page 417.

Bruckberg, 3rd April 1843.

How strange! Yesterday a judicial burglary was committed at my dwelling. They searched this home of a hermit, scholar and thinker for letters—*risum teneatis amici*—from students and for information regarding Students' Unions. Poor Germany! I must cry again and again, they would rob thee of thy last and only treasure—the honour of thy learned men. Is it then possible to inflict a greater injury on a man of notorious learning, a man who has lived for years in utter seclusion from the world, and has been in travail with a new principle of philosophy, than to implicate him in the darkness of secret societies? What else shall we live to see?

The philosopher may have been quite innocent. But curiosity seems to have led him to test strange experiences, for we certainly find him mentioned in queer company in a letter [2] of the revolutionary Michael Bakunin to Herwegh four years later :

Brussels, Summer of 1847.

The democratic alliance may really turn out well, but the Germans, the mechanic Bornstedt (later an officer in Herwegh's legion), Marx and Engels—and above all Marx, are doing their usual harm. Vanity, spite, gossip, arrogance in theory and faint-heartedness in practice, reflections on life, energy and simplicity, and an entire absence in action of life, energy, and simplicity—literary and philosophising mechanics and disgusting coquetting with them—Feuerbach is a bourgeois, and the word ' bourgeois ' has become a catchword repeated *ad nauseam*, but one and all, from the crown of the head to the soles of their feet themselves pettifogging bourgeois.

---

[1] Grün, *Feuerbach in seinen Briefwechsel und Nachlass.* (K.).
[2] Marcel Herwegh, *Briefe von und an Herwegh.* (K.).

In a word, falsehood and stupidity—stupidity and falsehood. It is not possible to draw one full free breath in such a crew. I keep away from them and have quite definitely declared that I am not going to frequent their communistic workmen's unions, and will have nothing to do with them.

In Austria the minuteness of censorial regulation exceeded even Prussian rigour. Among the posthumous papers of a Vienna censor were found certain ' private instructions regarding the censorship of the daily press, even withheld from the censor's staff.'[1] They ran as follows :

The visit of members of the Imperial House to suburban theatres is not to be mentioned in the press. . . .

The name ' Sophiensaal ' (called after the Archduchess Sophia) is not permissible, and must be altered in every case to Sophien-Bad-Saal. . . .

The price or monetary value of any article must not be mentioned in the papers. . . .

All articles relating to railways must be submitted to the Court officials. . . .

Everything relating to the erection of the monument to His Majesty Francis II. must be submitted separately.

Matter relating to Baden near Vienna is to be submitted separately.

To avoid personal attacks on the work of the stage-manager of the K. K. Court Opera-house, Schober, reasonable precaution is constantly to be taken. . . .

Articles which concern the nobility, the military or other similar outstanding professions, are always to be specially submitted to the police officials of the Court. . . .

The designation of Bachman as Proprietor and Editor of the *Wiener Zeitschrift* is a transgression and to be discontinued, and the words, ' Publisher and Editor ' are to be substituted. . . .

Corvin was associated in journalism with a clever fellow named Held, an ex-officer like himself, whose *Lokomotive* was far too pungent for the official taste and was soon suppressed. Among the dodges to which they resorted in order to circumvent or plague the censor were these. Between two apparently innocent paragraphs they would print some indiscretion sure to be struck out, so that the first and third paragraphs might be left in juxtaposition and thereby carry a message little antici-pated by the censor. Thus when they wished to score off the reigning Grand Duke of Weimar, a notorious blockhead, they first printed a note on the expulsion of Prutz, the poet, from Weimar, ' less owing to the will of the Grand Duke, than to the

[1] Wiesner, *Denkwürdigkeiten der österreichischen Zensur*, 1847 (K.).

influence of the Grand Duchess,' who was well known to be a Russian princess. Next followed a violent dig at Prussia, and then came a simple home chat sort of item : ' If you wish to keep a sheepskin from being spoiled place beside it a piece of Russian leather.' The censor would at once delete the paragraph against Prussia, leaving the Grand Duke in the desired association with the sheepskin. In shorter gaps Held would sometimes insert ' Cnsrchr,' *i.e. Censurscheere* (censor's scissors) with the vowels left out ; asked by a puzzled official what the curious word meant he told him solemnly it was a Cossack war-cry ! In longer gaps left by the censor he would print, to the delight of the intelligent public, childish poems and songs. Of the skill of the poets in slipping a poem through the censorship we have a good example from Prutz himself on page 200.

But no story at the expense of the censorship excels the following : [1]

AUTHOR AND 'AUTHORITY'

In critical articles an author deemed himself entitled amongst other things to invoke the ' authority' of Goethe and Schiller. The president of the governing council of Prague . . . in his bureaucratic exaltation knew only of civil and military authorities, and invited the Titan of the press to his office to reprimand him for his disrespectful terminology. When the man of letters wished to defend the expression, asserting that as in other spheres officials and officers of the first rank, so in the domain of German literature authors such as Goethe and Schiller, were unquestionably ' authorities,' the infallible official interrupted him with—' Authors, yes, but not authorities,' and taking up his pen he corrected the offending passage in that sense.

In this welter of reaction the noble protest [2] of Bunsen against a proposal still further to limit the freedom of the press comes like a breath of fresh air :

The freedom of the press is to the nineteenth century what spiritual freedom was to the Christian of the first century, and religious freedom to the sixteenth and seventeenth centuries. It is the political question of life and death in our time, the question that wrecks governments and reduces kingdoms to dust, or gives them the strength to rise. The fight for the freedom of the press is a holy war, the holy war of the nineteenth century. The result is as indubitable as it was in the first and second centuries or in the sixteenth and seventeenth. The drawing-room aphorisms to which we are treated on the subject are innocent dreams which do not

---

[1] Von Helfert, *Die Wiener Journalistik im* 1848 (K.).
[2] *Aus seinen Briefen, usw.*, ii. (K.).

touch the fringe of the reality. The times demand a common right and not privileges ; the power of the written word is no more dependent than the spoken word on office and dignity, rank and title. Privileges not only inspire hate, but in the sphere of journalism lead to helplessness, as is exemplified in states where the censorship prevails. All in opposition to the privileged, nothing in their favour, is believed.

Gustav Freytag,[1] writing in 1870 of the censorship in the thirties and forties, gives a faithful account of its effect not only on style but also on character, and with this striking passage we may take leave of the subject :

Young men of the present generation know the censorship only by hearsay. At none of the inflictions of the old Bureaucratic State have so many ink-pots been thrown, or thunderbolts so loud been hurled from the platform. But the most vehement complaints against the censorship have given but an incomplete reflection of the misery, dejection and bitterness with which this tyrannical, insolent, and heavy-handed governess imbued the soul of the people. She made the author a rebel and the reader vindictive. No foe to the monarchy could have invented a better means to set people against their ruler. For monstrous seemed the arrogance, intolerable the egotism which undertook to prohibit people from forming a judgment on their own concerns, and to choke every free word in the throat of the speaker. Even a well-meaning government always seemed to a man with pen in hand a pedantic, narrow, malevolent schoolmaster, and it was just the spirit of spite and malice developed in the scholar by repression in school, that the author felt at the criticism of governmental authority. . . . Every word an author wrote on any question of the day was attended by a feeling of humiliation ; he was in a condition of perpetual irritation, the effort to give publicity to a judgment of his own constituted a continuous feud between craftiness and unreasonable authority. He had daily the temptation ironically and with dagger-point concealed to stab where he dare not fight with open words ; slyly to envelop what was none the less a malicious insinuation. In a similar way millions of German readers grew accustomed to reading between the lines, and to amplify the text in an obnoxious sense. On the other hand, where an author could let himself go without fear of punishment, his zeal boiled over in grossly exaggerated expression ; since a man dare not go to the heart of a matter, he sought the assistance of general, high-faluting, passionate forms of speech. This destroyed the character of many a man, the style of many. Even to-day, in the case of men who served their apprenticeship under the censorship, it is possible occasionally to recognise some of the characteristics of the censorship style, the nervous reticence, the little barbs of wit and the phrase-making.

---

[1] *Life of Carl Mathy.*

M

CHAPTER IV

PHILOSOPHY AND THE MOB

THE philosophers who reflected best the spirit of the age were Feuerbach, the materialist, one of whose letters we have just enjoyed, and Strauss, the rationalist. They were two of the new philosophers who, as the brilliant epigram quoted or invented by Treitschke puts it, Hegel'd the Bible, and Bibled Hegel. Both published books that expressed in the uncompromising language likely to catch the ear of men ready for change, and as eager for freedom from religious convention as from political repression, views that promised a new religion, a new theology, and a new Christianity corresponding to the strong, new state that agitators were extolling to the clouds, and constitution-mongers setting down on paper. Feuerbach's *Essence of Christianity*, and Strauss's *Life of Jesus* raised a storm in theological circles, the effect of which extended to all Protestant countries. George Eliot,[1] publishing under her maiden name of Marian Evans, startled parsonages and manses in this country with English translations of the two books. According to Feuerbach, theology is anthropology; God and Heaven are man's own creation, for the terms are only the expression of his own longings and aspirations. His book is divided into two parts, ' I. The true or anthropological essence of religion,' and ' II. The false or theological essence of religion,' and the argument is well illustrated by quoting a few of the

[1] In a letter from Munich, dated 16th July 1858, Strauss gives an interesting glimpse of George Eliot : 'I had here a charming encounter with the English translator of my *Leben Jesu*, now the wife of Mr. Lewes, who wrote Goethe's life. When she heard of my being here they both came to call on me, but failed to find me. When I went the other morning to return the call I found her alone. I once before caught a glimpse of her, as Miss Evans, in Cologne, but then she could hardly speak German at all. Now she's getting on with it better. She is in the thirties, anything but beautiful, but has an almost transparent complexion, with an expression full rather of feeling than intellect. Between a man and the lady who acts as his translator there must always be a sort of mystic union. As I was leaving the good soul said, " When I came in I was so happy that I could not say a word." ' '

178

titles of the sections in the appendix in which he enlarges on particular points, e.g. ' The religious emotions purely human,' ' God is feeling released from limits,' ' God is the highest feeling of self,' ' In God man is his own object,' ' Anthropology the mystery of theology.' The crudity of the book in places is remarkable. ' I would rather,' says the author, ' be a devil in alliance with truth, than an angel in alliance with falsehood,' and now and again he appears to take a perverse delight in parodying himself, as at the end of the preface to the second edition of his book, where he declares after giving a list of his writings :

In these works I have sketched, with a few sharp touches, the historical solution of Christianity, and have shown that Christianity has in fact long vanished, not only from the Reason but from the Life of mankind, that it is nothing more than a *fixed idea*, in flagrant contradiction with our Fire and Life Assurance companies, our rail-roads and steam-carriages, our picture and sculpture galleries, our military and technical schools, our theatres and scientific museums.

Here, again, is another provocative passage, very German in its uncompromising, challenging tone :

The Greeks looked at Nature with the theoretic sense ; they heard heavenly music in the harmonious course of the stars ; they saw Nature arise from the foam of the all-producing ocean as Venus Anadyomene. The Israelites, on the contrary, opened to Nature only the gastric sense ; their taste for Nature lay only on the palate ; their consciousness of God in eating manna. The Greek addicted himself to polite studies, to the fine arts, to philosophy ; the Israelites did not rise above the alimentary view of theology ; ' At even ye shall eat flesh, and in the morning ye shall be filled with bread ; and ye shall know that I am the Lord your God.'

This crudity, which blunted the point of his terse and epigrammatic style and dulled the edge of his most ingenious arguments, made him an easy mark for the theologians who hurled at him the saying *Mann ist was er isst*, ' man is what he eats,' to show the depths of his materialism. The saying was not his but another's. ' Feuerbach,' says Höffding in his *History of Modern Philosophy*, ' was an eager student of physiology, and wrote an enthusiastic review of Moleschott's *Lehre der Nahrungsmittel* (1850) in which the following passage occurs, " The doctrine of foods is of great ethical and political significance. Food becomes blood, blood becomes heart and brain, thoughts and mind-stuff. Human fare is the foundation of human

culture and thought. Would you improve a nation ? Give
it instead of declamations against sin, better food. Man is
what he eats.'' And he adds that if the people had better
nourishment (peas instead of potatoes) a future revolution
would have a better chance of success.' This quotation from
Moleschott reads like an extract from one of the fulminating
reports discharged by the medico-materialistic department of the
English Board of Education. But all of Feuerbach is not crude,
and it would save much ink and paper if materialists of to-day,
whether doctors or social reformers or professors of the hybrid
science of anthropology and folk-lore, before setting out to
shock the simple-minded with what they fondly imagine to be
new notions of God and religion, were to sit down with a
wet towel round the head and read Feuerbach's *Essence of
Christianity*.

A more subtle and, in the theological sphere, more effective
controversialist was Strauss, ' the David with the deadly sling '
in Heine's phrase, who came boldly out with his *Life of Jesus*
to slay the four Evangelists like so many Goliaths, and to reduce
gospel history to myth. ' On his critical apparatus,' says some
German quoted by Klein, ' the historical Christ evaporated.'
His book became far better known in this country than Feuerbach's, and there is no need here to enlarge upon its influence.
But the attitude of Strauss towards politics deserves some
attention, for his published correspondence contains letters
which not only reveal his fastidious nature, but show also the
incompatibility in a sophisticated age between the study and
the forum, the introspective, somewhat selfish philosopher and
the expansive politician with inflated chest and straining eyes.
Strauss could not remain quite unmoved in so agitating a
time. In 1847 he even felt constrained to publish a satire
at Frederick William's expense, *A Romantic on the Throne
of the Cæsars*, in which he drew a cunning parallel between him
and Julian the Apostate. A letter [1] of his is printed on page 244,
in which he gives his cheerful impressions on first hearing of the
February revolution in Paris. But six weeks later, a month
after the revolution in Berlin, his mood has changed. He had
been urged to accept a seat in the Würtemberg chamber and
join his old fellow-student, Friedrich Vischer, a professor of
æsthetics, in working for the commonwealth. He writes scorn-

[1] For Strauss's letters, see Zeller's *Ausgewählte Briefe*.

fully of the mob, and indicates an incompatibility of temperament between his friend and himself :

HEILBRONN, 13*th April* 1848.

I was just thinking of writing to you when your letter arrived.
It is good that you have not misunderstood my dread of our meeting. So far as I am concerned, what I feared was less difference
of opinion than incompatibility of temperament. It is clear that
the movement of these days has touched us both just on the spots
where our dispositions are opposed. In you all that is chivalrous
and martial, all that makes politically for the common weal has
been stimulated and inspired with new life. These mean nothing
to me, as no one better knows than you, so I could only be deeply
and disagreeably touched by all that has happened. A nature
like mine felt much happier under the old bureaucratic regime
(*Polizeistaat*), when at least peace reigned in the streets and one
never came across an excited man or new-fangled wide-awakes
and beards.[1] In society one could talk a bit about literature and
art and curious people and other such themes ; one could let oneself go. That is no longer possible. The best men you meet are
now impossible and I go frankly no more into the world. So I am,
and have been ever since this business began, unwell and uneasy,
and as for some time you appeared to feel quite the contrary there
was reason to fear a clash [if we met]. Your experiences, however,
in Stuttgart have reconciled us so far as this is possible to two
such diverse natures. You and yours can accept the new times
and the new forms of government, which is not the case with me.
I learn to recognise myself in these days more clearly than ever
before as an inheritor of that age of individual development typified
by Goethe, and its limitations I neither can nor will overstep.
Towards this outpouring of the Holy Ghost on Jack and Jill, towards
this wisdom of the gutter, I can only take up an attitude of bitter
irony and contemptuous scorn. ' Odi profanum vulgus et arceo '
is and remains my motto. An assembly of such I could not bring
myself to attend even as a mere listener. For this reason I cannot
dream of going to Stuttgart, to bring myself before people's minds,
so to speak. I want no seat in either the German or the Würtemberg parliament. Even if I had any capacities for either, such
surroundings are not suited to my nature. And when you preach
to me of the common weal, I maintain my gospel of individuality
and say : Only when and where I feel at home, only where I am
satisfied with myself, can I give satisfaction or happiness to the
world. Even that cursed article in the *Mercury*, which these doings
have wrung from me, was only written in self-defence. I read as
few papers and speak with as few people as possible, but the stuff
penetrates into one's chamber, and one is obliged to make some
effort to get rid of it. Things are, of course, in your case otherwise
and better. You have a ticket for the future, which I have not,

[1] See page 407.

and it would be most desirable for you and the cause that you should be elected for Frankfort. But these elections, it appears, are altogether in the hands of the agitators. Should you appear, who can talk like you ? You have had long practice in extempore speaking and can doubtless make good. You must indeed be content to find your ideas standing cheek by jowl with Scherr's communism and Zimmermann's nonsense. I cannot aid you in society, for society I do not frequent. As to doing it in some paper or another, I shall watch for an opportunity. It is a pity you have done the same for me, for were it known mean men would think meanly about it. You have mentioned me to ministers ! But I do not want office. Least of all in these times. At any rate so long as I have a crust of bread to eat.

A year passes. Vischer has gone gaily on, and proceeded from the Würtemberg chamber to a seat in the National Assembly at Frankfort, of which we shall hear much in Book v. ; Strauss has been elected to the Würtemberg chamber, and been called upon to resign his seat, has stood for Frankfort and been defeated. Still more scornful is the tone of the letter he addresses to his friend on 24th February 1849 ; he is driven to use the final word in German, the word ' hate,' to express the strength of his dislike to the politics of the day, the mob-rule of parliament ; he twits his friend ironically with the poverty of his efforts as a legislator ; and he analyses the differences between his own and his friend's characters as ruthlessly as if both had found place in the gospel narrative. As an expression of the pride of intellect, tempered to steel in the academic forge, the letter is not easy to match.

MUNICH, 24th February 1849.

There ! I thought I should not get off so cheaply with you ! I wanted to sneak clear of our political differences like a cat, but here you come like a kind of honest John (*Biedermann*) and drag me into the thick of them. Indeed our cat and dog coquetting is more significant of us both than one imagined, and if we once have our portraits painted for Hardegg's gallery of Ludwigsburg notables, they will have to include these animals as they used to include an emblematic ox or lion in pictures of the evangelists.

That I can and will keep clear of these concerns, while you cannot, appears to rise simply from the fact that I have freed myself from them while you are still in their toils—from the fact that I simply say : ' Politics are a field quite foreign to both of us ; you have as little effective to do in Frankfort as I in Stuttgart ; and one from one leaves naught.' I recognise the fact, say I, and you do not. You say you would burst if you were not in the thick of it, and this I believe. But it proves nothing as to your aptitude, but only the existence of an instinct, often innate in imperfect natures like ourselves, which only mocks us and never leads to any fruitful result. You have helped in the accomplishment of many things such as the abolition of gaming tables, but that is no particular reason for going to Frankfort; they were doomed in any case. But the national militia law—that is your hobby-horse, and I have no judgment to pass on it, for I can only take up an ironical attitude with regard to it. You will say it is a case of the fox and the grapes; and that I must accept with submission. You allow that you don't feel very comfortable in Frankfort and that is quite enough for me, for I stick by the axiom that every man is happier in fulfilling the task he has a vocation for. Your refusal to recognise this equality between us is based on the fact that you have been dragged into politics willingly and I unwillingly. You wanted to take part in deliberations, came forward out of inward bent for it; I was put into the shafts by others; the Ludwigsburg people got on my softest side—my good nature—and on these grounds I accepted a rôle that seemed to me even then an unfortunate one. As the well-merited penalty of such conduct the kindly disposition of the Ludwigsburg people changed round in a way that rendered my continuance in the position impossible. You, on the other hand, seem to me like a man who as a painter was great and might have taken the lead in this line, and yet had a fad for music and preferred to play sixth fiddle in an orchestra or tinkle on the triangle rather than play the leading rôle in his own art.

Our natures are alike in this that they lean towards art and science. The differences in this unity I might express by saying that you are a scientific artist and I an artistic man of science, *i.e.* art is to you a subject for scientific treatment, and science to me a subject to which I strive to lend the grace of art. From this I can easily deduce the reason why politics should be for me a forbidden field. Goethe writes somewhere, I believe to Madam Stein, after many failures as a statesman, that he would no more dabble in anything that was not as much within his powers as the writing of a poem. That is it! Who indeed would paint pictures on a surface which others next moment would tread upon with their four bearish paws? Add to this the all too great sensibility of my nature by virtue of which I am irritated by daily converse with those whose doings I hate and who, I know, hate me. If this rendered me unsuitable in any case for political and parliamentary activity, present day politics excite my absolute repugnance to everything savouring of revolution and the unfettered action of the mob. This repugnance is quite natural; it is the shivering of a creature plunged in an element in which it cannot exist. Under Russian despotism I could still, though with clipped pinions, exist, but mob-rule would annihilate me. And so I hate all that leads to the latter, hate as I never hated anything before, because never have I met before anything so absolutely the end of all things. However much the reasonable politician may be ' out ' to tame this element, he can only call, like Mephistopheles :

' Be calm, kind element ! ' He must of necessity live in it to some extent himself, dare he not, like me, at the worst reject it with horror. In this you would not fail. Your combative disposition would come to your aid, but in the end you would be the loser, for, as you yourself say, it is the blind (and unclean) powers that turn the scales.

The political side of your nature I consider an outgrowth to be pruned which I put into the same category as my intermittent taste for versification. . . . You whom nature has destined to be a protagonist in your own sphere will not be able to attain to even the position of a tritagonist amongst that crowd of shouters.—You are not happy in your political activities ; you choose especially those matters, such as the militia bill, that appeal to your æsthetic side, a side which in politics can only be an unimportant side.

. . . I shall by no means assert that your stay in Frankfort will profit you not at all. But I expect to see the fruits of it, not in the paragraphs of the future constitution of the empire but in part 3 of your *Æsthetics* . . . I have just noticed that to-day is the anniversary of that glorious French revolution which everybody now in his heart regrets !

From the exalted plane of philosophy we now descend to view the plight of the common people, the mob, as the philosopher calls them. The early forties were years of distress, occasioned by a series of bad harvests as well as by causes moral and economic, and it is not surprising that this period afforded the seed-plot in which germinated the ideas of one of the many gifted Judæo-Germans of the century, Carl Marx, the man who has done more, perhaps, than any other to make the distribution of wealth the great social problem of modern days. The case of the Silesian Weavers in 1844 may be given as the most striking example of the misery that many had to endure ; a misery accentuated in the case of these weavers by the cruelty with which the wealthy mill-owners ground the faces of their work-people. The story has been made familiar in modern days by Gerhart Hauptmann's fine drama, *Die Weber*, in which he draws on childish memories of his native Silesia. A poem called ' The Bloody Assize,' to the powerful influence of which Treitschke bears testimony, circulated throughout the miserable district, and when a man was seized and locked up for singing it before the windows of the proprietors of the worst establishment, the crowd became a mob, and stormed and sacked mill after mill. Economic misery at this time was not peculiar to Germany ; we too suffered from it ; and it must be admitted that Frederick William exerted himself to the utmost to relieve the distress. But the rioting was only ended by the usual Prussian expedient, the firing of soldiers on the crowd. Our distress in England certainly did not evoke so bitter and so poignant a poem as this ' Bloody Assize.' Not even Heine for all his art could in his song of ' The Weavers ' with its

> A curse on the King, the rich man's king !
> No balm can he for our misery bring ;
> He 'll wring the last groat from the poor man's hand ;
> We 're shot down like dogs by royal command,
> Poor weavers, poor weavers !

rival the effect of the artless accents of the people.

' THE BLOODY ASSIZE ' [1]

Sung by the Silesian weavers to the tune ' There stands a Castle in Austria '

> Here in our midst there sits a court,
> The direst in the nation,
> Where men are sent to death in sport
> Without a condemnation.
>
> Here mortals suffer anguish slow,
> Here torture-chamber moaning
> And endless wails the horrors show
> 'Neath which the poor are groaning.
>
> Here Zwanzigers the hangman play,
> While Dierig's deeds are nameless ;
> Both the unhappy workers flay,
> Both unabashed and shameless.
>
> Devils with more than Satan's gall
> Increase the poor man's burden,
> And rob him of his little all.
> His curses be your guerdon !
>
> You 're of all wrongs the fountain-head
> Which workmen now are bearing ;
> Daily the wretched crust of bread
> From hungry lips you 're tearing.
>
> You think potatoes for the poor
> Suffice, while every glutton
> Amongst you daily sits at your
> Repast of beef or mutton.

---

[1] Zimmermann, *Blüte und Verfall des Leinengewerbes in Schlesien* (K.).

The weaver bears his web to you,
  You scrutinise it nearly,
And if there be one thread askew
  You make him pay it dearly ;

For half the sum of his poor wage
  Goes back into your purses,
And, if he murmur, in a rage
  You drive him forth with curses.

Of no avail to beg or cry,
  For deaf to all, you brutes, you
Say to the weaver : ' Go and die
  Of hunger if it suits you ! '

Oh say ! is not his bitter need,
  His misery unending,
Without a crust of bread to feed
  His dear ones, most heartrending ?

Speak not of hearts ! The cannibal
  Has none within his bosom ;
Ye who devour men, soul and all,
  Are savages more gruesome.

The wealth for which you damn your souls
  Grim death will from you sever ;
'Twill melt like fat upon the coals
  Where you shall roast for ever.

For you, when once your days have flown,
  To the poor's great Defender,
Trembling before the great white throne,
  Your true account shall render.

For you there is no righteous God,
  And neither Hell nor Heaven,
And conscience has no chastening rod,
  And life no holy leaven.

Your only aim is at your ease
  To grind the poor men's faces,
And many other villains please
  To follow in your traces.

The first in line is Fellmann, who
  Cuts down the weaver's wages,
And in his turn puts on the screw
  With cruelty outrageous.

Of Hoferichter's robber band
    There 's only this needs saying :
They flay the weaver with high hand,
    And wealthy grow by flaying.

If one of us the courage shows
    To tell them why we hate 'em,
His recompense is bleeding blows,
    And prison walls await him.

Herr Kamlot-Langer, so-called, too,
    (*You* are the best of judges)
Must take his place among this crew ;
    The meanest wage he grudges.

For work they fling at us we take
    A pittance most unholy,
And all the profits that they make
    Are sweated from the lowly.

And e'en the few who pity those
    That suffer from your dealing,
And cannot altogether close
    Their hearts to human feeling—

E'en these your competition dire
    Compels the rest to follow,
And crush us deeper in the mire
    Where we already wallow.

Who would have thought in days gone by
    That these vile personages
Would one day flaunt their dignity
    In stately equipages ?

And who found private tutors then
    In linendealers' houses,
Housekeepers, maids and liveried men,
    To serve them and their spouses ?

It was impossible to withhold at the conclusion of the last chapter a tribute of admiration for the vigour shown by Prussia in nursing, during a period of discontent at home, dreams of an adventurous foreign policy. Still more remarkable is the fact that from 1818 onwards, despite Metternich and Austrian jealousy, through all the network of inter-state rivalry, un-advertised by their King, ignored by the loud-voiced champions of unity and liberty, a talented group of official economists worked on relentlessly to make Prussia the centre of a German Customs Union, and thus to lay the real foundation of the German Empire, and to do as much as Bismarck to win the Imperial crown for the Prussian king. The idea was not Prussian in origin. It was first advocated in the early days of the Federal Diet by Friedrich List of Augsburg. Biedermann claims that some reform of the kind was forced upon Germany by the ruinous competition of English goods. England had profited by Napoleon's continental blockade to develop her industries, and when the blockade was raised, proceeded to flood Germany with her wares. List sowed the seed, but, as we shall see, the wily Prussian official reaped the harvest, and List died a disappointed man. His ideas outran the officials'; in the forties he was for initiating a campaign for commercial supremacy, and for Protection as well as a Customs Union ; he demanded for the mercantile marine of Germany a common flag, a common consular service, colonies and a regulated system of emigration. All of these demands, save the last, were satisfied by Bismarck in the next generation, but in 1846 List, treated with ingratitude by official and commercial circles alike, and suffering financially, was left to take his life with his own hand. To revert, however, to the history of the *Zollverein* itself, despite List's eloquent advocacy internal jealousies prevented the Diet from making any headway with the scheme, which meant nothing less than free trade between all German states. Then Prussia took the matter up independently. The first step was to abolish all customs dues within Prussia itself, and this was achieved by a law passed in 1818, for which the credit is due to K. G. Maasen, a native of Cleves and a disciple of Adam Smith. Maasen's hope was not only to free Prussian industry from within, but also, and by that very act, to give it a chance against English preponderance. Professor Pollard says in a striking passage : [1] ' In reality the law of 1818 was one of the earliest and greatest triumphs of the principles of Adam Smith ; for the corn laws and the navigation laws were still in full play in England. Maasen is now almost forgotten ; but the free trade petition from the City of London, presented by Alexander Baring (afterwards Lord Ashburton) to the British Parliament in May 1820, spoke of the " shining example which Prussia had set the world." '

[1] *Cambridge Modern History,* x. p. 355.

The work thus initiated by Maasen was taken in hand by F. C. A. von Motz, Prussian Minister of Finance from 1825, who with infinite tact and patience negotiated treaty after treaty, bluffed the Federal Diet, circumvented attempts to found rival unions, such as that of Hanover, Saxony, Hesse-Cassel and others, and wore down the sullen opposition of the South-German States. The following striking figures are given by Biedermann and Klein : whereas in 1818 the Prussian Customs territory comprised ten million inhabitants, in 1836 twenty-five millions, and in 1842 twenty-eight and a half millions of Germans were united in Prussia's *Zollverein*. Upon this laboriously erected structure of free trade between German states Bismarck was, half a century later, to place what he claimed to be the coping-stone of protection against non-Germans in general and England in particular.

The *Zollverein* became a popular institution in good time, and the lively intelligence of Hoffmann von Fallersleben did justice to it :

THE ZOLLVEREIN

Leather, salmon, eels and matches,
Cows and madder, paper, shears,
Ham and cheese and boots and vetches,
Wool and soap and yarns and beers ;

Gingerbread and rags and fennels,
Nuts, tobacco, glasses, flax,
Leather, salt, lard, dolls and funnels,
Radish, rape, rep, whisky, wax ;

Articles of home consumption,
All our thanks are due to you !
You have wrought without presumption
What no intellect could do ;

You have made the German Nation
Stand united, hand in hand,
More than the Confederation
Ever did for Fatherland.

There remains to be mentioned an ominous event that took place in Berlin on 19th April 1847, eleven months before the revolution itself. This was the riot known as the Potato War.

About a year before the revolution, *i.e.* on 19th April 1847 food riots broke out in Berlin. In the year of grace 1847 a great rise of prices took place throughout the country, but in the capital it attained an unheard-of height, in consequence of usurious speculations by the farmers in the neighbourhood and the small retail dealers ('hucksters') in the city. . . . A 'metze' of potatoes cost six silbergroschen and sometimes even more. So came it that on 19th April in the forenoon, a number of women attacked a gibing hawker in the market-place at the Oranienburg Gate, belaboured him violently and scattered his potatoes and vegetables throughout the market. This incident gave the preliminary impetus to further actions of a like kind. The crowd of market women, reinforced by other poor women, street boys, and apprentices, who gathered quickly in thousands from the Rosenthal suburb—the so-called Voigtland—rushed like a tidal wave through the streets of Berlin from one weekly market to another, repeating the spectacle in each. . . . On the 21st it dawned on the horde of women which had now divided into several bands, that extortion was not confined to the market-places, and so they now turned against bakers, butchers, and grocers (in Berlin called *Materialisten*). From this moment the whole affair began to look much more dangerous. For though the crowds which passed round the city whistling, roaring, shrieking, singing and uttering noises of every kind, were composed chiefly of the fair sex, their leaders were mostly men. The process adopted was simply to clear out the shops where comestibles were on sale, and to bid good-bye for ever to the owner, if he complacently allowed himself to be robbed of his property. In the contrary case, however, his windows were broken, everything smashable was smashed, and he himself beaten black and blue. In the bakers' shops in particular bread was weighed, and if the fivepenny loaf was found to weigh more than three pounds . . . the owner was shaken by the hand, a joyous hip-hurrah! was raised before his door, and the crowd passed on without confiscating anything. Indeed such a baker was then insured, for a notice was written in chalk on his door stating that he gave good weight, and this notice was always respected in subsequent forays. . . . On 22nd and 23rd April, however, the movement grew more extensive and better organised, so that on the fourth day the authorities decided to intervene. Military detachments, chiefly cavalry, patrolled the streets, laid about them occasionally with the flat of their sabres, arrested the noisiest demonstrators, and so restored peace and order almost in a day. When the city was quiet again, the Philistine wit came to the fore again, and christened the movement the 'Potato War,' because it had begun with an attack on potato dealers. Berlin, in the eyes of the carpet slipper citizen, had now had its 'revolution' as well as Paris, and when the first news of the February revolution (in 1848) reached the ears of the beer-house politicians they smiled knowingly, and gave it to be understood that they had seen this sort of thing before.[1]

<hr>

[1] Augerstein, *Die Berliner März-Ereignisse im Jahre* 1848 (K.).

CHAPTER V

POLITICAL POETRY OF THE FORTIES

THE political poetry of the forties was of first-rate importance, for the poets fanned the flame of discontent more effectively than the demagogues, and much of their work was fine in quality. Specimens are freely given throughout this book, wherever a poem irradiates a popular mood or an event, but it is well to devote a little attention to the poetry of the time as constituting an event in itself. Excluding Arndt as of a former generation, though he did in old age write one or two fine poems inspired by events, the six important political poets of the forties were Grillparzer, Freiligrath, Heine, Herwegh, Hoffmann von Fallersleben, and Geibel. Of these Grillparzer, the Austrian, Geibel, and Heine stand somewhat apart. The former was far too great a poet—the greatest German poet since Goethe, many count him—to limit his range to concerns of the day however engrossing, under the delusion that they were, as they seemed, all-important. His melancholy nature and hard life, long unrewarded, led him as much to introspection as to contemplation of events. But so imperious was the spirit of the age that the bulk of political verse and epigram (all his poetry is packed with the stuff of epigram) he wrote is considerable, and a number of examples will be found scattered among these pages as they come in their appropriate place. A man of his nature could be neither for nor against revolution. His epitaph on Metternich, printed on page 264, is as bitter an epigram as any one could let fly at the politician he least admires, but at the beginning of 1848, when the rumblings of approaching disturbance could be heard, he wrote :

> Evil draws near, sad watch my thoughts must keep ;
>   And ruin follows if none makes a stand ;
> Folly's loud laugh I hear, and I must weep,
>   For, ah, the stake is mine own Fatherland !

In a memoir [1] on the year 1848 Grillparzer thus explains his
aloofness from the March revolution of that year in Vienna :

This seems to be the place to justify my lack of enthusiasm for
freedom. As despotism has blighted my life, or at any rate my
literary life, it may be supposed that I am able to appreciate freedom.
But in addition to the fact that the movement of the year 1848
threatened to destroy my fatherland, for which I had an almost
childish love, it seemed to me that no moment could have been
more unfavourable for freedom than that one. In Germany,
which was always dreaming of progress, the whole scheme of education and culture had taken on such a character of incapacity,
unnaturalness, exaggeration and at the same time conceitedness,
that there could be no thought of anything reasonable and moderate.
And yet it was a hundred to one that literature, at any rate in
the beginning, would stand at the head of the movement ; in the
beginning, I say, because it was precisely the impracticability of its
theories that made inevitable a flinging open of the gates to the
baseness that existed in the second ranks. Freedom requires
common sense and self-control above all, and it was precisely those
qualities that were lacking in Germany. In spite of its censorship
Austria had not been able to hinder the spreading influence of
German literary absurdities, and if the Viennese dreamt of ' absorp-
tion in Germany,' it was chiefly because they hoped to be able
to pour great spoonfuls of the German scientific brew without any
trouble down their throats. Another reason why I was condemned
to passivity was this : if I had said, ' What you take to be wisdom
is nonsense,' no one would have believed me. But the chief reason
was that I was old, and only Youth accepted the credentials of
Progress.

Geibel was not a revolutionary, and indeed a poem of his
against Herwegh won him high favour in courtly circles. A
smooth facility, not unlike Longfellow's, of writing verse which
did not soar, but hovered above the commonplace, made him a
favourite German poet throughout his long life. He lived long
enough, indeed, to celebrate the triumphs of the Franco-German
war. One piece, from his *Nachlass*, is worth quoting, because
it gives a fine view of war, one which is not exclusively German,
but is not as true as those who admire it could desire :

> Ay,
> War is a horror, but a blessing also,
> In that it lifts the ban of littleness
> From off our souls, gives us once more to know
> For certain what in life is sound and true.

---

[1] *Franz Grillparzers Werke*, Deutsche Verlags-Anstalt, Stuttgart und
Leipzig.

The empty, wordy strife of formulas
Dies down ; *things* come into their own
And preach aloud : what gives the State increase,
Freedom, lies not in legal instruments,
Though subtly drawn, but in the sympathy,
Unchartered, 'twixt a people and their Prince,
That makes them joyful side by side to stand
For Fatherland, and, if needs must, to fall.
Away flies what was sham, for he alone
Counts as a man whose strength is shown in deed.
The weakling's nerveless hand resigns the helm,
The strong lays hold, and pilots undismayed
Through stormy seas the vessel into port.

Heine's critical and ironic sense prevented him from throwing
himself with enthusiasm into the cause of reform. Few men
suffered more than he from tyranny and the censorship ; his
romantic tendencies were towards another world than that of
his time, and constant contact with hard earth only aroused his
sardonic humour. So that for concise and bitter satire it is not
easy to find his equal. The verse from his *Deutschland* is well
known :

Russia and France possess the land,
Great Britain rules the sea,
Ours is the cloudy realm of dreams
Where there 's no rivalry.

He could never bring himself to believe that German demagogues
and corybantic poets would ever rouse the German Philistine to
action. Indeed his view was not unlike that of his racial as
well as political countryman, Börne, as set out on page 57. One
brilliant example of Heine's satire has been given on page 148.
Here is another short piece in which he satirises the blustering
swashbuckler student of the period who played so great a part
in riot and revolution :

DOGMA

Oh beat the drum, and show no fear,
But kiss the pretty vivandière ;
Of all our wisdom that 's the sum,
The secret of all books is there.

So drum the people out of sleep,
Sound the reveille with tuck of drum ;
Behind the drums to march along,
Of all our wisdom that 's the sum,

N

That's Hegel's whole philosophy,
    The secret of all books is there,
And this I know because I'm wise,
    And, what is more, a drummer rare.

Almost cameo-like is the satirical picture of Germany in the
forties to be found in his ' Night-watchman's Arrival at Paris ' :

' Night-watchman with long progressive legs,
    You look so startled, run so fast !
How fare the dear good folks at home,
    Is the Fatherland made free at last ? '

'Tis well : we're quietly getting on,
    We're strictly moral but growing stout,
And gently, surely, by peaceful ways
    Germany's turning inside out.

We're not superficial like men in France,
    Where freedom's only worn outside ;
'Tis in our being's very depths
    We Germans love of freedom hide.

Cologne Cathedral's finished now,
    To Hohenzollern zeal 'tis owed ;
The Hapsburgs sent a purse of gold,
    Stained glass a Wittelsbach bestowed.

The constitution, to make us free,
    The kings have promised us to sign,
And kingly promises are worth
    The Niblung-hoard deep in the Rhine.

The Rhine so free, Brutus of streams,
    No one dare ever from us steal !
The Swiss, they hold it by the head,
    The Dutchmen bind it heel to heel.

And God will grant a fleet to us,
    Our patriots' superfluous strength
Shall sail the sea in German ships :
    The fortress-ban's repealed at length.

Spring comes, the bursting pods rain down,
    We're free to breathe where nature's free !
And be my whole edition seized,
    The Censor melt in air you'll see,

The two great revolutionary poets, who worked for revolution,
who did not believe that things could be as they should be with
anything short of revolution, and who consciously strove to
rouse the people to claim their rights, were Freiligrath and
Herwegh. Hoffmann von Fallersleben, a poet of lighter touch,
deserves to be ranked with them because he is the author of
Deutschland, Deutschland über Alles, and because of the volume
and popularity of his endless stream of songs, many with the
true ring of the folk-song, and many too with a genial touch
of satire, which roused people to laugh at, rather than rave
against Bumbledom, princely, military, and bureaucratic alike.
An invaluable source for a knowledge of the character of these
German poets is Baechtold's *Life of Gottfried Keller*, greatest
of Swiss poets and novelists. To Keller the circle of German
political refugees at Zurich was familiar, and he had a poet's
sympathy with the poets among them ; as a neutral he saw,
though with no unkindly eyes, their weaknesses. Freiligrath
began life in commerce, and during a long exile in London he
returned to commercial pursuits. Beginning his poetic career
as one of the strongest of the sentimental poets of his country,
he held out for some years against the revolutionary view, and
accepted a pension which earned for him the taunts of Herwegh
and R. E. Prutz, one of several of the band of revolutionary
poets who rank only lower than the highest. But soon after
reaching his thirtieth year he threw up his pension and went
over to the revolutionary side, with the result that he had to
live for many years in exile. Fierce, almost savage, as are some
of the examples of his poems to be found in this book, it is a
characteristic of another side of his nature that among the
poetical exercises of his life in London were translations of
Hood's ' Song of the Shirt,' and ' The Bridge of Sighs,' the
latter an exquisite version. Keller wrote on hearing of his
death in 1876 : ' Freiligrath belongs to the few of whom we
cannot believe that they are really gone from sight, on whose
death one asks oneself anxiously, has one nothing to reproach
oneself for, has one never given them pain, but is at once
reassured by the thought that they could never have given the
slightest occasion for it with a nature so happily endowed.'
He had in his mind Freiligrath's most famous lyric, of which
a rendering is here given. It is worth reading in connection
with the savage lines, ' The Dead to the Living,' printed on

page 317. The two pieces show how near in the German heart lie the fountains of rage and of tears.

'O LOVE SO LONG AS LOVE THOU CANST'

O love so long as love thou canst,
O love so long as love thou mayest,
The hour will come, the hour will come,
When by the grave in tears thou prayest.

Bethink thee how thy heart aglow
Feels love and all its stirrings sweet,
So long as yet another heart
Sends back a warm responsive beat.

And who unlocks his breast to thee—
O give him love, and love again;
Be every moment one of joy,
And not a moment fraught with pain.

Therefore guard well the unruly tongue,
Hard words they are so easy said—
O God, it was not hardly meant,
But he, he goes and tears are shed!

O love so long as love thou canst,
O love so long as love thou mayest,
The hour will come, the hour will come,
When by the grave in tears thou prayest,

And kneeling by the mounded earth
Thou hid'st thy troubled, streaming eyes—
They'll never see thy friend again—
Where dank the graveyard tussocks rise.

Thou call'st to him: Look up at me,
Who have thy grave with tears besprent:
Forgive me that I hurt thee so,
O God, it was not hardly meant!

But he, he hears and sees thee not,
Comes not, tho' eager be thy plea;
The lips that kissed thee oft, no more
Can say: I've long forgiven thee.

He did! forgave thee long ago,
Tho' many the burning tears that fell
For thee and for thy bitter words:
But hush! he sleeps; with him all's well.

O love so long as love thou canst,
O love so long as love thou mayest,
The hour will come, the hour will come,
When by the grave in tears thou prayest.

Hoffmann von Fallersleben is in another way as attractive
a figure as Freiligrath. He was not of aristocratic birth, but
dubbed himself as such by adding to his own name that of his
birthplace. Literary history and Germanic philology were the
subject of his studies. In 1835 he was appointed professor at
the university of Breslau. But his academic studies could not
absorb his attention and wholly divert his sensitive eyes and
ears from the living present. Steeped as he was in the study
of folk-songs he found in the writing of folk-songs a means of
expression for his own criticism, racy to a degree and almost
always genial, of the shams and the abuses that so often
characterise the governance of an official and police-ridden
people. In 1840 and 1841 he published two volumes of *Un-
political Songs*. He was promptly dismissed from his chair,
and sent wandering from place to place, moved on by the police
from one town and district to another the morning after arrival.
But the policy of the authorities was a foolish one. The poet
was not punished ; he enjoyed his nomadic existence, that of
the scholar-gipsy, the wandering minstrel, and the vagabond
gentleman with his pilgrim-scrip, beloved of novelists. The
poet was not silenced ; on the contrary he gathered an audience
in every inn, restaurant, wine-shop and beer-cellar he entered
on his wanderings, and there enthroned in clouds of tobacco
smoke, he thundered out his humorous songs throwing ridicule
on law and order as understood by the governing classes, or,
glass in hand, told stories by the hour that made his hearers
laugh till their sides ached at the stupidity of princes and their
subservient ministers. In 1848 he was rehabilitated, granted
a pension and given a post as ducal librarian which enabled
him when the whim seized him, to grasp his pilgrim's staff and
set off on a spell of the haphazard wandering that had grown so
dear. Paul Lindau, in his *Gesammelte Aufsätze*, gives a vivid
account of the sudden descent on him at Elberfeld of the roving
jovial Hoffmann in his old age. The old man, with his bright
eyes, cheery countenance and great shock of hair, kept the party
up all night while he drank wine and trolled in a rich deep bass

voice song after song, and reeled off tale after tale, some of them twice.

Many a piece by him finds its place in this book, but two more of his light-hearted jests may be given here, and a single example of his art of song-writing for children. In this sphere his gift was not short of genius.

A TRAGIC HISTORY

(18. 5. 1840)

Last night, 'tis said, the general woke,
  The general stout and bold,
A midnight dream his slumber broke,
  And made his blood run cold.

In all his life fear had no part,
  No danger made him stare,
It was a dream that made him start,
  A dream exceeding rare.

Tell me, why should the general jump
  At that dread midnight hour ?
What made his heart work like a pump,
  His eyes in terror glower ? . . .

Was 't war and plague, or hunger's pang ?
  Was ' fire ! ' or ' help ! ' the cry ?
Treason, or murder's horrid clang,
  Or bloody mutiny ?

He dreamt—I know it sounds *énorme*—
  Its best the army wore,
But every blessèd uniform
  Had now two buttons more ! [1]

THE ETERNAL REVOLUTIONARY

Put the Springtide into prison,
  For a demagogue is she !
From the long long thrall of Winter
  She would dare to set us free ;
Wake us from the long night's darkness,
  Bid our slumbering eyes to see.
Put the Springtide into prison,
  For a demagogue is she !

---

[1] Of the importance attached in Germany to this item of military accoutrement we may judge by the fact that one of Bavaria's stipulations before consenting to the establishment of the Empire in 1870 was that the Bavaria army should retain its existing number of buttons.

Put the Springtide into prison,
For she sets the world astir ;
Waters murmur, woodlands whisper,
Things of feather, things of fur,
And the heart of man within him
Thrill in unison with her.
Put the Springtide into prison,
For she sets the world astir !

Put the Springtide into prison,
Keep King Winter on the throne,
For she is but a usurper,
He ' legitimate ' alone.
Springtide whispers ' revolution,'
Let her for her crime atone—
Put the Springtide into prison,
Keep King Winter on the throne.

A LULLABY

All is peaceful, all is still,
Sleep, my little one, thy fill !
Tho' the wind may rustle round,
Hush, my pretty one, sleep sound.

Close, oh close thy little eyes,
Like twin buds in Paradise !
When the morning sun shines bright,
They 'll unfold like flowers to light.

O'er my flow'ret watch I keep,
Kiss his little eyes asleep ;
Spring 's outside with all its joy,
Mother's heart is with her boy.

R. E. Prutz, play-writer and novelist, a north German
orn in Stettin, deserves to have his work illustrated here,
hough his fame has not been maintained like his comrades'.
He was a close friend of Herwegh's, but got his effects, not
y striking cymbals and gong, but by light, melodious verse
hich shows a genuine poetic feeling, and at times, as in the
econd of the pieces here given, surprises by the skill with
hich the climax is concealed to the very end. His most
mbitious effort, a satirical political play, *Die Politische
Wochenstube*, was hailed after its publication as a successful
ttempt to raise political poetry to the highest literary form,

and it secured for him the flattering attention of a charge of
high treason.   But it is tedious reading nowadays, and his hope
to play the German Aristophanes remained unachieved.

BURIDAN'S ASS

Clover and hay to right and left,
  Rich meadows stretching wide,
The ass stands there in misery,
  How on his choice decide ?
He snuffs to right, he snuffs to left,
  He turns him three times three—
O Buridan, O Buridan,
  Thine ass must stupid be. . . .

Freedom and slavery right and left,
  And both quite plain to see ;
But here we stand, and ever stand
  In dull neutrality.
Therefore far more contemptible
  And far more stupid we,
O Buridan, O Buridan,
  Than e'er thine ass could be.

BY NIGHT

Now fades the sun's last ray,
  Tall shadows bring the night,
The little stars shine out
  In points of twinkling light.

Down from the starry vault,
  And over hill and glen,
Freedom, on pinions soft,
  Sweeps through the haunts of men.

She visits all their homes,
  She knocks at all their doors,
In every sleeper's ear
  A whispered prayer she pours.

And all, both old and young,
  Her burning kisses stir ;
She has a light caress
  Even for the prisoner.

She tries the blade's keen edge,
Sees if the powder's dry ;
As the sands in the hour-glass fall
She counts them with jealous eye ;

Till the sleepers' hearts aglow
Dream but a single dream,
Of chargers that whinny and rear,
Of swords that flash and gleam ;

Till, laughing behind his bars,
His sides the prisoner shakes ;
Till, shivering in his palace,
A white-faced man—awakes !

The motives of ' blood ' and of ' hate ' are to be found in
Prutz as in Herwegh, though not in such rich profusion. An
example may be given which Herwegh would not have dis-
dained :

SULTRY WEATHER

Where's our content, and pose sedate ?
What pang gnaws in secret the soul ?
Why breathe not our hearts, like flaming coal,
But limitless love and limitless hate ?
Not grey be our colour, not grey !   Black or white :
That our strength and our will may prevail in the fight.

The world is growing all too tame,
We 've lost the noble art of rage ;
Therefore on foreheads grey with age
Sit but disgust and sullen shame.
From the blood's bubbling fountains, the source that is thine,
Send thy life through us pulsing, O Anger divine !

Before we go on to discuss the fiery Herwegh, and the problem
which a study of him involves, we may close this chapter with
an illustration selected not as a piece of political poetry, but to
show how amusing at times becomes the German instinct for
arrogance and self-assertiveness. Rückert, best known in
England as the author of a love-song set to immortal music by
Schumann, wrote a little piece on the meeting of Blücher and
Wellington after Waterloo. It will be familiar to all who
obtained their initiation into German through Buchheim's
Clarendon Press Readers. That genial old German pedagogue

selected it no doubt because he thought it good in itself, excellent in taste, and agreeable to his pupils :

> Old Blücher bold and Wellington,
>   As laurelled victors meeting,
> Knew each the deeds by the other done
>   And gave him hero's greeting.
> To Wellington said Blücher bold :
>   ' Youth has your laurels brightened
> On temples that more wisdom hold
>   Than those which age has whitened.'
> Said Wellington : ' O hero sage !
>   Thy soul with virtue glowing
> Has linked a head of hoary age
>   To heart with youth o'erflowing.'
> So stood the young man and the old,
>   Gripped hands and asked each other :
> ' We are a pair of heroes bold,
>   Does the world hold such another ? '

One can possibly imagine Blücher talking like this, but Wellington—no !

CHAPTER VI

VIOLENCE AND HATE IN GERMAN POETRY

GEORG HERWEGH was the standard-bearer of the revolution, 'the iron lark, the song-bird of war' as he has been termed.[1] In him revolutionary ardour burnt at a heat so white as to make him one of the select band of his country's great lyric poets. Two of his lyrics, indeed, appear by those of Goethe, Eichendorff, Heine, Novalis, Mörike and Platen in Richard Meyer's *Best Hundred Lyrics*. With Uhland, Justinus Kerner, and Mörike he was a Swabian, and he began his career, like other turbulent spirits, as a student of theology. To escape military service [2] he took refuge in Zurich, and there at the age of twenty-four published in 1841 his *Poems of a Live Man, Gedichte eines Lebendigen*. The bold, outspoken verses in which he preached the gospel of hate in rhythmic tones which rang like a gong, as Uhland's had like the clink of hammer on anvil, caught the ear of Germany at once. The instant success of the young poet was prodigious. Keller's account of his first reading of the book is worth giving : ' One morning, as I lay in bed, I opened and read the first volume of Herwegh's poems. The new and ringing tones gripped me like a trumpet-blast that suddenly rouses a vast camp of nations in arms.' And he goes on to tell how Herwegh's poems, with Grün's *Schutt*, made every fibre in his body beat rhythmically. So moved was Keller that he recorded his feelings in a sonnet as resonant as one of Herwegh's own :

---

[1] K. Breul in *Cambridge Modern History*, xi. p. 413.
[2] So Baechtold. Robertson in his *History of German Literature* gives the cause of his flight as an insult to an officer.

HERWEGH

O foaming draught ! Long have we thirsted sore,
Thou cup of gold, to taste a strong, new wine ;
In thy red heart we saw a vintage shine.
Oh how we drank, and, drinking, called for more !
Though stands Zwing-Uri's fastness as of yore,
Our age is dead, for dead men's bones a shrine ;
The sleepers bide the last dread trumpet's sign ;
But thou, to wake us, prince-like com'st before !
And yet, when after storm the rainbow gleams,
And all the powers of darkness take their flight
Back to the bourne whence come our evil dreams,
Then shall thy song, fierce summons now to fight,
Bourgeon in beauty under milder beams :
From Winter's grip Spring struggles to the light.

But there was to be no mild summer for this tempestuous spirit !
In 1842 Herwegh made a triumphant tour through Germany.
In the course of it he had an audience of Frederick William IV.
who had the curiosity of a child for exciting novelties, and it
was to him the King addressed his well-known remark : ' I
love a convinced opposition.' Musicians vied with one another
in setting his songs to music, among them Liszt himself. But
when a new journal he was bringing out was suppressed by the
Prussian government he wrote such a letter to the King that
he was summarily expelled from Prussia. However, on his
return to Zurich he carried with him a rich wife, daughter of
the Berlin banker Siegmund, who, when it came to fighting in
Hecker's rebellion a few years later,[1] showed herself a better
man than her husband. For many years the pair oscillated
between Zurich and Paris, with visits to Italy, Vienna, and
back to Germany, but he gradually lost touch with German
opinion, and his reputation as an active revolutionary did
not survive his performance with the Foreign Legion he led
from Paris to Hecker's support.

Baechtold describes his life in Zurich in no agreeable colours :
' The poetical revolutionary posed as a dandy, who was only to
be satisfied with the choicest of fleshly delights, drank only
champagne ("'tis my due" he used to say even later, to Keller's
disgust, when he was up to the neck in financial troubles), kept
servants in livery, and withal plotted revolution with shoe-

[1] See page 359 f.

makers' and carpenters' apprentices.' It was of the noisy
group of feather-brained revolutionaries collected at Zurich
that Keller wrote his amusing verses, ' Champagne ' :

> In our conclave polemical
> The corks were flying, and we sat
> Drinking concoctions chemical
> Which foamed at first and then went flat.

> We howled and shrieked and wept about
> The poor, dear proletarian's lot,
> Until our cash had given out,
> And not a farthing had we got.

> Then, sudden, came an old, discharged,
> Belated beggar, bowing low—
> On his misfortune we enlarged
> But not a stiver could bestow.

> Complacently we still went on
> Discussing what to beggars led,
> Enjoying every ' pro and con,'
> Then left him there and went to bed.

Wagner, who had been caught up in the revolutionary
whirlpool, and, like so many German suspects, found it convenient to live from time to time at Zurich, saw much of Herwegh
from 1850 onwards. ' Herwegh,' he says,[1] ' put on an aristocratic swagger and gave himself the airs of a delicately nurtured
and luxurious son of his times, to which a fairly liberal inter-
polation of French expletives at least added a certain distinction.
Nevertheless, there was something about his person, with his
quick, flashing eye and kindliness of manner, which was well
calculated to exert an attractive influence.' They became
close friends and Wagner soon realised that his ' showy and
trivial mannerisms ' were ' altogether alien to his original
nature.' He goes on :

He was the first man in whom I met with a sensitive and sympathetic comprehension of my most daring schemes and opinions.
[It is characteristic of Wagner's restless energy that in 1855 he
took his friend seriously in hand with a view to rousing him to
some enterprise worthy of his poetic gifts]. . . . I had worried
myself for a long time about him . . . trying to think that his previous efforts were merely introductions to really serious artistic

---

[1] *My Life* by Richard Wagner.

achievements. He admitted himself that he felt his best was still
to come. It seemed to him that he had all the material—crowds
of ' ideas '—in reserve for a great poetical work ; there was nothing
wanting but the ' frame ' in which he could paint it all, and this
is what he hoped, from day to day, to find. As I grew tired of
waiting for it, I set about trying to find the longed-for frame for
him myself. He evidently wished to evolve an epic poem on a
large scale, in which to embody the views he had acquired. As he
had once alluded to Dante's luck in finding a subject like the
pilgrimage through hell and purgatory into paradise, it occurred
to me to suggest, for the desired frame, the Brahman myth of
metempsychosis, which in Plato's version comes within reach of
our classical education. He did not think it a bad idea, and I
accordingly took some trouble to define the form such a poem would
take. He was to decide upon three acts, each containing three
songs, which would make nine songs in all. The first act would
show his hero in the Asiatic country of his birth ; the second, his
reincarnation in Greece and Rome ; the third, his reincarnation
in the Middle Ages and in modern times. All this pleased him very
much, and he thought it might come to something. Not so my
cynical friend, Dr. Wille, who had an estate in the country where
we often met in the bosom of his family. He was of opinion that
we expected far too much of Herwegh. Viewed at close quarters
he was, after all, only a young Swabian who had received a far
larger share of honour and glory than his abilities warranted
through the Jewish halo thrown around him by his wife. In the
end I had to shrug my shoulders in silent acquiescence with these
hopelessly unkind remarks, as I could, of course, see poor Herwegh
sinking into deeper apathy every year, until in the end he seemed
incapable of doing anything.

Almost the last glimpse Baechtold gives of the poet occurs
in the description of an orgy at the Swan Inn, Mühlebach, one
September evening in 1861. Keller was invited to the party,
the chief guest at which was Ferdinand Lassalle, accompanied
by the Countess Hatzfeld in a red blouse and white skirt.
Herwegh was there with his wife and son, and a crowd of
eccentrics. A Colonel Rüstow, an old Garibaldian, appeared
in a red blouse. On the sofa sat a Russian nihilist, Ludmilla
Assing, to whom the gentlemen paid constant court. Tea was
served first, and then came dinner. The women drank champagne
and smoked big cigars all night. Keller sat ill at ease, but
remained quiet. Finally, however, when Lassalle began, as
daylight dawned, to give a display of table-turning and tricks
of mesmerism and played his hocus-pocus over Herwegh's head
to send him to sleep, Keller went mad with rage, shouted out

'This is too thick, you blackguards, you swindlers,' seized a
chair and went for Lassalle. Women wept, men swore, and so
on and on— and out into the open air. Baechtold is probably hard on Herwegh. He drew on
Corvin, without acknowledgment, and distorted him. Keller,
at any rate, retained his admiration for the poet until his death
in 1875. There was a lovable side to the man, and it is note-
worthy that while Treitschke becomes epileptic when he has to
treat of Herwegh among the poets of the forties, Victor Fleury
writes kindly of him. Herwegh, we should remember, was a
scholar as well as a poet. He was a student of natural philosophy and of oriental languages. He interested Wagner in the
philosophy of Feuerbach and of Schopenhauer, and the latter
tells of an invitation he received from Wagner and Herwegh to
visit them at Zurich since they could not come to visit him in
Germany. He became as much at home in French as in German,
and he was deeply read in English literature. To Byron and
Shelley he addressed sonnets. The latter is certainly to be
accounted as a worthy tribute to the greatest of our revolutionary poets.

SHELLEY

To win his God he double forfeit paid,
Therefore the God he won was doubly dear ;
The Eternal never saw a soul so near,
No faith was e'er more strong and unafraid.
His pulse beat warm for all whom God hath made ;
Hope ever sat beside, his course to steer ;
And when his anger broke, the flame burnt clear
And tongues of fire on slaves and tyrants played.
A spirit of steel in fleshly body pent,
A glowing spark from Nature's altar sprung,
Whereat his England's vulgar scorn was flung ;
A heart made drunk with sweet celestial scent,
A father's curse, a woman's love he won ;
At last, a star in the wild waves fordone.

It is in connection with Herwegh, and another young poet
of the forties, Graf Moritz von Strachwitz,[1] who died at twenty-
five, too young to win the fame that must have become his due,

[1] In 1842, a year after the publication of Herwegh's *Gedichte eines Lebendigen*, Strachwitz published his *Gedichte eines Erwachenden, Poems of One
Awake*. Strachwitz was fond of adapting the striking titles of others ; thus
the title of his *Gepanzerte Sonette, Iron-clad Sonnets*,' recalls that of Rückert's
Geharnischte Sonette, Armoured Sonnets, both indicating a strain of
violence.

that it becomes natural to discuss certain important matters such as the German ideas of hate and of freedom, and the violence with which Germans allow themselves to express their most violent emotions. Herwegh's *Poems of a Live Man* contain a fine ' Song of Hate.'

Up and away, o'er flood and fell !
　Bright gleams Aurora's brow ;
To faithful, wife a last farewell,
　The sword 's our partner now.
And our right hands shall fall to dust
　Ere we our grip let go ;
Too long in love we 've put our trust,
　We 'll see what hate can show !

For love can win us naught we prize,
　Salvation 's not in love ;
Hold thou, O Hate, the last assize,
　Throned high our foes above !
On tyrants all thy sentence just,
　Then ours to deal the blow—
Too long in love we 've put our trust,
　We 'll see what hate can show !

Where throbs a heart throughout the land,
　Hate, like a pulse, beat high :
Dry wood there 's plenty here to hand
　Will make the red flame fly.
Freedom still lives, for shout men must
　As down the street they go,—
' Too long in love you 've put your trust.
　Now see what hate can show ! '

Let nought your steadfast vengeance sate
　While still lives tyranny,
And holier will become your hate
　Than e'er your love could be.
Oh, our right hands shall fall to dust
　Ere we the sword let go ;
Too long in love we 've put our trust,
　We 'll see what hate can show !

Still more violent are the sentiments expressed in his ' Cross from tomb and temple tearing.'

'CROSS FROM TOMB AND TEMPLE TEARING'

Cross from tomb and temple tearing
Beat to blades for freemen's bearing,
   God in Heaven will allow.
Truce to song ! Let all the singing
Iron be on anvil ringing !
   Steel is your redeemer now !

Oak and pine wood ask the nation,
In a green interrogation,
   'Must we grow o'er freedom's grave ? '
Nay, for freedom is undying,
And we, Hell itself defying,
   Our Eurydice shall save !

Germans, hearken to your seers,
Brazen are the present years,
   Breast of bronze your future need !
Sable death, our guerdon gory ;
All our gold, but sunset glory ;
   All our crimson, hearts that bleed !

Cross from tomb and temple tearing,
Beat to blades for heroes' bearing ;
   God in Heaven the work will bless.
From the throat of furnace roaring
Tongues of fire His grace imploring
   Win His steel new holiness.

Freedom first ! Let no man falter,
Lead no maid to marriage altar,
   Sow no seed and reap no corn ;
Till it see in gladsome gazing
Freedom's sun in Heaven blazing
   To no cradle babe be born.

Crape your cities' towers in sadness,
Till a new-born freedom's gladness
   Break its banners through the land.
Till, O Rhine, thy silver reaches
Trumpet freedom to their beaches,
   Weep thy wave on either strand.

Cross from tomb and temple tearing
Beat to blades for heroes' bearing,
   Christ's approving head will bow.
Freedom's sword is her apostle,
Tongues of steel preach freedom's gospel,
   Let yours speak for freedom now !

o

A fair match, however, for these two poems is Strachwitz's astonishing 'Calm,' not a political piece, but one indicating a mood commoner with the Germans than most other peoples. The poet strolls down from the hillside one lovely September evening to a Danish bay, golden in the sunset. Motionless on the still waters lies a frigate, black against the gold. These are the sentiments inspired :

CALM

Firm as a rock the waves astride,
 Her poise the frigate guards,
And mirrors in the sleeping tide
 Her tapering masts and yards.

The sea is like a looking-glass,
 So smooth the waves are rolled,
And sunset's glories, as they pass,
 Throw round a frame of gold.

O watery mirror, flawless thou,
 But, oh, how flat and stale !
Of thee my heart has had enow,
 Green sameness all thy tale.

O storm with hate of hurrying scud,
 Come down in driving mist,
And smite the mirror's glassy flood
 With fury-doubled fist !

Full in the midst with thunder sound
 Smite mirror, frame and all,
Till starred and shivered the crystal round
 In liquid fragments fall.

O tedious calm, thou stiflest me,
 When shall thy reign have end ?
Fore God, I 'll not put out to sea
 If thou my course attend.

Herwegh's 'Trooper's Song ' is fine, and the commencement of the second verse is German through and through.

THE TROOPER'S SONG

The gloomy night's last hour is come,
We gallop still, we gallop dumb,
 And Death keeps company.
'Tis cold, the morning wind is up ;
Come, hostess, quick, a stirrup cup
 Before we die !

O tufted grass, so fresh and green,
You 'll soon take on the wild-rose sheen,
　　When my red blood flows by.—
The first gulp drink I, sword in hand,
To thee, my hallowed Fatherland,
　　For whom I die.

The second gulp, fair Liberty,
Without a pause I toss to thee,
　　And drain the grape-juice dry.
This heel-tap here, for whom the toast ?
The Holy Roman Empire's ghost,
　　And may it lie !

Now bear my child the glass I smash—
The bullets hum, the lance-tips flash—
　　Wife of my heart, good-bye !
Up, and like lightning cleave the way !
　O trooper's joy, at break of day
　　To charge—and die !

And so with his ' Stanzas from a Foreign Land,' [1] a piece
remarkable for the opulence of its imagery.

O might I die as dies the afterglow
　When day's last ruddy beam fades in the West !
By such a death, scarce felt, I 'd lightly go,
　My heart's blood crimsoning the Eternal's breast.

O might I die as dies the falling star,
　In swift eclipse of undiminished light !
So would I painlessly, no shock, no jar,
　In heaven's blue depths sink silent out of sight.

O might I die as dies the flower's perfume,
　From chaliced rose or lily's lips outpoured,
Where zephyrs from each odour-laden plume
　Waft incense on the altar of the Lord !

O might I die as in the dewy vale
　The dew-drop dies to greet the morning sun :
Would God, that my poor soul like vapour pale
　Might greet his thirsty lips ere day were done !

---

[1] This song was set to music by Liszt, and appears as No. 6 in Part VI. of his
Collected Songs, issued by Kahnt of Leipzig.　In Marcel Herwegh's edition of
the *Poems of a Live Man*, published by Max Hesse, we are told that Liszt wrote
of the song to the Countess Caroline Sayn-Wittgenstein : ' Ce lied est le testament de ma jeunesse ! '

O might I die as dies the trembling note
Struck from some golden harp's vibrating string,
While in the great Creator's heart remote
Of earthly music heavenly echoes ring !

Thou wilt not die as dies the afterglow,
Thou wilt not, like the star, in silence sink,
Thou wilt not die like flowers that fade and go,
No morning-ray thy soul like dew will drink.

Yet die thou wilt, and dying leave no sign,
But misery must first thy manhood shake ;
To things insensate cometh death benign,
Our hearts, poor human hearts, in pieces break.

It will be noted that the glow of sunset suggests to the poet
his ' heart's blood crimsoning the Eternal's breast.' A rosy
sunrise suggests blood to him equally. The first verse of his
famous ' Reveille ' runs :

It was the lark, not the nightingale,
Fluttered skyward but now through the trees,
The sun's great orb in a crimson veil
Swings up on the morning breeze.
The day, the day grows bright—
The night,
The night in her blood must die !
Stand up if there 's one in the Light puts his trust ;
Ye sleepers, awake, tread your garlands in dust
And a flaming sword gird on to the thigh !

Only a German poet could have suggested that warm red blood
coursed through the veins of night, that grey and ghostly figure.
Again a match for Herwegh is Strachwitz, with his

' Flow my blood in music chanted,
Every drop of thee a song ! ' [1]

CALM THEE ! CALM THEE !

Calm thee, calm thee, swelling heart !
Though by storm thy course thou wendest,
And thy blood in battle spendest,
Downwards still thy way will part !
Though across the wild waves combing
Thou may'st see the far green shore,
See it after leagues of roaming,
Thou shalt reach it never more !

---

[1] *Blute drum in Melodien,*
Jeder Tropfen ein Gesang !

Calm thee, calm thee, swelling heart !
Hast thou hailed Fay Morgan beckoning,
By her star made out thy reckoning ?
Downwards still thy way will part.
Dreams on wings of hope ascended
Stand before thee clear as day,
But soon fades the vision splendid ;
What thou seek'st, too far away !

Calm thee, calm thee, swelling heart !
Hast thou heard the quiver rattle,
Stirred and breathed the breath of battle ?
Downwards still thy way will part !
Brazen heights of thy ambition,
Wouldst thou climb them, fall thou must.
Nought is left thee but contrition :
O that I were turned to dust !

Calm thee, calm thee, swelling heart !
Fiery hopes and stubborn fighting,
Then to fall, the end not sighting,
Is man's ancient, bitter smart !
What in life may not be granted
Speaks in death with accents strong,
Flow, my blood, in music chanted,
Every drop of thee a song !

Spend thee, spend thee, swelling heart !
From the breast's secretest dwelling
Send a stream of love a-welling,
Send it surging, wounded heart !
Let it flow, and end the story—
Ere it reach the sea so near,
From some pinnacle of glory
On the flood may fall a tear !

Let it not be urged that these citations are exceptional and unfair ; this book has many prose passages which show how steeped is the German nature in violence, expressing itself in violence both of language and thought. At times one can smile at it, as when Hermann von Gilm, chief poet of the Tyrol, sums up a husband's denunciation of the wife who cannot give him the love, the violent love, his German nature demands, with the lines :

Speak not to me of respect or admiration ;
Corpse-like the terms, why dig them up to view ?
Hatred or love 's the sole denomination
In which the coins your feelings mint ring true.

But we have begun to realise the danger of this violence, and we shall be the better able to deal with it when we recognise not only that the German nature is violent, but also that the German nation has been nourished upon hate as a virtue. Throughout history event after event has shown the German as conspicuous for brutality. In the tympanum above one of the northern doorways of Rheims Cathedral is a relief which tells the story how in 406 A.D. the King of the Vandals, about to strike off the head of S. Nicaise, was struck in the face by S. Eutropia, his sister. Whereupon, having struck off the Saint's head, the king murdered his sister. This violence is in the German blood. What we have now to learn is that it has been systematically fostered, and more systematically during the nineteenth century than in any other.

Professor Boutroux in his *Philosophy and War* has dealt very faithfully with Fichte. He points out how the philosopher in his famous series of ' Addresses to the German People,' delivered in 1808, in which he glorified Germans as the chosen people, and held up an ideal of freedom which implied (though he did not say so) the subjection of others, and a refusal to bend the knee to God, laid, unwittingly perhaps, the foundations of a structure of bureaucratic education which might have horrified him if he could now see its results. But we have elsewhere had enough of Fichte. Let us take Arndt, whose eminence as a poet was rivalled by his distinction as a writer of prose, and who was probably the greatest literary force in Germany during the first forty years of the last century ; Arndt, whose Christianity according to Professor Robertson [1] 'which reminds us of Luther's was sincere and manly,' whose ' writings, prose as well as verse, reflect the essentially religious character of the German revolt against Napoleon'; Arndt the hymn-writer, what may we learn from him ? In 1813 he wrote a poem entitled ' The Boy Robert's Vow,' of which the two following verses, translated almost literally, form part :

I swear a hot and bloody hate,
And anger that shall ne'er abate,
'Gainst Frenchmen all, the giddy crew,
Whose injuries my land may rue.

---

[1] *History of German Literature.*

> O Thou who, throned above the skies,
> Bid'st hearts to beat and suns to rise,
> Almighty God, be near me now
> And help me keep intact this vow!

Arndt *meant* that this was the right sort of doctrine to instil into a child. About the same date he published a pamphlet entitled *Ueber Volkshasse*, ' On a Nation's Hate,' subsequently expanded by the addition ' and on the Use of a Foreign Language.' In this essay occurs the following passage, which many will find it difficult to accept as a genuine extract from the work of any responsible writer :

A man who has the right sort of love must hate evil and hate it until death. That was Christ's way, who none the less was the meekest One and like a child of Heaven walked joyfully on earth. Know ye not how He rebuked and mocked the hypocrites, the Pharisees ; how He was angered when He saw the Temple built at Jerusalem profaned, and overthrew the table of the merchants and the money-changers and drove them out ? Can ye feel what a deep and exalted anger was His that enabled Him even on the cross to triumph over wickedness and sin ? Did He not say, I came not to send peace, but a sword ?

If a man seek to keep hate utterly from him, and will not arm himself against tyranny and wickedness, must not this tyranny lay hold on him and drive him perforce to oppress and to violate innocence and righteousness ? Therefore war against all outrage and unrighteousness ! Horror of slavery, since the slave is no man but a beast that crawls ; hate and revenge against all tyrants, for they would root out of the earth freedom and joy and every noble feeling and every Godlike thought ! Inspire this hate in your grandchildren and your great-grandchildren, and bequeath it as a pledge of virtue and of Christlike and human love. That is the true Christianity and the true humanity, the true old German loyalty and virtue. When in a hate so noble, and in so noble a war of revenge against injustice and outrage every sort of devastation sweeps over a land, and even all its inhabitants, proud champions of freedom, are undone in such a holy war, reckon it not, for ye cannot reckon it ; that ye must leave for God to reckon, yours is it to do your duty.

The true God is an angry and a powerful God who must always punish evil, and be displeased with indolent virtue and feeble cowardice, whereby all uprightness and freedom would vanish from earth. Because He is the God of love, therefore is hate pleasing to Him ; because He is a God of joy, therefore is courage pleasing to Him. But why oftentimes noble races succumb to inferior ones, and upright men to the perfidious ; why treachery and crime often appear stronger than fidelity and virtue—that we must not inquire of God, for His ways are past finding out,

There we have the old Adam, from whom has sprung within the space of a century so vast a progeny of hate. Comment on such a passage, save from a German, would weaken it, and there is German comment to hand. Paul Meinhold, who quotes the passage in a study of Arndt, published in 1901, says with unction in introducing it : ' Revenge and hate ! Are these feelings that can be justified in war ? How do they comply with the mild teaching of Jesus, "Love your enemies " ? Serious questions for the German soul, questions that cripple youthful energy, and the answer to which is decisive both for the character of war, and for its ends. Arndt met these scruples in his short essay " On a Nation's Hate." '

Arndt was not alone in preaching the doctrine of hate. His special contribution was the sanctification of hate. Others had glorified it, notably the dramatist Heinrich von Kleist, who in his patriotic drama *Die Hermannsschlacht*, written in 1809, had dowered the old barbarian, who slaughtered Varus and his legions, with all the attributes of pedantic cruelty and subtle treachery that his civilised descendants have so industriously acquired. ' Hate is my office, and revenge my virtue,' says Hermann when his wife, Thusnelda, pleads for the life of her would-be Roman lover, the young Ventidius ; but, out of refinement of cruelty, having left his fate in her hands, he reveals the Roman's faithlessness to her, and then reads his death in her eyes. ' Away, a she-bear has he made of me ! ' says Thusnelda to her maid, pleading for mercy for the young man, on whom her mistress in a paroxysm of rage lets loose the bear that tears him in pieces.

> My pretty one, a heroine I call thee !
> How greatly, gloriously hast thou kept thy word !

says Hermann, when husband and wife meet after their several triumphs of treachery and blood.

Among the rousing songs Kleist, like Arndt, wrote to stir up hatred of the French was one published in 1809, ' Germania to her Children,' the spirit of which is sufficiently indicated in the following verse :

> Every roadway, every homestead,
> Whiten with their bleaching bones ;
> To the fishes give the garbage
> Carrion crow or fox disowns.

> Dam the Rhine with piled-up corpses ;
> Choke him till his course he change,
> And, to mark another frontier,
> Foaming round the Pfalz he range.

So useful was this poem considered that in 1813 it was issued as a broadsheet. But in the interval its passionate author had shot himself, after shooting the woman he loved !

The lesson taught by men like Arndt and Kleist sank into the hearts of the generation to which it was addressed, and of each succeeding generation, gaining strength as years went on, until this doctrine of hate culminated in the orgy which has marked the second decade of the twentieth century. Sand, the murderer of Kotzebue, might, so far as his age went, have been ' the boy Robert' whom Arndt bade swear ' a hot and bloody hate.' The Follens were but carrying out Arndt's principles when they made the eyes of their young auditors in the lecture-room see red. Treitschke (*History*, ii. p. 543) makes merry in his German fashion over the importance given to the ravings of a sixteen-year-old schoolboy by their publication in the *Staatszeitung*. Disappointed by the results of Sand's achievement the ' young devil ' writes down his thoughts : ' O brave Sand, thou knewest not what dull oxen we were,' ' on every tree 'twixt here and Charlottenburg I 'd have one [of our princes] hanging ; I 'd breathe free,' and, finally, ' to kill the whole thirty-eight of them is a simple matter, the work of a moment.' From this young hopeful in the early years of the nineteenth century to the morbid young monsters who occupied the stage of Frank Wedekind's *Frühlings Erwachen*, and shocked Treitschke's old age, the transition provided by the scheme of German education was quite an easy one.

Leaving, however, out of account other ugly passions than hate, it is to be accepted as a commonplace not only that the passion of hate is rooted in the German nature, but that Germans know it and count on it. Bismarck, who must be allowed to have known his countrymen well, says in his *Reflections and Reminiscences*, c. xiii. : ' In order that German patriotism should be active and effective . . . the German needs either attachment to a dynasty or the goad of anger, hurrying him into action.' But Bismarck, like other Germans, forgot that anger and hate are capricious in their operation ; and the history of our own time may show that the goad of anger will suddenly destroy even the German nation's attachment to a dynasty.

We may conclude our discussion of a somewhat sultry theme, which is drawing uncomfortably near our own day, by working back to the poets of the forties, and by giving two full-blooded sonnets by Herwegh and Strachwitz respectively, from which we can form some idea of a self-respecting German's conception of freedom and the attitude he should take up to God :

FREEDOM

O Freedom, Freedom, not in blazing light
Where anthems echo through the princely fane—
Thy haunt 's the cottage of some lonely swain,
Thy choice, like Philomel's, the stilly night.
Thou shun'st the marble palace feast-bedight,
The revellers and the wine-spilt purple stain,
And in the poor man's hut, where tears like rain
On empty goblets drip, thou stay'st thy flight.
An angel, gliding through the prison gate,
Thou smilest on thy tortured votary,
Whose clanking chains make heavenly harmony.
Ah no, not thine the temple's haughty state,
To bid us sink our pride on bended knee !
Wouldst thou be Freedom if we knelt to thee ?

THE GOD OF FREEDOM

Ere God the Eternal's work on earth was done
His breath informed that child of Heaven, man's Soul,
Engend'ring courage like a burning coal,
Courage like flame, to fight till the end be won.
God said : ' Thou shalt not like a coward run
In flight before the press of teen and dole ;
Mid clouds of war that darkly round thee roll
Thou shalt bestride the coursers of the sun.
Thou shalt not sue the Almighty on bended knee,
Look upward to yon azure vault sublime,
Before the God of Freedom stand thou free.
Him crawling in the dust I may not see,
Him whom I made, the heir to dateless Time ;
Only the Free Heaven's arduous steep can climb.'

It is but a step from the sublime to the ridiculous, and it is one the German frequently takes. At a University Extension Meeting some years ago, Professor Erich Marcks, then of

Heidelberg, gave a lecture on Bismarck to the young people who flock to these gatherings like pigeons after corn, and telling them of Bismarck's deep religious feeling, he said : ' His soul needed a personal God as a staff to support his powerful and weighty personality.' [1]

[1] *Lectures on the History of the Nineteenth Century.*   Cambridge, 1902.

CHAPTER VII

THE BERLINER OF 1848 AND GLASSBRENNER
HIS CHRONICLER

To appreciate fully the events of 1848 in Berlin itself it is
desirable to form a mental picture of its population. The
latter was not simply divided into reactionaries and revolutionaries. There was a large middle-class in carpet slippers,
which looked on, sucking long-stemmed pipes with china bowls.
Between this class and the populace proper no love was lost.
The most lifelike pictures of Berlin life before the revolution
are to be found in the works of Adolf Glassbrenner,[1] who, under
the *nom de plume* of Brennglas, made it his mission to introduce
into German literature the men and women of the people who
had hitherto found no reflex in its pages. He came of middle-
class stock himself and was educated at a good school, but left
early to enter business. Here there was little scope for the gift
of wit and humour, of mimicry and satire in prose and verse,
which had distinguished him as a boy. His intellectual interests
stirred him to attend the lectures of the great philosopher of his
youth, Hegel himself ; but he emerged with his sense of humour
unimpaired, and a still livelier interest in men and things than
in ideas. He soon took to journalism, and poured out an interminable series of satires, skits, sketches, and homilies, which
caught the popular taste and made him one of the greatest
literary forces of the time. The literary school of Young
Germany, and the succeeding school of revolutionary poets,
headed by Herwegh, fired the professional classes and the
academic youth, but left the people cold. Glassbrenner
absorbed their message and transmitted it to the common folk,
for whom he felt a sympathy as keen as his contempt for the
flunkey of a German court, or the Philistine of the middle-class.

One feature marks the Berlin dialect, which he freely used,
viz. the prevalence of French words in it. This is not surpris-

---

[1] See Rodenhauser's *A. Glassbrenner.*

ing if the half-forgotten fact be recalled that Berlin owed its
initial prosperity to the influence and ability of the French
Huguenots who poured into it after the Revocation of the Edict
of Nantes (1685). Over fifteen thousand French refugees, on
the invitation of the Great Elector, settled in his dominions,
much to the annoyance of Louis xiv. At the end of the Thirty
Years' War the population of Berlin was only six thousand.
In 1688 it was twenty thousand, largely composed of French,
Flemish, and Bohemian elements. 'One man in ten was a
Frenchman,' says Daniel the Geographer. The proportion was
probably higher. In Frederick the Great's time French influence was paramount and the nomenclature of the streets and
places included many French names. The palace of 'Sans-
souci,' Gendarmenmarkt, Pariser Platz, Charlottenburg Allée,
Sieges Allée are cases in point, and the Berlin popular dialect
bristled with French words. Brav, amour, cour, flakkon,
populace, populär, conducteur, pomade, palais, terrasse, livrée,
nummer, restauration, cavalier, paradies, vesper, gondeln,
geniren, rentier and hundreds of similar words were found in the
Volkssprache, have remained, and have been carried to every
part of the German Empire. This knowledge of French was
not due as Lord Stratford de Redcliffe said to the German lady
' because the French troops had occupied the capital so often.'
It dates from an earlier day, and French names and terms
became so rooted in the language that all the efforts of the
German *Sprachverein* purists have not succeeded in eradicating
them.

From time to time Glassbrenner collected his sketches,
revised them and published them in volume form. A characteristic work of this kind was issued in 1847 under the title of
Berliner Volksleben. The introduction to this gives a statement
of the mission he had imposed on himself, and is worth comparing, from the point of view of style, with the irony of the Judæo-
Germans, Heine and Börne. Here are a number of extracts
strung together :

DEDICATION TO APOLLO

(*To serve as Preface*)

Celestial Jester of the World ! Most venerable Deity ! I here
present to your Highborn Worship my live figures of the people,
who in the year 1832 A.D. (I trust you understand this chronology)

sprang suddenly into German literature, and made way and room for themselves, most unceremoniously, amid the crowd of genteel ghosts who alone had hitherto held the stage. ' Ghosts ? ' Yes, ghosts of German literature you will find these figures that move through our elegantly pale and perfumed romances and plays. Instead of real men and women you will find shadow figures, phantoms of abstraction grinning with book-born souls and played-out sentiments. Was it not indeed necessary to make true men and women arise amidst this genteel rabble ? Was there not urgent need to emancipate the people in literature *first* ? ' Not in beer and brandy ' the enemy may say, ' but *in vino veritas* ' ! I can smile at the quibble, for the jurisdictio secularis of common sense will not let the joke pass. Are not beer and brandy the people's wine ? And is it not just such wine that any sane nature misses in the paper salons of modern plays and novels, where people have nothing to drink but that vile concoction tea, extracted from dried and withered leaves over which they have poured their own water ?

I know the frontiers of Art—they are the only ones that I respect. I have never been a smuggler—never striven to convey ignoble merchandise out of the realm of life into the region of Art. No, I never leave the most commonplace subject until, without loss of naïveté and truth, it has acquired shapeliness and charm ; and Your Well-born Self once told me that in moulding my glasses I ever sought to lend them that form which would turn the meanest liquor into wine. A pupil of Heine, am I ? No, I am no man's pupil ; my model is life.

> A spot of earth, however small,
> That little spot my own I call !

We are separated from the people by everything, by distorted custom and education, by money, by our speech, by our clothes and by that phantom of ' honour ' which leads the elect by the nose. Till we (the writers) join hands with the people and come to an understanding with them no true freedom is possible. The highest and most immediate task of literature is to teach the people to know itself, to awake it from its sordid daily round and teach it to enjoy interest on its immeasurable wealth. Not the despot and reactionary alone are to blame for the people's ignorance. No, those also are to blame who think that literature is for a caste, who seek the fulness of life in scrutinising a worn-out copper coin for an obliterated date, while a wealth of uncoined gold is lying at their feet ; who live and move and have their being in the mouldy atmosphere of the past, and turn their backs on the present and the future. Yes, and the critical and philosophical pug-dogs that bark at everything ungenteel, and the impudent flies that defile with their filth the mirror of God himself, and those intellectual midges that only dance in the sunlight in hope of sucking somebody else's blood.

It is just these imposing impositions, with all the defects and

none of the qualities of the German stock, who vent their pitying
scorn on a literature of the people. They judge high and low by
externals. They take the husk for the kernel. One can put the
question to them a hundred times : Before God, or, to use their
jargon, before the Absolute Idea, does a prince stand higher in art
and knowledge than the working-man ? They are silent and—
cleave to their folly. They will rather emancipate their horses
and dogs than the people, whom they call the mob. A shoemaker
with his cobbler's wax does more to make the world move than a
fool with his degree of Ph.D. The great Thinker on ' The World
and Time ' was right : the most insufferable, and most stupid, of
animals is a learned pig. The more doctors of philosophy, the
more patients ! ' True humane culture,' says Ludwig Börne, ' I
find amongst the people, and the real mob amongst the cultured.'

In conclusion I beg of thee, O world-rejoicing Jester, to read this
book of mine before some gay evening company at Jupiter's, and,
if it fails not utterly to please them, let fall a good word or two
anent my immortality, to wit : preserve me from it !

Glassbrenner had a passionate devotion for his native town,
and as a specimen of his sometimes glorified doggerel may be
given his ode to Berlin :

BERLIN

Though I see no soaring mountain and no flower-bespangled lea,
Yet the German oaktree's shadow veils the waters of the Spree ;
Though the golden grape is absent and the vineyard's mantling green,
Under thy dull smock both honour and nobility are seen.

Though thou hast not risen laurelled from a bloodstained field of fate,
Victory's goddess stands thine emblem on the Brandenburger gate ;
Though no sea to sordid venture and to greedy gain gives birth,
Yet the banner of thy spirit floats on all the seas of earth.

Though the simple robe thou wearest have but scorn as its award,
In the great heart of thy manhood is the spirit of the Lord,
In the soft hearts of thy women springs eternal innocence ;
And with pride I must regard thee, thou proud royal residence.

Though no nightingale thy woodlands consecrates with silver tones,
Yet the chisel of thy sculptors conjures anthems from thy stones,
And thy memory haunted palace soars majestic from the ground,
Gazing like a world-worn monarch mild-eyed on the world around.

And where'er the eye may wander tower buildings great and fair,
And all human art and learning reach their highest glory there,
For, Berlin, Great Frederick's spirit in thy heart is still aflame,
And to him thou look'st to teach thee to be worthy of his fame.

Looks a people strong and prudent, armed and armoured by their need
Straining resolute and restless towards the day-dawn of the freed.
Looks a people which though burdened with a legacy of sin
Still lifts up a head courageous and a glowing heart within.

So with all my heart I greet thee, city wondrous and sublime,
Now the golden seed-corn sowing of a golden harvest time.
Keep the laurel-wreath unwilted that the gods place in thy hand,
And let tears of joy bedew it from the German Fatherland.

And two of his photographic vignettes of the city by day
and night give some indication of the stuff he got the lower
middle-class and the working-man to read in prose :

BERLIN AT DAWN

It is four o'clock in the morning. The old watchman muffled in
furs, the pike-armed, horn-bearing announcer of the passing hour,
pipes out the end of night and leaves the dawning day to itself
and its whims. The silent washerwoman, with her cotton apron
and flapping bonnet, appears with the little lantern that lights her
way to ever renewed and never ending toil. The English gas
companies' myrmidons run up their little ladders and turn out the
street lamps, wondering why the sun should illuminate the world
gratis. The bakers' boys carry along in their rattling carts the
daily bread to the victuallers in the neighbourhood—their morning
rolls, milk buns and biscuits, and those ' salt-cakes ' which are
not cakes and not salt. The hands of the church clock continue
inexorably their Prussian progress. Peasant women with tired
faces stream in from the neighbouring villages in their wooden
carts ; the large carts drawn by horses, the small ones by tugging
dogs, bringing to the city those commodities the cow was created
to furnish. House doors begin to open with a creak as if they
objected to being disturbed so early. Labourers and workmen
are going to their work. The golden morning has come. The
houses wake up, shake the dreams out of their roofs, yawn through
their chimneys, open their window-eyes and stretch themselves
with rattling of bolts and locks. Every one takes up his daily
duty, drinking the last gulp of his morning coffee without a thought
that he is going to add another day to the history of the world.
How the latest bit of it looks we may learn from that serving-maid
of Clio dispensing from her basket the *Vossische Zeitung* and other
samples of the ' good ' and ' half-bad ' press. Long rows of cabs
' rush ' like snails to the railway stations. Shoeblacks, clad like
writers for the press in the rags they have begged, run with black-
ing and cane from one gentleman's lodgings to another, freeing,
alas, only their boots from filth, knocking the dust, alas, out of
their clothes alone. A black hearse jolts slowly along as if weary
of this always-the-sameness, its wheels creaking out their dismal

memento mori. Six black coaches follow in its train, for he who
is being borne back to mother earth was a successful man. The
highest aims of the Berliner's 'life' are decorations and funeral
coaches. 'Do that again and I'll knock your brains out,' shouts
angrily a carpenter's apprentice, wheeling a cart laden with a big
bedstead and a small cradle, to a cobbler's boy who has jostled him.
'That's something I couldn't do to you!' retorts the latter.
This cobbler's boy has more mother wit and understanding than
that arrogant 'Herr Councillor,' distant relation to some flunkey
in the employ of 'His Excellency the Minister,' more real brain
power than that 'Herr Professor' exhibiting out of a window the
portion of his body where his intellect ought to be, while from a
window in the floor above him protrudes the long pipe of a gentleman of means, gazing on the crowd below, wondering what can
be the aim in life of those who do not serve society in the capacity
of a gentleman of means.

BERLIN BY NIGHT

The little candles in the attic still light the poor citizen at his
hard work. Carriages dash hither and thither to balls and suppers.
The billiard-balls click in the restaurants. The glasses clink in the
taverns. There in a first-floor flat is gathered a gay company in
which a political toast has just been drunk with noisy joyousness.
The lighted clock on the Academy points to nine. It is a fateful
hour for the street-walkers, on whose diminution and reclamation
the police edicts have just so much influence as the censor's ban on
the so-called 'bad press.' The small fry, the newspapers and
pamphlets are strictly dealt with : books of twenty sheets are
exempt. Only the populace are under surveillance, the upper
classes can do what they like. And yet diplomacy, ambition,
hypocrisy, gentility are harlots compared with whose demoralisation and demoralising influence all the harlots in all the great cities
of the world are saints. The carillon of the parish church in the
Klosterstrasse casts far across the city the music of the hymn :

> ' We wander through this vale of tears,
> Oppressed by sorrows, pains and fears,
> Our sojourn here is brief ;
> God calls us from this night away
> To regions of eternal day,
> Where ceases every grief.

> The choiring saints in Heaven above,
> And blessèd souls on earth I love,
> They are my brothers all. . . .'

The night watchman appears. He cries ' Ten o'clock!' and
locks all the doors on his beat. Two policemen order two gay
rollers to take the cigars out of their mouths. The silence grows.

P

A doctor's carriage hastens by ; somebody wants scientific help to die. Somebody sings somewhere : ' O Freedom, it is you ! ' Here, in a ground-floor flat they are disputing about the German Catholics and free parishes. It grows ever more silent, dark and lonely. Now and then a carriage and pair swings swiftly homeward round the corner of a street. It strikes eleven ; then twelve. The last of the thousand cab horses jogs wearily stableward with hanging head. The last tobacco shop closes. In the taverns and beer-houses there is still noise enough. In the distance sounds faintly the music of a serenade. The stars twinkle, the world goes to bed and whoever has not to struggle with sorrow or care or pain sleeps. God watches.

Good-night !

Glassbrenner's stage is occupied by figures from the working and lower-middle classes, and the titles of his sketches give an idea of their scope. An Excursion into the Country, A Wedding Festivity, A Fancy Ball, and similar sketches depict with a skill sometimes worthy of Dickens scenes from the people's life. The dramatis personæ are all very similar. Those of the Wedding Festivity include, for instance, a master baker and his family, a young shopkeeper, a journeyman plasterer, cousin to the bride, a butcher friend and a maid-of all-work. Cockney-ism of the old Berlin type is the badge of all the tribe, a ready wit being a feature in some cases and a dull sameness of view regarding life and society an almost universal one. One acquires a vivid picture of old Berlin, the Berlin of a generation before the day when the old semi-Huguenot stock of Frederick the Great's time was swamped by the flood of blatant *parvenus* and *arrivistes* who have turned Berlin into the most vulgar, gaudy, godless, gilt and guilty capital in Europe.

The middle-class type is treated with contempt. The bourgeois is presented to us with a curious mixture of vulgarity, petty cunning and Sancho Panza-like simplicity, but the man of the people is redeemed by a sly mother-wit and a political *gouaillerie* denied to the class above him. How far Glassbrenner goes in caricaturing the former may be judged from the following picture of Herr Buffey at his daughter's wedding. 'Herr Buffey really lived in Berlin ' asserts the author. ' He was the pro-prietor of a small tobacco shop in the *Kommandantenstrasse* and the meanness of his actual circumstances were in curious contrast to his airs of importance.'

Herr Buffey (getting up from his chair in such a strange manner that he smashes two glasses on the table and upsets a bottle of wine over the cloth) : Doesn't matter a bit, I can afford it. What's use of bein' a man of meansh if I can't ? That's why I'm so happy. Ye've eckshpresht opinion 'bout ze wine—passed judgment, so to shay. I'll tell ye my 'pinion too, yes, I will. I'll make a speech. Der wine ish heavenly ! Der wine ish godlike ! Der wine ish gra-aschful ! Der wine ish shupernat'ral ! Der wine ish ver' brave ! Der wine ish inshpr-shpirin'. Der wine ish—der wine ish—(*sits down, and rises immediately*). B'shides when I want to have a weddin' I'll have one. I'm a man of meansh ! An' now I'm goin' to drink the health of my daughter and shon-in-law, without forgettin' my dignity. Zat's what I'm goin' to do ! An' whoever won't clink his glass with me's no good fellow. An' if it's a lady she's a bad woman—yes she is ! Now, Hoch !—nay that'll not do ; everybody must drink wi' me. I'm the bride'sh father, an' I can afford it. I've got the coin. Now, Hoch ! my daughter an' shon-in-law. Dat's all right ! Now I'm goin' to propose another toast : Long live the newly married couple ! Hoch ! again, Hoch ! An' third time, Hoch ! (*He sinks down in o his seat and closes his eyes.*)

But what gave Glassbrenner his importance as a force in pre-revolutionary Berlin was the art with which he instilled into the populace the ideas of constitutional reform and of German unity agitating so many of the intellectuals of Germany, chafing under all the pretentiousness of princely rule, the caste system, military caste, official caste, land-owning caste, on which it rested, and the instruments of oppression, notably the purblind censorship, which it wielded. With the intellectuals the middle-class Philistine was only a secondary object of attack, and there they made a profound mistake. The comparative failure of the revolution showed the strength of German Philistinism ; no seed of divine discontent had been implanted in that fat and greasy soil. For Glassbrenner to attack this middle-class Philistinism quite as keenly as he did any portion of the Prussian or the Metternichian systems shows his shrewdness.

For an example of the ceaseless fun he poked at the government of the day, let us take his description of the chaff scattered round a fallen horse in the streets of Berlin.

THE FALLEN HORSE

Hodman. Here, driver ! If I'm not mistaken your horse has fallen.

Driver. Pity he didn't fall on your head, and then we'd have had oats in plenty !

Bricklayer. Cabby, cabby, oblige me by lettin' your horse lie : he 's long sown his wild oats, and wants a rest. This Andalusian steed is busted.

Street Arab. Good Lord, what beautiful bones, but, Mr. Coachman, you forgot to put your Arab's flesh on this morning.

Haberdasher. Ye 're mistaken, my son ! This is no Arab, but a pure blood-horse, sire Hector, dam Birchpiper.

Newsboy. Look here, I 've six copies of the *Staatszeitung* ; put them under your patriotic gelding, and the leading articles will make him sit up. Even a horse could not stand them. *(The horse struggles to his feet.)* There, I told you ; he got a fright ; he 's a knowing beast !

Next, let us listen to a party of wood-choppers, an important class in Berlin, discussing emigration to America over their midday meal :

Flöter (cutting himself a piece of bacon). I was at Perlewitzen's last night, an'. . . .

Habermann (reaching for his bottle of schnaps). What are ye alwiz doin' at Perlewitzen's ?

Flöter. W'y we alwiz 'ave a game of ' solo,' the four ov us ev'ry Thursday reg'lar ; only none ov us generally turns up. An' as there was nothin' else to do I read the paper ; what else can ye do when there 's nothin' sensible ye can be at ? I was readin' about folk goin' all the time to America. The devil only knows what 's takin' them there. Don't it say somewhere : stay at 'ome an' . . . munch, munch, munch . . . to earn an honest livin' ?

Sherwitzky. Seems to me, that 'ere proverb 's a bit stupid. First, there 's countries where ye can't earn a livin' at all, and then there 's, or I 'm thinkin', countries where maybe ye can't earn enough to live. So long as ye 've somethin' to bite an' the police leaves ye alone, 'tain't very pleasant to leave yer own country.

Flöter. An' are there no police in America ?

Habermann (drawing the cork from his bottle). God forbid ! There 's freedom in America. Ye can smoke as much as ye want to, an' stick dibs in yer weskit pocket ev'ry day in life.

Flöter. Ye don't say so !

Habermann. Don't I ! The servants sit at the same table as the quality, an' bolt the same grub, an' when a chap 's got a dib to spare he can go to the theayter wiv'out any police sargint to tell 'im when to clap 'is 'ands. But I fear America won't be a free republic much longer.

Flöter. W'ye so ?

Habermann. There 's too many Germans goin' across !

Flöter. W'y don't any Americans come to Germany ?

Habermann. Aye, Sherwitzky my son, what can ye say about that ? An' the Americans can read in our royal newspapers 'ow 'appy we Germans are ! 'Tis a wonder to me 'ow the Americans can be so silly an' not come across to share our luck.

Scherwitzky. Listen now, if ye think the Americans are silly
·e 're barkin' up the wrong tree. Look at the way they knocked
ense into the English !
Flöter. D' ye mean they knocked sense into the English or the
·nglish into them ?
Scherwitzky. Nobody could knock sense into you !
Flöter. A sheep's head like you couldn't any way !
Scherwitzky. I 'll try. (*Clouts him playfully over the head.*)

Both on the literary and political side Glassbrenner's supreme
·chievement was his adoption of the Peep-Show Man as a
·ehicle for the expression of his criticisms of men and things.
·Ie won thus a permanent place in the history of German letters,
·r he founded on his Peep Show a new literature. Just as in
·he days of ancient Rome extreme candour with regard to their
·asters was a recognised privilege of the slaves during the
·aturnalia, and as the spectators at a Spanish bull-fight could
·url with impunity the most drastic criticisms at their auto-
·ratic rulers whether of the Crown or of the Inquisition ; so in
·re-revolutionary days in Berlin a certain freedom, despite
·olice and censorship, was enjoyed by a class of popular writers
·ho produced the so-called Peep Show Literature. Glass-
·renner was the first to use this fictitious character for that type
·f keen political criticism later embodied in those *Witzblätter* of
·hich *Kladderadatsch* became the most shining example. The
·llowing specimen of Glassbrenner's peep-show criticism shows
·is art at its highest :

THE PEEP SHOW

Dorothea (*the Peep-Show Man's wife*). Heavens ! How cold it
to-day. Folk might imagine themselves in Siberia !
The Peep-Show Man (*an old soldier with a wooden leg*). Do you
·ink so, beauteous fifty-year-old partner of my lot ? Well there
· a touch of Siberia about Berlin to-day. The difference is that in
·iberia they hunt sables and in Berlin they hunt authors. (*To
·e passer-by.*) Walk up, ladies and gentlemen ! Here you can
·joy the world-history of the past year, with kings and emperors
·rown in, for the sum of one halfpenny—and a very fair price it
· too. Don't be afraid ; only three persons can look on at once,
· there is no ' unlawful assembly,' and my patter is of such an
·cessively loyal nature that you run no risk of being arrested
·r listening to it. Now here, ladies and gentlemen, here you have
· picture of the statue recently erected to the memory of the late
·vered Emperor Francis of Austria. The erection of this monument

was a work of great difficulty for they could find no solid foundation for it. His Majesty was just such a great and exalted sove reign as the rest of them. Under the paternal rule of this great monarch, who always had the good of his country at heart, the present thirty kreuzer pieces were first coined, being worth six kreuzers apiece. When dying this great monarch bequeathed ' all his love ' to his ' dear people,' while his own relatives were cut off with fifty million thalers! This touching and unforgettable trait of a royal and imperial heart will inspire other sovereigns for generations to come.

Here, ladies and gentlemen, is Donna Maria da Floria, the present Queen of Lisbon, where the earthquakes come from. She has upset the constitution because she feels ' happy in the love of her people,' and the constitution induced her happy people to object to her way of loving them. His Highness, her Coburg-prince consort, is standing beside her and approving thoroughly, because you see, he came from Germany. Under the table you see the constitution and through the window you can see the sun setting in all his majesty. That is the queen with the golden crown on her head, and those bare-headed people standing round are her supporters.

Boy at the peep-hole. But where's the happy people ?

Peep-Show Man. They're nowhere to be seen! And now ladies and gentlemen, we see His Majesty the King of Denmark sending his ' open letter ' [1] to the ' ocean-bounded ' [2] Schleswig Holsteiners, telling them he means to be king of the ocean-bounded too. The ocean-bounded forget themselves so far as to be displeased and then Germany gets displeased, and then the King of Denmark gets displeased, and so everybody is displeased.

First Boy. What do the Schleswig-Holsteiners want ?

Peep-Show Man. They want to be German.

Second Boy. Is that all ?

First Boy. I thought they wanted to be free ?

Peep-Show Man. That's their affair ; you can't have everything

First Boy. And what's the end of it all ?

Peep-Show Man. Oh, we sing ' Schleswig-Holstein ocean-bounded ' and nothing happens to anybody.—And now, ladies and gentle men, you see a picture of the New Year 1847. You will observe that the upper part of 1847 is too fat ; he has a paunch like a parson while the limbs that support him suffer from emaciation and decay of the bone and sinew. In his right hand he holds a whip and in his left a rotten potato [3] in place of the imperial orb. Herewith is the world history at an end !

A petty official at one of the peep-holes. Good day ! (*He retires backwards.*)

First Boy. Look at that chap walking backwards.

Second Boy. Of course, he's a courtier !

---

[1] See page 157. [2] See page 189.
[3] See page 157.

The Peep-Show man goes off singing :

> Oh, a Prussian am I, and my flag black and white,
> Is a badge of the struggle 'twixt darkness and light.
> That my fathers for freedom of yore fought and fell
> Is a fact that no man from the present could tell.
> Theirs was the day of do and dare ;
> Ours is the day of grin and bear ;
> And if I don't like it, I must not complain,
> Born a German was I and a German remain.

It was on this world depicted by Glassbrenner that the storm burst in March 1848. Those who dreamed, like Uhland, Görres, Glassbrenner, and many another noble spirit, of a German state and a German parliament based on the suffrages of the people, reckoned without Germany's dynastic tradition, without the Prussian army, without the official caste and its blind inert allies, strong only in their dull passivity, Herr Buffey and his kind. Some of these dreamers of the forties lived on to 1870, and, rubbing their eyes in the sixties, persuaded themselves that Bismarck had made their dreams come true. Not among these was Glassbrenner. He remained an idealist in the non-German, non-Hegelian sense, and kept a warm heart for mankind. ' Our good angels,' he wrote in 1870, ' show sympathy neither for Germany nor France. 'Tis for the war they weep.' And again : ' This war is a glorious one for us, but—a war ! ! While one is proud to be a German, one is ashamed to be a Man.' He fondly dreamed that United Germany, now at last to be achieved, might express its will through a parliament whose constitution the people should fashion for themselves. And when he found that government alone was to draw up the constitution for the new Empire, he sang in December, 1870, a last complaint that showed his principles were still those of 1848 :

> They build, and build, and never rest,
> Our masters, O how wise !
> They 've stone and timber of the best ;
> They 'll plan some grand surprise.

> The house doth like a palace grow,
> When looked at from afar,
> But seems, as people nearer go,
> A barracks, bolt and bar !

BOOK IV

REVOLUTION

1848

CHAPTER I

FERMENT THROUGHOUT GERMANY

WE have now reached the month of March 1848, the *mensis mirabilis* of revolution in Germany. In that single month, and following on the Paris revolution of February, were crowded more exciting events than in any month before August 1914. King Ludwig of Bavaria had to abdicate, and King Frederick William IV. of Prussia had to bow bare-headed before the mutilated bodies of the men his soldiers had shot down in the streets of Berlin, and to ride round the city in a motley procession with the revolutionary colours on his arm, and, at his own request, flaunted before him. Metternich, the indispensable found dispensable, barely escaped from Vienna with his life, and had to make his way by devious paths—to England. Lola Montez, King Ludwig's Egerian mistress, had to fly—to England. The Prince of Prussia himself, the *Helden-kaiser* of 1870, had to shave his chin and, in disguise, to seek refuge from Berlin—in England. England, the asylum which, in headlong flight from Paris, Louis Philippe had sought a few weeks earlier!

To describe the crisis in each of the German states would be an endless task, and we shall not attempt it here. The main centres of interest are Vienna and Berlin, and of what took place there, and particularly in Berlin, we shall give an account detailed enough to satisfy even an Irish appetite for what, not to give offence, we may call sudden change. Nevertheless before we stand awed by the humiliation of Hapsburg and Hohenzollern, and watch the red torch of revolution light up the sluggish waters of the Spree, it is well to take a cursory glance at the situation in this eventful month of Germany in general, and, then, to indulge ourselves for a chapter in the contemplation of another passion than hate as it ran its violent German course in the Bavarian capital.

By rights the revolution should have begun in Baden. The

population was the most excitable in south Germany, and had been kept at boiling point for years by emissaries from German Switzerland, which most of the agitators expelled from Germany during the days of reaction had found a convenient *point d'appui* for operations in the Fatherland. How high were the demands of the extremists in Baden, led by Hecker and Struve, may be gauged by a broadsheet [1] setting out the programme adopted at a democratic conference at Offenburg in the autumn of 1847 :

A general arming of the people, with free choice of officers.

A German parliament freely elected by the people.

Every male German, as soon as he is twenty-one years old, to be entitled to a primary vote, and eligible as an elector. For every 1000 inhabitants an elector to be nominated, and for every 100,000 a representative in parliament. Every German without distinction of rank, position, means or religion, to be eligible as a member of this parliament as soon as he has completed his twenty-fifth year. The parliament to meet in Frankfort, and to draw up its own rules of procedure.

Unrestricted freedom of the Press.

Complete liberty of religion, of conscience, and of teaching.

Administration of justice in accordance with the national character, and trial by jury.

Universal German citizenship or franchise.

Just taxation according to income.

Well-being, education and instruction for all.

Protection of labour and the right to work.

Adjustment of the unfriendly relations existing between Capital and Labour.

Popular and economical government.

Responsibility of all Ministers and State officials.

Abolition of all privileges.

Against the extremists the authorities had the support of a strong liberal party, headed by Bassermann and Carl Mathy, one of the few attractive personalities of the time ; and this party, which succeeded in weaning the commonplace Grand Duke from police measures to some sort of constitutional government, proved a bulwark which the desperate efforts of the revolutionaries, when they did get going, could not for all the assistance of a mutinous soldiery wholly overcome. A fairly liberal government had been installed in 1846, and when

---

[1] Facsimile in Blum.

the news of the revolution in Paris arrived at the end of February 1848, the ministry, by the timely concessions of freedom of the press, trial by jury, and the institution of a National Guard, met popular demands more than half-way. The saviour of the situation was Carl Mathy, who showed that a man of moderate opinions and clear intellect, and dowered with the cool courage of conviction rather than the bravado of excitement, may play as conspicuous a part in the moment of crisis as any hero of the barricades. On 27th March, the moment the news arrived from Paris, the radicals convened a public meeting at Mannheim. Mathy took the chair and himself spoke in favour of a petition to the recently established constitutional authority, the Diet, in favour of a popular army, freedom of the press, trial by jury, and a German parliament. This petition was to be presented to the Diet at Carlsruhe on 1st March by a monster deputation gathered from all parts of the country. The Diet was thus to be taken by storm. Mathy hurried away from the meeting at Carlsruhe, represented the imminence of the danger, and by infinite address succeeded in winning from the government on the 29th the necessary concessions in advance. The sitting of the Diet on 1st March, when the concessions were announced, was a tumultuous one. Inside were the radicals, furious at the prospect of being baulked of their demonstration, outside the gathering crowds of their supporters. Hecker demanded the suspension of standing orders, in order that the petition should instantly be presented to the ministry. Angry cries from within, and the roaring of the mob without, supported him. For a brief space the chamber showed signs of weakness. But Mathy rose to his feet and declared calmly that standing orders required the petition to be referred for consideration, and the chamber was not going to allow itself to be overborne by the mob. The effect of his intervention was electrical ; members recovered their heads ; the psychological moment for revolution was past.

Thus, by the early surrender of the government, the populace were deprived of the opportunity, dear to the south German, for a revolutionary rising. But the rank and file were not to be robbed altogether of some sort of violent demonstration. Here and there peasants rose against their landlords, and, disappointed of any disposition on the part of the government to harry the people, the people in country districts proceeded to harry the Jews. The persecution that followed is thus described in the *Allgemeine Zeitung* of 9th March.[1]

A general persecution of the Jews has begun in the open country. The fugitives are making their way in groups to the towns, more especially Mannheim, where their friends reside. This popular movement takes no heed of our politicians' theories. In Bruchsal the mob of assailants, exclaiming, ' Down with the King of the Jews ! ' marched to the house of Brentano, the ultra-liberal deputy, in order to wreck it, as Brentano himself said to-day in the chamber. The intervention of the military put an end to the tumult.

In the radical party were many Jews, so that the leaders of the party of progress were not a little disconcerted by the recoil upon many of their friends of the popular forces they had themselves unchained a few days earlier. They joined with the leaders of the constitutional liberal party in issuing a spirited protest.[2]

MANNHEIM, *8th March* 1848.

With deep pain, which all true friends of popular freedom and the fatherland share, we learn that the days which fill the hearts of all honest citizens with lofty enthusiasm, the days which are to free all our people from the oppression and servitude of decades, nay of centuries, are to be profaned by blind rage of destruction, and by endangering the persons and property of our fellow-citizens of the Jewish faith, and that the shining banner of liberty is to be sullied by disgraceful excesses. . . . Fellow-citizens, we know that we speak in the name of all of you when we say : It is the sacred duty of every man of honour, who will not shamefully abuse the name of freedom, who will not misuse its name for the gratification of other passions, it is the sacred duty of all friends of liberty and the people to oppose with all their energy such an atrocious proceeding. Only servants of Reaction or those led astray by them can lend a hand in persecutions of the Jews, such as were never known in a free land, but only too well known under a despotism.

Dr. HECKER. HELMREICH. von ITZSTEIN. von SOIRON. L. WELLER. M. SACHS. CARL MATHY. FR. BASSERMANN.

It must be conceded that since the revolutionary period, and especially under the latest of the Hohenzollerns, the position of Jews throughout Germany has improved.

Saxony, like Baden, had to wait for her revolution until March was up. Trouble indeed threatened, for the King at first proved obstinate when the Paris news brought the usual demands ; his notion of dealing with the situation was to invoke the aid of the Prussian arms. Dresden itself, which

[1] Klein. [2] Klein.

was to break out in May, remained quiet. Leipzig was the centre of what movement there was in March, and there, in the centre of the German book-trade, the reform immediately pressed was the abolition of the censorship. Among the leaders of the agitation was Robert Blum, the great orator on the radical side, of whose tragic fate in Vienna we have to read in Book VI. From the following declaration [1] which appeared in the *Allgemeine Zeitung* of 8th March, it appears that even the Leipzig censors themselves were in revolt against the censorship.:

We the undersigned called on Professor Dr. Marbach at 4 o'clock P.M., in the first place to induce him to resign his office as Censor. Dr. Marbach declared that he could not reconcile an immediate resignation of his office in these grave times with his sense of duty. He, however, read us a memorial presented by the local censors to the cabinet as a whole, in which they expressed themselves against the censorship and its pernicious effects, and represented earnestly to the cabinet how undesirable they considered its continuance. Leipzig, 4th March 1848.

> ROBERT BLUM.
> Dr. HEINRICH WUTTKE, Chairman of the Authors' Union.
> E. M OETTINGER, Editor of the *Charivari*.
> Dr. ARNOLD RUGE.

If the fall of Louis Philippe did not move the King of Saxony, the news of the Vienna revolution brought him to his knees ; the censorship was abolished, a fresh Diet summoned, and a new ministry, with a strong liberal element, installed.

In Hanover the despotic Ernest Augustus forestalled serious trouble by concessions liberal enough to satisfy perhaps the least progressive of German states. And similarly with Würtemberg under its strong-willed king, though he had first to strike with the mailed fist.

Of common action by the government of the different states there was none. Local traditions and local differences, fostered by dynastic jealousies, which nourished German particularism, prevented the various currents of opinion from merging in one great stream. Of the extraordinary condition that resulted Klein gives a lively picture :

Often indeed the governments found themselves in a degrading situation ; ruling princes were objects of intense animosity but were allowed to retain their thrones ; the people were in general

---

[1] Klein.

more grim and extravagant in word than in deed. Every imaginable conception of the future form of the empire penetrated and crossed every other, whether designed on the French, Belgian or, especially, the English model. A German republic was freely and frankly dreamed of. Every one was prating and advising. ' Every one felt that in such times as those he must give vent to his ideas.' The glory of wearing a red feather in a shapeless wide-awake, of girding a sabre round one's waist, of marching out on guard with bugle and drum—the exhilaration of playing the propagandist, the fresh excitement maintained by hosts of newspapers, pamphlets and broadsheets, the suddenly revealed prospect of a new and always a ' free ' future, every emotion which is usually associated with violent personal activity, and now with combined political activity as well, all these coalesced in that high-flown, quasi-philosophic phrase-making which is characteristic of the German nature. Whenever a minister of the old regime was petitioned out of his job, ' the waving of the World Spirit's wings could be felt in the air.' A mode of speech was evolved which, in the ceaseless effort to find expressions worthy of the stupendous events taking place in the world, was often absurdly inappropriate to the pettiness of local happenings. This phrase-making degenerated, too, into coarseness and intemperance, especially in Baden, where the excitement reached its climax. . . .

Duke Ernest II. of Saxe-Coburg-Gotha, Prince Albert's elder brother, quotes in his *Memoirs* a correspondence between his people and himself which may serve as an illustration of the curious dialogues that took place in most of the lesser German states between princes and peoples. Strangely mediæval is the language used by both :

PEOPLE TO PRINCE

Concord between Prince and people, unity of all Germany, is now the cry which rises from all the well-intentioned men of the Fatherland, of the German Press and the German Confederacy. If this cry is to find an echo in the German people, as find it it must, the Press must be free, the German Confederacy must be national. But the Confederacy is only national when it is an organ of the efforts of all Germany to bring about an intrinsic unity, when it is, in the full sense of the word, representative of the German people, as well as of the German princes. Only under these conditions will an arming of the people fulfil its aim, that of preserving peace in the interior and defence against anything exterior.

Most Gracious Duke, most honoured Prince ! if it were only a question of the preservation of concord, between your Highness and your people, of a truth everything would be well with us. Your Highness has, through your noble reign, earned the thanks of your whole country. The strongest link is that which binds all those belonging to the land, particularly the Coburg Representative Assembly, to your Highness. But it is now a question of the highest and most noble possession of a great nation. The national existence of the Fatherland, that the whole German people may stand facing a common foe together like one man, can only be reached through the fulfilment of the long cherished wish and the just demands of all races of Germany for national institutions— a fulfilment which also lies in the hand of Your Highness as a member of the Confederacy.

We therefore lay this most humble declaration with confidence before our Most Gracious Duke and Sovereign, that during the next few days we shall unite in all the petitions for freedom of the Press, representation of the people in the German Confederacy, arming of the people and trial by jury, which come to our knowledge in all parts of Germany, being convinced that the Fatherland can be secured from outside dangers, and rejuvenated internally by means of the adoption of these institutions.

In consideration of the present pressing state of affairs we think, however, that it will greatly help to reassure the country if the Assemblies stand by our Most Gracious Prince. We, therefore, most humbly beg your Highness most graciously to order the immediate convocation of the Representative Assembly.

PRINCE TO PEOPLE

Burghers of my residence of Coburg, the address of the 6th of this month sent me by you affords me the welcome opportunity of expressing to you my most entire satisfaction at the quiet and lawful behaviour which you have shown during these days of universal political excitement. For the sentiments of true attachment which you expressed therein receive my warmest thanks. All this must indeed constitute a favourable omen of the promised concord.

To strengthen this concord between me and my people more and more shall be the object of my most earnest endeavours. The confidence with which you have as freely and openly expressed your wishes, as I like you to do, does my heart good ; I shall do my best to justify it. I have decided to assemble the representatives of my Duchy of Coburg on the 2nd of next month, in order to deliberate with them as to what, in this serious moment, the interests of the country demand with regard to the interests of all united Germany.

Meanwhile I shall have prepared a law to lay before them respecting the adoption of complete freedom of the Press. The latter entirely agrees with my principles, and I will gladly warrant it. A plan for a law respecting the alteration of section 79 of the Constitution will also be proposed to them, so that the right of petition and the right of the people's assembly may be freely exercised. I have already long since recognised the superiority of openness and publicity in the administration of justice by means of trial by jury, and the necessary preparatory measures for the adoption of this mode of administration were already ordered by me during the last year. My Duchy of Coburg shall also share in this institution so consonant with the times.

I will very gladly lend a helping hand to the adoption of the policy of arming the people, which lightens the burden of the standing armies of the Confederate States, and affords the necessary defence for the safety of the Confederacy. I shall hold a consultation with regard to this with the allied German Princes. Until then, wherever it will be possible to establish the universal arming of the people, I shall gladly allow a guard of burghers in the towns. A proposed law for the taking of the oath by the military on the constitution will be laid before the Assembly.

As a man of German sentiments and filled with the warmest love for the Fatherland, I most willingly joined the Confederate Princes, who recognise the representation of the German nation in the Confederacy to be the most effective means of strengthening Germany and furthering her common interests. I have already instructed my envoys to the Confederate Diet to support the proposal of a universal German Parliament as strongly as possible.

Burghers of Coburg, may these declarations furnish you with a proof of my great willingness to fulfil wishes which accord with the real wants of the times. Stand by me further with tried faithfulness, that we may maintain public quiet and order in these uneasy times. I confidently place them under your protection.

Of the broadsheets flying around, one [1] published at Mannheim in March 1848, and republished in Berlin, on the German, the revolutionary, colours is among the most striking :

Black, Red and Gold, these are the colours
We Germans proudly bear on high ;
Black, Red and Gold, these are the colours
For which in fight we gladly die.

The Black betokens death to tyrants
Who laughing nailed us to the tree ;
And Red's the blood we poured as offering
For Justice and for Liberty.

But Gold is freedom's blossoming
That men, their duty done, may see ;
So fly on highways and on by-ways
The sacred German colours three.

Black, Red and Gold, these are the colours
Fill every German eye with pride ;
Black, Red and Gold, with that fair harvest
Teems all the German countryside.

---

[1] Friedländer Collection, City Library, Berlin.

As for the press, L. Häusser, the historian, and himself a Liberal, wrote thus of the Radical press in the *Allgemeine Zeitung* : [1]

It may be much cheaper to join in the usual halloo, and to swell the crowd of those who court the people ; there are therefore, as Börne says, still plenty of worthy people to grasp the horny hand of an honest man. Since journals here and there have begun to put themselves outside of, and above, public opinion ; since the whole trashy crowd of literary pauperism and nihilism is hanging on to others who hang on to the cause of a sound and free development of the people, and talks so big ; it is high time in the name of the most important interests of German freedom to lodge an energetic protest against any alliance with frivolity, crudeness and ignorance.

Duke Ernest, from whom we have quoted above, was not without a sense of humour. Heavy and involved might be the German he wrote himself, but he had a keen eye for these defects in others, and he gives in his *Memoirs* a choice example from the *Coburg Gazette* of the extravagant language admitted by Klein to be characteristic of the German nature. It would indeed be difficult to match in any language but German a sentence like this : ' Disgrace and shame to the enemies of the Fatherland, who wish to scatter a seed of princes' teeth in the cleared fields of our time, without reflecting that this Cadmus seed must itself produce a generation of strangling despots ! ' And the Duke goes on : ' The republican local sheets were all edited by a breed of unpolished creatures who favoured their readers every day with the craziest appeals for, and provocations to, civil war, all couched in crude language and full of the most vulgar spirit imaginable.'

Two extracts,[2] from *Fliegender Blätter* and another comic paper of the time, give us some indication of the peasants' point of view :

BEAUTIFUL DREAM OF A THURINGIAN PEASANT

I wish that I could be the Prince, just for a few months. I would then have all those stags in the Schwarzburger game enclosure slaughtered, and the dirty old church in the Black Valley pulled down again. No hare would be allowed to show itself in the country ; and then I would abolish the Governments and the Consistories, also the soldiers and those taxes. I would get our

---

[1] Klein.　　　　[2] Facsimiles in Blum.

schoolmaster to do the writing that might be necessary—it wouldn't amount to much, and I would finish up by giving the Town Bailiff a good hiding.

THE DUKE WANTS 'THE BEST'

Bailiff. Well then, farmers, now you have heard that the Duke wants nothing but the best *for* you.

A peasant farmer. Yes, we have known long enough that he wants the best *from* us, but that is just what we 're not going to give him.

Illuminating flashes on the attitude of the intellectuals of Germany in the early days of revolution are given by the letters from philosophers and poets which follow. In dealing with Germans it is well to begin with the philosophers, for, as will be noted, they think much of their comfort, and to keep them waiting might irritate them. We give a letter from Strauss[1] to an old fellow-student named Rapp, pastor at Enslingen, and one from Feuerbach [2] to his wife :

HEILBRONN, 29*th February* 1848.

What sort of an effect has the fall of Louis Philippe, and the proclamation of the republic, made in Enslingen ? . . . The news surprised me very much as the Roman soldier did Archimedes. A French criminal process, of which full reports are given in the *National* . . . had been keeping me for several days from other papers. So I was sitting on Saturday at work over my extracts . . . when my servant came in and handed me the special edition of the *Mercury*, which gave the announcement of Louis Philippe's abdication, and I was not a little astonished ; but I had to finish my article on the *affaire Léotade* before giving myself up to the impression of the still more astounding news that came with every post. What times are beginning, my dearest Rapp! And I believe that at the bottom of it all we can only gain. I at least do not know anything worth mentioning that I could lose. During the night after the news reached us of the proclamation of the republic this was my first thought when several times during the night I awoke. . . . After all it is only the realisation of our most youthful wishes, of our inmost thoughts. It may be that amidst the events which await us we may long for the tranquillity of the days of yore ; it may be that we are getting too much exercise, as we have hitherto had too little. It is also true that too much in this way is better than too little—and also pleasant if one understands oneself rightly. Good-bye, Citizen Rapp—don't tell any one you have been a Court Councillor and remain as good in the new era as in the past.

---

[1] Zeller's *Ausgewählte Briefe.*
[2] K. Grün, *L. Feuerbach in seinem Briefwechsel.* (K.)

LEIPZIG, *3rd April* 1848.

It is a time when everything is at stake. For the safest mortgages no ready money is to be had here. On all sides bankruptcy or at least temporary suspension of payment, because every one wants to feather his nest and buries his talent, *i.e.* his money. Wigand [Feuerbach's publisher] has to collect about two hundred thousand thalers from one thousand firms. He will think himself lucky and well out of it if even half of it is paid by Eastertide. . . . One must now limit one's self to bare necessities and be content if one has even a morsel of bread. . . . My winter coat oppresses me in this heat, and I really hesitate at this time to buy myself a new one.

Of the poets' letters the first is by Freiligrath,[1] the second is by Gottfried Keller,[2] the Swiss, and the third is addressed to Herwegh by Robert Prutz.[3]

FERDINAND FREILIGRATH TO ARNOLD RUGE

LONDON, *6th March* 1848.

Where deeds and events agitate the minds of men, verses are naturally superfluous. When History herself, when Demos is in the act of composition, the poet can for the time and without blushing keep silence. What matters the reflection of the immense world-epic in the mind of the lyrical bystander ? Nevertheless, in the feverish joy of the first news I dashed off the enclosed [a revolution poem]. I have flung two thousand copies at the . . . Rhine. . . .

As far as I am personally concerned for the moment, let me say that I was on the point of embarking for Boston with wife and children (at Longfellow's invitation), when this glorious storm burst forth which has retained me for the present.

GOTTFRIED KELLER TO WILHELM BAUMGÄRTNER

HEIDELBERG, *12th March* 1849.

There is considerable ferment among the people here once more. But I hardly wish anything to break out in the near future, at least I should not like to be in Heidelberg during a revolution, for I have nowhere seen a more coarse and more depraved proletariat than here. No one is sure of his life at night, if he crosses the street alone ; the most impudent beggars almost devour one and at the same time these unfortunate creatures continually mutter

---

[1] A. Ruge's *Briefwechsel und Tagebuchblätter.*
[2] Baechtold's *Life.*
[3] *Briefe von und an G. Herwegh.* (K.)

threats about the Republic and Hecker. The so-called 'Leaders' are of the same stamp, namely, the editors of the small and local newspapers. I never came across more narrow-minded and more brutal fellows than the German republicans of the second and third rank ; all the evil passions—envy, revengefulness, bloodthirstiness, mendacity, are nourished and instilled by them in the lower classes.

ROBERT PRUTZ TO GEORG HERWEGH

DRESDEN, 12*th March* 1848.

Yes, old friend, the world is changing, and at last our golden ideals descend from the heights and walk and dwell among us. You, indeed, are at the fountain-head [in Paris] and drink in deep draughts the refreshing stream of a renewed and freed public life : do not, however, think too meanly of or esteem too lightly these isolated drops and streamlets in which freedom trickles to us here in Germany. . . . At the moment I am living in the most doleful spot in all Germany, Dresden, the land of the cake-devourers, the most washed-out, colourless, flabby generation in Germany : a people like a wet sponge, neither Guelph nor Ghibelline, merely idle gapers who still believe that all this is happening merely 'outside,' and merely that they may have an interesting newspaper to read every morning while drinking their miserable thin coffee !

We have pointed out that the outbreak of revolution found the various German governments quite unprepared for common action in self-defence. But there was common action, and that during the first week of March, on the side of those reformers, the first plank in whose platform was the unification of Germany. On 5th March there met at Heidelberg a conference of fifty-one 'friends of the Fatherland.' This conference was due to the tireless exertions of Heinrich von Gagern, a member of the Hesse-Darmstadt chamber, who had conceived the idea of settling constitutional difficulties in Germany and the question of unification by means of a representative assembly, elected on a popular basis by the nation at large. This self-constituted committee represented more than one shade of opinion, for among the fifty-one 'friends of the Fatherland ' was Hecker, fresh from his abortive attempt to stir up trouble at Carlsruhe. The conference proved to be one of the utmost importance, for, before separating, it elected a committee of seven to make arrangements for summoning the preliminary parliament at Frankfort, which in turn developed into the national assembly, that first German parliament, of whose fortunes we read in Book v. But even at the outset the rift between moderates and extremists, that did so much to frustrate the efforts of the Frankfort assembly, declared itself. The conference did not pass without an encounter between Gagern and Hecker.[1] Gagern had earnestly warned those present to beware of the dangers threatening from a new republican Confederation of the Rhine with France, and had exclaimed, 'I also would be a republican if the German people resolved upon a republican form of government. I can be a republican, for I have learned to live simply ; but I will have no mob rule and no coquetting with the mob.' Hecker retorted : 'I want freedom, complete freedom for all by whatever form of government it is to be attained. But no freedom, if it is to be only for the privileged or for the rich ; I am in a word a Social Democrat ! '

[1] Klein.

CHAPTER II

THE LOLA MONTEZ SCANDAL IN BAVARIA AND ABDICATION OF LUDWIG I.

THE revolution of February 1848, which drove Louis Philippe, the citizen-king, from Paris, set a light to the tinder of revolt against absolutism and reaction which had been accumulating in central Europe for thirty years. Nowhere were people more ready to believe that any change meant reform than in Bavaria, for there, beside the customary grounds for political dissatisfaction, existed the public scandal of the ascendancy of that brilliant adventuress, Lola Montez, over King Ludwig I.

Lola Montez, born at Limerick, was the daughter of a British father and a mother of Spanish descent. For a time she enjoyed the advantages of a strict Presbyterian up-bringing at Montrose, but was later exposed to the more meretricious influences of Paris and Bath. A run-away match, in itself creditable enough to her, terminated, like all her marital adventures, unhappily. After a chequered career as a dancer, a Spanish dancer she described herself, she captivated King Ludwig of Bavaria and was installed at Munich as his favourite, and indeed as his political Egeria. For a year she dominated the government of the country, and directed it into liberal channels, but Bavarian democrats were insensible to her charms, and were not prepared to rise in her defence against clerical intrigue and outraged middle-class sentiment which combined against her. The unfortunate woman was born too late ; she had the beauty, the wit and the courage to become one of the great romantic figures in the galaxy of fair women of the past; but these have become rarer since the invention of printing, and the development of the newspaper press has rendered wellnigh impossible the appearance of a halo of romance round the head of frailty however

248

beautiful. Out of no disrespect to a great institution is made the suggestion that Fancy cannot possibly play about a person who commits so commonplace an action as to write a letter addressed to the Editor of the *Times*. This Lola Montez did in a fatal moment. The stern guardian of European morals had published a scathing leader taking her to task on 2nd March 1847, and on 18th March appeared her dignified and quite unromantic reply, extinguishing her last chance of immortality. Even Helen's wizardry could not have survived an exculpatory note to the *Lacedaemonian Herald*, or whatever a newspaper circulating in Sparta would have been called. Marlowe would never have been moved to inquire :

> Was this the face that launched a thousand ships
> And burned the topless towers of Ilium ?

In place of the tributes of countless poets she would have had to put up with those she doubtless received from Paris, and these were probably no better than Ludwig's rhapsodies to his mistress.

Fraser's Magazine made a feature of its foreign correspondence in the forties, and there is no more authentic contemporary account of the situation in Munich during the reign of Lola Montez than is contained in an article which appeared in that Magazine in January 1848. The writer begins with a lively description of the estimate of Bavaria formed by foreign politicians of the time, and of the wretched character of its political system :

Bavaria, it would seem, is regarded as the Boeotia of modern Europe. Both the country and the inhabitants have certainly acquired a bad reputation. They are either spoken of with a sneer, or are passed over altogether as utterly unworthy of consideration. ' What do I care about Bavaria ? ' says the politician. ' It is a country sunk in moral apathy ; in diplomacy, it is a nonentity ; the people are mere slaves of the caprices of a king, who, in his turn, is ruled by the whims or the passions of a woman, whose oddities have made her the subject of European scandal. What are Bavarian affairs to me ? '
One thing seems to be universally admitted—that, although in an economical sense the administration of public affairs was benign, and the people were rendered substantially happy, yet in all that related to political freedom, and, *pro tanto*, to personal liberty, the utmost jealousy was manifested. Bavaria exhibited an absurd

parody of the Austrian system. A paternal government was
seen for ever with a sugar-plum in one hand and a rod in the other ;
and the latter was laid on too often and too vigorously. During
many years that followed the system of contraction, the government of Bavaria, although it had at its head a man whose abilities
as a minister are cheerfully acknowledged even by his most inveterate
political opponents, degenerated into a low, petty, grinding tyranny
—a system of exclusion to all who did not bow down before the
priesthood—a system devised and executed with a devilish ingenuity
—until, at last, it became intolerable to all but the favoured few.
Were we to enumerate even a few of the obstructions offered, at
every turn, to the natural development of enterprise or the expression of opinion, the reader would not credit us. Whether it be
just or not to attribute the then existing state of things to the
Jesuits, it is admitted by all but the parties interested in proving
a negative that the whole country, through its guiding minds, was
under the influence of a priestly tyranny, which found its virtues
in petty persecutions.

He proceeds to give an equally lively description of the popular
estimate of Lola Montez herself :

The popular notion of Lola Montez, judging from newspaper
paragraphs, presents her as a beautiful specimen of an embodied
fury. Her past public career is supposed to have consisted of
several attempts to dance at different opera-houses, where, not
being sufficiently admired, she vented her disappointment on the
audience, by indulging in expressions and gestures only to be
heard or seen at Billingsgate, or in the purlieus of Covent Garden.
Passing over the asseverations, from personal observation, of
mutually contradicting scandalmongers, as to her birth, parentage,
and education, she is generally regarded as a person who has led
a very scandalous and dissipated life ; who has been mixed up with
English *roués* and French *littérateurs* ; who has figured in public
trials ; and who has altogether denuded herself of the privileges
of her sex, by having lived the life more of a man than of a woman.
So much for her antecedents. As to her present position, the
popular idea is that she has acquired a pernicious ascendency over
the King of Bavaria, whom she holds in subjection by a low influence. For her way and manner of life, it is supposed that she
walks about Munich with a large and ferocious bull-dog, whom she
deliberately sets upon those persons whom she has not herself
the physical power to beat. This dog, it seems, has a peculiar
instinct for worrying Jesuit priests ; and so sagacious is he that,
even now that the Jesuits are ostensibly expelled, he can detect
the abhorred principles under the most profound of clerical dis-
guises. Further, it appears that the chief occupation of Lola
Montez is to stir up the disaffected and demoralised population
against the constitutional authorities : that she seizes every occa-

sion to outrage public decency [1]—as, for instance, by going to
the opera, or by walking for exercise, or riding for pleasure, through
and about the city, and a variety of other offences against good
order ; which she occasionally relieves by spitting in the face of a
bishop, thrashing a coalheaver, smashing shop-windows, or breaking her parasol over the head and shoulders of some nobleman
adverse to her party.

And he leads up to a sober estimate of the woman's character
and position which is probably to be accepted as just :

> Lola Montez has many of the faults which history has recorded of
> others in like situations. She loves power for its own sake ; she
> is too hasty, and too steadfast in her dislikes ; she has not suffi-
> ciently learnt to curb the passion which seems natural to her Spanish
> blood ; she is capricious, and quite capable, when her temper is
> inflamed, of rudeness, which, however, she is the first to regret and
> to apologise for. One absorbing idea she has which poisons her
> peace. She has devoted her life to the extirpation of the Jesuits,
> root and branch, from Bavaria. . . .
> As a political character, she holds an important position in
> Bavaria, besides having agents and correspondents in various
> courts of Europe. The king generally visits her in the morning,
> from eleven to twelve, or one o'clock : sometimes she is summoned
> to the palace to consult with him, or with the ministers, on state
> affairs. It is probable, that during her habits of intimacy with
> some of the principal political writers in Paris, she acquired that
> knowledge of politics and insight into the manœuvres of diplo-
> matists and statesmen which she now turns to advantage in her
> new sphere of action. On foreïgn politics she seems to have very
> clear ideas ; and her novel and powerful mode of expressing them
> has a great charm for the king, who has himself a comprehensive
> mind. On the internal politics of Bavaria she has the good sense
> not to rely upon her own judgment, but to consult those whose
> studies and occupations qualify them to afford information. For
> the rest, she is treated by the political men of the country as a
> substantive power ; and, however much they may secretly rebel
> against her influence, they at least find it good policy to acknow-
> ledge it. . . . Her creation as Countess of Landsfeld, which has

---

[1] In March 1847, the mean and fussy Dr. Singer of Reuss, who favoured
Bodelschwingh with the letter quoted on page 152, furnished Prince Wittgen-
stein at Munich with such scandal as he could rake up about Lola at Ebersdorf.
According to his account, she had been brought four years earlier from London
to Germany by the Prince of Ebersdorf (the hero of Hoffmann's skit on page
169). ' She was four weeks in Ebersdorf, drank at least four bottles of strong
red wine and champagne, and when she was a trifle elevated ran after even
the menservants. Then she tried to set the dogs on the peasants. Thereupon she was speedily removed [to Dresden], but she shrieked and fought so
fiercely, that it took four men to get her into the carriage.'—Manteuffel's
Memoirs, Unter Friedrich Wilhelm IV. by H. von Poschinger, i. p. 17.

alienated her from some of her most honest liberal supporters, who wished her still to continue, in rank as well as in purposes, one of the people, while it has exasperated against her the powerless, because impoverished, nobility, was the unsolicited act of the king, legally effected with the consent of the crown-prince. Without entrenching too far upon a delicate subject, it may be added, that she is not regarded with contempt or detestation by either the male or the female members of the royal family. She is regarded by them rather as a political personage than as the king's favourite. . . .

We do not attempt in any way to palliate or justify the kind of connection subsisting between the King of Bavaria and his favourite. All we have proposed to do is to explain the actual relations of the parties, and to counteract those false statements by which, we repeat, the cause of morality can never be truly served. A few words more, and we dismiss the subject. The relation subsisting between the King of Bavaria and the Countess of Landsfeld is not of a coarse or vulgar character. The king has a highly poetical mind; and he sees his favourite through his imagination. Knowing perfectly well what her antecedents have been, he takes her as she is, and, finding in her an intellectual and an agreeable companion, and an honest, plain-spoken councillor, he fuses the reality with his own ideal in one deep sentiment of affectionate respect.

With this account given in *Fraser's Magazine* it is interesting to compare the report of one Hineis, an Austrian spy in the service of the Vienna Ministry of Police, which is quoted by Klein :

A single feeling appears to burn throughout Bavaria and every class and individual, and that is contempt and hatred of Lola, save in the case of the new party, who also thoroughly despise and recoil from her, but appear nevertheless to owe her a debt of gratitude. From Schärding where I entered Bohemian territory, all the way to Munich, and from there to Salzburg where I left it, there prevailed in this connection one universal feeling, one temper. Officials of the provincial courts whom I happened to meet in Munich, and those too from different districts, assured me it was the same everywhere. Whatever beer-house or tavern or place of public resort one entered, one heard people everywhere talking about this scandal, or could easily succeed in inducing them to do so by touching the string in question, when one at once heard horrible things and exaggerations of what has really taken place. In Munich itself one hears less, since the recent establishment of a secret police service has rendered the people timid, especially towards strangers.

How deeply the national pride in Bavaria feels wounded by the relations of this person to their king is indicated by the universal nickname applied to Lola : 'The Country's Mistress.' I did not observe any political excitement amongst the masses in Bavaria, nor did I find any particular comprehension of the present political tangle existing in that country, nor did any one appear particularly interested in it. Lola, mischief-making bigots, and beer prices seem to be the only handles by which the Bavarian populace can be set in motion. The peasant speaks of the dearness of the times, prices of grain, of the hibernation of seeds, and the permission granted by the king to export grain into Switzerland and to France—a circumstance which gives rise to a great deal of resentment against the crown, and that too in the most diverse classes of the people, it being constantly pointed out that Austria has increased the export duty on grain. The Munich middle and lower classes talk about Lola and the king's infatuation for her, about beer prices, local affairs and incidents, the grain trade and food-prices, about the export of grain—questions of earnings and trade. There were also complaints that the king had forced on, or occasioned, the erection of so many public buildings at the expense of the citizens of Munich, that their very considerable municipal capital had been entirely swallowed up and a debt of eight thousand gulden incurred. In the official world there is many-sided restlessness, connected, however, for the most part with the individual and personal interests affected by the latest changes in the ministry. . . . The Civil Service, and especially the lower branches, seems entirely devoted to the king. Amongst the military the relations of the king with Lola excite great vexation and disgust, and are discussed in the most scandalous fashion. As this fact eventually reached the ears of the king the officers were informed at a suitable moment that it was the royal pleasure they should refrain from all conversation and comment on the matter. Since then the officers talk no longer about the king and Lola, but of a certain ' Herr Maier ' and his ' Pepi,' merely substituting these names for the former.

Military loyalty on the other hand has not in any way been shaken, if exception be made of the grave action of the Prince Carl Cuirassier Regiment at the last Lola riot, where it is said they did not by any means execute the orders given them but fraternised on the contrary with the public. This is in no way to be wondered at, if one casts a glance at the circumstances and organisation of the military in Bavaria. . . . In barracks the private is quite alone and withdrawn from the direct supervision and influence of his officers, since the adjutant alone lives in barracks, while the other officers are quartered in private houses.

In ale-houses, taverns, bars and coffee-houses and other public resorts you find the military and civilians all mixed up together without any distinction whatever, and fraternising perfectly with each other. They drink and play together, tease and chaff one another in terms so crude and forcible that they border on insult ; in short the demeanour of the military towards the civil element is as if they both belonged to one and the same caste. In service the soldiers' manners are perfectly free and easy. You can without any fear debate with the sentinel at his post, ask for information, which is fully and readily given, and a tactfully offered gratuity for the service rendered is accepted on the spot. In short there exists such a commingling of military and civilians that in critical cases the Bavarian military can hardly be reckoned on to effect anything in Munich against the common people and general public there, more especially if Lola should give occasion to renewed disturbances.

As an illustration of Munich wit at Lola's expense may be given the summary of her ' Lord's Prayer ' published as a broadsheet,[1] and only one of several documents of the kind, which show that the taste of that artistic city was no more delicate seventy years ago than it is in these days of ' Simplicissimus ' :

Our Father, in whom I have never believed throughout my life, thou who dwellest in a certain Heaven, in *loco secreto* as men say, all's well with me. Hallowed be thy name, so far as I am concerned, for to me every one is good and righteous if only he hold by me. Thy kingdom come, when thereby are understood my polished diamonds, my bags of gold, and my unpolished Alemannia corps. . . . Thy will be done, if thou wilt destroy my enemies, if thou enthronest over them not freedom but the blue devil. . . . Give me this day . . . champagne and truffle-pasties, pheasant and what there is of good and dear, for I have a cursed good stomach. . . . Forgive me my debts, in the measure in which I forgive not my debtors. . . . Lead me not into temptation, again to return to this land, for even were I bullet-proof they might seize me, put me in a cage and charge six francs for a sight of me. . . . Amen !

Certainly the King made no concealment of his admirations. A lover of art, his munificence made Munich the city of palaces, theatres, monuments, museums and galleries admired of travellers until the frontier was closed in the summer of 1914. But he was a poet as well. A respectable volume of his poems is published, but it does not contain his passionate addresses to Lola by name. These the infatuated monarch handed about freely, and they spread through Munich, and from Munich through Europe. The article in *Fraser's Magazine* gives literal translations of several. Of one of them, a sonnet, a version is here given, possibly as distinguished as the original :

> If for my sake thou hast renounced all ties,
> I, too, for thee have broken with them all ;
> Life of my life, I am thine, I am thy thrall ;
> I hold no compact with thine enemies.

---

[1] Facsimile in Blum.

On me their blandishments can win no prize ;
I answer not the sly seducer's call ;
Love lifts me up and will not let me fall ;
With thee, through life, my earthly pathway lies.
United as the body to the soul
Even till death my self with thine is blent.
In thee I find fulfilled my long felt need ;
Wounded and worn, thy sight has made me whole.
Of all my passing fancies I repent,
For in thine eyes at last true love I read !

One of his passing fancies appears to have been an Italian, for
Blum gives the original of a couple of what the King ' called
distiches,' in which the royal poet declares to his Lolita :

Drops, thin drops of delight, and an ocean of bitter bewailing,
    Were the Italian's bequest.—Happiness, joy unalloyed,
These were thy gifts to a heart and a soul and a spirit enraptured !
    Daughter of Spain, in thee love I discovered, and life !

Before the appearance of the beautiful and fascinating dancer
the King had been in the hands of a clerical ministry conducted
by Abel. His mistress exerted her utmost to shake his confidence in this Jesuitical instrument of government, as she
termed it, and with success. Provoked by the scandal of Lola's
growing influence, the Abel ministry, in February 1847, sent in
their resignations, accompanied by a memorandum [1] in which
their reasons were clearly set forth :

There are moments in public life, when to men who have been
called by the inestimable confidence of their king to the leading
posts of public administration in its various branches there remains
only the grievous choice, either to renounce the fulfilment of
their most sacred duties undertaken under the seal of sworn faith,
loyalty, devotion and warmest gratitude, or in the conscientious
fulfilment of those duties to disregard the painful danger of incur-
ring the displeasure of their beloved sovereign.—The undersigned
faithful and obedient servants of your Majesty found themselves
placed in this situation through the grant of Bavarian nationality
by Royal Decree to the Señora Lola Montez, and, as they are all
of them incapable of betraying those sacred duties they are bound
by oath to your Royal Majesty to fulfil, they could not therefore
flinch in their determination. . . . Since the month of October
last the eyes of the country have been fixed on Munich, and opinions
have been formed in every part of Bavaria on what is passing here
and forms the almost exclusive subject of conversation in the family
and in public, and these opinions have led to a state of feeling which

---

[1] Klein.

must be described as most serious. It is clear that reverence for the monarchy in the minds of the people is in process of effacement, for nothing is heard but expression of the bitterest blame and loudest disapproval. The national sentiment is at the same time most deeply wounded, because Bavaria believes itself to be governed by a foreign woman whose reputation is branded by public opinion, and in view of many facts nothing can eradicate this conviction. [Abel adduces, as examples, that the Bishop of Augsburg had shed bitter tears, and that the Prince-Bishop of Breslau had written a letter in which he gave expression to 'his decided disapproval of what was going on.'] . . . Foreign newspapers publish daily the most painful anecdotes and the most degrading attacks on your Royal Majesty. The annexed No. 5 of the *Ulmer Chronik* contains a sample of this. No vigilance on the part of the police can prevent these papers from being introduced. They are distributed broadcast and devoured with avidity. One and the same feeling prevails from Berchtesgarten and Passau to Aschaffenberg and Zweibrücke, nay throughout Europe, and in the cottage of the poor as in the palace of the rich. [The Crown itself was, he said, at stake, for even the army threatened to waver in its loyalty.] . . . What your most loyal and obedient signatories with broken hearts and in deepest reverence venture to lay before you is not the opinion of visionaries, it is the melancholy result of actual observations which they could not fail to make for months past in the daily exercise of their functions.—VON ABEL, VON GUMPPENBERG, GRAF SEINSHEIM, VON SCHRENK.

The result was the instant dismissal of the ministry. 'I have turned off all my ministers; the Jesuitical regime has ceased in Bavaria' said the King. More complacent successors gave way on the naturalisation question and Lola was recognised as Countess Landsfeld. By the end of 1847 she succeeded in getting installed, under Prince Oettingen-Wallerstein, and Berks, a creature of hers, a ministry which was wholly subservient to her. But riots began in town and university. Among the students Lola had a rowdy band of adherents who formed themselves into the 'Alemannia' Corps. In one riot the leader of this corps, a Count Hirschberg, struck right and left with a dagger. The King treated the disorder in university circles as a case of mutiny, and on 9th February closed the university. Then town and gown joined hands and there was a march on the palace. The King capitulated, the university was to be reopened at once, the Alemannia Corps disbanded, and Lola banished. On the 11th she fled from Munich, taking refuge with Justinus Kerner, the Swabian poet, doctor, and student of 'magnetism and spiritual possession' at Weinsberg,

later to become also Metternich's place of refuge. A letter [1] of
Kerner's, dated 19th February, gives an account of her :

> WEINSBERG, 19*th February* 1848.
>
> Lola Montez arrived here yesterday, and I am keeping her in
> my tower pending further orders from Munich. Three members
> of the Alemannia Corps are keeping watch and ward. It is very
> annoying that the king should have sent her to me of all people,
> but he was told that Lola was ' possessed ' and that he ought to
> send her to Weinsberg to have the devil exorcised. It is interest-
> ing all the same. Before I proceed to treat her magneto-magically
> I am submitting her to a severe fasting-cure. She receives daily
> but thirteen drops of raspberry juice and a quarter of a white
> wafer-cake. Say nothing about this to any one ! Burn this letter !

In a later letter he says : ' It is astonishing how much she has
wasted away. Theobald applies the magnetic treatment to her,
and I make her drink asses' milk.'

But the departure of Lola and the reopening of the university
did not allay the ferment. The hated and despised Berks-
Wallenstein ministry was still in power. A section of the
nobility endeavoured to guide the King to reasonable measures
of reform, and on 1st March Prince Leiningen wrote to him : [2]

> 1*st March* 1848.
>
> Circumstances so pressing as the present and so threatening to
> the immediate future of this kingdom, and therefore to our whole
> dear Fatherland, have not existed for a very long time, perhaps
> never ! Just at this critical moment, too, the confidence of all
> classes of your subjects in your Majesty has been most deeply
> shaken. This is the truly treasonable work of those creatures who
> are now insinuating themselves between your Majesty and your
> people. It is especially [resented] that your Majesty should retain
> as an adviser such a man as that substitute for a minister, von
> Berks, whom public opinion has branded with the deepest contempt,
> because he betrayed those on whose shoulders he mounted to power.
> Your Majesty has been completely deceived regarding the causes
> which have occasioned so much dissatisfaction and bitterness.

A conflict seemed inevitable, and Prince Wrede was on the
point of ordering the troops to fire on the crowd, when the King
showed signs of yielding. A visit of his to the theatre accompanied by the Queen on 9th March is thus described by a courtly
journalist in the *Allgemeine Zeitung* : [3]

---

[1] Justinus Kerner's *Briefwechsel mit seinen Freunden*, ii.
[2] Klein.   [3] Klein.

R

Our king appeared yesterday for the first time since the events of February by the side of the queen at the theatre and was greeted by his loyal people with an enthusiasm the house has seldom witnessed. At the conclusion of almost endless cheering the entire audience struck up the National Anthem ' Hail to our King, all hail ! ' and sang three stanzas to the accompaniment of the orchestra. Cheer upon cheer concluded a demonstration of homage such as never emanated from more thankful hearts.

A royal proclamation was published, summoning the Estates for 16th March, to consider the popular demands, including the question of a parliament. And on 20th March the King abdicated in favour of his son, Maximilian II. In the newspapers appeared the King's pathetic ' Farewell,' [1] an effusion of the royal poet himself :

> Forlorn and far and sadly
> Out of your world I go,
> For free and great and gladly
> Alone to rule I know.
> This heart that loved you dearly
> Ingratitude touched nearly,
> And filled with bitter woe.

> The nobles who reviled you,
> And wove my crown of thorn,
> Have fooled you and beguiled you,
> And put us both to scorn,
> Glib courtiers smooth and lying,
> Priests their own faith denying,
> My crown from me have torn.

> A soul which loved the beauty
> That art to life can lend,
> Held it a kingly duty
> To be art's greatest friend.
> The son succeeds the father,
> Round him, Bavarians, gather,
> And loyal hands extend.

So ended somewhat flatly the royal romance and the Bavarian revolution. It is to be hoped for reasons of sentiment that the story is true of a secret return of Lola, disguised as a boy, to take a last farewell of the King. *He* passed to affluent retirement ; *she* took the road trodden by so many Continental fugitives in days of trouble, the road to London, ultimately to

---

[1] Blum.

pass to America, and to die a penitent's death in New York. It was only by accident that Metternich did not cross the Channel in the same boat with her. In a letter to his daughter he unctuously congratulates himself on his escape :

THE HAGUE, *9th April* 1848.

If the Chartist movement had not prevented my embarking yesterday morning at Rotterdam I should have arrived this morning in London, in the company of the Countess of Landsfeld (Lola Montez). She proceeded to that city by the very steamer that I too desired to take. I thank Heaven for preserving me from such contact.

CHAPTER III

THE MARCH REVOLUTION IN VIENNA AND FLIGHT OF METTERNICH

COMPLICATED as was the situation in Germany proper all through the period from the War of Liberation to the revolution of 1848, the tangle was far more intricate within the Austrian Empire. In Germany the problem was twofold, how to bring about a political union of all the separate German kingdoms and dukedoms, each with its dynastic individuality and its particular interests and traditions, and, when a basis was arrived at, to decide which of the two possible powers was to be the head of any new body corporate, Austria with the halo of the old empire still shedding a pale lustre on the heads of the Hapsburgs, or Prussia with its well-disciplined army of soldiers and officials. Within the Austrian Empire itself was a third complication as serious as either of the other two, how to keep welded together as one empire the Austro-German, the Hungarian or Magyar, and the various Slav elements. Thus the growing strength of national feeling, which slowly but surely was working for German Unity, threatened the Austrian Empire with disruption. From 1813 to 1848 the German element in the Austrian Empire, Vienna in a word, shared all the aspirations of the German peoples, but the Magyars and the Slav races were animated not by German, but by Magyar or Slav enthusiasm. And what of the subjected Italians of Venetia and Lombardy ?

Metternich had done marvels in balancing one interest against another, and in maintaining at least a moral, or immoral, ascendancy for Austria in the counsels of Germany. His extraordinary powers as a manipulator undoubtedly did much to preserve the peace of Europe, and that claim, which is made for him, may be freely conceded. A similar claim was freely advanced, and in England up to 4th August 1914, for Kaiser William II. ! But manipulation is not enough for statesmanship, unless the hand is guided not only by a clear brain, but also by a heart that beats with some generous impulse. In Metternich's case the brain was clear and acute, but the heart was cold. And his unscrupulous use of the police, the informer, the eavesdropper and the spy as essential elements in the system of repression which he built up, left him at the last without a friend even in court circles. Francis I. had supported him heart and soul in his famous system. But his successor, Ferdinand, good-natured but weak physically and mentally, imbecile[1] some style him, epileptic others, was but an encumbrance. A vivid picture of Austria before the revolution is given by Hübner, the conservative diplomat, in his *Memoirs* : [2]

It was a sad time. On the throne sickness, alongside the monarch two old men, one of whom, although in full possession of his faculties, was deprived of all influence ; the new spirit which Francis I. had combated by every means creeping into the higher circles of the government ; the governing power falling more and more into the hands of insignificant people, that is to say, into the hands of a bureaucracy still honourable and respectable, but without authority, without discernment, without guidance and already more or less won over to the ideas which it was their duty to resist. Although distant thunder announced the approach of the storm, there was no one capable of leading the perplexed into a right path or of reassuring and inspiriting the discouraged. There was no word which spoke to the hearts, to the noble instincts, or to the higher feelings of the nation. Nothing but silence and stagnation.

The February revolution in Paris brought matters in Vienna to a climax. Italy indeed had risen in January against Austrian oppression. Riots in Milan were followed by similar scenes of disorder all over Venetia. For Vienna the push-off, as it were, came from Hungary, with a ringing speech by Kossuth, delivered in the Diet at Pressburg on 3rd March :

The future of our Fatherland is not assured so long as the system of government in the other provinces is in gross contradiction to all constitutional principles, so long as the State Council which has charge of the common affairs of the Monarchy continues, in its elements, its combination and its tendency, to render homage to absolutism. The immobility of the Government condemns the Diet to regular tread-mill work, and makes all the endeavours of the people's friends fruitless. From the charnel house of the Vienna System a pestilential air blows towards us, which paralyses our nerves

---

[1] 'The next thing to an idiot' was Palmerston's term for him.
[2] *Ein Jahr meines Lebens.*

and lays its ban upon our enthusiasm. The source of all the evil lies in the preposterous policy of the Austrian ministers, for whom it may possibly be painful to see one piece after another of the house fall in which has been built up during a long life, but who compromise the future of the dynasty by their obstinate adherence to their system. Where the foundation is faulty, a downfall is fated and inevitable. It is for us to save the dynasty, to attach its future to the fraternisation of the different races in Austria, and for the evil binding force of bayonets and bureaucratic oppression to substitute the firm cement of a free constitution. . . . In the most intimate fusion of the different provinces of the Monarchy are to be found the guarantees of peace, the support of the dynasty, the safeguard for our freedom. We therefore seek to surround the imperial throne with constitutional organisations, and to obtain the grant of a constitution to all countries within the Austrian Empire.

Petitions poured into the palace from all sorts and conditions of people, liberal members of the Estates, commercial, industrial, trade and professional associations, but the lead in the actual outbreak of revolution was taken by the university. Again and again throughout this book will be found examples of the astonishing part played in revolution by the universities all over Germany. The German student has a long record behind him of unruly behaviour. Emil Reicke in his monograph on *Der Lehrer* tells of an aristocratic student at Altdorf about the end of the sixteenth century, who distinguished himself at sixteen years of age as the leader of a gang of rowdies who murdered the son of a respectable citizen. Another exploit of his was to tie up his servant, for some dereliction of duty, to his chamber door, and then to lash out at him with a strap for a whole hour. This young savage rendered the name he bore illustrious, for he was none other than the youthful Wallenstein. Nowhere at this time were professors and students more hot-headed, or elaborately organised and attired than in Vienna. They formed themselves into a very close resemblance to an army, and if accounts from German source of the doings of the 'Academic Legion' are not enough, the reader will find a very vivid picture of the plumed and helmeted swashbuckler crowd of undergraduates, tutors, and professor in *Austria in 1848-49*, by W. H. Stiles, United States Charg d'Affaires at the Court of Vienna. On the evening of 12th Marc the Kaiser gave audience to two of the professors, who presente a statement of the demands drawn up by the students, but n

xplicit answer was returned. Next day, the 13th, on learning
he disappointing result of the audience, the students formed
ip and marched to the Landhaus where the Estates were in
ession. In the courtyard Kossuth's speech was read aloud,
nd the excitement of the crowd of students and citizens rose
o fever point. The rumour spread that the people's delegates
vere imprisoned. The Landhaus was stormed, and the members
f the Estates with difficulty forced their way to the palace.
Meanwhile, all over the city the citizens had risen like the
tudents, and tumult reigned, met by volley-firing on the
rowd by the troops under Archduke Albrecht.

Meanwhile, in the midst of this welter of riot and confusion,
he supreme authority under the Kaiser, the State Conference,
a select body of Archdukes, with Metternich and Kolowrat,
Chancellor in charge of the financial administration of the
Empire, met to deliberate. Their deliberations were short and
harp. A civic deputation had demanded Metternich's retirement. This was the solution of the crisis in every one's mind,
ind now in Metternich's own. With good grace he yielded at
nce, and the body politic suddenly found it had to do without
ts indispensable head. It still lived.

Metternich fled from Vienna on the following day, the 14th,
ind it was not until after a wandering flight, attended at times
vith danger, that he reached London on 21st April. A strange
glimpse of his flight, and of the man himself, is afforded by a
etter [1] from Justinus Kerner, who had sheltered Lola at
Weinsberg.

WEINSBERG, *April 2(?), 1848.*

I sheltered Metternich in my tower, the one in which Count
Helfenstein was imprisoned before his execution by the peasants.
He thinks that is a bad omen. It makes him feel uneasy and to me
his whole conduct is alarming, particularly his present shameless
pretence of liberalism. He asserts that it was only his wish that
Germany should become a republic, a wish that he has always
cherished, that made him adopt this anti-liberal system ; only in
his way was it possible for Germany to rise up in such might and
power. That is his work, and he did it intentionally in this way.
He did not rest until I put a red flag on my tower. He promised
me a butt of the best Johannisberger, but by the time his letter
reached Johannisberg, the cellar had been confiscated by the Nassau

---

[1] *Justinus Kerners Briefwechsel mit seinen Freunden,* ii. There is no
mention of this episode in Princess Metternich's *Diary.*

people.[1] So I must content myself throughout with declarations of favour which are never fulfilled. That is the fate of poets, as Schiller has already said.—*N.B.* Metternich plays the violin very well. There is an old one of Niembsch (the poet Lenau) in the tower. On this he keeps on playing the 'Marseillaise,' and whistles a spasmodic accompaniment in the moonlight.

Few more bitter epitaphs have been earned than that devoted to Metternich, on his retirement, by Grillparzer :

In this dark vault, too late for his renown,
Autocracy's Don Quixote lays him down.
Falsehood and truth he twisted to his will,
Deceived first others, then himself, with skill ;
Into grey-headed fool from rogue he passed,
For he believed his own fond lies at last.

Though Grillparzer wrote these scathing lines under the impulse of the moment, he was not without a feeling of respect for Metternich's great talents, and in a memoir on the year 1848 he wrote of his fall :

Later on the armed power at last took steps. The people were fired upon. Whoever gave the order, it brought the monarchy to the edge of the abyss by giving to a riot of street-boys the character of a revolution. It went on from that point without a stop, all the more so when Prince Metternich was dismissed. After all, and in spite of all his mistakes, he was the only one who would have had the sense and the energy to put a limit to the onward movement and to mark out its path. It was necessary to sacrifice some one, but it would have been sufficient to make a victim of Count Sedlnitzky, the Police President, who was universally hated and was really responsible in the main for all the evils. . . .

Hurried though Metternich's flight was he yet found time to write farewell letters to Kaiser Ferdinand, to the Czar, and to Frederick William. This last, together with the King of Prussia's reply,[2] deserves attention. In reply to Metternich's somewhat stilted phrases, the King's natural heartiness is remarkable. And what an impression his letter leaves of the confusion and bewilderment of those fateful days in Berlin, which followed 18th March, and of the King's busy buzzing brain !

[1] Prince Metternich got back his cellar ultimately, or formed a new one. Bismarck sampled his wines on a visit in later years.
[2] *Mémoires, etc., de Metternich publiés par son fils*, v., vii., pp. 609-12.

METTERNICH TO KING FREDERICK WILLIAM IV.

VIENNA, 14*th March* 1848.

Sire, I cannot resign myself only to make my voice heard by you from the midst of another life. It conveys to you nothing but assurances of my unalterable attachment, of a respect which could not have its being without affection, and the most sincere wishes for the personal happiness of your Majesty, of your kingdom and of the whole German Fatherland.

The 13th of March has put an end to my career of more than half a century, a career filled with the direction of public affairs and a ministry which has lasted for thirty-nine years. I have retired from active life with the firm conviction that I am no longer in a state to continue the struggle I have maintained in the field of domestic politics. The consciousness of having never failed in my duty accompanies me in the life which ought to be the portion of a private individual, and which to-day is more agitated, more troubled than any other.

May God preserve to your Majesty the full powers of your high intellect! May your Majesty deign, on your part, to continue the favour, I dare to say the affectionate sentiments which, during many years, have filled my whole being, and left no room for pride!

May I be permitted, in these grave circumstances, to renew to your Majesty the expression of the unalterable devotion and the profound respect with which I am and always shall be, etc., etc.

METTERNICH.

KING FREDERICK WILLIAM IV. TO METTERNICH

(*Autograph Letter*)

POTSDAM, 18*th April* 1848.

My very dear, most honoured and well-beloved prince, can you imagine that I only read the day before yesterday your letter of the 14th March, that letter so touching in its simplicity, so moving from the date it bears? An evil chance brought this about. The Minister Baron von Arnim handed me your letter on the 24th or 25th of last month, during a very important and very animated ministerial conference. This conference became stormy especially towards the end; I left the hall after having spoken for some time, and in my preoccupation left the letter on the table. I confess that with my head full of worry and annoyance, I had forgotten the letter. But after having returned to my peaceful Potsdam, I recalled my forgetfulness with pain, and on my first visit to Berlin I tried to recover the letter, but in vain. I assure you, my dear prince, that I was inconsolable and that I nearly sent you some sort of a reply, confessing the whole extent of my fault, of course. And then the day before yesterday I found a packet of papers quite in

order, that had been carried off at the time of our removal from
Berlin, and, to my great surprise, I saw your letter folded in one
from Arnim. Reading those lines so noble from beginning to end,
I felt my heart fill with admiration and regret, and tears came to
my eyes. Who would not exclaim : ' What a man ! ' and : ' What
a time this is not to appreciate such a man ! '

I have firm confidence in God. He will change this melancholy
situation and He will know how to reassert His authority, and that
perhaps sooner than we think. Meanwhile I have patience ; *but
I have also good hope*, and my hope will not be deceived. If you,
my very dear prince, and the dear and devoted princess, share the
same sentiments, I consider you happy. You have both professed
the Christian faith in the splendour of your power. It will bear
beautiful fruit in affliction, and religion, I hope, will shorten your
days of sadness.

The sentiment of my Estates, if you except the greater part of
the Rhenish provinces, *is not unsatisfactory* ; even in Brandenburg,
in Pomerania and in Prussia, in the plain of Silesia and in the
larger part of Saxony and of Westphalia, it is *quite excellent*. There
are only some large towns which are *disaffected*, and Berlin, where
good feeling is abroad and gaining strength, though still unfortunately passive, presents great dangers ; it is a town without discipline, without respect for authority, which knows neither order
nor obedience, though there is only one opinion of the good services
of the Civic Guard. There is probably another coup in contemplation for Holy Thursday (like that of 18th March). One cannot
predict that it will fail for want of actors, but that is probable. If
it succeeds, that may seriously alter the whole trend of things !

I do not know, my very dear prince, if you are still in Holland
or already in England. If you can let me know (by a safe hand)
your opinion, so valuable in my eyes, on the situation, you will
make me very happy. My personal relations with you will always
be the same as formerly ; they are even rejuvenated, bound closer,
made firmer by our common misfortunes. I feel for Austria the
same sentiments as in 1840. I will loyally do my best to ensure
for her hereditary emperor the hereditary dignity of head of the
Holy Empire. The Emperor must again become the titular head
of the German nation. A Cæsar at the side of this Augustus, as
elected sovereign of the Empire of Germany in particular, seems
inevitable. But I do not wish to be this Cæsar. My ambition is
to become ' generalissimo of the Empire ; ' but before these fine
dreams can be realised, with the aid of God we must surmount
many obstacles ; *at spes non fracta*.

I lay at the feet of the princess the homage of my respect and
my admiration. My good, admirable and suffering Elise feels, as I
do, a lively and sincere affection for you, like to that which I have
expressed for the princess. She has charged me to express to you
both as emphatically as possible, her profound sympathy and her
devoted attachment. The manner in which you both may receive

the expression of our friendship will be the most fitting response to my assurances and those of the queen.

May God keep you, my dear prince. May He preserve you to see better days in this world. Accept, I beg you, the expression of the high consideration with which I remain your Highness' devoted friend. FRIEDRICH WILHELM.

A singularly vivid account of the course of revolutionary events in Vienna between 5th and 17th March, is given in a diary[1] kept by Count C. Fr. Vitzthum von Eckstädt,[2] Secretary to the Saxon Legation. One can follow the scene breathlessly :

VIENNA, 5th March 1848.

A troubled, sinister mood prevails here in all circles. The Paris revolution has illuminated the obscurity of our position like a thunderbolt. The suburbs are said to be in a very irritated state. The lower middle class is in manifest fermentation. The most pernicious rumours are being circulated. It is as if there were a scheme to force the state into bankruptcy shortly. The Exchange Bank for bank-notes was almost besieged yesterday. . . . The coffee-houses are filled with inquisitive people. The newspapers containing the Paris news are read aloud to groups of twenty or thirty people. One reasons and ' prattles,' as we say here, almost the same as in Berlin during the last Diet. Discontent is general, and I only fear it is not recognised by the authorities as it ought to be. . . . Meat has risen by two kreutzer, and the day before yesterday a mob assembled in the street under the windows of a Jewish banker, who was giving a ball ; no one should dance, they said, while the people have no meat. . . . Meanwhile it is to be foreseen with certainty that we shall wade through streams of blood.

Sunday, 12th March. In Metternich's salon. Quiet and security. Little anxiety. . . . The people are contemplating demonstrations. Archduke Ludwig wants to place a guard over the Estates House : Count Montecuccoli advises the contrary. Precautionary measures are taken. Count Sedlnitzky (Minister of Police) engages one thousand men for the secret police and thereby reassures himself.

Monday, 13th March, 8 o'clock. Great procession of students to the Estates House. Masses of well-dressed people surge about in the streets.

---

[1] Klein.

[2] Count Vitzthum was one of the best diplomatic memoir writers of last century. He became Saxon Minister in London in 1853, and in an introduction to the English edition of his *St. Petersburg and London*, Henry Reeve quotes Disraeli as saying of him : ' If I want to know something about Austria and Germany, I do not ask the Austrian ambassador nor the Prussian, but the Saxon minister.' A friendly view of Metternich is given by Count Vitzthum in vol. I. chap. xii. of the book just mentioned. Of this chapter Reeve remarks : ' A Prussian critic, very hostile to Austria says, " this is a picture of perfect truth . . . and one of the finest pieces of modern historical literature." '

10 *o'clock*. The Estates meet in the Landhaus, more numerous than ever before. The autograph letter (with empty promises) is rejected as insufficient, and a motion for a petition is introduced. A students' deputation composed of twelve members tears up the letter and the petition of the Estates.

11 *o'clock*. The wishes of the people : (1) Freedom of the Press, (2) Freedom of teaching, (3) Right of association, (4) General representation, responsible ministers, (5) Open court, oral procedure, trial by jury.

12 *o'clock*. Great procession. Montecuccoli at the head of the students marches into the palace with the deputation from the Estates. At the same moment a deputation of citizens obtains entry to the palace. Meanwhile the streets assume a threatening aspect. Popular orators are surrounded by groups of people. Some of the shops are closed in the Graben, Herrengasse and Schauflergasse. Four battalions stand at the gates of the palace. Artillery is brought up and loaded. The chancellery is surrounded by troops. The cry ' Down with Metternich ! ' is heard on all sides and becomes the watchword.

1 *o'clock*. Movement of troops in the Freiung and the Michaeler Platz. All shops are closed. The gates of the (inner) city are closed for traffic, and no one is admitted. The excitement spreads. Finally a Hungarian battalion is sent to the Herrengasse and attacked by students and people. A mob marches to the chancellery and demands the dismissal of Prince Metternich. Another forces its way into the Landhaus and smashes the windows and furniture.

2 *o'clock*. The guard in the Herrengasse is reinforced. Archduke Albrecht seeks to pacify the people. In vain. He is received with stones. After repeated warnings a sharp volley is fired. Four killed, two wounded. A body is carried to the Archduke Albrecht.

3 *o'clock*. No news of the deputation. Indecision at the palace and the chancellery. Archdukes Albrecht and Wilhelm ride through the streets. The excitement affects everybody. Bayonet attacks. Several victims. There is talk of fifty deaths.

4 *o'clock*. It is said that the news of the reception of the deputation is to come at 5 o'clock. The street fighting gets hotter. The streets leading into the Juden Platz in the neighbourhood of the arsenal are provided with barricades. The people are repulsed. The arsenal is saved. The Schotten Gate and the Stuben Gate are captured by the inhabitants of the suburbs.

5 *o'clock*. The Civic Guard sounds the alarm and takes up arms. A deputation of ten officers (of the Civic Guard) goes to the palace. A kind of truce is arrived at. The officers of the Civic Guard demand (1) the immediate removal of the military from the city, (2) arms for the students, (3) resignation of Prince Metternich, and, with regard to points 2 and 3, their fulfilment by 9 P.M. In return for this they undertake to guarantee the orderliness of the city, with the threat that if points 2 and 3 are not conceded by 9 P.M.

the Civic Guard will place itself at the head of the rising. Discussion at the palace ; Estates and citizens take part in it. Sedlnitzky, Minister of Police, completely paralysed.

6 o'clock. Excesses by the rabble in the streets. Sentry-boxes destroyed. Windows are illuminated ; those not illuminated are smashed. Patrols of Civic Guards and students march through the streets. The Graben, the Kohl Market and the Michaeler Platz are specially thronged.

7 o'clock. The police-station near the palace threatened by a mob. Three police soldiers fire from the windows. Three of the Civic Guard fall. Great bitterness. Excesses in the suburbs.

8 o'clock. The rabble march through the streets in dense masses. In the suburbs the imperial stables are attacked, and the Hungarian Grenadiers defend them. Great butchery. Continued vacillation at the palace. Unwillingness to make any concessions.

8.30. Archduke John calls attention to the fact that only half an hour remains. The resignation of Prince Metternich decided upon. Count Brenner and Archduke John undertake to disclose it to him. Prince Metternich resigns.

9 o'clock. The news runs through the streets. Separate patrols announce it formally at every house.

10 p.m. to 2 a.m. From now onwards separate groups march through the streets rejoicing and shouting ' Hurrah.' Demonstrations of approval before Count Montecuccoli. He is, *à tort ou à raison*, the Lamartine of the moment. Some popular orators advise the people not to be content with the two concessions, the resignation of Prince Metternich and the arming of the students.

Tuesday, 14*th March,* 2 *a.m.* The illuminations are extinguished. Excesses in the suburbs. Several factories are set on fire.

8 o'clock. Dense masses of people march through the city. The students are armed.

9 o'clock. Cockades and ribbons appear. The cry for freedom of the Press becomes general. The soldiers guard only the palace and the chancellery, and camp on the glacis. Even the cannon have disappeared from the inner city.

10 o'clock. The white ribbon is more in evidence that the red-and-white and the red ribbons. That means freedom of the Press.

11 o'clock. Meanwhile nothing is made known as to the concessions actually granted. Discontent in the streets is as great as the indecision in the palace. Grotesque processions march through the city. Speakers explain the importance of the freedom of the Press.

12 o'clock. Archduke Albrecht resigns. It is said that thousands of citizens have sworn that he shall die, because an unfounded [1] story is in circulation to the effect that he was the first to give the order to fire. Prince Windischgrätz is Civil and Military Governor of the city. Count L. Wrbna is associated with him.

---

[1] Klein says, 'not altogether unfounded.'

1 *to* 3 *o'clock*. The whole city has the appearance of one left entirely to itself. The most fabulous rumours contradict one another. The Estates hasten through the streets in uniform, giving assurances that the wishes of the people are conceded. In the palace, where citizens are present, there is much discussion about the term ' National Guard ' ; the thing itself may be granted, but not the name.

3 *o'clock*. At last the concession of a National Guard is announced. People crowd to register themselves. The arsenal supplies weapons. Meanwhile more proclamations are torn down.

4 *o'clock*. Great discussion among students. Terrible discontent. An attack on the palace is agreed upon. The white ribbons disappear. The most critical moment of the day. Pickets of Hussars are visible. Fresh troops in the palace. Fifty cannon.

5 *o'clock*. Freedom of the Press proclaimed. Great rejoicing. Count Hoyos commander of the National Guard. . . . A request is made that the Kaiser should appear before the public. Prince Windischgrätz gives his word that his Majesty is too unwell.

6 *o'clock*. Great meeting of students. It is resolved to be content for the present with the concession of freedom of the Press, and to send a detachment of three or four hundred students to the suburbs to pacify the people there. Prince Metternich, with his family, leaves the city.

7 *o'clock*. General illumination. It is raining. All is quiet.

Wednesday, 15th March, 8 o'clock. The city awakes in great peace. News is received of the fighting in the suburbs, where the National Guard and the soldiers have put the mob to flight. Artillery has been used. There is talk of four hundred dead. A hundred of the National Guard are said to have fallen. A *comité permanent* of twenty-four members meets in the Town Hall.

Friday, 17th March. All is quiet here. The people show a moderation which is remarkable. . . . The old order of things in Austria has set. *Sic transit gloria mundi !* . . .

The students, it has to be admitted, played a useful part in allaying disorder once they had, as they thought, secured their ends. Adolf Pichler, author of *Das Sturmjahr 1848*,[1] tells us : ' Our first duty that night (13th March) was to appease the wrath of the people, who allowed themselves to be peaceably guided by us only, if at all. . . . At the stroke of 7 A.M. (on the 14th) we split up into patrols. I was assigned to the Favoriten district. When we arrived the people were just attacking the Treasury buildings. Advance at the double ! The mere sight of us restored peace. . . . Our persuasion was everywhere sufficient to prevent pillage and arson.' And the same writer gives us a picture of the personal loyalty of the

[1] Klein.

Viennese to their Kaiser, who on the 14th abolished the Censorship by the simple decree : ' His Imperial, Royal, and Apostolic Majesty has been graciously pleased to order the abolition of the Censorship and the immediate publication of a Press Law.' Says Pichler :

For the evening (of 14th March) a great procession through the city was announced, since there was a desire to rejoice heartily over the happiness that had been achieved. How shall I describe the magical glory and bliss of that night ! When I think of it even now my eyes are filled with tears : of joy for the glorious elevation of our spirits in those hours—of sorrow for the approaching end of it all now (autumn 1848), when strength gives place to weariness and enthusiasm to empty phrases. What a wealth of love for the Kaiser was revealed at that time ! Even when the revolt had broken out, and was raging with the utmost fury, not a single hostile word was ever uttered against him ; but now the rejoicing reached the level of a spring tide ; as devout Christians bow before the Sacrament, so was his picture, crowned with flowers and carried about by students, everywhere acclaimed.

That night of the 14th Dr. L. A. Franzl wrote a song which became instantly famous. Baron von Helfert prints it in his invaluable collection of Viennese poetry and doggerel in 1848, the *Wiener Parnass*, and tells us that 100,000 copies were distributed, and that it was set to music nineteen times :

THE UNIVERSITY

Lo, who be these so proud in bearing ?
The bayonets flash, the flags fly free.
They come with silver trumpets blaring,
    The University !

The daylight hour at last is breaking
Our hopes and prayers have yearned to see ;
'Tis your young hearts to light awaking,
    O University !

When Kaiser Joseph came in thunder
To bind the tongue's sweet liberty,
Who dared to burst the bonds asunder ?
    The University !

Our tongues wake with the lark to singing ;
O hear their dithyrambic glee !
Heart calls, and heart sends answer ringing,
    All hail, the University !

Where spirits of the dead are beckoning,
The dead who died for freedom, see—
With the first victim paid her reckoning
The University !

And when our sons in reverence finger
Each glorious page in history,
On thy name, writ in gold, they 'll linger,
Our University !

A glowing account of the position on 2nd April is given by Pichler :

Sunday, 2nd April. What a joyful surprise; the black, red, and gold flag is floating on St. Stephen's tower in the morning air. It seemed like a dream and a fairy-tale to me. During the night men came to the university and handed the flag to the detachment of students on guard with the request that they should put it up. Twelve of them sprang up, climbed the stairs of the tower, and then in the darkness of night clambered out on to the crockets and hoisted the symbol of German unity. That is how the story generally went.—Very early in the morning we hastened to the university. We saw two more German flags hung out in the street ; with what enthusiasm were they greeted ! Viennese women had sent us these banners. How great and noble the women of Vienna were in this excited time ! The flame of liberty was at its purest in their hearts ; they loved liberty with the supreme love of woman, with all their soul. We at once decided, after singing, ' What is the German's Fatherland,' to march to the Stephansplatz. The blue sky of spring shone down upon us, the flags streamed and waved in the procession, the air was full of the sound of bells. How impressive and how powerful were the tones of the German anthem ! Then to the statue of the last German Kaiser—to Joseph ! . . . From there we went to the Palace Square. . . . Lovely women looked down from the windows. A student could not resist the impulse to lay his hand on the German ribbon and to call to them, ' Look, these are the colours with which you must adorn yourselves in future ! '—' Yes, yes,' they answered, ' so we shall.' And they waved joyfully to us. We came to attention in front of the palace. The Kaiser appeared at the window and was welcomed with rejoicing. (In reply to a short address by a student the Kaiser returned thanks ' with joyful emotion.') . . . Then the flag waved, we hastened to the palace gate, and a few moments afterwards the flag was fluttering from the window where the Kaiser had been standing shortly before. He appeared once more, went up to the flag and laid his hand on the pole, with the Kaiserin at his left hand. Students in their uniform surrounded them. The German Flag on the Imperial Palace at Vienna ! We extended our arms, emotion stifled every sound, there was only one thought and one feeling : Germany, Germany !

Count Vitzthum writing to his mother on the 7th was less enthusiastic :

Here we are driving a rudderless ship on troubled waters ; so far, however, tolerably well. . . . The male members of the high aristocracy here are mostly so uncultivated that nothing is to be expected from the class as a whole. Are there any *men* in the other classes ? It is perhaps possible, but who knows them ? Apart from a few men of letters, there are no names of any repute at all. The most depressing thing to my mind is the lack of any plan with regard to Germany. . . . The black, red, and gold flag flies on St. Stephen's tower, the Kaiser himself has waved it, and had it fixed on the palace—true, but what is the good of that ? In Italy war has broken out. Radetzky, a man of steel and iron, who though eighty-two years old thinks nothing of being in the saddle for fourteen hours, has had to evacuate Milan after five days' fighting, which is reported to have cost him four hundred and fifty men and the insurgents four thousand. . . . I am afraid that Charles Albert is staking his crown, just as Pius IX. is doing with his. Local opinion is reflected in a broad-sheet which is being sold at all street corners and is headed ' Against His So-called Holiness Pope Pius IX.' The Archbiship of Vienna, who was serenaded with tin can ' music ' the day before yesterday, has had the German tricolour hoisted to ward off any further disturbance before his palace. The Redemptorist Fathers were unceremoniously expelled yesterday. The National Guard could do nothing beyond covering their retreat. The nuns of St. Theresa, too, were honoured by a visit from Their Majesties the Sovereign People yesterday, and permitted to leave Vienna. All this happens so smoothly and so quickly that one hardly notices anything of it. The excitement is still great, and the Prater empty in spite of the beautiful weather. Tradesmen are doing very badly ; there are shops where nothing at all has been sold since 15th March.

Frederick Hebbel, poet and dramatist, who was born in Holstein, but married in Vienna and settled there, made in his diary the following sarcastic entry for 18th April :

Oh these dear Austrians ! They are now considering how they can unite themselves with Germany without uniting themselves with Germany. That will be hard to do, just as hard as if two people who wanted to kiss each other wished to turn their backs on each other at the same time !

Another revolution in the autumn was to be necessary before the air of Vienna could be cleared, and not in the manner desired by the fond enthusiasts of these days in March and April.

S

CHAPTER IV

REVOLUTION IN BERLIN

THE news of the Revolution of 24th February in Paris did not reach Berlin until a few days later, for the railway did not yet connect the two capitals, and the French had cut the telegraph wires. But on the 27th, Frederick William IV. wrote a letter to Queen Victoria in which he poured out his soul, and called upon Great Britain to join the European powers in a pronouncement which would show that the Great Powers of Europe were united against France. The full text of the letter [1] shows the state of agitation into which he was thrown by the news from Paris :

27th February 1848.

MOST GRACIOUS QUEEN AND SISTER,—Even at this midnight hour of the day, on the evening of which the awful news from Paris has arrived, I venture to address these lines to your Majesty. God has permitted events which decisively threaten the peace of Europe. It is an attempt to ' spread the principle of the Revolution by *every* means throughout the whole of Europe.' This programme binds together both these individuals and their parties. The consequences for the peace of the world are *clear* and *certain*. If the revolutionary party carries out its programme, ' The sovereignty of the people,' my minor crown will be broken, no less certainly than the mighty crowns of your Majesty, and a fearful scourge will be laid upon the nations ; a century (will follow) of rebellion, of lawlessness, and of godlessness. The late King did not dare to write ' by the Grace of God.' *We*, however, call ourselves King ' by the Grace of God,' because it is true. Well, then, most gracious Queen, let us now show to men, to the peoples threatened with disruption and nameless misery, both *that* we understand our sacred office and *how* we understand it. God has placed in your Majesty's hands, in the hands of the two Emperors, in those of the German Federation, and in mine, a power, which, if it now acts in union and harmony, with reliance on Heaven, is able, humanly speaking, to enforce, with certainty, the maintenance of the peace of the world. This power is *not that of arms*, for these, more than ever, must only afford the *ultima ratio*.

---

[1] *Queen Victoria's Letters.* John Murray.

The power I mean is ' the power of united speech.' In the year 1830 the use of this immeasurable power was criminally neglected. But now I think the danger is much more pressing than it was then. This power is divided among *us* in equal portions. I possess the smallest portion of it, and your Majesty has by far the greatest share. That share is so great that your Majesty, by your powerful word, might alone carry out the task. But the certainty of victory lies, subject to the Divine blessing, solely in our utterance being united. This must be our message to France ; ' that all of us are cordial well-wishers to France, we do not grudge her all possible welfare and glory ; we mean never to encroach on it, and we will stand by the new Government as by the old, *foi de gentils-hommes*. But the first breach of the peace, be it with reference to Italy, Belgium, or Germany would be, undoubtedly and at the same time, a breach with ' all of us,' and we should, with all the power that God has given us, let France feel by *sea* and by *land*, as in the years '13, '14, and '15, what our union may mean.'

Now I bless Providence for having placed Lord Palmerston at the head of your Foreign Office, and keeping him there at this very moment. During the last quarter of the past year I could not always cordially agree with him. His genuine British disposition will honour this open confession. All the more frankly may I now express the hopes which rise in me, from the very fact of *his* holding that office at the present moment ; for a more active, more vivid, more energetic Minister of foreign affairs, a man that would more indefatigably pursue great aims, your Majesty could probably never have. If at this grave hour he sets himself to proclaim that our forces are united ; if he himself utters his message as befits St. George, he will earn the blessing of millions, and the blessing of God and of the world will rest on your Majesty's sacred head. That I am your Majesty's and *Old England's* most faithful and most devoted brother and companion, you are aware, and I mean to prove it. On both knees I adjure you, use, for the welfare of Europe, ' *Engellands England.*'

With these words I fall at your Majesty's feet, most gracious Queen, and remain your Majesty's most faithfully devoted, most attached Servant and good Brother,

FREDERICK WILLIAM.

P.S.—The Prince I embrace. He surely feels with me, and justly appraises my endeavours.

Post scriptum, 28th, in the evening.

I venture to open my letter again, for this day has brought us news from France, which one can only call *horrible*. According to what we hear, there is no longer left a King in France. A regency, a government, and the most complete anarchy has ensued, under the name of the Republic—a condition of things in which, at first, there will be no possibility of communicating with the people, infuriated with crime. In case a Government should evolve itself

276 RHYME AND REVOLUTION IN GERMANY

out of this chaos, I conscientiously hold that the ' united word ' of the great Powers, such as I have indicated in the preceding pages, should be made known, *without any modification, to the new holders of power*. Your Majesty's gracious friendship will certainly not take amiss this addition to my letter, though it be not conformable to strict etiquette.

The fate of the poor old King, of the Duchess of Orleans, of the whole honourable and amiable family, cuts me to the heart, for up to this time we do not know what has become of any of them. We owe Louis Philippe eighteen happy years of peace. No noble heart must forget that. And yet—who would not recognise the avenging hand of the King of kings in all this ?

I kiss your Majesty's hands.'

Neither the compliment to England, the Angel-land, nor that to Palmerston, another St. George, prevented the new French Republic from receiving assurances of England's friendship.

On the 28th the Paris news was generally known throughout the city, and the first effect of it is thus described by one who lived through all this period in Berlin : [1]

All classes of people in Berlin like a pleasure that costs nothing or is very cheap. It is a pleasure of this kind to walk about in Unter den Linden in the warm spring sunshine from about 11 to 1 o'clock. There one sees elegant dandies and beggars as well, officers and students, unemployed workmen and pensioned Councillors of State, aristocratic ladies and fashionably dressed courtesans, children's nurses and wet nurses from the country—all with the same occupation and the same object, namely, strolling idly about, looking at the windows of the fashionable shops, rejoicing in the first green shoots of the glorious old lime trees and chestnut trees, or catching now and then the elusive strains of a march or waltz played by the military band on the parade ground at the King's Guard-house. On the 28th of February 1848, in spite of the beautiful weather, this pleasant lounging had suddenly ceased. True, there were many people in Unter den Linden and the Opera Platz that day as usual, but they were not promenaders. Little groups were seen everywhere, made up of men who put their heads close together and talked of prodigious things. If a gendarme went past perhaps they scattered a little or spoke quite low ; but at once a fresh company took their place, discussing the same things ; and from hour to hour the number increased of people who wanted to hear or tell something new. The news that stirred everybody was : ' In Paris a Republic has been proclaimed, Louis Philippe has been driven out ; who knows what will come of it ? ' . . .

---

[1] Angerstein, *Die Berliner Märzereignisse* (K.).

Political movement among the people suddenly became intensely active. All political clubs were animated and open-air meetings were held at the *Zelte* or booths, a pleasure resort between the river Spree and the Tiergarten, surrounded with beer-gardens and beer-houses, which had taken the place of the original refreshment booths. On the open space was a bandstand, and concerts were given on fine evenings. The *Zelte* became a very convenient resort for the noisy and thirsty politician anxious to air his views. But it was not only the restless elements of society that were moved to feverish activity, the City Fathers themselves were soon constrained to seek an audience of His Majesty.

On 5th March the King dismissed the Committee of the Provincial Estates with a speech [1] which irritated rather than reassured public opinion, even among the staidest of the middle-class, so arrogant was still his tone, so little responsive to the hopes and aspirations stirring all hearts :

Providence has permitted events to occur which threaten to shake the foundations of social order. German hearts, Prussian men, men of patriotism and honour, know the special and holy duty that such conditions lay upon them. In similar circumstances (1789) no people on earth ever gave a more elevating example than ours. But that makes it all the more necessary for us to act in the same way at this moment, since we do not want to be less loyal, less courageous, or less persevering than our fathers, or than we ourselves were as young men. Gentlemen, when you go home, give utterance to that which every man of common sense understands, and every man with a noble heart feels. Proclaim to every one this incontestable truth : ' Cease all party strife, concentrate on the one thing necessary, if we want to come with honour and prosperity out of the storm, which can be assuaged by our unanimity, our conduct, and our example, with God's gracious help. Range yourselves, like a wall of brass, about your King, your best friend, full of confidence in him ! ' . . . As soon as the measures which I must take for the safety and honour of Prussia and Germany require the support of my faithful Estates, and at the latest if and when—which may God in His mercy forbid—the general call to arms must be sounded (in the event of a French invasion) I shall again summon you, gentlemen, and your colleagues, the whole United Diet, to give me your advice and support, well knowing that the confidence of my people is my firmest support, and to show the world that in Prussia the King, the People, and the Army are the same from generation to generation !

---

[1] Klein.

On the 13th, Minutoli, Chief of Police, thought the aspect of things so threatening that he addressed in the afternoon the following memorandum [1] to the government :

Since nothing has happened to disprove the supposition that serious friction with the labouring class will occur to-day ; since on the contrary, the attitude of this class appears to be decidedly insolent and provocative ; finally, since it is also not improbable that scenes will begin in various parts of the city : it will be necessary to get ready for these various events. In any case, it will be necessary, on the first outbreak of disturbance,
(1) to garrison the Royal Castle,
and to give orders for
(2) a company for the Town Gaol,
(3) reinforcements of the guard at the Brandenburg Gate,
(4) a guard for the State Prison in Moabit ;
and
(5) to have cavalry available from seven o'clock in the evening, and to direct traffic for the Brandenburg Gate through the Dorotheenstrasse or the Anhaltstrasse, in order that these troops may make an impression on the intended gatherings of the people, or drive them apart, or surround them for convenience in making arrests. . . .
VON MINUTOLI.

The audience of the King which the Municipal Authorities had asked for the 13th was not granted until the 14th, and then the deputation received a far from satisfactory reply to their address, the gist of which was as follows :

When the temperature was at boiling point all round, it was of course not to be expected that opinion in Berlin alone would be below freezing-point, and when this was taken into account it was worthy of acknowledgment that in a city of such a size, where there was no lack of plentiful elements of disorder, there had been no considerable disturbance or disorder. . . . First of all, he was glad to be able to reply, with regard to the chief petition, that it had already been granted. The summoning of the United Diet had been decided upon several days before, and the Decree convoking it had already been signed. . . . He (the King) had taken for his watch-word : ' Free peoples, free princes ' ; only when both were free could true prosperity flourish ! . . . There was one expression in the Address that he must refer to, viz., the one that was directed against a gradual development of the constitution ; he was unable to agree with that unconditionally. There were certain things that could not be hurried, unless one was willing to face the risk of upsetting them. . . . ' Be bold and cautious ' was the motto of every good commander-in-chief. . . . He himself did not want

---

[1] Klein.

to forget that. The good old German way ought not to be disregarded ; the organization of the Estates was German too ; any one who strove against that was exposing himself to dangers.[1] . . .

That day, the 14th, attempts were made to build barricades ; these attempts were frustrated by cavalry, and the crowds became infuriated with the soldiers. Outrages increased and people took to plundering shops, particularly the gunsmiths', where they could help themselves to weapons.

On the 15th, Bodelschwingh, Minister of the Interior, who appears to have been, *pace* the Bismarckian School, a clear-sighted and noble-minded man, with more of the real statesman about him than most of the King's advisers, made a despairing effort to shake the King's obstinate adherence to his project of substituting for the parliament his people desired, and which his father had long promised, a glorified version of the Provincial Estates, of whose futility they were tired. He saw the imminence of danger to the crown of Prussia, but, more than that, he realised that Prussia's one chance of securing the hegemony in Germany lay in her King frankly accepting the necessity for Reform, and he sought to be relieved of his office :

MINISTER VON BODELSCHWINGH TO THE KING [2]

I ventured humbly to inform your Majesty last Sunday that it seemed to me absolutely necessary for Prussia, if she is to maintain herself and become the rallying-point for Germany, to approach the new work that lies unavoidably before her with fresh powers that have not already exhausted themselves in other ways. (That is to say, not with the existing Estates.) Since that time I have come to see that the necessity is thrice as urgent ! ! All German princes, almost without exception, are compelled to reform their ministries and to throw themselves into the arms of radicalism or ultra-radicalism ; God forbid that anything similar should happen with us ! But it can and will be avoided only if your Majesty undertakes the necessary reforms in this direction also, while there is yet time.

As will be seen in the next chapter Bodelschwingh succeeded, but too late. Within three days the vacillating mind of the King was perplexed by the letter [3] of advice he received on the 18th from his old intimate Radowitz, a letter which must be allowed

---

[1] A. Wolff, *Berliner Revolutions-Chronik,* i. (K.).
[2] Klein.   [3] Paul Hassel, *Joseph Maria Radowitz.*

to be a brilliantly able expression of the absolutist point of view :

VIENNA, 16th March 1848.

I implore your Majesty to view firmly all the possible issues of the present moment. . . . In all human probability a flood of petitions will burst forth, threatening demonstrations will come next, and rebellion will follow ; its decisive scene of action in all other states is the capital. Will your Majesty be able to combat it with force, and to the furthest extreme ? In this matter the sphere of duty is co-extensive with the sphere of possibility. If there is a reasonable possibility of actual victory, your Majesty will perform this duty, the hardest of all the duties that fall to the lot of a ruler, to the last step. This last step would be the necessity of leaving Berlin before the troops have degenerated in body and spirit through much street fighting. Experience proves that every prolonged military conflict in large cities leads to the demoralisation of the troops and their officers. For that reason it should be cut short as soon as possible. A withdrawal to Spandau, which such attacks cannot reach ; removal of the Government thither ; the troops brought in from a distance to be concentrated round the fortress ; the greatest care to be given to victualling them. Only the maintenance of civil order in Berlin to be left to the citizens ; any political action to be definitely forbidden so long as the rebellion lasts. Not until order has been completely restored should your Majesty make known whatever you deem useful politically, and then as an act of free will on your part. . . . It is only acts of free will that can save the essence of monarchy and perhaps contain within themselves the germ of legal development. The same measures, if obtained by force during an attempt at rebellion, would lead to the abyss of revolution.

Specimens of Radowitz's letters of advice to the King are interesting, e.g. on the 2nd April 1848, he wrote from Giewitz : ' I therefore most earnestly entreat your Majesty to take a purely temporising attitude for the present. Do not come forward with personal views and inclinations, however well grounded they may be.' And on 13th April 1848 : ' When the next few months are over and your Majesty comes face to face with the actual Diet, there will still be time to achieve great things by circumspect energy. Till that time comes, however, I implore your Majesty not to appear personally or actively anywhere, but to leave to your ministers, in complete accordance with the system of constitutional government that is already actually in existence, the sole responsibility for good or evil.' The day following that on which Bodelschwingh communicated with the King was marked by the first bloodshed in the streets of Berlin. The well-informed Chief of Police knew what was coming, and was in readiness. Here is his memorandum [1] of the 15th to the Berlin Government :

(1) The Castle Guard, a battalion and a squadron at the least, is to march from the Lustgarten to the Gate and remain concealed inside the courtyards.—I request that it be left to the people to make the attack ; all good citizens will remain away, the mob will yield or be destroyed.

(2) The conduct of the masses is no longer in doubt ; it is only a question of the moment when the outbreak will take place.— All are making for the castle.—The inner courtyards must be guarded, and the windows without bars looking on to the carriage-way as well.—The troops must be kept in barracks.—Students are expected to arrive from Leipzig by the next train. A squadron ought to be posted at the station. VON MINUTOLI.

Minutoli was an efficient and not unpopular official, for he discharged his duties sympathetically and with no high hand. It was probably on his suggestion that the City Council issued on the 16th a call for special constables, the form of which may be interesting in these days of special constables at home.[2]

For the last three days the property and persons of the citizens of Berlin have been in the greatest danger. The voice of the community has declared emphatically against disorder and indicated a willingness to assist. It has therefore been resolved that in every ward in the city a Committee of Safety shall be formed, composed of all the members of the local authority, who shall co-opt the most suitable and best known from the number of their fellow-citizens, and particularly high corporation officials and superintendents. The badge of the special constables is a black and white band worn on the left arm, with the word ' special constable ' stamped thereon, and a white staff. Disobedience to the orders of a special constable will be punished as offences against a member of the local authority or against a sentry. We have confidence in our fellow-citizens and in the population generally, and believe that they will extend to a measure, which has been adopted in the interest of public peace and order, consideration and support.

The confidence of the authorities was misplaced, for though some twelve hundred men of good position, including one hundred and twenty students, were enrolled, they were quite ineffective against the now excited populace, were insulted and dubbed ' undertakers,' and at times had to seek the protection of the soldiers at the nearest guard-house. In the afternoon a

[1] Klein.   [2] Quoted by Blum.

collision between the crowd and the military took place and first blood was drawn, and of this some account will be given in the extract from Carl Frenzel's reminiscences of these days printed in the next chapter.

For the time order seemed to be restored. The 17th was a day of perfect quiet, a fact which those who hold that the rising of the 18th was the artificial creation of a band of professional agitators from outside explain by the suggestion that a breathing-space was necessary to prepare for the great effort next day, whereby respectable citizens should be sucked into the whirlpool of revolution. If so the King was deceived, for he congratulated the government on the preservation of law and order :

BERLIN, 17*th March* 1848.

I commission you to express to all the troops, without any exception, who have taken part against the unruly mobs here in the last few days my full acknowledgment of the exemplary conduct, endurance, and discipline displayed by them.

CHAPTER V

THE BARRICADES

AT 6 A.M. on the morning of the 18th, Bodelschwingh sent an urgent summons to the Oberbürgermeister to meet the Chief of Police and himself at 8 o'clock. News had reached him of a great demonstration in front of the Castle planned for the afternoon :

In the night just past, I received a report from a district official (of the Gendarmen Market) that several volunteer corps, into which many Jews have forced themselves (originating with the ninth corps, he thinks) are preparing for a great demonstration to present Addresses at two o'clock to-day. Von Minutoli, the Chief of Police, also reports this preparation. As such a demonstration would be extremely unpleasant, especially to-day, when so much might develop here and really might affect the fate of Prussia, I esteem it my duty to take steps against it as far as possible, and beg your Worship to lend me your support. I should be specially glad if you could come to me this morning at 8 o'clock, with Moewes the Syndic if possible ; Herr von Minutoli is coming at that time too.

The King spent the morning feverishly at work in his effort to give form to the suggestions which had been made to him by Bodelschwingh on the 15th. He gave an audience to a deputation of the City Council at 1.30, as a result of which posters, above the names of the Municipal Authorities, were displayed all over the city, in the vain hope of allaying popular excitement. It was too late ; fighting had begun.

PROCLAMATION BY THE BERLIN MUNICIPAL BOARD [1]

The Municipal Board has been officially informed that an Act concerning the freedom of the press, based on most liberal principles, has already been irrevocably signed, and the Municipal Board

---

[1] Klein.

guarantees the confirmation of this government measure with all
its strength. Moreover, his Majesty is at the present moment
occupied in signing decisions which will permanently ensure the
well-being of the Fatherland. The Diet will be summoned for the 2nd April.

What took place on the Castle Square up to 2 P.M. is thus
described by an eye-witness : [1]

At 11 A.M. I found the city perfectly quiet and cheerful enough.
. . . In the Castle Square about two thousand citizens were assembled
in groups, all well dressed and very respectable people. . . . They
told each other of the urgent representations which the deputation
from the Rhine had made ; they said they had been informed of a
partial change in the Ministry, etc. I found the people in an
excited mood but not at all hostile. On the contrary, the groups
gave loud cheers for the King time after time. Quite in the background, at the corners of the streets leading into the Square, I saw
working-men and common people standing. A few came one by
one to the front, and when they saw the cheerful faces round them
they said, ' This sort of thing won't help us poor people at all ! '
Then citizens went up to them, quieted them and warned them not
to repeat the excesses of the previous days : that would not lead
to anything. All the shops in the Square were open, and ladies
had occupied the windows. The passages through the Castle were
open too ; a Council of Ministers was being held in the King's Cabinet.
Inside the Castle the troops from Potsdam were bivouacked ; they
were smoking and walking about the courtyard, mingling with
the citizens. Meanwhile the Castle Square was more thronged
than ever, and the people began to discuss the suggestion put
forward that it was absolutely necessary that the soldiers from
outside should leave Berlin, and that the troops in barracks round
about Berlin should withdraw as well. It was then quite plain
that great bitterness against the troops prevailed—a fairly instinc-
tive bitterness not affected by politics . . . and one that gave
cause to fear the worst. Further, about 1 P.M. the crowd pressed
unmistakably towards the porch leading to the King's apartments.
Troops had been posted to defend this porch. It must also be
mentioned that the staircase leading to the Royal Apartments was
only protected by a light wooden erection. About half-past one
the King appeared on the balcony and attempted to speak. A
gentleman with him, Herr Naunyn, the Burgomaster, if I am not
mistaken, said with a loud voice something to this effect :

It is the King's will that the Press shall be free ;
It is the King's will that the Diet be summoned at once ;
It is the King's will that there shall be a Constitution on the most
liberal basis to include all German countries ;

---

[1] Angerstein, *Berliner Märzereignisse* (K.).

It is the King's will that there shall be a German National Flag;
It is the King's will that all Customs barriers shall be done away
with in Germany;

It is the King's will that Prussia shall place herself at the head
of the movement. (It was the substance of the Decree of 18th
March.)

The enthusiasm that prevailed in the Square was so violent
that it might almost have been taken to be the result of intoxica-
tion. People of the most highly educated classes jumped up on to
vehicles in order to spread the good news. The King came out on
the balcony again, and was greeted with enthusiastic signs of
rejoicing; he waved his handkerchief. A gentleman, whom I
took to be Herr von Bodelschwingh, expressed the King's thanks
from the balcony, but at the same time made known his own wish
that there should be no more demonstrations. About this time I
left the Square and went to the Königstrasse to have my midday
meal there. I saw people embracing each other and crying for
joy; women at the windows waved their handkerchiefs; materials
for bonfires in the evening were carried through the streets, and
the citizens who met me shouted, 'We want to go to the Castle
Square too, we want to cheer our beloved King too.' It was two
o'clock; I was seated at a table in the ' Crown Prince ' restaurant
half way along the Königstrasse; collections for the poor were
made as a token of rejoicing; people from the city came in to
celebrate the joyful day at the table d'hôte; congratulations
went round on the fact that the great day of freedom and new birth
had dawned for Prussia too, and had dawned gloriously, without
the shedding of blood.

Then came the catastrophe.. Two shots were fired by the
soldiers on the crowd at the Long Bridge. The King always
stoutly maintained that the guns went off by accident, and
Prince Hohenlohe-Ingelfingen states in his *Memoirs, Aus
meinem Leben*, that the Emperor William himself told him in
1881 that he saw the guns go off with muzzles in the air :

The present Kaiser (William I.) at that time Prince of Prussia, was
observing the doings of the infantry from a window of the Royal
Castle, and saw how two rifles, with the muzzles pointed upwards,
went off. He exclaimed : ' Oh, there are two rifles just discharged
into the air ! I hope no one in the houses opposite has been wounded ;
all the windows there are full of people.' He told me this himself
once.

But Prince Hohenlohe goes on to add a detail to this story
which does not, to say the least, add to its credibility :

Furthermore the two soldiers whose muskets went off were discovered. Their sworn statements agreed with those of the men

beside them, that their guns went off, and that as they looked down towards the ground they saw street urchins who in the pressure of the crowd had cocked the guns and pulled the triggers. It was therefore a put up job on the part of the rioters, and answered as well as if the two shots had come from the rioters' ranks as a signal.

History is never able to decide on the truth or not of these accounts of 'accidents.' Anyhow, accident or not, the result was disastrous. The following is the vivid account of an eye-witness : [1]

At one moment everybody was rejoicing and shouting 'Hurrah !' and a few minutes later all was changed to yells of rage and cries for revenge. In one hour the appearance of the city was entirely different, its physiognomy quite transformed. 'To the church towers !' was the cry, 'To the alarm bells !' and the church doors were broken open by force, for no one would wait till the sexton arrived with the keys. . . . As if by magic barricades arose. At every street corner people gathered, young and old, of high and low degree, to build barricades. Stalls, carriages, omnibuses, cabs, heavy transport wagons, postal and brewery carts and scaffolding poles were collected by thousands of hands in all parts of the city. Even women and children took part ; the unity which prevailed in building was marvellous. All were equal ; e.g., two men would be seen dragging a beam, one a workman with a torn shirt and the other a well-dressed gentleman. The chief materials of the barricades nearly everywhere were torn up pavements, stone flags, beams, and the many boards and planks lying across the gutters, or carriages, carts, etc., which were upset. Beds, sacks of flour, and furniture were brought out of the houses ; every one gave willingly what he had, gates, doors, fences, palings, hooks, bars, etc. Everything was done in perfect order, and everywhere with the same remarkable speed and contempt of death. People co-operated throughout. . . . At that moment there were only two parties : citizen and soldier, the people and the troops. The women made coffee, cut sandwiches, and handed food out into the street for the workmen and the fighters. In the streets bullets were moulded and lance tips forged ; many zinc bars brought from workshops, lead and so on were cut up into small pieces to load the muskets.

And now will be given a vivid account of the fighting in the streets and at the barricades by an officer who took a prominent part in it, Prince Hohenlohe-Ingelfingen.[2] Hohenlohe at the time was a lieutenant in the Guards Artillery, aged twenty-one, attained subsequently high military rank, and in the Franco-German War was actually in control of the artillery attack on

---

[1] F. Steinmann, *Geschichte der preussischen Revolution* (K.).
[2] *Aus meinem Leben.*

Paris. He won as high a reputation in the literature as in the practice of his profession, and his straightforward account of the fighting on the 18th is the frankest and clearest record extant of the military operations and the behaviour of the troops —a far more adequate account than is given, for instance, by Leopold von Gerlach in his *Reminiscences*. But, to check his observations on other matters than the actual fighting, we shall follow up his account with the equally frank impressions of Carl Frenzel,[1] another young man of twenty-one, who lived through the scene as a civilian, to become not a general but a long-haired German author, and who, like Hohenlohe, subsequently published his recollections. The reader will then realise the sort of evidence on which the professional historian has to make up his mind when giving judgment on the character of a popular movement :

PRINCE HOHENLOHE-INGELFINGEN'S ACCOUNT

We were just sitting down to table. A plate of warm soup was steaming in front of me, and a glass of wine-cup was actually being served, when the Colonel shouted : ' Up, gentlemen, every one to his post ! '

We officers of the Horse Artillery, as we had to make for the Oranienburger Gate, sprang up and hurried off, so as not to leave the men at the gate, near Borsig's workshops, etc., without any one to take command. As we were about to leave the Barracks by the exit on to the Kupfergraben an old gentleman with white hair stumbled up to us and called out : ' In God's name, gentlemen, don't venture into the street. I 've been an officer, and know what danger is. I implore you. You 're all doomed if you go out into the street.'

For a moment we looked at one another disconcerted. I remarked that if we all went together it would take a powerful mob to hold back twelve officers from their duty. So we went down the Artillerie-strasse, and the old gentleman called after us : ' Alas, poor gentlemen ! '

In the Artilleriestrasse we came to a place where, by shoving vehicles together, a beginning had been made with a barricade. Seeing our number people left us in peace, and we reached without hindrance the batteries at the Oranienburger Gate.

Lieutenant von Kräwell had the most extraordinary experience. He went home first to the Schiffbauer Embankment, not far from the Unterbaum, mounted his horse and rode towards the barracks. On the way a barricade blocked the street. He was

---

[1] *Die Berliner Märztage*, Reclam.

faced with the muzzles of rifles and a loud shout, ' Go back ! ' He
said quietly, ' You fellows must be mad, I think. Don't you see
that I must go on duty ? ' Thereupon a gap was made in the
barricade with the utmost willingness, and when he had roughly
abused them because the gap was too narrow for his horse, it was
made larger and he passed through the barricade, which was closed
again behind him and guarded. It remained untaken, by the way,
for it was never attacked. The unimportant alley which it guarded
was not the scene of any of the fighting. . . . Consequently the
defenders of their fatherland there could say with good conscience
that they had not yielded ground.

In the barracks we awaited further orders. For my part I was
in great perplexity. Despite instructions my charger was not yet
at the barracks. Soon came the order that the battery to which
I belonged was to march to the Castle ; for all the other batteries
ammunition was to be fetched from the arsenal. The second
mounted battery marched off, and the above-mentioned Lieutenant von Kräwell rode with several teams to the arsenal to bring
the ammunition wagons. I was in despair at being unmounted.
I ran into the stable belonging to the battery and saw standing
there, ready saddled, the doctor's charger ; he had not arrived,
and I mounted the horse. But the old fellow stuck to his place,
like Trajan to his column ! . . . At this moment my servant arrived
with my charger. In the Friedrichstrasse he had fallen into the
hands of a crowd of rebels, who sought to claim the horse as fine
booty. My servant defended himself with the aid of my good
Roderick, . . . who kicked out and bit. With a broken martingale
my servant got through. I set the harness right as best I could,
sprang on my horse's back, and made as though I was off after
the battery. At the gate men shouted to me that outside the gate
there was a crowd of rioters. I ordered the gate to be opened, and
rode at a gallop right through the crowd, riding down several. A
student, a fair-haired youth, with a blue cap and a black, red, and
yellow sash, struck at me with his sword, but missed, and I looked
back with a laugh and waved him a friendly good-bye.

[Not long afterwards, about half an hour, Lieutenant von
Kräwell returned with the ammunition.]

In front of the barrack gates he was attacked by a mob. The
gunners rushed out of the barracks on foot and came to his aid.
He was struck in the face by a paving-stone, which knocked in
six of his front teeth, so that he fell backwards on to his horse's
crupper. A student seized the horse's bridle with his left hand,
and was just going to ' do him in ' with his rapier, when a gunner
aimed a blow at the student, who ducked his head to avoid it. At
that moment Kräwell recovered consciousness, and got in a smashing blow on the student's unprotected neck. The young fellow
collapsed. He lay ill for a long time afterwards, and in the end
died of his wound. He was a Herr von Bojanowsky. His father
or grandfather is said to have been aide-de-camp to Frederick

William III. The whole family was distressed over the young man's erratic behaviour.

Meantime, I had long been with my battery. I caught it up while it was still in the Oranienstrasse, and, as the Artilleriestrasse was closed by a barricade, we marched through the Montbijouplatz and across the Hercules Bridge . . . to the Castle Square. There we again placed ourselves in reserve. Soon we heard fighting and cries on all sides.

[An adjutant came galloping up to the battery with the news of grape-shot at the Oranienburg Gate, the first cannon-shot in the city, which accounted for half a dozen victims, with innocent spectators among them. Presently the other batteries from the Oranienburg Gate, now supplied with ammunition, joined Hohenlohe's battery in the Castle Square. Lieutenant von Kräwell had grown faint through loss of blood on the way, and taken sick leave. He rode quietly home, again had a passage opened for him through the barricade, and got unmolested to bed.

Before darkness came on Hohenlohe's captain was ordered to load two guns with grape-shot, and advance them to cover the bridge by the Bourse, in case the revolutionaries attempted an attack on that side. Hohenlohe was put in charge, and had been standing for about an hour when General von Pfuel, recently appointed Governor of the city, came up to him, and said he 'might as well' cross the bridge and fire a couple of shots at the Hercules Bridge, where a number of the insurgents were collected. The shots 'would have a good effect.' Hohenlohe very properly referred him to his commanding officer, who pointed out that his orders were given him by General von Prittwitz personally. The pair then made their way to headquarters in the Castle courtyard. Prittwitz was furious. The Hercules Bridge was occupied by troops, and he had forgotten to order Hohenlohe's two guns to be withdrawn ! Hohenlohe was promptly ordered to rejoin his battery.

His dry comment on the affair is that there were too many orders flying round, beginning with the expression, 'You might as well.' Had he carried out General von Pfuel's instructions and shot down his own comrades in arms, the general would certainly not have defended him, but declared that he had only expressed an opinion. Hohenlohe continues as follows :]

Opposite the Castle was the Breitestrasse, which was shut off opposite the Cölln town hall by a barricade, over which waved a large black, red, and gold flag, the colours of the revolutionaries. General von Prittwitz sent out a battalion to attack it. But a fierce and effective fire from the barricade, which wounded the commander, Lieutenant-Colonel von Falkenstein . . . among others, indicated the necessity of beginning the attack with artillery. A battery of twelve-pounders advanced. Then came an order from the King not to fire. The rebels had promised themselves to remove the barricade within an hour if they were not attacked. After an hour the barricade was twice as high and strong. . . .

T

This very barricade had, after all, now to be bombarded and stormed. Close behind it was the strongly held town hall. The rebels blazed away with every sort of fire-arm, from cellar windows and attic windows, and used projectiles of the most various and horrible descriptions. An unfortunate soldier was dangerously wounded with a charge of steel pens in the stomach. This maddened our men, already much excited by the wounding of Falkenstein. Long enough had they been compelled to suffer patiently the insults of the mob. Many times had they endured, standing motionless, a hail of stones. Discipline was strong enough to prevent any reprisals so long as the use of weapons was not allowed. In the preceding days it had repeatedly happened that the officer commanding, when the insolence of the mob had become unbearable, had given the order, when rifles were loaded, ' Present ! ' If the mob then took to their heels, the order to fire was not given, but ' Ground arms ! ' instead, and not a shot was fired, a test of discipline which is not always successful even on the drill-ground.

But when the order for the capture of the barricade came along, the troops were let go, and their rage found vent. The barricade itself was only weakly held, for in face of the preceding artillery-fire the defenders had mostly deserted it and established themselves in the adjacent houses. Massed fire from the infantry made positions at window or in attic too dangerous, the barricade was stormed in a single charge, the doors of the neighbouring houses were smashed in, and the flood of soldiers poured into the rooms inside. The bulk of the defenders were posted in the Cölln town hall. In the large hall forty-seven so-called defenders of the Fatherland, well-armed, were collected together. As the soldiers pressed in and made use of bayonet and butt the cry rang out to them : *Pitié ! Vous êtes donc pire que les Russes.* Not one of these ' heroes of Berlin ' could speak German. Our fellows shouted : ' What ! we 'll show you how German 's spoken.' And very soon there were but forty-seven corpses. Ninety-seven bodies in all were removed from the Cölln town hall. . . .

During the taking of the Cölln town hall other corresponding columns advanced in radiating lines down the streets that called for attack. A lively resistance was offered in the narrow Königstrasse. Here there were barricades, one behind another, at every cross-road. Each barricade was first pounded with artillery, then stormed, and the adjoining houses taken in turn.

In the Friedrichstrasse again the resistance was marked. In particular there was a large house in which the rioters had taken up their position ; it was near a strong barricade, at the corner of the Mohrenstrasse, I think. This house was very well known to all of us. For whenever we marched past it with music on our way to drill, there always used to stand at one of the windows the actress, Fräulein Viereck, who was at that time famous both for her beauty and for her unrivalled artistic achievements. The rioters had established themselves in her apartments as well, and because they had reasons for reproaching her with a preference for aristocrats in uniform they wanted to murder her. The terrified actress was forced to escape by a back stair in very incomplete attire (a dressing-gown). She found safety and shelter for the night in the apartments of an acquaintance of mine, who had never known her personally before, and who for his part spent the night fighting in the streets.

In this house resistance was chiefly maintained by Poles and students. Fusiliers of the second Guards Regiment forced their way in, the Hun-like,[1] white-bearded Lieutenant-Colonel von Rauchhaupt at their head. He hurried to the roof from which a hail of stones and gun shots had rained down on the troops. The moment he stepped on to the roof of the four-storied house a student standing above fired a pistol at him. Rauchhaupt seized him by the collar with his fist and hurled the lad right down on to the street. The Fusiliers pressing behind did the like with the rest of the garrison on the roof.

Countless other scenes of the same kind took place. I have only given such accounts as agreed, although derived from various sources. Everywhere, in obedience to their orders, the soldiers took in a flash streets, houses, and barricades. Nowhere did the weak, irresolute opposition detain them for a moment, though many of the houses had been long and systematically prepared for defence. Windows were found blocked with sods in which loop-holes were contrived. These pieces of turf were several days old ; so they had been brought there long before. And of all this our police had had no suspicion (?).

The resistance of the rebels was not in the least heroic. They shot, as has been said, murderously, but in hand to hand fighting they were mostly cowards. The majority of those who fought was made up of a foreign rabble and working men from the dregs of the people, clothed with rags, only in shirts, generally open in front, and linen trousers, and intoxicated to madness. Remains of the drink served to them were found. It was brandy mixed with a decoction of tobacco. The last makes men mad and bloodthirsty when drunk. Not one Berlin citizen was to be found among the combatants. Of the class of intelligent and educated Berliners there were only a few students and other perverted youths, who were really eager for some exploit. Only these, like some well-dressed Poles and Frenchmen, showed courage.

The noise on that evening was terrible. The hoarse shouts of the men fighting, the unbroken rattle of infantry fire, and in addition, as a bass part, the deep roar of the guns, which when they were fired smashed the windows of neighbouring houses into dust, so that a rain of glass fell on to the gunners' heads and made them look as if they had been sprinkled with flour, the continuous ringing of the alarm from all the bells of the churches occupied by the rioters, the darkness, which threw the conflagrations into relief—all these things made the evening full of horror. It is true that the noise of battle is much greater,

---

[1] This epithet indicates little objection on the part of a Prussian officer to be called a Hun.

that fighting in towns and villages in time of battle is just like such street fighting as far as the noise and the conflagrations are concerned, and that the risk to life is much greater—but street fighting in your own country in the midst of peace has something indescribably weird about it, rather like the raging of an earthquake. One does not know who and where the enemy is. The tricks of the rioters, and the semi-murderous character of their actions, are frightfully loathsome and provoke rage and cruelty. It would have been well if the gentle and impressionable mind of the King had not been exposed to this noise and the direct impressions of it all. But in his apartments at the corner of the Castle Square and the river Spree he heard the terrible noise at first hand ; and then came the thought that he was fighting against his subjects, whose happiness was the object of his life! Such a night was bound to affect him deeply.

If we are to believe Prince Hohenlohe-Ingelfingen the revolution was, as the King always averred, no spontaneous rising of the citizens, but the mere explosion of the passions of the lowest dregs of the population, instigated by a handful of Polish and French incendiaries. He even suggests that not a real Berliner was engaged. Rather different is the view suggested by Carl Frenzel.[1] He admits that after the King's announcement on 14th March of his intention to summon the United Landtag, there were still alive in the city the embers of insurrection ; and he tells of a visit of his to the *Zelte* on the evening of the 13th, and how narrowly avoided was a collision between soldiers and the crowd both there and, later, in the heart of the city :

I do not mean to say that there was no revolutionary spirit in the city—that there were not individuals and even whole groups who, from love of disorder and rowdyism, did not in their hearts long for barricades and insurrection. But these unruly elements would have been easily repressed by the body of citizens, backed as it was by a garrison of ten thousand men consisting entirely of picked troops, had this same civic community not been embittered by five long days of mistaken measures and forced, more or less against their will, into that passive resistance which, on the morning of the 19th of March, brought matters to a decision.

On the evening of the 13th March this change from peace to war had taken place. On that day especially fiery speeches were to be made and energetic resolutions carried. The evening was mild and there was no wind ; the moon stood in the quiet sky. Unter den Linden was as full of people as on a Sunday afternoon. All were making for the Tiergarten. . . . To-day the Garden and the Platz (the *Zelte*) were already closely thronged with people ; they all

---

[1] C. Frenzel, *Die Berliner Märztage*.

pressed towards the lighted windows, but after every step the movement was blocked by the crowd. . . . It was proposed that the
speakers should come out and speak from the bandstand. But in
the moonlit night we had no longer any time or leisure for a popular
assembly of that kind with impassioned speeches. Some of those
who were standing farthest away on the roadway began to cry, ' The
soldiers ! The soldiers ! ' And soon enough the clatter of horses'
hoofs was heard ; then several squadrons of the Cuirassier Guards,
with swords drawn, charged the crowd and the *Zelte*. The people
cursed and shrieked, but did not think of resisting. The whole crowd
turned about and made for the Brandenburg Gate. The Cuirassiers
wheeled round as well, and accompanied us on both flanks and in the
rear. Force had not been used so far, and no one had been wounded,
but feeling grew more bitter when the Pariser Platz and Unter den
Linden were reached. There the crowd was twice as large, and the
Cuirassiers rode up closer, and drove the masses to one side at various
points, in order to clear the way for themselves. . . . Our own
momentum and the pressure of the soldiers drove us down the Linden
. . . towards the Castle Square It was impossible to come out
from the crowd as long as the cavalry were at our side and on our
heels. With every moment the danger increased of things assuming
an aspect of strife and violence, even if the people had in fact done
nothing to provoke it either actively or by their unruliness. In the
open space before the Castle the collisions were more numerous, and
the pushing and struggling began to look ugly. The narrow street
was made still narrower by a high scaffolding, which jutted far out in
front of the Eosander Gate of the Castle and had been put up for the
erection of a high dome on the chapel. ' If that could be set on fire ! '
cried some one in the crowd suddenly. All eyes were turned to the
scaffolding, to the planks, poles, and beams, which loomed up
gigantic in the darkness. But others told the speaker to be quiet,
and gave warnings against acts of violence. ' The King is sure to
make concessions,' they said, ' we don't need any revolution.' ' Down
with the soldiers ! ' cried others ; ' down with them ! ' repeated the
crowd in threatening tones which showed firm determination and
gave no promise of peace. Once the Castle Square had been reached
the thousands who formed the crowd had an opportunity of dispers-
ing through the Brüderstrasse and the Breitestrasse and over the
Long Bridge. Before ten o'clock in the evening the usual calm had
once more come over the town.

[He goes on to tell of the natural result of these experiences on the
average citizen :] Before the clock struck ten, the peaceful aspect of
the city had been restored. But in hearts and heads there still raged
alarm, exasperation and combativeness. The government had
needlessly aroused the latent hostility between soldier and citizen. I
cannot recall, looking back on my youth, any unpleasant incident in
which officers took part against civilians. Their mutual relations
were, it is true, of the coolest ; on the side of the civilians there
reigned an unconquerable mistrust and on that of the officers arrogance

and disdain. They were not precisely at daggers drawn, but the barriers which separated nobility and commoners were most acutely felt in intercourse with officers. The citizens of Berlin became conscious of these sombre feelings on the evening of the 13th of March.

[On 16th March Frenzel was in the Castle Square and witnessed there the first actual collision between the military and the public Despite even this provocation he declares that the dominant feeling in the city was peaceable, and he denies emphatically that either Polish or French emissaries were at work among the proletariat :]

On Thursday, 16th March, late in the afternoon, I was in the Square in front of the Opera House by the bronze statue of Blücher. Round about stood people talking eagerly. Any one who came along joined one of the groups automatically. The King's promises were eagerly discussed. The news of the revolution in Vienna and of the flight o Metternich encouraged and inflamed opinion among the people Should Berlin remain behind Vienna and be content with the meagre concessions of the Government ? We had no hated Minister who embodied the old system so completely in his own person as Metternich did, and whose dismissal we could demand as a satisfaction for freedom. Bodelschwingh, Eichhorn and Savigny were far too unknown to the people, and too indifferent, to arouse their wrath. But they had something before their eyes that continually insulted, injured, and enraged them. ' Away with the soldiers ! '—the people concentrated their demands in these words, and the cry grew more and more violent. So it was on that afternoon. The new Guard-house had in those days no railings to protect it in front and at the sides. The crowd pressed forward, and there was no obstacle between them and the soldiers. There were not many people shouting out or making an uproar ; the great majority were gobemouches and idle spectators In front there was a struggle. We saw one of the police with the white band on his arm run into the Guard-house. It may be tha those who were threatening him wanted to follow him, or that th officer thought himself in danger—there was a short roll of drum and, as no one moved from the spot—a volley. Two were killed and several wounded. Then the horrified people scattered in all directions yelling, groaning, and cursing. The soldiers did not advance any further. I was driven towards the side of the Prince of Prussia' palace. For although the crowd had taken to flight the crush wa very great. When we came to a stand, an old, well-dressed man a my side flung his hat on the ground, either in wrath or in the reaction of fright, and wrung his hands aloft. ' Prussians fire on Prussians, he cried, and the tears ran down his cheeks. The sight made an indelible impression on me. How typical as an expression of th situation this slight incident was, I naturally did not grasp till much later.

The populace had, doubtless, during all these days done man improper things, but when one considered fairly the excitement and restlessness which were so continually renewed by the quick and constant succession of tidings from France, Austria, and all th

German cities, it had really committed no deed of violence, no revolutionary breach of the law. The Berlin people had not even yet
conceived the idea of a contest with the military. Had this, as was
maintained later, been intended, very different preparations would
have been made for street fighting, and very different weapons
provided. In all the encounters which had hitherto taken place, the
only weapons made use of by the rioters were boards from the gutter-
crossings and paving-stones from the street. This dominating trait
of peaceableness revealed itself on Friday the 17th of March when it
was strong enough to restrain every outburst of passion. In spite of
the arrival of the deputations from Silesia and the Rhine Province,
which were to ask the King to abolish the censorship immediately and
hasten the meeting of the United Parliament, in spite of the previous
day's casualties, which seemed to cry for vengeance, Berlin remained
quiet. No gatherings in the streets either by day or night. In out-
of-the-way alleys where neither police nor soldiers were to be seen,
nothing stirred. No insurrectionary councils were held in church,
factory, or beer-house. No suspicious figures either Polish or French
were seen distributing five-franc pieces amongst the workers. Berlin
was wrapped in the deepest calm.

[Then Frenzel gives a clear story of the revulsion of feeling that
took place on the 18th following on the two shots by the Long Bridge :]
People congratulated each other on the peaceful course things had
taken, but one refrain sounded shrill and sharp through every one's
thoughts : ' Away with the military ! ' Not a word was raised in
favour or defence of the soldiers. ' We citizens,' it was declared,
' will keep watch and ward over our city and maintain order ; not
again shall it be entrusted to those young and supercilious officers.'
In their happy confidence all were convinced that the King also would
consent to the removal of the troops.

In the unusually warm and sunny March of that year the 18th was
one of the most beautiful days with a sky of cloudless blue and sunshine like May. The citizens of Berlin were making ready between
noon and two o'clock to give the King a great demonstration of
loyalty on the Castle Square. When the high school classes closed
at noon, the town was still intoxicated with joy. Not till three
o'clock did I hear in the Rosenthalstrasse, where I was then living,
wild shouting, tumult and cries for weapons. The people were
rushing to the Haack Market, some terrified, some snorting with fury.
The most defiant were brandishing bludgeons, crowbars, or hatchets
in their hands. The fateful doings on the Castle Square were re-
counted with the most fanciful exaggerations : the infantry had shot
down and the dragoons sabred the citizens waiting to shout ' Long
live the King ! ' Many were killed and wounded. And to establish
the truth of this—who in such an hour would have thought of it ?
Gusts of panic alternated with bursts of fury. Anger and hate filled
all hearts. If the military wanted a fight, now they should have it !
My first thought was to go to my mother, who in the perfect quietness
prevailing at noon had gone to a friend's in the Königstrasse to hear

and see something of the procession in front of the palace. But I could not get through the Spandauerstrasse. Everywhere torn up pavement, gangways lifted from their places, overturned wagons and handcarts !

[From an attic window in the house of his uncle, right in the heart of the disturbed district, Frenzel looked out and listened all through the night :] When dusk set in, the air began to be filled with low wailing and the clang of ringing bells. They sounded from every church all the evening—all through the night. Sometimes there was a short space of silence and then the tocsin began again. From the attic windows in front we could see right away over the Weiden-damme Bridge and on the other side to the Linden. The moon shone calm and full in the sky. The greater part of the troops were moving gradually away from our part of the street towards the Halle Gate. Obviously there was fighting going on there. Dull sounds of shouting and musketry reached us. The sentinels who had remained in front of our houses were not numerous. But neither in our house nor the next, which we communicated with across a little courtyard wall, was there a single weapon. It was not discipline or courage or clever leadership—it was the unarmed condition of the people which gave the troops the advantage from the very start. On the other hand the populace refused the soldiers any kind of food or drink. . . .

Later we could hear the distant thunder of artillery. No one thought of sleep, and towards midnight the sky to the north of us was lighted with the red glare of conflagrations. The populace had set the military workshops, foundry and sheds on fire. Uncertainty regarding the course and outcome of the struggle gave rise to hourly increasing anxiety. The occasional silence and the cessation of the firing seemed to us even more weird than the noise of the fighting.

Morning dawned at last ; in its early light the troops were withdrawn to barracks and the cannon rolled away from the streets. I left the house with my brother after eight o'clock. We walked along the Friedrichstrasse towards the Halle Gate. Till we reached the Behrenstrasse no traces of the insurrection and the fighting were to be noticed. How unpremeditated the whole battle of the barricades had been could be recognised in the fact that no attempt had been made to raise a barrier at this, the narrowest part of the street. From the Französischestrasse onwards the pavement of the roadway had been torn up for a great distance. We climbed over the ruins of the first barricade at the Taubenstrasse. It had been under artillery fire. From here on to the Leipzigerstrasse the effects of the fight were seen in the burst and shattered windows, the doors torn off their hinges, the ravaged pavement, the smashed up carriages and omnibuses. The dead and wounded had long before been carried into the houses. There were few people in the street. With wan and distorted faces they talked in low voices to each other of the scenes of terror they had come through. Beyond the Leipzigerstrasse the soldiers had not advanced, and here, towards one in the morning the last shots had been fired. It had taken them almost ten hours to get this length from the Linden. Of their losses nothing was known ; regarding their exhaustion, anger and brutality, where they had forced their way into houses, all accounts agreed.

But there is no doubt, from the numerous accounts left by persons of respectable condition who actually took part in the fighting, that the rising was a spontaneous one and that good citizens did take part in it, though no doubt a body of Polish revolutionaries was at work in Berlin as in every centre of possible disturbance in Germany at this period. Gerlach comments on the small damage inflicted on the military by what Prince Hohenlohe would have us to believe was a well-prepared revolutionary force. ' The light losses of the troops, 18 killed, 26 missing, 204 wounded, are explained by the fact that stones are only a dangerous weapon when skilfully thrown, that tiles hardly ever inflict a serious wound, that the rebels were cowards and shot badly, e.g., they stopped firing in the Königstrasse as soon as one of them was wounded, and that the houses were only defended at the entrance and occasionally, out of desperation, on the top floor.' Some doubt is thrown on what Gerlach says when we read a letter which Varnhagen von Ense, soldier, diplomat, critic and biographer, and one of the chief figures in the literary life of Berlin, wrote to Kerner on 28th March 1848. His story at any rate affords little evidence to support the King's contention that the revolution was the work of the rabble !

That the attack on unarmed citizens, calling out ' Long live the King ! ' arose through a misunderstanding, cannot be accepted. . . . The quarter in which I live was closed by barricades which were victoriously held by a small number of heroes against several attacks. Under my windows a half company of foot-soldiers collapsed beneath the dreadful hail of stones that rattled down from the roofs. Never have I seen greater courage, more resolute contempt of death, than in these young men, who were beaten down and lost beyond all hope of rescue ! . . . Well-bred students in fine clothing, menservants, apprentices, youths, old labourers, all went to make up a single company and vied with one another in courage and endurance. Nothing of the sort had I hitherto experienced as an eye-witness ! And I am glad to have been through these experiences !

These accounts, written from various points of view, give a vivid picture of the Berlin revolution at its height. The actual fighting, though fierce, was not of long duration, but its importance was heightened by the collapse of King and government described in the following chapters. Until the troops were ordered to withdraw they proceeded with the task of clearing the barricades. As prisoners were taken they were conveyed to the Castle, and Prince Hohenlohe tells us how they were received there :

Our soldiers grew very bored. It was not possible to keep them standing at attention the whole time ; they stood at ease instead. When it grew cool, they walked with short steps to and fro, and when darkness came, it was impossible to see whether each one was at his post. But soon there was entertainment enough, even for them ; for all who had been taken prisoners in the barricade and house fighting were brought under orders—though it seems incomprehensible—to the Royal Castle and assembled there. At first our fellows were amused at the sight of this dissolute and hopelessly drunken mob of blackguards, many of whom, even when they were surrounded by soldiers, delivered incoherent speeches, under the impression that they were at a meeting of the people. But then wounded soldiers too were brought to the Castle. The sight of them filled our gunners with wrath, and the less prospect they had of avenging the blood of their comrades by any action of their own the angrier they became. But when a soldier was carried past whose whole face had been scalded with boiling oil and another who had been wounded by a charge of steel pens, when they learnt that the sentry at the Bank had been attacked by hundreds to one, overpowered, and killed, then their rage knew no bounds, and they did not understand why any prisoners should be taken at all. The drivers with knout or whip, and the gunners with sabre or side-arms, encircled every batch of prisoners, and did not take their eyes off the accompanying squad for a moment, awaiting a chance of getting in a smart blow at the prisoners to make them feel their hatred. Here and there a prisoner may have been torn from his guards to be covered with blows. We officers endeavoured in vain to check these excesses. In the dark we did not recognise our men.

How the news of the fighting in Berlin reached Potsdam is thus told by Roon, later the well-known Field Marshal : [1]

In the afternoon some news of a fight in Berlin reached Potsdam, but we did not think there was anything in it. Princess Carl was coming in the evening, so Roon and Prince Friedrich Carl went to the station, and as the train was coming in they saw a carriage full of ladies of the court, all in tears. Their account of what had happened was hopelessly confused. Late at night, about 12 o'clock, the order came to send as many loaves as possible to Berlin. Roon and Prince Friedrich Carl themselves ran round, and commandeered all the post-horses and the Royal horses, and bread from the bakers as well. At 5 o'clock in the morning the wagons set off, accompanied by a squadron of Uhlans and two companies of Rifles on the wagons.

---

[1] *Preussische Jahrbücher*, Bd. 63, Heft 6, 1889 (K.).

CHAPTER VII

WITHDRAWAL OF THE TROOPS

MEANTIME, what was going on inside the Castle ? Here accounts differ, and the King's apologists make out the best case they can for the King, listening in anguish all the early part of the night to the sounds of firing between his soldiers and his people, and to the sensational reports that reached him from one source and another ; and bewildered almost out of his senses for the rest of the night, and next morning, by the multitude of his counsellors, his brother and the soldiers and police, his ministers and the deputations, and well-meaning individuals representing the City Council, the university, and this or that section of the citizens themselves. Klein says : 'The King had to stand his ground against impressions which would have had a powerful effect on even stronger nerves than his. His conduct can be understood only when one never loses sight of the fact that the King was fully aware of the bearing that the rising must have on his plans as regards Germany, for he had himself already taken the first step towards constitutional government before the street fighting began. That, in the event, a catastrophe happened, and that his own person and crown suffered the deepest humiliation, is only to the very smallest extent his own fault. The weakness of the King lay in his political attitude towards Germany. War to the knife was bound to deprive him of all German sympathy. But the legends that have arisen do not give a true picture of his behaviour on that eventful night.' The reader will be able to form his own judgment, for the evidence on one side and the other will be placed fully before him.

The military attitude was quite firm. Of General von Prittwitz we have an account, given by Count von der Goltz to Perthes : [1]

[1] *Preussische Jahrbücher*, Bd. 63, Heft 6, 1889 (K.). Prince Hohenlohe-Ingelfingen is not so favourable in his judgment of Prittwitz.

During the whole night of 18th March General Prittwitz was either in the Castle itself or in the immediate neighbourhood. He was quiet, cold, resolute and clear-headed as he always was ; he gave each adjutant the most detailed instructions as to what his particular body of troops had to do ; he had a very exact knowledge of local conditions in Berlin, and knew precisely, even in the night, the position of each detachment. There was no general in whom the troops had so great confidence as they had in him. When Count Goltz came from the Castle to the Gendarmenplatz, where several commanding officers were standing, he was asked : ' How are things going in the Castle ? ' ' Well ' ; he answered, ' Prittwitz has the matter in hand, and you know what he is.'

And of the Prince of Prussia, Leopold von Gerlach tells us : [1]

We stood in the Castle Square till a quarter to nine. At last I spoke to the Prince of Prussia near the big lamp-post. I told him I was glad that fighting had begun again ; this time we had our foes opposite us, and not in our midst as they had been in the morning. He was of the opinion that the King now had the right to take back all the concessions he had made.

The accounts of the King's attitude given to Perthes [2] by Roon, Pourtalès, and one unnamed, are as follows :

No regular plan of any kind for reducing the city could be drawn up on the 18th, because the King would not agree to anything. It was only with difficulty that he was persuaded to sanction the capture of an essential position, and his sanction had to be obtained afresh for each case. And every time he cried, ' Well, yes ! only don't fire ! ' and yielded only when it was explained that the troops could achieve nothing without firing. On the previous day the King had several times said loudly, ' The streets are mine ; I will keep them ! '
(ROON.)

Minutoli (the Chief of Police) kept bringing frightful stories to the King and thereby brought him into a feverish state. Twelve men, he said, were assembled in an inn . . . and had pledged their word to murder the King. (POURTALÈS.)

In the night of 18th March the King could not be persuaded to give an order ; he lay with his face in his hands, and after every shot he started up, exclaiming, ' No, it cannot be ; my people love me ! ' The Queen fell at his feet, and implored him to make an end to the fighting.

Bodelschwingh stated that in the evening of the 18th and the morning of the 19th the King had been on the point of losing his reason. (ROON.)

---

[1] L. von. Gerlach, *Denkwürdigkeiten*, i. p. 137.
[2] *Preussische Jahrbücher*, Bd. 63, Heft 6, 1889 (K.).

Klein declares that Roon was not an eye-witness and had only hearsay to go upon, and against his tale sets that of Gerlach. ' In spite of the great strain of the previous days, and in spite of the quite unexpected outbreak of passion on the part of the opponents of the Government ' the King ' did not lose for one instant his calm and kingly demeanour.' . . . The King replied to the civic deputation ' admirably and in a dignified manner ' and when the princes wanted to take part in the discussion stopped them with the remark : ' When I speak, no one must say anything in addition.' In particular, Klein quotes as against Perthes' account of the Queen's demeanour, based on anonymous information, Gerlach's statement : ' The King had been frightfully worried by deputations and bad advice. The Queen was quite firm and said, " If only the King does not yield." ' Here, however, Klein seems to overreach himself, for the King himself agrees with Perthes' anonymous informant. The last sentence of his address ' to my dear Berliners,' written with his own hand on the night of the 18th, runs : ' Your loving Queen and sincerely true mother and friend, who lies prostrate with pain and grief, joins with mine her heartfelt and tearful supplications.'

Rellstab, a newspaper editor who saw the King on the morning of the 19th reports : [1] ' His appearance after the frightful night that made history must have deeply affected every one, even one with whom it was a daily custom to have dealings with him. I was quite alone with the King. He appeared unstrung, but quiet and composed. His glance was full of kindly feeling.'

The main alternatives before the King were these, either that he should, as the military party wished, retire to Potsdam and leave the army to reduce the city, or that he should, as most of his miscellaneous civil advisers desired, yield to the popular clamour, order the retirement of the troops from Berlin, and entrust his person and the restoration of order in the capital to a Civic Guard. He sought, and rightly enough, a middle course ; as will be seen he found one, but faltered and was lost. On that dreadful night he composed his famous address ' To my dear Berliners,' in which he proposed a withdrawal of the troops, save from certain specified centres, conditionally on the barricades being cleared away.

He sent the address early on the morning of the 19th to

---

[1] *Zwei Gespräche mit Friedrich Wilhelm IV.*

Bodelschwingh with the following letter, Perthes' notes [1] to which are appended :

19th March 1848. Early Morning.

MY DEAR BODELSCHWINGH,—If you find the following address to the inhabitants of Berlin satisfactory, and if you expect nothing detrimental from the same, have it printed immediately and distributed in many thousands of copies. May God be with you and with us all! Make any correction of my bungling work that may seem proper to you.

Perthes reports in his *Political Notes* :

' Bodelschwingh (without making any alteration whatsoever in the manuscript and) without showing it to Prittwitz, took it immediately to the printer Decker. As compositors were lacking, Decker himself and his brother-in-law, Captain Schaetzler, put the first part into type until compositors were procured.'

Prittwitz, an irritable and passionate man, when he saw the appeal, cried out, ' If I, when on the defensive, cannot act on the offensive, the King himself may defend the town, I cannot do it.' (General von Griesheim.)

The address [2] itself was as follows :

By my decree of to-day's date, summoning the Diet, you have received the pledge of the sincere disposition of your King to you and to the whole German fatherland. Yet the public joy with which I had been greeted by countless true hearts had not died away, when a crowd of malcontents introduced seditious and insolent demands, and swelled in numbers as well-intentioned people withdrew. Since their tumultuous advance, even to the doors of the Castle, rightly gave rise to suspicions of their wicked intentions, and since insults had been hurled at my true and brave soldiers, it became necessary to have the Square cleared by cavalry, advancing at a walking pace and with sheathed weapons, and two infantry muskets were accidentally discharged without hitting any one— thank God! A band of miscreants, consisting mostly of strangers, who for a week now, although searched for, have known how to keep out of the way, have distorted this circumstance by obvious lies in the furtherance of their wicked projects, and have filled the excited minds of many of my true and dear Berliners with thoughts of revenge on account of blood which had presumably been shed, and so have become the gruesome authors of bloodshed. My troops, your brothers and compatriots, have then only used their weapons when they were compelled to do so by many shots fired at them in the Königstrasse. The victorious advance of the troops was the necessary sequel.

It now rests with you, the inhabitants of my beloved native

---

[1] *Preussische Jahrbücher*, Bd, 63. Heft 6, 1889 (K.).
[2] Facsimile in Blum.

town, to prevent a greater calamity. Take note, your King and truest friend therefore affirms, by all that is holy to you, the unhappy misunderstanding. Return to ways of peace! Clear away the barricades that are still standing, and send to me men full of the old genuine Berlin spirit, with fitting words in which to address your King, and I give you my kingly word that the troops shall be immediately withdrawn from all the streets and squares, and that the military occupation shall be confined to the necessary buildings —the Castle, arsenal, and a few others, and even there only for a short time. Listen to the paternal voice of your King, inhabitants of my faithful and beautiful Berlin, and forget the past as I intend to forget it, and will do so heartily for the sake of the great future which—by God's blessing of peace—will dawn for Prussia, and through Prussia, for Germany.

Your loving Queen and sincerely true mother and friend, who lies prostrate with pain and grief, joins with mine her heartfelt and tearful supplications.

Written during the night of the 18th March 1848.

FRIEDRICH WILHELM.

By 7 A.M. the Address was posted up, and the references to seditious malcontents and foreign agitators aroused indignation, for people knew them to be untrue. The bulk of those who fought were plain, honest citizens; ruffians there were, sedition-mongers there were, but in general those who fought had risen spontaneously.

In the Castle itself the scenes of the previous day were re-enacted; individuals and deputations tendered advice. Naunyn, the burgomaster, headed a deputation which urged the avoidance of further bloodshed, and solemnly undertook that if the troops were withdrawn peace and order should be restored. After a consultation, at which soldiers, the Prince of Prussia, Bodelschwingh and Count Arnim were present, the King decided to put in force the compromise indicated in his Address—troops to be withdrawn as barricades were cleared, the Castle, the Arsenal and other public buildings still to be held by the military. But then came, apparently, another hurried conference, and a secret one, between the King, Bodelschwingh, and Count Arnim, at which the King either did give, or was understood to give, a fresh order for the unconditional evacuation of the city by the troops. This fresh order Bodelschwingh announced in the hall where the Prince of Prussia and the rest were still collected. The Prince protested, and was told passionately by Bodelschwingh: 'The King's order may suffer no alteration or interpretation.' In the confusion the evacuation of streets and squares by the troops began ; it could not, once started, be arrested, and the King's personal humiliation was soon to follow. Those who nurse the delusion that the late Kaiser William i. was not an able man, but a mere creature of Bismarck's, may be surprised when they read the very competent account [1] of all these scenes of confusion which he wrote during his exile in London to his sister, the Tsaritsa :

LONDON, 28th March 1848.

At last it was decided that the proclamation issued by the King during the night must be carried out, that is, that in every case where a barricade was removed by the populace, it should be regarded as an offer of peace and the troops opposite the said barricade should be withdrawn. With this answer, which appeared to meet with the complete approval of the many deputations, those who had taken part in them withdrew, taking with them many copies of the proclamation which they were desirous of distributing in all parts of the city. Peace reigned, and not another shot was heard at this period. All the more unsettled was it in the Castle ; uninvited people came and went, in order to give advice. . . . It was somewhere about eleven o'clock. Minister Count Arnim, to whom the King had offered the presidency of the council on the 18th, arrived. Then came a deputation of persons unknown (Burgomaster Naunyn was present) who announced that on the other side of the Königstrasse three barricades had been removed by the people. (It proved later that this announcement was absolutely false.) I proposed to have this substantiated by officers, but instantly there was an outburst of something like the delirium of victory—the orders of the King should be respected at once ! So that I was not listened to, although I still said, that, if things were as they announced, the troops must naturally retire from the spot, according to the terms of the King's proclamation. Suddenly M. von Bodelschwingh came into the room (the dining-room), where the deputations were accommodated, and where we were all collected ; his face was flushed, and he shouted out, ' As the barricades are disappearing, His Majesty orders the troops to be withdrawn from all the streets and squares.' I immediately interrupted him, and said that this was contrary to the wording of the Royal proclamation, where it was stated that at any spot where a barricade was removed the troops facing the barricade would be withdrawn. The minister thundered at me : ' The King's word may suffer no alteration nor interpretation.' I continued and asked if it were to be understood that the squares of the Castle were included in the term ' all squares,' since these were the only squares where the retiring troops could be formed up. Minister B., however, threw at me once more the same words and then gave the order : ' Now

---

[1] von Petersdorff, König Friedrich Wilhelm IV.

be off, gentlemen, and ride to deliver the King's orders, the troops are to withdraw with bands playing.'

From that moment I did not see M. von B. again ; these were the last words he spoke as a minister. I sought the King in what used to be the Countess Reden's ante-room, but did not find him ; I found, however, Count Arnim writing. I asked him, ' Where is the King ? What are you doing then ? ' He replied, ' I am forming the new ministry,' and I read the names Auerswald, Schwerin. I said, ' That is quite like Paris, like Guizot, Thiers. Wait a bit.' ' No,' was the answer, ' there is only time enough.'

When I entered the King's cabinet off the hall I did not find him there either ; returning to the dining-room I found him just coming in ; he saw the general consternation and we described to him the scene with Bodelschwingh. He assured us that he had given no other commission or order than what was contained in the proclamation, and the mistake must be immediately put right. At the same moment, however, the 3rd Battalion of the 1st Regiment of Guards, with drums beating, was already coming over the Kurfürsten Bridge, next, that of the Alexander Regiment followed by a mob of people. The King ordered the bridge to be occupied and defended ; it was too late, and impossible. The troops moved to the courtyards of the Castle and to the Cathedral Square. When the bridge remained unoccupied, I said to Arnim, ' Now we 're lost,' for I foresaw everything that would follow.

I went to the troops, etc. When I returned to the Queen's room I calmed the disconsolate group I found there by saying that all the troops were still at hand, and that they were loyal. All at once I heard the beating of drums ; I rushed to the window and saw the 1st Guards Regiment marching out of the first gate across the Castle Square amid the hurrahs of the people ! Instantly came from all sides the cry, ' The troops are leaving the squares.' I asked War Minister von Rohr if he had given the order, and he replied, ' On the contrary, I have given the order that the troops should bivouac around the Castle.' Then some one entered and said : ' Count Arnim must have given the order, since he declared that half measures were useless, and therefore the troops must move into barracks.' The said von Rohr seized his hat, threw it on the table, and exclaimed, ' Count Arnim must answer for it,' and I cried to him, ' All is lost ! '—That Count Arnim had not given that order, and used these expressions, he assured me himself soon after my return.

The withdrawal of the troops was a melancholy business, and here is Prince Hohenlohe's account [1] of what his own regiment, the Guards Artillery, had to endure :

His Excellency General von Jenichen, Inspector of the 2nd Artillery District, at that time the most celebrated of artillery

---

[1] *Aus meinem Leben*, i.

U

officers, a hero of 1813, placed himself at the head and rode with us, as if he were returning from an inspection. The old man was deformed, crooked, I believe from a wound received in war, and just as highly esteemed as feared. He rode right up to the entrance to the barracks and allowed the troop to file in past him. Here it was that the hardest trial of the day awaited us. The crowd, from the lowest dregs of the work-people, surrounded the general, shouting and yelling while we marched in. A fellow in rags had fastened on a pitchfork a handkerchief steeped in blood and flourished it, especially under the nose of every officer who marched past, and at times even under the nose of the general. The latter sat silent, like a marble statue, on his horse. His example induced us all to suffer everything, and restrained the sword-arms of the soldiers who would most willingly have charged the mob. When the last man amid the frenzy, abuse, and curses of the crowd had moved into barracks, General von Jenichen quietly rode home alone, paying no attention to the fiendish noise around him.

We deployed in the barrack-yard, unlimbered and led the horses into the stables ; the buildings were crammed with the sovereign people, who stood insolently about us, smoking bad cigars, staring at and handling everything. A kind of stupor had come over us. In order to get rid of this rabble one of us had a happy thought. He went to the newly formed Civic Guard, which had taken possession of the guard-room in the barracks, and said to their leader that we considered it our duty to make him cognisant of the fact that there was powder in the limbers of our guns, and that the people were standing about smoking. At any moment the barracks might be blown up. We were quite indifferent, and desired nothing better after the abuse we had just suffered, but it would be a pity for so many brave men from the people to be lost. With hair standing on end the Civic Guard immediately fell upon the mob, and drove them out of the barracks with blows from the butt-ends of their muskets. We were now again in the closed barracks. We officers embraced each other, sobbing. We knew not what else to do. It was the expression of impotent despair. The barracks presented a motley spectacle. The doors were kicked in. The officers' quarters, in particular, were wrecked and the furniture destroyed. Three officers lived in the barracks. We others were dismissed to our quarters when we had provided for the horses. Our comrades in barracks offered us civilian clothes. I refused the offer, for I hoped to be struck dead on the way by the rabble, and this seemed to me the best that could happen to me. Lieutenant Groschke was of the same opinion and we went together. He lived in the Georgenstrasse, I in the Dorotheenstrasse, at the corner of the Charlottenstrasse. As we passed along the streets, closely packed with the crowds, we had the feeling that we were going through a madhouse. At one moment we were embraced and kissed, at the next moment we were insulted and stones were thrown at us. One man barred my way and said, sneeringly, ' Well, has your Highness had a very bad time for once in his life?' We went dumbly on, as if all that passed had nothing to do with us. On the bridge, coming in our direction from the other side, was Captain von Gerschow on his way from the barracks in the Kupfergraben to his residence in the Carlstrasse. A fellow cried to him, ' Dog! there you have your reward,' and discharged his gun point blank at him. He missed him, however, and killed a poor old woman behind. We continued on our way, for now nothing roused us from our dazed condition.

Count Lüttichau [1] tells of an experience of the 8th regiment :

When I left the Castle, there was on the Castle Square a huge crowd of men, every one in a state of great excitement. Music, which tames the most savage animals, was, I thought, a means to be applied here, and I ordered the trumpets to sound cheerily. Scarcely had the music begun when every one became furious at the gaiety of the music, declaring it a mockery of their brothers who had fallen. Funeral music was the universal demand, to the accompaniment of the most fearsome threats. In the confusion the trumpeters played a sacred anthem, which found general approbation, but in my turn, despite all the threatening protestations of the populace, I instantly stopped it. Instead, folk-tunes and other melancholy airs were played, and these calmed the excited mob.

H. V. von Unruh, a well known engineer, and active in railway matters, later president of the Prussian Diet, states in his *Reminiscences* that ' the troops were in no wise demoralised ; discipline was perfectly maintained. Nowhere was obedience refused, not a single soldier went over to the defenders of the barricades.' But it was impossible that Prussian soldiers, when their blood was up, should restrain the violence of their nature even with their own countrymen. The barbarities inflicted on a party of five hundred and seventy civilian prisoners conveyed from Berlin to Spandau on the morning of the 19th, are described in the following account [2] by one of the victims, an artist named Ludwig Pietsch, who lived to be attached as draftsman and writer of reports to the staff of the Crown Prince Frederick in the Franco-German War. Pietsch's was one of a host of similar depositions made public by the sufferers :

About eleven in the evening of 1st March, and after a violent struggle which began on the roof and ended on the ground-floor, I was arrested with four men in a house in the Gertrautenstrasse which had been stormed. We were almost choked by the Grenadiers, and under a shower of blows from the butt-ends of their rifles dragged

---

[1] A. Wolff, *Berliner Revolutionschronik,* i. (K.).
[2] *Adalbert Roerdanz, Ein Freiheits Martyrium* (K.).

down the stairs to the Gertrauten Bridge, whence we were led, in company with many other prisoners who had already been brought there, to the Castle. As to our ill-treatment on this journey I shall preserve silence. The rage of the soldiers whom we had hard pressed from the roofs justified it in any case. In the Castle itself we were received by the musketeers already drawn up there with general abuse of every kind, and with blows from the fist and the butt-ends of their muskets. A wounded soldier in a forage cap, and with his left arm in a sling, pressed forward towards every new arrival, and with the words, ' You dog, you have got nothing from me,' struck him a blow with his fist. The officer who had arrested us showed himself humane so far as he possibly could, for he sought to restrain his soldiers by word and deed in their ill-treatment of us. It was just the reverse with the officer we found here. A young lieutenant, standing on a chair, called to the men : ' Grenadiers, how could you bring in any more such dogs ? Strike them dead on the spot ! ' Whereupon the grenadier who was holding me replied quite sadly, ' Ah ! if we had only known that, Lieutenant.' After we had been visited by the Commissary of Police, who wrote down our names, professions, etc., we were dragged through a lane of soldiers and thrown into the Castle cellars ; we were visited once more and then packed together, several hundreds of us, in the deepest recesses. A wonderful company ! Students, citizens, merchants, workmen, apprentices, artists, some with frightful wounds on the head and faces covered with blood, standing or cowering together on the damp stone floor, and still in many cases carrying on an unruffled conversation about the different events of this lovely afternoon. Once a guard standing outside fired into the midst of us through the cellar windows, it may be because some one approached too near the windows, or for pure pleasure. At four o'clock we were taken into the Castle yard and, escorted by the Pomeranian Grenadiers and Uhlans, the procession started off down Unter den Linden for, as we thought, the Moabit Prison. Before the Brandenburg Gate we were joined by a new troop of prisoners, mostly chained together in twos. They had passed the night in the Ministry of War. We were now drawn up in rows of four men close behind one another, so close that each man almost crushed his toes on the heels of the man in front, while at the same time his own heels were being damaged by the man behind. On each side of the procession grenadiers marched in double file. We had almost reached the Great Star when we first learnt that Spandau was the goal of our frightful journey, and this robbed us of the last comforting hope. From now onwards we had to suffer the most refined torture. The word is hard but true. A deliberate malice and ferocity, which stand unique in the modern history of civilised states, were shown to us. The front men were goaded into a trot by blows from the butt-end, and the rear ranks were forced to follow them by thumps and blows on the head from the musket, and blows in the face from the fist. ' Get along, you dog ! ' ' Flay them ! ' was the continual refrain. Any one who offered prayers or excuses was sure to get a blow across the mouth and nose. More especially was this brutal treatment aimed at the wounded. At my neighbour, who had received a bayonet thrust through the upper thigh and several blows from a musket on the skull at the Cölln town hall, and whose hair, face, and coat collar were soaked with blood, a soldier dealt a well-directed and fearful blow with a gun barrel on the fresh wounds, so that the powerful young fellow collapsed with a cry, and a fresh stream of blood gushed over his face. It was with difficulty I dragged him along. Near to him a young carpenter's apprentice, with a most gentle expression, was tortured in a still more revolting manner. Almost every five minutes he received a blow, accompanied by expressions such as, ' You dog ! you have perhaps honest parents, why did you not go to bed ? ' etc. After a little time the soldier took a drink from his bottle (each soldier carried one in his haversack)—' Would you like a drink too, my son,' he asked laughingly, and when the poor young fellow raised his head he struck him an upward blow on the nose which made it bleed. A Munich student, whose tall form, noble demeanour and well-carried head appeared particularly to annoy the gentlemen, received incessant blows on the nape of the neck from butt-ends and fists, which, however, did not for one moment disturb his imposing calm. The grenadier striding along at my side was on the whole somewhat gracious ; he limited himself to a few blows on the thigh, in the back, and a blow with the bayonet on the temple. To make up for this, however, he sought to compensate me by the most witty remarks ; here are a few, for the exact words of which I can vouch : ' You dogs, did you really think we were Parisians ? No, we are Pomeranians ! Such a dog must indeed have no brains in his head, such a traitor to his country must have a bayonet thrust in his guts, a bullet would be wasted—You dogs want freedom of the Press. There you have it ! ' Once there was a shot fired behind us ; it was said that a man who could go no further and had stumbled had been shot. Those who stumbled in front of me were brought to consciousness by kicks and bayonet thrusts. The officers at times allowed these things to go on quietly ; at times their lukewarm command to cease this ill-treatment had no effect. I could go on recounting frightful details, but enough of these terrible memories. In Spandau we were driven along at the trot like a flock of sheep to the shambles. We thought, too, that we were actually going to be shot when we were drawn up on the open square of the citadel ; we thought that the people had been crushed and that a military dictatorship prevailed in Berlin. In those terrible moments we would have preferred death to the cold, narrow casemates into which we were thrown, five hundred and seventy in number.

Of the childish satisfaction of the populace at the apparent success of the revolution, a broadsheet,[1] which Klein describes as ' the first product of the free press in Berlin,' gives a pathetic

[1] Friedländer Collection, City Library, Berlin.

illustration. On the sheet was a vignette, two hands clasped in sunshine above clouds, and these doggerel verses :

Hail, O ye laurelled band,
Sons of the Fatherland !
 Hail, again Hail !
Nought but your weapons' might
Wins us fair freedom's right,
Leads us to fortune's goal !
 Hail, ever Hail !

'Tis not your mounted knights
Guard the steep slippery heights,
 Where princes dwell ;
Love of the Fatherland,
Grip of a freeman's hand,
Anchor a prince's right
 Like rock in sea.

Sacred the fires that glow,
Quenchless the lava-flow
 For Fatherland !
Men stand we side by side,
One man, the prince, our pride,
Gladly we fight and bleed
 For Folk and Land.

Science and Industry
Haughtily, lustily
 Rear high their heads.
Peace wins, like war, renown,
Each finds its laurel-crown
Stored for it faithfully
 In the Folk's breast.

Clasp then, O Prussian Land,
Firmly with heart and hand
 The German Folk !
Take glory for thy guide,
And nurse the sacred pride :
A German Folk to be !
 Hail, Germany !

Blum gives a facsimile of the marching-song of the revolutionaries, the music of which starts off with a suspicious resemblance to the ' Marseillaise ' :

Forward, forward, band of brothers !
Forward boldly to the fight !
Where 's the fool with scorn who smothers
Liberty, our sacred right ?
For the best that life can lend us,
For our darling Fatherland,
Stand we ready to defend us,
Pledge we head and heart and hand.
Forward ! Forward !
With God for Fatherland.

Backward, backward never gazing,
Let us leave what leave we must ;
Destiny's bright star is blazing,
A new world rises from the dust.
Foolish hopes and women's weeping
Have our hearts too long unmanned.
Up, the future 's in our keeping,
Make it good with sword in hand.
Forward ! Forward !
With God for Fatherland.

' Men are brothers, free and equal '
Gleams the motto on our shield.
Only cowards fear the sequel
While they still have arms to wield.
Life or death, let either beckon,
We 'll go forward hand in hand ;
Life and death as nought we reckon,
If we free the Fatherland.
Forward ! Forward !
With God for Fatherland.

Fontane's comment [1] on the withdrawal of the troops was
shrewd and true :

As we were walking up and down we saw a crowd of men gesticulat-
ing wildly as they came across the Alexanderplatz. At the head of
this crowd of cheerful countenances strode a fine figure of a man.
' He is bringing a message ' was the cry instantly, and in fact when
he was quite close to our side barricade, on the woody and rocky
landscape of which [2] I had taken up my position, he stopped in order
that he might inform the rapidly increasing crowd in a distinct voice
that all was conceded (conceded was at that time a favourite word),
and that his Majesty had given the order for the withdrawal of the
troops. The troops would leave the town. The distinguished

---

[1] *Cosmopolis*, iv. (K.).
[2] This particular barricade was largely built up of scenery and other
theatrical properties.

gentleman who brought this message, was, if I remember rightly, Privy Councillor Holleufer. There was great jubilation. They had won the victory, and the carpet-slippered element (naturally there were brilliant exceptions), which had held back the day before or had sneaked away, now put in an appearance, in order to embrace one another and to exchange with us, yea, even fraternal kisses. The whole was a Rütli scene [1] set for an epilogue, where men, after the event, took their oath to freedom, which, if it were there at all, had been cared for by quite other people. Many showed themselves quite earnest over it ; but personally I was only feeling wretched. I had, not to speak of myself and household, during the hours from midday to midnight seen only a handful of courageous people—all of course men of the people— who had arranged the whole business. At our corner in particular was an oldish man in a soft hat and with a pointed beard, whom by his entire demeanour I was forced to take for a gun-smith, and who now and then, advancing from the cover afforded by the side street, stepped up to the barricade and there discharged his presumably well-aimed shot. Otherwise there was nothing but noise, much cry and little wool. If the troops were now falling back, it was no hard-earned and thereby consolidated victory on the side of the populace, but merely an imperial favour, which at any moment could be withdrawn if it so pleased him who had made the present. And while I still stood there regarding the joy of my fellow-men and still shaking my head, I already saw in my mind the day dawning in natural sequence, when, in fact, seven months later the same battalions of the Guards marched in and took away the ten thousand guns from the Civic Guard, with which during the summer they had not been able either to gain freedom or bring about order. I could not get rid of the feeling that everything which was there called a victory, was nothing but a something taking place by the condescension of the authorities, a something to which had been given, without compulsion, this triumphant issue on the side of the populace ; and I for my part was convinced more than ever of the invincibility of a well-disciplined troop opposed to any mob, even of the bravest men.

Two further comments on the events of the 18th, those of Rudolf Gneist, an eminent jurist, and of C. F. Hebbel, the poet and dramatist, are worth reading. Gneist had said, in speaking on a motion in the Prussian Diet for the formal recognition of the revolution, ' that the 18th March, as with the tap of a magic wand, had given to the nation its long and shamefully withheld freedom, the consciousness of its independence and rights, and that it had unquestionably established the equality of the nation in relation to the crown.' In his *Berliner Zustände*,[2] published in 1849, he wrote the following passage which is not

---

[1] *Vide* Schiller's *William Tell*.　　　　　　　[2] Klein.

wholly spoilt by the tone of German self-complacency which infects it :

In this sense the revolution of March 18 is indeed perfect, and the wonderful part of it is the revolution in heads, hearts, thoughts, and sensations that has so wrought upon us, that even the most obdurate bureaucrat and lord-in-waiting has suddenly to acknowledge and preach principles which a year before he would have listened to only with a shudder. A revolution in this sense, in which the element of brute force plays only a secondary rôle, is only possible in Germany, in the predominantly ideal mind of the nation, and its danger lies less in the renewal of barricades than in the vagueness and unsteadiness of these ideas themselves. I do not wish to belittle the personal merit of those who took part in the fighting. It is justly meritorious to manifest one's patriotic enthusiasm in a speech, in an applauding assembly or by a banquet, but to die for an opinion is also something. It has frequently been maintained that among the fallen were dozens of thieves who had known the inside of a gaol. Privy Councillors were certainly not among the number ! If that assertion were true, Death has made those men honourable.

This chapter of confusion, delirium, and brutality may be closed on another note, with Hebbel's noble words [1] on the sacrifices of the revolution :

It is a tragic, inevitable necessity that victims must be sacrificed when principles clash, and the individual through whom they fall bears, just because of the inherence of this necessity in the scheme of things, only a relative guilt. This fact is realised, as soon as the passion which the circumstances of the moment bring with them has passed, by a nation, just as much as by the individual ; and the nation is great enough to forgive and forget a guilt which in fine might have been incurred by one individual just as much as by another, but, I admit, only on the essential condition that guilt is recognised, that it is not disowned, and that it is not laid to the charge of the poor ordinary man—the unwilling instrument.

---

[1] Klein.

CHAPTER VII

THE KING'S HUMILIATION

THE order for the withdrawal of the troops had gone forth, and in rage and shame officers and men left the city and their King, their war lord, who was now to lay his troubled head on the bosom of his people. Of the humiliations he had to suffer, this and the following chapter will give a vivid account. The first humiliation, his abasement in the courtyard of the Castle before the bodies of the victims of the 18th, was so sharp an experience that it seems to have aroused a perverse exaltation in him. He certainly behaved afterwards as if he enjoyed wallowing in his shame. The experience of a Hohenzollern ' crawling on his stomach,' to use his own phrase to Ranke,[1] was novel, and he evidently managed to execute the manœuvre as if he enjoyed it. To the German historian the catastrophe of those days was not the murder of civilians and soldiers in civil war on the 18th, but the pitiful display of the King himself on the afternoon of the 19th, and the following days.

Of the extraordinary scene in the courtyard of the Castle on the afternoon of the 19th, the following is the story given by Carl Frenzel :

That day I spent the hours about noon in both courts of the Castle, along with many hundred others, whom the great human tide had pushed and squeezed from the Breitestrasse and the Long Bridge across the Castle Square right into the Castle ; high railings did not, as they do now, protect the entrance. Until late at night people came and went quite unhindered, from the Lustgarten as well as from the Castle Square, across these courtyards, in order to shorten the way from the Linden to the Königstrasse. Only the Eosander gate was at that time closed by a hideous palisade. Frederick William IV. inhabited the part of the Castle on the Spree side. The corner windows which look towards the Long Bridge and the monument of the Great Elector were his favourite post. At the foot of the staircase leading upwards from the entrance arch-

---

[1] See page 142.

314

way to his apartments, which were shut off at the top by a simple glass door, an old woman had taken up her stand with cakes, apples, and oranges. Sentries in any number were only posted on state occasions. Now and then a lackey or a carriage appeared in the courtyard or the gateway. At other times nothing was to be seen of princely magnificence. On March 19 the populace raged and fumed in the courtyards. . . . Meanwhile dead bodies were brought into the Castle on planks, biers, and handcarts, now surrounded by a bloodthirsty-looking group, now by pale and sobbing men. Then all took off their hats and caps, a lane was formed, and the most affected sang a chorale. In the courtyard where the Castle guard was stationed, and opposite to it, the bodies were laid out; a wagon, however, with six or seven frightfully disfigured corpses, had been drawn into the inner square of the Castle. The rage and the grief of the crowd at this sight beggars calculation and description. They all cried out for the King. He appeared on the inner gallery at the top of the winding staircase. During the singing of the hymn 'Jesus, my Trust' the corpses were held up towards him and the Queen, who was leaning on his arm. I have a hazy recollection that he had a grey mantle over his general's uniform. More distinctly has the memory remained with me of a feeling to which a man in my immediate neighbourhood gave expression in the words, ' My God, suppose some one now shot him ! ' And this anxiety was fully justified by the passionate excitement of the masses. Many still had weapons in their hands, which they had used in the fight, and their faces and clothes carried traces of the fighting, dirt and blood, swellings and gashes. Who was there in the Castle to make an attempt to resist them ? Of the Guild of Riflemen, the only armed force in whom was vested a certain authority over the crowd, there were scarcely a dozen in the courtyards. A full company was expected. . . . They were to take over the protection of the Castle and the King. But a long time passed before they arrived. Luckily new speakers and new scenes continually cropped up to occupy the crowd. The good-natured temperament of the inhabitant of Berlin took its course ; it occurred to no one to storm the winding staircase or to break the glass door before the royal apartments. In these hours the Prince of Prussia was the most hated of men. On him was laid all the blame for the ' conflict between brothers.' Many, with curses and maledictions, called out his name. When, however, somewhere about two o'clock, a lady dressed in black got into a carriage, holding tightly by the hand a lad 'twixt boyhood and youth—coachmen and attendants without marks of distinction—and drove away at a walking pace through the crowds, and out by the gate leading to the cathedral, not a hand was raised, not a threat, not an insult was hurled at her. It was the Princess of Prussia with our Crown Prince, our Fritz of never-dying memory. Soon after, the company of riflemen marched into the Castle with military precision. They were welcomed with boisterous cheering. Apparently all fear of violence and pillage was now over. As if to show the King how secure he was in the guardianship of his citizens the arrangements made by the leaders of the riflemen were obeyed without any opposition. Then, too, as citizen after citizen came back with the first weapons from the arsenal, evidence that the arming of the populace was a reality, there was nothing but hurrahing and joy— ' all men become as brothers where thy gentle wing alights.' In the evening many houses in the town were illuminated.

Klein gives, to relieve the picture, an amusing episode related by Werner Siemens,[1] the celebrated inventor, who was at the time an officer engaged in the artillery workshops. He had, as a civilian, entered the Castle with the crowd :

The terrible scene took place on the balcony of the Castle. . . . Then came a saviour in the nick of time in the person of the young Prince Lichnowsky. He addressed the crowd in a clear and distinct voice from one of the tables set up in the middle of the Castle Square. He said that his Majesty the King had in his great kindness and graciousness put an end to the fight, since he had withdrawn every soldier and had put himself unconditionally under the protection of the citizens. All demands were conceded, and every one could return home in peace ! The speech made an obvious impression. To the question of the populace whether everything would really be conceded, he answered, ' Yes, everything, gentlemen.' ' Smoking also ? ' shouted another voice. ' Yes, smoking also,' was the answer. ' In the Tiergarten too ? ' was further asked. ' Yes, smoking may be indulged in in the Tiergarten also, gentlemen.' That was decisive. ' Then we certainly can go home ' was heard on all sides, and in a short time the crowd left the Square in a serene frame of mind. The presence of mind with which the young prince—probably on his own responsibility—bestowed the concession of free smoking in the streets of the town and in the Tiergarten perhaps prevented further serious misfortunes.

But in these extracts we have not the full story. Here is the description of the final scene given in his *History of the Revolution* by Blum, who bases his story of what passed during these eventful days on reliable sources ; so close a friend of the King as Gerlach confirms it in his account. What he tells us may be accepted as trustworthy. In response to cries 'The King must come out ; he must see the bodies,' Count Schwerin and Prince Felix Lichnowsky appeared on the balcony and begged the crowd to allow the King to rest, and, above all, to spare the Queen. They were answered by shouts : ' If the Queen could

---

[1] *Lebenserinnerungen.*

bear the news that the troops had fired on the people, she 'll
be able to stand our salvoes of joy and our cries.' Others
roared out, ' If the King does not come out, we 'll have the
bodies carried up to his room,' and the biers were raised in
readiness to be borne up the great winding stairway. ' Then the
King appeared on the balcony, the pale trembling Queen on
his arm. " Off with your hat " thundered the sovereign people
from below, and the King bared his head. The horribly
mutilated bodies were raised high towards the balcony. A
thousand oaths of vengeance were yelled aloft, and bludgeons
and weapons were brandished. But this was not humiliation
enough for the Crown of Prussia, so hated by the rioters. For
now rang out the imperious cry : " The King must come down
into the courtyard to inspect the bodies ! " The King did
indeed come down, he knew not how, and bowed himself, bare-
headed, before the lifeless, disfigured bodies. The Queen fell
fainting, and had to be carried up the stairs. The Crown of
Prussia had suffered an humiliation which left far behind it the
shame of the days of Jena and Tilsit.'

A few months later, when all the revolution had won seemed
lost, Freiligrath, in savage indignation, wrote his bitter lines,
' The Dead to the Living,' in which, as with corrosive acid, he
burnt in a picture of that scene :

THE DEAD TO THE LIVING

Each with a bullet in his heart, and forehead gaping wide,
You raise us on our blood-stained boards above the human tide,
High in the air with wild uproar, that each set face of pain
May prove an everlasting curse to him that had us slain !
That he may see us day and night, awake and in his dreams,
Whene'er the Bible meets his eye, or the foaming goblet gleams !
That ever deeper on his soul the sight may branded be,
And nevermore, howe'er he strive, he may that horror flee !
That every torture-twisted mouth and every wound blood-red
May haunt him still, and make him quail, upon his dying bed ! . . .

So was 't ! With bullet-shattered breast and forehead gaping wide
You raised us on our cranky boards near the balcóny's side.
' Come down ! ' and down he reeling came, reeling to our poor bed.
' Hat off ! ' He took it off, he bowed. An actor, yes, but dead,
Dead as a marionette ! How blank the lily-livered look !
The army meantime left the town, the town we dying took ;
' Jesus, my Trust ' you sang o'er us, for so the hymn-book says,
' Cold Steel my Trust ' had surely made a royal hymn of praise.

The morn it was that followed hard the night that sealed our doom.
And so in state, triumphantly, you bore us to the tomb.
And we! Though bullet and the sword our skulls had cracked and
  seamed,
The cheerful light of victory on our grim foreheads gleamed.
We thought : high was the price, but good the cause for which we bled,
And stretched us quietly to rest, each on his narrow bed.
Out on you! Were we not deceived ? Four moons their course scarce
  run,
Your coward hands have fooled away what we so stoutly won!
The rights our death secured for you in fumes they disappear—
Oh, all and everything we catch with our fine and ghostly ear!
All that on earth betides doth shake, like waves, our ghostly frame :
The folly of the Danish war and the latest Polish shame,
The rebels' outcry fierce and loud in the stubborn countryside,
The tramp of soldiers marching back, with the Prince in all his pride.

Then treason here, and on the Main, ay, treason kept by gold—[1]
O People, is it only peace your leathern aprons hold ?
Doth not war lurk within their folds, that ye may shake it out,
A second war, the last great war, 'gainst all the brutal rout ?
The Republic be your battle-cry to drown yon clanging bell,
Whose tune 's midsummer madness. O turn it to a knell!

In vain! You 'll have to dig us up from the earth in which we lie,
And raise us on our blood-stained boards once more towards the sky ;
Not now as then to bare our wounds before that man of shame.
No, show us in the market-place, and spread our gory fame
Through every hamlet in the land ; and then our rebel crew
Lay out on biers in Parliament, for members all to view!

O grisly sight, for there we lie, hair fouled with grass and mire,
And faces wasted half away—even we the Land's desire !
And as we lie, aloud we cry : ' Ere we could quite decay,
Freedom in your stout leaders' hands, Freedom has passed away.'
Soon fell the corn whose shoots were green in March when we were slain,
But Freedom's crop the Reaper cut before all other grain.
A scarlet poppy here and there escaped the scythe's keen blade ;
O had a spark of flaming rage in all the land but stayed !

And stay it will! Tho' low our state this comfort have we left :
Too much ye won, too soon, and now of too much are ye bereft.
Too much of scorn, too much of shame, are heaped upon your head :
Wild Rage must rankle in your hearts—trust us for that, the Dead !
For you she stays ; wide eyes awake, occasion prompt she 'll meet,
The Revolution half-achieved to nurse and make complete ! . . .

---

[1] The allusion is to the payment of members in the first German Parliament
at Frankfort on Main.

Meanwhile, until the hour shall strike, forget not our complaint,
Wherewith we 'd grip your sluggish hearts, in the pursuit so faint.
Be ready aye, and stand to arms, that the soil in which we lie,
Stretched stark and stiff, may all be free beneath the open sky,
And never again by that dread thought our sleep may broken be,—
You once were free, who slaves are now, and to eternity !

That night, the 19th, the question was discussed of the King's leaving Berlin for Potsdam. According to Perthes' reports,[1] the discussion ran as follows :

Roon : Prittwitz came to the King with the statement that even without further help he could keep the town in the same condition as it was for still 24-36 hours. General Neumann declared to the King that if things came to the worst the King could leave the town in the midst of his troops with bands playing. The King answered that if things came to the worst he would do so.

Pourtalès : In the evening of March 19, or rather at half-past eleven at night, the King was to leave Berlin and drive to Potsdam. Count Pourtalès, the father, had drawn up the plan for the secret departure ; Albert Pourtalès was to help him in carrying it out ; the King had fallen in with the plan. Albert Pourtalès was standing with his carriage in front of the Brandenburg Gate ; in the Castle Pourtalès senior conducted the Queen, and the King was to go with them on foot to the Brandenburg Gate. The King staggered aimlessly through several rooms, in order to go away, then he turned round just as aimlessly, and did not go.

General Dobeneck : According to another witness there stepped up to the King, when he was already on the stairs, Count Arnim-Boitzenburg, with the words, ' Never yet has a Hohenzollern withdrawn before danger ! ' Whereupon the King gave his cloak to his valet and turned back.

Perthes : According to another source, not divulged, Arnim's words were, ' Your Majesty would be the first Hohenzollern to flee before his people.'

Count Oriola : For two nights Oriola and Major (Edwin) von Manteuffel (later Governor of Alsace) slept before the door of the King, in order, if need be, to be cut to pieces for him.

Roon : The state of feeling among the Staff at Potsdam was shocking ; on the one side rage, on the other side, however, the determination to fetch the King from Berlin, cost what it might. Plans were thought out, to carry him off even against his wish. The individuals for this were told off even down to the junior officers. Roon said on March 23 to Harry Arnim, nephew of the Minister

---

[1] *Preussische Jahrbucher*, Bd. 63, Heft 6, 1889 (K.).

(later Ambassador in Paris), that he could inform his uncle that the King must come to Potsdam, at any cost; that steps were about to be taken of which the consequences could not be predicted.

Leopold von Gerlach describes [1] Arnim as dead against the King's going, and gives a lively picture of the King's indecision, lasting for days :

On the Monday evening I drew Count Arnim's attention to the fact that on the following day there would be no more troops in Berlin. ' I know that,' he answered, ' thank you.' He opposed the King's departure in every way. As early as the Sunday evening the King and Queen desired to drive to Potsdam. ' Arnim does not wish us to go,' the Queen said. Their Majesties were already on their way to the carriage, which I believe was standing at the exit by the Court Dispensary. On his way the King felt scruples which also affected the Queen : ' if you consider it wrong, you must not do it.' On the Monday, says Uhden, the King had been quite decided to set out. Everything was prepared, he and Massow with him. The King said to him, ' I am forced here to make one concession after the other ; I must be off to Potsdam ; I have just been obliged to liberate the Poles. Come with us, tell Bodelschwingh to come too, and all that are still true to me shall forgather there.'

Next day, the 20th, the wretched King had to proclaim an amnesty [2] for political offences :

I have already said yesterday that in my heart I have forgiven and forgotten. In order however that no doubt may linger whether I include my entire nation in this forgiveness, and because I should not like to feel that the newly dawning future of our Fatherland is troubled by painful recollections, I make known herewith :
Pardon to all those who have been charged with, or sentenced for, faults or crimes connected either with politics or the press !
My Minister of Justice, Uhden, is charged with the immediate execution of this my amnesty.   FRIEDRICH WILHELM.

Among those pardoned were a number of Poles, and their release was made the occasion for inflicting still further humiliation on the King :

Towards one o'clock the Public Prosecutor appeared in the State Prison, and in a solemn address announced to the Polish prisoners that they were free. A carriage, held in readiness, thereupon took up the two most important prisoners, Ludwig von Mieroslawski who had been sentenced to death, and Dr. Libelt who had been sentenced to four years' detention in a fortress. . . . The liberated men were received with jubilation by a crowd that had swollen to huge

---

[1] *Denkwürdigkeiten*, i.   [2] Klein.

dimensions. The horses were taken from the carriage, and the latter was drawn by men. Following it came all the released Poles on foot and with bared head. Von Mieroslawski held the German flag. A Polish flag, which had been made by ladies in the prison the moment the men were set free, waved from the carriage. Throughout the entire journey handkerchiefs and flags fluttered from all the windows, and garlands of flowers were flung to the liberated men. A vast crowd followed the procession. The first halt was at the University. The students, drawn up in arms, received the Poles in front of the University. The volunteer force on service at the main guard stood to arms and saluted. Mieroslawski and Libelt, the former in French, expressed their thanks and swore, in the name of the free-minded Polish nation, peace and friendship to the Germans and protection against the Russian power. ' The Polish flag,' said Mieroslawski, ' will wave side by side with that of Germany!' [1] Boisterous applause from the crowd greeted this statement. The fêted men were almost squeezed to death by the cheering crowd. . . . There was another halt on the Castle Square, in front of the windows of the King. After long-sustained shouts of joy the King appeared on the balcony, surrounded by the Ministers Count Arnim, Schwerin, and Bornemann. The monarch, the *Spenersche Zeitung* tells us, greeted them visibly delighted, thanked them repeatedly and raised his forage cap three times, a proceeding which secured round after round of applause. Count Schwerin then began a speech from the balcony somewhat in the following terms : ' His Majesty is greatly pleased that you have come to thank him for his generous act of kingly grace, and that he has been present to accept those thanks.' This was greeted with fresh applause and a resounding cry from the throng of Poles. Count Schwerin continued : ' His Majesty trusts that the Poles, now that they have seen how political prisoners are treated in Prussia, will cling to Prussia and its royal house.' The strongest assurances were then offered by the liberated men.[2]

A month later, 20th April 1848, the young Bismarck gave expression to his indignation at the liberation of the Poles ' sentenced for treason ' by writing to the *Magdeburger Zeitung* : [3]

The liberation of the Poles sentenced for treason is one of the gains of the fight in Berlin in March, and is certainly one of the most substantial. The men of Berlin have liberated the Poles with their blood, and have then drawn them in triumph with their own hands through the streets. As thanks for this you find the liberated men soon afterwards at the head of bands which requited the German inhabitants of a Prussian province with pillage, murder, slaughter,

---

[1] According to Klein, Mieroslawski a few days later headed an insurrection in Posen.

[2] A. Wolff, *Berliner Revolutionschronik*, i. (K.).   [3] Klein.

and barbarous mutilation of women and children. Thus once more has German enthusiasm been used to its own detriment to pluck foreign chestnuts out of the fire. I should have found it explicable if the first impulse of German strength and unity had given vent in demanding Alsace from France, and in planting the German flag on the tower of Strasburg. But it is more than German good nature if we, with the chivalry of Roman heroes, are enthusiastic, of all reasons, because the German states are deprived of the best of what German arms have won in Poland during the course of centuries.

But a more sensational, if quieter, incident than the proceedings connected with the liberation of the Poles occurred also on the 20th, viz., the flight of the Prince of Prussia, ' Prince Grapeshot ' as he was called. On his head was turned the fury of the crowd, who remained obsessed with the belief that it was he who was responsible for all the bloodshed. The charge was unfounded, but there is no doubt that had he been in his brother's shoes on the 18th the troops would never have been allowed to leave the city, and, cost what it might in lives, the revolution would have been stamped out by every resource of the military machine.

Perthes gives the following report [1] by his son Frederick William, later Kaiser Frederick III., of what went on in the Crown Prince's palace on the afternoon of the 19th.

During the afternoon of March 19 the Prince of Prussia's residence was like an inn. People of all sorts and conditions came and went. Towards evening some one came and said that a deputation would arrive which would demand of the Prince his renunciation of the succession to the throne. The Prince then wrote to the King, ' If I can help you by staying here and by renouncing my right of succession, tell me so and I will do it ; if, however, I cannot help you by so doing I will leave.' The King desired him to leave, and the Prince and Princesses drove away secretly in the evening to Spandau ; their children went to Potsdam, where they stayed with Curtius and von Unruh.

A full and vivid account of the Prince of Prussia's flight is to be found in von Petersdorff's *King Frederick William IV*. The writer of this account was the Countess Oriola, lady-in-waiting to the Princess of Prussia, and daughter of Bettina von Arnim-Brentano, the lively little person who, at the age of seventeen, sent word to the elderly Goethe that she burned with love for him, as Mignon for Wilhelm Meister, and pursued him for years

---

[1] *Preussische Jahrbücher*, Bd. 63, Heft 6, 1889 (K.).

with this wild Mignon fantasy. The Countess herself was an attractive personality. She was one of the beauties who gladdened the late Lord Redesdale's youth, for in Vol. I. of his vivacious *Memories* he speaks of meeting in the Prince of Prussia's household at Coblentz (after the Prince's rehabilitation) the Princess's charming lady-in-waiting ' Countess Oriolla, a beauty who preferred maiden meditation to matrimony and would not be won.' He goes on to tell of a 'Herr von Steinäcker, a rather melancholy man, who worshipped the ground on which Countess Oriolla's pretty foot trod ; it used to be said that he proposed to her once a month, and, on being once a month refused, would take to his bed love-sick, disconsolate, emerging at the end of twenty-four hours to resume his duties.'

Here is the Countess Oriola's story :

The crowd demanded the surrender of the Prince of Prussia, the bloodhound, who had desired the military to fire on the populace. The other brothers of the King (Carl and Albrecht) had already betaken themselves to Potsdam with their families. There, too, had already gone the children of the Prince of Prussia with their tutors. The Prince and Princess were still in the King's anteroom with a number of loyal friends, among them Princes Adalbert and Waldemar, awaiting what might happen there. Thoughts of the French Revolution and of the irruption of the populace in Versailles and the Tuileries might quite well be in every one's mind. Then the Prince was called to the King. An ominous silence fell upon us. When the Prince returned, he immediately turned to the Princess. It was the King's wish that they should leave the Castle. The Prince could not contribute to the protection of the King, since the hatred of the masses under prevailing conditions had directed itself against him, and his presence could only aggravate the situation of the King, instead of being useful to him. A carriage was procured, a four-seated hackney carriage. To whom it belonged I do not know. I heard say that it had been stationed in front of the Court chemist's, and was brought round to us. We left the Castle by a side staircase. On the steps some soldiers, with dejected looks, were lying about, and these their officer tried to rouse. The Princess, Prince, Countess Hacke, and I got into the four-seated carriage. The carriage drove along the Linden as far as the Brandenburg Gate without any interruption. The street was empty and quiet. In front of the Brandenburg Gate directions were given to the coachman to drive to the house of Privy Councillor von Schleinitz. Countess Hacke was a friend of the family, and it seems to me probable that she was the first to suggest a direction. Their Highnesses were here received with great commotion, and the events of the day were discussed ; then as the next step it was decided to dismiss the carriage which had brought us from the Castle, and to procure another one, in which their Highnesses were to be driven to the citadel of Spandau incognito. The Princess wished to dismiss us two ladies. She commissioned Countess Hacke to take her jewels from the palace in Berlin to Weimar, and, besides, to place Herr von Schleinitz, the Counsel of Legation, who lived in the town, in possession of all that had happened and get him on the following day to come himself secretly to Spandau, to consult with the Prince how to establish in this way communications with the King and come to some well-considered decision as to the next step ; he was also to bring with him the Princess's first lady of the bed-chamber, Fräulein von Neindorff, with some toilet necessaries, for we had nothing with us but the clothes in which we had left the palace at early morning. The Princess turned to me with the injunction to return to my mother, who lived in Berlin, and whom I had left for the first time only a few days before. This, however, I refused, very decidedly, to do, as I held it to be my duty to stay with the Princess : ' If your Royal Highness won't take me inside the carriage, I 'll soon manage to find a seat outside.' So the matter was arranged. The Princess, Prince, and I as the third got into the coach that had just been engaged. I saw that the Princess pulled a bracelet off her arm and slipped it on Frau von Schleinitz's as a souvenir of the occasion.

I remember nothing of any disguise for the Prince. When we arrived at Spandau, the Prince called a halt in front of a little inn, and said that he thought it would be better if he alone should drive up to the citadel, and that the Princess and I should wait in this inn until he sent the carriage back to bring us. The one thing that remains in my mind of the halt there and the following journey to the citadel is the wonderful sunrise on the way. Such an extraordinary contrast in its exalted beauty with the scene we had been through and the acts of human error and passion ! In front of the citadel we were naturally received by the Prince and the officers. One was the afterwards celebrated generalissimo von Steinmetz, and a staff-officer von Düring, and we were cared for, as far as could be, with military hospitality.

Never shall I forget the moment when the troops ordered to quit Berlin arrived, in disorder and without arms, and the Prince, from the main room of the citadel, whence he dared not show himself to the soldiers, saw his Guards Regiments arrive in this state. He drew back from the window, and tears ran down his cheeks. In the course of the day Baron von Schleinitz arrived for a first conference, and Fräulein von Neindorff with the much desired toilet requisites, and the news came from Berlin that the Castle, and their Majesties within it, had been confided to the protection of the Civic Guard, and that admittance could only be obtained by presenting a permit with the Berlin coat-of-arms. The palace of the Prince of Prussia had only been saved from pillage and destruction by the fact that the students had placarded upon it the words ' National Property.' Meanwhile the news had spread among the rioters that the Prince of Prussia had found refuge at Spandau, and this had been sufficient to bring about at that place a meeting of the people, with the popular leader Jung at the head, in order to demand the surrender of the Prince. What was to be done ? To allay popular feeling, as well as for the safety of the King's situation, every new excitement was to be avoided. So the Prince must go abroad for a time. Next, a motive for this must be found. A commission from the King must be the reason for his going away. Councillor of Legation von Schleinitz must come to an understanding with regard to the details with the King, and bring along with him the necessary instructions under seal of secrecy. Since the presence of the Prince in the citadel of Spandau was discovered, he could no longer stay there. The next night their Highnesses must escape unnoticed. Two officers of the garrison owned a boat ; this was carried on the shoulders of trustworthy artillerymen to the bank opposite the Pfaueninsel, whilst Lieutenant von Tietze, disguised as a coachman, drove a closed four-seated carriage—which the Prince, Princess, your humble servant, and the waiting woman entered at the citadel—through the town to the spot where the boat awaited us. Whilst we were crossing the streets we could hear coming in our direction the noise of the mass meeting in the market-place, where the democrat Jung was making a speech. Unnoticed we drove past, and out of the town. The road lay somewhat higher than the water. We were obliged to descend the slope to the landing-place for our boat. The Princess insisted herself on lending a hand to carry down the travelling bag. A mild night. with a wonderful moon, favoured us. So the short crossing was easily effected. The house of the court gardener, Fintelmann, lay on the Pfaueninsel near to the shore. One of the officers who had rowed us sprang ashore in order to call the gardener and warn him. Then, after repeated knocking, we heard the grating of a window, and soon afterwards a man appeared in a dressing-gown, trembling with fear, for which he was not to be blamed too much considering all the reports from Berlin which had reached him on the quiet island. He plucked up courage at the sight of the exalted guests who desired his hospitality, accompanied us into his gardener's cottage, and conducted the Princess and me into a nice room, where she lay down on the sofa, and I on some cushions on the floor. The Princess busied herself with throwing cushions from the sofa to swell my store. A sort of ball-game followed, the Princess throwing me one of her cushions and I throwing it back, until at last the lassitude of sleep overcame us, for this was our third sleepless night.

It was not long before Schleinitz came from Berlin as ambassador with the expected order, by which the Prince was commissioned to make a report to Queen Victoria on the latest occurrences in Berlin, and to leave immediately for London. Herr von Oelrichs, of the Grand General Staff, was appointed to accompany the Prince, and was to arrive on the following day (March 22) on the Pfaueninsel and to depart with his Highness. There appeared also Prince Carl, from the Castle at Potsdam, as well as the Prince's children with Prince Frederick William's military governor, General von Unruh. And now the details of the Prince's journey were discussed. The Princess wished to go with him. It was also proposed to take the children. Old General von Unruh expressed himself quite resolutely against this, which meant that the whole family of the heir-apparent would be leaving the country. The Prince admitted that he was right, and it was decided that the Prince alone, with Herr von Oelrichs, should set out the following day. On the other hand it was decided that the Princess should return with me to the Castle at Potsdam, where a great portion of the King's family was already The following day was the birthday of the Prince. How joyfully has this day been celebrated later as a national festival! This time there was nothing like a festival to be detected. In order at least to call forth a less sorrowful impression, I had brought to me from the garden a bouquet of the first spring flowers. The kind wife of the gardener lent me a gay-coloured dress (for I was still wearing court mourning from Berlin), which was intended for a full round figure, and in this disguise I stepped up to the Prince, to offer my congratulations and little bouquet, the only one, I believe, on that day. In the afternoon the Prince, in civilian clothes, departed with his attendant in a simple hired carriage. At a station where the horses were changed, they thought they were recognised by the attention with which they were regarded by the people standing about, and as a result the memory of Varennes forced itself upon them involuntarily. The gentlemen said to the people that they would walk on ahead until the horses were harnessed and the carriage caught them up. However, they quickly cut across the fields to a homestead on their way, which they soon recognised as the vicarage of the hamlet. They made themselves known to the pastor, and the latter quieted their fears and assisted them to maintain their incognito. As for the rest the Prince, without further incidents, reached the coast and England. The Prince was received most cordially by Queen Victoria.

It is a pity to spoil in any detail the Countess's story but it is extremely doubtful whether, when the mob made for the Prince of Prussia's palace, the words ' National Property ' were chalked upon its front to save it from plunder as she, and others, suggest. As a matter of fact, it was occupied by a weird Commission of Petitions, presided over by three convicted criminals, who, with a retinue consisting of whole families, made free of His Royal Highness's living-rooms, kitchen and cellar.[1] The Countess

---

[1] Hans Blum, whose account is fully confirmed by Frederick William' letter of 1st April to his ministers :—

POTSDAM, *in the night of the 1st April*, 1848.

MY DEAR MINISTERS CAMPHAUSEN AND VON AUERSWALD,—The unlawful occupation, by a number of unauthorised persons, of my brother the Prince of Prussia's property and palace, is an act of brutal violence without parallel in

states that she remembers 'nothing of any disguise' of the
Prince, though she tells of Lieutenant von Tietze being disguised
as a coachman, and speaks later of the Prince setting out 'in
civilian clothes.' Petersdorff informs us that according to
Gerlach the Prince was in mufti, but that Varnhagen and
Bernhardi say that he put on a suit of Vincke's. As a matter
of fact on the morning of the 19th he had had his beard shaved
in Berlin, and this was reason enough why he should not allow
himself to be seen by his troops ordered out of Berlin. His
shaven chin was not a sight to cheer his dejected Guards ! That
shaven chin figures enormous in a popular caricature, entitled
'How William, not the Conqueror, arrived in England,' where
his reception by our little Prince of Wales is depicted. The
general belief was that he donned *en route* a postilion's dress.
Another caricature represents his arrival in this garb at a
junction where he encounters as fellow-fugitives Louis Philippe,
Louis Napoleon, Metternich and Lola Montez. Possibly he
changed into von Tietze's suit ! A third caricature of the
period may be mentioned, for its general interest. This represents Queen Victoria standing on tiptoe as ' The Guardian
Angel,' with Louis Philippe and Metternich clasped to her
bosom, and the Prince of Prussia fluttering to her arms.

To conclude this chapter may be given the sober impressions
of the state of feeling in Berlin on 20th and 21st March formed
by Victor von Unruh :

> I travelled there (to Berlin) in order to get a knowledge of con-
> ditions, hunted up an old engineer who was better known than I
> in the machine shops and foundries, visited the workshops and
> various beer shops, attended the distribution of arms to the im-
> provised volunteer force, and spoke with many workmen. I was
> also present when the liberated Poles marched in front of the Castle,
> discharged pistols loaded with blank cartridges, and raised cheers
> in response to which Schwerin made a speech from the Castle
> balcony. Such occurrences appeared very revolutionary, there
> was certainly great excitement, and the former ministers were
> roundly abused ; but animosity against the dynasty I could find

---

the history of Germany or Prussia. This open scandal must now cease. I
demand and order as King and head of the Family that within the next few
days no stranger be suffered to remain in my dear, unhonoured, dishonoured
and maliciously slandered brother's house, and that the latter be quietly
made over to Court Marshal Count Pückler and Court Councillor Bork, both
of whom are in my brother's service. . . . I charge you both to prepare
the transfer of the house at once. Its protection by the Civic Guard must
continue for the present.

nowhere, nor could my companion. It was thought that the King was badly advised, but that he was full of good intentions, and no one doubted but that now things would turn out well. Among the workmen, of whom many had been in the fighting, no selfish motives were to be traced, no envy against the moneyed class. As is well known, less was stolen at that time than at any other time. Property was perfectly safe, women and children moved about the streets, all the shops were open. The members of the Magdeburg rifle corps and other citizens who returned from the great funeral of those who had fallen had quite the same impression. Many pitied ' the good King.' ' He grieved us very much, he did appear so very dejected ' was the expression one heard. Even Berlin humour was not lacking. Immediately beneath a shell which had stuck fast in the casing of a pump in the Breitestrasse had been affixed the Royal proclamation of which the heading was ' To my dear Berliners.' A gendarme on whose back some one had written in chalk ' National Property,' was allowed to pass by with a laugh.[1]

---

[1] von Unruh, *Erinnerungen* (K.).

CHAPTER VIII

THE KING DRINKS THE DREGS

By assuming the pose of constitutional leader of Germany on 21st March the King sought to extricate himself from the tangle of humiliation in which he found himself involved. So strangely constructed was his mind that it is quite possible he deceived himself into the belief that he was, after all, playing a noble part in enduring the trouble of the moment for the sake of the great German nation, and was turning even his humiliation to what seemed, in his feverish brain, profitable account.

On that day he issued a decree [1] ordering the Prussian army to wear side by side with the Prussian cockade, black and white, a cockade with the German colours, the accepted revolutionary colours, black, red, and gold :

Since I am devoting myself without reservation to the German cause, and since I see in the co-operation of Prussia a decided advancement of the same, I hereby decree that the army shall immediately wear the German cockade side by side with that of Prussia.

He followed this up on the same day with an 'Address [2] to My People and the German Nation ' :

Thirty-five years ago, in days of extreme danger, the King spoke with confidence to his people and his confidence was not put to shame ; the King, united with his people, saved Prussia and Germany from disgrace and humiliation. With confidence I speak to you to-day, at a moment when the Fatherland lies in the greatest danger, and to the German nation among whose most noble branches my people may count itself with pride. Germany within is the victim of a fever and can be threatened on more than one side by danger from without. Salvation from the doubly pressing danger can only be got by the most intimate union of the German princes and peoples under one leadership. I undertake to-day this leadership during the days of peril. My people, which does not shun danger, will not forsake me, and Germany will attach itself to me

---

[1] Klein.   [2] Klein.

with confidence. I have to-day accepted the old German colours and ranged myself and my people under the venerable banner of the German Empire. From this day onward Prussia is merged in Germany. . . .

Heinrich von Arnim, late Ambassador at Paris and now Foreign Minister, drafted this decree, according to the following story given by Perthes,[1] who also gives Count Pourtalès' estimate of this Arnim : ' To understand Heinrich von Arnim completely, one must know that he consists of four parts. He is firstly a brave man, secondly a pious man, thirdly an intelligent man, fourthly a fool ! He who is not acquainted with the fourth part in him does not know him at all.'

The proclamation of March 21 had been drawn up, and certainly with expedition, by Heinrich von Arnim, shortly before he submitted it to the States Ministry. The draft is in Arnim's own hand ; at the place where the published proclamation reads ' From this day onward Prussia is merged in Germany,' there are many alterations in Arnim's draft. Arnim says that in connection with this passage he always had in his mind Hegel's thought that a thing should be preserved in itself in order to live on as the germ of some new and greater thing. For that reason he had said ' Prussia will be immanent in Germany.' [2] The other ministers had not grasped this. He had explained it from the Hegelian point of view ; whereupon the reply had been that one or other of Hegel's pupils might understand it, but the nation would not understand it. Then it had been changed and changed, finally Count Arnim-Boitzenburg had exclaimed, ' We can certainly put " Prussia is merged in Germany." ' The others had agreed to this, and so it was Boitzenburg who introduced the notorious expression into the proclamation.

The King confirmed this Address by a proclamation [3] to the German Nation, anonymous but doubtless official, which was stuck up, early on the 21st, as a poster in the streets :

A new and glorious history begins for you to-day ! You are from now onwards a united and great nation, strong, free, and powerful in the heart of Europe !

Prussia's Frederick William IV. has, relying on your heroic help and your spiritual regeneration, placed himself at the head of the United Fatherland for the salvation of Germany. You will to-day even see him on horseback in your midst, with the old, the venerable colours of the German nation. Hail and blessing to the constitutional Prince, to the leader of the united German peoples, to the new King of the free, regenerated German nation !

---

[1] *Preussische Jahrbücher*, Bd. 63, Heft 6, 1889 (K.).
[2] *Preussen wird in Deutschland aufgehoben.*
[3] Facsimile in Blum.

On this piece of folly Wolfgang Menzel, the diplomat, makes the following bitter comments : [1]

This colossal folly filled me with all the greater indignation, as the King had only just promised me that he would have nothing printed, referring to the German nation, without letting me know of it beforehand. . . . The ministerial manifesto, which proclaimed the new King of the Germans, was usurpation in its crudest form, and must naturally give offence to all non-Prussians. The latter might have had less to say if the usurper had stepped upon the scene in the panoply of victory and full consciousness of power and had inspired fear. But after a deplorable defeat, after the humble surrender of the crown to the ' press-gallery ' and the rabble the usurpation could only appear still more laughable. I was somewhat angry, for the thing was too bad. (Menzel was summoned to the Minister of Foreign Affairs, Baron von Arnim, the ' Parisian ' or ' red ' Arnim.) Arnim was all fire and flame, really flattered himself, as it appeared, on being the man of the moment, and on having brought about a monstrously great and world historic fact. However, I was not in the mood to spare him in the slightest. I said to him that one could not have spoken in the name of the King more clumsily and tactlessly to Germany. . . . By return of post protests from all sides against Prussia's new policy and undisguised sneers at the unfortunate King would arrive in Berlin. . . . Moreover the sympathies between South-west Germany and Prussia, the nourishing and strengthening of which had been the object of my coming here a week ago, were no longer in existence and had been, for a long time to come, torn asunder by the usurping attitude of Prussia.

Menzel's misgivings were justified, for Klein relates that at Stuttgart, shortly after the proclamation, a figure representing the King was first riddled with shot by the democrats and then thrown into the flames, and that similar pranks were played in Munich. Hebbel gives an account [2] of the feeling in Vienna :

An Austrian knows what a constitution is, and understands too the significance of the fact that his own Kaiser granted one earlier than the King of Prussia. So the latter's proclamation, to the effect that he ' now ' wishes to place himself at the head of Germany, aroused peculiar thoughts in the mind of an Austrian when he read it in the Berlin papers yesterday ; and to-day, when the Vienna paper publishes a detailed account of the scenes of atrocity and terror in Berlin, the proclamation fills him with indignation.

Baron Stockmar of Coburg, Prince Albert's old mentor, wrote on 31st March (*Denkwürdigkeiten*, p. 487) :

---

[1] *Denkwürdigkeiten* (K.).
[2] *Augsburger Allgemeine Zeitung*, 30th March 1848 (K.).

The poor King of Prussia has made a sad mess. Never has he made a move or a concession but it was too late, nay, when it would have been better had he done nothing. Metternich and the Russian Emperor were the bane both of him and of Germany. Had he but listened to Prince Albert's letter of 1846, how simple, how easy it would have been for him to have taken another course in the Cracow affair, and how safe, how glorious, how great would his position have been at this moment—master of a power sufficient to uphold all Germany! In Germany no one will hear of him now : ' Rather the Emperor of Austria or the King of Bavaria.' Thus it is we Germans confound the cause with the individual!

On this eventful day the King was to suffer a humiliation as deep as that which he had endured in the Castle courtyard on the 19th. To suffer it! He seemed positively to enjoy riding through the city in a motley procession, and wearing the revolutionary colours. We have given their popular interpretation on p. 242, and Jahn's on p. 21 ; we may add here Freiligrath's as given in his poem 'To the Black, Red, and Gold,' written in London,

> ' Powder is black,
> And blood is red,
> But yellow 's the hue of flickering flame ! '

Of this amazing performance of the present Kaiser's great-uncle, the following is the description given in Wolff's *Berliner Revolutionschronik* [1] :

A large number of men had collected in the Castle Square when at 10 o'clock the King stepped on to the balcony, and cried to the crowd that he would immediately appear among them on horseback. At the same time he expressed a wish that some one might bring him a tricolour German flag in order that he might carry it as his standard. The King appeared soon afterwards, towards 11 o'clock, in the courtyard of the Castle at the entrance to the winding staircase. He was on horseback, wearing the uniform of the 1st Guards Regiment and his helmet, a broad band with the German colours on his arm ; he was surrounded by the Princes present in Berlin and by the Ministers, the latter in civilian dress. All were wearing the German colours. The King, greeted with cheers, first of all spoke the following words to those standing around : ' What you see here is no usurpation. I desire to thrust no rulers from their throne—everything is directed only to the restoration of the unity of Germany—this unity is endangered in isolated places, in Breslau for instance one speaks of treason, and treason and German do not go well together—I desire unity and order.' (Thus runs the original report in the *Spenersche Zeitung*.)

---

[1] Klein.

Amid the jubilant cries of approbation which followed these words a procession was formed, full of strangely contrasting elements. The Ministers, Count Arnim, Schwerin and von Rohr, Lieutenant-General von Neumann and Count Oriola, with Assistant-Judge Friedberg, representing the Minister of Justice, all on horseback and with the German colours on their arms, formed the advance-guard, which did not trouble to keep its proper formation ; a civic guard, following on foot, carried the tricolour flag which the King had had handed to him. In front of the latter, on both sides of the King, rode two citizens. A coach proprietor and poor-law guardian from the Mittelstrasse cleared the way for the King's horse. There was also one Urban, a veterinary surgeon, who had gained a reputation as one of the brave defenders of the barricade in the Alexanderplatz, as a popular orator and as negotiator with General von Möllendorff. He was a stately figure with long black beard and uncovered head, and he moved about, at first on foot, in the immediate vicinity of the King, holding in his hand an imperial crown painted (on card-board). Later he was seen entering the Castle on horseback side by side with the King and General von Neumann.—The procession halted first of all at the Castle Square, where the King again made to the assembled crowd a speech similar to his former one, and received the same approving cheers. From here the procession passed the precincts of the Castle—from the windows bunting was waving as on the previous day to greet the triumphal procession of the Poles—as far as the new Royal Guard-house. The garrison of the Civic Guard stood to arms ; the King rode up with a salute and said : ' I see you here on guard, I cannot express enough in words what I owe you— believe me ! ' Then, when a voice cried at the moment ' Long live the Emperor of Germany ! ' the King replied, apparently vexed : ' No ! No ! That I will not, may not have ! '

After the procession had wended its way in the direction of the Behrenstrasse and had passed by this street and returned by Unter den Linden, a further halt was made at the University. Here the procession was headed by the Chief of Police, von Minutoli, who had joined it in the Opera Square. Three students in advance bore to the King the Imperial banner. In front of the University were the Rector and Vice-Rector at the head of the students, drawn up in line. The King extended his hand to both professors and then, at a short distance from the space in which the foundation stone of the monument of Frederick the Great had been laid, made the following speech : ' My heart beats proudly that it is my capital in which such a powerful sentiment has held sway. This day is a great one, a day never to be forgotten, a decisive day. In you, gentlemen, lies the germ of a great future, and when, in the middle or at the end of your life, you look back upon it I charge you to remain mindful of this day. Students make the greatest impression on the nation and the nation on students. I wear colours which are not mine, but I attempt thereby no act of usurpation. I desire no crown, no overlordship, I desire Germany's freedom, Germany's unity, I desire order, that I swear before God ! (the King here raised his right hand to heaven). I have only done what has so often happened in the history of Germany, when powerful Princes and Dukes, if order be trodden underfoot, have seized the banner and placed themselves at the head of the entire people ; and I believe that the hearts of the Princes will beat in unison with mine, and that the will of the people will support me. Note that, gentlemen ; record it that I am no usurper, desire nothing but German freedom and unity. Tell it to the studious youth absent ; it grieves me infinitely that they are not all here. Tell it to them all ! ' The students raised a boisterous cheer and clashed their arms together. Amidst the cheering of the accompanying crowd which had gradually attained enormous dimensions, the procession bent its way across the Castle Square, through the Königstrasse to the Alexanderplatz, in order to make, on the return journey through the Breitestrasse, one more halt at the Cölln Town Hall. Here also the King felt constrained to address the town councillors and Civic Guard gathered at this spot. The conclusion of his speech ran : '. . . Citizens, I know perfectly well that my strength lies not in the arms of my certainly strong and brave army, my strength lies not in my well-filled treasury, but only in the hearts and the loyalty of my people. And those hearts, that loyalty, you will present to me, is it not so ? I swear to you, I desire nothing but good for you and Germany ! ' The procession soon after this ended with the return to the Castle.

According to Wolff [1] a statement of the King, during this ride, with regard to his brother was made public in July 1848, in a supplement to the *Lokomotive*, the paper edited by Corvin's friend, Held :

In July 1848 a statement of the King concerning his brother Prince William was made public by means of a poster. The placard bore the heading, ' A characteristic of Aunt Voss, *née* Lessing ' (Special Supplement to Held's *Lokomotive*). An eye-witness of, and participator in the procession of the 21st gives in the placard the general sense of the words of the King concerning his brother as follows : ' And now, gentlemen, do what you can to quash a rumour that burdens my royal brother with very heavy consequences. My brother is—out and out—a soldier. Gifted with the most modest and open character, he does not understand how to flatter the masses or how to make himself beloved. I can, however, give you the most sacred assurance that he it was and none other who gave his full assent to the new path that we have recently entered upon, and which we considered it right to take in the interest of the happiness of our people. . . . I give you the highest that a King can give. . . . (The King is said to have spoken these words with emotion and in a voice almost choked with tears.) I

---

[1] Quoted by Klein.

give you my kingly word of honour : My brother is innocent of all
the proceedings which are imputed to him by some malevolent
persons. I declare these assertions to be the meanest slanders,
spread by evil-minded people in order to bring about hostility
between my beloved nation and my house.'

In February 1849, Gerlach sat next the Queen at luncheon
one day. He found her very amiable and talkative. ' She
told how the King had said to her the 21st March, the day of
his ride round, had been the most terrible day of his life, though
she had never imagined it was quite so bad as that.' A naïve
remark ! That the King was not at this period always in
complete possession of his faculties seems to be clearly indicated
by the following circumstance : [1]

No one was thinking of the recall or return of the troops to the
city, when, scarcely half an hour after the King's official progress
through the city, the veterinary surgeon Urban, accompanying the
tailor Eckert, another of the same kidney, appeared at the office
of the chief of police and produced to the astonished head, von
Minutoli, an autograph letter of the King in the following terms :
' I willingly acquiesce in the wish of veterinary surgeon Urban that
he should lead back immediately to Berlin the troops lying at
Potsdam and in the neighbourhood, namely, the Kaiser Alexander
Grenadier Regiment.

Given under my hand on the 21st March 1848.
FRIEDRICH WILHELM.'

Next day the King had to drink the very dregs of the cup of
humiliation, as Germans of the Bismarckian era must hold.
He had to acknowledge, bare-headed, the passage to the grave
of the victims of the 18th :

Berlin presented on the morning of March 22 the appearance of
a town preparing itself beforehand for an unusually grave solemnity.
The public offices remained closed. Only very few shops were
open. On the front of the houses and from the windows waved,
side by side with the German flag, huge weepers of crape. Black
flags were hoisted on the gates and fluttered from the battlements
of the Castle. Men were wearing crape round their arms or hats,
the women appeared in black clothes on the balconies, at the
windows, and in the streets. The spectators were ranged on the
foot-pavement on both sides of the street ; a crowd larger than
the eye could reach covered the Castle Square from the Gendarmen
Market as far as the grave in front of the Landsberger Gate. In
front of the new church was erected a platform decorated with
crape and flowers, on which were arranged the coffins (183). At

---

[1] Steinmann, *Die Revolution in Preussen* (K.).

midday the different sections of the Civic Guard, students, artisans and corporations moved from their various rendezvous and took up the positions allocated to them. The Guild of Riflemen, whose duty it was to discharge the volleys over the grave, the municipal council and the town councillors adorned with their golden chains, and the clergy of all creeds joined in the procession. In the new church the evangelical clergy, Bishop Neander at their head, stood before the altar, to receive the mourners. During the hymn ' Jesus my trust ' the people left the church and approached the coffins (in the Gendarmen Market). The officials of the Lord Chamberlain had sent a head-gardener and workmen to arrange the floral decorations, which had been furnished with the greatest readiness from the Royal gardens. The mourners were given fresh bouquets. Before the procession proceeded on its way the clergy delivered their funeral addresses on the square in front of the new church. Those who were to deliver the addresses, the Evangelical clergyman Sydow, the Catholic chaplain Ruhland, and the Jewish Rabbi Sachs came forward in turn. Sydow spoke in front of the altar of the catafalque : ' Bear forth our brothers, who have fallen in the fight which has had such blessed results for the Fatherland, and which is destined now to throw a bond of love and unity around the whole German Fatherland. Let all the feelings which agitate the breasts of one and all sink in awe before the dead. Think of the will of God which rules the destinies of man and guides everything for the best, which directs the bullets in the battle and gives and takes life. . . .' The chaplain of St. Hedwig, Ruhland, said : ' The Catholic clergy also greet in the name of their Church the mortal remains of those who are henceforward to rest in mother earth. If this grave become the sign of union for all, if from this one grave is to go forth for ever the gospel of unity to all our dear German Fatherland, if this one grave is the passage to the resurrection for us all—then be blessed, you who stand around me here as corpses (!) . . .' The Rabbi Sachs closed the religious ceremony with the following words : ' . . . It was not Death, that made equal all those who rest here, but the strength of life, the power of an idea, a passionate enthusiasm which tore down all the barriers and obstacles that separated man from himself, man from man. It was the power of a conviction, a rising of the noblest feelings and thoughts, which impelled the deceased into the death struggle : they were the worthiest ends for which they strove, and towards which they advanced at the hazard of life ; it was free self-consciousness, the right of man to use his powers unhindered and untrammelled, which they helped to gain by fighting for the Fatherland.'—The coffins were then raised and the procession moved off. At the moment when the head of the procession reached the second gate of the Castle the King, surrounded by ministers and adjutants, stepped on to the balcony ; two flags covered with crape were lowered from the balcony and the tricolour between the two was also dipped in salute. The King saluted the dead, by taking off his helmet and remaining with bared head until the coffins had been carried past. The head of the procession had already reached its destination, the Friedrichshain, when the end of the procession had scarcely begun to move. It took close on three hours before the separate parts of the procession had congregated in the Friedrichshain. . . . When the coffins had been lowered, the clergyman Sydow delivered the address in memory of the dead, taking as his text the words in the New Testament : ' Verily, verily, I say unto you, except the corn of wheat fall into the ground and die, it abideth alone ; but if it die it bringeth forth much fruit.' . . . After Sydow's sermon Bishop Neander pronounced the benediction. The flags were lowered in the usual military fashion and the Guild of Riflemen fired their farewell volley. With this the official ceremony was concluded.[1]

In the *Vossische Zeitung* of 23rd March appeared a pronouncement of His Majesty on the burial :

His Majesty the King has, in reference to the funeral ceremony which took place yesterday, made known and expressed his most complete admiration ; the sublime demeanour of the inhabitants of Berlin has not only exceeded all and each of his expectations, but is also the best gauge of the worth of the high spiritual exaltation of the people which is the fruit of the fight in the memorable days of last week.

The soldiers killed in the street-fighting were buried without honours paid by the King. Adjutant-General von Natzmer's account [2] to his wife of the scene at their burial is worth reading :

The soldiers who had fallen in the street-fighting were buried on the 24th March in the Invalidenkirchhof. The funeral procession set out at five in the morning from the military hospital at the Brandenburg Gate. Since disturbances and insults were feared during this solemnity precautionary measures had been taken. Bodies of police had been stationed along the streets to be traversed and at the churchyard itself. The garrison had left the city several days before. . . . The procession went down the Luisenstrasse and through the New Gate to the Invalidenhaus. In the streets and especially in the windows many men were to be seen ; great crowds of people had already collected in the churchyard and it was believed that hostile demonstrations would be made there by the heroes of the barricades. In the streets the people maintained a quiet demeanour, and from the windows the liveliest sympathy was manifested to the funeral procession. At the Invalidenhaus Lieutenant-General von Held and General von Jaski stood at the head of all the Pensioners drawn up on parade, who saluted the dead. The eighteen coffins

---

[1] A. Wolff, *Berliner Revolutionschronik* (K.)
[2] von Natzmer, *Unter den Hohenzollern* (K.).

were lowered into one big grave and at the last moment were covered with flowers and garlands thrown from all sides.

The chaplain of the garrison, Ziehe, delivered an address and gave his benediction to the dead. The people remained throughout orderly but indifferent. When the religious ceremony was over, the Infantry General von Natzmer stepped on to the mounded earth above the grave and expressed in a short speech the thanks of the King and Fatherland to the fallen heroes—to the heroes who had sealed their oath of fidelity to the King with their blood and their lives, etc. This speech, in spite of its very decided tendency, was received by the people present with the greatest enthusiasm, the very people who at this time never encountered a military uniform without insulting it. For that reason it has been formally intimated to the soldiers that they should refrain from wearing uniform. On the occasion of this burial all the officers naturally appeared in uniform ; General von Natzmer, in order to express quite openly the highest respect to the fallen warriors, appeared in full general's uniform with the ribbon of the Order of the Black Eagle across his breast. This was the first public function since the revolution at which men were not shy of courageously expressing their true convictions. If people had gone on consistently in this way, much would certainly have been left undone and much would have become better. But unfortunately many—who spoke bravely and defiantly after the happy change in things—did not step forth with the same courage in those days !

On the 25th the King paid a visit to Potsdam, to reassure his troops, and Gerlach gives in his *Denkwürdigkeiten*, i. p. 148, the speech addressed to the officers, from the account of one of them.

I am glad to be once more in your midst. Rumours are current that I have not been quite a free agent. I have come over here for that reason, and intend to pass several days in Potsdam during next week ; my presence is the best proof of the contrary. I have moreover come to speak with you about another matter. There have also been rumours circulating in Berlin that among the troops, among the officers in particular, a *coup* was in contemplation : I beg you to refrain from all demonstrations, firstly out of regard for me, secondly out of regard for the Fatherland, thirdly so as not to dissipate the strength which we may need against foreign enemies, whereby the whole of Europe may be endangered. All my strength is claimed by the German Fatherland at this decisive moment, when Germany is in the greatest danger of falling into fragments. To attain this object I shall shun no sacrifice ; as early as the 17th and 18th, and even earlier, everything was ready, and no power in the world would have forced me to act otherwise, if I had not considered it necessary for the welfare of the German people. The conduct of the troops was noble beyond all praise ; to my last hour I shall remember it to your advantage. Troops which have accomplished that will accomplish the unsurpassable against a foreign foe. I am not aware whether the condition of Berlin is now known to you ; it is quite an abnormal condition. There is no authority, no magistrate, no town-councillor, and yet by the goodwill of the citizens property and person are protected. My person has never been more secure, and I could not have believed that the inhabitants of Berlin had such attachment for me. Individual orators, thirty to forty, even up to fifty, who have attempted to make speeches and to rouse public feeling, have been arrested by citizens, youths of fifteen up to old men of sixty. I have got together a fairly large body of troops, and have so disposed the army along the railways that they can be ready instantly, on a sign from me, to meet the contingency of the rabble rising against the citizens and the latter failing to get the mastery. In such an event they are to support the citizens, so as to suppress such a rising. As things stand, however, I do not think it will be necessary. Only in case the citizens should desire it, would I go more closely into the question of the return of the troops.

Leopold von Gerlach adds : ' After a pause, during which General von Rohr whispered something to the King, the latter said, " But that 's impossible to misunderstand. Don't misunderstand me. What I meant is that my person since the moment the troops left Berlin has never been safer than now." ' Klein says : ' According to the report of the *Vossische Zeitung* the much-quoted words of the King concerning his personal safety were " I have never been freer and more secure than when under the protection of my citizens." Bismarck, who was present when the speech was made, quotes in his *Reflections and Reminiscences* the words in the latter form, and remarks in addition : " At the words : ' I have never been freer and more secure than under the protection of my citizens,' there arose a murmuring and a clanking of scabbards such as no King of Prussia in the midst of his officers had ever heard before, and, I hope, will ever hear again." The *Vossische Zeitung* was of another opinion. It remarks at the end of its report : " The Royal words bore a message of peace and reconciliation to all hearts. The joy over the King's visit has brought about a happy and contented state of mind among all the inhabitants of Potsdam, as well as among the soldiers." According to its report the King's speech at a specially significant part was certainly to this effect : " There does indeed rule among the citizens of Berlin an excellent spirit that is unparalleled in history ; I desire therefore that the staff of officers may likewise embrace the spirit of the time, as I have embraced it, and that from now onwards they also may prove true citizens of the state as they have proved themselves true soldiers." '

The painful impression left by this speech is well indicated by what Prince Hohenlohe-Ingelfingen, who was present, says :

Why then had we fought for him ? Why then at the news that his life was endangered, if we went on fighting, had we silently suffered abuse and insult ? Sixty-five officers of Guards regiments had been actually insulted by the populace, and had sent in their papers, for it was then the generally accepted idea that an officer could not continue to serve, if he did not wipe out an actual insult by the blood of his opponent—and they, out of respect for the King's command, had undergone with stoicism that experience ! In the midst of those 'dear Berliners,' who had cudgelled us, did the King feel just as safe as in our midst ? In the midst of those Berliners who had insulted him, jeered at him, who had overwhelmed him and the Queen with the most filthy speeches, just as safe as in our midst ? What, was he then not safer with us, safer at least from outrage and insult ? Such was the impression that the speech made ; it grieved us deeply, and was more humiliating than anything we had suffered up to that time. We did not know how sorely the King suffered himself in consequence of his untimely yielding on the 19th March. It was kept back from us that, immediately after the speech, when he had left us, he broke down weeping in a side room and sobbed : ' O my God, my God, must I say that to my brave officers, who have fought so bravely for me ? ' We had only the one feeling, that we, after we had done all we were bidden, suffered and endured all that man could, were disowned by him for whom we had done everything. A kind of stupor again took possession of us, and every one of us made himself familiar with the thought of seeking a new profession. For we all believed that, in logical sequence, the time was not far distant when every professional officer would be declared useless. I for my part thought of learning farming.

The angry feeling among officers was fully shared by the rank and file. They could not forgive the humiliation of their withdrawal from Berlin, and that at the King's command. A song of extraordinary bitterness, first sung by the Second Guards regiment, expressed their indignation with true Prussian arrogance and intensity. Three verses of it run as follows :

> Prussians were we, our colours black and white ;
>   Once more our ensign fluttered in the van,
> As for their King his true ones fell in fight,
>   Fell for their King rejoicing, man by man.

We saw without dismay
Our comrades borne away,
Then like a dagger-thrust the order came :
' Prussians no more, Germans henceforth your name ! '

And yet with love we waited on the throne,
Firm in our faith and in our conscience clear.
His was the gratitude to virtue shown—
To us, his Prussians, deaf the kingly ear !
Then severed was the band
That bound the Fatherland,
When he repulsed the faithful with disdain,
He broke our hearts, and snapt his staff in twain. . . .

Black, red, and gold are flaunting in the sun ;
Dishonoured, our black eagle claws the sand ;
Here, Zollern, here thy course of glory 's run,
Here fell a king, but not with sword in hand.
O fallen star, no more
Our eyes thy light adore !
What thou thyself hast done, Prince, thou shalt rue,
Nor find another, like a Prussian, true.

Bismarck, in his *Reflections and Reminiscences*, tells the story of how he was cruel enough some years later to read these verses to the Prince of Prussia at Babelsberg. ' Thereupon,' he says, ' he broke into a violent fit of weeping.'

With all his fine intellectual qualities, his kindliness of disposition, his romantic enthusiasm, his cowardice, there was in the King an element of roguery of the sort which seems peculiar to rulers and politicians because to them comes continually the opportunity for its exercise. On 30th March he wrote to Camphausen, one of his ministers : ' So long as Berlin remains unpurged of the Camarilla of the clubs and of the blood-thirsty rabble I cannot, nor will I, return thither.' The next day he said [1] to a deputation from Berlin : ' The people of Berlin have behaved so nobly and magnanimously to me as would perhaps be impossible in any other great city in the world.'

Unruh [2] again gives a useful summary of opinion, which shows very clearly the weakness of the King and his government during the scenes lasting from 18th to 22nd March :

The surging masses of people in the streets on the 19th and 20th everywhere respected the name of the King, and security of pro-

---

[1] A. Stahr, *Die Preussische Revolution* (K.).
[2] *Skizzen aus Preussen's neuester Geschichte*, pp. 22, 26, 27.

perty and person prevailed generally ; the shops, even those of the goldsmiths and jewellers, were open. The people showed itself ripe for freedom. The country was in joyous mood ; the officials and a section of the aristocracy complained and distorted facts. . . . The small number of republicans did not dare to venture out with their flag. Still more favourable was the position in the provinces. From the uppermost ranks of society down to the labourer no one desired to hear anything of the overthrow of the dynasty, every one held firmly to the constitutional throne ; odd people here and there of republican tendencies were obliged to conceal carefully their opinion. The deposition of the King in Berlin would have raised a storm in the provinces. Line regiments and Landwehr, citizens and peasants would have marched immediately on Berlin. Every town, every district would have declared for the Monarchy. This was the best shield of the Monarchy. The feeling of the country could not have been unknown to the Ministry. Neverthe- less steps ought to have been taken at once for the formation of a powerful and organised executive authority, which could deal energetically with any mob goaded on by individual agitators. What happened ?   On March 19 and following days pretty nearly every one who wanted arms had been allowed to have them. . . . The twenty-five thousand armed men were to organise themselves, and to make their own regulations. Truly, people were more re- publican than the oldest republicans ! Yet no, they were only weak, without energy. Anarchy was to organise itself without any leadership.

And of the Civic Guard to whose protection the King had entrusted his own person, and the life and property of his lieges, Gneist gives an amusing description : [1]

That an armed force without discipline is just as much an im- possibility in the North American republic as under Russian despot- ism could not be brought home to this volunteer force. They mounted guard everywhere with untiring perseverance. But any military development, even the capacity to execute merely a move- ment in close order, was lacking. Especially dangerous, as is well known, was their rifle-practice. They drilled at times, showing exceptional zeal when there was a band. At night patrols traversed the town. I have taken part myself in such as a member of the Civic Guard and of the Corps of Students. Nothing speaks louder and more distinctly for the good sense of this capital than the circum- stance that no harm ever happened to the patrols. Occasionally a man's musket was taken from him, but even that did not happen frequently. For the rest the organisation was as democratic as possible. Officers had certainly been chosen, but naturally with the proviso that they should be removed as soon as anything irre- gular happened. The generalissimo also stood on the same trustful

---

[3] R. Gneist, *Berliner Zustände* (K.).

footing. Nevertheless confidence and harmony were wanting. . . . Every one was very angry, for instance, at the attempt ' to place the will of companies in a sort of tutelage under the will of commanders.' . . . Briefly, it was the long-desired self-government now finally realised, and even if the commands, Slope Arms! Order Arms!, were obeyed, this took place, nevertheless, with the full conviction that the question should really have been decided by a show of hands. . . . Moreover where individuals were gifted with incontestable personal courage, such could only become dangerous to themselves on the occasion of combined movements involving large numbers. Fortunately things seldom came to that. Almost daily, it is true, in many districts, the alarm was simultaneously sounded by bugle and drum, indicating the danger of a riot somewhere or other. Nevertheless the good-natured temperament of the populace gave such incidents as a rule rather the character of an altercation, over which certainly a good deal of time was wasted ; and when, as a matter of fact, the Civic Guard did arrive on the scene, too late as a rule, they had all the less to do, since in the meantime little had occurred. . . . The exaggerated zeal of the first few weeks, during which the Civic Guard lapsed at times into the rough ways of the Gendarmerie, disappeared with time. Only the goodwives of Berlin had to complain of the frequent recurrence of calls for twenty-four hour spells of duty. Since there was no reckoning with certainty on a given number of men presenting themselves, it was continuously necessary, particularly in case of night alarms, to summon whole battalions. Still, the trembling Andromache always saw her courageous hero return, after a few hours, cheerful and uninjured.

BOOK V
THE FIRST GERMAN PARLIAMENT
1848

CHAPTER I

THE PRELIMINARY PARLIAMENT—HECKER'S REBELLION IN BADEN

THE question may well be asked, what had become during all this time of tumult of the Federal Diet at Frankfort, the recognised organ of the great German Federation established as a result of the Congress of Vienna ? We have watched its activity up to the accession of Frederick William IV. in 1840, seeing how ruthlessly it set itself to repress every attempt at constitutional reform within the German states, and to stamp out every spark of popular enthusiasm. The outbreak of revolution found the Diet itself as impotent as Metternich. The agitation among its members at the end of February and the beginning of March 1848, led to the adoption on 1st March of the following resolution : [1]

The German Federal Diet, as the lawful instrument of the national and political unity of Germany, appeals confidently to the German governments and the German people. The Federal Diet, empowered by the constitution to provide for the safety of Germany, both internally and in its relations with foreign powers, expresses its conviction that the national safety at home and abroad can remain unimpaired only if the most unanimous co-operation of governments and peoples, and the closest agreement between all races in Germany, are preserved with conscientious loyalty in all German countries. . . In the name of our common fatherland the German Federal Diet therefore urgently calls upon all Germans who have the well-being of Germany at heart—and other Germans there are none—to endeavour with all their might, each in his own sphere, to secure the continuance of the harmony that now exists, and to see that law and order are maintained unimpaired everywhere. . . . The assembled Diet confidently places its full trust in the respect for law, the ancient loyalty, and the mature insight that the German people have always shown in the most critical periods of their history.

A few days later, on the motion of the Prussian plenipotentiary

[1] *Corpus juris Confoederationis Germanicae*, ii. (K.).

at the Diet, it was decided to adopt as the colours of the Federal
Diet the now popular black, red, and gold. A more serious step,
with the avowed object of drafting a German constitution, was
taken by the appointment of a committee, consisting of seventeen trustworthy persons selected by the Outer Diet or General
Assembly, who were to act in an advisory capacity with the
seventeen members of the Inner Diet. On this advisory
committee were men of conspicuous ability and the highest
standing, e.g. the historian Dahlmann (Prussia), Schmerling
(Austria), the historian Droysen (Holstein), Professor Gervinus
(the Free Cities), the poet Uhland (Würtemberg), Friedrich
Bassermann (Baden) and Max and Heinrich von Gagern
(Brunswick and Nassau). The committee set to work early
in April, and within a week Dahlmann produced, with the aid
of the eminent jurist Albrecht, a draft constitution. Of this
draft Sir A. W. Ward says : [1] ' " Dahlmann's Constitution," a
historical document of the highest significance, accepted the
principle of a hereditary sovereign head of the Empire : it
further proposed a two chamber system, giving seats in the
Upper Chamber, by the side of the reigning Princes, to one
hundred and sixty-one notables, to be chosen in part by the
Governments, and in part by the Diets, of the several States.
For the rest, while army, diplomacy, and customs were to be
Imperial concerns, there was left to the particular States a
measure of independence sufficient to satisfy the demands of
historical tradition. As to the extent of the Empire, both East
and West Prussia were to be included in it, together with part
of Posen, but only the Cisleithanian dominions of the House of
Austria.'

This scheme, though approved by men of practical common
sense, such as the Prince of Prussia himself, Bunsen, and Usedom,
the Prussian plenipotentiary at the Diet, came to nothing.
Austrian jealousy and Prussian lukewarmness were fatal to it.
Vienna knew well enough that in Dahlmann's mind the only
possible hereditary sovereign of the Empire was the King of
Prussia, while Frederick William iv. had a fantastic rival
scheme of his own, of which we shall hear later, in which
he combined the Austrian Kaiser as Roman Emperor with
himself as German King. The task of devising a German
Constitution was to be taken out of the Diet's hands and

---

[1] *Cambridge Modern History*, xi. p. 162.

assumed by a body known as the German National Assembly or Parliament, sitting at Frankfort, whose strange unofficial origin was only possible at a time of such agitation and stress.

Liberal opinion in the south and south-west of Germany had tended to unite in the opinion that the essential preliminary to a settlement of the vexed questions of German unity and constitutional reform, was the calling together of a National Parliament. Heinrich von Gagern, a German patriot of the school of Stein, and the son of Stein's old friend, who had fought at Waterloo, and was a conspicuous figure in Hesse-Darmstadt, was the man who set going the movement that resulted in the actual assembly of a National Parliament. We mentioned on page 246 that as a result of his efforts, which were brought to bear not so much on the Princes as on the Estates, some fifty liberal members of various representative assemblies, met on 5th March at Heidelberg, and decided to press their Governments to bring about as soon as possible the popular representation in one Assembly of all the States making up the German nation. A committee of seven, including Gagern, was appointed to advise and act also in the matter. On the 12th this committee issued invitations to the various Estates to attend a Preliminary Parliament, known as the Fore-Parliament. The outbreak of actual revolution in Vienna and Berlin helped the promoters of the scheme, for the Governments were not in a position to oppose it. On 31st March the Fore-Parliament, some six hundred strong, met at Frankfort and began its stormy sittings, stormy because, in the words of Ranke, ' as if by some natural law the fermentation of all elements which seethed confusedly in Germany came to an eruption. A two-fold doctrine could be distinguished : one, under French influence, against the existing governments ; the other, of an exclusively German character, for a general, a national union.' H. Laube, dramatist, critic, novelist, who suffered much under the censorship, sat in the Fore-Parliament and in the National Assembly, and wrote in *Das erste deutsche Parlament* the brightest history of its proceedings, gives us (p. 5) his impressions of public opinion at the moment :

Three points remain in my memory from my spring journey to Frankfort. Firstly, Halle, the peaty-yellow beauty, was covered to such a degree with black, red, and yellow flags that luckily I saw nothing more of it than these colours. Twenty-one years ago I had on this 'risky business' sat for six weeks in the lock-up on account of my partiality for these 'criminal' colours, and fourteen years ago the spacious prison had scarcely room for us 'black, red, and gold' criminals. To-day 'Prussia is merged in Germany,' and what was then a crime, is to-day a merit. . . . Secondly what was told me at Naumburg as a bit of news sounded serious. An old Prussian officer had shot himself that morning, because he could not bring himself to eclipse with a black, red, and gold one the old Prussian cockade, the colours of Old Fritz and of the wars of Liberation. It appeared to me that many people could not understand this tragic incident. I understood it perfectly and heard in the third place with astonishment, that all the people in my third class carriage never called these colours the German colours, but always the colours of Liberty. This was instructive. Our political and national unity was no immediate concern of the nation, freedom was more popular than unity, revolution more popular than reform. The masses are never otherwise, that I had learnt from the theatre ; they desire strong contrasts. And so it is. It was for this freedom and nothing more that the people of the lower classes had risen in revolt. These classes alone were revolutionising top and bottom, guided by leaders who had some presentiment of their aim, but could not define it. Unity came in the second line of the fight, and those who fought and fight for it are those who know pretty well what they want, or who at least know pretty well what they do not want. Liberty and equality, on republican lines if possible, became the revolutionary solution ; liberty and unity, on monarchical lines if possible, the solution of the party of reform.

And the aspect of Frankfort on the day before the inauguration of proceedings is thus described by Ludwig Bamberger [1] in the *Mainzer Zeitung* :

FRANKFORT, *30th March.* 3 *o'clock.*

Great Heavens !—Shouting ! Firing of guns ! Frankfort swims in black, red, and gold, and has a provisional-delirium ! They overdo themselves to such an extent with hope and feelings of triumph that the victory itself might almost be a thing of secondary importance. Things here have the appearance of an innocent Whitsuntide festival. Houses decorated with evergreens, carpets and flags, streets full of well-dressed people. Elegance enough, but terribly few of the common folk. Germans of all districts and kinds flock together, some of them the sort but lately expelled, and others the sort to be driven out in the future. . . . Side by side with republicans, their beards on their chests and their hair brushed back, walk models of courtly fashion with moustaches turned upwards and hair brushed forcibly from back to front. Respectable citizens in their smoking-caps, surrounded by their admiring wives and children, stand in front of their doors and with serious looks discharge their

---

[1] Ludwig Bamberger, *Politische Schriften von 1848-1868* (K.).

guns into the air. Old and young look out of the windows with a knowing expression, which signifies : ' It is certainly a memorable time ; what silly whims people have ! Amusing too, in a measure, provided they do not play some mad prank. . . .' A troop of Sachsenhäuser riflemen made a good impression ; men in green blouses and grey felt hats, not washed and combed, but covered with dust, tanned and bearded. On the shoulder they carried petitions of a sensible kind—each a good double-barrelled gun—Up to noon to-day two hundred and forty-six deputies had been enrolled. . . . What is to be expected of the Assembly is no better known here than elsewhere—far too much well-wishing and far too little good-nature. A debate which was arranged last night at the Weidenbusch is said to have been a heated one, for the republicans almost came to blows with the constitutionalists. In this crowd of strangers things appear more republican than I believed. At least the republicans speak out whilst the others remain silent. There is much fear in the Frankforters' breasts. ' Are you also for the republic ? ' is the question put with pale face to every newcomer, and one feels really important, to be consulted about one's opinion with such strained and anxious looks. Behind the gay flags beat quaking hearts. ' Rates of exchange,' asked at table an imposing individual with a big moustache, who looked more of the fire-eater than the gold-bug, ' what are the rates of exchange ? ' ' None ! ' was the answer. That facetious remarks should be heard on all sides may be imagined : ' What then can be done with the princes if they are dethroned ? ' asked one.—' Just so, there's the rub,' earnestly replied the other. ' Historic ' and ' organic ' are trump-cards in argument ; ' Wash my furs for me, and don't wet 'em ' is the brief import of all the fine speeches, and ' That cursed French Revolution ! ' the quiet thought of many good souls. . . .

The wild republicans were in a minority but they were led by Struve and Hecker, the two Baden irreconcilables, forceful and fiery, of whom Laube [1] gives vivid pen-portraits :

Struve is of middle height and has a wizened monkish head of the Slavonic type. He is indeed the monk of the German Republic, belonging to one of the mendicant orders, who despise the luxury of high-thinking, who are looked upon with contempt by the higher orders, but who will unfailingly, without passion and in a simple belief in the law of necessity, hurl these members of all the higher orders into the abyss of death, so soon as the sovereign hour strikes for the modern orders of mendicant friars. Related to the Russian Struves, and therefore sharing in the unpopular ' von,' he has had on repeated occasions the troublesome duty of declining the title of ' Herr von Struve ' and remarking untruthfully ' My name is Struve ! ' . . . ' He eats nothing but vegetables ! ' say his friends, and when his bloodless and boneless condition is considered, it is quite be-

---

[1] *Das erste deutsche Parlament*, i. 22.

lievable. So too he appears not to smoke, and the skull sparingly covered with thin hair, the parchment-like skin on his forehead, the far-away expressionless little eyes, the dismal beard, the lymphatic colour of the face, the whole get-up like an overcoat in which cut has been as much despised as shape—everything points to the Rousseau-Robespierre trend, poor in thought, thirsting after concepts wide as the world, satisfied to play the leveller, but strong in the exact knowledge and calculation of penny-wise riches.

Quite different is Hecker and nearer to the plain man, the sensual man. He is a meat-eater and a full-blooded, healthy man. There is directness here, when he comes forward, shakes his long brown hair from his face and begins to speak in a strong baritone voice. One instantly realises that a man is speaking who does not come from the office, nor from studying the *Contrat Social*, but from a circle of robust individuals, who desire a thorough change in the life of the state. . . . 'The day of movable goods and chattels has come,' he used to say, and nothing is immovable any longer, neither capital nor property, once firm as a rock. . . . His attack is poetical and not really socialistic ; it springs from quite a human impulse, not from the insistent conditions imposed by dogma. . . . He appears good-natured, negligent, a rollicking student, as it were. He reminds students times without number how long he has held his seat in the Baden Assembly, and by that is shown, apart from everything else, his stimulating influence on the young men of Western Germany. These form quite a different sort of revolutionary youth from the so-called young revolutionaries of the North, particularly of Berlin. To the youth of the West and South-west the will and the way to appreciate these abstract logicians and their conclusions are strange. They refuse to give out their hearts to them, and the coldness of mere formal inference is deeply repugnant to them. . . . So he stands between the prosaic school-master Struve and the heartless logicians of the North, a solitary figure without further tie than the bond forged by a common enemy, a representative of the natural Revolution.

The republican minority endeavoured to bring up for discussion a scheme for a republic on the model of the United States, but they were voted down, and a resolution adopted to leave the question of the future Constitution of Germany to the National Assembly itself, when duly elected in accordance with a law passed by the Federal Diet providing for direct election to a single chamber. The Fore-Parliament broke up on 4th April, but not until a resolution had been passed, appointing a committee of fifty, from which Hecker and Struve were excluded, to keep an eye on the Federal Diet until the National Assembly was in being. Resolutions were futhermore passed dealing with two national questions agitating the public mind, Poland, and Schleswig-Holstein. The incorporation of the latter in the German Federation and the restoration of Poland were recommended. These thorny questions, particularly that of Schleswig-Holstein, contributed later to the break-up of the National Assembly. Hecker and Struve took their defeat with bad grace and hurried off to the south of Baden, to stir up an insurrection of which we shall hear more presently.

Meantime, it will be well to have the views of Frederick William IV. on liberalism and reform, and also his fantastic scheme for the future government of a United Germany. One of the most remarkable of his letters to Bunsen was that in which he records his judgment on the Berlin revolution and on liberalism : [1]

POTSDAM, 13th May 1848.

I have something on my conscience against you, my dear, true Bunsen, and it must out, for I am your true friend. When we were still revelling blissfully in those disgusting pot-boy riots, you wrote to me in one of your replies that you had formed the firm conviction that the belief in conspiracies was a phantom ; there were no conspiracies nor had there been ; the simple fact was that a consensus of people's minds and of the spirit of the age had produced the phenomena which the Metternich school so emphasised and exploited. That was the import of your words. At this blind faith my hands fell limply at my sides. I had no suspicion that the evidence against it was to be written for us in such a sanguinary manner on the houses of Berlin—for do you know that in Berlin for more than a fortnight everything had been systematically prepared for the most infamous insurrection that has ever dishonoured a town. Stones for the stoning of my loyal soldiers had been collected in every house in Berlin itself, in Cölln, in the Neustadt and the Friedrichstadt. These had been seen arriving for a long time, and turf-sods too, in order to serve as a breastwork against the fire of the troops ; and this peculiar demand for stone and turf is not to be explained away. Further, in the main streets communication was established from garret to garret, so that advancing or retreating troops could be harassed from end to end by shooting and stone-throwing from the roof windows. It has been proved that over 10,000 men—possibly twice that number, but this has not been authenticated, of the most horrible rabble had flocked into the town and had been concealed, so that the police with their small means could not discover them. Among them were the scum of Frenchmen (men from the galleys), Poles and South Germans, especially Mannheimers, but also soldier-like groups, men with the look of Milanese counts, wholesale merchants, etc. A rich merchant of Mannheim met his

---

[1] *Briefwechsel Friedrich Wilhelms IV. mit Bunsen.*—Ranke.

Z

death in the Königstrasse, after a company of my god-like 1st Guards Regiment had spared his life and he attacked them again in the rear with an axe. Among the criminals of ' the great days ' to be buried were from thirty to fifty of whom no one knew a word, neither native land, nor name, etc. From Paris, Carlsruhe, Mannheim and Berne I know officially, from the Diets themselves, that the chiefs of the insurrection on the 18th March declared openly : ' Berlin falls to-day ! ! ! ' Hecker to wit, Herwegh and many others of the Rascals' Union.

For this reason therefore I put the question to you, dear friend : Do you still persist in your agreement with Niebuhr never to believe in a conspiracy ? God grant, No. And yet I cannot assume the responsibility for this ' no.' I have that against you on my conscience. That I must tell you.—But why cannot I assume the responsibility?—Answer: Because there are unmistakable symptoms indicating that you are in the fetters of liberalism.

Liberalism, however, is a disease, just like disease of the spine. The symptoms of the latter are, for example, that the strongly convex and prominent muscle of the thumb and fore-finger becomes concave by pressure ; (2) that an aperient constipates ; (3) that an astringent medicine purges, and, at a later stage, (4) that the legs can be raised without one's being able to walk. And all the while such a patient can be accepted for a long time as healthy by others and by himself.

In this way liberalism works on the soul. The evidence is denied ; that consequences follow from causes existing clearly for a long time is rejected as superstition. Schön (the liberal *Oberpräsident*) does not even believe to-day that Napoleon was in Moscow. The spirit of the age is accepted as a grandiose apology in circumstances where God does not merely recommend but actually commands the confession of sin. A man believes that he is paying due homage to progress, is taking a part in it and—backwards it goes full speed, into ruin. The most shocking outcome of supreme ungodliness is, forsooth, the struggling of the collective feelings of man to what is noble, to the light. Black is called white, darkness light, and the victims who succumb to a sinful, God-cursed frenzy are almost or entirely deified. For the spirit in them (convicts, galley-slaves, Sodomites, etc.) struggled courageously upwards to the sky ! But enough of this blasphemy. I have mentioned the last stages in the spiritual, as in the physical, disease. Far be the thought from me to consider you, dear friend, on the road to serious illness.

But you do appear to me attacked, for the disbelief in conspiracies is the first infallible symptom of that liberalism which dries up the soul. And of that you have yourself borne witness against yourself. Niebuhr [1] died on conversion from liberalism and disbelief in con-

---

[1] The last letter but one that Niebuhr wrote was to Perthes, the publisher, father of C. T. Perthes. In it he said : ' Never has Germany been so untrue to herself as now ; and, since the revolution in Poland, not only is salvation by her own strength hopeless, but there is no room, which yet there should always be, even for a miracle to re-establish order in human affairs.'

spiracy. You must become converted and live, for me, for your generation, for the church of God. But sickness is not to be joked with. I only know one medicine against it : ' The Sign of the Holy Cross on Breast and Forehead.'—Translate that into the evangelical, the eternal truth, and so you have the remedy, which stands close to you, thanks be to God ! May God the Father give you his blessing.

FRIEDRICH WILHELM.

Bunsen replied neatly enough to this letter, contrasting the ' spinal marrow complaint of liberalism ' with the ' cataleptic trance ' which might be said to have prevailed in Austria, and he suggested that, when the noises of the streets and the excesses of corner-boys were over and done with, the king himself would realise ' how easily one can control the age in which one lives, if one speaks the language of the present, as it issues from a recognition of the actual conditions which God has established.' How far from the present was the king's style of speech and thought may be judged from an unofficial circular [1] of his on the constitution of the empire, which he was moved to write on receipt of a memorandum [2] from our own Prince Albert :

. . . Let the Roman Emperor again be recognised as the honoured head of the German nation. Let the Roman Imperial Dignity be restored, and, as up to the year 1806, indissolubly with the Hereditary Empire of Austria—if one wishes *pro honoris causa*. Let him still retain certain distinguishing honours. I am entirely for the election of a separate overlord of the German Empire. Let the same be called, if he be, as I hope to God, elected for life and then— a German through and through—be also recognised as the highest authority of the realm (and is not regarded *à la polonaise* as the plaything of the ambitions of grandees)—let him be called ' King of the Germans '—as of old. I desire that the Kings of the Confederation (who in their title should again associate themselves with the Electors) should alone take part in the election, but afterwards summon the other reigning princes for their assent. Both the affair of a few hours,—the Kings and Grand Dukes perhaps in the so-called Conclave of the Cathedral of St. Bartholomew at Frankfort, the Princes in the choir. Thereupon let the Roman Emperor be approached, and reverentially be requested to confirm the election. That can be done at the same moment by an Elector invested with

---

[1] Ernst II., *Aus meinem Leben.*

[2] The full text of Prince Albert's memorandum will be found in vol. i. pp. 439-446, of Sir Theodore Martin's *Life of the Prince Consort.* The latter portion of that volume, and the earlier part of vol. ii., afford ample evidence of the prince's liberal views in regard to Germany.

full powers. Then as of old let the people into the Cathedral that its acclamations may complete the election. Soon after let the German King be anointed and crowned (exactly as the Roman Emperor on his accession), and certainly, if he is a Roman Catholic, by the Archbishop of Cologne, who should become Chancellor of the Empire —if he is an Evangelical, by an Archbishop of Magdeburg who should be appointed Primate of Germany. By this placing of the Imperial Roman Dignity on the head of the Austrian Hereditary Emperor, Austria is for the first time assured to the German Empire. Austria is for ever won for Germany, and with her the most beautiful of Germany's earliest dominions assured to the new (old) Empire,— the Tyrol, Lower Arlberg, Upper and Lower Austria, Styria, Carinthia, Carniola, and Istria. If Austria does not wear the highest crown, an obeisance on the part of Austria before the elected German ' overlord ' is not to be thought of when she recovers in some measure her prestige. And who could despair of it ? The Diet of Princes seems to me to be an uncommonly sound idea. Only I picture it as split up, like the old Imperial Diet, into a college of Kings, Grand Dukes, Dukes, and Princes. Strengthened by the mediatised princes and counts (partly man by man, partly in groups) the Diet of Princes would form every three years the German Upper House of the Imperial Diet, of which the Lower House would be the House or Curia of Deputies to the Diet. Only I recommend most urgently that in the relation of the Upper to the Lower House it should never be forgotten that reigning Princes form its nucleus and among them two great powers (the Lord be merciful !).

After this interlude of Frederick William IV. and his opinions we may turn to the Assembly's worries over the Polish trouble, and Hecker's insurrection in Baden in which the fiery poet, Georg Herwegh, with his German Legion from Paris was to play an inglorious part as active revolutionary.

In April and May a Polish insurrection gave a good deal of concern. Prime movers in this were the Polish clergy and the Mieroslawski who was the darling of revolutionary Berlin, and was escorted in triumph through the streets when released from prison on 20th March. The Poles had been promised a reorganisation of the province of Posen, and proceeded as if this meant a reorganisation by the Poles and for the Poles, to the detriment of every German settler. Prussian troops only restored order after some hard fighting, for, as Sybel says, ' the Poles displayed as great bravery against the troops as they did a brutal cruelty against defenceless Germans and Jews.'

Baden was the hotbed of republican revolution ; its southern boundary marches with that of Switzerland, and it was overrun with emissaries from revolutionary exiles who had found refuge across the Rhine. After Hecker and Struve's exit from Frankfort trouble was looked for, and a striking illustration of the cleavage that had arisen between liberals and radicals in Baden is afforded by the arrest at Carlsruhe of Fickler, a republican leader on his way to join the rebels, by Mathy, the liberal leader, whose moral courage we have already had cause to admire.

The trains to Constance and Mannheim cross at Carlsruhe. As Mathy, early on the morning of April 8, came to the station, he recognised Fickler in a compartment on the way to Constance. He stepped up to the carriage : ' Stop ! where are you going ? ' Fickler answered timidly : ' That has nothing to do with you.' ' I know that you wish to go up there.' ' Yes, and I want to show you what we can do.' ' You are not going, you 'll stay here.' ' You won't stop me.' Thereupon Mathy hailed a policeman standing by and called on him to arrest Fickler. The policeman grew pale with fright and was not in a state to carry out the order. Fickler shouted vehemently to the railway officials and to the guard : ' Get the train away ! ' Mathy, however, stepped up to the stationmaster : ' You must not let the train depart before the arrest of Herr Fickler.'— ' My God, I have no instructions from the government ! '—Mathy : ' On my responsibility ! '—There was a great commotion and much excitement among the passengers ; finally a commissary of police was fetched and he ventured, with hesitation, to make the arrest.[1]

Of the ' bar-parlour republicans,' who were to be Hecker's leading supporters, Ludwig Haüsser [2] gives an unflattering picture :

No more repugnant phenomenon has appeared in our days than a republicanism which unites in itself all the vices of Cataline and his crew and does not possess a single republican merit ; which deprives itself with officious readiness of all national feeling, throws itself on the neck of all nations and in cosmopolitan heedlessness sympathises rather with Slavs, Italians, Magyars than with the Fatherland. Robespierre and Danton and all true Jacobins of the nineties were in the first place Frenchmen, and side by side with magnificent crime they could still feel the stirrings of a great patriotic impulse ; our bar-parlour republicans have learnt a number of catch words from their models, but the one which raised their predecessors above the ordinary and common is lacking to them.

Otto von Corvin's picture [3] of the proceedings of Herwegh

---

[1] Freytag, *Carl Mathy.*
[2] *Denkwürdigkeiten der badischen Revolution* (K.)
[3] *A Life of Adventure*, by Otto von Corvin.

and his committee at Paris, in connection with the German Legion there, is no more attractive :

The sessions of the committee took place in a public-house in the Rue Montorgueil, and the chiefs of the sections were also admitted, in which capacity I attended. These sessions, however, thoroughly displeased me, for in this democratic committee nothing was less to be found than a democratic spirit. No discussion was possible, for every remark which did not agree with the views of the president was at once put down in the most insulting, dictatorial manner. Herwegh was in this respect even worse than Bornstedt, and I was so disgusted with the whole thing, that I resolved to retire from it if an alteration could not be effected.

The legion soon became very discontented. Most of its members were labourers, who had given up their work to leave for Germany, and were obliged now to live on their savings. They clamoured, therefore, for the departure of the legion, and grew almost rebellious. They had in general changed much for the worse, and the authors of this change were Louis Blanc, Bornstedt, and the committee. Louis Blanc turned the heads of the French, and Bornstedt those of the German labourers. They flattered them in the most foolish manner, and made them at last believe that the whole Revolution had taken place exclusively through them and for them, and that their fists were worth far more than the cleverest heads. Many labourers who had, until then, been modest and industrious people, now became conceited fools, expecting the government to take care of them if they were not inclined to work.

Bornstedt was our Louis Blanc, but he exaggerated everything, and even adopted the dress and manners of the labourers, with whom he lived in cynical intimacy. He managed that labourers should be elected members of the committee, by which means he flattered their vanity and increased his own influence ; for these members were all his creatures, who voted with him under all circumstances without reflection. The ideas of liberty, equality, and brotherhood, which he taught our men, produced in them a spirit which was opposed to all order and discipline. In a military expedition, it is necessary that the chiefs should be considered as something exceptional ; but it is impossible to achieve this, if its members are told every day : ' Your leaders are no better than you are ; they are in your service, and those who strive to distinguish themselves from you by their acts or behaviour are aristocrats.'

One may have ideas of liberty, equality, and brotherhood very warmly at heart, without trying to equal the less educated in their language and manners, and to manifest brotherhood by drinking gin with every blackguard, and calling him ' thou.'

Herwegh increased the evil by his peculiar views. He had once run away from Würtemberg because it was contrary to his feelings to become a soldier, and he had a spite against soldiers. When I urged military order, he would go almost into fits, and, stamping with his feet like a naughty boy, he would cry, *Ich will keine Gama-schenknechte,* 'I want no pipe-clay orderlies!' I was compelled to let things go on as they would, and they went very badly.

It is bare justice to the poet to give Corvin's detailed account of him that follows, for Klein and others have done their best to keep alive the fables that the governments were only too ready to spread in order to make him appear merely an object of contempt. Nor should we dispense with the amusement to be derived from the concluding remarks on Frau Herwegh :

Notwithstanding his unfitness for the position he had assumed, I had become attached to Herwegh for his amiable qualities ; and after due consideration, I resolved not to forsake him, thinking that I might still be of use, notwithstanding the unpromising aspect of affairs.

Herwegh is a poet, and has all the faults of one—faults which are virtues in a poet. His life is a life of imagination ; poems are his actions. Such intellectual actions are very useful in preparing people for real action, but it is a great mistake to place a poet at the head of an important undertaking.

Herwegh took the greatest interest in all these political movements, which owed their origin in part to his stirring poems. However, his thoughts always soared, just because they were poetical, over the common realities of life, on which he looked with anger and disgust, and to which he would not concede any rights. Though he hated details, he frequently occupied himself with them and then he became mean. He could endure deprivations and fatigues without complaint, though his health was delicate ; but he became furious if asked to do things which another would do. In general he acted only when compelled to do so, never from his own impulse. He possessed not the least presence of mind ; but when the right moment had passed, he set his fancy to work, and then knew very well what he ought to have done.

His inclinations were despotic, as I have found to be the case with many democrats. Reasonable objections he answered with spiteful passion. He never liked to give explanations, because his ideas had no certain outlines. He wanted people to catch his ideas, as it were, and was glad when any one shaped them into a distinct form. Practical men who had observed him long, and who had within themselves no appreciation of his value as a poet, were ready with their judgment of him : ' a poet, a dreaming, ambitious, soft-minded fellow, who is good for nothing whatever ! '

After having given a sketch of our leader's character, I must also speak of Frau Herwegh. Emma Herwegh was the daughter of the Berlin banker Siegmund. On first acquaintance she did not make a favourable impression on me. I believed her to be affected, and forward and pert in her manner. This, however, was not the case. After a time, one became used to her manner and learned to respect her for her many good qualities. She was not a dreamer like her husband, but far more practical. She was full of energy, resolute and courageous ; she never lost her courage, even in the most difficult situations, and was not frightened when facing the utmost danger. She never feared and never cared for herself, but only for her husband, whom she loved with the most affectionate devotion and of whose talents and reputation she was proud. She was a good wife and mother. Herwegh knew her value, and did not feel happy away from her. He said he had no luck without her.

Frau Herwegh was at this time about twenty-five years of age, not pretty, but agreeable. She had a good figure, and was of middle height, had light auburn hair, and light blue or grey eyes.

She had resolved to accompany her poet on his expedition in behalf of liberty, and to put on man's clothes for the purpose. It was long before she could make up her mind as to the shape of her hat, and whether she must cut off her hair, or how she should arrange it. I am not sure whether that important affair was not discussed in committee, but it is a fact that all of us were asked our opinion about it.

A letter from the poet himself to Hecker, in March, reveals his foolish optimism. As a matter of fact the French Government did nothing for the German Legion but lend a little money, and Gottfried Keller's account to Baechtold, on Corvin's information, of this financial transaction shows the incredible naïveté of the poet turned active revolutionary. Flocon, Minister of Finance, asked the agitator : ' How much do you want ? ' ' Six thousand francs,' replied Herwegh. Flocon paid the trifle, shrugging his shoulders.

PARIS, 15th March 1848.

The Germans here are beginning to organise and to arm, and there is every reason to hope that in a short time a body of four to five thousand men, drilled and officered, will be at the disposal of Germany, ready to march to the appointed place at the first signal from abroad that the help of a disciplined German army is necessary or desired.

Negotiations have been begun with the Government here ; you may count with certainty on an important and perhaps extensive participation of the Poles in France in the event of a partial or general insurrection. There is a good prospect, if it is necessary and desired, of quickly winning to our cause the German section of the Foreign Legion, which is inured to hardships, etc. The feeling among the Germans here is warlike, and as soon as the first corps had been marched off, thousands, and perhaps tens of thousands, would follow, organised and drilled (in order to be able to resist regulars in case of need). Cologne, Frankfort, and the Grand Duchy of Baden are the points to which they direct their chief attention. . . . Should, however, the contrary event happen, it would not be

possible to contain any one here, and no doubt the French Democratic
Government (even if not officially) would offer a hand in making
them efficient in the use of arms and ready to march out.
The inhabitants of Paris themselves would be ready to support
this with joy, since the selfish motive arises of getting rid of many
thousands of artisans who are competing against the French. I
do not doubt for a moment that, if we to-day received a signal to
rise, we could stand on the frontier thoroughly equipped within
eight days. . . . There will be no lack of efficient officers, and as
soon as the number enrolled is big enough a proper war council
will be placed at the head. The help of the Germans in Paris may
be counted upon at all times, and it would be wrong to slight them,
since many of them have fought during the three great days (the
February Revolution), and all have seen how a revolution is made,
and what a people can do.[1]

On the 12th April Hecker proclaimed a republic, and next day
set off with his followers on a long and toilsome march, through
rough country and foul weather, from Constance to Kandern.
On the 19th he came, with a force of twelve hundred, into
contact with the Hessian and Baden troops, two thousand
strong, and after a short fight on the 20th was put to flight.
At the very commencement of the fight General Gagern was
killed, not treacherously but by the sort of accident common
enough in irregular warfare. Hecker himself gives [2] a vivid
account of the incident, though Klein asserts that the first
shots were fired by the irregulars.

Thursday, the 20th April dawned. . . . Willich [one of Hecker's
lieutenants] had occupied the heights on both sides of the road
behind Kandern and the road also. I was standing by a little
troop on the mountain, when some one called out that Gagern
wished to speak to me. I went on to the road, where a lieutenant
of cavalry came towards me, and repeated this information. I
descended the path accompanied by several of the republican
leaders, and met Gagern in the middle of a bridge in front of the
town of Kandern, where he said to me : ' You, that is the republicans,
must lay down your arms.' This I naturally refused to do, whereupon he continued : ' You are a shrewd man but also a fanatic.'
To this I replied : ' If devotion to the liberation of a great nation
is fanaticism, then there is a fanaticism on the other side which you
serve ; however, I have not come here to debate about that, but
ask if you have anything else to communicate to me.' Thereupon
he retorted that he would attack with all his strength, to which I
answered : ' And we shall know how to meet such an attack, and,

[1] *Briefe von und an Georg Herwegh* (K.).
[4] *Die Erhebung des Volkes in Baden im Frühjahr*, 1848 (K.).

for the rest, will you allow us (the leaders) first to return to our corps?' His reply was 'Certainly.' After this dialogue a Baden staff officer cried out to me : ' I implore you to desist !' With that the parleying and the first act of the business came to an end.

At this stage the irregulars retired to the Scheidegg Pass, the troops following them. Eight to ten soldiers soon stepped forward from the foremost ranks of the Hessian troops, evidently with the intention of a friendly meeting. When this was noticed Gagern rode forward, and one or more higher officers likewise advanced. The soldiers fell back into the ranks, after he had called out something to them ; the order was given to fire, file-firing followed and it was only now that firing came from the republican side. . . . Only after firing had begun on Gagern's side did our people fire ; Gagern fell, and almost at the same moment others fell with him, wounded or dead I could not decide.

Hecker escaped to Switzerland. Struve's contingent was dispersed at Steiven, and Struve, though taken prisoner, managed also to escape.

Of the part played by Herwegh's German Legion Corvin's account is not without entertainment. The legion was assembled near Strasburg where Herwegh and his wife joined them. Klein tells us that an old sergeant-major, one Carl Börnstein, ' who had made cartridges and wore a big moustache on his corporal's face and knew how to hold his tongue significantly,' was placed in command with the more capable Corvin under him. Hecker was reluctant to accept the assistance of Herwegh's contingent, and it was only after the energetic Frau Herwegh had gone ahead to interview him that he gave his assent to their crossing the Rhine. Before the legion could effect a juncture with Hecker news came of his defeat, and Corvin's energies were directed to getting the force safe into Switzerland. But it was intercepted at Niederdossenbach by a small force of Würtemberg troops, whose first volley dispersed the legion helter-skelter. Here is Corvin's account :

On the Saturday before Easter, 1848, we started at four o'clock in the morning. When everything was ready, I took a fancy to convince myself whether our boxes containing the guns were in the train ; and indeed they were not ; they had been left in the barracks ! When I reproached Börnstein, he told me that he had given his orders to Colonel Löwenfels. I convinced him, however, of the necessity, under prevailing circumstances, of himself looking to our arms. The train was stopped, and our commander had to walk to Strasburg to arrange that our arms should come at least by the next train. . . .

Many of my myrmidons were tailors—a most excitable race !—who had never before handled a gun. When firing at my command, they were so frightened at the dreadful noise they made, that some sank on their knees, and about a dozen ran from the ranks and crouched behind the shrubs. At break of day, my valiant tailors returned to their quarters much admired by their comrades. . . .

Herwegh accompanied the expedition as a kind of political missionary, but *in partibus*, for he had indeed nothing to do, but marched always ahead with his wife, who looked like a half-grown schoolboy. She wore trousers of black cloth, a blouse of black velvet, with a leather belt, which was ornamented with two small pistols and a dagger, probably intended to protect her poet in case of need. On her head she had a broad-brimmed black hat, without cockade or plume.

At Niederdossenbach the Würtemberg troops were encountered, and Corvin thus continues his story :

I had placed my men behind me in a kind of hollow, where only their bayonets were to be seen. When the skirmishers in the field saw the Würtembergers emerge from the wood and prepare to attack my left wing, they ran back as fast as possible to procure some cartridges, or at least gunpowder, which was dealt out by Herwegh and his wife (who were seated on a cart), though to little purpose, as there was not even paper to carry it in, or to load with. This rushing back of the skirmishers, together with the sight of some wounded men, made these men in the hollow rather uneasy, as they were not able to see what was going on before them in the field ; and when the volley of the enemy, which, however, could not hurt them, rattled against their bayonets, they were seized with a sudden panic. They made to the right-about, and, like a herd in a stampede, ran back about five hundred paces.

This panic was, however, pardonable. Men, tired as they were, who had not eaten anything worth speaking of for two days, and who moreover had no cartridges with which to answer the fire of the enemy, could not feel in very good spirits, especially when hearing one of their commanders cry out loudly to them to run, as Börnstein did when I saw him for a moment. He stood somewhat to my right behind an oak-tree, nominally looking through his glass at the enemy, but his orderly said he stared at the tree and shook awfully. This volley had frightened him out of his wits, though he was safe behind the oak. Running past me, utterly scared, he urged me to run also, which I did not feel inclined to do. Two reliable men, who had carried back a wounded comrade, found Börnstein in a sheltered place some hundred paces in the rear, and on asking him with astonishment what he was doing there, he answered : ' You do not imagine that I am going to let them kill me, do you ? ' And to an officer who saw him tear off all the signs of his office, he said, ' As my plan has not been carried out, I resign my command.' He was the first of those who joined his fellow-coward Löwenfels in Strasburg, and took thither the news of our disaster. . . .

A French drummer showed more pluck. He beat his drum assiduously, though it was riddled by as many holes as his blouse. He remained unwounded, however, stood about ten paces from the Würtembergers, making faces at them, and calling out, ' *Ah, les gredins! ah, les gredins !*' He was taken prisoner. . . .

An old soldier who passed me said sadly, ' This is the fifteenth time that I have been in battle. I was never wounded before, but now I am done for.' He had received one shot in the thick of his leg, and another through his arm, above his wrist ; but the bullet seemed to have passed between the two bones, for he was still able to take his aim quite coolly, and to bring down an enemy. This old soldier implored me to order a retreat, as nothing could possibly be done without cartridges. I came to this same conclusion myself with a very sad heart. Some thirty of our men were killed ; I do not know how many were wounded. Several of the fugitives who tried to save themselves by swimming were drowned in the Rhine ; one was hanged by the Würtembergers in the wood. They were exasperated by their losses, which equalled ours, and behaved with a cruelty which I never could have believed possible from Swabians, who are said to be so very kindhearted. One of the carts with the wounded fell into their hands : they murdered not only the wounded, but even the innocent peasant-driver, and killed the two horses also ! . . .

The Herweghs were not with us ; they had succeeded in reaching a village and in finding kind people who concealed them. The papers of that time abused Herwegh much, and told many untruths of his cowardice. They were all inventions. Herwegh had nothing to do in the battle-field ; he and his wife remained on a cart, distributing gunpowder. It was said that he crept under the splash-board, and remained there during the whole fight. A great number of caricatures represented him in this situation, and the name of Herwegh and splashboard became so closely connected, that it will stick to him all his life, though I have done all in my power to contradict the ignominious report. Even if he had felt an inclination to creep under a splashboard, he could not have done so, as the common farmer's cart on which he was seated had none.

Thus does Corvin dispose of the malicious report, one that the ' good press ' in Germany has kept alive, that Frau Herwegh carried off her husband safely to Switzerland in the carriage in which they had remained discreetly in the rear through all the fighting. As a matter of fact they did escape, as did Corvin, on foot, but with great difficulty, for they only got across the Rhine disguised as peasants.

Robert Blum, the democratic leader, who was shot by the

Austrians in the autumn, as will be told later, wrote to his wife on this abortive enterprise :

FRANKFORT-ON-MAIN, *3rd May* 1848.

Hecker and Struve have betrayed their country from the point of view of the law—that is a detail ; but they have betrayed the People by their mad rising ; the People has been checked in the midst of its victorious progress ; that is a horrible crime.

The Committee of Fifty appointed by the Fore-Parliament, to watch events until the National Parliament was elected, discussed, after Hecker's insurrection, the question of establishing a parliamentary army. On this Frederick William IV. sent to Camphausen, his minister, one of his characteristic notes : [1]

POTSDAM, *5th May* 1848.

The audacity of the ' Committee of Fifty ' in Frankfort with their army of ten thousand men, whose leaders they desire to nominate, surpasses, by God, the limits of the incredible. I hope confidently that Prussia will not allow Germany to be subjected to this insult ; beside the insult there is obvious danger involved. It can be seen that they actually wish to play at a *Gouvernement provisoire.* Where have we got to ? We must at last say, and firmly : ' So far and no further ! ' Speak out, dearest Camphausen, for the welfare of Germany, for the fame of Prussia and for your own, which of a truth I wish you from my heart.

---

[1] *König Friedrich Wilhelm's IV. Briefwechsel mit L. Camphausen,* p. 56.

CHAPTER II

OPENING OF THE NATIONAL ASSEMBLY

OF the state of exaltation in which many of Germany's intellectuals of high official, diplomatic, academic and legal position found themselves on the occasion of the opening of the Frankfort Parliament we have a remarkable revelation in a, memorandum which, on 6th May 1848, Bunsen sent, together with a draft constitution, to Henry Reeve of the Privy Council Office, a confidant of foreign diplomatists in London, and, later, editor of the *Edinburgh Review* and the *Greville Memoirs* :

> *Saturday morning, 6th May 1848,*
> *half-past seven o'clock.*

With heart and mind thus prepared, you have taken the Draft and its great object into consideration ; you have conceived both in their relative import to the world's history ; you render justice to both,—and yet you have not attained to a belief in our future.

What is with you essentially opposed to this is your rigorously conservative view as to the origin of the present Constitutional movement. You say poetically, ' The truly animating principle comes from above—the shades of Endor rise out of the abyss.'

Let me follow up this idea, in order to convince you that our struggle for freedom has rightly originated—that is from the Spirit —*descendit cœlo*. Was not its beginning indeed from above in the minds of the great thinkers, who, from Lessing and Kant down to Schelling and Hegel, have, in conflict with the materialism of the past century and the mechanism of the 'present, proved both the reality and essentiality of reason, and the independence and freedom of moral consciousness, and have thereby roused the nation to enthusiasm for the ideal of true liberty ? And did not poetry and the fine arts take the same way ? What is the signification of Goethe in the world's history, if not that he had a clear intuition of those truths, and the art of giving them due utterance ? Wherein consists the indestructible charm of Schiller's poetry, but that he has sung as hymns to the supernal, preternatural, those deductions of philosophy ?

Now to proceed to the time of our deepest depression, and of our highest elevation,—from 1807 to 1813. That which now *would* and *should* and *must* enter into life, was then generated, in the midst of woe and misery, in blood and in prayer,—but also in belief in that ideal, to the true recognition and realising of which the feeling of an existing fatherland and of popular freedom is indispensable. Truly prophetical (as the truth must always be) are the words of Schenkendorf in 1813, *Freiheit, die ich meine,* etc., and *Wie mir deine Freuden winken,* etc. And also Arndt with his grand rhapsody, *Was ist des Deutschen Vaterland?* and Körner's melodies of death, and Rückert's songs, brilliant and penetrating as steel! All that may sound to the foreigner as mere poetic feeling : but to us, who then pronounced the vows of early youth, it was a most holy and real earnest, the utterance of overflowing hearts. And thus it remained to us ; and our children learned from us to repeat the vow ; and when we lay twenty-five years long in heavy bondage, when the very freedom of speech was suppressed, then through all suffering the spirit of liberty took refuge in the sanctuary of knowledge,—but, not as was the case with our fathers, to expatiate in untried regions, and seek freedom only in contemplation and speculation, but to fetch down the highest blessings of common life, as the poets of the former generation had in a vision beheld them, and as Scharnhorst and Stein and Niebuhr and Wilhelm von Humboldt had grasped them in will and wish. Then was the younger generation instructed by persecuted men, that liberty is ancient and tyranny modern, and that to liberty alone belongs that legitimacy which unsound politicians have used as a weapon for her destruction. Then it was that English empiricism, French abstractions, and the feeble imitation of both in the new Constitutions of Southern Germany, were compared with history and with the true ideal—and a higher standing point was aimed at and gained for all. Thus did the year 1840 find us ; but the hopes which the year brought were not finally realised. King and people (as Beckerath finely expressed it in the year 1844) spoke wholly different languages, and lived in different centuries. The path became dark, and when the lightning and storm had ceased, the old state of things had vanished. Since then, seventy-three days have passed, and we are living, and the Draft of a Constitution was accomplished before *seventy* of those days had elapsed.

Descendit cœlo, if ever that could be said of a popular movement named in history—in the humble form which is ever assigned to the Divine, revealed in humanity. Dragged in the mire by knaves, hung round with bells by the weak-minded, schooled by the ignorant, the work of liberty has not been crushed by any class of enemies. As a heavenly birth she is making her way through foaming waves, and, in the power of the Spirit, she has lifted her foot out of the depths, to place it upon the rock of law and right—a position well earned by her forty years' wandering through the desert, amid the raging of nations, the vain fears and imaginations of Princes, the scorn and mistrust of France and of England, actual insurrection, and latent anarchy.

Descendit cœlo.—Our Draft of a Constitution, the firstfruit of

German political energy, is not a *Déclaration des Droits de l'Homme*, it is not one of the numerous transcripts of the parchment Magna Charta upon Continental blotting-paper—it is not the aping of the American or even of the Belgian Constitution ; it is as peculiar as the nation to which it offers a form. A nation! rather, many nations : no nation, and yet a nation! and, so may it please the Almighty, a great and a free nation! not one of yesterday, but of a thousand years of fame and of suffering. I cannot claim from you the enthusiasm I feel for the work which is the weighty subject-matter of the Draft in question : but I crave belief in it from you, for the very same reason that you, the true disciple of Burke, demand confidence in your own political faith.

I am ready to give up to you the Committee of Fifty, and the seventeen ' men of trust,' and the entire Diet : but though the Fifty, and both assemblies of seventeen were blown to the winds like the free corps of Herwig and Hocker,[1] yet the rock around which they collected will remain,—that is, Germany and the German people, even though humbled and torn in pieces for a thousand years, to many a mockery, to all an enigma !

On the 18th May at three P.M. took place the inauguration of the National Assembly. There was a solemn procession, there were flags, ringing of bells and firing of salutes. For a place of meeting the *Paulskirche*, the church of St. Paul, was set apart. Laube's description [2] of it is as follows :

The Paulskirche was a round temple, the central portion of which was surrounded by pillars. In this central portion the first German representatives of the people sat in the pews, facing the pulpit-like rostrum at the south end and the presidential daïs behind the pulpit, with a background of red curtains bordered with black and gold, and decorated with the double-headed eagle of the Empire. High above the presidential daïs they confronted a romantic picture of Germania, a figure full of austere innocence but with little force of character. Behind this central space, the kernel as it were, and therefore behind the pillars mentioned above, there still rose in the shape of an amphitheatre to the windows four rows of seats, forming a ' mountain,' in wait for its ' montagnards,' [3] which it found later on the north-west side. For the moment these ' mountain ' seats were swarming with spectators, who looked over the heads of the members of parliament sitting right underneath them, as good as saw their cards, felt their pockets, and whispered in their ears as if they were the People's prisoners. Woe to the prisoners if they did not pose as free, quite free ! High up, around the rim of

---

[1] So in Baroness Bunsen's *Memoir of Baron Bunsen*, ed. 1868, vol. ii. p. 180. Obviously Herwegh and Hecker are intended.

[2] *Das erste deutsche Parlament*, I.

[3] Extreme party in first French Revolution, occupying elevated position in chamber of assembly.—*Concise Oxford Dictionary*.

the temple, on a level with yonder Germania, ran the main gallery
which accommodated fifteen hundred to two thousand spectators,
to listen and to cheer. It was an imposing spectacle of the Sovereignty of the People.

For parliamentary purposes it was a very inconvenient
building, gangways were narrow and the free space very
limited. There was no provision for committee-rooms, and,
what was scarcely less important, as Robert von Mohl tells us,[1]
for refreshment-rooms :

Great pains were taken with the lighting and heating. The
only trouble was that there was little unoccupied room for gangways and for a free space in the centre, and even what there was
was unnecessarily encroached upon by seats for privileged visitors.
For this reason communication between the members was very
difficult, so that one could hardly make inside the hall the personal
acquaintance of those who sat in another part of the House, and
the opportunity for a brief exchange of ideas, for inquiries and
concerted action, scarcely existed. Still worse, almost intolerable
indeed, was the fact that, as you would expect in an isolated church-
building, there were no side-rooms. There was no question of
committee rooms ; these were hired in the town, some of them at
a considerable distance. Hence no hurried meeting of a committee,
such as was often necessary, could be held. Not even the President
nor the Ministry had private rooms ; a consultation or hasty conversation had to take place in the open air, whatever the weather,
in the square in front of the church. I remember having a discussion here in the pouring rain with Privy Councillor ——. Inconvenient, and in the result indecent, proved the circumstance that
there was no space to install a refreshment-room within the House
itself. . . . There was nothing for it but to pay a call at one of
the public-houses in the adjoining streets, the result being that the
continual coming and going from House to drinking-shop did not
offer an edifying spectacle to the man in the street.

The parliament began with three hundred and twenty members,
but in some states the elections had been delayed, and the
numbers finally rose to five hundred and eighty-six. Among
the personnel were many of the most distinguished men in
Germany, but lawyers were, unduly perhaps, represented, and
also another class of doubtful advantage in a would-be sovereign
assembly, viz. officials. The professorial and academic class,
as was to be expected in Germany, was there in strong force.
Few great landed proprietors or captains of commerce and
industry found seats. Klein makes out as good a case as can

---

[1] *Lebenserinnerungen*, ii. (K.).

be established for the constitution of the Assembly and for the work it accomplished :

The Frankfort Parliament was an assembly of the best brains of the nation. It has often been repeated that in the Church of St. Paul mere theorists with no knowledge of the world set about founding the German Empire. Still this is only conditionally true. Men experienced in higher politics, in so far as they had served in the former cabinets, were simply not eligible for election. Thus an indispensable element was, admittedly, weakly represented. The ninety-five barristers might certainly often handle political questions in a casuistical way ; but opposed to them were one hundred and twenty-four administrative officials and a hundred judicial officials. The one hundred and four ' savants ' numbered in their ranks historians like E. M. Arndt, Dahlmann,[1] Droysen, Biedermann,[1] Duncker, Gervinus, Friedrich von Raumer, Stenzel, Waitz; among the constitutional lawyers were Robert von Mohl, Karl Welcker, Zachariä, Georg Beseler. Then came a number of practising lawyers. Among the great representatives of German national science and culture were numbered Jacob Grimm and Ludwig Uhland. Twelve men of letters, eighteen of the clergy (including Döllinger), fifteen doctors, ten soldiers, thirty-four landed proprietors, thirteen manufacturers and merchants completed the round of the professions represented. In proportion landed property, commerce and industry were feebly represented. But after all there sat in the Church of St. Paul representatives like von Beckerath, Bassermann, Gabriel Riesser. The task was a colossal one. The zeal and tenacity displayed in the worst, most hopeless situations were on all sides admirable. Strong men in the one year of the German Parliament became grey and decrepit through anxiety, contention and worry. Their Palladium, the sovereignty of the people, concealed also within it a terrible responsibility. The leaders were thoroughly conscious of it. And if the men of the extreme left overwhelmed the majority with derision, history has not agreed with them. The majority, which created a central authority, fundamental laws, a constitution for the Empire ; which voted for a Prussian Hereditary Empire ; which finally, when the revolution once more broke out on the question of the constitution of the Empire, dared to take upon itself the reproach of treason, because it saw behind this new revolution the onset of reaction in arms,—this majority justified itself.

Of the spirit which inspired the elections throughout Germany we have a clear and impartial statement from R. Haym, in his *Die deutsche Nationalversammlung* : [2]

It was in accordance with a radical electoral law that the people had cast their votes for the National Assembly to meet on the 18th May in Frankfort. The elections were coloured by the circumstances.

---

[1] The historian often quoted in this work.   [2] Klein.

The method of election removed every barrier against eligibility, and the vagueness of view on the task of the Frankfort Assembly which floated in electors' minds favoured the exclusion of every selfish consideration. Thus an opening was afforded for intelligence and talent ; of less account was mere business-like acumen ; a man's political faith determined the result. Feeling in the separate countries gave the preponderance here to a republican bias, there to an avowal of adherence to constitutional monarchy ; and it could also be seen in the assembly that in Baden the republican idea had gained most ground, and in Prussia least. The net result, however, was that the republicans were in the decided minority.

As in the Fore-Parliament, so in the National Assembly itself, the cleavage between monarchists and republicans became evident at the very outset. But as weeks and months passed intermediate parties formed themselves, and finally there were at least six parties clearly distinguishable, who took their names from the hotels, inns and other places where they foregathered, the ultra-conservatives on the extreme right (*Milani*), the right (*Casino*), the right centre (*Landsberg*), the left centre (*Würtemberger Hof*), the left (*Teutsche Hof*), the extreme left (*Donnersberg*). The broad distinction between those who sat on the right and those who sat on the left was that the former desired, more or less, that recognition should be given to the existing governments, while the latter held, in moderation or immoderation, the doctrine of the sovereignty of the people. It was from one of the moderate sections, the right centre, that most of the ministers were drawn. Clearly in such a House the claim that every question that came up was discussed from almost all possible points of view may be conceded.

The first step taken by the Assembly was to elect a president, and the choice naturally fell on Heinrich von Gagern, whose character and standing, as well as the exertions by which he had done so much to bring the Assembly into existence, marked him out for the post. Gagern announced on accepting the presidency : ' We are to frame a constitution for Germany, for the whole realm. The call and the capacity demanded for this work are inherent in the sovereignty of the nation (tumultuous applause).' [1] Later he gave expression to his ambitions for a united Germany : ' I have conceived of the sphere of the

---

[1] All extracts from speeches in the Assembly, save where otherwise stated, are taken from the official stenographic report, to which the author has had access.

German people as a great and a world commanding one. Men may jeer at the idea, and cynically deny that a people can have such a vocation ; I believe in it and would lose the pride of belonging to my race, were I obliged to give up the belief in such a higher destiny.'

Robert Heller who wrote a series of sketches of personalities in the Assembly, *Brustbilder aus der Paulskirche*, thus describes him :

The secret of Gagern's gift for leadership lies in the moral respect that he inspires, and in the manly dignity to which even his silent gestures give eloquent expression. His talent for presiding is certainly not nearly so great as his disposition for it. . . . He recoils before no expression of opinion, he respects even the most irregular course of an opponent ; but in the presence of what is false or malicious or mean he lacks the calm to win the mastery. The mean suggestion may come from any quarter, but Gagern cannot get over his natural aversion from it. . . . Anger, which then lends a wonderful beauty to his face with its bold and lofty brow, bushy eyebrows and firm mouth, is . . . irresistible in its impact. For with the externals of authority is united the far stronger force of a moral decision. But passion is a magnet, which instantly arouses everywhere a passionate reaction, and then requires the full strength of one of Gagern's *Quos ego* to allay the storm let loose.

Finer than this is Gustav Freytag's noble tribute : [1]

There were at Frankfort many talents worthy of the nation, and the display of intellect, knowledge and political insight was so brilliant, that Germans have been glad to recognise in it the high capacity of their race. The fame of none of the men of 1848 shall suffer disparagement, but one of them, Heinrich von Gagern, seemed to his contemporaries the embodiment of all in the way of great resolve and noble passion that revealed itself in that Assembly. And a later generation will look back with love and sympathy on the sovereign ruler of the fine and impetuous spirits of 1848, that tall form standing 'twixt dawn and daylight in the crimson rays of the rising German state, a vision that like a poet's fancy could not endure in the cold illumination of a work-a-day world. So pure and full of youthful innocence was his idealism, so great his confidence in the goodness of the German nature, so loyal his sense of honour, so proud his moral strength, and almost irresistible his appeal to the emotions ! . . . He was wont to regard the world with a kingly eye and to maintain his own free judgment against the most arrogant. Many fine virtues too were his : much courtesy of heart, and unaffected joy in the display of his powers, and withal a notable delicacy of feeling which often remains with the man reared in a sheltered station

---

[1] See his *Life of Carl Mathy.*

in life, and cheers so gaily or depresses so deeply, according as fortune is fair or foul, the best of our knightly class.

On the day of Gagern's election there was an emotional scene in the House, very German as a spontaneous and open expression of strong feeling. Its occasion was the appearance of the poet Arndt on the scene. In Heller's description of the old man we forget for the time the apostle of hate : ' What a picture of an old man is father Arndt ! Light white hair wreathes his crown and still soars gaily upwards, his cheeks laugh with health and his eye with sunny thoughts. His memory is enriched with the same indestructible freshness, and thus there sits, full of vigour and high esteemed, on the right side of the House, the embodiment of all the erudition and experience with which the three last quarters of a century could endow a man of genius.' The report of the ovation to Arndt runs as follows :

Venedey (Cologne) : Gentlemen, this morning a man stepped on to the rostrum and, without saying a word, stepped down again. It was Arndt, old and grey. I think we owe it to him to say that we did not know who it was.

Many voices. Up ! On to the rostrum ! (Arndt ascended the rostrum.)

Arndt (Bonn), ascending the rostrum amid tumultuous cheering and applause : I do not feel flattered but touched by this recognition of one who plays his part as the representative of a great and noble Folk, in sympathy with whom, in commemoration of whom, I at least have lived and worked from my boyhood. The services and achievements of an individual are a trifle ; he counts no more in the millions of thoughts and sensations, in the spiritual development of a great nation, than does a tiny drop of water in the ocean. That I am standing here, a grey-haired old man on that side the bourne where work can be done, was my feeling when I rose—as it were a good old German conscience, the one I acknowledge. (Tremendous applause interrupted the speaker.) That I should dare to rise among so many men, among so many young men, whom I have had the good fortune to know,—that also I owe to a good old German conscience. He who believes in the perpetuity of his Folk . . . (Here the speech was lost in tumultuous applause.)

Drinkwelder (Krems) : I desire to propose the nation's thanks to Arndt for his song *What is the German's Fatherland ?* It has encouraged us in the day of oppression and it has made us one.

Soiron (Mannheim) : I have only one little amendment to propose. We wish to thank him not for his song, we wish above all to thank him for what he has actually done for the whole of Germany. (Three rousing cheers resounded in the Assembly and on the rostrum.)

Jahn (Freiburg a.d.U.) : My worthy German gentlemen, there was a time when we were reared on Arndt's songs. We beg of him to add to his swan-song yet one verse more. We have often sung his song *Was ist des Deutschen Vaterland?* . . . and we have often asked ourselves : *where* is the German's fatherland ? And now, when a ' Germany ' is no longer in question, we would beg of him to add yet a verse, the one which Germany's present situation calls for. (Tempestuous applause.)

Two comments from London on the German situation at this moment find here an appropriate place. On the 17th May Bunsen wrote to Usedom, Prussian plenipotentiary at Frankfort : ' Peel said to me three weeks ago : " Let not Germany attempt to speak a word in European politics for six weeks—not till you are constituted. You speak in the feeling of a future in which we do not believe." ' [1]

The Prince of Prussia wrote to Leopold von Gerlach from exile :

LONDON, 16*th May* 1848.

Warmest thanks for your kind letter of the 5th inst. Ay, what has become of Prussia since we spoke for the last time by that battery beside the street lamp ! Who could suspect that twelve hours later the old Prussia would be buried, a quite new one arise. What my relation will be to this new one cannot yet be seen ; to resist it, not to give my services to it, appears impossible ; under what conditions I can do so, time must show. With a constitution such as the Constituent Assembly has devised, and with a king so circumscribed, how can I remain there, for all the constancy of my desire to return to the Fatherland ? . . . My banishment, if one wishes to call it so, I bear with all the courage and strength, which my clear conscience's [*sic*]. That I should be persecuted as the supporter of the old Prussia, and of the old army I count as an honour ; for I knew and dreamt only of an independent Prussia, a great power in the European Political System, and for such a Prussia no other constitution was suited. For the new Prussia merging itself in Germany a new constitution is surely necessary. Whether the expansion was necessary for our position as a great power, which we still were early on 19th March, I do not know ; it has, however, been announced, and the business has since been directed by fifty people at Frankfort-on-Main, who get their authority from themselves. So stands everything topsy-turvy. Our (United) Diet was a reasonable arrangement, even if very many hearts were broken. Do write at times to your Prince of Prussia.[2]

As soon as the Assembly got to business two committees were appointed, one of thirty members (including Dahlmann,

---

[1] *Memoir*, ii. p. 182.   [2] L. von Gerlach, *Denkwürdigkeiten*.

the draftsman of the Federal Diet's Constitution Scheme) to
draft a National Constitution, and one of fifteen, to report on
what was recognised to be the most pressing practical question
of the hour, viz. the establishment of a provisional executive
authority, pending the final settlement of the constitution.
But in the consideration of these questions, as of the third
great problem which the Assembly had to face, viz. a settlement of the fundamental rights of German citizenship, the
Assembly was constantly and violently interrupted by happenings within and without, of the sort which give professional
politicians so frequently the opportunity for assuming the air
of good men struggling with adversity. On one of these
happenings from without, the Schleswig-Holstein question, we
must touch before describing, in the next chapter, how the
question of the supreme executive authority was dealt with.

Christian VIII. of Denmark died on 20th January 1848,
leaving as a troublesome bequest to his successor, Frederick VII.,
the scheme to incorporate into Denmark proper the Duchies of
Schleswig-Holstein, hitherto only united with Denmark by the
personal bond of a common king. He desired to refer the
question to a joint commission representing both Denmark
and the Duchies, but his hands were forced by the violent
agitation which broke out in Copenhagen, and among the
Danes in Schleswig, for the immediate incorporation of Schleswig.
On the other side, the German party demanded provincial
estates for the Duchies, freedom of the press, right of public
meeting, and entry into the German Federation. The king
proclaimed on 21st March the incorporation of Schleswig in
Denmark, and this was met by the establishment on the
German side of a provisional government, including the
hereditary Prince Frederick of Schleswig-Holstein-Noër (the
Augustenburger, to quote the family name familiar in later
days) and two prominent political leaders, Count von Reventlow-
Preetz and Wilhelm Beseler of Schleswig. War began, and the
Prince invoked the aid of Prussia. This was only reluctantly
granted by Frederick Wilhelm IV. : he felt on the one hand the
danger in revolutionary days of encouraging any movement
that had even the appearance of rebellion against a crowned
head, but on the other hand German public opinion was over-
whelmingly on the side of the Duchies, and Prussia's hopes of
hegemony in Germany depended on a due recognition of

German sentiment. The situation was complicated by the jealous attitude of Russia, Great Britain, and France, each with its own reasons for sympathising with the Danes. However, the German Federation gave its formal recognition to the provisional government, and when the Prince von Noër was defeated at Flensburg, and Schleswig was occupied by the Danes, General von Wrangel took command of a Federal force consisting of Prussians and Hanoverians. Wrangel stormed the Danish fortifications at Schleswig, and after occupying the north of the Duchy unopposed carried the war into Jutland by the capture of Fredericia. Here Frederick William called a halt. He was fearful of the Tsar's anger at his support of a subject in rebellion against his king, but he had also to complain of lukewarmness on the part of German governments generally. For all the popular enthusiasm on the side of the Duchies, the King of Prussia found that he was expected to carry on the war alone, and, at the same time, to bear the brunt of bitter complaints from all the towns on the Baltic sea-board which were suffering from the Danish blockade. In the end a seven months' armistice was arranged at Malmö, under the stipulation, not that the *status quo ante* should be re-established, but that the provisional government should be replaced by a joint government conducted by nominees of Prussia and Denmark, presided over by Count Carl Moltke, a Danish sympathiser.

When news reached the National Assembly that the Prussian troops had been withdrawn from Jutland, and that negotiations were in progress for a truce with the Danes, Dahlmann, as became the scion of an old Hanseatic family, hotly espoused the cause of the Duchies. He was one of the strongest men in the Assembly, and, like Jacob Grimm, one of the famous seven of Göttingen. Heller says of him : ' Dahlmann's iron will kept to the right, and all the more impressive was his intervention in the question of the armistice at Malmö. He won over allies from a section of the House not as a rule easily persuaded to approve forcible, even extreme measures. But the strongest ally in his cause was the tall, stiff, embittered-looking man himself, with his concise style of speech, with the weight of his solid and absolutely genuine personality. His indictment cut men's consciences to the quick,'

In a debate on the Schleswig-Holstein question on the 9th June, Dahlmann spoke as follows :

Grant a short hearing to a man who, without boastfulness, may say of himself that he has dedicated the best efforts of his youth, a loyalty lasting the span of a man's life, to the Schleswig-Holstein question. . . . We, the movers of this motion, have begged of you to preserve the honour of Germany. . . . Do not believe that those men who have so much to say about the whole balance of European power being upset if all Schleswig, united to Holstein, enter the German Federation, that these men deserve a tittle of your confidence. By such an event the European balance of power will not in any way be convulsed, indeed not even disturbed. The same men, however, who maintain that, will not, if we succeed in the matter of our constitution, in the founding of a new and all-embracing constitution for our Fatherland, be idle in raising their voices with redoubled strength, to cry in the midst : ' This means upsetting the whole balance of European power,' and the men, who say that, will then be right. For, to be sure, the then existing balance of power in Europe will be upset, if our Germany rises from a weak, submerged community, from a Federation treated abroad with contempt, to dignity, honour and greatness. (Cheers.) But this derangement of the balance of power in Europe we desire to have and to maintain, and on this upsetting of the balance of power in Europe we mean to insist until the last drop of our blood has been shed. (Cheers.) If you fool away in the Schleswig-Holstein question a cause which is good and right, a fatal blow will be struck at the root of the German question. You will do what the honour of Germany demands, and may the plans of those who count on the persistence of the weakness and degradation of our German Fatherland come to nought ! (Cheers.)

The debate ended in the adoption of the resolution moved by the historian Waitz : ' The German National Assembly declares that the Schleswig question, as an affair of the German nation, comes within its scope, and demands that energetic measures be taken to bring the war to an end ; but insists that in the conclusion of peace with the Crown of Denmark the rights of the Duchies of Schleswig and Holstein, and the honour of Germany, be safeguarded.'

The serious issues of this question for the National Assembly we shall see.

CHAPTER III

ELECTION OF ARCHDUKE JOHN AS REGENT

THIS chapter will consist mainly of an extract from the official report of the debate, lasting from the 19th to the 28th June, which resulted in the election of the Archduke John of Austria as the provisional executive authority for the Germany to be united, so men fondly imagined, by a Constitution that still lay on the knees of the gods. The debate is worth reading, partly as a piece of lively debating in itself, partly for the opportunity it affords of comparing a German with a British parliamentary discussion. To clear the ground, and facilitate an appreciation of the debate and of the men engaged in it, the report will be prefaced by some account of the speakers quoted. Of the president Gagern, Arndt, and Dahlmann probably enough has already been said.

Robert Blum, the most popular leader on the Left, came of humble stock at Cologne, and raised himself by his own efforts to a position of political importance. He settled at Leipzig as secretary and treasurer to the theatre there. But his ambitions drew him to politics, and the gifts of a born orator soon made him a prominent figure among radicals. He turned bookseller in 1847, and issued a political journal, the *Vorwärts*, which, with other publications, helped to spread free ideas. So high was his position as a political leader when the Fore-Parliament was formed that he was elected its vice-president. Of his disastrous mission to Vienna during the October revolution, which resulted in his being shot by the Austrians, we shall read on p. 498. A not over kindly description of him is given by his colleague Robert von Mohl : [1]

For some time much more was said and written about Robert Blum than the real importance of the man demanded ; later he was more forgotten perhaps than he deserved to be. I shall attempt

---

[1] *Lebenserinnerungen*, ii. (K.).

to give a picture of him as I learnt to know him by experience and observation. I not only heard Blum on the platform, but also sat with him on more than one committee, and I thought him a remarkable enough person to keep constantly in view. Well, I do not hesitate to say that I gained only a very moderate opinion of Blum's talent. I willingly grant that he knew the lower classes of the people, and how to move them to the very depths, and to rouse them quickly. Further, he may have possessed the gift of forming a party and making it effective. And no one could gainsay his outstanding rhetorical gifts, and his untiring industry in the development and the exercise of them. Finally, I concede him a nice judgment, which restrained him from going further than he could see was safe, and did much to save him from the blunders which otherwise are easily committed by a person of incomplete education who wishes to conceal this defect. But he not only lacked the knowledge of a statesman but also the vision of one. . . . He prepared everything with great care beforehand, chiefly pompous expressions and sesquipedalian words ; and he never spoke without beginning with a pretty picture and ending with a thundering peroration. As for the thoughts in between there were practically none, and never once did he bring his excitement of the passions to a head; but always swung round as if to tone down his effect. Withal he did not realise how far he might have been carried had he let himself go. . . . It is quite possible that he made the journey to Vienna, which ended so disastrously for him, with a feeling that he had to play a new rôle and win a reputation for courage if he wished to maintain his position in the party.

Prince Felix Lichnowsky was a choice example of the aristocratic and dashing Prussian officer, of a type as much at home in a ballroom as on the parade ground. An episode in his career was service under Don Carlos, by whom he was made a general. He entered the Assembly as a member of the Extreme Right, but modified his views and joined the Right Centre. A description of his brutal murder in the autumn of 1848 will be found on page 417. Of him Mohl says :

It would take us too far to depict this man, wonderfully endowed by nature and terribly spoiled by society, even only as he showed himself during his stay in Frankfort. . . . On the platform he made a striking picture. It was not knowledge that distinguished him. Hundreds in the Assembly were more learned. Nor was it the outlook of the born statesman. . . . It was not his voice nor his diction ; the former was not strong enough, the latter not always correct. Least of all was it moral dignity ; how could the latter be compatible with such vanity, such egotism and such a life ? No, it was his verve, his composure, the very extravagance of his life, his defiant insolence, his aristocratic assurance and his beauty.

Lichnowsky trembled with impatience until he could pick a quarrel with a front bencher on the Left, or attack some principle hitherto considered inviolable ; and the greater his excitement the more brilliant the display of talent both in substance and form. An interruption, a shout from the gallery, were for him a stroke of good fortune, for on those occasions he found his happiest expressions. He carried on a highly annoying guerilla warfare, which brought him to an early and gruesome death.

Klein gives an amusing example of his method of guerilla warfare :

The rules of the House required that every speaker before beginning his speech should give his name. Naturally well-known speakers omitted to do so. But as often as such a speaker rose on the Extreme Left, perchance Robert Blum, Lichnowsky called out with a drawled nasal twang ' Name,' and the best known man in the House was obliged to give his name.

Carl Vogt, who sat on the Left, was a well-known scientist, becoming in 1847 Professor of Natural Science at Giessen, his native town. He was a materialist, and one of his declarations in the Assembly brought a deluge of ridicule upon him :

I am for the separation of Church from State, but only on the express condition that what is termed the Church shall be destroyed ; only on the condition that what is termed the Church shall disappear without a trace from this earth, and betake itself to its home in Heaven. Yes, to the Heaven of which we shall learn something after our death, but of which we may spare ourselves the knowledge so long as we are on earth. . . . In relation to this question I stand on a totally neutral standpoint, so absolutely neutral, that I may almost say it is no standpoint at all.[1]

Mohl's [2] judgment of him is severe :

Few members of the Assembly could compare with Vogt in clear, incisive reasoning, quickness of grasp, biting wit and retentive memory. He scintillated with intellect and life. Moreover he was a born orator : mastery of speech, a resonant voice, presence of mind, calmness in moments of flaming passion, nothing was lacking ; and it was very seldom that he failed to entertain his hearers and keep their attention keenly alive. . . . But there can really be no doubt about Vogt's bad qualities and their influence on his actions ; he himself took not the slightest trouble to cloak them. . . . He received the general recognition of his talents, which he could rightly

---

[1] The German shares the Irishman's aptitude for bulls. Klein quotes a deputy of the Saxon Second Chamber, who said on 13th February 1849 : ' I do not know the motives of the government, but I object to them.'
[2] *Lebenserinnerungen*, ii. (K.).

claim ; but he could make no further headway, for his intellectual gifts were unhallowed by moral worth. His influence on German affairs was only a detrimental one.

Carl Mathy, we may say again, was one of the finest types to be found in the Assembly. He was born at Mannheim, and his liberal opinions led to his spending the years 1834-1840 as a refugee in Switzerland. But he was not an extremist, and of his courageous action in thwarting Hecker and Struve at Carlsruhe, and in arresting the revolutionary Fickler we have read. He became ultimately President of the Baden ministry. A striking sentence of his, in debate in the National Assembly, is the following : [1] ' When I hear the flattery which is now so frequently lavished on the masses, the virtues which are attributed to them to their own embarrassment, I might be permitted to find such flattery not less unworthy than kneeling before the throne of a crowned head.'

Arnold Ruge, one of the leaders of the Young Hegelians, the grim door-keeper of the Hegelian school Heine called him, was an advanced republican and sat on the extreme Left of the National Assembly. Despite his revolutionary fervour he was not loved by Herwegh who wrote of him to his wife in 1847: [2]

This Ruge gets coarser and coarser the more important he grows, and the fulsome gang, which he has . . . as good as organised, is on a par with him in the matter of meanness and stupidity. He is sinking in a veritable slough of conceit. Nothing more weary, stale, flat and unprofitable under the sun than he and his crowd have I encountered, even amongst ' Young Germany.' Heaven knows that it is with no great pleasure I declare that in their direction too I can cast nothing but a glance of contempt. . . .

He was an industrious propagandist, and wrote and published much in the way of dramas, poems, philosophical essays, and radical journalism. In 1849 he had to take refuge in London. In 1850 he settled at Brighton, where he gained a living by teaching until his death in 1880, and conducted a voluminous correspondence with his old friends in Germany and other Germans domiciled in England. He devoted his pen to the cause of Prussia in 1866 and 1870, and was rewarded with a small pension, partly, no doubt, through the good offices of his

---

[1] Klein.   [2] *Briefe von und an G. Herwegh* (K.).

old friend of unregenerate days, Lothar Bucher, later Bismarck's right-hand man.

Like many men of violent opinions, which they endeavour violently to force upon other people, Ruge posed as a pacifist. In 1850 he wrote from Brighton to an International Peace Congress at Frankfort claiming that in the National Assembly he had moved a motion in favour of European disarmament and arbitration by a Congress of all nations, and he proceeds :

> The admiration of war, the war superstition in the German nation, is like the reverence of children for lions and tigers. Education fosters this superstition. Rude and vicious men like Alexander, Sulla, Cæsar, Charles XII., and Bonaparte are praised as heroes. All authorities enjoin admiration of war and devastation. Thoughtless historians admire war. Admiration of war is spread abroad by superstitious journalists. Even philosophers have participated in it, and they called the great Kant, who proclaimed eternal peace, an enthusiast.[1]

We now proceed to give a summary of the important debate on the establishment of a provisional executive authority, which led up to the election of the Archduke John. The extracts are from the official stenographic report edited by Professor Wigard, Leipzig, 1848. Klein has been followed in the choice of speakers, but his excerpts have been amplified where this seemed desirable in the interests of an English reader :

> *Ruge (Breslau)* : The point at issue is : do we desire to be without masters, that is, do we desire to be free men ? The honourable member who is sitting near me (turning to Arndt) has said that it would be a misfortune to be without masters. I respect my friend and compatriot but still believe that he has on this occasion pronounced a great inexactitude. For the North Americans who have no master, the Swiss who desire no master, and the French who have expelled their master, are without masters. My friend Arndt has said that the French have been wrong, but he will not say that the Swiss have been wrong.
>
> *Arndt (Bonn) (speaking from his seat)* : But Arndt will say that the French will soon have another master. (Laughter.)
>
> *Ruge (Breslau)* : Please compose yourselves, gentlemen, and permit me to say to you, that I don't believe it. . . . The main question is, whether we have the right to set up a master again. Gentlemen, the only thing that we Germans have done up to the present is to overthrow despotism. That path we must pursue ; we

---

[1] *Briefwechsel und Tagebuchblätter*, ii. p. 116.

must go forward and overthrow despotism where it still exists.
. . . In the whole of Germany we have no master. . . . That is the
basis on which we stand. . . . The basis is the republic, and the
republic is this Assembly. It has only the right to decide on a
republican basis, which it is itself ; it has not the right to reach after
something outside itself. . . . That power is foreign to it, and not
to be found in this hall. The German nation is here. If we reach
out beyond it, we reach out beyond the German nation. (Laughter.)
This is assuredly no laughing matter, and in him who laughed at it
I see the *facies Hippocratis* ; [1] the future will judge him. It is a
laugh of mockery, but also the laughter of a death-struggle.[2]

The President : I do not think you have the right to apostrophise
the Assembly in this manner.   (Disorder.)

Ruge : I only addressed a remark to an individual who laughed
sarcastically at me.   (Disorder.)

The President : That is beside the question. If Herr Ruge had
paid more respect to the injunction of his predecessor, which was
received with applause, to leave out all feeling of bitterness, we should
not have been so often interrupted.   (Hear, hear.)

Ruge : Constitutional monarchy is a fiction. That King of
England who denied his responsibility, Charles the First, proved
later that he was only too responsible. But free countries in 1848
will not have responsibility on the basis of 1649. . . . Irresponsibility is an irresponsible concept. There is no more irresponsibility.
Every one is responsible ; and after the events that have taken
place in Berlin and Vienna you will allow that I am right. . . . You
stand at the parting of the ways : if you turn from the path of
legality, if the great feeling of the nation, the feeling for unity and
freedom, is not recognised, then will your path be that of illegality.
And, gentlemen, . . . the spirit of the age bends to its will even
those who acknowledge it not, so that you too, I hope, will be
forced even against your will to found the One German Republic.

Blum (Leipzig) : The proposal for a Directoire is nothing but the
warming up of an old dish. A Directoire does not give us what we
want, viz. : a federal state, but merely the old federation of states,
with all its separate interests and divisions. . . . We have had,
as time has gone on, many references to the Revolution ; we have
been warned to close its maw ; and we have been told we were
hurrying on to a Reign of Terror. . . . We can probably assign
to the Revolution, which is an accomplished fact, yet another goal
if we seek to do it justice. Some one drew a comparison yesterday between liberty and love of wife, and a newspaper in the country
that borders on our own, a French paper, has recently maintained
that the German people has become too old to win in bold and

---

[1] ' Hippocrates, b. 370 B.C., in his work *Prognostikon* : a face bearing on it
the signs of approaching death, admirably described by him in his work.'—
Zoozmann's *Zitatenschatz*.

[2] The laugher, according to Klein, was Prince Lichnowsky, subsequently
murdered by the mob.

manly embrace, and to clasp inseparably to its heart, that most lovely of brides, Liberty. We have seen how terror can bleach the hair in a single night, how it can make a man old and grey. How can the heart become otherwise under a thirty years' tyranny, and how can it become otherwise than old during a generation of servitude ? And yet an old heart can love, and it loves more deeply, even if less passionately, than a young heart, because it has the consciousness that the spring of love comes to it only once again. It will step into the lists for the chosen one, not with the enthusiasm of youth, but with the fully developed strength of the grownup man. Do not hand over the bride of our thoughtful German People to its worst, its deadliest enemy, Force. (Cheers from all sides. Applause in the galleries.)

Prince Lichnowsky (Ratibor) : The word ' republican ' has been repudiated by the Left with a certain coyness, I may say, especially during the early days of the debate, when in particular it was a question of these republicans presenting us with a uniform republic. As Herr von Radowitz pronounced the words *une et indivisible*, Herr Wesendonck retorted that no one was thinking of a *république une et indivisible*. I am glad to hold entirely the same opinion as he, and believe that no one thinks of bringing into existence a republic stretching from the Russian to the French frontier, and centralised in Frankfort. I believe it is impossible, since Frankfort happily has not 1,000,000 inhabitants, and since the various races with us are not fused to the extent they are in the case of our neighbours. It is also impossible on other grounds which you will excuse my· stating after seventy-five speakers. . . . If I could persuade myself that all forms of constitutional government would disappear if every German state were allowed to do as it pleased, I would admit that the whole of my Fatherland desired the republic, and I would bow to it, even if in grief. Yes, I would bow before the collective will, for I do not belong to those who, as Herr Lassaulx says, have loved the republic as a dream of youth ; I do not belong to these, and have never admired them. (Hear, hear.) And so I should bow my head in grief. . . . But I cannot assimilate the thought, I cannot possibly resign myself to the thought, that the great majority of our nation wishes to have a republic. . . . I am not going to harangue you here on the affection entertained for certain of our princes ; there may be sovereigns in Germany who have no claim to affection ; there are some whose mediatisation I should not regard as a misfortune. (Laughter.) I speak therefore not of a man's love for his sovereign. I speak of the monarchical principle, and if by the will of God the four and thirty German sovereigns and their families were removed at one and the same moment from the earth, I am convinced that people would join hands and set new ones at the head of this land, even if not in such profusion. (Laughter from the Left.) I understand your hilarity, gentlemen. If I had said the reverse my friends would have laughed. (General laughter.) . . . Herr Ruge tells us that when a country has been bereft of its rulers (this expression leaves a disagreeable taste), it never submits to a ruler again. I cannot understand how any one can get this idea in his head, since the one and only Directoire with its five members led, on the 18th Brumaire, directly to the Consulate and the iron dictatorship of Napoleon. . . . I am fully persuaded that our business here is not to cut and clip a fundamental principle to this shape or that, but to secure the greatest possible consensus of opinion, a majority that will save us from the misfortune of agreeing on nothing at all. So far as possible, to the uttermost limit, will we extend our hands to you, but do not insist . . . on our reducing to the rôle of an executor him whom we set at the head of our land, to face foreign countries and factions at home ; do not insist on that, but think of all other free countries, which serve you as models, think of North America, where the President has a veto which he often exercises with the approval of his country. . . . Now I turn to my friends . . . and implore them to go with me so far as honour and conscience will allow, in order to avoid the terrible misfortune of dissension at such a moment as this. (Hear, hears, and applause from all sides.)

Vogt (Giessen) : We have been told here (pointing to the Right) : We love our princes.—That is an individual opinion which I do not wish to dispute. Gentlemen, I do not take the standpoint of the great Englishman who said over there : ' You can only get hold of a Prince by the neck.' Nor do I take the standpoint of the poet who said : ' Too long in love we 've put our trust, we 'll see what hate can show.' [1] But this I must say, ' To love our rulers does seem to me to be going rather too far ! ' (Laughter.) Gentlemen, we do not love them, for they betrayed and deceived us after the year 1813 ! When the people had staked their blood and their all on liberation from French despotism, when thousands were lying on the battle-fields as a guarantee for the pledged word of Kalisch, which promised representation of the people, which promised freedom of the press, they paid no heed to these sacrifices, for they broke the word which they had given. When in the year 1830 Liberty was knocking at the door and shook the German system to its foundations, yes, then too were promises given ! But after a few years the prisons were crammed ; for the second time they did not keep their word ; again they committed a breach of faith ! And now we stand on the threshold of a third period ; we shall again have promises ; we are here to secure the realisation of the nation's liberty, and now, as always, we are to give a display of our credulity ! No, gentlemen, we are generous, but credulous we are not. Gentlemen, we have been told that it is the same whether princes and governments choose the Sovereign of our Realm or whether we choose him ; the same persons would appear. I shall admit that ; but he whom we elect, and he whom the govern-

---

[1] See Herwegh's ' Song of Hate,' p. 207.

ment elects, is on the day following his election no longer the same person ; for the man who is chosen by us is the man of the people, the man of our trust, and he who is chosen not by us, or who is chosen by the help of governments is the man of our mistrust. (Hear, hear.) I grant that this mistrust may be undeserved, gentlemen, but it will be there and you will not be able to eradicate it. . . . Let me direct your attention to the future ! We have all insisted on a strong central authority. What is a strong central authority ? Gentlemen, the central authority that we fashion finds its strength only in this Assembly, and in the People who elected it. . . . If a small majority is availed of to create a central authority opposed to the clearly defined principles for whose defence we stand, then will such an authority find that we are its foes. . . . I want no half measures, I want nothing indecisive, and I do not want them precisely because I believe that we must be clear we are not giving to certain sinister forces, that still exist in the fatherland, a hold whereby they may undermine our decisions. Therefore, gentlemen, I quote to you, without dropping my voice, a saying of Machiavelli's —I do not exactly admire that statesman, but I quote you his saying—' Peoples have often been false, and Princes have often been false ; but never have Peoples been so false as Princes.' (Tempestuous applause.)

Mathy (Carlsruhe) : I cannot . . . play with the names of republic and monarchy. Gentlemen, as regards the proposed arrangements I care not whether they are called monarchical or republican ; I am only concerned whether they are necessary, whether they are good, whether they are suitable to our purpose. . . . The republic, as it appears to us here, is not the true republic which has been so faithfully depicted to us from his own observation by an honourable member from Austria. It is that state of being without a master which has no relevance to the case of free men, but only to the case of liberated slaves ; for among free men every one understands that he is his own master though he recognises one absolute overlord, the will of the people and its expression, the Law. (Hear, hear, from the Right). . . . But I am not surprised that propositions of that kind are advanced. . . . I am not surprised that there should be a disposition to translate the autocracy of a crowned individual in terms of one elected by acclamation. . . . I should not be surprised at anything still more remarkable, for a nation does not pass suddenly from a condition of prolonged tutelage to that of determining its own destiny, without strange leaps. The passage was too rapid, the emotion too violent, not only for novices and recruits in politics, but also for men who though they have reached maturity are corrupted by the enjoyment of long peace. . . . The German people in the mass, as a whole, has hitherto maintained a praiseworthy attitude, and the Assembly— the vast majority of it—has shown that it has not forgotten the first condition of enduring freedom, a wise moderation and self-restraint, that it understands how to take the right measures demanded by the fatherland in an hour of urgent need and of danger. It will observe that condition on this occasion also, and should the governments of individual states fail to follow the example of loyal duty towards the whole fatherland which the Assembly, I doubt not, will give, then, gentlemen, then would a bold stroke for sovereign power not only be permitted us, but be forced on us of necessity. . . . Nothing entitles us yet to go to extremes ; we have still the hope that a great majority will declare itself for the installation of a provisional authority, a majority from which will emanate decisions corresponding, if not to the wishes of every individual, nevertheless to the general interests of the nation. (Hear, hear.)

President von Gagern : . . . Who is to create the central authority? Gentlemen, I deal the bold stroke and I say to you, we must our-selves create the provisional central authority. (Prolonged and loud cheering.) The majority of this Assembly appears to have come more and more to the view, which I share, that the future central authority must be placed in the hands of a Regent with responsible ministers. . . . If we desire such a Regent, as undoubtedly is the case according to the majority, the man has been found, a man of high standing, who has shown himself worthy of the nation's support for the highest office, and a man who will continue to show himself worthy. We must choose a Regent from the highest sphere ; for in circumstances such as the present there is no private person, as perhaps individuals or even parties have thought, who could assume the office. (Hear, hear, from the Right.) . . . Gentlemen, seeing that I have argued this question fully before you, I cannot be reproached (turning to the Left) with having surrendered the principle of the nation's sovereignty. . . . Assuredly there will be found in my proposition no surrender of this principle even if my opinion should be, as indeed it is, that this exalted personage must be a prince, which you also may concede, not because of, but despite the fact that he is a prince. (General and repeated cheering, and applause in the Assembly and in the galleries.) Gentlemen (address-ing the whole Assembly), many bitter things have just been said of our princes ; I have not been reared in this hatred against princes, and the love of mankind was always more dear to me. (Loud cheers from the Right.) But, gentlemen, to bear hatred against whole generations, without designating the individuals who may to some extent deserve hatred, is not magnanimous. (On the Right, and in the galleries, repeated and prolonged cheers.) . . . Let us unite so far as union is possible ! Let us sacrifice what must be sacri-ficed in order to obtain, and to lighten the passage towards, better conditions. . . . We do not compromise liberty, and we consti-tute the unity of our nation and fatherland, for which we have yearned so long. (Tumultuous and prolonged applause from all sides of the Assembly, and from the galleries.)

Dahlmann (Bonn) : For a whole week the strife of speeches has continued, a stress of intellect worthy of its object. . . . Things in Germany have reached a point when men abroad are already beginning to fix the date when she will become entirely the prey of parties. People expect of us all the train of follies and crimes that have stripped the French revolution of the tender blossoms of freedom. In Russia they give us a term of three weeks, *i.e.* after that period Germany will be lost through internal dissension. The statesmanlike wisdom of England allows us a somewhat longer term ; they are satisfied to allow us six months. Let us disappoint these sinister hopes. Establish a firm central authority and then face courageously anxiéties and threatenings from abroad. Hold to your wise resolves ; they will re-echo through the continent, and carry the conviction that Germany has ceased to waste her best forces in the service of a despotism, may it threaten from above or from below. (Tumultuous applause.)

The result of the election held on Friday, 30th June 1848, was the return of Archduke John of Austria as Regent. President Heinrich Gagern acquainted the Assembly with the result in these words : ' The result of the election is as follows :

John, Archduke of Austria . . . 436 votes.
Heinrich Gagern (Darmstadt) . . 52 „
Von Itzstein . . . . . 32 „
Archduke Stephan . . . . 1 „

twenty-seven members abstained from voting, therefore the total number present was five hundred and forty-eight. I proclaim, herewith, John, Archduke of Austria, Regent of Germany ! (Three cheers echoed in the Assembly and the gallery, all the bells were set ringing, and salutes were fired.) May he retain the love for our great Fatherland which he has shown at all times, may he be the founder of our unity, the guardian of our liberty as a people, the restorer of order and confidence ! Once again, Long live the Archduke John, the Regent ! ' (The Assembly as well as the gallery joined in the toast.) Many South Germans had voted for Heinrich von Gagern, among others Ludwig Uhland and Fr. Th. Vischer ; for Itzstein among others Robert Blum, Wilhelm Jordan, Carl Vogt. A deputation was to inform the Archduke John of his election as Regent. The law of 28th June assigned to the Overlord the executive power in all matters affecting the security and welfare of the German Confederation ; the supreme direction of the armed forces ; the representation of Germany abroad (ambassadors and consuls) ; the Regent was to take no part in the work of drafting a constitution ; he was to be irresponsible ; the ministry nominated by him was to be responsible to the National Assembly ; the Federal Diet ceased to exist. The National ministers whom the Archduke John had appointed were announced to the Assembly on the 15th July : Anton von Schmerling, Austrian Ambassador to the Federal Diet, Minister for Home and Foreign Affairs ; Johann Gustav Heckscher, Minister of Justice ; the Prussian Major-General Eduard von Peucker, Minister of War.

Laube's impressions [1] of the moment probably represent the enthusiasm of the majority of the German people when the fact was known that the National Assembly had settled the first thorny question before it, and that its choice had fallen on the man who was popularly supposed to be the most democratic of royalties.

Germany has a common head ! This thought exercised its charm on old and young. Only the body remains to be recovered. No, it may still be there, though its numbed limbs may have to be set in natural motion. In particular two of its greatest and most important limbs, Austria and Prussia to wit, may at last be at our disposition again. Prussia, as a Prussian Power pure and simple, may be broken by the revolution, but may again be serviceable to Germany, and Austria transmits her influence through her most popular Archduke.

The summer of 1848 saw us then at the summit of our idealism. This idealism gave so much happiness that it is impossible to make it a subject of reproach ; it was so intoxicating that even reasonable people lost their balance over its claims on the future, and it was bound to render much more difficult the building up of a really durable future. For he who thinks he possesses a million, considers himself robbed and injured when he finds as a matter of fact that he only possesses half a million.

The election of an Austrian archduke was a political blunder, for Prussia's jealousy was at once aroused ; but a sentimental attachment had drawn people to him. This dated from 1842 when he was the guest of the King of Prussia at the festival in connection with the laying of the foundation stone of the nave of Cologne Cathedral. He was said to have proposed at a banquet the following toast : ' No Prussia, no Austria ; a United Germany, as firm and as free as its mountains ! ' Such a toast assured him the reputation of a German patriot, while his democratic sympathies were attested by his marriage with the daughter of a keeper of post-horses.

[1] *Das erste deutsche Parlament.*

To this sentimental attachment Justinus Kerner, Uhland's old Swabian comrade and the befriender of Metternich and Lola Montez, gave poetic expression :

TO THE ARCHDUKE JOHN

(*June* 1848)

Son of the mountains, huntsman bold,
    Keen thine eyes the future view.
With God's help thy purpose hold ;
    Thine be comrades staunch and true.

Princely corridor and hall
    Thou hast paced with halting feet,
Readier scaled some rocky wall,
    Where an eagle thou may'st greet. . . .

Guided has thy hand the plough,
    Tended thine own garden plot ;
In Tyrol no courtiers bow,
    Simple peasants shared thy lot.

Lead us, thou, from gloom to light,
    Give us breath of mountain air ;
Tyrolese are we to fight,
    When we hear thy trumpet blare.

Fan thy temples silver-grey,
    Soaring gaily ever higher ;
Till it come, thy glorious day,
    Eagle-eyed our youth inspire !

And again, on a changed note, after the murder of Lichnowsky and Auerswald :

ENOUGH !

Thou with the Hapsburgs' lofty brow,
    And heart that nurses love alone,
Back to thy valleys and hills of snow,
    And here let outraged nature moan.

Here where the tumult's victims bled,
    Where murder's bloody ensign flew
O'er Auerswald and Lichnowsky dead—
    This is no longer place for you. . . .

Shake from thy feet the dust, and go,
    Wash from thy hand the horrid stain,
And drink, where living waters flow,
    The spirit of the hills again.

The Archduke entered Frankfort on the evening of the 11th July. Next morning a jubilant procession escorted him on foot, as befitted a personage with his simple tastes, to the *Paulskirche*, where he was to assume his office by giving assent to the law instituting a provisional Central Authority. After Gagern's address of welcome, the Regent made the following declaration:[1]

Let the haste with which I have come here, in order to appear in your midst, be to you the most convincing proof of the high value I set on the dignity of Regent which you have conferred upon me, and on the confidence manifested to me on this occasion by the representatives of the German people. At this moment, when I assume the office of Regent, I repeat the declaration that I will keep and cause to be kept, to the renown and welfare of the German Fatherland, the law governing the establishment of a Provisional Central Authority, which has just been read out to me. I declare at the same time that I shall dedicate myself wholly to this office, and shall without delay beg His Majesty the Emperor to release me, in accordance with the communication of the Imperial Diet to which I have already agreed, from further attendance in Vienna. (Long sustained and thunderous applause and 'Long live the Regent' from all sides of the Assembly and from the gallery.) In this world (turning to the President and offering his hand) we may not do things by halves ; if we have made up our mind, we must give ourselves up entirely to that to which we are called, namely, to the German Nation. (Loud and prolonged applause.)

What Hecker and the revolutionaries thought of all this jubilation may be judged from a letter[2] of Hecker's to Frau Herwegh :

MUTTENZ, 11*th July* 1848.

Things look gloomy, my honoured lady ; Liberty hides her head, and I am drawn homewards to the West of America, to the home for which I have yearned for fourteen years. That the privileged betrayers of the people in Frankfort have manufactured a provisional Kaiser, of the race which has only produced . . . an irresponsible Kaiser, not bound by the resolutions of the Assembly ; that they have given us a revival of what was said and done at the Congress of Vienna, the whole of the 1813-15 farce of acting and lies ; all this is known to you. But that the republicans have been defeated at the elections in Austria and Hungary ; that the heroes of the Vienna barricades, that the whole crowd of Simple Simons hailed the Regent with loud hurrahs (Corruption, Corruption !) ; that though our fire-spitting 'manifestos' and 'Addresses to the German Nation' were applauded with jubilation, men's hands fell listlessly

---

[1] Laube, *Das erste deutsche Parlament.*
[2] *Briefe von und an G. Herwegh* (K.).

by their sides ; that in a word the spirit of the people is willing but the flesh continually weaker ; all that pierces us to the heart you do not know ; and it is well that you do not know it. For any one who is not the dupe of his own enthusiasm, or a short-sighted fool, can clearly see that Germany is on the high way to become monarchical, not thirty-four times over but thirty-five times. Unhappy nation, poor fatherland ! If a shock does not come from without, if red breeches do not cross the Rhine, the nation will not rise. A great period has swept rapidly over a diminutive generation, and the spirit of the age shakes angrily its pinions and turns away its face from a despicable race.

The Executive Authority and the Ministry formed by the National Assembly were from the first but a make-believe government. And yet the Assembly survived the snub it received when it called upon the Army to render homage to the Regent. Austria protested against the demand ; Prussia simply ignored it !

CHAPTER IV

DEBATES ON FUNDAMENTAL RIGHTS, ON POLAND, AND ON HECKER'S ELECTION

No better fortune than had attended the Federal Diet was to favour the National Assembly in its efforts to produce a workable and acceptable scheme for a Federal Empire or State. The moment the question was seriously approached the jealousy between Prussia and Austria broke out, between Great Germans and Small Germans, while the red republicans of the extreme Left were watchful to seize every opportunity of spoiling the best-devised schemes that retained any of the trappings of Monarchy or Empire. This vital question was therefore by force of circumstances driven into the background, and through the hot summer months of 1848 the members of the Assembly toiled at the task of formulating the fundamental rights of German citizenship. This task, continually interrupted, as we shall see, by occasional and violent debates on questions of immediate urgency, was too much even for German patience. Laube is driven to exclaim : [1]

> During these endless proceedings the Left called out continually, ' You are betraying freedom, you repulsive men of the Centre ; you are more hateful to us than the reactionaries of the Right ; you are betraying the great age which might enable us to clear away every vestige of tutelage and slavery. Shame upon you ! . . .' Between these two extremes, between ill-considered outcry and sarcastic silence, came and rose the flood of amendments, came and rose the flood of speakers—the German parliament seemed to be foundering in speechifying, scholastic wisdom and endless waste of time. A civic crown for him who can keep silence in this morbid, impractical craze for words ! So say all of the better sort.

And the old poet, Arndt, surrounded by a crowd, who could

---

[1] *Das erste deutsche Parlament*, ii.

not see the wood for the trees, inscribed in the Parliament Album the verses : [1]

> You grope for light where lights by thousands shimmer,
> And cry : Good friends, show us the faintest glimmer !
> Bathed in a sea of light you beg a candle,
> The light into its several beams refining
> Before you 'll own its radiance round you shining.
> Ye fools and blind, who thus God's gifts mishandle !
>
> No thunderbolt of war, the foe to shatter,
> Is he who bids his captains idly scatter
> To count their men by lance or stirrup-leather :
> Rally as one, to count heads is but harmful !
> Here for your garlands are flowers by the armful.
> In Fame's panache who tells each separate feather ?

Of the kind of speeches that streamed on in their interminable course, examples may be given in two naïve extracts from the deliverances of Jacob Grimm, who represented very vigorously the professorial element in the House :

We Germans, as no one will dispute, are an industrious and orderly people. But these praiseworthy qualities often degenerate with us into defects. We have—I must say it—a great, a decided tendency to pedantry ; I have even declared on another recent occasion that had pedantry remained undiscovered in the world, a German would have invented it. The defect lies here, that we are all too much inclined to cling to the trivial and small, and therefore to allow the substance to escape us. The well-known aphorism,

> 'Acting first, and thinking after,
> Has furnished food for scornful laughter,'

this aphorism can seldom be applied to us Germans in political matters ; rather might another be applied to us :

> 'Rich in counsel, poor in deed,
> Is our musty German creed.'

Grimm gives in a further utterance a fine illustration of the very defect to which he has been calling attention.

It is clear to me also, that the nobility as a privileged class must cease to exist ; this has been for a few generations the judgment of the spirit of the age, and now it can furnish eloquent testimony in support of its judgment. The nobility is a flower which has lost its smell, perhaps too its colour. We seek to exalt freedom as the highest. How then is it possible for us to add something even higher ? Therefore for this reason, surely, since freedom is the

---

[1] Klein.

centre of our being, nothing more exalted ought to exist beside her.
. . . The greatest German, who achieved our religious liberty,
Luther, came of humble stock and so is it thenceforward through all
the following centuries. You will see continually that the majority
of the great enlightened intellects belonged to the middle class,
although first-rate men did make their appearance among the
aristocracy, as Hutten's name has already been cited. In later times
I recall Lessing, Winckelmann, Klopstock, Goethe, Schiller, all
commoners, and it was a case of spoiling the middle class, that a
' von ' should be stuck on to the names of the two last. Thereby
they were not made a hair's breadth taller. . . .

After all that I have said so far it can only appear to me that the
nobility must die out, but I do not think that it need be extirpated
with its titles and its memories ; these may ᵗemain, and for us
commoners too who are just as eagerly attached to our own fore-
fathers. . . . No, something quite different, viz. that in future he
(the nobleman) shall forego his privileges, and in all matters with
which rank is concerned be on an equality with every other man.
But that those privileges persist we have often, and up to the most
recent date, painfully experienced. It was not only the right to wear
golden spurs, or to allow one's finger-nails to grow longer, an appanage
of the Mandarins as well, which were the subject of discussion
earlier ; there were privileges that interfere most acutely with our
habits and manner of life.

I come to the question of decorations. . . . I am sincerely devoted
to the Monarchy. There are high-hearted kings, and the King whom
I serve is full of the noblest human sympathy ; he has ever desired
Germany's welfare and will never desire anything else ; on that I
can firmly rely. But at the same time I nurse the conviction that
our princes will soon have the self-denial to renounce all Byzantine
and Chinese finery, return to the simplicity of ancient days, and
distribute no orders to civilians, since they seem originally to have
been intended for the army alone. For them, for warriors, let them
remain ; their right to them I cannot seek to dispute. It is something fine in the heat of battle to have won such a distinction, and on
it the soldier's eye is naturally set, but, among civilians, what does
a knight mean, who never mounts a horse, or a commander of this or
that Order, who has nothing to command ?

It must be admitted, however, that the National Assembly
did, in the fullness of time, complete their labours under this
head and formulate the fundamental rights of German citizenship; and no more striking example can be given of the grimness
of German tenacity. Sir A. W. Ward gives in the *Cambridge
Modern History*, xi. p. 167, a valuable summary of them :

Every German is a citizen of the Empire. No German State shall
in the administration of civil or penal law make any difference
between its own subjects and those of any other State. Before the

law there exists no distinction of classes. The rights of all citizens are equal ; the duties of all are the same : every man is bound to serve the Empire in arms. Personal freedom is inviolable, and no man may be arrested except on a judicial warrant which gives the cause of his detention and is communicated to him within twenty-four hours after his arrest. All Germans have the right of freely expressing their opinions by word of mouth, in writing or in print ; the right of free petition ; the right of public meeting. Every German State is to possess a Constitution with a popular representation, and to this representative body the ministers are to be responsible.

The work was still-born, for, as Sir A. Ward says, ' though the *Grundrechte* were, on 27th December 1848, proclaimed as law by the *Reichsverweser*, and though on 28th March 1849, they were incorporated in the constitution of the Empire, the larger states (Austria, Prussia, Bavaria, Hanover) neither proclaimed them as law, nor treated them as having the force of law without proclamation.'

We may now retrace our steps to consider two of the urgent questions that interrupted the course of debate on fundamental rights, the question of the reception of the German portions of Poland into the German Federation, and of their representatives into the Assembly, and the matter of the rebel Hecker's election to the Assembly. ' The Poles,' said Laube, ' were utilised (by the Left) partly as a lachrymal gland, partly as a poison-bag.' The outstanding speech delivered in the debate, towards the end of July, was that of Wilhelm Jordan of Berlin, an author by profession, who entered the Assembly as a radical, but on the Polish question deserted his sentimental party and their policy of an independent Poland, and after this speech joined the Right Centre.

Wilhelm Jordan (Berlin) : It were inhuman and barbarous to lock one's breast to all sympathy at the sight of the long passion of such a people, and I am far removed from such want of feeling. But it is one thing to be thrilled by a tragedy, and another to seek as it were to undo the tragedy. . . . To seek to re-establish Poland simply because her fall fills us with well founded grief, that I call a piece of weak-minded sentimentality. (Bravo from the Right, hisses from the Left.) It is a pleasant change for me once in a way to hear this tone from this side of the house. (Laughter.) . . . You say, ' Political sagacity counsels, justice demands, humanity insists on the re-establishment of a free Poland.' . . . We are to declare war against Russia, in order to wring from Russia the independence of Poland. It is a crusade against Russia that is preached to us. . . . Hatred between nations is a barbarism that is incompatible with the culture of the nineteenth century, is downright nonsense. Certainly, the Russian people are not hateful! . . . Our hatred can only be directed against the system under which Russia groans. . . . I say, ' The policy which calls to us " Set Poland free, cost you what it may! " is a short-sighted policy, a policy of self-forgetfulness, a policy of weakness, a policy of fear, a policy of cowardice.' It is high time for us, once and for all to awake from this dreamy self-forgetfulness, in which we have raved over all possible nationalities, while we our- selves cowered in shameful bondage and were stamped upon by all the world, to awake to a wholesome national egotism, to say the word right out for once, which in every question places the welfare and honour of the fatherland uppermost. I admit without pre- varication, our right is none other than the right of the stronger, the right of conquest. Yes, we have made conquests. . . . In the West we have only been conquered ; in the East we have had the great misfortune ourselves to make conquests, and thereby have given whole swarms of German poets occasion for moving Jeremiads over the various nationalities which have had to succumb to the pressure of the German race. (Laughter from the Right, hisses from the Left.) Yes, gentlemen, you will perhaps hiss me still more, for I have the courage to set my face against a commonplace over which German Liberals have been fussing for nigh a generation. I have the courage to defend an act of cabinet policy dating from a time when there was no other policy, because the political and national consciousness was astir nowhere but in the brain of Absolutism ; yes, I have the courage to tax with ignorance or falsification of history those who regard the partition of Poland in a light so des- perately dark, that they have no other designation for it than that of an infamous scandal. (Prolonged hissing from the Left.) . . . Prussia can treat the accusation quite calmly when she is charged with complicity in the murder of a people. She can maintain a proud silence, and allow her work to speak for her ; for this affords eloquent testimony that she has worked more effectively for the reanimation, or rather creation, of a new Polish nation than those fine gentlemen who turn up like stormy petrels wherever there is a chance of stirring up a war or an insurrection, in order to win the chance, amid the general shock, of raising a new conflict. . . . I am persuaded that in you the principle still lives : ' Freedom for all, but the strength and welfare of the fatherland above everything ! ' (Prolonged and tempestuous applause.)

On 7th August the Assembly had to make up its mind whether it would allow Friedrich Hecker, the leader of the Baden in- surrection, who had been returned by a Baden constituency, to take his seat in the House. The heat with which the question was debated reminds one of the scene at Westminister when the question of Mr. Bradlaugh's admission was under discussion. Simson of Königsberg, a charming personality and a great lawyer, who, from 1879 to 1891, presided over the Supreme Court of the Empire, delivered the speech that made the greatest impression. Mohl says of him :

It is impossible to speak in too flattering terms of Simson's conduct in the chair. If he had not an imposing exterior like Gagern, a generous nature had bestowed on the more slightly built man a beautiful voice, and an engaging aspect brimming with intelligence. . . . His peculiar composure, acquired perhaps by painful struggles within him, his dignified courtesy and lofty impartiality, made a personal insult to him or an act of disobedience to his ruling almost impossible. But his mere conduct of the business was masterly. . . . It is impossible to calculate the amount of time and useless irritation that he thereby saved the Assembly.

Simson's speech on the question of Hecker's admission or rejection ran as follows :

Simson (*Königsberg*) : The one question that ought to be raised in connection with Hecker's action is this : In what relationship has Hecker, by his action, placed himself to this Assembly, to which he seeks admission in virtue of his election at Thiengen ? And here the answer seems to me infinitely simple : Hecker's deed may have given him the entrée into all the Halls of Honour and Fame in the world—entry to this hall of ours it has closed to him ! . . . You have heard to-day from the South-west that the summons to Hecker would allay people's feelings ; speaking for the North-east I reply that any one, who knows more of our common fatherland than the few square miles about him, must hold the firm conviction that this high Assembly has only to take Hecker to its bosom and it will not merely hamper and cripple its authority, which is, despite all that may be said, only a moral authority, but will utterly and at a single blow destroy it. (Cries from the Right : Hear, hear ! Very true !) His reception would suffice to reduce this Assembly in the eyes of the overwhelming majority of German districts and races, despite their manifold characters, to an absolute impossibility ! (On the Right : Very true !) . . . Were this the place to apply to the deed of which we speak the measure of our judgment as individuals, the majority of the Assembly would profess the view that regards men struggling in the stress of life, and imputes the greater half of their guilt to the unlucky stars. This is a view, with regard to which I maintain, unreservedly and at all costs, that it is in the present case my own. . . . In the light of our political judgment, which alone is germane to the matter, the fact remains, say whatever one may against it, that Hecker has drenched the sacred soil of our fatherland with blood, that he has shown the foreigner the doorway into German territory. In place of the eternal ordinances of Law, which after temporary eclipse shine ever the brighter, he sought to plant the banner of Force. Therefore he cannot find a seat among men to whom our people has entrusted the founding of unity, the strengthening of her freedom by way of counsel, of moderation, of wisdom and of patience. Only after long and earnest atonement can place be found for him again upon German soil! (Loud cheers from the Right and Centre, hisses from the Left.)

Hecker's election was declared invalid by a large majority. Rebuffs such as this were mortifying to the extremists of the Left, and as in the Fore-Parliament, so in the National Assembly, many of them had to be faced. Carl Vogt wrote to Herwegh on 2nd August : [1]

FRANKFORT, 2nd August 1848.

Our position here becomes ever more trying. The Right and the Centre are veritable *conservateurs bornés* of the past, and of a truth it is impossible to get anything into the brains of these numskulls except by knocking a hole in the cranium. The most pitiful rôle is played by these poor wretches who have been freed from chains and bonds, Eisenmann, Jordan, etc., the student-heroes of 1830, the Hambachers of '30 ('32) and others. Most of them are whole-hearted aristocrats, and most of them indeed for romantic reasons ; they fear that poetry will go out of life when they have no aristocracy, no princes, no castles, palaces, soldiers and ensigns. Then come the money-bags, which are beginning to fill, and which are best represented by Bassermann and Mathy. How is one to do anything with these people ? Our German Michael himself has become quite flabby ; he grumbles no more, but since he has placed himself under the wing of a John Lackland, is delighted with his God, and dreams only of coupons and good harvests. Indeed I am compelled really to despair of any fresh political stir among the people before the end of the potato harvest. . . .

Very interesting just now are the particularist squabbles, which may perhaps lead to a breach between North and South Germany. The Prussians are thoroughly determined not to subordinate themselves to a central authority, and now that our Frankfort War Minister has issued orders for an allegiance parade, there is a hellish row among the Guard and the Junkers. They won't have anything to do with the Hapsburger, won't pay homage, want only their ' guid king, etc. etc.'

Hecker, despairing of further opportunity in Germany, sailed for America in September. He settled there, and in later years found vent for his restless activities in the Civil War. There was something attractive about the man. He had many of the qualities that go to make a successful leader, eloquence, contagious good-humour, and courage ; certainly he had not that ' judgment ' which enables politicians less gifted to succeed.

[1] *Briefe von und an G. Herwegh* (K.).

He sacrificed a brilliant career, as advocate, for his republican opinions. There is a fine side to him revealed in the passage with which begins his account of the disastrous march from Constance : [1]

On Sunday, 9th (April), at daybreak, I said good-bye to my wife in Mannheim, to her who in joy and in sorrow had stood truly and sincerely by me, at whose side in undisturbed domestic happiness I had so often found rest and compensation after the struggles of public life, and impressed a kiss on the foreheads of my three sleeping children. Filled with a confidence surely founded on belief in a just cause, and principles which had inspired the youth and the man, I relinquished a brilliant career, carried away and exalted by the idea of fighting, of conquering or of dying, in the cause of the liberation of our glorious race, and of co-operating in its release from the servitude of a thousand years. Travelling day and night through Rhenish Bavaria, France and Switzerland, I reached Constance on Tuesday, the 11th, towards 6 o'clock. On Thursday, the 13th, in the early morning the general order was given at Constance ; the men in arms were drawn up on the market place, four drummers in front ; many of them, who even the day before had borne themselves very resolutely, slipped away. Others promised to come after us. The wet weather exerted a paralysing influence on many, for the fact that the rainy season was setting in was very prejudicial to reinforcements. But those who took the field were merry in mood, and stout of heart, and remained so from the beginning to the end. The women, old and young, showed themselves to be more courageous and more enthusiastic than the men. . . . To the lively beat of the drums, with hundreds accompanying us, we marched out of Constance across the bridge. . . . Appeals for recruits were made by envoys in the neighbouring districts, especially on the island of Reichenau, which is inhabited by a bold, daring race, good rifle shots. . . . The blue sky smiled from rifts in the rain clouds, at our side the clear glorious lake, and the Alps so far away, so free ; in front of us Hohenstaufen, Hohenhoben, Hohenstoffeln, Hohenkrähen and Hohentwiel. A world full of old sagas and songs, of forgotten legends, lay before us. Old chronicles tell of the despotism of the German Emperor and feudalism, of Fridolin the preacher of Christianity in Reichenau, of priestly deception and the burning of Johann Huss. And we marched out with the banner of the German republic ; we wished to exterminate the despotic remnants of the Middle Ages, and found the free state. Men's voices made the air ring with songs of battle and the white sea birds hovered around our heads. . . .

The affection for him, and hatred of Prussia, felt by many are expressed in a farewell poem by G. Sulzer which was pub-

[1] Fr. Hecker, *Die Erhebung des Volkes im Baden, 1848* (K.).

lished as a broadsheet.[1] Four of the seven stanzas run as
follows :

FAREWELL TO HECKER, SEPTEMBER 1848

Hecker, farewell ! How sore the spirit labours !
   The words are wrung like blood from a stricken heart ;
Peace art thou seeking far from friends and neighbours,
   Leaving for us the longing and the smart.
Thy loyal friends will nurse for thee their sorrow.
   Man's treachery our leader from us stole ;
And yet 'tis they who should our pity borrow,
   The traitors with the canker in their soul !

What here remains for those whom thou art leaving,
   Thou the sole anchor of our hopes and prayers ?
Wilt thou escape the net the Prussian's weaving
   Round us with lies, false promises and snares ?
Hope is there still, our day is not yet over ;
   Changeless the sun pursues his ancient way,
And if at even the clouds his brightness cover,
   Splendid he rises to hail the new-born day. . . .

Patience ! for soon the yeast will work from under ;
   With its own hands Reaction digs its grave ;
Not even the Prussian king can stay the wonder,
   Germany's fame will shiver sword and glaive.
Glowers the Dane, to profit by disorder,
   Covets the land that German lives have won ;
Hail Holstein, hail, and all the Baltic border !
   We 'll keep the oath we Germans swore as one. . . .

Now fare thee well ! Our hopes go with thee roaming ;
   Fortune attend thee o'er the ocean's swell ;
We shall stand fast, for all the Prussian's foaming—
   Lo ! at his feet yawns wide the mouth of hell.
Take for a pledge this happy expectation,
   Nurse it with joy on far Columbia's strand ;
Soon, brothers all, we 'll build one German nation,
   Then, O our loved one, back to thine own land !

---

[1] Facsimile in Blum.

CHAPTER V

THE BUILDING FESTIVAL AT COLOGNE, AND THE LIGHTER SIDE OF LIFE IN THE NATIONAL ASSEMBLY

An interlude, not without its significance, in the labours of the Assembly was the festival in connection with the building of Cologne Cathedral. Here the members of the National Parliament met the King of Prussia, and the relative importance of King and National Parliament was made disagreeably plain to the latter. The completion of the vast building was an enterprise due to the Hohenzollerns, as Heine sang :

> ' Cologne Cathedral 's finished now ;
> To Hohenzollern zeal 'tis owed ;
> The Hapsburgs sent a purse of gold,
> Stained glass a Wittelsbach bestowed.'

The choir had stood since the thirteenth century, with little more than the foundations of a nave, as a monument of the church-building zeal of the period. Even then inflated German arrogance played its part. The design of the choir was appropriated from Amiens, but the building was to be Amiens on an even vaster scale. There was little real church-building zeal in the spirit which moved Frederick William IV. to resuscitate, in 1842, the scheme for the completion of the nave. He was partly moved by romantic enthusiasm, but partly also, and mainly, by the vision of a grandiose edifice, the greatest of its kind, which should stand as a symbol of the ambitions and the power of the German nation as a whole. The pile may be regarded as a temple of Moloch rather than a Christian church. The political aspect of the undertaking was well recognised. Grillparzer's fine comment on it is as follows :

THE BUILDING OF COLOGNE CATHEDRAL

> Why build the house before the guest is there ?
>   Union dwells not in homes of wood or stone ;
> Deep in man's heart she lays his feelings bare,
>   And those who love soon make their union known.

Like whirling leaves your boastful pamphlets come,
　And if they stir the surface they do well ;
The fish, as is their nature, still are dumb,
　And swim cold-blooded underneath the swell.

More than a prince's whim the people need ;
　First give them something worthy to defend,
With name of German more than name concede,
　And then to what men can our wills we 'll bend.

When rights are lost that princes hold in fee,
　And every German feels that loss his own,
As with the French and British you may see,
　With us a nation's sense is fully grown.

Long since, that union might persist for aye,
　Men built for them the monstrous tower of Babel ;
Though speech was one, by tribes they went astray ;
　That consecrated tower is now a fable !

Very striking also are the concluding four verses of a long
ode on the subject of the completion of the cathedral by the
East Prussian poet, Gottschall. The allusion to a German as
distinct from a Christian God shows that this is no new conception in the German mind.

Let us be one in pride, and strong in deed—
　To Freedom rear another haughty dome,
But, building for our weal, of this take heed—
　A new-born age wants not another Rome !
'Tis but a foolish wizard's empty boast,
To conjure up the dead past's vanished ghost.

'Twould sweep us Germans on its stormy way,
　And sink our souls in dungeons dank and cold,
That endless stream of monks from cloisters grey,
　Like mushrooms after tempest plump and bold,
Or poisonous foxgloves with their spreading roots,
Who 'd strangle Freedom's young and tender shoots.

Oh, fair our mediæval heritage,
　Could we but turn it to the people's good !
But let us not forget that our new age
　A godhead new worships in hardihood ;
'Tis Freedom's vestal fire that now we serve,
And while it burns our faith shall never swerve.

> Build our Cathedral, hail its topmost tower
> Mirrored majestic in the flowing Rhine !
> So may it stand, symbol of German power,
> Ay, and of German Unity the sign.
> But stones of shattered Bastilles must we use
> To build the church our German God will choose.

Laube gives a significant account [1] of the King's reception
of the members of the National Assembly :

The King of Prussia, for whom people had foretold an unfavourable
reception, was not yet there.   He did not arrive until the following
evening at the Deutz railway-station, and it was understood he
would not cross the Rhine by the bridge but by steamer.   So it
came about, and indeed with the thunder of cannon on all sides.   The
windows rattled with the discharge of the guns, and a comparison
with the previous day's reception of the Regent brought home to
every one that he who now arrived was still the War Lord in this
country.   One knows how the discharge of massed artillery rouses
men's hearts, and therefore one cannot draw conclusions from the
reception given by the spectators.   Regent and King met on the
roadway and embraced like two men the sincerity of whose manner
and emotion is natural.   One had to wait until they were separated
before one could judge of the feeling for the King.   An hour later
this was possible.   The King and the strength of all Prussianism was
in the Government Buildings, received the authorities, and desired
also to receive the members of the Parliament.   When they arrived
they found the street packed with spectators, and it was clearly no
feeling of opposition that filled them ; it was an assumed, or genuine,
enthusiasm over the arrival of the Prince of the Land.   Government
buildings bristled with uniforms, and what was to be seen and heard
here did not correspond in the least with what had been read every
day for months in the newspapers of the declarations of the democratic Parliament of Berlin, the democratic sentiments of Berlin
and Breslau.   Here all matters of form, and the feelings one heard
expressed, were as monarchical as ever.   Members of Parliament
could scarcely find room to get in, and were obliged to stand one
behind another, three or four deep, in the room where the King
desired to receive them, and where he must therefore receive them
as a featureless crowd.   He walked in, helmet in hand, and Heinrich
von Gagern welcomed him in dignified terms, conforming to the
then proud status of the Parliament.   The King interrupted him to
take leave of the Regent who passed, at the very moment, from a
room at the back through the reception chamber.   The interruption
was short and apparently accidental, but gave much displeasure.
Gagern himself, full of assurance and dignity at a social function, then
proceeded calmly with his address and brought it to a close.   The

---

[1] *Das erste deutsche Parlament.*

rôle of mere listener seemed difficult for the King ; he interjected one or two observations, but now, when Gagern ended, kept silence, and permitted the latter to present members to him as he passed round, close to the semi-circle. It was the merest formality, for the ranks were too deep, and Gagern could only give the names of the foremost. Then the King placed his helmet on a table close by, made with his hand, in which he held a handkerchief, a gesture of introduction or invitation, and spoke fluently and quickly in a flexible tenor voice a few words on ' eye to eye acquaintanceship,' and how attentively he was following proceedings in the *Paulskirche*. Unexpectedly he then raised his voice of a sudden, and, in direct reference to Gagern's address, to the ' bold stroke,' [1] and to the national sovereignty which the *Paulskirche* claimed, added in clearly articulated tones : ' Do not forget that there are still Princes in Germany, and that I am one of them.'

Therewith he turned himself to go, and one of the Prussian officers, who was a member, raised a cheer, which was taken up vigorously by the numerous company in all the rooms.

In this chapter, which is, as stated, by way of interlude, may be introduced Laube's account of the lighter side of the National Assembly's activities at Frankfort. As a relief from the boredom of interminable debates on fundamental rights members took to caricature. Artists joined forces, and soon the shop-windows of Frankfort were displaying lively sketches of the weaknesses, eccentricities, and absurdities of the great men assembled in the *Paulskirche*. German caricature is often coarse and brutal, but it must be admitted that many of the skits produced at Frankfort were as witty as can fairly be demanded : [2]

Caricature soon announced itself in the art-dealers' windows. But people did not recognise its meaning as a symptom : they still nursed the belief they were a reflection of the French Revolution of 1789. During the actual onset of that revolution it would have occurred to no aristocrat to popularise the speakers of the ' mountain ' by his drawings, as Herr von Boddien, a tall and gallant Prussian cavalry officer began to do with his colleagues in the *Paulskirche*. He sat on the Right, and held the gentlemen on the Left as even then so little dangerous, that he placarded abroad as a canary-bird one of the grimmest of their peer-killers, who was far from content with the abolition of privileges of rank, a certain Herr Rösler, a school-teacher from Öls. Close shorn, red-haired, beak-nosed and dressed in yellow nankeen, he aroused, spectacles and all, as ' The Imperial Canary

---

[1] The ' bold stroke ' was Gagern's capture of the Archduke John, and his audacity in proposing his election as Regent. The expression itself was Carl Mathy's.

[2] *Das erste deutsche Parlament,* ii. p. 95.

Bird ' (' sings little, talks much, lives on his salary ') general amusement, though through no merit of his own. Similar ' imperial offices ' were distributed daily, and the stream of caricatures swelled like the Nile. Schlöffel (a radical) as the Hyena of Parliament ; Blum as Sir Robert, who grasps brotherly the proffered hand of a French general, whereupon the entire French army instantly disbands ; Eisenmann (of the Right) equipped with telescope on telescope, who cannot discover, and finally does discover, Reaction ; Moritz Mohl, who seeks to bring forward a resolution against the emancipation of the Jews, and on whose shoulders the heavy Israelite Riesser sits so much at ease, that the evil-counselled Moritz, bent double, groans from the tribune : ' It becomes pretty heavy, this resolution.' Crushing was the caricature of Vogt with the title : ' No standpoint whatever.' [1] As a tramp, hatless and with knotty staff, he wanders through the air, a pair of strangled conservatives for knapsack on his shoulders, a city collapsing in ruins and flames beneath his feet. First and foremost fall the church towers left and right, and all the great buildings into the bargain. He had on the constitutional church question quite naïvely announced : ' Here I can say that I stand really elevated above all parties, on a standpoint so absolutely neutral that I can almost say it is no standpoint at all.'

Presently, however, all caricatures were eclipsed by the invention of a type as brilliant as any that ever pointed a moral for politicians in Germany or elsewhere, one Herr Piepmeyer.[2] Laube tells us : ' A caricature developed into the actual creation of a character and thereby became classic. Such was Piepmeyer. In him a new species was represented. The modern weaknesses of politicians were combined in his single figure ; and therefore this figure, at least in its main features, cannot be passed over by the historian. It is just such times as ours, when a great reform is called for, and, favoured by chance, a great revolution is in course of simulation, that can and must produce a Piepmeyer, the unprincipled hero of principle, the slave of freedom, the creature of popularity, the knave with the gift of swelling phrases.' [3] The following is Laube's account of the gentleman :

Before the election Piepmeyer has convinced one section of his constituents of the strength of his opinions in favour of a constitutional monarchy, and, in another corner, another section of the purity and vigour of his republican principles. He is elected unani-

---

[1] See page 380.
[2] *The Opinions and Performances of Herr Piepmeyer*, by J. H. Detmold, with illustrations by A. Schrödter.
[3] *Das erste deutsche Parlament*, ii. p. 107.

mously. It is not until he enters the *Paulskirche* that he feels any uncertainty as to whether he shall take his seat on the Right or the Left. In this condition he makes the acquaintance of a journalist who clears up many things for him. An inclination towards the Left suggests itself as timely, and is confirmed. He buys himself a parliamentary hat and gives it, by treading on it, the necessary parliamentary shape. In explanation it will suffice to say that the fashion in hats generally corresponded during the years 1848 and 1849 with the prevailing principles in politics. The tall unbending chimney-pot hat disappeared with the March Revolution and made way for the soft felt, yielding to every impression. The higher the tide of revolution rose, the more curly the brim of the hat, and the lower the tide sank in the year 1849 the stiffer again became the hat's material. Hand in hand with the hat went the beard, the luxuriance of which was a symptom of the luxuriance of freedom. Piepmeyer, no longer a mere lad, decided to allow nature a free hand in this regard and soon acquired the aspect of a devil-may-care sort of man. Meanwhile he hands Robert Blum his album, who inscribes in it the line ' Be ever faithful and sincere ! ' Then his friend, the journalist, calls his attention to the fact that Germany still lacks an exclusively national drink of its own, and, with that, plunges him into the birth-pangs of a great political idea. ' The problem is to devise a drink that preserves the right mean between wine, beer and brandy, and thus on the one hand takes account of the inclinations and tendencies of the various German stocks, and on the other recognises the idea of German unity.' He makes expensive and not altogether dis-agreeable experiments. To his horror he hears that the ' Politico-Economical Committee ' is engaged on the same business, and there-fore may easily forestall him in the discovery. Moritz Mohl, Philipp Schwarzenberg, Lette and Eisenstuck (well-known Economists) have great weight in this dreaded Committee ; the burning desire asserts itself in Piepmeyer to become member of a Committee for which he feels himself thoroughly cut out. He manages to contrive at least an entrance into the Registrar's office. There sits, working alone, a man in a grey overcoat and with a blond head of hair. Even from the back he recognises in him the inexorable Professor of Political Economy, Moritz Mohl, and steps up on tiptoe, so as not to disturb Archimedes and his circle ; he wants only to read and to enjoy the Registrar's labels. He reads : ' Military concerns,' ' The Ill-treatment of Cabin-boys by Sailors,' ' The Immortality of the Soul,' ' Various Measures against Bugs : N.B. To be dealt with confidentially,' ' On Intercourse with Men,' ' An Improvement in Scissors for cutting Paper. Report by Freiherr von Wordy,' ' The Constitution of the German Nation,' ' Measures for the Pacification of Mexico,' ' Improvements in Braces for Trousers,' ' The Like in Heavy Ordnance,' ' The Relationship between Church and State,' ' The Education of Children of both Sexes.'—Admiringly he passes all this in review, and withdraws, happy and envious, as quietly as he had come. The endless reading of newspapers is so disturbing ! To-day he feels impelled to consider ' whether in view of most recent developments it will not be expedient to range his political convictions rather more to the Right ; to-morrow whether expedience does not call for a move rather in the direction of the Left.' Meantime he has again and again sent up his name to speak, but only just as the discussion is closed and the exasperated Gagern is within his rights in closuring him. Conscientiously he announces this to his constituents every time. Finally, however, he does reach the Tribune for the first time—only to support a motion that has already been withdrawn. This he announces to his constituents, and also to his wife. Nevertheless he burns the midnight oil, and sits in his shirt-sleeves practising a speech before the looking-glass, with the appropriate turns of phrase and gestures. In particular the following expressions, and corresponding attitudes, commend themselves to him ;—I challenge the National Ministry ! We desire to have regard to the wishes of the People. From my point of view. The Convention, gentlemen, the Convention ! Reaction, undisguised Reaction ! A treacherous Camarilla, a brutal Soldateska ! No hand's breadth of German soil ! Heaven's opening eye of Freedom !

Scenes at his club follow, with conferences over indispensable ' questions.' It is on questions that Piepmeyer concentrates his energies after he has with dubious success delivered a speech, in connection with which he has pleaded with Herr Wiegard for a suitable number of ' Hear, hears ' and ' cheers ' in the shorthand report. Questions, after all, are the most interesting line. The Democratic Union of the town where he resides (Rederkosa), whose general influence tends to drive him further and further to the Left, attaches, on principle, great importance to questions. . . . The questions asked by Piepmeyer of Rederkosa soar not only into European politics, but even to World politics. He has become quite at home with his constituents, and wishes to let them know, not merely through some commonplace division list, but also, more piquantly, by newspaper advertisement, that at Frankfort he has ' arrived,' and sits well on the Left ; and so he rises to ask, in reference to the discovery of gold in California, ' What steps has the Government taken to prevent a depreciation of the gold in the coffers of the State ? ' . . .

The name of Piepmeyerei was soon given to a quality which is in truth always present as a weakness in human nature, but is only conspicuous in times of mild terrorism. Whoever had not the courage to become unpopular played the Piepmeyer. In the course of the debates on fundamental rights this weakness revealed itself in a hundred ways. A conception of freedom, a worthy conception, dear to every friend of man, was propounded in a wrong context or impudently exaggerated, as happened daily in the course of every debate ; it was set ablaze with filthy, reeking combustibles, with sulphur and pitch and nasty resin—and who had the courage to repudiate it under the hisses and cries of shame from the chirruping grasshoppers ? Not the poltroon on the left Centre ; not the short-sighted, nor the feather-brained, who does not see or will not learn how deeply a fundamental word strikes its roots : they all played Piepmeyer. The Left terrorised the left Centre, and the left Centre terrorised many a weak soul on the right Centre. It was Piepmeyer here, Piepmeyer there ! Just so, but in the reverse direction, travelled intimidation from the Right, when established Authority stood with the reins of terror in her hand. Piepmeyer is, in a word, the antithesis to the man really independent, really free, him who allows himself in voting to be diverted by neither praise nor blame, by neither reward nor punishment.

A racy view of Germany in the summer of 1848 is given in a letter [1] from Michael Bakunin to Herwegh :

Germany exhibits the most interesting and the most remarkable of spectacles ; not a sham-fight, (but) a battle between shadows that take themselves for realities and yet feel every moment their utter feebleness, and involuntarily show it. The official reaction and the official revolution compete in futility and stupidity, and you have, as well, all the hollow philosophic-religious-political-poetical-comfortable-ponderous phrases which, after haunting our German brains for so long, now come to light. . . . The collapse of Austria is for us Slavs, and indeed for the whole revolutionary party, a vital concern.

This chapter of miscellanies may end with a letter [2] from poet to poet, Justinus Kerner to Uhland, which illuminates the situation at the time as it existed in countless little towns all over Germany :

WEINSBERG, 29th July 1848.

To a sovereign representative one must write on foolscap. In addition to the Polish plait of the politician, which you have now to take your part in unravelling, I send you here yet another, a poetical one. . . . How things stand with my politics you can gather from the fact that when I was lately at Schönthal, and strolled about the ancient corridors of Romance, I prayed God He might bring to life again the Abbot and all his monks, and allow them to chase all the school-boys in their gymnastic kit to the devil. ' Now you know me ; I cannot be otherwise.' On the other hand I have given a son (Theobald Kerner) to the world who holds with the red republic and Herr Hecker. Ten town-drummers, who are learning the drum, drum before my little house from six in the morning to six at night to cheer my labours. Surely this alone may enable one heartily to excuse this beautiful period of German freedom and unity, wherein one man applies a boorish compulsion to another, and people have

---

[1] *Briefe von und an G. Herwegh* (K.).
[2] *Kerners Briefwechsel.*

one another by the hair. 'Tis good, old fellow, that we're now turned sixty years old ! Perhaps I may still come, in company with the deceased wig-maker Gross, from Tübingen to Frankfort, in order to inspect for myself the tousled pig-tail of the German realm, unless Cavaignac hews it asunder beforehand, or some other Melac, which in league with the cholera is possibly the one radical cure.

CHAPTER VI

THE ARMISTICE OF MALMÖ AND THE REVOLUTIONARY OUTBREAK AT FRANKFORT

THE news of the armistice arranged at Malmö came with a great shock to public opinion all over Germany; but the National Assembly at Frankfort was peculiarly affected, for there, but a few weeks earlier, Germany's honour had been pledged by solemn resolution as guarantee for the rights, as understood in Germany, of the two Duchies. It was recognised that Prussia had sheathed the sword practically at the dictation of Great Britain, France, and Russia; it was forgotten that Prussia had been left by other German states without active support. Shame took possession of the German people, and shame, in a people nourished on hate as a virtue, cannot exist without resentment. Twin objects of resentment, now, were the Prussian Government and the National Assembly.

Laube describes [1] in graphic language the announcement of the armistice in the *Paulskirche*, and the impression it made :

What a terrible thunderbolt it was when on the 4th September at the very beginning of the sitting, the then Minister of Foreign Affairs, Heckscher, suddenly appeared on the tribune, pale and with nerves evidently unstrung, to announce that an armistice had been concluded at Malmö, and that certainly the terms contained not unimportant deviations from the substance of the stipulations which the Central Authority had attached as conditions to its sanctioning a settlement. Dahlmann interpellated the National Minister and concluded:—' You have, however, received the conditions of the armistice through official channels. I venture to remind you of one thing only : on the 9th June, not three months ago, it was resolved here in the *Paulskirche*, that in the Schleswig-Holstein question the honour of Germany should be guaranteed—the honour of Germany !.' This was the lightning-flash in which the storm brooding over the Church discharged itself, and so violently, that not a heart in the vast room was untouched, and that all rose from their seats in

---

[1] *Das erste deutsche Parlament*, ii. p. 189.

tempestuous applause, as without adding a word more (the speaker) stepped down among the deeply moved assembly. That oft-abused expression ' The honour of Germany ! ' Here it was genuine.

In the debate next day Dahlmann concluded his speech as follows :

Is not then the Schleswig-Holstein question a German question ? If so, let me tell you what has weighed infinitely more, infinitely heavier, with the whole Committee than Schleswig-Holstein. It is the consideration of our universal German Fatherland. . . . What is it that has made the Englishman so great ? It is assuredly not his world-dominating fleet, assuredly not his glorious and wealthy conquests in every quarter of the globe ! One fact, one quite simple fact has made him great : every single Englishman counts for England as much as all England ; every single Englishman counts for England as much as the whole Fatherland—and in our case there are many hundreds of thousands !—It was in a spirit of fore-boding that I said to you on the 9th June, ' It is not this isolated question of Schleswig that rouses so many efforts, so many attacks upon us, but it is the Unity of Germany (Loud cheers from all sides). This new German might, which has never yet been seen so long as Germany has existed, which has its centre here in the *Paulskirche*, and over which the confidence of the whole German people keeps watch, this new growth is to be nipped in the shoot ; had people the power it would be disintegrated on all sides, and finally broken to bits (General applause). If at the first trial that approaches us, at the first sign of danger, we bow ourselves, pusillanimous at the outset, in the face of foreign powers, then never will you raise your heads proudly again (Loud applause). Think on these words of mine. Never ! (Renewed applause.) Certainly it is not despotism, of that I am sure, but anarchy, that will rule within these walls, and far outside them, and they will fall who now believe in their madness that they triumph over us (Loud applause, and commotion). I have spoken. May His hand prevail, Who knows how to guide the counsels of men to right conclusions ! ' (Exceptional, and long-continued applause.)

Finally, after the most heated of debates, in which there were symptoms of the threatening revolt, Parliament accepted the armistice. Ludwig Simon, the radical of radicals, had exclaimed : ' We too, for we know how to honour the services of great men, dwell with pleasure on the portraits of the Great Elector and Frederick the Great. But the Great Elector and Frederick the Great would turn in their graves could they learn how their memory has been abused, to trample Germany in the dust before Denmark ! '

On 17th September, the day after the final resolution of the

Assembly accepting the armistice, a revolutionary assembly was held on the Pfingstweide, a large meadow outside the city gates. The following is Klein's summary of the account given in Brockhaus's *Die Gegenwart* :

At a late hour on the evening of 16th September, in a darkened house, after agitated debate and much disorder, the Parliament had by a majority of twenty-one certainly not approved, but had allowed to stand, the Armistice of Malmö. After 8 P.M. the President of the Assembly announced the result of the voting. The *Paulskirche* shook with a heartrending, ear-splitting uproar, in the Assembly, the rooms underneath, and the gallery. Amid the tumult strange figures called people to a conference in the Stadtallee ; on leaving the house representatives of the majority and, in the confusion, also of the minority, were jeered at, insulted, and driven to flight. The West-end Hall, the meeting-place of the moderate Left, was cleared as if by Vandals ; the mob that had marched there from the Stadtallee searched for old Turnvater Jahn, who only got quit of their attentions at the risk of his life. Similar scenes of destruction began at the Englischer Hof, where the mob were after Heckscher, who, on the fateful 18th September, escaped death as by a miracle. The halloa of the wild huntsman rang through the city ; law and authority were powerless. Several leaders of the most radical clubs of Frankfort improvised a united meeting, and resolved to issue invitations for a general gathering of the people on the following day (Sunday). . . . This assembly of the people was held at 4 P.M. on the Pfingstweide, a large meadow in front of the Allerheiligen Gate, and right against the arrival platform of the Hanauer Railway-station, which brought ominous reinforcements. There may have been from ten to twelve thousand men brought together, some out of curiosity, but many carrying cudgels, pistols, and the red feather in the hat. The ringleaders were the representatives Zitz and Schlöffel, and the ' colporteur of barricades,' Germain Metternich. Then came the resolutions : ' To use leaded type,' to threaten the majority of the National Assembly with loss of house and life, in order to induce them to clear out. Even that seemed too mild for those who were blind with rage. The leaders of the chorus, among them a young man from Schleswig-Holstein, crossed the T's for them. Make barricades of your bodies ; disperse the betrayers of the people, the National Assembly ; away with the ' money-bags,' the *Bourgeoisie* ! Even the Left must go, for they play havoc, they and their half-measures ! Only the extreme Left can, shall, and must guide the movement to its goal : And so the ' resolution ' was finally adopted by a show of several hundred hands and several thousand cudgels ; the majority of the National Assembly were declared to be ' traitors to the German people, to German freedom, and to German honour ' ; the German Nation was to be instructed in this sense ; but before all things this ' resolution ' was to be ' communicated by a deputation' to the National Assembly itself. Sympathisers from outside were expressly enjoined to remain in the city next day in order to ' give weight to' the resolution. A section of the wild crowd marched afterwards to the Deutscher Hof, the meeting-place of the Left, to demand their withdrawal *en masse*. As they came storming on, Vogt waved them back ; Venedey remonstrated with them on the heinousness of their assault. Both were jeered at, Venedey especially.

Next morning the mob attacked the *Paulskirche*. Some such attack was expected, and arrangements had been made to summon troops from Mainz. The mob, however, acted too soon, and found the north side of the building unguarded. Laube's account[1] of this exciting scene ends with the rescue of the Assembly by Prussian troops. Nothing could show more clearly the powerlessness of the ' first German Parliament,' a body without even the means of self-defence.

Some belated representatives, Riesser among them, came from the north side and made for the doorway. The mob seized the opportunity and pressed after them. Riesser turned round in vain to hold them back ; the crowd shoved and forced him with them through the first door, and through the second, only two steps further on. Behind this second door there is another small space about two paces in width, separated from the interior of the Church by a glass door without fastening. The torrent of men had forced its way into this space when some of the Parliament servants noticed what was happening, and hurried up to support the resistance of Riesser. Several représentatives who sat next to the glass door on the left and right, did the same, and so the Assembly, deadly still in a moment, became aware of the incursion. It was about ten o'clock. Gagern rose in the full strength and beauty of his commanding presence—with his keen eyes he could plainly see the tumult behind the glass door—and called on members to keep their seats without any sign of disquiet : he expected that they would face in dignified silence the attack that threatened. Any one who had risen resumed his seat ; only the ladies on the lower seats reserved for spectators on the south side of the Church began to make their escape. The tumult at the glass door lasted only a short time. The servants and several representatives succeeded in pushing back the first ranks of the aggressors, men of the rabble, behind the middle door, and in securing this by a little bolt that was fortunately on it. Then began the attack on this middle door, which the mob endeavoured to force, or smash in. It was much weaker than the first door, which gives on to the street, and a wooden panel yielded under the thrust and the blows. The crack grew

---

[1] *Das erste deutsche Parlament,* ii. p. 272.

wider under the weight of the pressure applied to it, so that one could see through it, and it was improbable that the weak bolt would long withstand the force against it. We sitting there above were prepared every moment for the inrush of the torrent. The colossal figure of the historian Gfrörer, sitting, as it happened, in the neighbourhood of the door, never made so fine an impression in the *Paulskirche* as at this moment. He stood, armed with his stick, right against the glass door, evidently proclaiming that every intruder would find in him a redoubtable obstacle. Now the door is yielding, is the cry—despite the fact that every man's weight on our side was propping it—now it's bursting !—then all at once the noise of blows and shouting outside ceased, the pressure relaxed, and we saw that in the Diplomats' Gallery, which was further west on this side, every one was pressing to the windows. Something new must be taking place outside. Gagern called out : ' Leave the windows, gentlemen.' ' No comedy here ! ' called a voice from the Left. Blum's, I think. ' No comedy outside ! ' rejoined a voice from the Right.

For the rest there was silence, and as Gagern had firmly detained on the tribune, all through this mysterious interlude outside the walls, the member he had called upon to speak as to standing orders, so he continued undisturbed his duties as President : ' Three proposals have been brought forward, which I shall proceed to put to the vote.' The help without came from the Prussian troops. Although far from the scene of the incursion, the officer had none the less observed what was going on, and had made his men fall in and march down. Still the mob had not given way. Every moment they expected to see the door fly open ; then inside we go, thought they, despite the soldiers ! In the wild disorder their work would then be cut out for them, to hunt out who were representatives, who were of the people. The officer had ordered the crowd to disperse. They yielded not. He had made his men load. They yielded not—the doors might fly open any moment—' Fix bayonets ! Charge ! ' he had ordered at last ; and the bayonet-charge had scattered the mob, and forced even those who were storming the door to beat a retreat.

Then followed fighting in the streets, of which Laube's account[1] is as follows :

There was continual rattle of musketry, and an elegantly dressed young man came up to us on the Zeil with the remark we had better not go beyond the bend of the street, for even outside the ostensible line of fire thoughtless bullets wandered here and there. As proof he displayed his smoke-blackened cigar, which had just been knocked out of his mouth by such a bullet and spoiled. The cigar, as the saying goes, had drawn only too well, and the young man was somewhat excited by this merry turn. We saw the wounded being carried past ; we saw adjutants galloping by, particularly a slim

---

[1] *Das erste deutsche Parlament,* ii. p. 287.

young Austrian who was got up as for a dance with his close-fitting white tunic and scarf of black and gold, his képi and feathers, and white kid gloves twisted in the reins of his horse. Boddien too, high on horseback, dashed past along the Zeil right into the fire-zone, and we heard that he was helping to direct the attack on this side. They made slow progress, either to spare bloodshed, or because there were too few troops. . . . The Darmstadt guns arrived, and drew up in the Horse-market and by the main guard-house ; Darmstadt troops, wide-awake, intelligent, smart-looking fellows, marched on from another street, and greeted their guns with a rousing cheer. The guns got ready to rattle down the Zeil. Then came an anxious pause ; day declined more and more. All waited in suspense, wondering whether (the truce) would last longer and spoil a decisive result. The artillerymen sat on their horses in front of and near the cannon, and waited likewise ; then we heard suddenly the command ' Forward ! ' and again ' Forward ! ' and yet a third time, ' Forward ! ' and off at a trot went cannon and escort down the Zeil. The effect after such a feeling of sus-pense was so great, that the numerous spectators, certainly for the most part hostile to the insurrection, broke out into general cheer-ing. We heard the cannon pull up away down on the Zeil, and listened to hear if the thundering report were to follow. Simul-taneously we thought we heard far over there to the south, rather in the direction of the Old Bridge, a fresh volley of musketry. ' Those are the Darmstädter Rifles,' cried one of us who had come back with news from the Eschenheimer Gasse, ' they 're working their way with marvellous courage and skill through the barricades, right up the Fahrgasse, in order to join hands with our fellows.' ' So the truce is up ! ' ' Up ! ' The Left threatened Heaven and Hell if more civilian blood were spilt, and laid the whole responsi-bility on Schmerling. ' I 'll bear it,' he replied from behind the table in his dry Austrian way, ' and Boddien and Deetz are on the spot, and——' Then thundered forth the first report from the Hessian cannon.

It was the most extraordinary case of a revolutionary battle that you can conceive. The insurgents fought against authorities which were actually constituted as the result of universal suffrage ; therefore the glamour and the savour of an outraged feeling of justice, forced to acts of violence, was wanting. But those attacked defended themselves with troops, whose authentic masters had been but shortly before the opponents of those now assailed, and probably in a short time would be so again.

On this street-fighting we have an interesting sidelight in a letter from Schopenhauer,[1] the one brightly written letter in this book from a philosopher, and the only one not informed with the idea that a German philosopher's mere existence, like

[1] *Schopenhauers Briefe, 1813-1860.*

that of Stevenson's lover, is not only a thing creditable in
itself, but also of advantage to the world at large :

FRANKFORT-ON-MAIN, 2nd March 1849.

Things with me are as of old : Atma [Schopenhauer's poodle]
sends best greetings. But what experiences we 've had ! Just
think, barricades on the bridge and the ruffians standing right up
against my house, aiming and shooting at the soldiers in the Fahrgasse, whose return volleys shook the house : suddenly voices and
a great row at the closed door of my room : I, thinking it is the
sovereign mob, jam the door with the bar : then come alarming
blows against it : finally the clear voice of my maid, ' It is only
some Austrians.' I opened at once to these worthy friends : twenty
thorough Bohemians in blue trousers came tumbling in, to fire
from my windows on the sovereign people : soon, however, they
bethink themselves 'twill go better from next door. From the first
floor the officer reconnoitres the mob behind the barricade ; at
once I send him the large pair of opera glasses, with which you once
saw the balloon.—And ψυχῶν σοφῶν τοῦτ' ἐστι φροντιστήριον ! (What
a temple of thought for spirits of wisdom !)

That afternoon two members of the National Assembly,
Prince Lichnowsky and General von Auerswald, both of them
aristocrats who had developed liberal sympathies, were brutally
murdered outside Frankfort by Hessian villagers on their way
to the city. They had ridden out to make a reconnaissance ;
for Hessian troops were expected. On encountering the
threatening mob they endeavoured to escape, but chose their
course ill. Finally they took refuge in a market-garden, the
owner of which offered to conceal them, but their horses
betrayed them. Laube's accounts [1] of the murders and of the
funeral of the two victims are fine pieces of descriptive writing,
and contain passages of real eloquence :

Hardly had horse and rider disappeared in the gardener's cottage,
when their enemies were on them, like sleuth-hounds on a horse's
track. ' The horses are in here ! They must be here ! ' And the
garden was surrounded, and the house searched. In the house
itself people came with the utmost good will to the fugitives' assistance. Auerswald had been given a dressing-gown, to lend him the
appearance of one living in the house ; Lichnowsky had been taken
into a cellar and concealed there behind a lattice partition. In
vain ! Auerswald, who would probably have been recognised by
no one, and who was actually murdered without people knowing
whom they were slaughtering, did not remain in his dressing-gown
calmly in the open room like an inmate, but fled to the loft, and

---

[1] *Das erste deutsche Parlament*, ii., 303, and *Erinnerungen* (K.).

was found there. He was hauled down the stairs and fired at.
Without further parleying the mob dragged the stunned man outside
the cottage, through the very gate by which he had entered the
garden, and there on the little bridge right against the garden gate
he was struck down like a wild beast. His dying body rolled over
into a dry ditch. A woman brutalised by politics, who is said to
have been a woman writer, struck at him with her umbrella and
incited the maddened crowd of men to kill him.

Probably Lichnowsky heard all this. The cellar was so shallow
that only a few steps led down to it, and it was past the cellar door
that Auerswald was dragged. Now came the cellar's turn. There
were three lattice partitions there side by side. Lichnowsky was in
the middle one and had thrown himself on what is called a fruit-shelf
at the back. This fruit-shelf was broken, and he was thus really
hidden, for the board faced a person looking in, and concealed any
one who had slipped down against the wall. But fate played a
spiteful game with him : a corner of his coat hung over the board,
just enough to be seen. The occupant of the house who had to open
the cellar for the bloodthirsty crew, endeavoured to deceive them
with regard to the existence of the middle partition : he opened that
on the right and that on the left, and the ruse succeeded. They left
the cellar with curses, and the prisoner could breathe again. But
the *two* horses that were found in the cow-house spoke too strongly
for the fact that the second fugitive must also be to hand. The
house was searched again from top to bottom, and so the mob
visited the cellar for a second time and—discovered the middle door.
The gardener's lad, who had to strike a light, endeavoured to prevent
them from breaking in the door without more ado, and was wounded
in consequence. They broke open the door to the accompaniment of
the cries of the young lad, and stepped in. Nothing ! No one was
visible, but wait—there ! They caught sight of the corner of a coat ;
the victim was found. As the unhappy man came out he addressed
in this awful moment some earnest words to his persecutors, to the
effect that he was ready to use his best efforts to help the people.
To no purpose. They dealt with him as with Auerswald, but a man
of superior station, Dr. Hoddes by name, arrived on the scene from
Bornheim close by, and succeeded in starting the idea that Lichnowsky should not be killed at once, but conveyed to Bornheim.
There he might serve, in the appropriate expression of the moment,
as a hostage, a ' Prussian ' prisoner as against some rebel who had
been taken by the Prussians in the city. In accordance with this
plan for postponement, the grisly crowd conveyed him across the
little bridge, right past Auerswald's corpse. From there a narrow
avenue of poplars, with a broad footpath, led across the meadow to
Bornheim. They had got about three hundred paces down this
avenue when one of the murderers lost all patience and grabbed at
Lichnowsky's clothing. Lichnowsky turned to defend himself and
gripped a gun-barrel that was pointed at him, the scuffle became
general, and blows descended on him, rained on him ; he was hacked

to pieces. ' Out of the way, there ! ' shouted several ; way was made, and the bullets rattled on the collapsing orator of the *Pauls-kirche*, on the representative of the German Parliament, who had incurred the displeasure of the sovereign people of one small townlet. There on the meadow, which lies high, and gives a view on the right, over the Taunus, and on the left, over Frankfort and its ancient Cathedral, there he lay, the man who had so long been fortune's favourite, weltering in his blood, in sight of the beautiful world to which he clung so keenly, and could not live, could not die. With savage jeers the murderers went off. Dying slowly, for the breath left his body with no less obstinate reluctance than his soul the earth ; dying in agony, he was carried back to that unlucky cottage in the garden. There he dictated his will. ' My heir is my brother Carl—no ! I revoke ' he said with breaking voice—and this is the most lovable incident I know of in his life—' I revoke ! My heir is the Duchess of Sagan.' She, the former Duchess of Dino-Talleyrand, was one of the richest women in the country, and he was, people say, loved by her. Late at night, still amid the rattle of musketry, he was carried to the hospital in town, and there it was not until close on midnight that he passed away, a victim of political hatred. Even to-day I hardly believe that he lives no more, although I saw him with my own eyes laid in the grave. He belonged to those men who seem gifted with everything for this world, and this world only.

THE FUNERAL OF LICHNOWSKY AND AUERSWALD
ON 19TH SEPTEMBER 1848

The bodies of the murdered men, Lichnowsky and Auerswald, were buried in the cemetery. The cemetery was packed with people. All members of Parliament were there, next to the coffins ; behind us were people sympathetic and defiant, the latter in deep masses. One could see by their faces that resentment was stronger than pity. Parties stood here in broad daylight side by side. There was a feeling of awe as Wilhelm Jordan began the funeral oration. He above all was the object of the hatred of the men of the barricades, who were there among his hearers ; for he had first belonged to the Left, but had later severed himself from them and their extra-vagances. And he of all others delivered the funeral oration. He spoke in chilling tones, but hot anger pulsed through his words. He threw the responsibility for this atrocity on the soul of the insurgents in menacing tones. One thought that at any moment the terrible, uncompromising indictment might drive the audience he was accusing to an outbreak, to a fight over the still open graves. This feeling lay like a monstrous ink-black thundercloud over us. We marvelled at Jordan's cool defiant courage, and yet trembled before every new biting word, lest it might discharge the storm and the lightning flash spread destruction. All was still, as still as death, when he finished. The clods of earth rolled down on to the coffins ; we heard this comfortless noise from far, and each one of us departed in silence through the staring crowd, pondering in his heart how heavy a task is the moulding of a new form of government, and what a price has to be paid for it.

The outbreak was stamped out in a few hours, but light is thrown on the aftermath, in the shape of prisoners and their treatment, by Robert von Mohl : [1]

A service of another sort (than the carrying through of certain financial measures) was this : in all probability I saved a number of men from death by suffocation, and so spared the Assembly and the National Ministry an unheard-of scandal. Late at night on 18th September, and thus after the victory over the insurrection had declared itself, but before the complete cessation of the fighting, as I was passing the main guard-house on the Horse-market I saw that prisoners were being brought there from all sides by soldiers, and summarily thrust into a cellar beneath the guard-house. I wished to know what was going on there, and in company with some officers who happened to be on the spot went down to the cellar, or, to speak more correctly, intended to go down, but was stopped on the stairs from going further by unendurable heat and a frightful stench. There were hundreds of men packed together in the narrow room, who were calling for air, for water, for medical attention, and were only withheld from breaking out by the muzzles of the guns of their numerous guard. That help must be found here, and quickly, was clear ; but no one knew what to advise. There was no place in the city capable of guarding securely so large and, in part, so desperate a body of prisoners. Therefore I decided to telegraph to the Governor of Mainz, and ask him to take charge of the prisoners. On the prompt arrival of a favourable reply I went to the General Officer commanding the troops, General Nobili, arranged with him for the military transport of the prisoners by rail, and had the satisfaction after a few hours of seeing the cellar entirely cleared. The sight of any one as he was brought out into the fresh air showed most clearly how urgent had been the need for help. In the prison within a fort at Calcutta known as the Black Hole, one hundred and forty-six Englishmen were thrown by the Bengalese in the year 1756, and after a very short time only twenty-three came out alive. I have not the slightest doubt that the scene of the Black Hole of Calcutta would have been re-enacted had the prisoners (I believe there were six hundred to seven hundred of them) been left in the hole over night. Too much reliance could not have been placed on sympathy from the side of the soldiers, who were embittered in the highest degree by the losses they had sustained, and the treachery with which much of the fighting had been conducted.

Two comments on this September outbreak, both from

[1] *Lebenserinnerungen* (K.).

members of the Assembly, but taking different points of view,
are worth quoting, with Heller's characterisation of the speakers.
The first we take is that of Gabriel Riesser, a Jew, who ultimately became, in 1860, as Councillor of the High Court, the
first German judge of the Jewish faith. Of him Heller says : [1]

> Gabriel Riesser, a lawyer from Hamburg, and sent to Frankfort
> as representative for Lauenburg, belonged heart and soul to Judaism.
> We have to ascribe it to the reaction after oppression that at every
> point in our agitated quarter of the globe, in Paris and Genoa, in
> Vienna and Venice, in Berlin and Anhalt-Dessau, the Jews played
> a conspicuous part in the reshaping of affairs. Here to the good
> of the cause, there to its prejudice, but always with effect. We
> know of old that they possess zeal and intelligence in a degree which
> the German race in particular may well take as an example. We
> know too that they are, if seldom creative artists, very often
> masterly virtuosos. But to those among us who ascribe to them
> all qualities rather than that of amiability, we may venture to
> present the figure of Herr Riesser as that of a man whose amiability
> carries absolute conviction. Modest, in spite of his remarkable
> gifts, full of assurance, but only in a good cause, and a patriot. Of
> the cosmopolitan watering down of races, of the lamentable policy
> of generalisation and disintegration, which the Jews, as a result
> of the consciousness of their homeless condition, have introduced
> first into literature and then, working from the side of the Left,
> into parliamentary chambers, there is not a drop in Riesser's blood,
> not a thought in his brain. The wrongs which the race he loves so
> passionately, and defends with so glowing a sense of honour, have
> had to submit to in Germany, have not made him waver for one
> moment in his belief in, his devotion to, our Fatherland. Such
> characters are worthy of a share in the task of laying its foundations.

When the question of a law for the protection of the Assembly,
and of the officials of the Central Authority, was under discussion
in October, Riesser said :

> I cannot wipe away from my mind the impression of these events
> like dust from my feet, and when a man (Vogt) tells us that even
> passion has a right to have its say in politics, then we can claim
> that there is some good in the passion of indignant Justice. . . . I
> declare solemnly that I fear death not at all, but I do fear crime. I
> fear it not only for the sake of its victims, but also for the sake
> of its instigators and its instruments, for the sake of the Fatherland,
> whose honour it undermines, whose freedom and future it endangers.

Against this we have to set Ludwig Simon-Trier's declaration.
Klein quotes his entry in the Parliament Album : ' Frankly the

---

[1] *Brustbilder aus der Paulskirche.*

" democratic Monarchy " involves a fundamental contradiction. But it is precisely out of the actual existence of fundamental contradictions that further life is developed.' Heller's description of him is as follows :

Freedom without limits, without law, and without end, is his dream, his life, his ideal. Others stick the red cap on their heads as a fashion, the style of which pleases them, or as a piece of adornment which lends one at the present time an air of courage and advanced opinions ; Ludwig Simon alone wears it as a priestly tiara, in virtue of whose sanctity he is no longer himself, but the instrument of a mystic power. . . . The lava-stream of one of Simon's speeches discharges itself like Vesuvius to the accompaniment of thunder and lightning. The vivid flashes of sheet-lightning against the dark cloud fascinate the eyes, and even if the elemental force of destruction does give us a shudder of dismay, we still cannot gainsay it a certain admiration.

When summoned with others for examination as instigators of the insurrection, Simon said, much as all rebels say when rebellion has failed, but with more genuine eloquence than many :

You ask for the grounds of the insurrection. The insurrection is the result of the Revolution that was disowned. . . . We might now be a State had we seized the right moment, had we at the time of our coming together, when all pulses beat in sympathy and union was the goal, seized the moment enthusiastically, and so moulded in Frankfort the heart of Germany. Now, as a State, we are lost. We are now at best a University, where, in my judgment, a very tiresome lecture on politics is being delivered. . . .

We have seen the blossoms of freedom, but the evil spirit of old wandered nightly through the fields and poisoned the blossoms, and the people, betrayed, wring their bleeding hands after the fruit that is lost ! This is the real cause of the spasms that shake the whole German Fatherland.

Robert Blum wrote despairingly to his wife : [1]

FRANKFORT-ON-MAIN, *4th October* 1848.

In the National Assembly we are the victims of malicious persecutions, reduced to the most doleful position by the populace and their stupidity, treated as enemies and outlaws by the democrats in their folly ; thus we stand more isolated than ever, and have neither ahead of us nor behind us any hope. During these last weeks forces have been squandered and madly destroyed which, had they been more wisely combined and more carefully expended, would have sufficed to transform entirely the destinies of Germany. Never

---

[1] Klein.

have I been as tired of life and of work as I am now ; were it not a shame to desert one's comrades in misfortune, I would collect what I have left and either emigrate, or buy a mill or something of the sort in some quiet peaceful valley in South Germany, and never return to the world.

But we have to bear in mind that amid all this tumult and talk the strong Centre party kept its head. The tenacity with which some of its members held to the ideals which had forced Prussia to the front, despite the weakness and follies of Frederick William IV., is well illustrated by the remarkable letter [1] from father to son which is now to be given. The writer was one Adolf von Zerzog, of whom Mohl speaks as ' that glorious strong man, Zerzog of Regensburg, the incarnation of independence towards those above and those below ; hard-hitting, healthy common sense made flesh ; in speech and literary form of classic solidity, but with thoughts and turns that remind one of Jean Paul or of Shakespeare ; in outward appearance almost a savage, but with an intelligence cultured and well-informed.' A true type this of men who exist in Germany, men who are not easy to beat down ! He was, says Heller, a fine example of the Bavarian of the tougher sort, a man of intellectual culture but with the rough and powerful build of a peasant and a mountaineer. A country squire, he was informed with the soul of a people ' that lives on familiar terms with wind and weather, that shouts lustily with full lungs on the mountain side, that toils after the plough in the sweat of the brow, that hunts the wild game of the forest.' In his youth he had suffered under the persecutions of 1825, but sat in the National Assembly as a moderate. He was not a frequent speaker, but distinguished himself whenever he did give tongue by the strength of his voice, answering to his name as if he were shouting across the Danube. His constituents once ventured to send him an instruction. His reply was : ' The only intimation I receive from you or any one else is " God bless thee, Zerzog, and we trust we find thee well ! " '

It may well be that you will not live much longer, as your fathers did, the glorious life led by a host of young companions, honourable, lively and gay ; in the innocent enjoyment of God's beautiful world, and in full strength to enjoy it. Our universities shall be our pride for all time. Never was the nurture of knowledge more free ; nowhere more free this self-government of young men, free, like

---

[1] Given *in extenso* in R. Heller's *Brustbilder aus der Paulskirche.*

one to another in nature and in culture, knowing no law but that of courage and honour, untroubled by the heavy demands of the time and the prosy anxieties and needs of the Philistines, and carrying over into the life-struggle that awaits it an unbending and a generous heart ! Therefore you can still tell by looking at an old greybeard whether he was once a ' man.' And what a man ! See how his old eyes still flash over stories of the good old time and his dear companions ! Did the police and their pig-tails, the Jesuits and their wiles, officials and their stuck-up airs seek to harry our lives, we ourselves bothered ourselves not a whit, we leapt gaily over the knobbly fence, and if one of us was left hanging, did it matter much ? We paid our tribute to the time of ferment, but honourably and like university men, not with a grandfatherly grin of wisdom, or the wrinkled pretentiousness of a philosophical seven-months child.

The whole world has gone mad, and that Youth alone should retain its senses is hardly to be hoped for—but Youth shall remain youth and not bear the aspect of a disgusting, decrepit, untimely monkey-pup which dances to the pipe of a dirty knave, who maintains it is ' the spirit of the age.' One would think that it needs mighty little wit to see that one who has learnt something must know it better than one who is only setting about learning ; one would think that only a precious noodle would assert ' what we have not experienced and tested we understand better than what we have experienced and tested.' I have the fixed unyielding conviction that these are great donkeys ; but they don't believe it themselves, and you can see and hear any day how some whiskerless young cub, who will readily admit to you that he is not nearly equal to the work of a senior clerk, is ready to set up to govern and save the German Nation, and that with a vengeance !

There they sprawl, these coxcombs, like staff-officers, and patch together intolerably insipid addresses full of laboriously tortured phrases ; revel in the consciousness of their greatness and significance ; and perhaps have not the slightest idea how sick at heart and stomach grows every reasonable being when he witnesses such a farcical to-do, such disgustingly arrogant, unseasonable buffoonery, too contemptible to be angry with, too sad to laugh at. I cannot allow it that thou shouldst become so miserable a fool ! That a student like any one else should worry himself over the weal and woe of the Fatherland, that must be, and is all right ; not, however, in the fashion of a pert young cock-sparrow, but heartily and naturally. And when the day for action comes his place is not in the office of a starveling journalist, not in the clubs of crazy, rapacious Republicans, not in the Assembly of envy-ridden Democrats and salaried poltroons, but out there in the field where beat the soldiers' honest hearts, which heed not the wrangling of the pedants, nor the cowardly demagogues yapping out their lies.

It is for the old to sit in council and for the young to fight, but not the other way round. What are we to think now when this

student or that instantly demands a civic crown if he has spent a
fortnight on guard, instead of in a drinking-shop, and brags about
sacrifice and risking his life, if he has once had to chase a mob of
the riff-raff down a street or two ?

You young men belong to the Fatherland, but not the Fatherland to you ! When you are needed, you will hear the call, and
then shalt thou, my son, not stay indoors. There is no blood, then,
too precious to pour out !

Learn something ! I have learnt too little, and this often comes
home to me painfully ! Thou art not rich, and mayst even become
poor, for there is nothing more certain in this world than death.
Robbery and theft shall prevail as righteousness, so will the red
republic have it ; and it is not yet clear whether there is enough
courage and insight in the country to prevent madness and wickedness obtaining the mastery. . . .

Take care of thy health ! Without it the wealthiest is a miserable
wretch, with it the poorest a Croesus. A sickly fellow is soon half
way to a bad fellow, for the thought that one can only play the
Tantalus, when all earthly happiness, all the joy and glory in the
world are brimming to one's mouth, makes a bitter heart. He who
has the misfortune to be an invalid and bears it with a smile, has
only become a man by mistake, and was meant for an angel. . . .

Make no debts ! Borrowing makes sorrowing, is a proverb since
the world began. Debts make lies, dependence, enmity and strife,
a strife that brings no honour. He who has debts is no longer a
free man, and many a fine fellow has become a scoundrelly cur in
the progress from debt to vacillation, from vacillation to deceit, from
deceit to theft, disguised, it may be, by another name, and so on
until he reaches the abyss. Then it is he who has the finest sense of
honour who falls quickest, for 'tis he who is shaken most by shame
and regret, and loses most easily control over head and feet. . . .

Be no ruffler, but let no imputation lie on thee. He who suffers
an insult will soon deserve it ! Allow thyself to be called a scoundrel
for eight days, and on the ninth the whole world will believe that
thou art one, and on the tenth thou wilt be treated as a scoundrel.
The man that is not ready to spill his blood for his honour, has not a
drop of true German blood in his veins. He's a bastard ! For the
custom of duelling is not, as clever men say and write, a relic of the
barbarism of our fathers, of which their sons in the folly of to-day
cannot rid themselves. No, it is a good, honourable and manly way
to settle a dispute, when it is not about property and money and
things that can be weighed and measured, and for particulars of
which we can apply to books or magistrates, but about a thing that
lies deep in the heart, and deepest of all in a German heart. Such
is honour, a strange and wonderful thing, of which the greatest
philosophers know but little, not so much, at any rate, as a simple
woman, good and pure ! I have heard and read much of the folly
of duelling said by lawyers and Christians, and men of the world
and professors, but one lesson they have not taught me—how I am

to distinguish prudence from cowardice. Lay on, then, in God's name, when the right time comes, and boldly, for I would rather see thee buried than despised as a coward. But be on thy guard against an unrighteous quarrel and thoughtless and wanton behaviour ; a clear conscience makes strong the arm, but any doubt as to the justice of thy cause helps the enemy. Mark that, and mark too what thy fencing-master says to thee. God be with thee and good courage !

The troubles at Frankfort echoed loudly in the provinces. The revolutionary refugees in Switzerland, always gazing with strained eyes across the frontier to Baden, judged this the opportunity for a fresh attempt to raise the republican standard. Struve, Hecker's associate in the abortive rising in the spring, headed a party which suddenly appeared in Lörrach on 21st September and proclaimed there a German Republic. To the short but bombastic proclamation [1] was attached, with the names of Struve and Löwenfels (another of the Hecker crowd), that of Carl Blind, once well known in London.

CALL TO THE GERMAN PEOPLE !

The fight of the People with their oppressors has begun. Even in the streets of Frankfort-on-Main, the seat of the powerless Central Authority and the garrulous constituent Assembly, have shots been fired on the People. Only the sword can still save the German People. If the reaction wins the day in Frankfort, Germany will be sucked dry and enslaved, in the course of so-called law and order, far more frightfully than could happen in the bloodiest of wars. To arms, men of Germany ! Only the Republic can guide us to the goal for which we are striving. Hail to the German Republic !

> In the name of the Provisional Government : GUSTAV STRUVE.
> Commanding Officer, Head-quarters : M. W. LÖWENFELS.
> Secretary : CARL BLIND.

LÖRRACH, 21st September 1848.

The revolutionary force was easily broken up at Staufen, and Struve was captured ; but the rebellion had been marked by conduct little in keeping with the lofty profession of its leaders. Ludwig Häusser's account [2] of it, based on documents used at the trial, runs as follows :

The crisis in Frankfort, which had been occasioned by the armistice of Malmö, seemed to the refugees the favourable opportunity, and so

---

[1] Facsimile in Blum.
[2] Denkwürdigkeiten zur badischen Revolution (K.).

Struve broke into Baden on 21st September and proclaimed ' the German Republic ' in Lörrach. He came at once too early and too late. Too late because the bloody decision against the Revolution had already been arrived at in France ; too early because things in Baden were not yet so rotten, so unstable that such an expedition could hope to meet with much success. Rather had the atrocities of 18th September produced a noticeable reaction, and Struve's raid was not calculated to wipe out this impression. There was such a mixture of bombast and baseness, of Jacobin affectation and commonplace robbery, of ridiculousness and revolting outrage in this three-days drama, that a propaganda in its favour was not to be apprehended. From the moment when Struve's band marched into Lörrach, brutally abused those who resisted or displeased them, robbed not only public coffers but also private people in the meanest fashion, and raised all bad characters to official positions, to the moment when, to use the revolutionary leader's own account, the combatants at Staufen fled ' like beasts of the field that seek trembling their holes on the approach of a thunder-storm ' ; to the moment finally when the Struves, husband and wife, bolted with 16,700 florins, to be arrested by a guard of citizens—all this together made so deplorable an impression and roused so much resentment that the whole revolutionary party seemed at first to be overcome. The ' Republicans ' of April (under Hecker) had behaved like feather-brained adventurers, those of September like robbers and footpads.

That Struve was at least less dangerous to the revolutionary cause in prison than out of it, seems clear from a letter written late in the year to Frau Herwegh by Theodor Mögling, one of Hecker's associates : [3]

STRASBURG, *4th December* 1848.

I am glad that the Baden government have arrested Struve. This is real good luck for us, as Struve would have done us still more harm. In this way he is useful to us as a martyr, and can do no harm now. His wife is still in prison at Freiburg, but is said to be in charge of an amiable examining magistrate.

We must now suspend our account of the fortunes of the Frankfort Parliament, and, before opening the final act of its dramatic history, consider what had been going on in Berlin and Vienna while the National Assembly was in deliberation and debate at Frankfort.

---

[1] *Briefe von und an G. Herwegh* (K.).

BOOK VI
THE AFTERMATH OF REVOLUTION
1848

CHAPTER I

CONFUSION AND EXCITEMENT IN BERLIN

AFTER the turmoil and bloodshed, and the humiliation of the King of Prussia in March 1848, until 10th November, when the King forcibly broke up the Prussian National Assembly, the aspect of Berlin was one of the most extraordinary that any capital city ever presented. Among the King's desperate expedients to save the situation was a change of ministry, and we have read on page 305 of his brother Prince William's wrath when he found Count Arnim-Boitzenburg in a room in the Castle quietly drawing up a list of new ministers. The will that imposed itself for the moment was that of von Bodelschwingh, the man who had counselled the King to reasonable concession before the storm burst, and had dared to beard the Prince of Prussia himself when he endeavoured to stop the withdrawal of the troops from Berlin. But the rush of events soon showed Bodelschwingh that a liberal ministry under Count Arnim, even with the introduction of one or two well-known business men and commoners, new to the state service, would not command confidence. On the 25th Arnim resigned, and on the 28th the King brought himself to entrust one of the commoners, Ludolf Camphausen, no aristocrat, no soldier, no bureaucrat, but an ex-president of the Chamber of Commerce at Cologne, and the man who made the bold speech in the United Diet in January which is quoted on page 151, with the formation of a new government. His, then, was the impossible ' task of reconciling the old order and the new. He did not lack courage. The King's departure to Potsdam, where he lay in the bosom of the army, excited a not unnatural suspicion of his designs among the populace. The suggestion was made that it would be just as well for the King to separate himself from his Guards, and this was actually communicated to him by Camphausen. The royal reply[1] to the suggestion ran as follows :

POTSDAM, 27th April 1848 (Evening).

You let fall a word to-day that has since lain heavy on my heart ; a word it was of mistrust respecting my Guards. I conjure you, my dear Camphausen, to let no one persuade you it is justified ; do not listen to any such suggestions ; reject them with severity. First, because such a suspicion is as unfounded and unfair as anything in this world could be. My Guards are faithful unto death, and the justifiable effervescence against the cowardly and impudent Berlin talk regarding their behaviour on the 19th is calming down amongst the troops, in proportion to the growing and well-deserved contempt it meets with in Berlin itself. Take measures, I beg you most urgently, to secure the appearance of good patriotic articles in the papers—articles in which such genuine Prussian sentiments will be found as will prove agreeable and beneficial to both citizens and troops. Again, my best of Camphausens, I must remind you that there is a certain limit to concession which no Prussian king, who is born a soldier and who has, as I have, shared in fifteen battles, can go beyond without dishonour. To such concessions would belong, above all, acceptance of the impudent proposition that I should separate myself from my brave, beloved and loyal Guards at the bidding of Berlin, or rather of a minute minority of its population ! ! ! That would be morally my death, for in the opinion of the whole army, who on the 18th cheered the heroic bravery of the Guards so enthusiastically, I should cease to be an officer. Then indeed I should be of no account. It struck me you supposed I was surrounded by numerous troops. It is easy to put you right on this point. . . . The Fusilier Battalion has gone to Kremmen, near Fehrbellin, to protect the mayor against his own mad municipal train-bands. . . . Now promise me, my dear Camphausen, that you will never lend an ear to such insinuations as those suggesting my separation from my Guards, the best troops in the world. Such suggestions would be in vain. For I shall submit to the worst rather than do anything which would dishonour me in the eyes of those splendid fellows, of the whole country, so excellently disposed, even in those of the majority, believe me, of the Berliners themselves, and lastly in my own.

Of the general spirit of excitement in the city Gneist[2] says :

The unquiet physiognomy of the capital was almost entirely due to the alliance between the educated and the uneducated classes. . . . It was the reaction against preceding conditions. The old government knew nothing worse than ' excitement.' The police-governed

---

[1] See Erich Brandenburg's König Friedrich Wilhelms IV. Briefwechsel mit L. Camphausen, where other letters to Camphausen quoted are to be found.
[2] Berliner Zustände (K.).

state regarded as the most dangerous quality a man could possess the ability to cause ' excitement ' ; and were it the noblest and most joyful excitement in the world it was as ' excitement ' a subject of grave suspicion. Now, on the other hand, excitement is sought for its own sake. It is believed that the life of a free state is nothing but excitement.

And of the efforts of the people to organise themselves Wolff [1] gives an amusing picture, in his account of the disputes that arose among every sort of union or association of masters and work-people, over the division of the spoils of the popular victory :

The number of societies for the protection of trade defies computation. Each individual craft, every kind of calling claimed the ' fruits of victory ' as its alone by right. The purveyors of food-stuffs in Berlin demanded that the inhabitants of any street should be obliged to buy off traders in that street only. The retail fruit-dealers turned against the wholesale fruit merchants, and then retailers in general against the wholesale middlemen in general. The hackney-cab owners demanded the abolition of the ' omnibus monopoly.' The furniture dealers fell out with the committee of unincorporated master cabinet-makers. ' The Union of German Cooks in Berlin ' in an address ' to high, and highest society' entered the lists, to combat the injustice, ' founded on prejudice,' of employing French cooks in preference to German. ' The time has come when Germany can cook its own soup. And a powerful broth it will be. In your Frenchified cuisine many a thing is cooked that revolts the German stomach.' The waiters, the grocers' assistants, the landlords, the milliners, the seamstresses and hairdressers all claimed public attention to their grievances. ' What is this freedom ? ' is the modest inquiry of ' several lady hairdressers' in the *Vossische Zeitung*, ' if girls are to be debarred from hairdressing which is rather an occupation for women than for men ? ' The master and journeymen wig-makers did not share this view : ' We can by no means stand quietly by and see . . . so-called lady hairdressers poaching on our preserves, to wit the heads of our lady customers.' The shop assistants propose to close at eight o'clock instead of ten, and are supported by the ' Union of Young Business Men.' From the 9th till the 13th April, placards summon meetings of landscape gardeners, paperhangers, barge-owners, others interested in water transport, mechanics, silk-workers, butchers and carpenters ' incorporated ' and ' chartered,' hotel-keepers, etc. Even the civil service officials begin to bestir themselves with a view to improving their depressing lot. A general meeting of ' Privy-chancery secretaries, Chancellists, Day-clerks and Assistant-writers,' appoints a committee of ' Allied Law Clerks.' So too

---

[1] *Berliner Revolutionschronik*, i. (K.).

unions are formed of 'Temporary Clerks in all branches of the Civil Service,' and 'Magistrates' chief clerks.' The railway and Post Office officials apply to their chiefs for an amelioration of their lot, the latter calling for the dismissal of the Post-Master General, Schmückert. Nothing perhaps affords such direct evidence of the bonds from which the workaday world had to free itself, as does this attempted social union of all sections.

Socialistic demands were not wanting, similar to those in Paris after the revolution of February 1848, which led to the ruinous establishment of State Workshops and the bloodshed that followed their abolition in June. Unruh [1] tells us :

> Less than nothing was done in behalf of administrative authority ; great building operations were begun close to Berlin, and in order to satisfy at least the masses fifteen silver groats were paid as daily wages per man, not only to the Berlin unemployed, but to strangers who were attracted thither against the wishes of the promoters. Daily wages without any specified quantity of work, without any strict supervision or any means of providing it, and this too in a great town where thieves and vagabonds mingled with honest workmen, is demoralising in the most peaceful times. To pay such high wages for idling in a time of revolution is bound of itself to call a revolutionary horde into being. The demagogues were no longer obliged to fix a place of meeting, they always found their audience already assembled at the scene of the building operations ; and by no means a languid audience either, but sturdy, powerful men on whom the authorities had bestowed a lotus-eating existence at the expense of the state. There could be no better testimony to the mild sentiments of the population than the fact that this proceeding did not aggravate the revolution, which still remained a matter of street brawling.

Klein states, further, that 'On 30th May a great crowd of unemployed workmen assembled in front of the Cölln Town Hall. Two representatives of the workmen presented themselves to the Minister von Patow and demanded a written declaration that the Minister would secure them work " to-day " or " immediately." He promised that he would do his best and caused money to be distributed " on account " to the assembled workmen, upon which the latter dispersed.'

In the autumn a German Democratic Congress was held in Berlin, and a scathing report of its proceedings is given by a writer who might have been expected to be sympathetic, the distinguished criminal lawyer, Temme,[2] who sat on the

---

[1] *Skizzen aus Preussens neuester Geschichte.*
[2] Temme, *Erinnerungen* (K.).

extreme Left in the Prussian National Assembly, was ultimately dismissed the public service, and ended his days as Professor of Jurisprudence at Zurich :

In Germany there has never been, I imagine, a more senseless, conceited, or uncultured assembly. These creatures claimed to represent the German people, its rights, its liberties, and its honour ! I went once for half an hour as a spectator and out of curiosity. I never in one half-hour experienced so much that was nonsensical and crude. . . .

When I entered, the deputies of the various districts were busy reporting on the political sentiments of their respective neighbourhoods. Naturally the German people demanded in all quarters ' the German Republic one and indivisible,' the expulsion or hanging of all princes and everything else that made part of the catchword vocabulary of the street democracy. Loud cheers from the assembly greeted every speaker. Then there appeared on the tribune a small and insignificant young man, Rudolf Benfey of Göttingen. He was the Deputy of the Democratic Union of a district, I think, in Thuringia. He began by stating that he was a good republican—hear, hear, and cheers greeted the announcement. He had heard with great interest the declaration of republican sentiments announced from so many districts by previous speakers. Hear, hear, and cheers ! He wished nothing more than that this should be the sentiment of the whole German people. More hear, hears, more cheers ! But——but ——a low growl went through the Assembly. But, continued the speaker, he for his part must confess—— Must confess ! The growl had grown into a snarl. . . . Confess ! What had he to confess ?

Rudolf Benfey continued quietly from the tribune that he had also news from many other districts in Germany, and according to these the matter was not just quite as the previous speakers had represented it. Only a small part of the German people was so far ripe for the republic.

A fearful tumult broke forth ; the squat postal secretary (one of the chief rowdies) giving the signal for it. ' Lies ! Slander ! ' he shouted, ' the German people do want the republic, the one and indivisible red republic ! ' He hit and thumped and banged on the floor with his stick so that chairs and benches trembled. With him shrieked and shouted and raged all in his neighbourhood, soon the half and then almost the whole House. The president—I think Bamberger from Hamburg—at last succeeded in restoring order. Rudolf Benfey spoke on, and assured them that he must unfortunately go so far as to declare, with respect to the district that he represented, that there they would have nothing to do with the republic. A new tumult, a raging one at that. ' Lies ! Slander ! The German people will have the republic. Leave the tribune ! Apologise ! '

. . . Rudolf Benfey left the tribune. ' He must get up again. He must apologise,' they cried. ' He has insulted the German

nation, the representatives of the German republic one and
indivisible.' The president called the assembly to order, and to
conduct themselves in a parliamentary manner. 'Parliamentary
manner!' they cried, 'Oh, yes! oh, yes! divide! divide!' 'What
are you going to divide on?' asked the astonished president. They
looked at one another dumbfounded. Thereupon the squat postal
secretary roared in a voice of thunder : ' What are we going to vote
about ? That the German people by a great majority desires a
republic.' The president stood thunderstruck : ' How can we vote
on that ? ' But they yelled like raving maniacs : ' Resolve that
the nation wants the republic—the one and indivisible—the red !
Divide ! Divide ! ' There was an uproar like Bedlam let loose.
The president left the chair ; he was heard to say he laid down his
office and they might choose another president. A name was
mentioned. I have forgotten it. It was received with acclamation :
' Yes, let him be our president ! ' The individual named assumed
the chair. ' Divide ! Divide ! ' was bellowed again. And the
president called for a division on the following resolution : ' That
the German Democratic Congress assembled in Berlin resolves, that
the German nation desires a republic one and indivisible.' It was
adopted ' by a majority approaching unanimity.' A roaring storm
of applause followed. I left the hall. It was impossible to remain
any longer. I had grown so heavy and sick at heart. There were
so many educated men there taking part in an outburst of lunacy.
Many, it is true, never returned to it. Many were, it is true, only
cured of their madness at the next sitting. On that occasion the
assembly tried to give practical effect to its nonsense. In its deliberations on the solution of the social question it gave paragraph
three or four the force of a resolution : ' That the tenant shall no
longer pay rent to the landlord.' What scornful delight might those
in Potsdam take in scenes like these !

In this condition of ineffectual effort and immoderate demand,
it is not surprising that the consciousness dawned on many that
some strong hand was required to produce order out of chaos.
The cry arose for a Great Man. Gneist says : [1]

In this situation, when for want of reliable leadership all was
uncertainty and wavering, a widespread cry arose for an energetic
ministry. This became the catchword of the day. ' A great
statesman,' and he alone, could and must rescue us from this
condition, and for him the population wailed as for a new Messiah.
. . . Every one was shouting for ' an energetic ministry' but at the
faintest attempt at energy a cry of ' Murder ! ' was raised, just as a
wounded man in his fever shrieks at the slightest attempt to lay a
healing finger to his wound. The most violent resentment was
excited some three months later by an attempt made to reintroduce

---

[1] *Berliner Zustände*, 1848 (K.).

the ordinary street-police. . . . Prussia, in the whole course of her history, never suffered from such a complete stagnation of the functions of government as she did during these months. There was a complete paralysis of an apparently healthy body. Finances and administration both in fairly good order, the army victorious over its enemies, no loss of material resources ; and yet absolute powerlessness in head and limbs ! Every class, high and low, was permeated by a complete want of confidence in officialdom, and officialdom had lost all faith in itself. Every attempt at reconstruction was, however, met by the cry ' no more tutelage ! ' Only one form of confidence was present in plenty, and that was everybody's confidence in his own judgment. In all grades of society every one suddenly developed into a statesman. No creature, however much of a cipher in matters political, but had acquired the clearest convictions of the ministry's incapacity. No expression, at least, of appreciation or excuse has ever come to my notice.

But in place of a strong ministry, or a great man, Berlin had to put up in the meantime with the Civic Guard, whose quality may be judged from the following anecdote related by Prince Hohenlohe-Ingelfingen : [1]

Berlin at that time presented a strange spectacle. It was less animated than formerly. Strong detachments of the Civic Guard patrolled the streets. Political order was very strictly maintained. The Civic Guard were in civilian costume with top-hats, which, with the regulation rifle and bayonet, formed a ludicrous combination. Instead of the usual double guard at the Brandenburg Gate there stood on one occasion a burly butcher with his top-hat. He was terribly bored. It was noon. His equally substantial wife brought him his midday meal. While he was dining in the sentry-box, his wife shouldered his musket and marched up and down his beat, and the street-urchins sang to the air of a well-known polka :

> Come, proud Guards, oh come back here,
> Back once more to Berlin your town,
> For the noble volunteer
> Will no more march up and down.

All this time there was a certain nimbleness of wit alive in Berlin, which may surprise those who refuse to the Germans the smallest scintilla of that quality. It was on Sunday, 7th May 1848, that the first number of the well-known comic paper *Kladderadatsch* [2] appeared, and the following are some of the amusing and topical items to be found therein :

[1] *Aus meinem Leben.* i.
[2] Facsimile in Blum.

KLADDERADATSCH NO. 1

BERLIN, 1st *May* 1848.

> When blossoms oped to Springtide's balm
> Their bright eyes wet with dew,
> My sweet and careless livelong calm
> Had its ' eye-opener ' too.

The times have come a cropper ! The spirit of things has upset convention ! The wrath of Jehovah thunders through the world. The *Allgemeine*, the *Vossische* and the *Spenersche Gazettes* have ceased to appear—ditto the *Figaro* and the *Fremdenblatt*.—General elections have begun—Princes have been overturned—Thrones are fallen—Castles razed—Women devastated—Lands outraged—Jews deflowered—Maidens plundered—Priests demolished—Barricades held up to scorn—Kladderadatsch !

Who, after this, would dare to cast a doubt on the colour, the tendency, the character of our paper ? This clear statement of our convictions will secure to us as co-workers men like Junius, Julius, Curtius, Gervinus, Ruppius and Nebenius ; Löwissohn, Löwenfeld, Löwenberg, Löwenthal, Löwenheim, Löwenstein, Löwenherz . . . Louis Blanc . . . Lamartine . . . Hecker . . . Struve . . . Herwegh. . . .

Citizens of Berlin, clear away the obstacles in the path of this journal ! Send out men full of the genuine Berlin spirit, who subscribe to Kladderadatsch !

A candidate for election, a banker withal, delivered himself of the following creed : ' Gentlemen, my motto for Berlin is : ' With God for King and Country ! ' For Frankfort : ' Do right and fear nobody ! '

NOTICE

Malicious competitors have for some days past endeavoured to spread a report that I desired to become German Kaiser, and intended at an early date to retire from business. Those who know me more intimately will know what to think of it. To strangers and visitors, however, I beg to recommend, for the future as heretofore, my large and well assorted stock of Night-caps and Pants.

LEVY HEYMANN.

CASTLE SQUARE.

' DOWN WITH ALL THE SCRIBBLING CREW ! '

> On this earth no peace nor quiet,
> No surcease of row and riot,
> Till its literary hacks
> Into banishment it packs ;

Till it teaches better manners
To these filthy faction-fanners :
My advice, Berlin 's to you,
' Down with all the scribbling crew ! '

Priests who 've lost their reputations,
Lawyers sacked for malversations,
Officers for drink cashiered,
Porters, pensioned, old and ' cleared.'
All the shady, sordid party
Call themselves the ' Literati ' :
My advice, Berlin 's to you,
' Down with all the scribbling crew ! '

With the Lindens' shade behind them,
Strolling in the sun you 'll find them,
A seedy crowd of real curmudgeons
With napless hats, but sticks like bludgeons,
Hoping some one will be willing
To advance the nimble shilling.
My advice, Berlin 's to you :
' Down with all the scribbling crew ! '

Citizen A. B. KIELSTEIN.

Here is an advertisement [1] of the period :

ELECTION CIGARS

O yes !   O yes !

Ordinary Elector Cigars

Real well-matured Palatinates (small local brands) 6 for a Groat.
The popular old Hamburg-Manillas, Original Bundles of *Ten*
for two Groats.

Electoral College Cigars

Hamburg and Bremen Manufacture
7 to 20 Thalers a Thousand.

Member of Parliament Cigars

Genuine Imported Havanas

(Members of Parliament must indeed act patriotically, but they
must also sample the best that foreign countries can offer, in
order to relieve our need accordingly). . . .

W. FÄHNDRICH and Co., Cigar and Tobacco Dealers,
50 Charlotte Str.

---

[1] Friedländer Collection, Berlin Library.

And here is a remarkable broadsheet[1] sold in the streets:

THE RAGMAN'S SONG

Rare Berlin broadsheet. Lithographed border (A ragman fills his bag) and lithographed text. Printed by R. Kretschmer, Berlin. Delt. O. L.

Doomed has me the Heavenly Father
Rags upon this earth to gather ;
So you hear me loud and clear,
Calling ' Rags ! ' both far and near.

Hear me calling bright and breezy :
Bring your rags however greasy :
Royal rags, brocaded gold,
Beggars' rags, and rags untold.

Orders, ribbons, stars and garters,
Sackcloth, shirts of saints and martyrs,
All must fill the Ragman's sack,
All must join his rascal pack.

Buckram bold and fustian lowly,
Priest and prelate's vestments holy
Reeking of the incense still ;
All is grist to Ragman's mill !

All the great we greet in wonder
Are but rag-dolls stuffed with plunder !
Tatters all, and shreds and patches,
In his net the Ragman catches.

Shining silks and satins showy,
Inky crapes and laces snowy,
Cap of folly, crown of state,
Reach the Ragman soon or late.

Edicts royal, ministerial,
Acts and bills, and law material,
Scraps of paper, old and new ;
All make malt for Ragman's brew !

Ruffians' ' rights ' and vermin-eaten
Privileges must be beaten
Into pulp for paper white,
For the Charter of the Right !

---

[1] Friedländer Collection, Berlin Library.

But the most valuable document of all is a satirical pamphlet styled the *Text-book of Demagogy, Lehrbuch der Demagogie,*[1] directed against the radicals, of which Klein gives a full account. 'The terms,' he says, 'appearing in this "lexicon" are not inventions but really occur, of course distributed over a wide area, in the publications and speeches of those days.'

EPITHETS

There are many adjectives which do not get worn even with the most constant use, as for example : indigenous, supreme, democratic, reactionary, mediæval. Others on the other hand cannot be used now at all, because, through frequent use, their original impress has been lost. Such are : liberal, servile, opportune, and indeed all the stock phrases of the moderate liberals.—We may here be allowed to give a varied and heterogeneous list of expressions collected from the choicest stump oratory of the day for the benefit of youthful aspirants : lunatic, vile, lickspittle, crawling, mean, jejune, scoundrelly, antediluvian, worn out, putrid, threadbare, lamentable, trite, currish, imbecile, enslaved, wretched, cowardly, contemptible, whining, hireling, catspaw, hostile to the people, worm-eaten, rotten, tottering, decrepit, riddled, mediæval, plaguestricken, mouldy, leprous, brutish, bloody, egged-on, lethargic, enervated, narrow-minded, extortionate, hypocritical, intriguing, jeering, brutal, arrogant, snarling, cannibalistic, bestial, welldrilled, crazy, shameless, immense, gigantic, death-defying, heavenstorming, colossal, horrifying, incorruptible, misinterpreted, slandered, despised, crucified, terrorised, racked.

ACHIEVEMENT

This is one of those great words which cannot be vulgarised by the most frequent use. It cannot be too often availed of, any more than such expressions as : ' It is too late ! '—The Revolution is knocking at the door,' etc. Planetary adjectives to this sunsubstantive are : sacred, glorious, eternal, gory, dearly-bought, hard-won, inalienable.

THE MINISTERS

Popular synonyms for the Ministry are : camarilla, servile bootjacks to the princes, lickspittles, cancer on the commonwealth, bloodsuckers, retrogrades, courtisans, apostates, garotters of freedom, gallows-birds, sophisticated diplomats, assassins of freedom, princes' whipping-tops, backstairs intriguers, time-servers, diplomatic sneaks, hypocritical word-spinners, venal minions.

[1] Published by G. Wiegand, Leipzig, 1848.

PASHA

A name for any and every Oberpräsident, Landrat or Military Governor; in place of it Satrap or Landvogt may be suitably made use of. Judge-pasha indicates the Judge presiding over a court of justice; and so Communal-pasha stands for Burgomaster, School-pasha for Head-master. Other Turkish and Russian words are popular in this connection, such as ' Vizier' for minister, ' firman ' or ' ukase ' for an Order in Council, ' Knäs ' for prince, etc.

CLAPTRAP

Besides the words and terms indicated in the foregoing paragraph we can recommend the following as telling phrases : forward to the fray ; now 's the time for resolution ; the country is in danger ; we still have steel ; now or never ; to the barricades, the throne is tottering ; the bullet must decide ; are we to be trodden underfoot ; event follows event like avalanche on avalanche ; tinder for the revolution ; armoury of freedom ; souls of sweet lavender ; the spirit of the age ; speaks in thunder ; lamblike patience of impotence ; poisoned breath of autocracy ; pesthouse of despotism ; smoking ruins ; dramatic fury of a risen people ; incorruptible tribune of the people ; ashes of a world ; genius of our era ; dragon's teeth sown by old official mountebanks ; magic charm of freedom ; deeds of violence that stink to heaven ; sequestered rights of man ; death-rattle of slaves ; renegade rule ; honour of a dynasty of beasts ; regulation drill-sergeant-like graces ; Christo-German stupidity ; death-struggle of despair ; roaring, blood-dripping wild beasts ; food for worms ; noble and manly defiance ; ploughing wrinkles in the forehead of world-history ; baby's comforter ; enervated quill-driver ; arena of enthusiasm ; pulse-beat of the age ; sublime survey of the world ; churchyard peace ; breath of freedom ; close atmosphere of prison ; food for the guillotine ; furies of Civil War ; night of superstition ; pride of silence ; monster of the Prime ; beasts of the Central Court-Martial with their thick, tumid, tiger-lips.

Finally, a few extracts may be given from a paper called *The Rowdy, Krakehler,*[1] which appeared for the first time on Thursday, 18th May 1848, ' on the 60th day after the first misunderstanding (the two shots fired by soldiers on the crowd on 18th March[2]).' It was published by Ernest Litfass, 6 Adler-strasse, with the motto ' Peace is the last duty of a citizen, but the first is : Ready with your blunderbuss ! ' The programme of this journalistic effort is thus succinctly stated : ' The aim of the Rowdy is wholly and solely a Row.'

[1] Facsimile in Blum,   [2] See page 285,

Here are some of the *Krakehler's* ' unofficial ' *communiqués* and notices :

God is the first of revolutionaries, for He invariably favours revolutions with the most glorious weather, but generally treats coronations, swearing-in days, and levees with a deluge of rain.

Something has got to be built in Berlin to signalise the return of the Prince of Prussia, but people are not yet agreed whether this shall take the form of a triumphal arch or a barricade.

Against the ministerial proposition, that the Prince of Prussia shall be summoned home, the inhabitants of Berlin have raised an objection that has cost the life of three quite innocent window-panes.

The Civic Guard has been suffering of late from flatulency and an affection of the drum-skin. So serious is its condition that the services of Veterinary-surgeon Urban [1] have been requisitioned.

My friends and acquaintances are requested to take notice that my voice, though I have been compelled recently to shout more than usual, has lost nothing of its strength,
BAUER, *Privy-counsellor of Confusion.*

---

[1] See page 333 f.

CHAPTER II

THE PRINCE OF PRUSSIA'S RETURN, AND GENERAL WRANGEL'S REVIEW IN BERLIN

THE King's courage gradually revived. He began to realise that the country generally was not at the back of the Berlin democracy. Evidence no doubt reached him (we know from Bismarck it did) that the peasantry in Prussia were ready to rise against the capital. Robert Prutz published in the *Konstitutionelle Klubzeitung* [1] on 9th May a striking letter which had come his way :

We peasants in West Prussia warn you Berliners that if you don't soon restore order and decency in your damned hole, and restore our beloved King to his just rights, we peasants will come to his help in a way that will strike you scoundrels blind and dumb. Dogs that you are, you have freed the treacherous Polaks and hounded them on to us, to burn and slay as they are doing. You have betrayed and butchered our sons and brothers of the Guards. That will be remembered to you, especially as you are always talking big, and are yet too cowardly to tame your own rabble. Then, too, you blackguards, you plundered the State's treasury ; and other national property, to which we have contributed, you have wantonly destroyed. That you shall make good to us. Your barbarity has driven the Prince of Prussia to flee the country, and if you don't see that he is restored to his rights and his country by the 24th May next, you will make acquaintance with the West Prussians, and your city of robbers' caves will be fired in a hundred places at once. We peasants are not going to feed you any longer, to be ruined by you and your brood. Remember the 24th May ; we 'll teach you to ape the Frenchmen's monkey tricks.

As a pendant to this homely utterance may be given the cheering message [2] received by the King in May from a higher circle, a Count Asseburg and his friends. The document is a good example of the unctuous language in which German

---

[1] Facsimile in Blum.
[2] Poschinger's *Unter Friedrich Wilhelm IV.* (Manteuffel's *Memoirs*), i. p. 16.

loyalty among the aristocracy has been educated to express itself.

Your Majesty knows that throughout all the turmoil, perplexity and change of the immediate past a large proportion of your subjects have remained unaltered in their loyalty towards the person and the house of the exalted father of their country, and will remain unaltered, if God grant His aid.

If we, the undersigned, hazard the opinion that your Majesty must find a precious consolation in this indisputable fact, then the firm resolve, of whose existence in us we have been becoming conscious in these days, viz. to sacrifice for your Majesty, joyfully and without hesitation, our lives and our property, gives us a standpoint from which we can look back with mind at ease on a past that has seemed to imperil our dearest interests.

A particular circumstance has rendered it impossible for us hitherto to reconcile ourselves with what has happened. That is the uncertainty which still continues with regard to the return of your Royal Highness' exalted brother, the Prince of Prussia.

From the decree issued by your Majesty to the Ministry of State on the 11th instant we have seen to our indescribable delight that his Royal Highness has been summoned to return without delay to the fatherland. In this connection we cannot enforce silence on our feelings, but find ourselves irresistibly impelled to lay at the feet of the throne the thanks of us all,

> because the first and most exalted Prince of our dear Kingly House, the Viceroy of our loyal Pomerania, the pride of our army, the benefactor of our arms, will soon be granted us again, and therewith his strong arm and wise counsel be restored to the fatherland. . . .

This missive was promptly despatched by the King with the endorsement in his own royal hand : ' To the Home Secretary with the injunction to have it published in the papers at once.'

An opportunity for testing the King's courage soon presented itself. The United Diet, which had held its first meeting on 11th April 1847,[1] held its last on 10th April 1848. But it left the field to a successor in a Prussian National Assembly, much as the Fore-Parliament at Frankfort had arranged for the assembling of the Frankfort Parliament. This much the Berlin revolution had effected, that neither the King, nor the conservative Camarilla about him, dare dispute the validity of this Assembly, which was to meet on 22nd May. Among those elected to it was the Prince of Prussia himself !

Since his flight from Berlin on 22nd March the Prince had

[1] See page 150.

been living quietly in London. Bunsen [1] wrote of him on 29th March as follows :

LONDON, *29th March* 1848.

The Prince came to breakfast with us all at 10 o'clock, and was very amiable. Frances (Bunsen's wife) had fetched in an arm-chair and placed it in the centre of one side of the table, but the Prince put it away himself and took another, saying, ' One ought to be humble now, for thrones are shaking.' Then I sat on one side of him, and he desired Frances to take her place on the other.

Again, Bunsen [2] wrote of the Prince to his father in April :

He is making the best impression in all quarters with his gallant bearing and keen intelligence. For his part, he is learning much from his conversations with leading English statesmen, and the questions they put to him, particularly Peel. He is about to take daily lessons from an educated Englishman in the English language and literature, and the English constitution.

On 7th April the Prince wrote a manly letter [3] to Otto von Manteuffel :

LONDON, *7th April* 1848.

. . . What we have gone through since last we met ! There's no use in crying over spilt milk ! Prussian hearts may grieve for many a long day over what has happened, but it cannot be undone, and may every attempt to do so be given up ! To accept the new Prussia with resignation, and to help in its reconstruction, are now the task of every patriot, however repugnant it may be to aid in the erection of a second-class power, where once a great power stood proud and independent ! It is a great grief to me to be unable to serve my country in this crisis, and to show by deeds, still more than by my known principles, that I have been most shamefully slandered, and have been the victim of a miserable intrigue. I am nevertheless proud to be pointed at as a representative of that old régime, for I knew no other duty than to see that Prussia was maintained in that high position in which history and her monarchs had placed her. It has already been declared that she is no longer to hold that position, since she is to be absorbed in the German Empire. So, institutions may suit this new Prussia which would never, I am convinced, have suited the old one. The future will show that I am prepared to devote all my energies, if indeed I am permitted to do so, to the welfare of my fatherland in its new shape also. In a responsible ministry cannot indeed be any place for me !
Your   PRINCE OF PRUSSIA.

---

[1] *Memoir of Baron Bunsen,* ii. p. 171.
[2] *Briefwechsel Friedrich Wilhelms IV. mit Bunsen.*
[3] Poschinger's *Unter Friedrich Wilhelm IV.* (Manteuffel's *Memoirs*), i. p. 19.

The King's general state of agitation in the past had been pitiful, but he wrote on the morning of the 12th to Camphausen in true Hohenzollern style :

SANS SOUCI, 12th May 1848.

DEAREST CAMPHAUSEN,—You have doubtless been already informed of the nice project to hold a ' demonstration against the ministers,' of which my faithful Hensel (Painter and Chief of the Artists' body) has notified me.   I conjure you and your colleagues, as your best and most faithful friend, not to allow yourselves to be in any way disturbed or impressed by this project, if indeed it be realised.   The solution of the situation is for us : Courage, steadfastness and a glance at the well-disposed country.   Berlin is not Paris, nor is the Mark of Brandenburg France.   Reflect that to give way one step is to put the succession to the throne and therefore the throne itself in question.   Above all, then, for God's sake let none of you think of giving way.   It would be unpardonable to do so in the face of any Berlin demonstration ; in the face of this one it would be a felony.   It would be to renounce the throne. Tell these criminals that you will answer for yourselves to the Diet, but not to them.   Should the matter become threatening, which heaven forbid, then leave the city and come to my side, where your place is in the hour of danger.   I am like a rock in the determination to meet, arms in hand, any demonstration which questions the succession.   God be with you ! <i>Vale.</i>

FRIEDRICH WILHELM.

The King's change of mood continued, and on 30th May he wrote [1] to Bunsen, twitting him with his scepticism as to the revolutionary spirit abroad in Europe :

POTSDAM, 30th May 1848.

A new 18th March is being organised in Berlin.   An immense number of Polish and French rabble are hiding in taverns, cellars and courts.   The brood of liars is fearfully active, and French money is in currency, chiefly in the form of five-franc pieces, as in the days of March (hear ! hear !)   In short, if the <i>coup</i> planned is not wrecked by the cowardice of the rabble, and the bayonets of the Civic Guard, you may look out for great doings.   Has it not struck you how the revolutions attempted or carried through in Berlin, Paris, Vienna, and Naples were all fixed for the same day ? That is grist for my mill.

The same day he wrote to Camphausen, revealing the fact that he had now brought himself to the resolution to reduce Berlin by force, if necessary :

[1] Ranke, <i>Briefwechsel Friedrich Wilhelms IV. mit Bunsen.</i>

SANS SOUCI, 30th *May* 1848.

I trust you do not for one moment doubt that any day something serious and of a revolutionary nature may break out in Berlin. I credit you with having reckoned the chances of this in advance, and settled amongst yourselves as to the moment when you will rally to me and gather round me. Then the solution must be the subjugation of Berlin. This will certainly prove, if successful, an immeasurable boon to our country, its present and its future. I do not of course waver for a moment in fulfilling all the promises which can possibly be fulfilled. We must, however, reckon with the chance of a considerable minority of the Diet taking part in the revolutionary movement. I expect the return of my brother will be the signal for the outbreak of this long-prepared movement. . . .

The Prince desired to return to Berlin and take up his election to the Prussian National Assembly, and the Ministry supported him ; the King consented. The news of the proposed return of the Prince roused the slumbering elements of revolution. A mob from the *Zelte* [1] made for Camphausen's residence on 12th May, and demanded the withdrawal of the resolution in favour of the Prince's return. Says Klein : ' Schwerin and Camphausen promised that the matter should be reconsidered by the Council of Ministers. Thereupon the crowd retired peaceably to the *Zelte*. Towards midnight, however, disorders broke out before the palace of the Prince of Prussia. The old inscription, " The Property of the Nation," was put up again and the windows were smashed in. The leaders of the populace, Held and Jung, succeeded in persuading their followers to go home. No worse violence occurred. The Ministry decided finally that, when the constitution of the country was being discussed, the heir to the throne could not fitly be absent. He must not, however, enter Berlin before the opening of the Constituent Assembly, and must publicly declare before his arrival that he accepted the new institutions.'

More serious was the action taken on 30th May by the Civic Guard, instigated by the mob, in preventing the execution of an order of the Minister of War for the removal of rifles from the Arsenal. In the confusion the crowd managed to carry off a piece of artillery. Next day the King wrote furiously to Camphausen :

---

[1] See page 277.

SANS SOUCI, *1st June* 1848.

DEAR CAMPHAUSEN,—Let me know by Count Kanitz what is being done against yesterday's unprecedented attack by the educated and uneducated mob on my provision of weapons for the army. I demand, as I am King by the Grace of God, the despatch of these arms . . . most urgently needed by the army, and on the delivery and use of which depends perhaps the success of the next battles. I demand furthermore the return of the stolen gun. Fortified by the declarations of the Diet, we can go ahead with confidence and talk straight to this mob. Berlin is a festering boil which must be cut sooner or later if the State is to aspire to better things, as it is my earnest wish it should.

Finally, before we leave for a few pages this letter-writing King, we have a remarkable letter of his to Camphausen, dated 6th June, in which he gives some of his ideas for righting public opinion :

SANS SOUCI, *6th June* 1848.

MY DEAREST CAMPHAUSEN,—The state of things is becoming so serious that I hold it to be my first duty to obtain an exact account of the condition of affairs, through whose fault things have come to this pass, and what means, if any, are available and can be fitly employed to check the evil. . . . The Berlin populace has grown accustomed to see go unpunished gross blasphemy, most insolent interference with the King's majesty, licence and disorder, calls to resistance and disobedience, shameless lying, revolting placards, outrageous club-domination and, for some days past, to hear the streets desecrated by the cry for a republic, and the complete subversion of existing institutions. To-day the Clubs have advertised a meeting ' to inspire the provinces with the right (!) spirit.'—And all this is calmly endured by Auerswald (Minister of the Interior) without lifting a finger or even a pen to prevent it. . . . I hereby demand and command that the Ministry of State take measures to counteract with the greatest energy this licence, these outrages, and this open if incipient treason in Berlin and elsewhere ; and that effective means at last be taken in hand, in the most active and zealous fashion, to wit : speech, writing, popular propaganda, placards, meetings, pictures, pamphlets, formation of good clubs, despatch of envoys to the provinces, suitable appointments, vigorous steps for the final restoration of the Berlin guard to the Military Authority, reinforcement of the Berlin garrison, summons (under penalty) to the clergy of all denominations to preach not peace alone but also good order, obedience, and loyalty.

Fuel was added to the King's wrath by such incidents as the assault [1] on Arnim, one of his ministers :

---

[1] Steinmann, *Die Revolution in Preussen* (K.).

The garden attached to the Conservatorium (the meeting-place of the National Assembly) and the building itself were invested by Civic Guards, and no unauthorised persons were to be found there. Outside this zone knots of people had gathered, when an elderly man, with long moustachios, wearing a cloak lined with white, lame and supporting himself with a knotty stick, came out of the Conservatorium, and as he approached the nearest groups and was asked as to how the voting had gone, replied harshly : ' What do you want ? What are you standing here for ? ' On receiving a reply as to what they wanted, he exclaimed still more roughly : ' That you will know to-morrow. Go home and get back to your work ! ' He was about to continue his way when a voice from the crowd cried : ' That is the Minister von Arnim.' Loud cries then arose and a dense crowd gathered about him, drawing ever more closely round him. ' Hang the fellow. Knock him on the head ! ' resounded amidst wild confusion. Cudgels were brandished in the air. Squeezed in amongst the crowd he was hustled hither and thither and there was no immediate hope of release for the minister ; he was really in danger, for no dissuasion by the reflecting element in the crowd was of any avail. Then a number of young men headed by some students found their way through to his rescue. ' Bring him to the University ! ' they cried. The crowd joined in the cry and rolled slowly towards the University buildings. In this way the University was reached and furnished an asylum to the minister.

It was in circumstances such as these that the Prince of Prussia returned courageously to his country. His letter [1] of thanks to Queen Victoria for the hospitality that this country had afforded him will be read to-day with mingled feelings :

BRUSSELS, 30*th May* 1848.

MOST GRACIOUS COUSIN,—I obey the impulse of my heart in seizing my pen, without any delay, in order to express to you my warmest and most heartfelt thanks for the infinitely gracious and affectionate way with which you and the Prince have treated me during my stay in London. It was a melancholy time, that of my arrival. By the sympathetic view which you took of my situation, most gracious Cousin, it became not only bearable, but even transformed into one that became proportionately honourable and dignified. This graciousness of yours has undoubtedly contributed towards the change of opinion which has resulted in my favour, and so I owe to you, to the Prince, and to your Government, a fortunate issue out of my calamities. So it is with a heavy heart that I have now left England, not knowing what future lies before me to meet— and only knowing that I shall need the strengthening rest and tranquillity which my stay in England and an insight into her institutions have afforded me in full measure.

---

[1] *Queen Victoria's Letters.* John Murray.

Offering my most cordial remembrances to the Prince, to whom I shall write as soon as possible, I remain, most gracious Cousin, your faithful and most gratefully devoted Cousin,

PRINCE OF PRUSSIA.

The Prince's reception at Potsdam by the Guards is thus described by Prince Hohenlohe-Ingelfingen : [1]

I believe it was on the 7th June itself that all we officers were summoned to Potsdam Palace, because the Prince of Prussia wished to speak to us. We assembled in the very saloon in which the King had addressed us after the March fighting. We awaited him in a state of the greatest tension. The fiercest hotspurs amongst us anticipated he would summon us to take up arms against Berlin. If no one, on quiet consideration, could regard such a thing as possible, yet all were enthusiastic to see again, after such painful events and three months' absence, the beloved Commanding General and Heir Apparent, so much abused and so unjustly disparaged. The doors opened and the giant form of the Prince entered. He was met by a thundering cheer which, however unmilitary such a spontaneous demonstration might be, was obviously a not disagreeable surprise. Overcome with emotion he at first stepped back a pace. As the cheering, however, continued one could see how much he was moved. He made a sign that he wished to speak ; there was dead silence immediately and we listened. Though the Prince's words were indeed those of a general speaking to his troops, who had suffered injustice with him and for him, as he for them, they did not quite realise the expectation which the hotspurs amongst us had cherished. In conclusion he said he would always consider himself the first and most obedient subject of the King. He said that the confidence in the King, which found expression in the greeting just accorded to himself, justified his own reliance on us, that we would follow with him the King, blind and unquestioning, in any way the King might think fit to pursue for the welfare of the country. Deeply moved, the Prince left us. Deeply moved, we streamed down the grand staircase to the Lustgarten. A small two-horse phaeton drove up to the little door on the Colonnade ; the Prince and his aide-de-camp entered it quickly, and were driven at full speed to the railway station. 'Where is he going ? ' 'To Berlin ! He will be assassinated.' 'He is only going to Charlottenburg.' 'No, he is going to the National Assembly in Berlin ! '

On the 8th, the Prince, amid shouts and yells from the populace, drove to the Conservatorium, where the National Assembly was in session. On his entry to the House members of the Right rose respectfully ; those of the Left called out amid hisses : 'Keep your seats.' The Prince's speech, which has something of the Hohenzollern touch, ran as follows : [2]

---

[1] *Aus meinem Leben*, i.   [2] Klein.

In virtue of my election to a seat in this House I am entitled to appear amongst you. I should have hastened hither yesterday had it not been the anniversary of an irreparable bereavement which retained me in the bosom of my family. (It was the anniversary of the death of Frederick William III.). To-day, however, I seize the first opportunity of expressing my thanks for the confidence which has called me into your midst, and rendered it possible for me to extend a hearty welcome to you, gentlemen, who have been sent here by every province of the country and every class of the community. The eyes, not only of Prussia but of the whole world are fixed on this Assembly of ours, for, through its intermediary, an understanding with our Sovereign must be brought about—an understanding which must decide for long years to come the destiny of Prussia and its kings. What a lofty mandate that ! The more sacred that mission the more solemn must be the spirit and disposition which guides our counsels. The establishment of a constitutional monarchy is the form of government which our King has designated as our aim. I shall devote all my energies to that task, with the loyalty and conscientiousness which my country has a right to expect from my known and proven character. This is the duty of every son of the fatherland, and mine, therefore, above all, who am the first subject of the King. So stand I here, once more amongst you, to aid you so far as in me lies in carrying out to a happy conclusion the task which has been entrusted to our care. May the sentiments I here express be shared and retained by all ; so will our labours be successful and redound to the well-being and safety of our beloved country. I trust my appearance amongst you may be of advantage in this connection, and that our united efforts may realise all that is hoped and expected of us. My other duties will not allow me to take part regularly in your debates, and I therefore request the president to have my substitute summoned. May all of us, gentlemen, be inspired with the motto and war-cry of Prussia so often tested and approved : ' With God for King and Country ! '

The mob's reply to the Prince of Prussia's audacity was to storm the Arsenal on 14th June, a performance the serio-comic aspect of which is well brought out in Gneist's account,[1] which, with Klein's summaries of certain passages, is given at length. It affords yet another example of the futility of a half-disciplined mob, always less dangerous than one wholly indisciplined.

The seed of this outburst lay in the curious idea of a universal arming of the people, a natural reaction against the former Prussian military exclusiveness. The idea was intensified by recollections of the defenceless situation of the populace on the 18th March, and

---

[1] *Berliner Zustände* (K.).

political inexperience and naïveté caused it to take the form of a demand that every voter should be provided with arms, this, of course, free of charge and ' at the Government's expense. . . .' Attention was called in vain to the fact that universal arming meant arming the reactionaries too, and that in future not the Democratic Unions alone, but the Teltower Peasants' League also, as well as the Prussian Union and the Junkers' Parliament, would turn out with pikes and drums, and that you would be arming error against reason just as much as vice versa. . . . All this was of no avail. To the democrats the *people* meant only the men who foregathered in the ' clubs' and conclaves of Berlin, and became known to each other as lusty partisans and fellow-champions of freedom. The other sixteen millions of Prussians did not exist for this brand of politicians. Without this key to the situation in Berlin it is impossible to understand either this, or the conduct of the National Assembly. For weeks the idea had prevailed that for reactionary motives Camphausen's ministry had withheld from the ' people' the weapons which were their due, had indeed dared to send the weapons away for the better arming of the King's soldiers elsewhere. As a matter of fact several consignments of arms had been despatched. An end must be put to such ' reactionary arrogance,' and each despatch of arms gave rise to disturbances. These, fomented by outside incitements, developed on 14th June into a battle royal. Many simultaneous rumours reached the populace to the effect that the Arsenal was to be actually cleared of arms, of which the ' people' were thus to be deprived. So while it was still light, noisy crowds began to gather round the Arsenal. . . . [It was a beautiful moonlight night between ten and eleven o'clock when Gneist in the Gendarmenmarkt received tidings that the Arsenal had been stormed.] On receipt of this news the companies (42nd, 43rd, 44th) drawn up in the Gendarmenmarkt marched off to that side of the Arsenal directly opposite the new Guard House. It was on this side that it had been broken into ; the doors and windows had been smashed in ; in front of the doorway rose a long fire-escape leading up to the window of the second floor directly over it. I had joined the last section of my own free will as a fugleman, and found myself, when we halted, in front of the fifth window from the door on the side we approached from. The scene, in spite of the beauty of the night, had something weird about it. Some torches burned dimly at the door. The interior of the Arsenal was in deep darkness, and only from a certain murmur could one guess that a great number of people were busy inside. . . . Then Captain Vogel [the same courageous leader who during the labour riots in October was the first to mount the barricade in the Ross-strasse and was dangerously wounded in doing so] hit on the happy idea of commanding the drums to beat in front of the door. The noise was infernal, for the rolling of the kettle-drums reverberated awesomely from the bare walls of the Arsenal in the stillness of the night—a noise it was which excited in all of us emotions which, if we cannot quite call them warlike, were in any case suf-

ficiently violent. This act was decisive. In a twinkling the scene
changed. Men who had been helping themselves to weapons began
to scramble out of the windows, and scurry away along the wall with
admirable celerity. Hardly five or six had got away when the
guards in my section were no longer to be held. They sprang forward to arrest the fugitives, and such was the zeal which fired us, that
three bold men rushed with prodding bayonets on a seventeen-year-
old boy who was disposed to debate the matter. I sprang in between
them ; but their intentions were not really so fierce after all. Other
great feats of arms we were unable, even with the best will in the
world, to accomplish. From this time a stream of men poured
continuously out of the windows. We tried to arrest the first of
these, but as we had not men enough to take charge of them all we
allowed anybody to run away that wanted to run away. But it
became more and more the rule for the fugitives to appear with a gun,
which they wanted to take with them as a keepsake. The majority,
however, promptly dropped the weapon on demand ; many were
quite surprised and hurt at such an unreasonable request ; others
began to argue the matter and had their ears boxed, upon which
they handed over the weapons. Very few, indeed, tried to force
their way through, but were induced by a prod in the ribs to give up
their rifles also. . . . [In the meantime several further battalions of
the Civic Guard and a battalion of the 24th regiment appeared on
the scene. The garrison of the Arsenal, two hundred men under the
command of Captain von Natzmer, had retired. The unfortunate
officer had been persuaded that the people was in revolt, that the
throne had fallen, that resistance merely meant immense bloodshed
and would in any case be hopeless. . . .] Fugitives were still constantly streaming out of the Arsenal, and the ground floor must have
been fairly well emptied when the line battalion marched up to the
roll of its drums. This was the signal for those on the upper floor,
one or two hundred people in all, to make themselves scarce as
quickly as possible. Every window was opened, and those inside
climbed out on to the broad cornice in front of the window-sills,
pressing each other along it to the fire-escape, down which some of
them proceeded to climb. Many of these, naïvely enough, carried
rifles with them, which they were of course compelled to give up at
the bottom of the ladder, mostly in exchange for a cuff on the side
of the head. At this time some guns were thrown down to the
pavement by those above, and one man fell headlong from the
cornice. These, however, were the only dangerous incidents that
occurred to my knowledge during the proceedings. I mention these
details, since I have been unable to find in the newspaper descriptions
any more unprejudiced presentation of the facts than was given of
the incidents in March. The crowd which entered the Arsenal
consisted of three classes. One of these, under the influence of the
' Arming of the People Swindle,' were convinced that they were
doing right in fetching the arms so unjustly withheld from them.
The second was formed of that exceedingly numerous class of

Berliners who are always to the fore, when it costs nothing, and there is in addition a chance of carrying something away. The third consisted of professional thieves, to whom the flags in the Arsenal were but so many pieces of gold-embroidered silk. If only this 'foam of the angry billows' had not cost the State some 50,000 thalers, and a few trophies of victory! The whole occurrence would have been impossible if the Civic Guard had been under one system and one commander.

After the storming of the Arsenal the Camphausen Ministry resigned, but the government did not pass into stronger hands; it was not until September that action was taken, and the task of restoring order intrusted to Count von Wrangel, fresh from his exploits in Jutland. The following was his Order of the Day on 17th September on taking up his appointment as Commander-in-Chief of all garrisons in the Mark: [1]

17th September 1848.

. . . It is my task to restore peace in these countries whenever it is disturbed and the forces of the well-disposed citizens prove unable to do so. . . . I firmly trust that I shall have no occasion to intervene with the military under my command, as I have every confidence that the civilians also desire the best for themselves and their country since it is their own hearths and homes that both they and we are called on to protect. There are, however, elements present in the country which desire to see it unhappy. They are indeed few in number but for that reason all the more violent in their demeanour, while good citizens hold back. To these latter I shall in the first place afford most vigorous support, to facilitate the maintenance by them of the public peace without which no lawful liberty is possible. . . . Soldiers, do not allow yourselves to be led astray by the speeches and proclamations which unknown persons address to you. Pay no attention to them, however flattering they may sound, and whatever future they may promise in high-sounding words if you will only consent to follow the advice they offer you. Listen, on the contrary, to my voice, the voice of your General who only wishes you well. Stand firmly by your officers as these will by you. Let no stranger element come between. Any reasonable wishes you may have you must bring before them in the way prescribed. No one will render you more assured help than they, for no one understands your needs better than they do, and no one is more thoroughly inspired with the desire to help you by word and deed. . . . My greeting to you is: 'Officers and men, hold fast by your confidence in one another and by your beloved Sovereign. Three cheers for the King!'

---

[1] Klein.

The general decided to hold a review in Berlin on 20th September. His reasons are stated clearly enough in one of his letters. 'The political circumstances here are hopeless. Things are left entirely to chance and no one whatever has the least idea what to do. Everybody feels that something drastic must be done, but nothing is undertaken to remedy this lamentable state of affairs, and to save the crown and country. There are a thousand ready to give advice, but no strong action is taken. So we are hurrying hopelessly to anarchy and the republic.' [1] The new head of the Ministry in September was a soldier, General von Pfuel, who had just completed the work of restoring order in Posen, and might have been expected to give Wrangel what administrative support he could. His courage failed him, and Wrangel held his review in the Minister's despite. The following is the account given in *The Nation in Arms for Democracy* [2] of the masterly manner in which, displaying a rare combination of firmness and tact, he discharged his self-imposed task :

Von Pfuel, Prime Minister and Minister for War, was in terror lest it should come to dangerous outbreaks and conveyed a request to von Wrangel not to hold the review in Berlin. The latter, who better understood the Berlin character, insisted on holding the parade in the city, and replied to the Minister of War's adjutant in the night of the 19th : ' Tell the Minister of War that you have executed his commission to the letter, but tell him at the same time that not with my consent shall the review be countermanded, and that I take all the responsibility. If the holding of the review in Berlin is, however, to be absolutely forbidden, I should be obliged if the Minister would have an Order to that effect made out and signed by all the Ministers. I cannot indeed recall my Order, but shall then forthwith resign the supreme command of the troops, and beg His Majesty's permission to return again to Stettin.' Early on the 20th arrived another message from the Prime Minister with an urgent warning not to hold the review in Berlin. Wrangel repeated his declaration, mounted his horse with his suite, rode slowly towards the Great Star and halted there, in order to give the troops time to take up their positions. Here the Commander of the Civic Guard, Colonel Rimpler, presented himself with his staff, delivered a somewhat lengthy address to the Commander-in-Chief, and then took his place in the suite.

When the troops were in review order, the Commander-in-Chief,

---

[1] Blum.

[2] *Das Volk in Waffen im Sinne der Demokratie,* a work published in 1887, by a Prussian Staff Officer (K.).

passing through the Brandenburg Gate, rode at a slow pace from the left flank along the front, greeted by the troops with loud and joyful cheers. The Linden was crowded with spectators, every window filled to the utmost, even the skylights and roofs had been occupied by those eager to see. The street-urchins had climbed into the branches of the trees. In the Lustgarten Wrangel assembled the officers of his staff around him, and made the following speech to them and the public pressing closely around him :

'Gentlemen, this is one of the happiest days of my life. I have already been greeted in such a friendly manner at the gates of the city by the staff of the Civic Guard, and met with a reception in the City such as might be called triumphal. I know it was not intended for me, but for the troops whom I have had the honour to command and to lead to victory in Schleswig-Holstein.

(*To the public*) : 'I shall bring these troops again to you if not immediately, then at an early date ; you may rely on that.

(*To the officers*) : 'Gentlemen, the King has accorded me the greatest proof of his favour and confidence in entrusting me with the command of the troops stationed in the Marches. I am to restore order where it has been disturbed and vindicate the law where it has been infringed. The troops are good, the swords are keen-edged, the rifles loaded.

(*To the public*) : 'Not against you, people of Berlin ! but for your protection, for the true freedom the King has given, and for the maintenance of the law (general applause). Does that please you, Berliners ? (Yes ! yes !) I am glad of it. For you, and with you, we shall come on the scene and act. How sad a place do I find Berlin again ; grass grows in the streets, the houses are deserted, the shops are full of wares that find no purchaser, industrious citizens find no work, nothing to earn, the artisans are stricken with poverty. This must all be changed, and changed it will be ; I bring you all that is good with good order. Anarchy must cease. This, I promise you, and a Wrangel has never broken his word !

(*To the officers*) : 'Gentlemen, it makes me very happy to see the troops in such good condition. You will keep them so. Good feeling between them and the civil population must be maintained.

(*To the public*) : 'They are of one blood with you, they have the same end in view, to uphold the greatness and fame of Prussia, to lay with you the foundations of German unity. They are your brethren, and you will never forget that in the army are your brothers, your kinsmen, and your friends.

(*To the officers*) : 'I am sorry, gentlemen, that I cannot to-day present the troops to His Majesty. Long live the King ! '

Some indication of the good-humour with which Wrangel's action was received is afforded by a broadsheet [1] which appeared after the review, taking up, in the Berlin vein of humour,

---

[1] Friedländer Collection, Berlin Library.

Wrangel's reference to grass in the streets of Berlin, and poking fun at the democrats :

At the end of this week, if the pleasing circumstances now prevailing permit, a great Auction of Berlin Street-Grass will be held at my address. The exact time I reserve for decision, but now beg to announce that every purchaser will receive as a gift the picture ' How a Short Man rides through Long Grass.' The proceeds, after deducting expenses, will be devoted to providing powder and shot for the Sovereign Linden Club.

Gustav Müller, Marienstrasse 1a.

CHAPTER III

GENERAL WRANGEL EJECTS THE PRUSSIAN
NATIONAL ASSEMBLY

THE Prince of Prussia's return had passed over without provoking a revolution, and General Wrangel had held his review in Berlin without any conflict with the Civic Guard. The King's growing confidence nerved him to take a firmer stand in face of the swelling arrogance of the Prussian National Assembly. Whereas in the case both of the Fore-Parliament and the Frankfort Parliament the extreme Left was always in a minority, and the tendency as time went on was to move from the Left nearer to the Centre, in the case of the Prussian Assembly the tendency was just the reverse and the move was towards the radical side. Of the extreme republican section Unruh said that to them ' the American republic was not nearly republican enough and not nearly democratic enough.' However, as against the Assembly and its frothy resolutions, strong support was afforded to the King by the so-called Junker Parliament, a ' Union for the Protection of Property,' which had been formed in August, and in which the young Bismarck played an active part.

In October the Prussian Assembly began the discussion of a draft constitution. Nobility was declared to be abolished and the words ' by the grace of God ' were expunged by resolution from the royal title. A Hohenzollern's wrath at a resolution so sacrilegious may be imagined, and Frederick William IV., the Hohenzollern who, but seven months before, had reeled down from his apartments into the castle courtyard and bowed bare-headed before the mutilated bodies of the victims of 18th March, who had ridden through the streets of Berlin, with the revolutionary banner in front of him and the revolutionary colours tied round his arm, now spoke out in the tones of his great-nephew. When the Assembly and the Civic Guard presented themselves at the castle on 15th October, the King's birthday, to offer their congratulations, his reply [1] was short and sharp :

What you say to me bears, it is true, the appearance of devotion and obedience, but the appearance only. The proceedings in the National Assembly, which I summoned in full reliance on the loyal sentiments of my subjects, give me proof of the views and principles by which they are actuated. They leave no right untouched, the most sacred thing is not safe from their attacks. They have impugned my God-given right to the crown ; they wish to take from me what I hold by the Grace of God ! For this no power on earth is strong enough.—I shall faithfully maintain it as I have inherited it from my ancestors. Tell this to the gentlemen who sent you. Tell them that I shall re-establish peace and good order in the country, that ample means to do so are at my command. Tell them that disorders and those who incite to disorders, wherever I find them, I shall combat and crush, and that for this I feel myself, by God's grace, strong enough.

The Assembly was unaffected by this rebuff and pursued its radical course, stimulated by the excitement caused by the news from Vienna, where the revolutionaries and the army were at grips. Waldeck, the extremest of the radical leaders, who had been very active in connection with the Assembly's proposed ' constitution,' brought up for debate a resolution demanding that the Ministry should ' immediately devote all the means and energy at its disposal to the protection of popular freedom now threatened at Vienna.' Crowds surrounded the House, and Pfuel, the head of the Ministry, was mobbed. Powerless in the situation, the Pfuel Ministry resigned on 1st November, and the King resolved to select [2] as the new ministerial chief one who would stand no nonsense, a cavalry general and a Hohenzollern, Count Brandenburg, natural son of Frederick William II. With him was associated Otto von Manteuffel, a trained bureaucrat with the qualities that the soldier sometimes lacks.

The Assembly at once voted an address to the King, in which the dismissal of this Brandenburg Ministry was demanded. Unruh, who led the deputation charged with the presentation of the address at Sans Souci on 2nd November, gives the following account [3] of its reception :

---

[1] *Das Volk in Waffen im Sinne der Demokratie* (K.).
[2] On the young Bismarck's advice.—*Sybel*, i. p. 254.
[3] Victor von Unruh, *Erinnerungen* (K.).

At first the King would not receive the deputation, but finally decided to do so. Having made a deep bow to the King, I stepped up to a table in the middle of the room on which stood a lamp and read out the address clearly, but in a respectful tone. The King, who had already shown signs of impatience during the reading of the address, took the paper out of my hand when I had finished, turned on his heel and went to the door. Just as he reached it Jacoby cried after him : ' That 's the misfortune of Kings ; they don't want to hear the truth.' This scene made anything but a favourable impression on all the members of the deputation ; indeed the impression was a very painful one. There were signs and exclamations of disapproval which could be caught by the King's adjutants, who still remained in the room and were also astonished, but remained perfectly courteous to the deputies. Jacoby's expression also violated parliamentary conventions, one of which is that, in the case of a deputation such as this, no one must say anything save the official speaker. Later Jacoby was praised to the skies, not only by radical papers but also by liberal ones, for this conduct of his at Sans Souci. He, they said, was the only man who had dared to speak openly before the King. We may leave posterity to form its judgment on the incident, which, however, passed exactly as I have related and produced the impression described on all those present. None of the latter said a word in approval of Jacoby. Had the King at the conclusion of the reading of the address, which thus constituted a speech to himself personally, consented to answer or engage in any discussion, then it would have been seen whether the president had the courage to express his opinion respectfully but frankly. On the other hand it seemed to me and others present, that to shout something at and behind the back of the retiring King was not a dignified action, but rather a piece of revolutionary affectation. In the course of the next few days it was clearly seen that the National Assembly was in no way inclined to revolutionary measures.

Next day came the news that Vienna was in the hands of the troops, which was thus announced in a supplement to the *Neue Preussische Zeitung* : [1]

BERLIN, 3rd November 1848.

Vienna has been in the hands of the troops since yesterday morning.—' Florisdorf, 1st November. During the past night Vienna was taken by storm ! Most of the leaders of the Academic Legion and the crowd fled like the cowards they are, and left those they had misled to their fate. . . .' So falls the rule of anarchy and the red republic. The forces of law and order have conquered. May the hydra never raise its accursed head again !

On the 9th Count Brandenburg announced to the Assembly that it was prorogued until the 27th, to meet then, not in

---

[1] Friedländer Collection, Berlin Library.

Berlin, but at Brandenburg. The excited Assembly, now a
Rump, for it was deserted by almost all members on the Right,
decided to continue its sittings in Berlin, and passed a resolution
refusing the payment of taxes it had already voted. But
Wrangel was at hand, ready to hold a second review in Berlin.
The following was his Army Order next day, prior to his entry: [1]

1. Although the troops marching into the City may expect in
general a friendly reception, it is nevertheless possible that their entry
may encounter opposition at certain points. Where this occurs, the
troops must behave with the greatest tranquillity and moderation,
but, as a last resort, overcome the opposition by force of arms.
Every incident of the kind must at once be reported to me.

2. The quarters will during the first few days leave much to be
desired ; but the soldiers are to be instructed to content themselves
with what is provided, even when this means bivouacking in a bare
room with straw for a bed.

3. The soldiers are to be warned against committing any excesses,
and must all be in their quarters at nine o'clock P.M.

Prince Hohenlohe-Ingelfingen gives a racy account [2] of the
actual entry of the Guards Artillery into the city :

We began to move. The batteries marched between the two
battalions. Suddenly ' Halt ! ' ' Aha ! Now for the order to
attack. Right you are, there comes an adjutant galloping up.' ' Is
the battery to advance ? ' ' No, the band must march at the head.'
So the drum-major's staff of the Janissaries' band was to lead the
forlorn hope through the Schönhauser Gate. The same farce was
played at every other gate. Several battalions of the Civic Guard
stood at each gate ready to defend it. The leader of this imposing
body had hastened up to our troops and declared he could not suffer
us to enter, and was prepared to defend the gate with his battalions.
The music of the Triumphal March into Paris drowned his words.
' For God's sake, order the troops to halt ! ' he shouted. A terrible
noise of big drums, kettle-drums, fifes, etc., was the answer. ' Make
them halt, Colonel ! ' Head shaking and music are the answer.
' You don't surely wish to cause frightful bloodshed ? ' More head
shaking and more music. ' I shall oppose you.' ' Oh don't make
yourself ridiculous ! ' ' I protest against your entry.' ' I don't
mind.' ' If I use force, will you then use force too ? ' ' You can
see that for yourself.' ' Very good ! I yield to force ! ' he cried with
a flourish, and hastened off to order his force of civilians not to oppose
our entry.

Wrangel quietly surrounded the Theatre Royal, where the
Assembly was listening to a message from Count Brandenburg,

[1] Klein. [2] *Aus meinem Leben*, i.

declaring null and void all resolutions passed since the proro-
gation. An account,[1] based on Wrangel's own description,
indicates the ease with which he broke up this Assembly, the
elect of the people :

At ten o'clock General von Wrangel rode from Charlottenburg to
the Brandenburg Gate, thence round the town to the Kreuzberg,
whither the Grenadier Guards brigade had been summoned, and at
two o'clock he marched at their head through the Halle Gate into
the town. The march was directed to the Gendarmenmarkt where
the battalions formed up in column and piled arms. The artillery
was stationed in the Mohrenstrasse and Markgrafenstrasse. The
Civic Guard stood along the Charlottenstrasse up to and round the
Theatre Royal. The General rode along part of the front and greeted
the Civic Guard, which, however, made no response. Hisses and
whistles sounded from the crowd further off. On the way from the
gate to the square the populace looked on in sulky silence.

General von Wrangel, having returned to the troops in the Mohrenstrasse, dismounted and sat down on a chair which was fetched for
him out of a house. Soon afterwards the Commander of the Civic
Guard appeared, bare-headed, accompanied on his right by the chief
of his staff, Duncker, and on the left by his aide-de-camp. He
declared : 'The Civic Guard is resolved to protect the freedom of
the people and the dignity of the National Asembly and will only
give way to force.' The General answered in a quiet and friendly
tone : 'Tell your Civic Guard that the force is already here, and that
I with my troops will guarantee to keep order; the National Assembly
will leave their hall within fifteen minutes, and then the Civic Guard
will retire also.'

Major Rimpler went back to the Civic Guard at the Theatre. The
time fixed had not yet elapsed when the deputies began to come
down the steps of the Theatre in pairs, and accompanied by the cries
of the crowd, passed on in procession to the Taubenstrasse and
disappeared. The Civic Guard vanished just as quickly and leaving
as little trace of its whereabouts. The Charlottenstrasse and the
precincts of the Theatre had emptied like magic.

Two days later, on 12th November, a state of siege was
declared in Berlin. Wrangel's pronouncement was sufficiently
drastic in its terms : [2]

In pursuance of the decree by the Royal Ministers of State whereby
the City of Berlin and the adjoining district for a distance of two
miles from the town are placed in a state of siege, I order as follows :

1. All clubs and societies for political objects are to be closed.
2. No gathering of persons in the streets and public places must
exceed twenty individuals by day, or ten by night.

---

[1] *Das Volk in Waffen im Sinne der Demokratie* (K.).
[2] Facsimile in Blum.

3. All public-houses must be closed at ten o'clock P.M.

4. Posters, newspapers or other publications must not be printed, sold in public, or posted on walls, etc., until permission to do so has been granted by the police authorities.

5. All strangers who cannot give a satisfactory account of the purpose of their stay here are to leave the City and its precincts within twenty-four hours, on pain of expulsion.

6. All strangers arriving with arms are to be disarmed by the guards.

7. The Civic Guard is by Royal Decree, dated 11th inst., disbanded pending reorganisation. This reorganisation cannot be effected during the state of siege. . . .

Von Wrangel.

There can be no doubt that Wrangel's success was due to his extraordinary combination of uncompromising firmness and genial tact, which of themselves conquered the crowd. Prince Hohenlohe-Ingelfingen [1] claims that he soon became a most popular old gentleman :

Wrangel was at that time decried as the most frightful tyrant and oppressor, the Gessler, Tilly and devil of Berlin. This terrible personage, however, soon revealed himself as the most popular old gentleman who had ever lived there. At first he received anonymous, threatening, and incendiary letters. One day it was announced to him that if he and his troops had not withdrawn from Berlin by such and such a date, his wife would be hanged at Stettin on that day at three o'clock to the minute. This was his dinner hour, and as he sat down to table on the day indicated he looked at his watch and remarked : ' It is three o'clock. I wonder, have they hanged her ! Hardly, I imagine.' The incident is said to have occurred on the occasion of his march to the Gendarmenmarkt and the threat only referred to this.

Order was restored in the city as if by magic. A leaflet [2] was issued, as some sort of appeal to the people, in behalf of the National Assembly :

. . . At this grievous moment, when the constitutional representatives of the people have been scattered by the bayonet, we call on you to cling fast to the liberties already won and which we pledge ourselves to maintain with all our strength and with our lives, but never for a moment to over-step the bounds of the law. The calm and resolute attitude of a people ripe for freedom, will, with God's help, achieve the victory for freedom !

Another,[3] by the democratic clubs, gave vent to their feelings :

---

[1] *Aus meinem Leben*, i.
[2] Friedländer Collection, City Library, Berlin.
[3] *Ibid.*

GENERAL WRANGEL

who is in open opposition to the meeting of the nation's representatives and therefore to the whole Prussian nation, who has attempted to hinder by the bayonet the National Assembly in the discharge of its legal obligations,

This General Wrangel we, in conjunction with all other honourable citizens of the state, declare to be *a traitor to the people*, who having put himself outside the law has no claim to the law's protection. The Democratic Club. The Democratic Unions of the Royal Capital.

A feeble attempt was made, not in Berlin but on the Rhine, to support the strike against taxes called for by the Prussian Assembly. An amusing report [1] of what took place at Bonn is given by Carl Schurz. Schurz was concerned in the Baden insurrection of the spring of 1849. He was conspicuous among revolutionaries for courage, resourcefulness, and strength of character. Captured at Rastatt he effected a most adventurous escape, but returned boldly to Germany in 1850, and rescued from prison at Spandau his friend, the poet Gottfried Kinkel. Ultimately he took refuge in the United States, where he rose to high distinction both as a statesman and as a general. His *Reminiscences*, published in 1909, make up one of the most interesting personal accounts of the revolution of 1848 in a crowded literature. The stories of his escape from Rastatt and of his rescue of Gottfried Kinkel are as good as much that is to be found in Casanova's adventurous record :

The democrats in Bonn, among whom we students played a prominent part, were zealous in demonstrating their determination to support the Constituent Assembly. The declaration that we would refuse the payment of taxes coming from the students looked somewhat like a huge joke, because we had none to pay. The problem we had to solve, therefore, consisted in persuading other people to refuse to pay their taxes. We believed we could strike a demonstrative blow by stopping the levying of octroi duties at the gates on the foodstuffs brought to the town. We did this in driving the revenue officers from their posts, which pleased the peasants, who were at once ready to bring in their products free of duty. This led to conflicts with the police, in which, however, we easily had the upper hand.

Now it appeared to us necessary to seize upon the general machinery of the tax department. The next day, a committee, of which I was

---

[1] *Reminiscences of Carl Schurz*, i. p. 154: Doubleday, Page & Co., New York.

a member, appeared at the city hall to take possession of it. The Burgomaster received us with great politeness, and listened quietly to what we had to say to him about the authority of the Constituent Assembly and its power to stop the payment of taxes ; but he tried to amuse us with evasive talk. At last we became impatient and demanded an immediate and definite answer according to which we would resolve upon further measures. Suddenly we noticed a change in the expression of the Burgomaster's face. He seemed to hearken to something going on outside, and then, still politely, but with a sort of triumphant smile on his lips, said : ' Gentlemen, your answer you will have to receive from somebody else. Do you hear that ? ' Now we, too, listened, and heard the distant, but approaching, sound of a military band playing the Prussian national air. The music sounded nearer and nearer in the street leading up from the Rhine. In a few minutes it reached the market-place, and behind it came the heavy tramp of an infantry column, which presently filled a large part of the square in front of the city hall. Our conversation with the Burgomaster of course came to a sudden end, and we thought it very decent on his part that he permitted us to leave the building unhindered.

We may close our account of this peaceful ending to the revolution in Berlin with three documents, the first a letter [1] from that most amusing of revolutionaries, Michael Bakunin, to Herwegh :

KÖTHEN, 8th December 1848.

. . . ' J'attendrai, Monseigneur ! ' That is my reply to the triumphant reaction,—and Anarchy, the destruction of states, will have to come soon. But I have thought of you very often, and said to myself how right you were, when I saw near at hand how things stood in Germany, and what was going on there. I remembered the words you repeated so often to me in Paris before the revolution : ' The first revolution in Germany will have nothing encouraging for us, for it will be the victory of middle-class meanness.' How great is the meanness of the German Philistine I have now seen in its full measure. Nowhere is the bourgeois a lovable individual, but the German bourgeois combines meanness with smug comfort.

The second document [2] gives us a glimpse of the introduction of methods quite modern into the autocratic Prussian government. The brains of the Brandenburg ministry were furnished, as had been intended, by Otto von Manteuffel, who had played for some years before the revolution the part of fidus Achates to the Prince of Prussia, and who now showed his ability to

---

[1] Briefe von und an G. Herwegh (K.).
[2] Unter Friedrich Wilhelm IV., Manteuffel's Memoirs, by H. von Poschinger, p. 184.

play the same part in relation to his uncle. He was a man of firmness, courage, and some imagination. The revolution had taught him this much, that it is as well for even an autocratic government to take some account of the sentiments of the populace, and not to depend solely for information on the reports of spies and officials. Taking a hint from the *Arabian Nights*, he determined in the autumn of 1849 to explore like Haroun Al-Raschid, incognito, the haunts of the working man. The *Vossische Zeitung* of 30th October 1849 gives an account of the first of these expeditions, in the somewhat stilted language on which the political journalist still has to strut when called upon to write up a party favourite in hours of ease, felling timber, playing golf or shaking hands with the humble friends of his boyhood :

Great sensation has been aroused in the city by the circulation of the rumour of a ministerial adventure, which, if it is to be accepted as accurate, must do more than many governmental ordinances to confirm the judgment of all thinking people on the present adminis-tration. On Saturday, we are informed, the Minister von Manteuffel appeared, unexpected and unrecognised, in a humble lower-class restaurant, No. — Linienstrasse, which enjoys a democratic reputa-tion, accompanied by a man whose simple language indicated a man of the people. Who could even imagine that the Home Secretary would condescend to step down, in the literal sense of the term, among the people ? Who could recognise in the individual, who called himself Herr Müller, and appeared in plain clothing and in plain company, the Minister of State whom Prussia has so largely to thank for her salvation ? Even the striking likeness between Herr Müller and the minister was not calculated to lead the white-beer-drinking [1] politicians to divine that their new guest was his Excel-lency himself, and therefore conversation went on just as free and unconstrained as before. Herr Müller drank his white beer without ceremony, just like any one else, and in the pros and cons of discussion the prevailing tone was so unprejudiced and the general judgment so sound, that often Herr Müller was the speaker and all the others listeners. An instant had sufficed to win him all hearts, without his being recognised. And as he finally got ready to depart, his com-panion raised his beer-glass and cried out : ' Long live ,lawful freedom ! Long live the ministry that keeps watch and ward over this lawful freedom ! Long live his Excellency, the Minister von Manteuffel, who does not think it beneath his dignity to join a company of simple citizens, and appears among them not as Minister but as a simple citizen himself.' Then the scales fell from the eyes

---

[1] White beer, a sour, detestable drink, used to be popular in certain circles in Berlin, notably among cab-drivers.

of the pothouse politicians. A boisterous, thundering cheer from the assembly, three times repeated, showed his Excellency that he had won a welcome as man of the people, that the Minister, in his capacity anyhow as Herr Müller, was popular. The Minister expressed his thanks in the warmest terms for their applause, which seemed to him like a vote of confidence in reply to the vote of censure passed against him the previous year by the National Assembly from the stalls of a theatre, and promised, if possible, to pay another visit. He had come not as an eavesdropper, but as a listener, not as Minister, but as a citizen. A renewal of the boisterous cheering, with a grip of the hand from all who could reach the Minister of State, speeded his departure. This bare recital of facts needs no comment. The Minister has become a man of the people.

The third document is Victor von Unruh's summary [1] of the results to Prussia of the year 1848 :

If one asks himself now (1877) after twenty-nine years : ' What was achieved in Prussia by the struggles of the year 1848, and have they proved useful or injurious ?—and if one endeavours to answer this question as impersonally as possible, but still from the liberal point of view, one cannot deny that, in spite of the many and great mistakes which were at that time made on all sides, those events in the year 1848 laid the foundations of our political development and of our political conditions as they exist to-day ; conditions which no fair-minded man, and hardly even a Conservative, unless an absolute reactionary, would willingly exchange for those of 1848. Yes, even the reactionaries themselves would not be disposed to return to that time of absolute bureaucratic and arbitrary government. Certainly it would have been better if, long before 1848, the Government had lent a friendly hand in an absolute, necessary, organic reform of the state; but that, in view of the personality of Frederick William IV., was not for a moment to be thought of. . . . We were all in 1848 amateurs, not to say children, in matters political. We clung to Rotteck-Dahlmannish constitution-planning, and thought that everything desirable could be attained by judicious paragraphing. We had to learn by bitter experience that it is actual reforms in the existing State, and especially in its organisation, which are most effective in achieving a logical progress with as few sudden transitions and experiments as possible.

---

[1] *Erinnerungen* (K.).

CHAPTER IV

CONFUSION IN AUSTRIA AND VIENNA THROUGH-OUT SPRING AND SUMMER

VERY different from the peaceful ending of the revolution in Berlin was the case in Vienna. As pointed out on page 260 the constitutional and national questions raised by the revolutionary movement which culminated in 1848 were far more complicated in Austria than in Prussia and the other purely German States. The German element in Austria, with its centre in Vienna, shared all the enthusiasm for a united Germany that animated Prussia, Bavaria, Baden, Saxony, and the lesser German States. But the non-German elements in the Austrian Empire had their individual national aspirations. The northern Slavs, the Czechs of Bohemia, were nursing hopes of autonomy. The Magyars of Hungary, under the stimulus of their eloquent hero, Kossuth, were aflame for independence, for an actual severance from German Austria, though what they demanded for themselves they were hotly determined not to grant to the southern Slavs under Hungarian domination. For their part the southern Slavs, under the leadership of Jellachich and his Croatians, were equally bent on wresting their liberties from Magyar tyranny, and dreamed of a great Slavonic Illyrian state. The Galicians too had their fond hopes, and the Roumanians and Germans of Transylvania each a confused vision of what was due to them. And besides all these warring elements within the Austrian Empire proper were the subjugated Italians, the populations of Lombardy and Venetia, who rose under Charles Albert of Sardinia to free themselves from a foreign yoke.

Within eighteen months of the Vienna revolution of March 1848, the Imperial Government and the Imperial Army had to crush, and did crush, with Russia's assistance in the case of Hungary, northern Italy, Bohemia, Hungary, and a new revolution in Vienna itself. To give a clear description in detail of all the fighting and diplomatic dealing and constitution-mongering that went on within the Austrian Empire during 1848 and 1849 is a task surpassing the most intricate jig-saw puzzle yet devised for the recreation of the immature brains of the nursery or the exhausted intellects of the parlour. It is mercifully outside the scope of this book, where it is only necessary to tell so much, in the broadest outline, as makes clear the course of events in the October revolution in Vienna. Above all, the following considerations have to be borne in mind. So complicated was the situation, and so confused were the minds and emotions and passions of all concerned that the most astonishing paradoxes resulted in the attitude of men towards events. Thus the victory of Windischgrätz in Bohemia, when he reduced Prague by bombardment in June, and the victories of Radetzky in Italy were hailed by German radicals as triumphs of Germanism. They made, as they thought, for 'German freedom,' which, as has been pointed out before, takes no account of the freedom of others ! On the other hand, German radicals warmly supported the Magyars against the Slavs, and finally we have them heart and soul with the October revolutionaries of Vienna, the enthusiasts for popular government and German unity, in hailing the Magyars as allies against the Imperial Government and the Imperial Army, with their allies, the southern Slavs under Jellachich, Ban of Croatia. There was no longer a subtle-minded Metternich to direct the policy of Austria, but there were some cool heads around an impotent Kaiser, and the counterpoise of contending forces maintained for a time an unstable equilibrium. What finally tipped the scale in favour of the Imperial Government was the action of the Croatians under Jellachich in uniting their fortunes with those of the Hapsburgs as the one means of shaking themselves clear of Hungarian oppression. And so we have the crowning paradox that, whatever became of German unity, German predominance within the Austrian Empire was saved by the Slavs !

We may now take up the thread of events in Vienna after the March revolution. The Imperial Government had utterly collapsed. The National Guard and the Academic Legion were recognised by the Kaiser, and the government was ultimately in the hands of a Committee of Public Safety, consisting of members of the National Guard, students and citizens, who dictated their will to the Ministry. The army was powerless, for the two great generals of the day, Windischgrätz and Radetzky, were tied with all available forces, the one to Bohemia and the other to northern Italy. Only a small garrison was left in Vienna, and it was a rumour that drafts from this were being secretly sent off by Latour, the Minister of War, to reinforce in the autumn the army massed against Hungary, that led to the outbreak of the October revolution in Vienna. On 25th April the Ministry, under Pillersdorf, promulgated the brand-new constitution which was to be the fruit of the successful revolution in March. It provided for a two-chamber parliament, and ministerial responsibility to parliament. This did not satisfy the radicals of Vienna. The state of unrest in the capital continued, where the same sort of confusion, but in exaggerated form, prevailed as in Berlin. The chief elements of unrest were the students and the unemployed workmen with their wives and families, whom the government endeavoured to keep quiet by a series of doles. On 13th May a new governor of the city, Count Hoyos, endeavoured to rid himself of the interference of the National Guard and the students by dissolving the Central Political Committee they had set up. Thereupon a mob of discontented workmen and students, unchecked by the National Guard, marched on the palace on the 15th. They selected a deputation which forced its way into a meeting of the cabinet, and demanded the reinstatement of the Central Political Committee and a revision of the new constitution on the lines of a single chamber system and universal suffrage, with the further proviso that the army should not be summoned except on the demand of the National Guard ! Late that night the Kaiser signed all these concessions ; but two days later he left Schönbrunn for Innsbruck, on the pretext of a water-cure.

Naturally enough the Kaiser's flight did not mend matters, and suspicions arose of a reactionary camarilla hostile to the fine flower of democracy now scenting the university and the streets of the capital. The unfortunate Pillersdorf induced the Ministry to try again where Count Hoyos had failed ; they went for smaller game, not the Central Political Committee but the Academic Legion. The university was to close for the summer vacation on 26th May, and the Ministry chose that day to declare the dissolution of the Legion. The students resisted, and were backed by the dole-fed workmen of the city. A feeble show of force was made by the National Guard and a few regular soldiers, but barricades were erected, and the Ministry capitulated. From that day until the revolution which broke out in October was finally crushed by Windischgrätz and Jellachich, though there was still a nominal Ministry in office, the actual government of the capital of the Austrian Empire was entirely in the hands of the Central Political Committee.

It is a relief to turn for a few moments from this spectacle of civilian muddle to see how the armies of Windischgrätz and Radetzky were faring in Italy and in Bohemia. The former, after making the quite unfounded claim that he had restored order in Vienna, left for his command in Bohemia on 18th April, where there was plenty of occupation for him in watching the progress of the Czech national movement. Prague, the capital, was kept in a state of excitement early in June by a great Slav congress, which, however, like many other congresses, resulted in nothing more than a series of inconclusive resolutions. The Prague students, emulous of their brothers in Vienna, demanded arms, and when these were refused by Windischgrätz, they joined an excited mob in attacking his palace on the 13th. Windischgrätz, who became notorious for his slowness of movement, showed extraordinary restraint or nonchalance in his dealings with the rioters, even after his wife had been shot dead at a window.[1] As a result of negotiations he withdrew the army to the heights round the city, but this may have been a tactical move on his part to avoid the street-fighting which every soldier hates. He certainly succeeded in crushing the insurrection without it, for on the 16th some shots fired from the city gave him the opportunity of subjecting it to so effective a day and night bombardment that the place was absolutely at his mercy and surrendered unconditionally.

---

[1] Metternich heard in London of her death, and wrote on 26th June : ' The death of poor Élénore, that angelic creature, is a catastrophe that affects me very nearly. After the death of her mother [Princess Schwarzenberg, burnt to death in a fire at the Austrian Embassy in Paris, 1810], a death rendered so terrible by the circumstances that accompanied it, I devoted to the child a father's affection. She found an asylum with me in 1810 ; she was treated as one of my own children, and has always been regarded as such. The tragic fate of the Atridæ weighed on her though she deserved it not. I weep for her as if she were my own daughter. I mourn for her as the victim of a delirium, which, usurping the title of progress though it brings nothing but death in its train, does so much harm to-day.' *Mémoires, etc. de Metternich*, vol. viii. No. 1722.

The news of this success of drastic measures against revolution
was hailed by German princes and all supporters of the old order,
and their joy was heightened by the further good news that came
from Radetzky in Italy. This great soldier who, like Windischgrätz, had fought with distinction at Leipzig, was eighty-two
years of age when Lombardy rose in revolt in March 1848, but he
conducted the Austrian campaign with the dash and energy of a
young man. Count Hübner, a clever, middle-class protégé of
Metternich, who rose to eminence as a diplomatist and understood England better than most of his countrymen, gives in his
Ein Jahr meines Lebens an amusing glimpse of him at this time :

Radetzky, what an amiable old man ! In spite of his eighty-two
years he has preserved the activity, the cheerfulness, the nimbleness
of a stripling. He exercises a remarkable charm over the army.
13th (March), Monday. Great military dinner at the Field-marshal's
with all the chiefs of his army : the Wallmodens, Carl Schwarzenberg,
Calm-Gallas, Wohlgemuth, Wocher, Schönhals and tutti quanti !
In my character as civilian, the only one of my kind, the Field-
marshal had placed me beside him and took pleasure in heaping
dainties on my plate with his own hand. On his right sat his contemporary, General Wallmoden. ' Look,' said Wallmoden to me,
' how his hand trembles ; he is getting old, very old.' This said,
he fell asleep at my side. Now came the venerable Radetzky's
turn.—' Look, look,' said he with a wink. ' He still wishes to play
the gallant, raves about the beautiful sex and snores at table.'

After five days street-fighting, Radetzky was compelled to
abandon Milan on 23rd March, and fell back on Verona and
Mantua. Here for a time he seemed unable to make any impression against the King of Sardinia, but in the very moment
of defeat at Goito, on 30th May, he wrested victory from the
Italians. His army was still intact, and within little more than
a fortnight he captured successively Vicenza, Treviso, Padua,
and Rovigo. Before the end of July he had routed the Piedmontese at Custozza, and on 8th August he re-entered Milan in
triumph. His final victory over Charles Albert and the Italian
patriots was to be at Novara in March 1849. There he virtually
destroyed the Piedmontese army, and was enabled again to
place all northern Italy under the Austrian heel.

Even in a Vienna reduced to a state of anarchy, the intelligence of Radetzky's brilliant achievements early in June could
not fail to arouse some enthusiasm. And this was voiced by

Grillparzer. To Windischgrätz the poet had nothing better to
offer than an epigram :

> Windischgrätz, to whom compare you
>   In speech that for the plain man caters ?
> Old Metternich I do declare you
>   If not in stockings, still in gaiters.

But to Radetzky in June he addressed the tribute of an ode :

TO FIELD-MARSHAL RADETZKY

> Here 's to my general ! Now strike home ;
>   Not only fame for thy fee !
> Thy camp encloses Austria,
>   Her separate members are we.
>
> By foolishness and vanity
>   Came our collapse and fall,
> But when thou leadest men to war
>   The old fire glows in all. . . .
>
> Whom God as Slavs and Magyars made,
>   They 'll quarrel not for a word ;
> They 'll follow a German battle-cry :
>   ' Vorwärts ! ' be the call, it is heard.
>
> On help from all, at need of all,
>   Are founded Kingdom and State,
> For only in death man stands alone,
>   In life and in strife finds a mate.
>
> Shoulder to shoulder 's the lesson
>   Thy glorious victories teach ;
> In union of all comes victory,
>   With happiness for each.

This poem was hailed by the army with an enthusiasm which
proved embarrassing to the poet, who had to defend himself
from the charge of conversion to reactionary principles by an
epigram at the expense of the military :

> Field-marshal and Sergeant-major, both
> To praise the sword are nothing loth ;
> Had they the art to versify,
> Like brandy to the soul 'twould fly.

But though contingents from many of the varied races making
up the Austrian Empire fought in Radetzky's army, this fact

in itself was no proof of Czech or Magyar loyalty to the empire, and the revolutionary mob at Vienna soon forgot the foreign triumphs of Austrian arms in their hatred of the Austrian government.

On 20th June Hebbel made a gloomy and enigmatical entry in his diary, which points to the apprehensions tormenting men of moderate opinions :

The very pavement of the state and of society is being rooted up. I have a curious feeling about it. It seems to me as if ancient experiences were the basis of the building which is now being demolished, won out of conditions which are now again approaching ; as if every paving-stone bore the inscription on the upturned side : ' we indeed know that this is a paving-stone, although we have stamped upon it as it were the image of a god. Take heed how you will succeed without paving-stones which men esteem as more than paving-stones.'

Towards the end of August the curse of public doles, whereby the Minister of Public Works had endeavoured to pacify the crowds of unemployed workmen by the provision of nominal work at a daily wage, came home to roost. The state of the exchequer forced the Ministry to economise, and they reduced the daily wage they had been paying, with the result that a bloody conflict was provoked on 23rd August between the workmen employed on the Prater and the municipal guard. Hebbel's account of this in the *Augsburger Allgemeine Zeitung*, and his reflections, were as follows : [1]

To-day, Wednesday, matters came to a crisis, and, alas, did not, as on the day before yesterday, pass without victims. The circumstances were these. Early this morning, the workmen who were assembled in the Prater at their regular place of employment, instead of going to work as usual, gave vent to their discontent by making a mud doll, which was said to represent the Minister of Public Works, and burying it ceremonially with characteristic rites. Thereupon, they grew more and more inflamed, tumultuous scenes took place, and two men, belonging to the guard, who had mingled with the crowd, apparently in order to induce peace, were killed, according to one account, by hanging, according to another, by strangling. Meanwhile, the alarm had been given to the National Guard, near the Leopold suburb, and they turned out in great numbers. The working people began to march into the town, carrying flags before them, and at the beginning of the Jägerzeile, on that open space stretching out on all sides, an encounter took place. The number

---

[1] Klein.

of killed and wounded is so very variously stated that I will say
nothing about it ; I myself saw three workmen, who had been shot,
lying where they fell.

Who is to blame ?   Certainly not the working men, for they are
good fellows at core ; but the fools who, heedless of the true nature of
things, and disdaining the only proper standards of what is just and
practicable in a world of realities, inoculate them with their own
crude, socialistic dreams, and also the speculators, who are im-
measurably worse, for they wish, by an upheaval of the masses, to
bring about a rise for their benefit.   I know very well that under
some circumstances bloodshed is not too high a price to pay, and
would willingly have endured to see it flow in streams in March when
the most sacred of causes was at stake.   But to-day I could not look
upon those three corpses mentioned above, without heartrending
pain, for I could not but say to myself : They have, it is true, taken
it upon themselves to commit acts of violence, but they were en-
snared in error which they themselves could not recognise as such,
and from every standpoint they are to be pitied.   The guard, into
the bargain, as I heard from very reliable testimony, gave itself
licence to act with roughness and severity, and indeed, on its return
march into the town, hoisted green boughs as if coming from a famous
battle.   I had also cause on this occasion to admire the sound sense
of the middle classes, still so hardly oppressed, and for whom nothing
is done.   ' The whole thing,' said an artisan to me, ' lies at Metternich's door.   If, ever since 1815, he had gradually undone our strait-
waistcoat button by button, how far we should have been on the
road to freedom by now ! '   With that, he deeply deplored the fate
of the Emperor Ferdinand.   ' It ought to have happened to old
Franz,' he added with flashing eyes, ' if I could wake him, I would
raise him up to-day ! '

A month later, on 28th September, came the atrocious
murder of Field-marshal Count Lamberg at Budapest, which
precipitated the crisis in Vienna itself.   The count, himself a
Hungarian magnate, and well-disposed to his countrymen,
had been sent there by the Austrian Government in a last
desperate effort to avoid a conflict between the Magyars and
the Croatians.   On the one side stood Kossuth, who had
inflamed Magyar fanaticism to the highest pitch, and by his
extravagances, including a proposal to make the Palatine or
Viceroy, Archduke Stephen, King of Hungary, had forced the
latter to resign his office ;   on the other stood Jellachich,
straining at the leash, panting to be at the throat of the
oppressors of the Slavs.   Lamberg's mission was to take over
the command of all troops, Hungarian and Croatian alike,
and arrange an armistice.   Kossuth carried a resolution
through the Hungarian Diet on 27th September, calling on

the Hungarian army to refuse all recognition of Lamberg's authority. The unfortunate man arrived next day and proceeded to Buda (the ancient city on the left bank of the Danube) to present his credentials to the president of the Hungarian Ministry, Count Batthyány. But Batthyány was away. He went on to the residence of the general commanding the fortress. A mob followed him there, and though he escaped them, he met a horrible death a few minutes later, on his flight across the bridge to Pest. Here is a contemporary account [1] of his murder :

While this was going on at the fortress, the alarm was sounded in both cities, all gateways were barred, the National Guard turned out, and the streets surged with people, both volunteers and peasants. . . . The unfortunate Count Lamberg, who had come to Buda without escort or guard, trusting in the inviolability of a Royal Commissioner, had meanwhile procured a vehicle and was driving over the pontoon-bridge to Pest, to gain the secure protection of the law. At the middle of the bridge stood a troop of the National Guard and men bearing scythes . . . with a few members of the Academic Legion of Vienna at their head. These stopped the fiacre and recognised Count Lamberg. One of them stepped forward with the question : ' Who are you ? ' ' Royal Commissioner, Count Lamberg,' was the steady answer. ' Then go to hell ! ' yelled the student, and split open his skull. And then followed a scene which is difficult to depict. The half-dead Count, bleeding terribly, was pulled out of the carriage and dragged along the bridge—the trail of blood could be followed right into the town. He was stabbed with bayonets, his limbs cut off with scythes, his body was slashed, so that the intestines gushed out. Arrived at the wide Bankgasse the corpse of the murdered and mutilated man was taken possession of by the mob. He was pulled and dragged hither and thither, all his clothing was literally torn into shreds, they stamped on him with their feet, spitted him on bayonets, and exhibited the corpse to the devilishly jubilant multitude. . . . At last the mob reached the hospital. A rope was tied round the neck of the body of Count Lamberg, now hardly recognisable as a human form, for the last shreds of the stomach had been torn away, and in this condition he was on the point of being hanged on a lamp-post. The National Guard prevented that ; the dishonoured corpse was carried into the *Invaliden Palais* and thence conveyed during the night to the Rochus hospital.

The excitement this abominable crime aroused in Vienna was tremendous. It was not indignation against the Hungarian murderers that stirred the German revolutionaries of Vienna. What moved them was the example Hungary had afforded of a

---

[1] Dunder, *Denksc . ift über die Wiener Oktober-Revolution* (K.).

short way for dealing with any hated representative of the Imperial Government. And in little more than a week they showed themselves as brutal adepts in the art of murder as the mob of Budapest. The prelude to the bloody outbreak of the October revolution in Vienna was sounded in a poem which appeared in the *Politischen Studenten-Courier* on 4th October, and is reprinted in Baron von Helfert's *Wiener Parnass* :

À LA LANTERNE !

They will not learn, they nothing learn,
These courtly high-born peers !
In vain the clanging trump of doom
Assails their stubborn ears.
    That only after bloody throes
    Doth Freedom's dawn expand
    To golden light, dispelling night,
    They cannot understand.
So, since the high-born will not learn
A fresh, new age is nigh,
Then hang the high-born gentlemen
High on the lamp-posts, high !

They nothing learn, they never learn,
In royal robe and crown ;
The avenging hand of destiny
Strikes them with blindness down.
    They dream 'tis still the ancient time,
    That, by their royal nod,
    The people's blood shall dye their robes—
    Kings by the Grace of God !
Because these tyrants merciless
The people's rights defy,
Give them short shrift and hang them quick,
High on the lamp-posts, high !

My German people, would you learn
The road to your salvation ?
Then let not Freedom, stifled, die
'Neath indolent stagnation.
    At dark, on guard, they challenge ' Blood ! '
    The watch-word of the foe ;
    They forge new chains, inflict fresh pains—
    Their blood, their blood must flow !
Though checked and crossed, with dauntless will
Your purpose glorify,
And hang them, tyrants, priests and slaves
High on the lamp-posts, high !

CHAPTER V

THE REVOLUTION IN VIENNA

THE trouble between Austria and Hungary had long been brewing, and had gradually forced into the background the constitutional struggle which was the ostensible justification for the revolution in March. The promised Reichstag, which was finally to settle this problem, was indeed opened towards the end of July by the Archduke John, a few days after his election as Regent by the German National Assembly at Frankfort. A striking feature of this Reichstag was the variety of languages and dialects in which debates had to be conducted, the Germans actually forming a minority in the assembly. This fact in itself is evidence enough of the difficulties that faced pan-German Austrians in their efforts to make common cause with their German brothers in the effort to secure not only constitutional reform, but also German unity. The Reichstag referred to a committee the question of the new constitution that was to govern the empire, and devoted August to the one great purpose which it did achieve, viz. : the liberation of the peasants from the condition almost of serfdom under which many of them still suffered. But before the Reichstag could take up the thread of discussion on the constitutional question came the menace of the Hungarian revolt against Austria, and then the sudden rising of the mob in the streets of Vienna, and, like a thunderclap, the murder of Latour.

The Imperial Government had for months maintained a vacillating attitude between the Magyars and the Slavs, between Kossuth and Jellachich. They recognised the advantages to be gained by keeping on friendly terms with Jellachich, for he might prove a useful ally if Hungary finally rose in rebellion, and with this in view they had appointed him Ban, or governor, of Croatia. His ascendancy there rested on a firm basis, for he was the son of a Croatian nobleman who had distinguished himself in warfare against the Turks, and he himself had gained some reputation as a soldier.　But Vienna had no wish to see all Hungary rise in arms to repel an invasion of the Croatians under Jellachich, for confusion in the capital must then become worse confounded.　Now, however, the murder of Count Lamberg forced the Government to abandon its temporising policy, the Imperial answer on 3rd October to Kossuth's virtual declaration of war was a declaration of war from the Austrian side, the dissolution of the diet at Pest, and the nomination of Jellachich as Viceroy of Hungary and Commander-in-Chief of the Imperial forces in Count Lamberg's place.

Grillparzer's epigram on Hungary was fine, but did not reflect the sentiment of revolutionary Vienna :

> You fought through cloud and night,
> To earth your foe did smite ;
> -At dawn the corpse you scanned,
> Lo ! 'twas your fatherland.

Indeed the Austrian declaration of war roused the utmost indignation among the German revolutionaries in Vienna ; they had kept in close touch with the forces of insurrection in Hungary and regarded them as friends and allies linked by a common hatred of autocratic imperial rule.　Their wrath rose to fever-point when they found the Austrian army committed to an attempt to crush Hungary by force of arms, and the aid of Slavs against Magyars invoked.　Latour, the Minister of War, became the especial object of their fury.　During months of disorder in Vienna, Latour had not interested himself in making public appearances ; he had confined himself closely to his duties of keeping the armies of Radetzky and Windisch-grätz supplied, and had done his work well, despite the enormous difficulties of the time.　Now, in the first week of October, the rumour, probably true enough, spread that he was sending reinforcements to Jellachich.　A mob rose, filled the streets on the 6th, and it became obvious that Latour's life was in danger.　The mob swarmed into the War Office, and Latour hid himself in an attic.　One of his aides-de-camp had escaped from the War Office to the Reichstag, where he announced the danger in which Latour lay.　Several deputies promised to take him under their protection if he would resign

his office. He did, but that did not save his life, as the following
account [1] of his brutal murder will show :

It was towards four o'clock ; the crowd was continually increasing,
the uproar growing louder and more violent, the ways thronged, so
that people were obliged to force their way through. Niewiadomski,
(Latour's chief aide-de-camp) tried to get through the crowd, as he
feared for Latour's life ; he had a paper in his hand, relating to
Latour's resignation, and he wished to go to the Reichstag in order
to report the danger in which Latour stood, and to crave help from
it ; but when the people about him read the contents of the paper,
which was freshly sprinkled with sand, he was seized, detained, and
pressed, under threat of death, to point out the whereabouts of the
War Minister, which he refused. After long demur, and under ever-
increasing threats, at last he pointed them towards an indefinite spot
as the place where the War Minister had fled for refuge. One
portion of the crowd dashed towards the spot indicated ; another
detained him as hostage ; he was thrust into a room which both
people and guard watched closely. [Nevertheless Niewiadomski
managed to escape to the assembly of the Reichstag.] Whilst the
foregoing was taking place in the lower rooms of the War Office, the
War Minister on the fourth floor was listening to what Smolka had to
say and receiving his proposition, whereupon he stepped out of the
dark passage and placed himself under the protection of Smolka and
Sierakowski [deputies], and an officer of the National Guard and
Academic Legion. Latour [while descending the stairs to the
courtyard] was certainly much jostled, but hitherto remained uninjured. In the courtyard, however, by the fountain, the throng
which happened to be there rushed upon the group, which was
driven hither and thither. In vain Smolka and Sierakowski, as
well as the afore-mentioned officer of the Legion and National
Guard, tried their utmost to protect the life of Latour, who stood
under a barred window ; they were forced away from him ; a
workman struck the War Minister's hat from his head, others began
to seize him by the hair, he tried to defend himself with his hands
which were already bleeding ; Captain Count Leopold Gondrecourt
shielded him with his body and bleeding hands. At last a Magyar,
dressed as a workman, struck him on the head with a hammer a
fatal blow from behind, and a man in a grey coat with a cutlass gave
him a cut across his face, another a bayonet stab through the chest,
and in this manner he received many other wounds with all kinds
of instruments, under which, with the words ' I die guiltless,' he
yielded up the ghost. At this a cry of joy from the people rang
through the air. . . . Thereupon the murderers attached him with a
cord to the window bars. Here the body hung for about ten minutes.
The cord broke in consequence of the outrages perpetrated upon the
corpse. Then they dragged him out of the courtyard—repeatedly

---

[1] Dunder, *Denkschrift über die Wiener Oktober-Revolution* (K.).

letting him lie, while flying at the cry of ' Soldiers,' and then again returning—to the square adjoining the court in front of the War Office, where they again hung him up with a cord to the gas-lamp before the main guard-house.   They stabbed and shot him ; he fell down ; they tore the clothes from the body and outraged the corpse in unheard-of cannibal fashion, for, naked as he was, they derided, mocked and practised every atrocity upon him ; they dipped their pocket-handkerchiefs in his blood, and leapt about exulting. . . . The Grenadiers stood, their weapons at their feet, at the main guard-house.   The captain on guard refrained by the Minister's last command from interference.   A fair young fellow, between seventeen and twenty years of age, with rolled-up shirt sleeves, in a white jacket and check trousers, apparently a brewer's or butcher's lad, carried out the hanging this time with the help of straps from two military cloaks.   Thus Latour hung until late in the night, first in dress-coat and shirt, then in vest, underclothes, and socks, lastly quite naked.

Hübner, the diplomatist, who walked about the streets for hours, despite the irritation caused to the mob by his tall hat and shaven chin, ' both of them characteristic signs of the reactionary,' gives the following brief account [1] of this display of the *furor Teutonicus* : ' The first blow was delivered by a workman with his hatchet.   Conformably to the great traditions of 1792 and 1793, the remains of the unfortunate count were dragged away and attached to a lamp-post standing in front of the Ministry.   The horrible mob of murderers, men, women and even children, all drunk with blood and wine, sang with their hoarse, shrill voices songs of mockery over the dead man ; they howled and danced, and, until late at night, circled round the lamp-post on which hung the mangled trunk of their victim.'

Against the mob the authorities, whether represented by the Ministry or the Committee of Public Safety, were powerless. The day after Latour's murder the Arsenal was stormed, and the city was reduced to a state of anarchy.   As for the Reichstag it was rent in twain.   The Slav majority declared its sittings transferred to Brünn.   The revolutionary German rump declared the Reichstag permanent, appointed a sort of Council, a body with no intelligible function, by the side of the students and others composing the Committee of Public Safety, clamoured for an amnesty, to include Latour's murderers, and demanded the withdrawal of the declaration of war against Hungary. The Kaiser, who had returned to Vienna in August, gave, during

[1] Hübner's *Ein Jahr meines Lebens.*

the night of the 6th, a gracious answer to these demands, and next morning made a second flight, this time to Olmütz.

Adolf Pichler, from whose record, *Das Sturmjahr*,[1] several vivacious extracts were quoted in Book IV., gives a good description of the Abbot of Unreason enthroned in the university at this period :

On the steps of the University Church sat the grimy railway workers, more prepared, as it seemed, for action than for speech ; each carried in his hand an iron rod, from five to seven feet long, having a handle at the lower end, by which to wield it more effectually, and its upper part forged into a sharp spear point. The University building repudiated every sign of its original purpose ; the serious spirit of learning seemed to have retreated for ever before the noise of barrack life. Straw was spread in the lecture-rooms, upon which soldiers and students, their weapons beside them, slept quite sociably ; portraits of eminent scholars, who once had here paraded their booklearning, gazed wondering down. One of them, with a prodigious full-bottomed wig, had had the face cut out, and the mask of a monkey inserted instead. On the spot where once stood the lecturer's desk, a wench, not even modest, offered cigars and poppy-seed cakes for sale ; in the middle of the hall a lively crowd of smokers lolled upon overturned benches, and made themselves merry over a little student who, in a trooper's cuirass with a huge helmet, looked like a mouse under a pot. Others flourished half-emptied tin cups of tithe-wine which some one had presented to the undergraduate body corporate. These were indeed the prompters of every measure which demanded vigorous enforcement, for the firebrands here took no rest and would certainly, if occasion failed, have seized the first opportunity to pick a quarrel. It is clear that the University of Vienna, had it continued under these conditions, would not have been adequate to even the most moderate of the demands which the state must impose on an educational institution for the cultivation of its citizens. All the joints were dislocated ; who could set the limbs ? There was indeed many a Hamlet who drivelled about the world-soul, but not one man to act with the force of inspiration. This was the heaviest accusation which lay at the door of the authorities of the past, that they had never trained the citizens for the state, by reason of their own cowardice and selfishness ; now the people were stirred irrepressibly, as to the blast of Oberon's horn ; those who blew it were seldom clean-handed, were either visionaries or, far more often, coldly calculating speculators.

On the news of the outbreak of revolution in Vienna, Jellachich relinquished for the time his designs upon Hungary, which for the matter of that he was beginning to find not so easy of accom-

[1] Quoted by Klein.

plishment as he had hoped, and marched straight on the capital.
He reached it by the 11th and commenced its investment.   But
even in such a desperate situation certain *convenances* had to be
observed by the fugitive Imperial Government ; it would hardly
do for Jellachich at the head of his Croatians to appear in the
streets of Vienna as the sole saviour of Austrian rule, and therefore on the 16th Windischgrätz was nominated by an Imperial
rescript commander-in-chief of the army of relief.   On the
revolutionary side there was bungling over negotiations with
Kossuth for the assistance of an Hungarian army, and when an
Hungarian army under Moga did cross the Leitha, and encountered Jellachich and his army, it was only to sustain a
disastrous defeat.   The revolutionaries, left to their own
resources, put up the sort of defence to be expected of a mob.
Their nominal leader was Messenhauser, a member of the
Reichstag, an ex-soldier, a popular orator, a journalist, and,
with all these titles to fame, an honest and courageous man.
But for jealousy and mistrust the genius of the defence might
have been the heroic little Pole, Bem, one of the most meteoric
of the many soldiers of fortune or misfortune his nation has
produced.   He fought with distinction under Napoleon in
Russia, won the cross of the Legion of Honour at Dantzig,
gained fresh glory in the Polish War of Independence 1830-31,
escaped to Paris, endeavoured to raise a Polish Legion to fight
for liberalism against reaction in Portugal, joined the revolutionaries in Vienna, organised their desperate but unavailing
resistance, escaped to Pressburg and offered his services to
Kossuth.   Despite his patriotism and his heroism he was unpopular with the democratic section of his Polish countrymen,
and Kossuth sent him off to Transylvania, where he performed
such prodigies with a small army as few generals have to their
credit, defeating again and again far greater forces of Austrians,
Russians, and Slavs.   He was finally crushed by overwhelming
numbers, and escaped, seriously wounded, to Turkey.   There
he turned Mussulman and died a year later, 1850, as Governor
of Aleppo.   He deserves a far wider fame than he has achieved,
for the variety and brilliance of his achievements are not easy
to parallel.   In the intervals between his military exploits he
played the part of a teacher of mechanics and the physical
sciences.   And the man who, after a victory over Jellachich,
indited the despatch *Bem Ban Bum,* ' Bem has defeated the

Ban,' [1] must have had a gift of laconic speech as remarkable as his genius for action.

Of the course of the March revolution in Vienna a vivid account was given from the diary of Count Vitzthum. One quite as striking is given in his *Narrative of Events in Vienna* [2] from September to November, by Berthold Auerbach, one of the most distinguished German writers of his day. He claims to give the world a faithful record of events as they presented themselves to his keen eyes during the October revolution. The extracts which follow tell us the thrilling story of the investment of the city, the violent but ineffective struggle put up by the motley crowd of revolutionaries with their oratorical, political leaders, their National Guard and their Academic Legion, a combination so futile as a whole, so treacherous in many of its elements, that even a military improvisator of the genius of Bem could make little of them, and, finally, of the inevitable collapse with all its attendant ignominies. The whole account is instinct with that note of actuality, that personal, human touch, which gives such value to Wagner's record of the revolution in Dresden.

EVENTS IN VIENNA
AUTUMN OF 1848

9th October.

An extraordinary excitement reigns in the city. Jellachich with his hordes turns out to be a real enemy, and a representative of barbarism. An eagerness for fight prevails everywhere ; the people want to sally forth, to attack and annihilate Auersperg and his troops, before he can unite with Jellachich. Others oppose this, saying that an army of the people is only strong in defence, not in an attack ; in the former case moral courage would avail,—in the latter, discipline alone, in which the people are deficient.

It is said that an artilleryman in the city declared his readiness to suffocate by means of sulphur-rockets Auersperg's troops, which are closely crowded on the Belvedere. People shook their head at this proposal : ' No, no, they are men like ourselves, and many of them our fellow-countrymen ! ' said a quiet-looking man. [3]

Groups are quickly formed on all sides ; a person addresses an acquaintance, and instantly a crowd gathers round ; they discuss matters, they relate things, they contradict one another, although

---

[1] Bem, *Chambers's Encyclopædia*.
[2] English translation by J. E. Taylor : David Bogue, 1849.
[3] The introduction by the Germans in the twentieth century of gas and gas-shells shows that they have in the interval got over this squeamishness.

perhaps perfect strangers. A member of the Academic Legion is sure to receive most attention. This Legion consists not only of students, but comprises all who have graduated, and who are connected with any literary or scientific calling. It is reported that the soldiers on the Belvedere sally out and barbarously maltreat the citizens who pass that way, especially the students. In the hotels and inns every one sits down at table armed ; we are completely as if in a large camp.

11th October.

There is great rejoicing in the ciy. Five hundred national guards have arrived from Brünn ; the Hungarians, it is said, are fitting out steamers, to hasten to the assistance of Vienna. The news spreads from one to another, in the streets, and every face beams with joy. . . . Many brave mountaineers have arrived to-day from Gratz and Styria, decorated with green and white ribbons, who have come, as one of them told me, ' for a fight.'

12th October.

In the afternoon I went with some friends for the first time to the Central Committee of the democratic clubs. . . . Dr. Tausenau, a man just turned forty, with a dark complexion, full features, and a rather pointed chin, who is said to possess, after Schütte, the greatest gift of speech, presided at a long table in the middle of the room. . . . Jellinek [1] also was present, the busy, political Magus from the North. . . . His transparent features bespeak great mental activity, while his rather emaciated figure is a living proof that abstractions do not make a man stout ; his manner is perpetually restless, his hands are always in motion ; one minute he rushes as it were on his opponent, and the next he starts back to fix his spectacles on the bridge of his nose. . . . Another remarkable man in this meeting was Dr. Frank, —a man of an imposing and powerful figure, as if formed for a suit of armour. There was a discussion to-day, whether, as a well-trained soldier, he might not be invested with the military command of

---

[1] As recorded on page 497, Jellinek was shot by order of court-martial after the capture of Vienna. The cold-blooded way in which a statesman can speak of the pawns with which he gambles is illustrated by the following dialogue between Metternich and Palmerston (Metternich's *Memoirs*, viii. p. 206) :
' Brighton, 17, 12, 48. A call from Palmerston :—
P. asked, '' What sort of a man is this Jellachich ? ''
'' I 've never seen him,'' I replied, '' which is not surprising, for that sort of *canaille* has never approached me and I 've never had any desire to look for it. All that I know of the individual is that he was a literary man and a Jew.''
P. (almost falling off his chair), '' Jellachich a Jew ! ''
M. '' Yes, a Jew ; but that 's not the reason why he was shot.''
Seeing my questioner more and more astonished, I asked him : '' But of whom are you talking ? ''
P. '' Why, of *Jellachich*.''
M. '' I beg a thousand pardons ; I thought that Jellinek was in question, and if you have been surprised by my answers, no less was I at the importance you attached to knowing what sort of a man this scoundrel of a Jew '''

Vienna. He and Messenhauser were the candidates of the democratic party. . . .

I took two horse pistols with me, in order to be armed like the
rest, and we went to the Students' Committee. . . . In the corridor
students were lying about upon straw, and glasses of wine stood on a
bench : large bags of tobacco and cigars, sent by the Municipal
Council for the common use, were being carried into the different
rooms. . . .

I had a desire to see the Croats [who had been taken prisoners]
and we were taken to the room where they were confined. . . .
Besides the evident consciousness of imprisonment, which did not,
however, seem to weigh heavily on them, their features had that
inexpressible cast of melancholy which is seen in the human face
when the powers of man's nature are not fully and freely developed.
Naturalists find this feature also among the higher species of
animals, especially among dogs. I say this without any intention
further than to explain what I mean by this melancholy cast of
expression. I confess that it gave me a feeling of sadness to see
these poor fellows, allured from their Steppes by a bold intriguer,
for mere mad purposes of murder and ambition. . . .

[Later] there was an uproar in the court of the Aula like the rising
of a storm. The dead body of a student was just brought in, which
had been found on the Belvedere after the departure of the troops.
The corpse was frightfully mutilated, the tongue was cut out, the
eyes put out, the mouth slit up to the ears, the nose cut off, the belly
ripped up. All the horrors that the frenzy of a monster in human
shape could devise had been perpetrated. And now there arose in
the Aula shouts and howling and heart-rending cries for vengeance,
such as I had never before heard. The women wept and wailed
aloud ; and the men—not students, not proletarians—raised their
arms and swore vengeance on the House of Hapsburg and Ferdinand
' the kind.' I saw one burly old man, the tears running down his
cheeks, crying out till he was hoarse, ' Vengeance on Hapsburg !
Thus the *good* Emperor has us murdered, because a single man has
been killed ! ' In the scene before me I beheld the flames of revolt
break forth in the breasts of the most easy-tempered people on the
face of the earth, and saw to what lengths their spirit can be driven
by infamous perfidy. ' To the Diet ! to the Diet ! ' cried several
voices, and instantly ' To the Diet ! ' resounded on every side.

Thither the dead body was borne, preceded by a black flag, that
the members of the Diet should see how the troops of the Emperor
dealt with his people. Schuselka came down, and pacified the
crowd with a few words. But when Prince Lubomirski set eyes
upon the corpse, the sight drove him stark mad upon the spot : ' O
Jellachich ! O Jellachich ! ' he is said to have exclaimed, before
the madness came upon him.

13th October.

Messenhauser has issued his first proclamation : he speaks of the
time as one in which ' every day fills a leaf in the world's history '

and again, ' We drown all sad reminiscences in the eternal stream of oblivion.' I cannot understand how such hackneyed phrases can remain in use ; but the more I observe those who read, the more I see that such humdrum expressions still produce an immense effect. These are a childish people, and moreover they are Southerners. . . . A report that Windischgrätz is collecting troops to march on Vienna inflames the people anew.

16th October.

Messenhauser has sent a long despatch to Jellachich, well meant but confused. It is said that Jellachich answered it very ironically by word of mouth. General Bem,[1] from Lemberg, who fought so bravely at Ostrolenka, has undertaken the military dispositions. . . .

On our way home we met two students on horseback, drest in white cloaks ; they were galloping to headquarters. Joyous youths, who are now radiant in the full possession of power and freedom to use it ! But will they hereafter work on quietly in the study, where no eye regards them ? Will they not weary of labouring day after day, for the benefit of their fellowmen, restricted within the close bounds of law ? . . .

The Hungarians are said to be now at all events near at hand : Messenhauser asserts it positively.

17th October.

Schuselka reports that a deputation of the Frankfort Left, consisting of Robert Blum, Froebel, Hartmann, and Trampusch, has arrived, and presented an address.

19th October.

After sauntering about the streets for a long time, we were attracted by a great drum to a tent in the square near the barracks. Here was a merry spectacle : at one end of the tent a full band was playing waltzes and military marches ; huzzas and clapping of hands formed the accompaniment. In the centre of the tent were tables covered with cloths, on which glittered pots of beer ; several men had writing materials before them, and nosegays of artificial flowers. As soon as the music struck up, an open space was formed on the left, and the young men danced and capered, shouted and sang together, or with the girls whom they caught up in the surrounding circle. . . .

Here then we are in a recruiting tent of the Garde Mobile. The music now stopped. A spare-looking figure, in a grey military cloak, and a black, red and gold band, with a student's cap on his head, beneath which peeped out a cunning-looking, one-eyed visage, paced round and round the tent, or rocked himself backward and forward, evidently to some air which he had in his head. Brandishing a sabre, he exclaimed, ' Come on ! come on ! a jolly life this, five-and-twenty kreutzers a day, and only enrolled for a month ! Whoever doesn't like it, can leave it again. Come on, my boys ! a jolly life this ! ' Occasionally he made a stop at some lad who stood looking on, and solicited him to enlist ; or he would go up to a girl,

---

[1] As soon as he was nominated intrigues against him began.

and promise to equip a regiment of petticoats : laughter and giggling went the round of the crowd.

. . . The behaviour of the Hungarians is revolting and mean : every day it is said that they come, and they do not come ; they are in advance of Bruck, behind Bruck, on the frontier, over the frontier —nothing more can be said.

22nd October.

Schuselka . . . announced [to the Diet] that Prince Windisch-grätz had sent the following manifesto to the Municipal Council. . . .

' Inhabitants of Vienna ! your city has been stained by deeds of atrocity, which fill the breast of every honest man with horror. It remains still, at this moment, in the power of a small but audacious faction, which hesitates not to commit any atrocity. Your lives, your property, are abandoned to the arbitrary power of a handful of criminals. Take courage ! Obey the call of duty and reason. You shall find that I possess the will and the power to free you from this thraldom, and to re-establish peace and order.

' With a view to attain this object, the city, the suburbs, and the surrounding country are hereby declared to be in a state of siege ; the civil magistracy is placed under military authority, and martial law is decreed against all who transgress my commands. . . .'

In a calm and impressive exposition Schuselka proceeded to show that . . . the Diet alone has the power, as in Paris, to decree a state of siege, for its own protection. Force must be opposed by the arm of the Law, and the Permanent Committee therefore proposes to the Diet the following decree :

' Whereas . . . the Imperial Manifesto of the 19th of this month guaranteed anew the full maintenance of all the liberties hitherto obtained, and in an especial manner the free deliberation of the Diet :

' The Diet declares the measures threatened by Field-marshal Prince Windischgrätz, of proclaiming a state of siege and martial law, to be *illegal.*'

23rd October.

A placard stuck up at the corners of the streets reminded us that a public meeting in the Aula had been convened by the students for this hour : Robert Blum was to attend and speak. . . . As we entered, Blum was in the middle of his speech. . . . I am very sorry that Robert Blum allows himself to be made a tool of by such men, who parade his intimacy, and to see him demean himself by showing off to the Viennese his powers of oratory. . . . The address was received with repeated hurrahs, at every powerful expression and clever turn of speech. The measured, pulpit-toned strings of words, which dropped off like beads on a rosary, allowed pauses for the hurrahs without causing interruption ; after each burst of applause the speaker quietly continued. Every minute he seemed to be coming to the end,—now— and now—there must be a close ; but no, there was always something more to follow. In conclusion he exhorted the people to courageous perseverance, adding that he and his companions were ready with them to conquer or fall.

24th October.

Whilst the shadows of the Commissioners of the Empire still figure on the street walls, Windischgrätz comes forward with undisguised brutality, and demands not only the general disarming of the people, but also the surrender of twelve students as hostages : his third mild and conciliatory demand runs thus : ' Several other persons, whom I shall select, are likewise to be given up.'

. . . Unhappily some excesses have occurred in the suburbs : armed persons are levying forced contributions. Martial law is proclaimed against these men.

The supply of water is cut off ; the fountains in the public squares are dry.

26th October.

The Tabor, the Pater, and the Augarten are occupied by the military. The Leopoldstadt is said to be incapable of holding out any longer. The country around Vienna is in flames.

27th October.

This evening I made the acquaintance of Messenhauser. His face, with its small black beard and dark eyes, has no great expression, his manner and conversation betoken an unassuming good nature. He shares that strange inconsistency of character which is only too common ; simple and unostentatious in ordinary life, he becomes bombastic and wordy as soon as he takes a pen in hand, especially in his proclamations. . . . He is an enthusiastic democrat, but this is by no means enough to justify his occupying any position above the common ranks.

28th October.

This then is the decisive day of battle. The distant roar of artillery is heard early in the morning ; the *générale* is beaten in all the streets, the alarm bell sounds from St. Stephen's, and as the call travels on the quick tread of cavalry is heard. . . .

The conflagration which raged around the city presented a fearful spectacle ; the whole sky was reddened by the flames. The high road and the Leopoldstadt are occupied by the troops : the city is crowded with fugitives from the suburbs.

29th October.

The fourth Sunday. The whole city has the appearance of a man worn out with fatigue, who sits down to take breath, but is instantly impelled on again by restless impatience. There is an armistice. It is said that the Municipal Council and the Council of War have determined on a surrender, and, as the conditions demanded cannot be fulfilled, they have requested Windischgrätz to march into the city himself and to enforce their execution. But the simple fact that this is said, and yet that no one knows the truth of the report, shows the hopeless confusion that prevails. . . .

The foul turn which passion takes, when its hopes are destroyed, was now visible : men whose names had before been mentioned only with the highest veneration, were now denounced as despicable traitors. ' Unmask yourselves ! ' exclaimed the National Guard and the (Academic) Legion one to another in a tone of bitter scorn.

30th October.

The surrender is determined on ; but the proclamation of the Commander-in-Chief announcing this, which was placarded in the streets, is torn down by armed men, and I see only fragments of it here and there. What will be the end of this state of things ? Already friends have actually to make themselves known, as we meet them in the streets, so altered is their appearance by clipping their beards and hair, and change of dress.

At noon the alarm was beaten again. What now ? The Hungarians are come—at this moment fighting is going on. No one will believe it, and yet who can wish purposely to deceive ? Every one again flies to arms. A wish I had long felt was now gratified ; through a member of the Diet I obtained permission to ascend St. Stephen's tower with him. We found there a great excitement. Near the belfry, close to the watchman's dwelling, telescopes were fixed, pointing in four directions. One person after another of those who were taking observations said aloud what he saw, and this was put down in writing in the little chamber. We were able to descry with tolerable distinctness the result of the battle : it was in the direction of Inzersdorf. I could plainly see the ' Imperialists ' load their field-pieces, the skirmishers lie down in the entrenchments, the cavalry drawn up, and from time to time wounded soldiers borne off. Messenhauser had already sent down the news, and spread it through the city on slips of paper, that a battle had been descried, that nothing decisive could yet be ascertained, but that the people must be prepared for all hazards. It was also announced that the battle was drawing further off. Below in the city there was an incessant beating of drums. We mounted higher up the tower to Messenhauser, who was taking observations from the wooden balcony near the summit. Messenhauser looked very much worn ; he repeatedly drew out his telescope, and then shut it up again. Some one present observed, ' The tragical watchword of our days, "*too late*," seems to hold good with the Hungarians.' Messenhauser nodded, without answering.

Messenhauser was in a very critical position : in the city he was called a coward and traitor ; and, actuated by a last enthusiastic hope, he was led, after the conclusion of the capitulation, to spread the news in print respecting the movements of troops outside the city, and, if not to command, yet to exhort the people pretty plainly to remain under arms. . . . We went to the University : a wild scene presented itself in the courtyard of the Aula. Piles of arms were heaped up, which had been brought thither from the suburbs and by the citizens. A large body of women had armed themselves ; and one in particular, with her hair drest *à l'enfant*, kept flourishing her right arm in the air, looking up to the stars, and exclaiming wildly against the cowardice of the men, who submitted to be shamed by women. This troop of Amazons marshalled themselves and marched toward the city. It was a disgusting farce.

31st October.

The night has passed over quietly. No certain information can be obtained respecting the Hungarians until near noon, when the fog has cleared off. The *rappel* is again beaten, and the alarm-bells rung.

A proclamation is issued, signed by Messenhauser and Fenneberg, calling upon the people to lay down their arms, as the Hungarians are defeated. Who has ordered the bells to be rung and the alarm to be beaten ? . . .

I again went up the tower of St. Stephen's ; there was dreadful confusion. . . . Several now entered the apartment of the watchman's wife, and taking a clean sheet hoisted it in place of a white flag. Soon afterwards came other people, exclaiming that we were all dead men, that the proletarians and military deserters would not allow the white flag to be hoisted, and would butcher all whom they should find on the tower as the perpetrators of the act. We left the tower to take care of itself and repaired to a neighbouring wine-shop. It was awful to hear the crowd under a gateway, amidst scornful laughter and the noise of artillery, shouting the song *Gott erhalte unsern Kaiser*, and in the pauses hooting and uttering the bitterest imprecations on the House of Hapsburg. In the vaulted wine-room, which was lighted with gas, we found a large assemblage of persons. . . . A glass door suddenly opened, and a new guest rushed in, exclaiming, ' The soldiers are here ! ' There was a death-like silence : at last a man called out, ' When they come, we shall bid them good-evening.'

 . . . On my return across the square ' Am Hofe,' I saw some men of gigantic figure—grenadiers—working with sledge-hammers by torchlight : they had destroyed the lamp-post on which Latour had been hung, and were now working to shatter and root up the stump of the post ; close by lay the pile of iron : at every stroke the crowd raised a loud hurrah. All trace of the barbarous act was to be swept from the earth ; and yet who knows how many of the very people who now stood by shouting, were equally vociferous at the sight of the murder ?

The houses were illuminated up to the fifth story, and everywhere white flags—curtains, sheets, etc.,—were hung out upon poles. Many of the honest citizens had tied white handkerchiefs round their left arms as emblems of peace. They conversed with the soldiers, who were drawn up in all the streets, and I continually heard expressions of compassion when the latter related the hardships they had suffered.

A great body of flames was rising from the Burg,—the library and church of the Augustines were on fire. . . .

I was in a cigar-shop, when a dark-featured soldier entered and demanded cigars ; a handful were given him. ' Do you also come from Windischgrätz ? ' said the shopwoman's little son. '*Nix deutsch !*' answered the soldier as he walked away.

'When you grow older, you can also learn Croatian,' said the mother to her boy, who understood nothing of what had passed. Poor child, he will indeed learn it, for from this very evening the word has gone forth, *Nix deutsch !*

Those people in the streets who were able to speak Czechish and Croatian thought themselves lucky, and entered into eager conversation with the soldiers ; but as soon as any one began to talk in ' good Viennese,' he received the general answer, *Nix deutsch !*

1st November.

There is quite a new population in the streets, a general unmasking. On every side the little attentions to dress, smart gloves and the like, are again to be seen,—luxuries which for weeks have been wholly unknown ; and what a quantity of beards and long locks have fallen since yesterday ! The German and Calabrian hats are exchanged for the ordinary, tasteless cylinder.

2nd November.

This afternoon Jellachich entered the city in triumph on his charger, surrounded by his staff, and accompanied by the Sereczans and Red-mantles. The Sereczans kept continually shouting, ' Vivat, vivat, vivat ! ' and I am pained to say that the cry was echoed by the people around. The Viennese have learned all kinds of exclamations, Eljen, Zivio, Eviva, etc. . . . Ladies in particular were waving their white handkerchiefs from every window, and saluting Jellachich, who bowed courteously on every side. He is a powerful man, with a countenance that bears the traces of an eventful life. The appearance of the Red-mantles is a mixture of the gipsy and the bandit : they wear a red cap on the head, and a long red cloak reaching nearly to the ground, with a hood of the same colour. A red jacket trimmed with lace, which in the officers' dress is of gold, an ornamental belt round the waist, in which are stuck pistols and a dagger, tight-fitting yellow trousers and red laced boots, compose the costumes of the Sereczans. . . .

The German flag has everywhere disappeared, and the black and yellow standard floats from St. Stephen's tower. No one passes without looking up at it, and many appear to regard this as the hardest measure Windischgrätz has inflicted on them : they loved the German colours though they were unable to stand by them. The statue of the Emperor Joseph, whose hand was the last to part with the German flag, now holds a black and yellow one in its place.

CHAPTER VI

THE MAILED FIST IN VIENNA AND IN HUNGARY

THE farce of government by a Committee of Public Safety, and an Imperial Ministry subservient to that Committee, was now over. The army had come into its own : Radetzky, Windisch-grätz, and Jellachich were the heroes who had saved the Austrian state. A new ministry was installed under Prince Felix Schwarzenberg, a cold, clear-headed, and determined aristocrat ; of whose ' swaggering, quality manners ' Bismarck speaks in his *Reminiscences*. He had done good service under Radetzky both as soldier and as diplomatist, and had now, for his first task, to restore order in the conquered capital.

Pichler [1] gives two graphic pictures of scenes in the city after its capitulation. First, a glimpse of the University and the Cathedral square :

At the University, this once so famous birthplace of freedom, all was waste, desolate and forsaken. On my return yesterday across the Cathedral square, I chanced to look up at St. Stephen's Tower : from the top, through the damp mist, fluttered the black and yellow flag, token of the triumph of military might and reaction. This was the end of the desolating drama, yet truly the starting-point of new and incalculable developments.

Then a visit to the mortuary where the victims of the struggle were laid out :

Because there was nothing else to look at, the inquisitive crowd streamed to the mortuary to view the fallen ; among them many a one who went with the nervous presentiment of finding there missing friends, just where they wished not to find them. The dead lay stretched in four rows upon the dirty floor, so beset by spectators that I decided to wait until the place of least crowding and pushing became clearer. Upon this surging mass the lunatic inmates looked down from the tower of the madhouse close by, some pale and silent, others jabbering of their delusions, which corresponded to nothing

---

[1] *Das Sturmjahr* (K.).

in either place or time ; sometimes a shrill yell rang out, followed by resounding laughter ; it was a dreadful scene. But most repulsive of all were the women, and not those only of the lowest classes : often with children in their arms, they thrust themselves everywhere forward, and lingered just in front of the corpses, from whose horrible mutilations even a doctor would have turned his eyes ; they were like the carrion flies of their markets. After a time I succeeded in getting nearer. . . . Several corpses showed traces of shocking ill-treatment, others with blue swollen faces still retained the cord round the neck, two—man and wife—were lying, quite charred, a heap of ashes, and beside them the head and upper part of a body. Most of them were young men, the expression of their faces showing that they fell in fight ; the brows grimly drawn, the fist convulsively clenched, the mouth half open ; to me it seemed as if I heard that line of the Roman poet :

> Exoriare aliquis nostris ex ossibus ultor !

Jellachich's views on the Viennese and on Germans generally are recorded by Count Vitzthum [1] to whom he said on 23rd November :

It is marvellous how throughout life, ever since my eighteenth year, the presentiment has accompanied me that I should one day be called upon to muster my troops before the walls of Vienna, and to converse, through the mouth of my cannon, with this cowardly and imbecile population. Things were different in those days, but they did not please me much better. And with these spatchcock-eaters I have at no time felt much sympathy.

' Individually I like the German very much,' said the noble Ban on another occasion, ' he is open, faithful, upright and loyal. But as a nation, the Germans at present are only fit for a madhouse.'

A few days later he said :

The Mongol [the Magyars] must be exterminated root and branch. When we have done with Hungary, it will be the turn of our present Reichstag. An end must be put to its hitherto shop-keeping policy. In Austria, for the immediate future, *this* (striking his sword) is the Reichstag ! Only so shall we attain the true freedom of which the Frankfort professors understand nothing.

The clearing up after the revolution was not so simple a business in Vienna as Wrangel had found it in Berlin. Procedure was of course under martial law, but what cruelty was shown is probably to be ascribed rather to Schwarzenberg than to Prince Windischgrätz, whose character is travestied in the following extraordinary broadsheet : [2]

---

[1] *Berlin und Wien* (K.).
[2] Friedländer Collection, City Library, Berlin.

BROADSHEET AGAINST WINDISCHGRÄTZ

Motto : He stays ! He will not go.
An oppressed people must make reprisals.   ' Thus the people ! '
The undermentioned, more accurately characterised as
Criminal

WINDISCH-PRINCE

Robber, murderer and incendiary as well as leader of a band of
robbers, murderers, incendiaries, and a mob of Croats and other
foreign rabble, is herewith arraigned, under warrant of arrest, by the
undersigned Upper Tribunal of the people, and solemnly declared
under the ban of the people's law, which we herewith bring to the
notice of all civilised nations of Europe. . . .

SENTENCE

The murderer, destroyer of towns and villages, Windisch-Prince,
treading the rights of the people under his feet, shall, immediately
after his apprehension, be tied up in the inner side of the newly flayed
skin of an ox, and in that condition be dragged to the usual place of
execution.   Then he will be favoured with death by hanging, and if
this is impracticable, by powder and shot. . . . The executioner
shall receive the head to be exposed in the cages occupied by blood-
thirsty hyænas in travelling menageries, so that coming generations
may always be given opportunity to recall the struggles for liberty
of a great nation.   The ox hide shall be thoroughly cured, and the
shameful deeds of the abominable tyrant branded upon it in fiery
writing, in order that it may be affixed to the pinnacles of the
Pyramids, so that the unbelieving may know the love of justice of a
long-enslaved people.

Description :   Name—Windisch-Prince.
Vocation :   Murderer and Incendiary-in-chief.
Age :   About fifty.
Appearance : Tigerish.
Hair :   Like that of the Siberian fox.
Height :   The height of Mephistopheles.

Special distinguishing marks. . . .   Carries usually on the left side of
his breast a number of metal flaps, and is always to be found in the
midst of his gangs.

Freedom City, on the River of Revenge, at the Day of Judgment.
The People's Upper Tribunal of the United Free German Land.
HERMANN TEUTON, *President.* NEMESIS. T.S.[1]

A vivid description of the reign of martial law is given by
Franz Bodenstedt in his *Memoirs, Aus meinem Leben* : [2]

First in interest for a time stood the long list of executions wherein
the victim was sentenced to death by hanging, but ' in default of an

---

[1] *Tod oder Sieg*, Death or Victory.
[2] *Aus meinem Leben* (K.).

executioner, was executed by Royal and Imperial riflemen by means of powder and shot,' this being officially authorised in the Minutes. . . . At that time, by the Danube, it was as if the value of life had lessened, like the value of Austrian paper money. Horrible stories were rife of the excesses and atrocities which the Croats were said to have perpetrated in the suburbs. I was sitting one day at table in Vienna with the greatly beloved Professor Bischof, Professor of Music, who told me of the festivities in which he had formerly taken part in the palace of Prince Metternich, whom he commended as an exceedingly amiable host, when a short, stout officer came in, and after politely greeting us, sat down opposite. He looked through the bill of fare, and said to the waiter : ' Bring anything that is ready ; I am hungry.' ' Will you not in the meantime drink a glass of Vöslauer with us, Major ? ' said the Professor, presenting me to him. The Major made no ado about it, and soon three glasses clinked together. I did not write down the conversation which followed, and will not recapitulate it, but will briefly give the substance of it, as it remains vividly in my memory.

Throughout the whole day the Major had been too agitated to eat, because he had been obliged, early that morning, to superintend the carrying out of two executions, which had made a profound impression upon him. The matter concerned two journalists who were to be made the targets of the Royal and Imperial riflemen, on the charge of having, through the newspaper *The Radical*, incited the people to revolt against his Majesty the Kaiser, and to offer armed resistance to his Highness, Field-marshal Prince Windischgrätz. One of the accused was Dr. Julius Becher, forty-five years old, of the Protestant faith, proprietor and responsible editor of the above named paper. The other was his coadjutor, Dr. Hermann Jellinek,[1] twenty-five years old, of the Jewish religion. Dr. Becher, a strongly built, vigorous man walked to his death with a firm step and quiet glance, wasting no words. But Dr. Jellinek, whose slender meagre form I have already described, tried with the help of lively gesticulations to make it clear to the Major that some error underlay the whole business. He said it was really not thinkable that a writer's life should be extinguished for an article published in order to teach the people about its rights and duties in a constitutional state. Furthermore, it was only the editor who was responsible for everything which appeared by his permission in the newspaper. The way in which the good-natured Major related all this in detail was deeply moving. One saw the unhappy figure of the condemned man standing vividly before one, and heard him exhaust all arguments in the effort to avert his heavy fate. As soon as he had convinced himself that all further talk was useless, he pulled himself together and cried, resolutely stepping back : ' Now, shoot me dead ! ' assuming at the same time a bearing which showed that moral strength did not fail him.

---

[1] See page 486.

' I cannot forget the expression of his face, as he collapsed under the bullets, and never has the execution of an order been so difficult for me as to-day,'—so the Major ended his story.

The most prominent victims were Messenhauser himself and Robert Blum.   The last-named had, as we have read in the entry from Auerbach's diary on page 488, arrived in Vienna on 17th October at the head of a deputation from the radical party in the Frankfort National Assembly.   There is reason to believe that Blum had undertaken this hazardous mission in order to retrieve his position as a democratic leader, shaken by the failure of his party in the Assembly, a failure for which no one with the merest elements of statesmanship in him could be held responsible.   The fault lay with the excesses of the revolutionary mob outside the walls of the *Paulskirche*.   On the day after their arrival the deputation, realising the hopelessness of the revolutionary prospects, resolved to return to Frankfort. It was too late ; escape from the city was impossible, and Blum threw himself courageously into the fighting line.   When arrested after the capitulation he claimed inviolability as a member of the German parliament.   Windischgrätz referred the appeal to Schwarzenberg at Olmütz, with the suggestion that Blum should be expelled from Austrian territory ; but Schwarzenberg at the instigation, according to Hans Blum's prejudiced account, of the newly created Baron Hübner, who cherished a personal rancour against Blum dating from his days of service as Austrian consul at Leipzig, insisted on his condemnation under martial law.   He was therefore shot on 9th November.   He died like a brave man.   His last letter to his wife is given in facsimile in his son's *Die deutsche Revolution*, and the blotted document runs as follows :

My treasured good dear wife, farewell ! farewell for time—some call it for ever, but that will not be so.   Bring up our—now only thy— children to be noble, then will they never bring shame upon their father.   Sell our little property with the help of our friends.   God and good men will help thee.   All that I feel melts into tears, therefore only once again : farewell, dear wife !   Consider our child to be a precious bequest which thou must make the best of and thus honour thy faithful husband.   Farewell, farewell !   A thousand, thousand last kisses from thy   ROBERT.

Vienna, 9th November 1848.   Morning.   5 o'clock.   At 6 o'clock I shall have passed away.

I had forgotten the rings ; I press the last kiss to thee upon the marriage ring. My seal ring is for Hans, the watch for Richard, the diamond stud for Ida, the chain for Alfred, as keepsakes. Distribute all other keepsakes according to thy own judgment. They come! Farewell! farewell!

Of the final scene, his execution, Sparfeld [1] gives an account :

In due accordance with martial law the court-martial sentenced Blum to death by hanging, but, in default at the moment of an executioner, the sentence was to be carried out by shooting with powder and shot. On Thursday, 9th November, at 5 o'clock in the morning, an orderly fetched a priest from the Schottenstift, and brought him to Blum. The holy man found Blum still without knowledge of his doom. At first Blum would not believe the priest, when he said that he had come in order to prepare him for death. But the Judge-advocate soon appeared and intimated to him the sentence of the court-martial, which he read aloud to him and then departed. . . . Blum appeared quite composed and said to the priest : ' You know I am a German Catholic, dispense me, I beg, from auricular confession.' The priest, a sensible man, assented, and gave him time to write some letters.

Hereupon Blum conversed for a long time with the priest. Then, in company with the priest and three riflemen, he was driven away in a fiacre under military guard. In the carriage he is said to have held his hand before his eyes for a moment and wept. When they came to the cavalry barracks in the Leopoldstadt, the guard was considerably strengthened, so that about two thousand men were present at the execution. Here they wished to put chains on Blum. But, rejecting them, he said to the officer, ' I will die as a free German. You will accept my assurance that I will not make any absurd attempt to escape.' The officer ordered the chains to be taken away, and the procession moved towards the Brigittenau, a meadow where trees grew, and in which the execution was to be carried out. It was nearly half-past seven o'clock. Blum alighted and asked an officer : ' Who, then, is to shoot me ? ' He received the answer that riflemen would do it. He responded : ' Well, I am glad of that, riflemen are said to shoot well. One got me here '—and with that he pointed to a spot below his shoulder, where on 26th October a bullet had grazed him. Likewise he forbade the binding of his eyes, but allowed it to be done when they pointed out to him that the riflemen would shoot straighter. With the words : ' I die for German freedom, for which I have fought. May the Fatherland keep me in remembrance ! ' he offered his breast to the bullets, which laid him low. His corpse was brought to the anatomical theatre in the Josephinum, and then was laid, with several others, in the Zähring cemetery.

Another account is given in an eloquent passage in Auerbach's *Diary of Events in Vienna* :

[1] *Das Buch von Robert Blum*, 1849 (K.).

'It is impossible—it is too horrible—they dare not—so many lies are told, one can no longer believe anything.' Such were the exclamations on every side when the news first spread that Robert Blum had been shot : and yet one person after another asserted that he had been told the fact by an eyewitness, or had heard it second-hand. One's hair stands on end at such an atrocity : it cannot be—they durst not have gone so far !

We could bear the suspense no longer : it was said that the corpse of Robert Blum was lying in the City Hospital ; I hastened thither with one of the deputies. The body was not there ; we were told that perhaps it might be in the Military Hospital ; none of the young medical men would accompany me thither,—so great was the fear of being subjected to a secret inquisition merely from inquiring after the dead body. It was night when I reached the Military Hospital : the courtyard and the lower rooms were filled with soldiers. The keeper of the hall in which the bodies lay was absent : a student, who was standing by, said to me, ' No one can enter now ; and,' added he, ' there is only the corpse of Robert Blum. . . . '

Then it is true ! and endless misery will spring to life from yon lifeless body. I heard further particulars of Blum's death. Until yesterday afternoon he had been a prisoner in the same room with Froebel : they were then separated. This morning at five o'clock his sentence of death was announced to him. He quietly said, ' It comes not unexpected.' The priest of the Schottenthor, in whose parish the prison of Blum was situated, came to receive his confession. Blum said that he was not in the habit of practising confession, and the priest replied that he was aware of it. Blum then wrote a letter to his wife, in which he exhorted her to bear her fate with courage and firmness, and to bring up his children in such a manner as not to disgrace his name, which was honoured by his dying for liberty. He then conversed with the priest on the subject of immortality. Three riflemen and an officer conducted him to the Brigittenau. In walking to the place of execution he stopped several times, breathing hard. He requested that his eyes might remain unbandaged. The officer replied that this could not be allowed, as it was done on account of the soldiers ; and Blum himself bound the handkerchief over his eyes.

A barbarous proceeding was then enacted, which shows the obsolete nature of the formalities that are still perpetuated. When the delinquent was ready for execution, the Provost-marshal, stepping up to the commanding officer, said, in the usual words, ' Colonel, I beg mercy for the poor sinner.' ' No,' was the answer. ' Colonel, I beg mercy for the poor sinner,' repeated the Provost. ' No,' was again the reply. A third time the Provost exclaimed, ' Colonel, in God's name and by His mercy I beg grace for the poor sinner ! ' Thereupon the Colonel said, ' With men there is no longer grace for him, there is mercy alone with God.' The word was then given to fire. Is it not a piece of inhuman barbarity to torment a dying man with such a farce ? As long as the prince, who had the power to grant mercy, was himself present at the execution, this formality had a meaning, it is now a mere mockery.

Blum fell pierced by three balls : one lodged in his forehead, the others in his breast. His last words were :—' From every drop of my blood a martyr of freedom will arise.' And his words will come true, but woe to those who compel the betrayed nations to win their freedom through streams of blood ! If the demons of vengeance are thus let loose, what power remains capable of restraining them ? Where will all this end, and what horrors may we still have to witness ! . . .

As I was leaving the Military Hospital, a troop of soldiers had just arrived. In the midst of them walked two men, carrying a bier, on the cover of which was a black cross : within it lay another man, who had been shot. Who may this be ? whose heart has ceased to beat ? I could not ask the soldiers,—their answer—I knew it— would have been, *Nix deutsch !*

' Last words ' as delivered by the dying are proverbially difficult to specify with exactitude. The versions given by Sparfeld and Auerbach differ. Hans Blum, the little boy to whom his father left his seal ring, and who lived to black Bismarck's boots, adopts a modified form of Sparfeld's version : ' I die for freedom ; may the Fatherland be mindful of me ! ' The friend to whom Robert Blum commended the care of his family, Carl Vogt, ' the impartial,' [1] did well by his charges. Public sympathy showed itself in the ready flow of subscriptions for the benefit of widow and children.

But Blum's murder, for so it was regarded, did more than stir up sympathy ; it raised a storm of indignation throughout Germany. The iniquity of the case was evident from the fact that Froebel, one of his colleagues on the deputation and equally guilty of taking up arms, escaped the death penalty. Messenhauser had been shot as a lesson to the Austrian Reichstag ; Blum was shot as a lesson to the German Parliament. The act was interpreted as the challenge of reaction to reform. Of all the outbursts of indignation none was more eloquent than Freiligrath's in lines that recall ' The Dead to the Living ' :

BLUM

'Twas two-and-forty years ago, upon his mother's knee
A seven-days child in fair Cologne cried loud and lustily ;
A child with broad and open brow, lungs filled with life and joy,
One of the People's right good sort, a cooper's sturdy boy ;

---

[1] See page 380.

He cried till all the barrels rang his father's workshop round,
And his mother smiled as to her breast the child she softly wound,
And rocked him in her arms to rest, the crooning waves along.
So sang the mother in fair Cologne her babe's sweet cradle-song.

To-day in this self-same Cologne, while roars the winter wild,
The deep-toned organ-pipes peal forth the requiem of that child.
She who still lives, the mother mild, joins not the funeral dirge,
The voices of a city-full in one great anthem merge.
They cry : O thou that bore him, nurse at home thy bitter moan !
Before thy God, O thou grey-head, pour out thy grief alone !
His City is his mother too, his City and one higher—
The Revolution lit by flames of all-consuming fire !
In secret yield thee to thy grief ; we 'll keep his memory green—
Thy Robert's requiem sings Cologne, the Revolution's Queen ! . . .

So honours now his native town the cooper's sturdy boy,
Him whom the Austrian tyrant's hands to death have foully done ;
The man who climbed on his own feet life's hard and steep ascent,
And fought his way with stalwart fist to Frankfort's Parliament.
No traitor he, a strong straight man, to-day as yesterday !—
Why grip ye not your swords, O ye who kneel and ye who pray ?
Why turn ye not to trumpets all, ye organ-pipes of brass,
Till shuddering to the murderers' ears God's judgment-summons
    pass ? . . .

A requiem does not spell revenge, vents not our righteous rage ;
But soon Revenge herself will step upon the sable stage,
Revenge herself in gloomy red, besprent with blood and tears ;
She will, she must and shall, declare she stays once she appears !
Then will the murdered victims hear a dirge of other sort—
You call her not, Revenge, she comes with Time for her escort !
Those others' crimes will summon her.   Then comes the tide full-flood :
Woe, woe to all whose murderous hands are stained with guiltless blood !

'Twas two-and-forty years ago, upon his mother's knee
A seven-days child in fair Cologne cried loud and lustily.
'Twas eight days since, a bleeding corpse, he lay on Austrian sand ;
To-day his requiem sings Cologne hard by Rhine's shelving strand.

When Schwarzenberg took in hand the government of the
distracted Austrian Empire he was as thorough as any admirer
of reaction could require. He insisted on the abdication of the
feeble-minded Kaiser Ferdinand, and the renunciation of his
rights by his brother, Archduke Francis Charles, and set on the
Imperial throne, in December 1848, the latter's son, Francis
Joseph, then a youth of eighteen, and until 1916, his eighty-
seventh year, the Austrian Kaiser. Further, Schwarzenberg

and the forces of reaction were determined that there should be nothing of the Federal State in the constitution of the Empire ; one man must be Austrian Kaiser and King of Hungary, absolute monarch of all lands and races that had hitherto counted as within the Empire. The revolutionary movement for constitutional reform had been crushed in Vienna itself, Radetzky was in a fair way to bring Lombardy and Venetia again under subjection ; there remained Hungary, and Hungary was not to be subdued until it was bled white. Görgei, Bem, and others did marvels by courage and military skill, and Kossuth by fiery eloquence, and the Hungarian resistance was long effective. The slow-moving Windischgrätz was superseded by the notorious Haynau, the very embodiment of ruthlessness, but the Austrian armies failed to reduce Hungary until the aid of Russia was invoked, and it was to a Russian army that Görgei, when further resistance was hopeless, surrendered in August 1849, at Világos. The savagery with which Haynau shot and hanged generals and statesmen who fell into his hands has made his name a byword for all time. In the autumn of 1850 Haynau had the assurance to pay a visit to London. There some irresistible call in his German nature led him to pay a visit to Barclay and Perkins' brewery. His reception surprised him, for as soon as it was known he was inside the gates the draymen went for him with dirt and brooms. He had to fly, with the mob at his heels, to the waterside, where he was rescued by the Thames police who rowed him off in a police galley. The Austrian Ambassador took up his case half-heartedly, but so incensed was public opinion against the ' Austrian butcher ' that he obtained scanty satisfaction. Lord Palmerston, then Foreign Minister, wrote to the Home Secretary, Sir George Grey, in a style which is probably less common to-day in correspondence between the Right Honourable This and the Right Honourable That : ' . . . the draymen were wrong in the particular course they adopted. Instead of striking him, which . . . they did not do much, they ought to have tossed him in a blanket, rolled him in the kennel, and then sent him home in a cab, paying his fare to the hotel.'

Haynau's barbarities in Hungary had in a measure, it is true, been disavowed by the Austrian Government—when it was realised what a feeling of resentment they aroused throughout the world ; but Schwarzenberg and his friends cannot shake off all responsibility for them, and it is well to remember that Francis Joseph began his long and gloomy reign, as he ended it, in blood.   With his accession the end of reform in Austria for many a year had come.   All constitutional concessions of 1848 and 1849 were taken away one by one ; Austria was once more an autocratic state, and free to devote her attention again to the struggle with Prussia for the hegemony in Germany.

BOOK VII
THE LAST ACT
1849

CHAPTER I

THE NATIONAL ASSEMBLY ELECTS A GERMAN KAISER

WE may now return to the National Assembly at Frankfort, and see how it is getting on with its task of building castles in the air. We left it at the end of September breathing hard after the murders of Lichnowsky and Auerswald, and the Frankfort insurrection, from which the elect of the people had been delivered by the troops of autocratic Prussia. The Assembly's moral authority was hopelessly shaken, but it took up again its rope of sand, and having provided a provisional central authority and settled the fundamental rights of the German people, now set about determining the form and content of its new German Empire, and choosing the august individual who, by its gracious will, was to preside over a United Germany. The consideration of these problems brought up at once ' the German question,' the rivalry between Prussia and Austria for the hegemony. The first difficulty to be solved was a vital one : how much of the Austrian Empire was to be admitted within the German pale ? The Austrian Empire consisted both of German and non-German elements ; were both, or only the former to be admitted ? In its discussions during October of this question the Assembly was influenced by the course of events in Austria, the revolt of Hungary, the fighting in Bohemia, the struggle in North Italy, the October revolution in Vienna itself. The collapse of the dual monarchy seemed imminent, and on 27th October the Assembly resolved : ' That no German country may be united with non-German countries to form a single state, and that where German and non-German countries have one overlord, only the union of independent states under one sovereign shall prevail between them.' These resolutions practically determined the exclusion of Austria from the new German Empire, for Austria, now under the forceful guidance of Prince Schwarzenberg, was equally determined that the Austrian Crown should be one and indivisible, embracing all lands and races hitherto comprised within the Austrian Empire. By the end of the year, Schwarzenberg made plain to the National Assembly that Austria was henceforward to ignore the first German parliament and its resolutions.

Among modern German historians the question has been discussed whose was the mind that first realised the necessity of proceeding to the unification of Germany by the exclusion of Austria. Evidence enough is given in the present work to show that the idea was foreign to the mind and sentiment of Frederick William IV. But was there any statesman who, having conceived the idea before the Frankfort parliament came into being, resolutely set himself to guide the policy of the King and his advisers, and also the National Assembly, in that direction ? The question has not yet been satisfactorily resolved, but a fair case has been made out for the keenest intelligence among the King's intimates, the subtle-minded Radowitz.

When the question forced itself to the front in the National Assembly, there were grave misgivings even on the purely German side over a line of policy which virtually excluded Austria from the German future. That sturdy patriot, a radical, but not a revolutionary, the poet Uhland, spoke eloquently against it. His style of speech is thus described by Laube : [1]

As a conscientious representative Uhland appeared daily in his place, and also several times on the tribune. The light-coloured eyes under fair eyebrows looked far away over the crowd into vacancy, his gaze caught no man's gaze, answered none, and like a hermit spoke the man in a harsh voice with the Swabian accent, up there aloft, as if no one heard him. No trace of the dramatic ! Slowly, with little pauses, the sentences rose one after another, and the *Paulskirche* soon accustomed itself to disregard the political tenor of his speeches, but to single out for applause the fine figures and similes, of which there was no lack when he spoke.

His speech [2] against the separation of Austria from Germany ran as follows :

It has been well said that the mission entrusted by Providence to Austria was to dominate the East and to carry to the East enlighten-

---

[1] *Das erste deutsche Parlament*, iii. 77.
[2] Notter, *Ludwig Uhland*.

ment and civilisation. But how can German Austria exercise this power if it is itself overpowered ? How can it light and enlighten if it is itself overshadowed and obscured ? Granted that Austria is called to be a lamp to the East, she has another and a higher function, that of ' an artery in Germany's heart.' Austria has been with us in the German Federation, and the pressure of Austrian diplomacy has weighed like a load on Austria herself, on us, and on every movement towards freedom in the individual German states. We would nevertheless not have let Austria go. We knew what we owed to her. But now it appears Austria is to be torn away. Now, when young as an eagle, with the fresh wounds of the March and May battles she approaches us to strike the new treaty of freedom ! It is said that ancient walls are indestructible because their lime was mixed with blood ; Austria has mingled its heart's blood with the mortar that is to serve for the new structure of German freedom. Austria must be with us and remain with us in the new *Paulskirche*. Gentlemen, you have only this instant passed a law protecting the personal freedom of the members of this House. Are you going to vote that a hundred and fifty representatives of the Austro-German people shall be driven into exile before your very eyes ?

On the Austrian side in the Assembly Giskra, an Austrian deputy, challenged the decision in these words :

It is a great moment ! The tree of German unity and freedom has already lost many buds, many blooms, but the tree of German unity and freedom is still putting forth roots in the ground. The roots lie bare : one blow,—and the tree of unity falls. The roots lie bare, the axe is raised. Strike,—if you dare !

And the war-worn hero Radetzky, no cabinet soldier, but the greatest of Austria's fighting men, declared : [1]

Look at the map and ask yourselves if it is really possible to tear the Germanic provinces of Austria out of a union of states in which they have been happy and prosperous for centuries. Is it seriously believed in Frankfort that this can be effected by a vote ? A true German heart beats in my bosom, but if this were to be the price of loyalty I should have to still its promptings. There is a great deal of babble in Germany about the danger of Pan-Slavism, but everything is done to give this spectre a body, for fury against it and loyalty to Germany have almost become identical terms. Austria with its non-German provinces numbers thirty-eight million souls. Let us hope this fact will not be forgotten in Frankfort, and that an all too rigid Germanism will not rob us of such an ally. Austria will separate from Germany sooner than from Austria.

But the die was cast, and, having determined on the virtual exclusion of Austria, the Assembly proceeded to debate the

---

[1] Carl Mathy. *Briefe von 1846-48* (K.).

question as to who was to be the overlord of United Germany. The official recommendation was that this honour should be offered to one of the ruling German princes. But amendments were numerous. Some were for a life-appointment; others desired the honour to be hereditary; others that it should only be for a term of years; others objected to its restriction to ruling German princes, and thought that all Germans should be eligible; and finally others proposed a board of five directors, with Austria and Prussia taking the chair every two years. A few examples of the opinions expressed in the Assembly are well worth quoting. Rümelin, later Chancellor of the University of Tübingen, spoke out in favour of the King of Prussia as hereditary sovereign :

I desire that the King of Prussia be hereditary King of the Germans in the more restricted German Federal State which we are here called upon to found.

We would rather stand at a forsaken, abandoned outpost of a German State, we would rather be the stepsons of a German fatherland than have no fatherland at all !

Uhland wanted an elective Kaiser :

Has then our political reorganisation issued from the monarchical, dynastic, aristocratic side of our foregoing German political life ? No ! indisputably from the democratic ! Thus the root is democratic, and the summit does not spring from the branches but from the root. It would not be conformable with the natural growth of the new-springing German oak if we wished to plant on her crest a nest of hereditary Imperial eagles ! . . . The Revolution and a hereditary Kaiser are like a youth with grey hair.

Yet still I lay my hand on the old open wound, the exclusion of Austria. Exclusion, that is the candid expression ; for if a hereditary German Empire, excluding Austria, were determined upon, it is difficult to see how Austria can at any time enter into association with Germany. . . . Many a time, when Austrian delegates have spoken in this hall, even when they spoke against my opinions, it yet seemed to me as if I heard a voice pealing from the Tyrolese mountains or from the Adriatic Sea. How narrowed will be our horizon, if Austria is separated from us ! . . . Finally, gentlemen : cast aside the hereditary principle ; create no ruling single State ; do not throw Austria over ; preserve the right of election, that precious privilege of the people, that latest effective sign-manual of the popular origin of the new power. Believe me, no head will shine resplendent over Germany which is not anointed with a full drop of democratic oil !

Welcker, who had been Professor of Law at Freiburg, who sat on the Right Centre in the Assembly, and who moved the final resolution in favour of the election of the King of Prussia as hereditary Kaiser, roundly dismissed all amendments based on republican sentiment :

As, in my eyes, a republic without republican virtue and culture appears merely a band of robbers, and as I do not find republican virtue and culture to any great extent in my people, I am convinced that, with a republic at this time of day, we are facing a serious situation, and, with the republic, are heading for military domination.

Dahlmann, as usual, caught and reflected the general feeling of the German nation in his powerful speech in favour of the Hohenzollerns :

A dynasty is of more account than an individual. In the Hohenzollerns of Prussia we can have a ruling house, but, more than that, with the worst and the best will in the world, no mortal can persuade us that we have not got it. There is absolutely no future possible for Germany without Prussia. . . . I will speak my mind, unheeding how unfavourably it is received on various sides. You will not put down the fire of anarchy in Germany, nor will you bank down this destroying fire either in the small states or in the middle-sized ones, or lastly in the large, even in the largest, of the purely German states except in one way, and only in this way, that you establish a powerful unity, and through this unity open out the path for that German national energy which makes for might. The path of power is the only one that will appease and satisfy the fermenting passion for freedom, a passion that has hitherto not recognised its own nature ; for it is not only freedom it desires, it is power, the greater half, which it has hitherto lacked, for which it craves.

At last Germany must as such enter the group of the great political Powers of the Continent : that can only come to pass by means of Prussia, and neither Prussia without Germany, nor Germany without Prussia, can find salvation. . . .

I condemn no man's vote ; but, so far as concerns myself, I should feel that I had broken with all that is patriotically dear and sacred to me, that I had broken with my fatherland, if I gave my vote otherwise than for German unity, for an hereditary crown on my German fatherland.

And Soiron, whose speech is singled out by Ranke as among the most significant, said : [1]

Our provisional central authority had all in its favour : the most popular of princes, public opinion, the shock administered to the stability of thrones by the Revolution, the National Assembly itself

---

[1] *Aus dem Briefwechsel Friedrich Wilhelms IV. mit Bunsen.*

—but it had no material power. Therefore it was, and remained, impotent. But that power may be lasting, it must be hereditary. Only under this condition is it possible that Prussia may be merged in Germany. Were the King of Prussia only overlord for life, Prussia would consolidate herself as a constitutional state, and make a federal state impossible. But were the King made hereditary Kaiser of Germany, then Prussian particularism would cease. We may anticipate that individual provinces will find the centre of their aspirations for unity not in Berlin, but in the seat of Empire.

A broadsheet [1] shows how the mocking populace discussed the question. Above is a caricature, representing a hurdy-gurdy man, wearing the German cockade, and a stout female, Germania, with a wreath on her head, who holds the ' fundamental principles ' in her left hand, and with her right points to a chequered chart on which are depicted the arms of all the German princes. Between these two figures stand Gagern and Simson as two ragged urchins singing the following song :

A NEW KAISER SONG

Who shall our German Kaiser be ?
Prince Reuss-Greiz-Schleiz-Lobenstein, *he* ?
Perhaps the Prince of Birkenfeld ?
Or Windischgrätz, now hero held ?
　　O no ! O no ! We all agree,
　　Some other shall our Kaiser be ! . . .

Who shall our German Kaiser be ?
A prince from Elbe or Rhine maybe ?
Perhaps a prince from Leuchtenberg,
Munich, Hanover, Würtemberg ?
　　O no ! O no : We all agree,
　　Not one of these shall Kaiser be !

Who shall our German Kaiser be ?
Too small are Hesse and Saxony ?
An Austrian of Hapsburg kin ?
A Hohenzollern from Berlin ?
　　O no ! O no ! We all agree,
　　Still mightier shall our Kaiser be !

Now tell us true, who shall it be ?
Whose hand shall stablish Germany ?
Whose brow deserves the dignity ?
Perchance the People's sovereignty ?
　　Ah, there again we all agree,
　　The People shall our Kaiser be !

---

[1] Facsimile in Blum.

The debate in the Assembly on the question promised to be interminable, but a final decision was precipitated by Austria's contemptuous attitude. Welcker, a staunch supporter of Austria, suddenly swung round, and. in an excited House moved a resolution in favour of the King of Prussia. The division was taken on 28th March 1849, and the two hundred and ninety votes cast were unanimous in favour of the election of the King of Prussia as hereditary German Kaiser. But two hundred and forty-eight members, including all the representatives from Austria, abstained from voting !

Before we deal in the next chapter with Frederick William's rejection of the offer, a rejection which administered the *coup de grâce* to the first German parliament, we have to glance at Bunsen's embittered view,[1] early in 1849, of the King and his entourage during this fateful crisis :

As I had quitted Frankfort with the longing desire to be enabled, there in the centre of German life, to live and act, so did I quit Berlin with a physical repugnance against the thought either of living or dying there. A general consciousness of dissatisfaction had come over me already in 1845, which in 1848 strengthened into disgust, and now were moral indignation, dejection, and grief fixed permanently in my heart. More than ever did I feel myself a foreigner in the chief city of my fatherland, repelled even in the very dwelling-house of my King. The ante-chamber countenances recalled to my mind the condition of 1806 ; there was no free spirit, no fresh and unshackled heart, no human sympathies among all those human forms there seated or gliding about. [An enumeration follows.] Lastly, X., . . . now the organ of Meyendorf for communication with the King, by means of whom the King was plied every morning with all the bits of intelligence that could be found likely to irritate and displease him,—at one time the rudeness of the Frankfort orators, at another the so-called insurrectional plans and utterances of Gagern ; again, the complaints of princes, of noblemen, and of the well-disposed, who felt themselves oppressed (no matter where they were), even mixing suggestions relative to the highest politics. Through this channel the Emperor of Russia transmitted menaces to the King, by word of mouth, and in writing ; and thus were formed within the King's inner Closet notions, plans, convictions, against which the Ministers vainly contended, and secret correspondences, which overruled politics and ruined diplomacy, Already in 1848 I had discovered traces of this system of by-play and suffered from it ; the malicious letter of Lady —— to Frau von Meyendorf came in this manner to the knowledge of the King ; but now I had penetrated further behind the scene, and could see and

[1] *Memoir of Baron Bunsen*, ii. p. 209.

feel the destructive effects of the political agitation ceaselessly carried on.   Of the Court in general the only positive characteristic, among many negations, was that of enmity to the popular cause.   Humboldt's presence was a consolation, as well as here and there a man of worth in office, known to me from former times.   The hatred of the official body, and of the party of nobles, *as such*, which had persecuted me now during full twenty years, came upon me in yet coarser distinctness than ever, as well as their incapacity and the narrowness of their views, which the exasperation of 1848 had but more strongly brought to view.   To Count Brandenburg I was drawn by his inartificial kindness, and his manly devotedness to the King ; but his entire previous course of action was a censure upon mine, as mine upon his.   The general impression made by countenances all around was that of choking from suppressed rage.   A real statesman was nowhere to be seen ; and what could such an one have attempted at Charlottenburg, in the present state of things ?   The King was resolved to direct all politics by himself alone, he would have a Dictatorship by the side of the constitution, and yet be considered a liberal constitutional Sovereign ; whereas he regarded the constitutional system to be one of deceit and falsehood.   The faithfulness, the discipline, and the bravery of the army, being the object of his just pride, he reckoned upon being able to unloose the political knot at last by means of the military ; for his noble heart was corroded by habitual exasperation from the events of the 19th and 21st March 1848, which was more and more transferred to Frankfort.   Often did more liberal thoughts and feelings emerge from the flood ; but the surrounding influences and the secret communications from Olmütz and Munich allowed not of their permanence.

However I struggled against the thought, I could not be blind to the fact that the noble King was preparing for himself and the country a dark and difficult future, which seemed inevitable ; humanly speaking, no help [appeared] to be within reach, at least as long as the King remained in Charlottenburg and Berlin.   He might have been compliant with a German Ministry of high intelligence, high station, and European reputation ; but never with one merely composed of Prussian, Brandenburgian, Pomeranian, and Saxon materials.   The idea that subjects, and those such as he felt to be inferior to himself both in abilities and experience, should direct his politics, should in any degree hinder his acting as he pleased, was intolerable to him.   What in earlier days, and even still in 1848, had appeared accidental and transitory with him, now assumed a fixed and fateful character ; and what was to my feeling the most painful, was that I could not perceive the same high and truly royal consciousness of right as existed formerly ; also that his energy in action bore no proportion to his resolute bearing and declaration of will ; that there were moments in which he might be said to sink exhausted rather than to yield to argument ; after which giving way his inward wrath was kindled.   I felt myself ever bound to him by affection and gratitude, but the bond of souls was torn asunder, the hope that I had founded upon him had been a delusion ; a nearer relation to him in the Ministry of the State had become impossible, or must have closed in an absolute breach.

All around I was aware of disesteem, mistrust, hatred, indignation, directed against the King, by which my heart was irritated as much as wounded ; he occasionally spoke of abdication, but the idea that the act was, or might become necessary, was in the heart of thousands. And this in the case of a Sovereign so rarely gifted, so noble minded, towering so far above his fellows ; born to be the beloved of his people, the jewel and ornament of the age !

Thus did I leave Berlin, resolved never willingly to return thither ; which feeling has been more and more confirmed. The four months which have since elapsed have only formed one course of mental suffering, anxiety, grief, pain, and vexation, with few glimpses of light ; and I must call them the most distressful and afflicting of my life.

CHAPTER II

FREDERICK WILLIAM REJECTS THE IMPERIAL CROWN

WHEN Bunsen wrote the gloomy memorandum quoted at the end of the last chapter he was a disappointed man. He had always been a warm advocate of constitutionalism in Germany, and had in London a strong supporter in the Prince Consort ; he therefore threw the whole weight of his influence with Frederick William on the side of the National Assembly. When it became clear in the autumn of 1848 how feeling at Frankfort was moving, he wrote [1] to the King :

LONDON, *Autumn* 1848.

If we come first to consider a new and final disposition of the Empire, I shall take the liberty of reminding your Majesty that in 1848 and 1850 a modern arrangement must be recommended and established, not because of but in spite of mediæval times. Your Majesty, to be precise, will have to beware of posing as an archæologist instead of figuring as a king and legislator of the year 1848 or 1850, and speaking the language of the century.

Frederick William's reply to this letter might have been written by his great-nephew :

POTSDAM, 13*th December* 1848.

You say (word for word as Herr von Gagern said to me on the 26th and 27th of this month) : ' You want the consent of the ruling princes ; very well, that you shall have.' But, my dearest friend, you are whipping a dead donkey. I want neither the *consent* of princes to the *election* nor the *crown* itself. Do you understand the words underlined ?

I shall enlighten you on the subject as briefly and clearly as possible. First then the crown is no crown. The crown which a Hohenzollern could accept, if circumstances rendered such a thing possible at all, is not one created by an Assembly born of revolutionary seed, even if offered with princely approval (*dans le genre de la couronne des*

---

[1] For this and subsequent correspondence of Bunsen with the King, *see* Ranke's *Aus dem Briefwechsel F. W. IV. mit Bunsen.*

pavés de Louis Philippe). No it must be a crown set with the seal of the Almighty, one which makes him who assumes it, after the sacred anointment, Sovereign ' by the Grace of God,' and that because (and *as*) it has made more than thirty-four princes Kings of the Germans by the grace of God, and gives the latest wearer his place in the ancient line. That crown which was borne by the Ottos, the Hohenstaufens, and the Hapsburgs, a Hohenzollern can of course fitly wear, for it honours him inexpressibly with its thousand years of glory. But the crown you unfortunately mean *dis*honours one inexpressibly, stinking as it does of the Revolution of 1848, the silliest, most stupid and the wickedest, if not, thank God, the most disastrous of the century. Such a fictitious coronet baked out of mire and clay is to be accepted by one who is a legitimate king by the Grace of God, and that too by a King of Prussia who has the happiness of wearing, if not the most ancient, at all events the noblest crown, and one that was not stolen from anybody ! . . . I tell you roundly : if ever that thousand year old crown of the German nation, which has now rested unworn for forty-two years, should again be conferred on any one, then it is I and my peers who are going to confer it and woe to any one who arrogates a right which is not his due !

There is little doubt that a majority of the German princes had come to the conclusion, despite the personal unpopularity of Frederick William IV. and a general suspicion of his restless temperament, that the military, bureaucratic and economic strength of Prussia so dominated the whole political system, that only under the hegemony of the King of Prussia could unity be achieved. This view is reflected in a letter [1] which Duke Ernest of Saxe-Coburg-Gotha, Prince Albert's brother, wrote to the King on 14th January 1849. The style in which the All-Highest is addressed is surely resplendent enough for any earthly potentate :

Most Illustrious, Most High and Mighty King! Most Highly Honoured Sovereign Cousin,—The Committee for the Constitution of the German National Assembly in Frankfort-on-Main has decided by a majority that an Emperor shall be placed at the head of the German Empire.

Only in this way can Germany attain greater unity, by means of which her elevation to higher political importance externally and the development of real freedom internally are secured.

I therefore hope that the future decision of the National Assembly will conform to this determination, but that the fate of Germany will be placed in the hands of a Prince who possesses will and strength thoroughly to fulfil his high calling.

---

[1] *Memoirs*, vol. i.

Your Majesty is henceforth intended by divine Providence to lead the German Fatherland to a happier future. Your Majesty will therefore have no difficulty in obeying the call to fill this high position, as soon as it has reached your Majesty.

I am expressing a wish which is certainly entertained equally by the majority of the Princes of Germany, and do not for my part hesitate to lay at the feet of your Majesty the assurance that I shall be pleased to see your Majesty at the head of Germany.

I beg your Majesty to accept the assurance of my distinguished regard and devotion, and remain, your Majesty's obedient friend, cousin, and servant,

ERNEST, D. of S. C. and G.

But Duke Ernest's intimate dislike of his ' Highly Honoured Sovereign Cousin ' is revealed in his comment on the situation after Frederick William had refused the Imperial crown. ' The King of Prussia,' he says, ' was not to play his double part in the Imperial dream of Frankfort without being punished for it. Severe humiliation lay without doubt in the lamentable way in which his election was laboriously brought about by his party in Frankfort, and in the really painful situation in which he found himself forced to refuse an offered crown of the most imaginary kind, with the appearance of feeling himself flattered thereby. . . . In reality Frederick William IV. could have no other feeling concerning the results of the long pains in labour of the Frankfort Empire than one of heavy defeat.'

Other great Germans endeavoured to move the King to accept the offer which it was certain would come from Frankfort. Among these was Arndt. His letter to Frederick William is described by Ranke as saturated with patriotic feeling. His chief argument was that Austria, though in her own despite, would attach to herself the elements of radicalism and communism, and wavering on the part of the King might lead to the red republic. The letter, says Ranke, was a mixture of childish importunity and the respect of a true subject. ' One saw in his silvery hair the blond locks of the child.' The King answered him as his ' well-disposed king and good friend.' His attitude is even more hostile to communists and red democrats than Arndt's, he styles them men of hell and of death. But it was not in them that he saw the real danger, for it was only on the rich soil of revolution that they had grown ; the danger was in revolution itself. And the National Assembly was hurrying down the very stream of revolution, seeing that it paid no

respect to the German governments. Its mission was to draft
a constitution and then come to an agreement thereon with
Germany's ruling princes and the free cities. Who had given
it the right to impose a Kaiser on the rightful governments ?
It had neither a crown to give nor to offer. The crown that it
offered him would be an iron collar, and would make him, the
ruler of sixteen millions, the slave of the revolution. Far from
him was the idea of accepting it. Were, however, a true and
properly constituted council of princes and people to offer him
the ancient, true, rightful, and thousand year old crown of the
German nation, then would he reply, as a man must reply,
when the highest honour in this world was offered him.

Bunsen received on 31st March the news of the final decision
of the Frankfort Assembly to offer the Imperial crown to the
King of Prussia. He wrote off to the King on the same day,
urging him passionately to accept the offer. Ranke admits the
force of his arguments and summarises his letter as follows :
' Refusal would be dangerous for the person and family of the
King, for the Prussian monarchy, and for the future of Germany.
The manifesto of Austria, according to which she was to have
thirty-eight votes for herself at her entry in full force into the
German Federation, while to the Germans only thirty-two
votes were to fall, made any further word unnecessary.
" Germany can in future only exist as a free Federal state side
by side with the Austrian joint-state, and only in the form of a
state with an hereditary overlord. Prussia has to choose
between this high position, and a wretched dependence on
Austria and Russia. Your Majesty may possibly delay for your
lifetime what must come. But come it will, for Germany's
passion to be a nation, and as such to confront foreign countries
in peace and war, is ineradicable." '

We have now to consider two documents of the highest
interest, the King's official reply to the deputation from
Frankfort offering the crown, and his answer to Bunsen's
arguments in favour of acceptance. It is seldom that one has
the opportunity of observing the attitude of kings and politicians both in dress and in undress, in relation to the same
occasion. Let us take the King's letter to Bunsen first, though
it is the later in date, for it gives the King in undress. This
letter, in which he seeks to prove the correctness and necessity
of his refusal, is styled by Ranke ' one of the most significant

documents for history that Frederick William ever penned.'
It was written in May 1849, at Easter-time, when, as the letter
began, ' the ringing of bells proclaims the advent of the Easter
festival.' After thinking for half a day over Bunsen's letters,
he had arrived, he says, at the sad conclusion that he could
not come to terms with his old friend. Between them was
discord, like the discordance between fish and bird. The
letter proceeds :

You are overborne by impressions of the Revolution of 1848.
You have given to the horrible bastard of man and devil an honest
name *Teutschland*. I, on the contrary, from the 18th and 19th
March 1848, until to-day, have seen in it nothing but a falling from
God. (O dear friend, do not take this in mockery ! ! !) I have
given his proper name to the atrocious bastard without wincing or
wavering. Next to the destruction of the sacred edifice of *Teutscher*
customs, organisations and laws, this, above all, has wounded my
heart, that the sacred watchword *Teutschland* has been, perhaps
for ever, held up to the scorn, the denunciation, the wrath of all
noble men of future days, that the word which for fifty years has
sent thrills of ecstasy quivering through my soul, has become the
catchword, ay, the pretext for all faithlessness, every violation of
oath, every infamy. And the name *Teutschland* is not invested
with the sanctity of God's name, which cannot be injured even by
the abominations of the Jesuits. And yet I love *Teutschland*, its
honour and fame and worth, with the love which one attaches to the
name of an incomparable mother. (And I know what that implies.)
. . . If the majority in the *Paulskirche* had been really in earnest
in the matter, common sense as well as a jot of respect for law and
a little of faith in the honesty of my official utterances would have
told those patriots to obtain first of all the assent of the lawful
authorities. I ask why not ? Have they then not asked themselves
that ? Everything has a cause. Then also this thing. Why not ?
To me (and, thank God, to all sound minds) the answer is not
doubtful. Because these patriots (!) wished thereby irrevocably to
confirm the Revolution, to establish the sovereignty of the German
nation, they would buckle a dog's collar on the fool, the King of
Prussia, which would fetter him indissolubly to the sovereignty of
the people, make him a bondsman of the Revolution of 1848 !
That, dearest friend, is the gist of the matter, the only excuse for
this contemptible business. *Grâces à Dieu ! c'était une finesse,
cousue de fil d'archal.* [It was a pretty little thing but a snare.] I
and my Ministry did not need any expenditure of mental effort over
such clumsy machinations, in order to discover their meaning.
Therefore I base my decision on the incompetency of the *Paulskirche*
deputation. The meaning of the decision is : ' I can answer you
neither yes nor no. One only accepts or refuses something which
can be offered,—and you there, you have nothing to offer : I shall

settle the business with my equals, or else good-bye to truth : against democracy only soldiers can avail ; adieu ! '

I hope that this decision which my honour and my name, my position ' as Prince by the Grace of God ' have constrained me to give, has been clothed in the requisite court-dress. What is hidden behind coat and shirt, you know as well as I. I can and may not alter it. And now may the matter proceed under God's guidance, Amen.

Now let us have the King in regal state, standing before his audience, with all the consciousness of a great actor playing a great part, or of a prominent statesman opening or closing a full-dress debate on some momentous occasion. It was on 3rd April that the King received the Frankfort deputation, including Arndt and Dahlmann, who announced to him ' that the Fatherland had chosen him, as the shelter and shield of its unity, freedom, and might, to be the overlord of the Empire.' The King's reply [1] was certainly an example of stately eloquence difficult to match, beside which the most grandiloquent utterances of his great-nephew are like sounding brass :

The message, as bearers of which you have come to me, has deeply moved me. It has turned my eyes to the King of Kings, and to the sacred and inviolable duties which devolve on me as King of my people, and as one of the powerful German princes. So gazing, the vision is cleared and the heart swells. In the resolution of the German National Assembly which you bring to me I recognise the voice of the representatives of the German people. This call gives me a claim, the worth of which I know how to value. It demands, if I follow it, immeasurable sacrifices from me. It lays on me the heaviest duties. The German National Assembly has elected me, among those eligible, as the man to found the unity and might of Germany. I honour its trust, express my thanks to it for me. I am ready to prove in act that those men have not been mistaken who based their confidence upon my devotion, upon my faithfulness, upon my love to our common Fatherland. But I should not justify your confidence, I should not meet the mind of the German people, I should not uphold German unity, if I contravened sacred rights and my former explicit and official utterances, by seeking to make a decision without the free assent of the crowned heads, the princes, and the free towns of Germany, a decision which for them and for the German peoples ruled by them, may have most critical consequences. It will therefore now be well to examine, in consultation with the governments of the individual German states, whether this policy will benefit the parts as well as the whole, whether the privileges proposed for me will set me in the position which such a call

---

[1] Klein.

demands from me, to lead with stronger hand the destiny of the great German Fatherland, and to fulfil the hopes of its peoples. But of this Germany may be certain, and you may proclaim it throughout its provinces : should it be in need of Prussian shield and sword against enemies abroad or at home, I shall not be wanting, even if uncalled. I will then go solaced along the way set for my house and my people, the path of German honour and loyalty !

Bismarck was of course delighted with the King's decision. On 21st April he spoke in the Prussian Assembly on the subject of the Frankfort offer, and his sentence on the Frankfort ' crown ' is well known :

The crown of Frankfort may be very brilliant, but the gold which gives genuineness to its brilliance must first be obtained by melting down the Prussian crown ; and I have no faith that a recasting in the mould of this Constitution will succeed.

The Prussian National Assembly itself had on 1st and 2nd April passed resolutions urging the King to accept the invitation. But the opinions of the moderate minority in that Assembly are reflected in Victor von Unruh's comment : [1]

The Second Chamber was convinced that the King would not accept the crown, nevertheless it held itself under an obligation to frame a resolution advising the King to consent to his election. As was expected, he declined it. The message, read out by Count Brandenburg in the Chamber, closed with the cry : ' Never, never, never ! ' which suggested to *Kladderadatsch* the well-known lines :

> Peevish folk, my heart bleeds so,
> Never, never, never, no !

It was then reported that the King had inquired of Humboldt, who was known to hold himself apart from all politics, as to what course he advised him. Humboldt was said to have answered : ' Your Majesty's great-uncle [Frederick the Great] would not have debated one moment.' The King's answer ran, so it was said : ' If I were my great-uncle, I also would not debate the question ; but I am not ! ' If this anecdote is true, it does the King all honour. The King was really not at all qualified, either in mind or gifts, to take such a work in hand and carry it through.

---

[1] *Erinnerungen* (K.).

CHAPTER III

SUPPRESSION OF THE NATIONAL ASSEMBLY

THE King of Prussia's rejection of the proffered crown knocked the bottom out of the always leaky vessel of government at Frankfort. It was the second heavy blow administered to the pretensions of the first German parliament, for after the vote of 28th March the Austrian deputies withdrew, and on 5th April Schwarzenberg recalled the Austrian Ambassador at Frankfort. The National Assembly had been impotent from its inception because it had no material force, and now no moral force remained to it, for the circumstances were such that one could not exist without the other. Nevertheless the remnant of the Assembly still pursued, under Gagern's leadership, the hopeless task of persuading the German governments to accept the constitution which so much of the legal, academic and other talent of Germany had at such prodigious cost of conference, debate and compromise produced. Despite efforts to conciliate Prussia by negotiations with L. Camphausen, the Prussian envoy, in the direction of modifying the constitution to suit Prussian views, the Prussian government definitely rejected the constitution on 28th April. The constitutional party was paralysed, and the ascendency in the Assembly drifted towards the extremists on the Left. On 4th May the Assembly called upon all German governments to enforce the constitution as one legally enacted, and announced that a new and duly constituted German *Reichstag*, for which the writs were issued, would be convened on 15th August. To this announcement the Prussian government's answer was the recall of all Prussian deputies to the Assembly. Events moved faster and faster. A few days later Gagern and his ministry resigned. The unfortunate Regent nominated on the 17th a new ministry, composed of elements so odd that it could only be regarded as a ministry *pour rire* ; the Minister for Foreign Affairs was a

General Jochmus who had previously been a Turkish Pasha, and before that, according to Sir A. W. Ward, a Hamburg merchant's clerk. Three days later Saxony ordered the Saxon deputies to withdraw, and sixty-five of the most distinguished members of the House retired of their own accord. These included Gagern, Simson, Mathy, Dahlmann and Arndt, the last named of whom gave expression to his sentiments in a poem as fine in feeling as anything he ever wrote :

MAY 1849

Away ! Our heroes' arms grow tired,
    And stricken sore the strongest fall.
A truce to life no more desired !
Away ! The death-knell tolls for all.

Away ! The hurrying moments flee ;
    Nor dog-like die a coward's death.
Proud dreams of Empire came to thee—
Bury them where none whispereth.

True hearts will know where hid they lie,
    Those dreams, and bring them back to light.
And though we fall, the victory
Will yet be ours in such a fight.

Mathy wrote [1] on 18th May to his friend Beckerath :

The attitude of the kings towards the Assembly and its work has disillusioned the men who sought to guide the unification of Germany along the path of peaceful development, and has thrust them from the stage upon which chaos, anarchic and demonic, is now advancing against the kings. Should they be victorious by means of their armies, they have so deeply wounded the best feelings of the nation, that their momentary victory over anarchy will not long establish their thrones.

The unrest in Baden has just as solid a foundation as the policy of the kings ; breach of oath on the part of a furious and misguided soldiery. Complete dissolution of the state has set in there, and that of society is in prospect. Würtemberg and the Palatinate have the same to expect ; a South German republic under a French protectorate must be reckoned as by no means an impossibility. Baden and the Palatinate of the Rhine are overrun with a rabble which receives reinforcements from Switzerland and Alsace ; Würtemberg and Hesse are still holding back ; for how long ?—that is uncertain.

---

[1] *Deutsche Revue*, viii. 1, 1882 (K.).

The staunch and stalwart Uhland remained, and composed a dignified [1] address to the German people which was issued in behalf of his colleagues and himself on the 26th. It ended as follows :

For these efforts to maintain the existence of the National Assembly and to bring the constitution into being we demand at this fateful moment the active co-operation of the whole German people. We are not provoking any breach of the peace, we do not wish to stir up a civil war, but we think it necessary in this iron time that the people should be capable of defending themselves and practised in the use of arms, so that if their right to the constitution and the popular liberties connected with it are threatened with force, or if there is an attempt to impose upon them forcibly any kind of constitution that does not proceed from their representatives, they may be able to repel the unjust attack. To this end we hold it urgently necessary that in all states that adhere to the constitution a national army should be rapidly and completely created and that with it the standing army should be pledged to maintain the Imperial constitution. . . . Above all things, our firm confidence in the manly pride and honour of our people, newly awakened to freedom as it is, makes us believe that they will never respond to an election held in accordance with an Imperial election law arbitrarily imposed, but only to one held in accordance with the law made by the Assembly which had the right to give the constitution ; and that when the appointed election day arrives there will be keen emulation simultaneously in all German districts to make use of or to acquire the universal franchise.

By the close of the month the pitiful rump of the Assembly, surrounded as it was by Prussian troops, had resolved to transfer its sittings to Stuttgart. There, on 6th June, the Regency was vested in a committee of five, which included the ' absolutely neutral ' Carl Vogt. This many-headed monster of a regency provoked an excellent epigram [2] by Carl Heinzen, which is quoted in Arnold Ruge's *Correspondence and Diary* :

> When first the German Empire stood,
> No Regent made its title good ;
> Then Regents five came,—in their day
> They ruled the empire quite away.

The quintuple regency issued on 7th June a manifesto [3] to the German people, an address reminiscent of Uhland's issued

---

[2] Notter's *Life of Uhland*, 1863, p. 323.
[2] Written in London, and, as he says, on the usual dull English Sunday afternoon.
[3] Facsimile in Blum.

on 26th May, and eloquent with that pathetic eloquence which comes to men on a great or desperate occasion, and deludes them into the belief that a high-sounding phrase has the effect of a ringing blow :

TO THE GERMAN PEOPLE

The provisional Central Authority, which has hitherto existed, has, in opposition to the duties laid upon it by the law of 28th June, stubbornly delayed to enforce the Constitution, and has disregarded all the resolutions of the National Assembly directed to that end. It has omitted, despite repeated reminders, to lend its support to the rising of the German Peoples in favour of the Constitution, and to proceed against the Governments who presumed to force on the German nation a constitution and an electoral law.

The Constituent Assembly of the German Realm has, for these reasons, in its sitting of 6th June resolved :

To relieve the hitherto existing Central Authority of its functions, and to set up a Regency for Germany, which shall exercise executive authority in all matters that concern the general safety and welfare of Germany.

We, the undersigned, are nominated by the representatives of the German nation to compose the Regency for Germany. To us are transferred the rights and duties of the hitherto existing Central Authority, the enforcement of the Constitution and the fulfilment of the resolutions of the National Assembly. For our conduct of affairs we are responsible to the National Assembly.

Germans ! We have obeyed the call of your lawful representatives, in firm reliance on the justice of our cause.

The condition of our Fatherland calls for prompt action. We have to save our Holy of Holies, the freedom and honour of the German nation, from the boundless encroachments of crude force. We shall do all that in us lies to avert civil war and to attain to German unity and freedom by ways of peace ; but, if this proves necessary in order to reach the goal, we shall oppose force to force. Hundreds of thousands from all parts of Germany have solemnly sworn to spend their blood and their treasure for the Constitution ; we shall call on them, in that event, to fulfil their manly promise.

Yet a special word for you, soldiers of Germany ! The law gives us the control of the whole armed force of Germany ; it delegates to us the nomination of the Commander-in-Chief. You, soldiers of Germany, will obey the law, whose armed defence you are. Officers, non-commissioned officers and men of the National Guard and of the Standing Army, be your rank what it may, you will vie with one another in the prompt discharge of the orders which we, and the Commander-in-Chief nominated by us, will deliver to you. You will be mindful of every soldier's motto : Loyalty to the law, obedience to its ministers !

After to-day, when the command over the national forces, which have hitherto owed allegiance to the provisional Central Authority, is transferred to our hands, every further act of obedience to the orders of the hitherto existing Central Authority will be punished as treason against the law and the German nation.

Germans ! In this fateful hour we appeal to you.

There is yet time, by our own strength, to save the greatness, the unity and the freedom of the Fatherland, to win for it honour abroad and peace at home ! There is yet time, again to establish under the guarantees of the German Constitution an order of things founded on freedom.

Peace and repose, the indispensable conditions required if industry and commerce are to flourish, will not return until the inevitable struggle between Absolutism and Freedom is settled in favour of Freedom. Stand by us, all, in the full power of will and deed ! A righteous cause is sure of victory.

STUTTGART, 7th June 1848.

The Members of the German Regency,

FRANZ RAVEAUX, CARL VOGT, HEINRICH SIMON, FRIEDRICH SCHUELER, AUGUST BECKER.

A few days later they declared the Archduke John, still at Frankfort a Regent in partibus, to be a usurper. But this effort was to be their last. The presence of so fantastic an organisation and its parliamentary rump at Stuttgart was distasteful to the Würtemberg government, who decided to disperse it on 18th June by the military in true Prussian style. The final scene is thus described in Notter's Life of Ludwig Uhland : [1]

At midday Uhland had sought one of his political friends, who still remained beside him in the National Assembly, but had not attended it during the last two days, and, in fact, to-day, wished no longer to attend. He found him at dinner. ' What are we to do ? ' he asked as he entered, a question which had half become a joke in the little circle. And again came the humorous response, ' Let ourselves go bust ! ' He sat down to the meal without sharing it, and was confidential and talkative as his friend had seldom seen him. The hour of the sitting (three o'clock in the afternoon) drew near ; suddenly they heard troops approaching the Fritzschen Reithaus, the meeting-place of the Assembly, not far off. Such an intervention Uhland had not then expected. He sprang up, his friend wished to hold him back ; he, however, hurried away with the words, ' No ! No ! I must be there ! ' and sent word to President Löwe, at that time living in the Hotel Marguardt in the Königstrasse, that in his opinion all the delegates who were at hand should betake themselves in procession to the Assembly Room, in order, if it had to be, that

---

[1] Page 335.

they should suffer in their persons the indignity of force. The President at first did not favour a formal procession, yet he realised, as he expressed himself in the Protocol published on the occasion, the last act of the German Parliament, ' that the Assembly, led by the first German poet, could not end better,' and the proposal was accepted. . . .

[Uhland and Albert Schott, the two senior deputies present, set the President Löwe-Calbe between them, and so the remnant of the delegates to the Frankfort National Assembly walked in procession to the Reithaus.   In the Hohenstrasse they came into contact with the infantry.   Twice Löwe asked the troops to give place.]   The incessant beating of drums overpowered his words, and the soldiers were ordered to advance, which, however, they did not do in any ruthless spirit, as all witnesses agree ; on the contrary, the advance, according to the impression of the commanding officer, appears to have been somewhat too hesitating, for he asked with a loud voice : ' Where 's the cavalry ? '   At this demand an infantry officer called to Uhland : ' Place yourself here between us, Professor ; here you are perfectly safe.'   Uhland did not avail himself of the invitation, but the cavalry, to whom an officer had communicated the above-mentioned inquiry, set off at a quiet trot.   The nearer, however, they came to the Langenstrasse, so much the more moderate became the pace of the horses, and when they reached the delegates, they were going at mere walking pace.   For the rest, the cavalry, like the infantry, seemed disinclined for violent measures, although orders rang out, and even the cry, ' Cut them down ! ' was raised several times.   Naturally, however, this restraint in the use of weapons of offence did not prevent the delegates from seeing each other soon scattered by the on-coming horses.   At this moment a delegate's oft-quoted words to the approaching horsemen must have been uttered— if they really were—' Would you ride down old Uhland ? '   The members of the National Assembly now turned about, rearranged as well as they could their ranks, which had been scattered by the cavalry, and walked back to the Hotel Marguardt, Uhland again in front with President Löwe at his side.

Thus was finally dispersed, like a mob at a street corner, the great Assembly of the German people on which so many fond hopes had been founded.   It did a great work, for the principles of personal liberty which it laid down were sound and the con- stitution it based on those principles was such as no Englishman who believes in his own constitution, as it stood until times comparatively recent, could disapprove.   The skeleton of the constitution was to be clothed with German flesh and blood, and informed with the German spirit of hate, and lust for power, but there were nobler elements in the German nature.   These would have been allowed more play in the German Empire founded on the principles adopted at Frankfort than has been the case in that built up of blood and iron from 1850 to 1870. The forces of dynastic tradition and strong centralised government, military and bureaucratic, proved too strong in 1848, and the German enigma of to-day is, will they survive the present struggle ? Like pious platitudes sound the comments of Laube and Sybel on the Frankfort fiasco. The former ends his history of *The First German Parliament*, so frequently quoted in this work, with the words :

> We strive not for sovereignty ; we strive for truth. History ought to say, and will say : 'Through unheard of obstacles and difficulties the first German Parliament sought and found for Germany political truth. You will never look upon its like again.'

Sybel, the historian of the founding of the German Empire, says : [1]

> Nevertheless it is no shame, but a glory, to be ahead of your contemporaries, and on that account, to be unsuccessful for the present, but perhaps to scatter the seed of a great future. This the National Assembly has done, and so maintains an honourable name in history. The impress which it left on the mind of the fatherland has remained indelible, and further, a happier after-time would not have won the success it did, if our first Parliament, in spite of all mistakes about methods, had not so clearly and with such strong emphasis, pointed the people towards the goal : inward freedom, outward unity.

There is more stuff in Gustav Freytag's summary [2] of the history and the achievement of this first German parliament. But even the author of the *Life of Carl Mathy* shows little sympathy with the national aspiration for popular as well as constitutional government which Prussia, by overthrowing the National Assembly, succeeded in checking so decisively for more than half a century :

> So long as there is a German nation, the path to unity that was opened out in the year 1848 will count as an expression quite unique, peculiarly German in its character, of national sentiment. The soaring thoughts of a small number of patriotic men crystallised into demands, and for the testing and execution of these demands a great assembly of elected representatives was summoned that took counsel quite independently of the existing governments and states. The governments so far acquiesced as to issue the writs for the elections in their territories. The assembly carried on its debates for a year.

---

[1] *Die Begründung des deutschen Reiches*, i. p. 320.
[2] *Life of Carl Mathy.*

During that year the souls of Germans in every quarter of the country were so dominated by the intellect, the nobility and the greatness of the assembly that neither on the side of the governments nor of dissatisfied factions was resistance hazarded against its policy or its resolutions. After a year the great dialectical process was completed, the essential constituents of the new state were ascertained, the non-essential eliminated, and a constitution was drafted and published by the assembly. Through the work of this year three great ideas were brought within the consciousness of the nation : Germany as a homogeneous Federal State with a strong central authority, the King of Prussia as overlord of the central government, and the exclusion from the new unity of the great territory of the Austrian Empire.

With these obituary notices from German sources it is interesting to compare Palmerston's,[1] communicated in 1850 to Lord Cowley, who had acted as British envoy at Frankfort :

German affairs are indeed come to a state of chaos. The only thing that seems pretty clear is that all parties are more or less in the wrong. But Prussia seems to bear away the palm in this respect. Her course has been, indeed, dishonest, inconsistent, and irresolute and weak. In regard to the Schleswig-Holstein question, she has throughout acted with the greatest duplicity and bad faith ; in regard to German affairs, her only object from beginning to end seems to have been her own aggrandisement, which, at moments when much was within her grasp, she had not courage or steadiness successfully to pursue. Her partisans try to make out that the contest between her and Austria is a struggle between constitutional and arbitrary government, but it is no such thing ; it is only a conflict between the two leading Powers in Germany as to which should be politically preponderant. We should have had no objection to see Prussia take the first place ; on the contrary, *a German Union embracing all the smaller states, with Prussia at its head, and in alliance with Austria as a separate Power, would have been a very good European arrangement* ; but when the Empire was offered to Prussia the King shrank from the hazardous position thus proposed to him, and declined to accept it until he should be asked to do so by the Sovereigns. That decided the question, for it was pretty certain that the Sovereigns would never trouble him with such a request. . . . Poor Bunsen is stung to the quick at the failure of all the fine schemes which he and Stockmar and Gervinus and Gagern and the rest of them had so loudly proclaimed as certain of success, and Bunsen accordingly shuts himself up and is seen by nobody.

The words we have ventured to italicise go to show that Palmerston was not so good a prophet as Heine, and that, after all, a statesman does not always see much further than the man in the street.

[1] Ashley's *Life of Palmerston.*

CHAPTER IV

THE REVOLUTION IN DRESDEN

THE obsequies of the National Assembly were far from peaceful. The mailed fist of Prussia had to strike, and blood was still to flow before the first great tragedy in the Trilogy of modern German history was complete. The first German parliament was suppressed, and the responsible leaders of the struggle for German unity and constitutional freedom under monarchical or imperial auspices had retired to their tents. But the extremists of the Left remained to occupy the field, and to carry on a desperate struggle for a far more radical change in the system of government than had yet commended itself to the mass of the German people. The pretext of the rebellions which broke out on the collapse of the Frankfort Assembly was the constitution that the Assembly had framed, but the real aim became the republic and nothing less. Of the perplexities which tormented the finer spirits among the rebels, those who fought for a principle and not for plunder and revenge, Ludwig Bamberger [1] gives a clear picture :

A movement of the people could only succeed in Germany if a sign appeared in the political sky which of itself, by its mere appearance, made to all the separate nationalities the same successful appeal : now is the time ! Such a sign—if any such were possible—must be afforded by a challenge to the National Assembly from the princes, and an appeal from the former to the people. That was the great question : will the whole of Germany rise ? It was that which the most hesitating, the most inveterate doubter was obliged to put before himself. Most clearly do I remember, of all the emotions of those fateful days, the painful perplexity produced in us by that question, on the answer to which everything hung. I was always of the opinion, and have on many occasions acted upon it, that nothing should be more deliberately weighed than a decision to give the signal for revolt. The people are quite ready to risk their lives, and in a moment there are thousands reduced to misery

---

[1] *Politische Schriften von 1848-1868* (K.).

or suffering persecution and exile. Besides this, every defeat naturally brings back that condition, already unbearable, which called forth the rising. I have asked myself the question many, many times since the sad outcome of the last movement : did the state of things justify the signal to join the rebellion in Rhenish Hesse ? And then I tried, as well as I could at this time, to realise the emotions of those days. It was not hope, no feeling of ecstasy, above all, no passionate state of mind that possessed us. With a heart full of unrest, but with a clear consciousness of an unavoidable ' must,' we were resolved for the uttermost step. Open war had been declared on the last scanty remnants of the gains of the so-called revolution ; the greatest danger was obviously there. It was asked : has this hazard of war any prospect of success ? And the answer sounded : yes, if the whole of Germany come in. But will it come in ? That was the momentous question. We had our serious doubts. The answer, however, to all scruples was so obvious, so imperatively categorical, that one could not do otherwise than join. This answer ran : if every one inquires and doubts, then a German revolution will never be possible. In Saxony the fight at that time fluctuated without decisive result ; it was uncertain whether Berlin would again maintain a passive attitude in the face of Prussian intervention. On the lower Rhine all was in ferment ; Düsseldorf, Elberfeld, Iserlohn in open rebellion ; then came the rising in Rhenish Bavaria, the call thence for help, one could no longer shilly shally, the people were fire and flame, confident that everywhere in Germany at that very moment the same determination a thousand times uttered, was being framed ; this forced the fateful word from our lips.

In Prussia a few mild demonstrations were easily stifled, and in Austria the course of the struggle with Hungary, engrossing enough, was uninterrupted by civil disturbance. It was in Dresden that the first serious revolt occurred. The King of Saxony had reconstituted his government on a more conservative basis, and steadfastly refused to recognise the German Constitution promulgated at Frankfort. The rebellion broke out there on 3rd May when the Arsenal was stormed, and the Parliament House occupied by the Gymnastic Clubs in arms. At half-past four next morning the King fled with the royal family and the ministry to Königstein, and a provisional government, consisting of notable rebels, Tschirner, Heubner, and Todt of ominous name, was set up. The military direction was in the hands of one Heinz, who had been a Greek officer, and by his side stood that stormy petrel of revolution, the Russian Michael Bakunin, whose racy personality lent a charm to any desperate enterprise.

The unfortunate Regent at Frankfort, left struggling in the air, endeavoured to get together a Federal Army to repress the insurrectionary movements threatening all over South Germany. But the one strong military force was Prussia's ; that force Prussia was determined to keep in her own hands to use at her own discretion ; and it was Prussia, at the direct invitation of the governments concerned, who stamped out the rebellions in Dresden, the Palatinate and Baden.

Richard Wagner, then holding the position of conductor at the Dresden theatre, was drawn into the revolutionary stream, to join his whimsical revolutionary friend, the Russian Michael Bakunin, and his story of a week as exciting as his own music is one of the most brilliant, if egotistic, descriptions of a revolution ever written. A long extract is given here, but the whole passage, commencing on page 473 of vol. i. of his *Autobiography*, ought to be read by those interested in the psychology not only of the German, but also of genius, where sometimes the psychological aspect is shot with pathological traits. At times the reader is curiously reminded of the voice of Benvenuto Cellini in his *Memoirs* :

Emergency deputations, nightly mob demonstrations, stormy meetings of the various unions, and all the other signs that precede a swift decision in the streets, manifested themselves. On the 3rd May the demeanour of the crowds moving in our thoroughfares plainly showed that this consummation would soon be reached, as was undoubtedly desired. Each local deputation which petitioned for the recognition of the German constitution, which was the universal cry, was refused an audience by the government, and this with a peremptoriness which at last became startling. I was present one afternoon at a committee meeting of the *Vaterlands-Verein*, although merely as a representative of Röckel's *Volksblatt*, for whose continuance, both from economic as well as humane motives, I felt pledged. Here I was at once absorbed in watching the conduct and demeanour of the men whom popular favour had raised to the leadership of such unions. It was quite evident that events had passed beyond the control of these persons ; more particularly were they utterly at a loss as to how to deal with that peculiar terrorism exerted by the lower classes which is always so ready to react upon the representatives of democratic theories. On every side I heard a medley of wild proposals and hesitating responses. . . . [Wagner left the hall in company with a young painter, Kaufmann.] I was on my way home, deep in conversation with this man, whose pale face and troubled look betrayed that he foresaw the disaster that was imminent, when, just as we reached the Postplatz, near the fountain erected from Semper's design, the clang of bells from the neighbouring tower of St. Ann's Church suddenly sounded the tocsin of revolt. With a terrified cry, ' Good God, it has begun ! ' my companion vanished from my side. He wrote to me afterwards to say that he was living as a fugitive in Berne, but I never saw his face again.

The clang of this bell, so close at hand, made a profound impression upon me also. It was a very sunny afternoon, and I at once noticed the same phenomenon which Goethe describes in his attempt to depict his own sensations during the bombardment of Valmy. The whole square looked as though it were illuminated by a dark yellow, almost brown, light, such as I had once before seen in Magdeburg during an eclipse of the sun. My most pronounced sensation beyond this was one of great, almost extravagant, satisfaction. I felt a sudden strange longing to play with something hitherto regarded as dangerous and important. . . .

On the 3rd of May I betook myself direct to that quarter of the town where I heard unpleasant rumours of a sanguinary conflict having taken place. I afterwards learned that the actual cause of the dispute between the civil and military power had arisen when the watch had been changed in front of the Arsenal. At that moment the mob, under a bold leader, had seized the opportunity to take forcible possession of the armoury. A display of military force was made, and the crowd was fired upon by a few cannon loaded with grape-shot. As I approached the scene of operations through the Rampische Gasse, I met a company of the Dresden Communal Guards, who, although they were quite innocent, had apparently been exposed to this fire. I noticed that one of the citizen guards, leaning heavily on the arm of a comrade, was trying to hurry along, in spite of the fact that his right leg seemed to be dragging helplessly behind him. Some of the crowd, seeing the blood on the pavement behind him, shouted ' He is bleeding.' In the midst of this excitement I suddenly became conscious of the cry raised on all sides : ' To the barricades ! to the barricades ! ' Driven by a mechanical impulse I followed the stream of people, which moved once more in the direction of the Town Hall in the Old Market-place. Amid the terrified tumult I particularly noticed a significant group stretching right across the street, and striding along the Rosmaringasse. It reminded me, though the simile was rather exaggerated, of the crowd that had once stood at the doors of the theatre and demanded free entrance to *Rienzi*. . . . I was able to press right into the rooms of the town council, escaping notice in the tumultuous crowd, and it seemed to me as if the officials were guilty of collusion with the mob. I made my way unobserved into the council-chamber ; what I saw there was utter disorder and confusion. . . .

On Thursday, 4th May, I could see that the Town Hall was gradually becoming the undoubted centre of the revolution. That section of the people who had hoped for a peaceful understanding with the monarch was thrown into the utmost consternation by the news that the King and his whole court, acting on the advice of his

minister Beust, had left the palace, and had gone by ship down the
Elbe to the fortress of Königstein. . . . At the same moment news
arrived from all sides that, in accordance with a previous compact,
the King of Prussia's troops would advance to occupy Dresden. A
general outcry immediately arose for measures to be adopted to
prevent this incursion of foreign troops. . . .

The Old Town of Dresden, with its barricades, was an interesting
enough sight for the spectators. I looked on with amazement and
disgust, but my attention was suddenly distracted by seeing Bakunin
emerge from his hiding-place and wander among the barricades
in a black frockcoat. But I was very much mistaken in thinking
he would be pleased with what he saw ; he recognised the childish
inefficiency of all the measures that had been taken for defence, and
declared that the only satisfaction he could feel in the state of affairs
was that he need not trouble about the police, but could calmly
consider the question of going elsewhere, as he found no inducement
to take part in an insurrection conducted in such a slovenly fashion.

The rest of the day passed in continuous negotiations over the
truce which, by arrangement with the Saxon troops, was to last
until noon of the next day. . . . On that day a certain Heinz,
formerly a Greek colonel, was placed in command of the armed forces.
These proceedings did not seem at all satisfactory to Bakunin, who
put in an occasional appearance. While the provisional government
placed all its hopes on finding a peaceful settlement of the conflict
by moral persuasion, he, on the contrary, with his clear vision
foresaw a well-planned military attack by the Prussians, and thought
it could only be met by good strategic measures. . . . The time
passed pleasantly enough. Elegant ladies with their cavaliers
promenaded the barricaded streets during those beautiful spring
evenings. It seemed to be little more than an entertaining drama.
. . . So I strolled comfortably home through the numerous barricades
at a late hour, thinking as I went of the material for a drama,
Achilleus, with which I had been occupied for some time. . . .

Early on Saturday, 6th May, it was obvious that the situation was
becoming more serious. Prussian troops had marched into the New
Town, and the Saxon troops, which it had not been considered
advisable to use for an attack, were kept loyal to the flag. The
truce expired at noon, and the troops, supported by several guns, at
once opened the attack on one of the principal positions held by the
people on the Neumarkt. . . .

It was irritating to me, while I heard the sharp rattle of fire, to be
unable to gather anything of what was going on, and I thought by
climbing the Kreuz tower I might get a good view. Even from this
elevation I could not see anything clearly, but I gathered enough to
satisfy myself that after an hour of heavy firing the advance artillery
of the Prussian troops had retired, and had at last been completely
silenced, their withdrawal being signalled by a loud shout of jubilation from the populace. Apparently the first attack had exhausted
itself ; and now my interest in what was going on began to assume

a more and more vivid hue. To obtain information in greater detail
I hurried back to the Town Hall. I could extract nothing, however,
from the boundless confusion which I met, until at last I came upon
Bakunin in the midst of the main group of speakers. He was able
to give me an extraordinarily accurate account of what had happened
Information had reached headquarters from a barricade in the
Neumarkt where the attack was most serious, that everything had
been in a state of confusion there before the onslaught of the troops ;
thereupon my friend Marschall von Bieberstein, together with Leo
von Zichlinsky, who were officers in the citizen corps, had called up
some volunteers and conducted them to the place of danger. Kreis-
Amtmann Heubner of Freiberg, without a weapon to defend himself,
and with bared head, jumped immediately on to the top of the
barricade, which had just been abandoned by all its defenders. He
was the sole member of the provisional government to remain on
the spot, the leaders, Todt and Tschirner, having disappeared at the
first sign of a panic. Heubner turned round to exhort the volunteers
to advance, addressing them in stirring words. His success was
complete, the barricade was taken again, and a fire, as unexpected
as it was fierce, was directed upon the troops, which, as I myself saw,
were forced to retire. Bakunin had been in close touch with this
action, he had followed the volunteers, and he now explained to
me that however narrow might be the political views of Heubner . . .
he was a man of noble character, at whose service he had immediately
placed his own life. . . .

At nightfall I found it impossible to make up my mind to go home
and leave my interesting place of refuge. . . . Thus I spent one of
the most extraordinary nights of my life, taking turns with Berthold
to keep watch and sleep, close beneath the great bell with its terrible
groaning clang, and with the accompaniment of the continuous
rattle of the Prussian shot as it beat against the tower walls.

Sunday (the 7th of May) was one of the most beautiful days in the
year. I was awakened by the song of a nightingale, which rose to
our ears from the Schütze garden close by. A sacred calm and peace-
fulness lay over the town and the wide suburbs of Dresden, which
were visible from my point of vantage. Towards sunrise a mist
settled upon the outskirts, and suddenly through its folds we could
hear the music of the *Marseillaise* making its way clearly and
distinctly from the district of the Tharanderstrasse. As the sound
drew nearer and nearer, the mist dispersed, and the glow of the
rising sun spread a glittering light upon the weapons of a long column
which was winding its way towards the town. . . . [They were
miners from the Erzgebirge.] Soon we saw them march up the
Altmarkt opposite the Town Hall. . . . Reinforcements continued
to pour in the whole day long, and the heroic achievement of the
previous day now received its reward in the shape of a universal
elevation of spirits. A change seemed to have been made in the plan
of attack by the Prussian troops. This could be gathered from the
fact that numerous simultaneous attacks, but of a less concentrated

type, were made upon various positions. . . . I felt a still deeper impression, however, when, towards eleven o'clock, I saw the old Opera House, in which a few weeks ago I had conducted the last performance of the Ninth Symphony, burst into flames.

On the following morning (Monday, 8th May) I tried again to get information as to the state of affairs by forcing my way to the Town Hall from my house, which was cut off from the place of action.

In the Town Hall I learned from Bakunin that the provisional government had passed a resolution, on his advice, to abandon the position in Dresden, which had been entirely neglected from the beginning, and was consequently quite untenable for any length of time. This resolution proposed an armed retreat to the Erzgebirge, where it would be possible to concentrate the reinforcements pouring in from all sides, especially from Thuringia, in such strength, that the advantageous position could be used to inaugurate a German civil war that would sound no hesitating note at its outset. To persist in defending isolated barricaded streets in Dresden could, on the other hand, lend little but the character of an urban riot to the contest, although it was pursued with the highest courage. I must confess that this idea seemed to me magnificent and full of meaning. . . . I now definitely abandoned all consideration for my personal situation, and determined to surrender myself to the stream of developments which flowed in the direction towards which my feelings had driven me, with a delight that was full of despair. [Wagner had first to convey his wife to a place of safety at Chemnitz. On their way they met both reinforcements and grim regulars marching on Dresden. On his return, he proceeds :] The nearer I approached the capital, the stronger became the confirmation of the rumours that, as yet, there was no thought in Dresden of surrender or withdrawal, but that, on the contrary, the contest was proving very favourable for the national party. All this appeared to me like one miracle after another. On this day, Tuesday, 9th of May, I once more forced my way in a high state of excitement over ground which had become more and more inaccessible. All the highways had to be avoided, and it was only possible to make progress through such houses as had been broken through. At last I reached the Town Hall in the Altstadt, just as night was falling. A truly terrible spectacle met my eyes, for I crossed those parts of the town in which preparations had been made for a house-to-house fight. The incessant groaning of big and small guns reduced to an uncanny murmur all the other sounds that came from armed men ceaselessly crying out to one another from barricade to barricade, and from one house to another, which they had broken through. Pitch brands burnt here and there, pale-faced figures lay prostrate around the watch-posts, half dead with fatigue, and any unarmed wayfarer forcing a path for himself was sharply challenged. Nothing, however, that I have lived through can be compared with the impression that I received on my entry into the chambers of the Town Hall. Here was a gloomy, and yet fairly compact and serious mass of people ; a look of unspeakable fatigue was upon all faces ; not a single voice had retained its natural tone. There was a hoarse jumble of conversation inspired by a state of the highest tension. The only familiar sight that survived was to be found in the old servants of the Town Hall in their curious antiquated uniform and three-cornered hats. These tall men, at other times an object of considerable fear, I found engaged partly in buttering pieces of bread, and cutting slices of ham and sausage, and partly in piling into baskets immense stores of provisions for the messengers sent by the defenders of the barricades for supplies. These men had turned into veritable nursing mothers of the revolution.

As I proceeded further, I came at last upon the members of the provisional government, among whom Todt and Tschirner, after their first panic-stricken flight, were once more to be found gliding to and fro, gloomy as spectres, now that they were chained to the performance of their heavy duties. Heubner alone had preserved his full energy ; but he was a really piteous sight : a ghostly fire burned in his eyes which had not had a wink of sleep for seven nights. . . . Bakunin [unchanged despite want of sleep] then gave me a short and precise account of what had happened since I had left on the previous morning. The retreat which had then been decided upon soon proved unadvisable, as it would have discouraged the numerous reinforcements which had already arrived on that day. Moreover, the desire for fighting had been so great, and the force of the defenders so considerable, that it had been possible to oppose the enemy's troops successfully so far. But as the latter had also got large reinforcements, they again had been able to make an effective combined attack on the strong Wildstruf barricade. The Prussian troops had avoided fighting in the streets, choosing instead the method of fighting from house to house by breaking through the walls. This had made it clear that all defence by barricades had become useless, and that the enemy would succeed slowly but surely in drawing near the Town Hall, the seat of the provisional government. [Bakunin proposed that the remaining stores of gunpowder should be disposed of by blowing up the Town Hall ! But he was overruled by Heubner and a Town Council excited to tears.] It was now decided that as everything was ready, the retreat to the Erzgebirge, which had originally been intended for the previous day, should be fixed for the early morrow. . . .

[Wagner gave an account of the reinforcements he had met on the way to Dresden, and had found at Chemnitz and also at Freiberg. He was commissioned to return to Chemnitz to convey the views of the provisional government, and to leave orders for the requisitioning of horses and carts wherever they could be found in the villages. Bieberstein accompanied him. Wagner despatched his business, and on his way back to Dresden was suddenly roused from sleep in his carriage by a noise outside.] ' What is the matter ? ' I cried. ' Where are you going ? ' ' Home,' was the reply. ' It is all over in Dresden. The provisional government is close behind us in that carriage down there.'

I shot out of the coach like a dart, leaving it at the disposal of the tired men, and hurried on, down the steeply sloping road, to meet the ill-fated party. And there I actually found them—Heubner, Bakunin, and Martin, the energetic post-office clerk, the two latter armed with muskets—in a smart hired carriage from Dresden which was coming slowly up the hill.

The revolution in Dresden, which cost one hundred and eighty-eight rebels their lives, was so thoroughly quelled that the state of siege which followed was a mild one. Several of the leaders escaped, but Bakunin was arrested at Chemnitz, whither Wagner had conducted him, and was sentenced to death. The sentence was, however, commuted to imprisonment for life, and he was handed over to the Russian authorities, by whom he was ultimately sent to Siberia in 1855. From Siberia he escaped by way of Japan and the United States to England. Thenceforward he lived chiefly in Switzerland, concerning himself with communistic propaganda, and was actually busy at Lyons in 1870 organising a rehearsal of the Paris Commune. His turbulent career did not end until 1876, when he died at Berne.

CHAPTER V

THE FINAL REVOLUTION IN BADEN

THE ever restless Grand Duchy of Baden, already the scene of Hecker's and of Struve's abortive risings, was the fierce battle-ground on which was fought out the last and most violent conflict of the revolutionary era in Germany. In the Palatinate an effort was made on 2nd May to set up some sort of a provisional government, but the scheme devised by Professor Kinkel of Bonn, to procure arms for the revolutionaries by storming the arsenal at Siegburg, a few miles from Bonn, resulted in a ridiculous fiasco. Carl Schurz, the revolutionary who, like many another of his associates, found in the United States the field denied him in his native land, gives a frank account [1] of this feeble affair :

Like the Spartan woman or the Roman matron of whom we read, my mother went to the room where my sword hung, and gave it to me with the one admonition that I should use it with honour. And nothing could have been further from her mind than the thought that in this act there was something heroic. . . .

Our commander, Anneke, mustered the crowd and divided it into sections. One of these was put under the command of Josef Gerhardt, who at a later period went to America and did good service as colonel of a Union regiment in the Civil War. Anneke found that his troop did not count over one hundred and twenty men, and could not refrain from giving bitter expression to his disappointment. Many of those who attended the meeting during the day had in the darkness slunk away when the signal was given to march. Patriotic impulses that in the morning were fresh and warm had cooled off in the many hours that elapsed between the first resolution and the moment for action.

Our column being formed in order, Anneke made a short speech, in which he set forth the need of discipline and obedience, and then the march began. About half an hour after our start one of the horsemen, who had remained behind, came up at a gallop with the

---

[1] *Reminiscences of Carl Schurz*, i. p. 172: Doubleday, Page & Co., New York, 1909.

report that the dragoons then garrisoned in Bonn were at our heels to attack us. This report should have surprised nobody, for during the day and the evening the preparations for our enterprise had been carried on so openly that it would have been astonishing had the authorities received no knowledge of it and had they not taken measures to frustrate the expedition. Moreover, we had forgotten to make the ferry behind us unserviceable. Nevertheless the announcement of the approach of the dragoons produced in the ranks considerable consternation. Anneke ordered our horsemen to hasten back and to reconnoitre as to the nearness and strength of the pursuers. Meanwhile our march was accelerated so that we might possibly reach the River Sieg and cross it before the arrival of the dragoons ; but in this we failed. Long before we approached the river, we heard not far behind us the trumpet-signal ordering them to trot their horses. Anneke, who evidently was not very confident of the ability of his men to face regular soldiers in a fight, halted our column and told us that we were evidently not in a condition to offer successful resistance to regular troops ; we should therefore disperse, and if we wanted to make ourselves further useful to the cause, we might find our way to Elberfeld or to the Palatinate, where he was ready to go. This signal to disperse was at once obeyed. Most of the men scattered over the surrounding cornfields, while some of us, perhaps twenty, stood still by the side of the road. The Dragoons passed us quietly at a trot on their way to Siegburg. There were only about thirty of them, not enough, therefore, to overcome us or even to force their way through on the road, if those of us who had firearms had offered an orderly resistance.

When the soldiers had passed by and only a handful of our band found itself together, a feeling of profound shame overcame us. The enterprise had come not only to an unfortunate but to a ridiculous and disgraceful end. Our column had taken to the fields before only a handful of soldiers, scarcely one-third of our number ; and this after the big words with which many had pledged themselves to the cause of German liberty and unity ! . . .

The fate of the provisional government in the Palatinate was settled by Prussia in a few weeks, and the Rhenish rebels who had courage and resolution enough, foremost among them Carl Schurz, had to make their way south to join the rebels in Baden. The Baden government had actually accepted the Frankfort constitution, but the republican party in the Grand Duchy had now obtained the ascendency, and of the savage spirit animating it a few quotations from the Baden press will give sufficient illustration. Abt, a radical-democrat, wrote of the liberal ministry of Bekk-Dusch : [1]

---

[1] Häuser, *Denkwürdigkeiten zur badischen Revolution* (K.).

The striking fact confronts one, that under the government of Bekk-Dusch, political liberty existed, as far as the State, under Continental conditions, could tolerate. This fact is irrefutable. After the agitation in March, freedom in Baden actually existed to a degree which marks the uttermost possibility which the State can tolerate without giving up its own existence.

And he went on to characterise the action of the Baden press as follows :

By [its] highly studied insolence, the press of Baden dissociated itself very much to its advantage from the loyal, courteous and honest attitude of the journalistic press of Würtemburg, which indeed fought against the principles of its opponents, but always treated their personalities with respect, instead of dragging them through the mud by unsparing, malicious, spiteful allusions to their defects and weaknesses.

Examples of this ' highly studied insolence ' afford racy reading. *The Republic*, a widely circulated paper published at Heidelberg, denounced the Frankfort Constitution :

[The National Constitution is] an abortion which is not worth a bean. Such a constitution we did not desire, nor will we defend it with life and property. It is too bad for the people, they can make no use of it. Michael, the National Constitution is of no use to thee, none at all ! And wouldst thou know what will profit thee ? A revolution in which thou wilt sit in swift judgment on thine enemies ! Consider it ! We will hold ourselves prepared, in order that we may be on the right side of the hedge when something turns up for us !

The Liberal ministers, Bekk and Dusch, came in for the grossest personal abuse, and the Grand Duke did not escape :

' In a short time not another dog will devour a morsel of Bekk, if he does not descend from his ministerial seat.'

' He [Bekk] already feels the sensation at the neck produced by a cord thrown round it and drawn tight, while one's legs dangle a foot from the ground. The windows of Herr Dusch, the Minister, have been smashed ; the smashing of his skull would have pleased us better.'

' The trumpery Ministry in Paris does not resign any more than our Baptist Bekk does, although the whole country has spit at him. In time to come, ministers and rulers will not resign their posts ; they will merely be beheaded.'

' There lived in the country a fellow named Carl Baden, a descendant of the former robber knights of Baden. One fine morning it occurred to the said Carl Baden to issue an order in which he prescribed that the ' people of Baden ' should send sixty-three people to Carlsruhe, to keep, to all appearance, an eye upon the Government, and to make all sorts of beautiful speeches ; this order was called a Constitution.'

These examples are given by Häusser in his *Denkwürdigkeiten zur badischen Revolution,* not as isolated examples but as typical of the journalistic tone. But what lent the rising in Baden its alarming character was the wholesale mutiny of the regular army. The Grand Duke was forced on 13th May to fly into Alsace, and the whole Duchy, including the important Federal fortress of Rastatt fell into the hands of the rebels. Delay in the grant of increased pay and other military grievances made the army an easy prey to republican agitators, among whom were old comrades who had taken part in Hecker's rising. A description of the mutiny at Rastatt itself is given by Förderer,[1] a student at the time of the mutiny, and later Catholic priest and dean. Förderer tells us that among the most effective agitators inside the walls of Rastatt was Struve's wife, ' a devil of a beauty,' whose intrigues were facilitated by the Governor's weakness for the fair sex. His account of the actual mutiny is as follows :

Discipline among the soldiers became continually slacker, and finally, at the end of May, a soldier named Stark, who had made a turbulent speech, was placed under arrest. A surging crowd of gunners, infantry, men employed at the fort, and others, assembled before the Leopold barracks, and peremptorily demanded Stark's release. The barrack guard, which ought to have driven the crowd away, did not carry out their duty, and so Stark was released by his Major. But it was Stark who declined to be thus set free. He thanked his comrade for a proof of friendship, but remarked that he would not repudiate his arrest in this manner. He said that was not the ' lawful way ' which one ought to follow. His Captain had placed him under arrest, and he it was who must release him again. . . . The Captain then set him free, upon which the rabble gradually dispersed. In the afternoon, however, the devil again got loose, when a report spread that Stark had again been arrested. At the Wilhelm Barracks, Colonel von Pierron, together with some other officers, drove the mutineers out of them with drawn swords. ｛These gathered later in tumult before Pierron's residence, in order to revenge themselves, but allowed their wrath to be appeased by the liberated Haas. Now, however, the crowd moved back to the Leopold Barracks. A Corporal Kehlhofer who had been arrested had to be released. He had, without leave of absence, stayed for more than eight days out of the garrison, and, therefore, after his return that day, had been placed under arrest. ' Out with Kehlhofer ! '

---

[1] *Erinnerungen aus Rastatt* (K.).

yelled the crowd. The commandant of the Guard, Captain von Degenfeld, had stationed himself with a reinforced guard before the door of the barracks. As his order to disperse was not heeded, and in fact the riotous mob were approaching the guard, some in the background throwing stones, he gave the command to charge and drive back the assailants. Only a few soldiers and one non-commissioned officer, named Rinkleff, obeyed. 'Fetch the cannon,' roared the enraged gunners, and ran off. The mutineers promised to go away, if the guard were withdrawn inside the barracks. Just at the moment this was happening stones were thrown at the officers, and Colonel Hofmann was severely wounded. At this critical moment Colonel von Pierron, with an adjutant, rode by, and the crowd suddenly turned against him; abuse, stones and sword-bayonets were hurled at him. A dragoon made a cut at him with his sabre, but only severed his horse's rein. The adjutant instantly seized the horse by the other rein, and dashed with the colonel through the howling crowd which now—it had meanwhile grown dark—surged again in the street. Here the lie was spread among them, that Captain von Degenfeld had stabbed a man. They rushed to his residence, happily without finding him. Pursuit was made after other officers, but in vain. Now the crowd dashed to Colonel Pierron's quarters, but, by good fortune, his landlord had hurriedly hidden him. The furniture, however, was destroyed in presence of his wife and sick daughter, and after that, the old flag of the regiment, which, riddled with bullets, bore token of the past loyalty and courage of the Baden troops, was carried off, and the crown on it torn to shreds in the street. This incensed some of the older soldiers, and they rescued the flag from such shameful insult, and took it to the Town Hall. The Governor, General von Clossmann, had appeared with a detachment of dragoons, in order to clear the square, but the dragoons were no longer to be relied on ; the General was somewhat severely wounded by stone-throwing, and was conveyed by officers to his quarters in the Castle.

On this and other similar occasions, a lieutenant of Dragoons, named Gramm, roused by the boldness of his bearing the admiration of all the well-disposed. Riding as if he and his horse were one, swinging his sword, he dashed into the thickest mass of men, broke his way through, and galloped along the streets, like the Knight of the flaming sword, so that the sparks flew. A splendid, knightly figure. At that time, a thing happened which my mind recalls vividly to this day. As the undisciplined soldiers poured in tumult through the streets, the Governor, General von Clossmann, appeared on foot with his adjutant Stölzel, and a drummer. When the latter stopped beating his drum, the grey-haired general addressed the soldiers, and asked them to return to obedience and discipline, otherwise he would be obliged to proclaim martial law. 'What,' cried a drunken fusilier, ' you will proclaim martial law over us ! You ——, we proclaim martial law over you !' I thought the General would draw his sword and split open the head of the insolent fellow. He did no such thing, however, but turned back sadly, with his escort. Assuredly, if he had done what I, as an excited and inexperienced student expected, he would have been massacred by the bestial horde. A few years later, in the years 1854-1855, I was curate at Achern, and occasionally visited the Sanatorium of Illenau. There, one day, I saw a man, huddled together, sitting on a step, dully staring before him. My companion informed me that this was General von Clossmann. Then I recalled that exciting scene at the corner of Poststrasse and Herrenstrasse in Rastatt ; I thought to myself, what a glorious end this old General would have had, if he had been murdered then by the mutineers ! Who knows whether such a sacrifice would not have borne good fruit.'

Of the utter demoralisation of the army no more convincing evidence could be furnished than the gloomy account of the disbandment at Bonfeld, in Würtemberg, of the remnants of the Grand Duke's escort. General Hoffmann and officers with twelve guns and a squadron of dragoons entered the place dog-tired. The inhabitants refused at first to tender any hospitality, and men and guns were lodged in the lower courtyard of the castle. An eyewitness describes the scene that followed : [1]

The officers cheered up their men, instilling the courage which was needed by the dragoons even more than by the gunners. Suddenly, at seven o'clock, a shot rang out in the castle garden near by, and a soldier was reported to have shot himself. ' A gunner ! ' some said, ' an officer ! ' cried others, and all ran to the spot. Anxiety on every face, the sky dismal, night coming on, the whole situation one of gloom ! There, in his blood, laid on his cloak as on a bed, lay the Grand Ducal artillery captain von Grossmann, a native of Mecklenburg, shot through the head. His men wept, and asked of one another, ' What are we to do now ? ' The officers threw themselves on their comrade and bore him into a summer-house, others cast reproaches at the citizens : the guilt of this lies at your door ; he could not bear to see his men shown the door by you, no hospitality offered them in spite of their exhaustion ; you deserve a whiff of grape-shot. The citizens stoods dumbfoundered and lost in thought, children ran about crying, an inexpressible feeling of awe came over every one. ' We have lost a battery,' said the General with tears in his eyes, and turned away ; I heard another exclaim, ' 'twould have been very handy for our men here '; ' that is the result of the unhappy condition of Germany, where there is no longer an understanding between man and man,' replied the local pastor. This event had a twofold effect ; it robbed the soldiers of all hope, and, in their despair a momentary danger from the stirred-up military instincts of the gunners really threatened us ; but sympathy had gained the mastery

---

[1] Bernhard, *Der deutsche Bürgerkreig in Baden*, 1849 (K.).

in the hearts of the citizens. They now took the soldiers one after the other to supper in their homes, and when, an hour later, the officers despatched to Heilbronn returned with some of the inhabitants of that place, most of them had found quarters. [General Hoffmann assembled his men very early next morning in the lower castle court.] Choice was given them whether they would remain with the officers, or go home alone, or retrace their steps in rank and file, though they, the officers, would not accompany them. Now ensued perplexity and distress, a military disorganisation of the most unusual kind, without any bustle. Down there, under the barest of escort, moved off the guns with their teams, on the short return journey over Fürfeld. Here above dragoons and gunners rode in and out amongst each other, they knew not whither, yonder a small band, here men wending singly to their various homes, with bag and baggage, weapons and horses. Many, many wept, at such an end, the further issues of which they probably foreboded ; a goodly number rode to the pastor's house to thank him with tears for yesterday's refreshment, which he had been first to give ; others made for other houses. . . . I had never before experienced the disintegrating feeling of a parting and loosing of old ties as then, when I saw these men ride away, so aimlessly and hopelessly. My guest, a valiant, upright officer of Dragoons, on the best of terms with his soldiers, cried like a child whose favourite toy has been snatched out of its helpless, unresisting hands. No helmet on his head, he carried it in his hand, and walked about like one lost, until he went out into the open. No blare of trumpets, no bugle-call, no shouting, no salutes, no neighing of horses—only a dumb moving hither and thither and a riding away. . . . At one o'clock all was quiet and deserted. . . .

On 1st June a provisional government was set up presided over by Ludwig Brentano, a lawyer from Mannheim, of whom Häusser gives an unlovely picture : [1]

With Hecker, Brentano had in common only the commonplace radicalism of a lawyer, otherwise very little. Of the impetuous, extravagant nature of the youthful tribune, a nature which carried others along with it, of his real fire, and his fascinating outward gifts, Brentano had nothing. He possessed an ordinary, one might say a common, demagogue's nature. Hecker's individuality, his appearance, his way of speaking, brought to mind moments when uncontrolled enthusiasm sways men's souls with all demonic power and irresistibly carries them along. Brentano exhibited only the poisonous demagogue's art of calumny and sophistry. Himself cold and egotistic, incapable of an enthusiastic emotion, without soaring thought, without ideas or ideals, Brentano displayed in his whole outward

---

[1] Klein.

appearance, his words and deeds, nothing but a lawyer's readiness of speech, the persistence of a partisan, the superlative craftiness of a pettifogger, the brazen forehead of a demagogue of the worst kind. His speech was cold and acrid, largely through personal rancour, venom and spite, set in an artificial heat ; his bearing, insolent to the utmost bounds, scornful, and full of personal gall, and when indeed rage and anger overpowered him, it was difficult to know whether the whole effect was more repulsive or uncanny.

The revolutionary government, conscious no doubt of the desperate prospect ahead of it, actually issued an appeal [1] calling on the French nation for assistance, and sent to Paris Carl Blind and others to further the appeal :

We call you, brothers of France : To the Rhine, to the Rhine ! The liberty of Europe is in danger, France must not fail at the post of honour ; forward in the name of Liberty, Equality, Fraternity.

The insurrectionary forces were at first placed under the orders of an ex-officer, a young man named Sigel, but after a few days Mieroslawski, the Pole who figured so often in rebellion, assumed the command. Of the inherent weakness of a revolutionary force the two following private letters afford amusing evidence : [2]

*Citizen Tiedemann to the chief commanding officer,
Citizen Sigel, on citizen Mögling*

LADENBURGH, 20*th June* 1849.

DEAR COLONEL,—I implore you not to leave such truly worthy but muddle-headed people as comrade Mögling in the first line, without any assistance, for he brings everything into confusion. He does not grasp the simplest military duties ; if on other grounds he must remain at this post, put at his side an experienced, capable officer. I have also written approximately the same to the General [Mieroslawski].

*Citizen Mögling to the chief commanding officer,
Citizen Sigel, on Citizen Tiedemann.*

NECKARHAUSEN, 20*th June* 1849.

DEAR SIGEL,—I beg you, summon the fool, Tiedemann, away from here, for although he causes much merriment in the garrison, he will be a common danger if we come to an engagement. If he

---

[1] Klein.
[2] *Deutsche Chronik für das Jahr* 1849, i. (K.).

spoils our chance of victory again, I shall have him inadvertently shot.

Nevertheless it was not without hard fighting that the Prussians crushed the rebels, but before giving an account of the final scene it is well to read two documents which tell the story of domestic agony involved in civil war. The first is an extract from the letter [1] of a Prussian Staff Officer, dated 26th June 1849 :

I wrote last from Altdorf on the 19th and will now look back again on the evening of this day, the last hours of which have so deeply moved me. . . . My host was the pastor of the place. He had been busy and friendly the whole day, but withal he seemed to me to be confused and broken down. After the orderlies had been despatched, I was still constrained, in spite of all demur, to eat supper and drink wine with the old gentleman. This last, and the company of myself, who, after all the work and excitement of the day, looked forward cheerfully to the next few days, made him more talkative. One word led to another. A confession seemed to be trying to force its way to the old man's lips, again and again he seemed to repress it. He led the talk to the declaration of martial law, to the treatment of prisoners, and at last he burst out with the words : ' I have two sons among the rebels. It breaks my heart. . . . Let them die an honourable death as soldiers, but not fall as thieves and murderers under martial law ! ' I sought to soothe him, I promised if either of his sons were taken prisoner, to do the utmost possible for him. I took note of their names, but in vain ; the old man, wringing his hands, or running them through his grey locks like one distracted, and now sobbing aloud with both hands hiding his face, could not compose himself, and at last left me, for I myself was moved to the depths. The maidservant then told me that one of the sons was owner of a business in a neighbouring small town, and unfavourably disposed towards every revolutionary movement ; the other on the other hand was a student, had come with several comrades, had ridiculed and mocked his elder brother who had betaken himself to his father, and at last compelled him to accompany them. Thus had the sons departed from their father ; the mother, upon the news that one of the sons had been wounded at Rinnthal, and had fallen into the hands of our troops, had hurried thither, in order, if possible, to save him.

The second is a letter [2] from Professor Tiedemann of Heidelberg to his son, then rebel commander of the fortress at Rastatt, and one of the parties concerned in the quaint correspondence

[1] *Deutsche Rundschau*, xxxii., 3 Quartel, 1882 (K.).
[2] Quoted by Klein.

quoted on page 547. His father's piteous appeal moved him not ; in August he met bravely death under martial law :

HEIDELBERG, 16*th July* 1849.

Thou art one of the few noble spirits who have of late been diverted from the right way, and carried along to the most questionable extremes by the ardent wish to help to achieve unity and freedom for the German people : recognise this and ponder over it. I adjure thee once again by all that is sacred, by faith in God, the righteous Rewarder of all, by the teaching of Christ in which thou wert brought up, by thy love to thy poor parents, and to the dear Fatherland, to forsake a path which will only bring eternal shame to the name thou bearest, and draw thee infallibly to the merited death of a criminal. Have mercy on thy old parents who stand at the edge of the grave, spare thy poor wife and thy little son, and, above all, consider thy good tender mother, who will not survive thy death. Beware of drawing down upon thyself the curse of the world, now and in the future, and of all thy contemporaries, whose life's happiness thou hast begun to destroy. Make an effort, if thou canst, to bring the misled and deluded soldiers who have broken their military oath, and who in their delirium trampled their flags in the mud, the flags under which thousands have fought, bled and conquered, and among them thy late uncle, the gallant Colonel von Holzing—make an effort to bring back these soldiers to their senses, and to their duty towards the Fatherland. Trust in the mercy of the Grand Duke, in whose breast beats a noble heart. I enclose the amnesty put forth in May by the Grand Duke, for the soldiers returning to duty ; communicate it to them ; the whole of Baden is occupied by the National forces, therefore every attempt to defend Rastatt is not only useless and mad, but even dishonourable and scandalous. Consider, that the death of every fallen warrior in or before Rastatt is a murder, and that this is chargeable upon thee, as Commandant. Beware of burdening the conscience. There is a beyond. Thou art wounded ; look upon thy wound as a warning from Providence, in order that another bullet, already cast, may not make a dis-honourable end of thy life. Shouldst thou be deaf to the prayer of thy old father and the entreaty of thy troubled mother, of thy wife and thy little son, then I can only regret that the bullet which wounded thee did not rob thee of life. Shouldst thou, enlightened by God's grace, come to the knowledge that thou art wandering in false ways, and shouldst thou, giving ear to my prayer be so fortunate as to put an end to the fighting round Rastatt, then I hope and wish that thou mayst find mercy. Leave then Germany and Europe as quickly as possible, and go to America, to thy youngest brother [1] who was misled by Hecker. The means for the voyage across, I will forward to thee by thy uncle in Bremen ; maintain thyself there by hard work on the land. It is the only way which, even on the

---

[1] He married a sister of Hecker.

happiest chance, remains open to thee. Once again I adjure thee, not to shut thine ear to the prayer and counsel of thy old father, and thy deeply troubled mother. . . . It depends on thee whether these are the last lines written by thy father's hand, which thou wilt ever see. May God enlighten thee, that is now the only wish of thy faithful father. TIEDEMANN.

CHAPTER VI

THE END

THE Prussian army, with its Federal auxiliaries, set out in June for the reduction of the Palatinate and Baden, under the supreme command of the Prince of Prussia. The force was in two divisions, one under General von Hirschfeld, which easily subdued the Bavarian Palatinate, and then joined the other division, under Generals von Peucker and von Groeben, which was operating on the right bank of the Rhine against Baden. These armies were superior in number, discipline, and equipment to the mutineers and rebels, under Mieroslawski and Sigel, opposed to them, and a few weeks sufficed to enable them to crush their German kinsfolk. Schurz has a significant passage [1] on the part played by Polish soldiers all through the German Revolution : ' The popular legend attributed to them not only extraordinary bravery, but also all possible military talent and exceptional familiarity with the secrets of the military art. It was as if a stock of generals was kept in store at the rallying places of the Polish refugees, especially in Paris and Switzerland, to be occasionally distributed for revolutionary enterprises in any part of the world.' Mieroslawski gained a momentary success at Waghäusel, but was routed in fight after fight which immediately followed ; by the end of June he threw up his command, and Sigel [2] with a remnant of six thousand men was in full flight for Switzerland. The field army thus disposed of, any insurgents that remained in arms were shut up in Rastatt. The fortress was closely invested and by 23rd July was forced by starvation into surrender. It is on the final scene that our attention must be concentrated. We shall see how the mailed fist of Prussia can strike at home. Dean Förderer [3]

---

[1] *Reminiscences of Carl Schurz*, i. p. 187 : New York, Doubleday, Page & Co., 1909.
[2] Sigel made his way to America, where he rose to be a general in the Civil War.
[3] *Erinnerungen aus Rastatt*, 1849 (K.).

gives a vivid picture of the scene inside Rastatt before its investment :

The real state of the matter could not be kept secret for long, as fugitives from the ranks of the regulars and the volunteers arrived in crowds. On 25th June the provisional government had left Carlsruhe and withdrawn into the Oberland. On the same day the remnants of the Baden insurrectionary force reached Rastatt in retreat, with all the semblance of a flight. What a picture did these confused, disheartened remnants present ! Men and horses lay in heaps, dead tired, on the streets, the soldier using his knapsack, if he had one, as a pillow for his head, the dragoon beside his horse, which stretched out all its four legs. It was a picture of misery. The next day (26th June), the general march was sounded for a long time through the streets, and called the dispersed companies together. Upon a great flat meadow between the Kehler and Ottersdorfer Gates Mieroslawski held a review of the fragments of his army which once was said to number about twenty thousand men, not reckoning women. Such, you must know, were also there. But what sort of an army was it ? Our Baden soldiers still looked fairly respectable, although their uniforms had gone through such heavy wear and tear. But the volunteers ! It is a pity that no painter was there to give to posterity a picture of them, at least of types of them. Before one legion rode a brazen hussy, wearing a riding dress of black velvet, a red feather in a hat like Hecker's, spectacles on her nose, two pistols in her red waist-band, a cavalry sword dangling at her side, and—a Baden dragoon riding behind her as orderly ! A well-merited disgrace ! No longer able to follow their officers, they now became the satellites to utterly unknown adventurers and despicable women. In almost every company of the rebel volunteer corps marched an insolent wench as so-called vivandière. . . . The standard-bearer of the Legion was an unforgettable sight. He was an old, small, scrubby churl, had covered his singular-looking head with a captured Prussian spiked helmet, and wore a faded blue blouse and grey linen hose which hung in tatters loosely round his thin legs ; in his red belt was stuck a pistol, at his side a huge cavalry sword. He carried the banner with a grandiose air, as if he were one of the highest dignitaries of the state. Weather-beaten ´grey-beards marched along, by the side of pale, half-naked youths. Of a uniform I saw no trace. The Rhenish Bavarian legionaries, who made the most fearful din, had a few small Corpus Christi cannon with them, upon which they cast martial glances. At this time spy-hunting was the order of the day. . . .

On the afternoon [of 29th June], I betook myself to a rampart in the neighbourhood of the Carlsruhe Gate, from which one could observe the highroad towards Carlsruhe, which leads through the Niederwald. In a short time, the Commander-in-Chief, Mieros-lawski, with an adjutant on horseback came up and directed his telescope towards the Niederwald. I stood hardly ten paces distant from him. On the Carlsruhe road orderlies rode hither and thither at full speed, ammunition waggons rolled thither and back, and we heard besides the incessant rattle of musketry and thundering of field guns. Suddenly a considerable number of Baden Dragoons, seemingly in flight, came dashing from the scene of battle towards the fort, ventre à terre as the French say, as if the Prussians were already upon their heels. Mieroslawski gesticulated violently with his arms, and cried repeatedly : ' Attaquez, cavalerie ! ' But the horsemen cared nothing for discipline or for the French curses of the Polack, as the people of Baden called him ; forward, only forward ! if you do not run, all is up ! Mieroslawski turned his horse and galloped to the town. I remained for a time and watched the retreat. It was wild confusion. The enemy had crossed the river Federbach, and was only stayed from the pursuit of our men by the great guns of the fort, which now began to play for the first time. They made a mighty rumbling which set all the windows of the town rattling. At the Town Hall I met all that were left of the Freiburg Academic Legion. . . . Among the University men lust of battle was not exactly at fever point, except in a Bavarian theologian. He was a splendid Swabian from the Allgäu, with a fresh complexion and flowing black hair. ' To-morrow we will sacrifice hecatombs to liberty,' he said with a confidence which was pathetic. On the following morning, this Academic Legion was posted behind the dam of the river Murg at Kuppenheim. Our brave Swabian stretched his head over the protecting dam in order to spy on the enemy, and suddenly fell speechless to the ground. A Prussian bullet had hit him in the head and brought the young life to a sudden end.

On 30th June the Prussians advanced across the Murg, and therewith the doom of the fort, and of the Baden revolt, was sealed. In the afternoon, Mieroslawski and his following, with the war chest, marched out by the Kehler Gate, ostensibly in order to collect his forces at Oos against the Prussians.

Other sensitive souls also slipped away, after first plundering the castle and taking away, among other things, certain Turkish weapons, deriving from ' Turkish Louis ' (the Margrave Louis of Baden). Komlossy, too, the popular tribune (an umbrella maker), succeeded in escaping. However, the Baden guard at the Kehler Gate soon grew suspicious, and allowed no more persons to go out. ' We must remain here,' so ran the order. On 1st July, a Sunday, the fortress was invested.

The adventurous Corvin had hastened to join the South German rebels, but found great difficulty in securing due recognition of his soldierly qualities. Competition for posts of command was severe, and against service on the platform and in the committee-room mere military experience could hardly hope for success. Ultimately he was given charge of a brigade at Mannheim. There he contributed much to the organisation of a resistance that kept the Prussians at bay for some days, directing with great skill an effective bombardment of Ludwigshafen. But the defence was outflanked, and Mannheim had to be evacuated. Corvin then made his way to Rastatt. Here he was disgusted with the state of confusion that prevailed, and, when he found the rebel leaders as busily occupied in arresting one another as in concerting measures against the enemy, he decided to resign his commission and escape from the mousetrap before it was closed on him. But a good dinner delayed his departure too long, and when he did endeavour to get away he was stopped at the gates and discovered that the place was completely surrounded by the Prussians. Next day he accepted with good grace the position of chief of the general staff that was offered to him.

Corvin's account of the siege gives just such a picture as one would expect of a military enterprise controlled by non-military chiefs. In this Baden insurrection, as has been mentioned, many soldiers, including officers, took part, so that in comparison with other revolutionary movements of the time it was less like the caricature of a rebellion. The garrison of Rastatt consisted of six thousand men ; and there were in addition to the artillery of the fortress several field batteries and a number of guns from the Palatinate. The nominal governor, however, was Tiedemann, a civilian for all his title of colonel.

The investment was completed on 1st July, and on the 2nd General von Groeben summoned the garrison to surrender. His letter ran as follows : ' The fortress is surrounded by my army corps ; two other army corps pursue the Free corps, who are fleeing and disbanded. There is no hope of relief. I summon the garrison to surrender the fortress, and, as a token of submission, to set the prisoners free at once. Twenty-four hours are given for reflection.' The mayor entered headquarters with a crowd demanding surrender, but Tiedemann threatened him with his sword, and Groeben was sent a refusal. Unfortunately Tiedemann had irritated the military as well as the townspeople, and the latter took advantage of the fact to stir up a feeling of disaffection against him. The result was the arrest of the governor by a party of soldiers, and he was only rescued from his ridiculous position by the address of Corvin, who showed not only courage but also some demagogic talent in composing matters, and inducing officers, in true German fashion, to embrace each other with tears in their eyes.

The unfortunate Tiedemann, distracted by a situation to which he was not equal, continued to provoke similar scenes, and by his vacillation to hamper the best efforts of the real fighting men. It was only the courage he showed under fire that rendered his position at all possible. Sortie after sortie failed, the bombardment of the town became more intense, provisions began to run short, beer also, which was quite as important, and on 18th July, in accordance with an invitation from General Groeben, Corvin and a Major Lang were sent out to ascertain the hopelessness of the position. They were allowed to proceed to Freiburg and to go on thence to Constance. Corvin was completely satisfied, for he found that the revolutionary army which was to relieve Rastatt had taken a different road, viz. that across the Swiss frontier ! On his way back he had an interview with the chief of the Prince of Prussia's general staff and pleaded for terms enabling the garrison at Rastatt to retreat from the fortress. He was told this was impossible, but that he ' must not conclude, however, from their refusing conditions, that the garrison would be treated barbarously. The great number of persons who had taken part in the revolution precluded over-severity.'

A council of war was summoned on Corvin's return and his report was read. The result of a short debate was that Corvin was directed to proceed on the 22nd to the Prussian camp and negotiate, if possible, a surrender on conditions. He took with him a letter in which the case for considerate treatment was well argued. ' The Grand Duke with his ministers left the country, and, by doing so, compelled the soldiers to obey the government installed in his place. The proclamations of the Grand Duke have been kept from the soldiers, as also the offer of pardon for all those who would submit . . . up to 15th July. . . . . Now that the provisional government has resigned, which has become known to the garrison only this morning, and that the Grand Duke claims his right to the government (which he seemed to have renounced by leaving the country), the garrison have not the slightest objection to submit to their lawful prince, and if he with an army of Baden troops stood outside the gates, the garrison would go out to meet him without any distrust. But the assurances of lenity given to us by the commander of the Royal Prussian forces are not satisfactory to the garrison until expressed in a more precise form.' Groeben received him kindly, and from all Corvin says he believed him to have been a kind-hearted man, who meant as a German honestly to do his best for a beaten German foe. But he could do no more than state that surrender of the garrison must be at discretion, though he would intercede for them and promised ' that everything granted to other troops who had surrendered before ' should be also granted to them. In that promise the sequel showed either that he had gone beyond any authority given him by the Prince of Prussia, or that a promise made by a responsible officer was to be repudiated as soon as convenient.

Corvin made his report that same day to a Council of War in Rastatt, and surrender at discretion was resolved on. His account runs : [1]

I explained my view of the situation to my comrades. I repeated verbally all the words of Count Groeben ; and, in reference to his promises, said I believed him to be a kind man and a gentleman, incapable of deceiving even an enemy under such circumstances. My comrades listened to me with earnest attention, for they knew that I was honest, that I spoke out my inmost thoughts, and that I had sense enough to judge of the circumstances. They resolved in consequence to surrender at discretion, and the great Council of War was to assemble on the next morning.

It was a solemn moment when all these brave men signed the record, knowing that they were signing their death warrant, for we no longer entertained any illusions with regard to our own fate, though some of us did not perhaps fear the worst.

When the session was ended, old Boening asked in a tremulous voice, and Lefebre put the same question with his eyes : ' But, Corvin, what will become of *us* ? ' I answered, ' We do our duty as men of honour. A good shepherd gives his life for his sheep.' The old man held his grey head with both hands, and with a heavy step left the room.

Next day, the 23rd, after the resolution of the Council of War had been confirmed by a sort of general council, Corvin was despatched with a companion to settle the terms of capitulation with Count Groeben. The first of these ran as follows :

The garrison submits at discretion to His Royal Highness the Grand Duke of Baden, and surrenders to the Prussian troops before

---

[1] *A Life of Adventure*, by Otto von Corvin.

the fortress. In doing so it claims the clemency of His Royal Highness, which has been granted to other troops under similar circumstances. Though the General commanding the Second Army Corps cannot give a precise promise, he will take care to fulfil that which he made yesterday.

It was also stipulated that arms were to be laid down on the glacis in front of the fortress, in order to save the garrison from the humiliating ceremony of laying them down in the presence of the Prussian troops. Officers and men were then to be received by the Prussians drawn up some distance from the town. Unfortunately it was not noticed by Corvin, or later, in the town, by Tiedemann or any other officer, that while the original document signed by Corvin and his companion was written down in Groeben's own hand the copy given them to take back was not signed by the general himself, but by von Alvensleben, a major on the general staff.

The terms of the capitulation were not observed. The Prussians received the garrison close to the gates, and no consideration was shown the officers, who, after the surrender, were abominably housed in the lowest casemates of the fort. Corvin did not waver in his belief that Groeben meant honestly but was over-ridden, and he admits that the rank and file of the Prussian army dealt considerately, in some cases even fraternised, with the men of the garrison. It was the high command, the officers and non-commissioned officers that were determined to make an example, to give a display of *Schrecklichkeit* as a crown to their work of suppression. Tiedemann had not taken the advice given him to burn all his documents, and after he was shot man after man was executed, including ' old Boening ' referred to on page 556, largely on the evidence furnished by his papers. Tiedemann, we are told, and those who followed him died like brave men.

One of the rebels, the brave and resourceful Carl Schurz, was determined not to hand himself over to the tender mercies of the Prussians, and he effected a daring escape, the story of which, as given in his *Reminiscences*, is well worth reading. Others were not so fortunate. Five who ventured the attempt were shot, and, as Corvin tells us, ' Major von Weltzien had the five corpses laid on boards, and carried to all the different casemates as a warning.' Corvin himself was sentenced to death, but the untiring exertions of his wife, of his courageous advocate, Dr.

Kusel, and, possibly also, the quiet influence of Count von Groeben, secured a commutation of the sentence to ten years' imprisonment in the House of Correction, a punishment which was ignominious enough, for it was attended with the loss of all civil rights. Six years were spent by him in solitary confinement, and then he was released, to escape with his wife to England and thence to the United States. One significant passage from the account he gives of his imprisonment is to be read :

The Prussians, especially the officers, behaved in Baden as if they had conquered the country. Their insolent and despotic manners were not at all liked, even by the Baden officers who had remained faithful to the old government. These had been living for many years under a constitution, and were shocked by the Prussian tyranny. Besides, North German roughness very seldom agrees with South German *bonhomie*.

Prisoners who never see a green tree or field for years are very excusable if they try to find means to get a stealthy peep out of their windows. This is forbidden, and if detected, is punished. It might have sufficed that the Prussian sentries should have been told to report such offenders, but they received orders to fire at them. Almost every day shots were heard in the courtyard, and many of the prisoners had narrow escapes. Of course the political convicts were very much shocked by such severity, and all the prison officers likewise. Complaints, however, were of no avail ; on the contrary, the soldiers were praised by their officers, and it was only a matter of regret that not one of the democrats was shot. Sometimes I saw the sentries crouch behind firewood piled up in the yard, watching the windows, with their muskets ready, as if they were sportsmen stalking deer.

Once I heard the report of a gun very near me, a cry, and then the tramping of many feet, which seemed to me to be carrying a heavy burden. I was afterwards told that it was a poor prisoner, who was employed to whitewash a cell. He was standing upon a step, just about to replace the window, when he was spied by a sentry, and shot through the breast. The poor fellow had strength enough to descend the steps, and to set aside the window, which he held in both his hands ; then he fell, and died a few days afterwards. This atrocity was inexcusable, inasmuch as the sentries had been warned not to fire at prisoners who worked as masons in the cells. Afterwards a red flag was stuck out from the windows of cells where masons or whitewashers were at work.

This was not our only grievance. The sentries pacing up and down the courtyard, near and under the windows of the cells, used to call to one another in the night. Becoming aware that this calling vexed the prisoners, who were awakened by it, the sentries amused themselves by shouting all night, to the great vexation of us all. One night the whole place was roused. They roared like madmen, encouraged to do so by a lieutenant who had just been visiting the guards. Several of the prisoners clambered to the windows, and one of the sentries shot at them without effect. At the same time, I heard one of the prisoners angrily exclaim at the man who fired, ' Hold your peace, you d—d bloodhound ! ' On the day following, when all the higher officers of the prison had left for their dinner, and only the recently appointed head-overseer was present, the Prussian military officer in command of the town, a major, appeared in the establishment, accompanied by several officers, corporals, and a patrol with loaded muskets ; two corporals had sticks in their hands.

Major von E. demanded from the head-overseer the delivery of the inmates of three cells he pointed out, and whom he accused of having, on the previous night, insulted the sentries. The head-overseer was perplexed, but did as the major ordered. By the noise in the courtyard the prisoners were attracted to the windows, in spite of the danger. The major, seeing this, invited them all to come to their windows, and see what he was going to do.

Three of the prisoners were then brought into the courtyard, and barbarously caned in presence of the major and his suite.

Dean Förderer's picture of the gloomy reign of martial law in Baden is as follows : [1]

Now, when I read the words ' martial law ' and ' court-martial,' I shudder. . . . The Prussians were in a hurry to bring this terrible ' law ' into action. Even on 7th August the first sitting of the court-martial was held. The Rastatt court-martial, which pronounced sentence in the name of the Grand Duke of Baden, consisted strangely enough only of Prussian military men, and, in fact, of a major, a captain, a first and a second lieutenant, a sergeant-major, a non-commissioned officer and a private. Only the public prosecutor, counsel for the crown, belonged to Baden. The government of Baden had, at the outset, divested itself of all authority over courts-martial. A verdict of martial law required no higher assent ; appeal against it was not allowed. It was only later, after the court-martial had acted in too bloodthirsty a manner, that a decision was come to that every verdict not given unanimously should require confirmation by the Grand Duke. The defence was usually conducted by lawyers from Carlsruhe, now and then by laymen also. Amongst the lawyers I have a pleasant memory of the Jewish advocate Strauss, who used to espouse the cause of his clients with great warmth, and developed brilliant eloquence. Counsel for the crown did not leave a good impression upon me, because I felt sympathy for the accused, and these public prosecutors sought with terrible tenacity to make the most of all that told on the side of the prosecution, and would let no milder considerations prevail. The sittings, which were held in the Castle, were public, yet one was obliged to get a ticket of

---

[1] *Erinnerungen aus Rastatt* (K.).

admission from the authorities. The verdicts were made public by street posters. . . .

Rastatt was then, one could almost say, a veritable battle-field. The soldiers who had the sad office of carrying out the death sentences often came pale as death out of the fortress moat. They say that only such soldiers were employed in this as have ' something on their sheet.' I do not know if that be true. At all events, it was a real punishment to be obliged to shoot down a defenceless man. The smoke of these execution volleys lay heavily upon the spirits of the inhabitants of Rastatt, although they had had to endure much from the victims. It may well be believed that many a one would have got off with imprisonment if martial justice had not acted so quickly. How many in that distracted time forsook the way of law and order who later became ' decorated supporters of law and order ' ! Had they fallen into the hands of the Rastatt court-martial, many of them would be lying in the old cemetery there. Truly, even the Nurembergers hanged no one, if they had not got him. Here they wanted to make examples of those whom they had. But the chief offenders were not in their hands. The death penalty fell with especial hardness on the common soldiers who could only have entered upon the precipitous path because in higher circles all was not right. *Quidquid delirant reges, plectuntur Achivi.* ' The sins of those in authority must be expiated by the common people ' ; every death sentence taught us that. Neither coffin nor mounded grave was allowed to those executed by martial law ; no sign was to mark the spot where these human bodies, lying in the cool earth, await the Resurrection. And even now, when the events of 1849 are accorded even in higher circles a more lenient interpretation, and all the surviving offenders of the time have long been mercifully pardoned, and indeed may be presented at court, there still lies a certain ban upon those graves. In the year 1873 friends and sympathisers of those who had been shot wished to set up a gravestone, in common memory of them. The Grand Ducal authorities of Baden had nothing to urge against the scheme, but the Royal Prussian Government vetoed it in the following decree :

GOVERNMENT SECTION III. Nr. 3523

RASTATT, *24th November* 1874.

Touching the erection of a monument in the cemetery of this place, in memory of those who were shot in the year 1849.

To the Grand Ducal District Government with the observation, most respectfully tendered, that in the case under consideration the provisions of local statutes do not apply. The bodies of persons executed belong to the Court, which alone is competent to decide how and where the interment shall take place, and whether a memorial is to be erected. As the present Governmental Court of this place is the successor of the former Baden Court-martial which, in its time, condemned the individuals concerned to be shot, permission to set up a memorial is refused.

The Governor,
Von Cayl, *Lieutenant-General.*

Prominent among those in Germany who resented this ' untiringly active Bloody Assize ' conducted by Prussia on non-Prussian soil, and who dared to raise their voices in protest, was Uhland, the true German hero of this half-century, who expressed his views in the following article in the *Observer,* a Würtemberg paper : [1]

MARTIAL LAW IN BADEN

The protests made by public opinion against the untiringly active Bloody Assize in Baden are not merely expressions of natural feeling or of political partisanship ; they are supported by a stern and deeply injured respect for law in general. It might well have been expected that German jurisprudence would have taken up this standpoint more emphatically and resolutely. The writer of these lines does not know what has been done in this direction in Baden itself, publicly and with the full weight of their names, by eminent jurists, representatives of the people, and delegates to the Reichstag, who have co-operated in framing the constitutional rights. . . .
That one State may not intervene in the independent jurisdiction of another is an undisputed principle of law. But that does not exhaust the legal bearings of the present case. When the subjects of one State are treated by the courts of another State in a way which is in contradiction to the constitution and the laws of the latter and to universal standards of law as well, then not only is intercession called for and justified, but *remonstrance* and *challenge* as well—the demand that those subjects shall not be examined and sentenced otherwise than according to valid forms of law. Is it consistent with the constitution of Baden, with the laws of Baden, to say nothing of the constitutional rights of the German people proclaimed by Baden, that the criminal jurisdiction of that country should be transferred by the Government alone—a case perhaps never heard of before—to the military power of another country ? Is it consistent with all this that the courts-martial should go on and be renewed from month to month, as if it were a question of the most immaterial extensions of time, when the conditions precedent to the establishment of any court-martial, viz. danger of war and insurrection, have so visibly disappeared that it has been possible to withdraw the greater part of the army brought in from outside ? Or can it be a *legal reason* for continuing the courts-martial that only by means of them can all those who are to be sentenced receive

---

[1] Notter's *Life of Uhland.*

sentence of death ? If the ministry of Würtemberg answers these questions in the negative, of which there can be no doubt, it must recognise it as its right and its duty to make not only intercession, but also, even though there be no definite prospect of success, a *remonstrance* and a *demand*. Delay is dangerous!

L. U.

Two somewhat conflicting accounts of the situation in other parts of Baden, Freiburg and Heidelberg, may be given to complete the picture of the Prussian triumph. The first is from the letters [1] of Henriette Feuerbach, mother of Anselm Feuerbach, the greatest of the dull German school of classical painters. Her account begins with an hysterical appreciation of the restoration by Prussia of order out of chaos, but ends in a sombre strain, at the mention of the word ' court-martial ' :

FREIBURG, Sunday [July 1849].

The Prussians have marched in, God knows, as angels of deliverance, at this moment. It had come to such a pass that I was almost obliged to weep for joy as we passed the first advance posts. They conduct themselves very humanely, and show great sympathy towards our poor army, raised from the people, which marched into the fire in such a desultory and irresponsible way, and yet were so gallant.

How things have been going here lately, cannot be described in the short space of a letter, also there are no words to express these events. The retreat itself I did not see, what they tell us of it borders on the fabulous. The wretchedness, the distraction of the poor victims who stood between their own executioners and the enemy were boundless ; they literally rushed about the streets in absolute dismay and destitution, half starved, in rags, in oddments of clothing picked up on the battle-field, they forced their way into the houses which were obliged to stand open day and night. The Foreign Legion was the most horrible spectacle. The people clothed them, providing them with underclothing and garments as far as every single house could, in order to stave off robbery. Now they are scattered in the mountains, and a trail of plunder marks their track. The barbarous brutality and the terrorism holding sway under our provisional government leave nothing more to be hoped and desired. The Prussian state of siege in which we now live has given back to us such abundant freedom, that we do not know how to behave ourselves under it. We need no longer tremble in anticipation of deeds of violence to life and property. People arrested are no longer dragged with cords to prison, and weakly eighteen year old boys can sit at home, and need no longer stagger about under the weight of a thirty-six pound gun. Oh ! those processions of the

---

[1] *Ihr Leben in ihren Briefen* (K.).

first levy—three-fourths of whom were always pressed men—were a sight to draw tears of blood. The fear of the Prussians was so great that even the wounded in the Hospital fled if their feet could still carry them. That was how the poor people were deluded in order to make them stand firm, as indeed our whole revolution has been a systematically raised edifice of all sorts of lies and lawyers' tricks. Our poor, poor beautiful country is bleeding to death of this wound, and those who led it into this abyss of misery, they enjoy now in a foreign land the golden fruits of their knavish tricks. Forgive me for writing to you in such an excited strain, I cannot help it ; the Prussian vanguard is just marching past the house, six thousand men with twenty cannon, into the Oberland in pursuit of the ' Army of Freedom '—how many poor innocent ones will these cannon strike down !

FREIBURG, 15th *July* 1849.

Everything is in perfect order and quiet, the garrison only twenty-five hundred men strong, the billeting very reasonable and carried out with courtesy and civility, the common soldiers behaving themselves as well-bred, well-mannered young men in houses where they are not received with ill-will, the authorities displaying the greatest consideration and forbearance. A traveller through our town will find there a joyous picture of freedom, greatly enhanced by the splendid regimental music ; nevertheless severe depression weighs down secretly our spirits, a depression which only few can resist. The general question, which every one perplexedly asks himself is, What will happen now ? Hitherto, not one single arrest has been made here, except of captured soldiers and volunteers, who are hourly brought in by troops, not bound and gagged, as last year, but decently, with a small escort. Whole files come voluntarily to submit themselves. But this mild condition of things cannot continue ; our state of war would then be a picnic. The court-martial began its work two days ago. God preserve us from a terrible harvest of martial law, my nerves could not stand that. It seems to affect the Prince of Prussia in the same way ; they say he will leave Baden after taking military possession, so that he may delegate the executions and the indemnity to Wrangel.

The second account is given in a letter [1] from the Swiss poet, Gottfried Keller, to his mother and sister. He tells how the Baden gunners shot their own wounded to save them from falling into the hands of the Prussians :

HEIDELBERG, 24th *July* 1849.

I do not recollect, dear Mother, whether I have acknowledged the receipt of your fifty gulden. If not, I forgot it in the tumult of war, which surged for a time around Heidelberg. Cannonading and

---

[1] Baechtold's *Life of Gottfried Keller*, vol. i.

musketry went on at a distance of about two leagues, and once or twice the enemy came up in front of the town, so that we saw them running round on the hill. They shot right into our streets, at a distance of two thousand paces, and a soldier fell dead, not far from me, on the bridge. Upon this we, who had no business there, found it well to move further away. The Prussians, you see, have sharp-shooters. I betook myself to my room, but things were still worse there. The people of the house removed their possessions for safety, because their house stands by the water. Close under my window were planted cannon, which were to keep off the enemy across the Neckar, who in the event of making a serious attack would probably take some account of these cannon together with the house in front of which they stood. Meanwhile, the Baden soldiers were obliged to leave the city, because a battle had been lost in the rear, and next morning, the Prussians marched in before sunrise. That, in short, is the whole business. If only you people would treat the Baden soldiers decently, for they are very honest fellows, and have offered a brave resistance. The Prussians have had to buy their victory dearly, in spite of their superior strength. The Baden gunners, in particular, behaved heroically. As it was very hot, they worked only in their shirts beside their guns, like bakers before the baking-oven, and all the time were active and of good cheer. They shot their wounded themselves, in order that they should not fall into the hands of the Prussians. Freedom for us Germans has been once again dished, but it will not remain so for long, and the King of Prussia will take good care not to tackle Switzerland. Probably the German princes will soon be flying at each other's throats. They have conjointly finished off the people, but now comes the settling of affairs at the funeral feast.

So ended the revolutionary struggle in Baden. Brentano, the head of the revolutionary government, had fled before the end of June to Switzerland, whence he issued a violent manifesto [1] to the people of Baden justifying himself at the expense of Struve and others, including the revolutionary assembly itself. ' At the very beginning,' he says, ' of our revolution hundreds of adventurers came into our country ; they boasted that they had suffered for liberty, they wished to receive the clinking reward out of our chests : one could scarcely go along the streets of the town of Carlsruhe for the press of uniformed quill-drivers trailing their cavalry sabres. These loungers battened upon your money, while your sons, who for the freedom of the Fatherland had faced the enemy's bullets, were forced to starve.' He denounces Struve in particular, ' whom the army despised on account of his personal cowardice. . . .

[1] Klein.

He had not the courage to walk to his hotel from the Town Hall.' Of the revolutionary Assembly he says : ' I believed that the representatives of the people, quite freely chosen, would support and strengthen my honest endeavour ; I deluded myself. An assembly whose majority consisted of incompetent, ordinary ranters offered the most lamentable picture of a popular assembly that ever appeared, trying as it did to hide its entire lack of insight and knowledge behind so-called revolutionary propositions which, passed to-day as resolutions, must be rejected again to-morrow as impracticable. . . .'

But it would be wrong to close this account of the revolutionary, republican struggle, into which nigh half a century of striving for constitutional reform degenerated, on so mean a note as Brentano's. It is fairer to take leave of the German revolutionaries of 1848 and 1849 in the words,[1] however rhapsodical, of Carl Schurz, the soldier and statesman whom Germany lost but America gained :

Since the Franco-German war of 1870 and the establishment of the present German Empire, it has been the fashion in Germany to scoff at the year 1848, dubbing it the ' crazy year,' and to ridicule the ' thoughtlessness ' with which at that time great political programmes were mapped out, comprehensive demands formulated, and far-reaching movements set on foot, to be followed by cruel disappointments and catastrophes. But did the German people of 1848 deserve such ridicule ? True, the men of those times did not know how to deal with the existing conditions, nor to carry to the desired end the movement so victoriously and hopefully begun. It is equally true that the popular movement was disjointed and now in retrospect appears in certain lights fantastic. But what reasonable person can wonder at this ? The German people, although highly developed in science, philosophy, literature and art, had always lived under a severe guardianship in all political matters. They had never been out of leading strings. They had observed only from afar how other nations exercised their right to govern themselves, and managed their active participation in the functions of the state, and those foreign nations the Germans had learned to admire and perhaps to envy. They had studied the theory of free institutions in books and had watched their workings in current newspaper reports. They had longed for the possession of like institutions and earnestly striven for their introduction into their own country. But with all this observing, learning, longing, and striving, the larger part of the German people had been excluded by the prevailing rigid paternalism

---

[1] *The Reminiscences of Carl Schurz*, i. p. 122 : New York, Doubleday, Page & Co., 1909.

from practical experience in the exercise of political self-government. They had not been permitted to learn the practical meaning of political liberty. They had never received or known the teachings which spring from the feeling of responsibility in free political action. The affairs of government lay outside the customs and habits of their lives. Free institutions were to them mere abstract conceptions, about which the educated and the seriously thinking men indulged in politico-philosophical speculations, while to the uneducated and the superficial they only furnished political catch-words, in the use of which the general discontent with existing conditions found vent. . . .

He surely wrongs the German people who lays solely at their and their leaders' doors the responsibility for the failures of the years 1848-1849, overlooking the tergiversations of the princes.

The memory of that 'springtime' should be especially dear to Germans because of the enthusiastic spirit of self-sacrifice for a great cause which for a while pervaded almost every class of society with rare unanimity. It is this moral elevation which, even if it some-times ran into fantastic exaggerations, the German people should prize and honour—of which they should certainly not be ashamed. My heart warms whenever I think of those days. In my immediate surroundings I knew hosts of men who were ready at any moment to abandon and risk all for the liberty of the people and the greatness of the Fatherland. We ought to respect him who is willing to throw away all, even life itself, for a good and great idea ; and whoever, be it an individual or a people, has had in life moments of such self-sacrificing enthusiasm should hold the memory of them sacred.

EPILOGUE

THE spring of 1848 had, as Sybel [1] puts it, demolished the old
Federal Diet : that of 1849 saw the collapse of the enterprise to
erect in its place a new form of central government. Thus the
situation in Germany at large was one of anarchy, or, to adopt
Metternich's epigram, in place of a plenum a vacuum was
established. At first sight one might suppose that the way
was clear for Prussia to assume the hegemony on her own terms.
She seemed to have the ball at her feet. Austria and Hungary
lay struggling like 'two dark serpents tangled in the dust.'
Prussia, through her *Zollverein*, which now comprised the bulk
of Germany, was the economic mistress of the situation ; her
bureaucracy had been elaborated into a machine, soulless and
with something of the power of a force of nature ; her army
had been called in to crush radicalism and republicanism in
state after state, and was preparing for a final triumph, under
the command of the Prince of Prussia himself, in the fiercest
revolutionary struggle of all, the last test of civil war in Baden.
But we have to reckon with the weakness and the scruples of the
fantastic genius on the Prussian throne, and the deep-rooted
jealousy and suspicion of the governments of Hanover, Würtemberg, Saxony and Bavaria, not to speak of the hatred of the
republicans whom Prussian arms had suppressed. The liberal,
but impulsive and excitable Bodelschwingh had long lost his
influence, Manteuffel was not clever enough, and it was on the
supple and diplomatic intelligence of Radowitz that the King
now leaned for advice. Early in the year the first draft of a new
Prussian scheme for a German constitution was circulated.
There was to be a German Union under Prussia's lead ; this
German Union was in turn to form a Union with Austria, for
protection from attack from without or within, and for the
promotion of national welfare and commerce ; two representatives each, from the German Union and Austria, were to form

---

[1] This brief summary follows in the main *Sybel*, I. iv. cap. 1 and 2.

a United Government and to control foreign policy by the appointment of all ambassadors and consuls.

These proposals were politely rejected on 16th May by Schwarzenberg. Austria, he said, could not subscribe to what was merely a provisional draft. Nevertheless the King, despite his chagrin, proceeded, at the instance of Radowitz, with a select conference of the more important states which he had summoned for the next day. In the vain hope of conciliating liberal as distinguished from radical and republican sentiment, Radowitz had taken as his basis the Frankfort constitution, but had modified it in a conservative sense. Direct election based on a wide suffrage was to go ; in its place indirect election was substituted, and the electors in first instance were to be divided into three classes according to their means. In the Reichstag there were to be two chambers and the budget was to be submitted both to the upper and the lower house. No legislative proposal was to have the force of law without the assent of the Imperial Government. The authority of the Imperial Government over the individual states was limited and defined, and the dignity of the princes received more scrupulous consideration. In place of an hereditary Kaiser appeared a College of Princes under the presidency of the King of Prussia.

At the first meeting of the Conference on 17th May there were present representatives of Austria, Bavaria, Saxony, and Hanover. The Austrian envoy withdrew after the sitting. The Bavarian envoy continued to attend meetings, but expressed continually his regret that he could only express his personal opinion, as he was without instructions entitling him to associate himself with any binding decision. Proximity to Prussia prevented either Saxony or Hanover from taking an independent line, and finally they subscribed, though only reluctantly and under pressure from Radowitz—the reservation in their minds that if Bavaria did not come in they would withdraw—to Prussia's new constitutional scheme. Thus came into being on 26th May the ineffective and short-lived League of the Three Kings.

A month later, by the end of June, Prussia was at the height of pre-Bismarckian power : she stood with her heel on the neck of revolution, and her courts-martial were busy in Baden inculcating the lesson of *Schrecklichkeit*. She could have forced through her scheme of reform had the supreme direction of her policy been in hands less august than those of the reigning Hohenzollern. Bavaria played, and successfully, for time in which to make up her mind. By the end of August the great wrestling match between Austria and Hungary was over ; with Russian assistance Austria had thrown her opponent, and her hands were now free to try another fall with Prussia for the German hegemony. Then Bavaria at last plucked up courage with Würtemberg, who had been holding herself coyly aloof, to intimate a formal rejection of the Prussian proposals. On 20th October the representatives of Saxony and Hanover announced their withdrawal from any further collaboration in the great Prussian scheme. So fell to pieces within five months the League of the Three Kings, and Prussia was left to gather round her at Erfurt twenty-eight of the smaller fry among German States, to form the Parliament which Radowitz had summoned to ratify the would-be German, now merely Prussian, Union.

Austria lost no time in preparing a counter-stroke. Schwarzenberg appealed to the old Federal Act of 1815 against the new German constitution promulgated by Prussia, and enunciated a rival scheme conceived in the Austrian interest. The affairs of Germany were to be controlled by a seven-headed Directory, representing Austria, Prussia, the four Royal States and the two Hesses counting as one, a Directory, be it understood, with no nonsense of popular representation about it to hamper autocracy and its bureaucratic nominees. This scheme, with a few modifications, notably the addition of a popular chamber *pour rire*, was readily accepted by Hanover, Würtemberg, Saxony, and Bavaria ; the Three Kings League of 26th May 1849 on the Prussian side had soon been converted into a Four Kings League on the Austrian side ! But Austria was satisfied with this display of her diplomatic strength. Her success in checkmating Prussia's scheme by a counter-scheme of her own encouraged her to come out with what she had really at heart,— no brand-new constitution for Germany but the restoration of the old Federal Diet at Frankfort which had surrendered its powers to the National Assembly.

Prussia's prestige, so high after her military display in crushing revolution in Dresden, in the Palatinate, and in Baden, was sinking fast, and was soon to fall to the level reached in March 1848. But whereas it was the King of Prussia who had then crawled on his stomach before the populace in Berlin, the fresh humiliation in store was to involve the whole Prussian nation. It was precipitated by two events, the renewal of the Schleswig-Holstein war and a constitutional crisis in Hesse.

The fateful armistice of Malmö, which had administered such a shock to the National Assembly, had expired in March 1849, and the war was resumed. The Central Authority at Frankfort, still in being at the moment, despatched a German army against the Danes, which won several successes, to some extent counter-balanced by the failures of the Schleswig-Holsteiners themselves. But Prussia again disappointed German hopes. She had claimed the right to act on her own in the matter of Schleswig-Holstein, and King Frederick William, tired out and disgusted by the whole business, yielded to pressure from Great Britain and Russia, and concluded in July an armistice with Denmark, and a year later an inglorious peace, which left the Duchies to their fate.

The trouble in Hesse-Cassel brought Prussia to the verge of war with Austria. In the heyday of revolution and reform in 1848 the hated minister Hassenpflug, loathed as a renegade of renegades, had been driven from office, and constitutional govern-ment was established. But in 1849 the Elector profited by the general triumph of reaction to recall Hassenpflug and under-mine the very constitution he had himself granted. Officials, judges, and the army supported the Diet in its resistance against attacks upon its prerogatives. The Diet appealed to Prussia as the head of the Prussian Union, and, apparently, not in vain. She announced her determination to maintain the Hessian constitution. On the other side Austria stepped forward to support the Elector and autocracy. Both Austrian and Prussian troops entered the little state, and stood facing one another. Shots were actually exchanged and it seemed nothing but a miracle could save open war. But the same miracle occurred as had occurred on 19th March 1848 ; the King of Prussia surrendered. The orthodox German explanation is that Prussia was not prepared for war, and had to withdraw in order to avoid the calamity of a military reverse. Certainly the Minister of War expressed this view and he was supported by the Prime Minister, the left-handed Hohenzollern, Count Brandenburg. The unfortunate Radowitz was left practically alone in the Ministry. He was ready to persist in Austria's despite, but the forces against him were too strong, among them the hostility and the sinister influence of Bismarck, now a real power. Bismarck's attitude was determined by various considerations, —genuine doubt as to Prussia's military strength, especially in view of the fact that Russia might be expected to support the Austrian case, a repugnance to the idea of Prussia's championing a popular, constitutional cause, and one associated with the year of revolution, and lastly, but not least, a personal dislike of Radowitz and a jealousy and suspicion of his policy. The King threw Radowitz over, and on his resignation appointed Manteuffel Foreign Minister. To placate Austria the Prussian Union was dissolved, and a conference arranged between Manteuffel and Schwarzenberg at Olmütz. There on 29th November 1850, Prussia made an abject surrender to Austria ; for the convention signed by Manteuffel conceded all her rival's demands.. The bitter feeling of humiliation left by that abject surrender was not removed from German consciousness until the great day of Königgrätz, more than sixteen years later.

Thus ends, with the humiliation of Prussia and the restoration of the Federal Diet at Frankfort, the first drama in the great trilogy of modern German history of which we spoke in our introduction. The second stage began in 1851, when Bismarck, the superman, was sent to Frankfort as Prussian envoy to the Diet, and by stress of intellect, force of will and ruthlessness in action led his country from triumph to triumph, until in 1870 Börne's prophecy came true : a man midwife delivered Germany of that abortion in a democratic age, the German Empire.

1870

Then think of our own day's heroes,
Of these Blumenthals and Fritzes,
Of the Herren Generale
Number this and number that!
Under Prussia's ghastly colours—
Sorrow's clout of black and white—
Ne'er burst forth achievement's larvæ
As the butterfly of song.
They perhaps their silk may spin
For a time, but die therein.

Just in victory lies defeat;
Prussia's sword proves Prussia's scourge.
Ne'er poetic inspiration
Springs from problems that they solve.
Deeds win no response in song,
If a people noble, free,
Beauty-loving, are transformed
Into staff-machinery,—
Bristling with the dirks of cunning
From the time that Herr von Moltke
Murdered battle's poesy.

So demonic is the power
That received our world to rule:
And the Sphinx, her wisdom guarding,
When her riddle's solved, is slain.

Cipher-victories are doomed.
Soon the moment's blast will veer;
Like a storm on desert-plain
It will fell the false gods' race.
Bismarck and the other old ones
Will, like Memnon's column-stumps,
Still on saga-chair be sitting
Songless to the morning sun.

Ibsen's 'Balloon Letter,' 1870. A. R. Anderson's
Translation, English Review, November 1914.

INDEX

DATE DUE

OCT 2 6 1997			

GAYLORD   PRINTED IN U.S.A

DD
207.5
L51
L

G

1

₍1970₎

282440   xxiv, 584p. 23cm.

    ı study in

character,

, AMS Press

Reprint of the 1918 ed.

1.Germany-History-1815-1866. 2.Germany-History-Revolution, 1848-1849. 3.Political poetry, German. 4.German poetry-Translations into English. 5.English poetry-Translations from German.   I.Title.